A Garden Book
For Houston

and the Texas Gulf Coast

Gulf Publishing Company
Houston, Texas

To Robert & Elizabeth:
Happy Gardening!
Lorna Hume Terrell Thomas
10-18-92

RIVER OAKS GARDEN CLUB

A
Garden
Book
For
Houston

and the Texas Gulf Coast

Fourth Edition

Library of Congress Cataloging-in-Publication Data

A Garden Book for Houston and the Texas Gulf Coast.

   Rev. Ed. of: A Garden Book for Houston and the
Texas Gulf Coast. 3rd ed. c. 1975.
   Includes index.
   1. Gardening--Texas--Houston Region. I. Terrell, Lorna
Hume. II. River Oaks Garden Club. III. Garden Book for
Houston and the Texas Gulf Coast.
SB453.2.T4G33 1989   635.9'0976   89-11748
ISBN 0-88415-350-9

"All animals on our planet (including us)
are guests of the plant kingdom.
No plants = no people or animals. It's that simple."
—Malcolm C. Shurtleff

*T*he validity of this quotation and the primary intent of providing gardening information suitable expressly to the climatic and soil conditions characteristic of Houston and much of the Texas Gulf Coast shaped the major purpose of this garden guide. The desired objective is to inspire the readers to improve not only their own grounds but also that of their broader environment, using methods beneficial to all creatures and vegetation.

The assistance of our secretary has been most generous as has been the offering of the many contributors here listed. The superb expertise in the editing and design by Doug Craig and Don Stalinsky transformed a duckling into a handsome swan. The encouragement and patience of my husband Arthur was unlimited. All contributed greatly to the pleasure I have experienced these last five years in writing and compiling this fourth revision of *A Garden Book For Houston*. I appreciate the opportunity given me by the River Oaks Garden Club. My hope is that some of my pleasure will be shared by the gardeners who may benefit from the contents.

—*Lorna Hume Terrell, Editor*

*The Forum of Civics, Home of the River Oaks Garden Club,
2503 Westheimer, Houston, Texas 77098.*

*"No Athenian should ever confess that he neglected public service
for the sake of his private fortune" a quotation from Pericles, a 5th
century, B.C. statesman, is carved into the stone facade. The
building began as the John Smith County School. It was purchased
and renovated in 1927 by Will Hogg to house The Forum of
Civics, "an organization to stimulate civic pride and to combine
many and varied forces for the betterment and beautification of
our city and county." In 1942 the River Oaks Garden Club
purchased it to be their home, dedicating it to the memory of Will
and Mike Hogg, the leaders of The Forum of Civics. Renovated
again in 1988.*

*The Forum and its gardens are open to the public.
For information call (713) 523-2483.*

Foreword

"Beautiful cities make better citizens."
—Will C. Hogg

*T*his Fourth Revised Edition is dedicated to the memory of Will C. Hogg, who recognized the need for gardening information adapted especially to the climatic conditions peculiar to Houston and its environs. Holding in his mind the motto, "Beautiful cities make better citizens," Mr. Hogg correctly surmised that with more complete horticultural information suitable to this city's micro-climate, the townspeople would improve not only their own little corner but the city as a whole. Sixty years have proven the truth of his concept.

When the Hogg family bestowed the copyright of this book to the River Oaks Garden Club in 1944, the ladies accepted the challenge not only to reprint but periodically to revise the book as circumstances necessitated. Gardening information is continuously being modernized.

As a member of the Garden Club of America, the River Oaks Garden Club is a non-profit organization. The proceeds from this garden book are designated to cover the expenses of the reprintings and revisions.

A Garden Book For Houston is one of the River Oaks Garden Club's gifts to the citizens of the City of Houston.

The monies obtained from the Club's fund-raising projects, such as the annual Azalea Trail in March and the Pink Elephant Sale, are returned to the community to support the objectives to which the River Oaks Garden Club is dedicated: contributing to the maintenance of the Bayou Bend Gardens, assisting in urban beautification, conservation and improvement of our environment, and the dissemination of horticultural knowledge.

With this Fourth Revised Edition of *A Garden Book For Houston and the Texas Gulf Coast*, the River Oaks Garden Club continues "to stimulate the knowledge and love of gardening among amateurs." May those who study this garden book find the pleasure described long ago by Charles Dudley Warner:

"To own a bit of ground, to scratch it with a hoe, to plant seeds and watch the renewal of life— this is the commonest delight of the race, the most satisfactory thing a man can do."

—*River Oaks Garden Club, Member, Garden Club of America, Zone IX*

Acknowledgments

With sincere appreciation to:

Members of the River Oaks Garden Club: President Advisors: Nancy F. Japhet, Mary Ellen F. Thanheiser, Carolyn S. Wimberly, Marilyn G. Lummis, Kay H. Symonds.

Garden Book Chairmen: Christy I. Manuel, who also served splendidly as editorial assistant; Lizinka M. Benton, who gave repeated encouragement; and Donna B. McFall, who served marvelously as editor, librarian, messenger, and listener as well.

Special appreciation to Sadie Gwin Blackburn, who wrote the AZALEAS chapter even while serving as First Vice President and then President of The Garden Club of America; to Suzanne P. Cain, who wrote ARRANGEMENTS FROM YOUR GARDEN; to Virginia V. Lawhon, who edited, advised, encouraged, and tracked down slides; and Elaine L. Colvin, for continuous assistance, especially with CONTAINER GARDENING.

Applause to Virginia V. Lawhon, Donna B. McFall, Kay H. Symonds, Bobby Jean R. Haemisegger, Lettalou G. Whittington, Christy I. Manuel, Honorary ROGC member Douglas S. Craig, and designer Don Stalinsky for the stunning cover of our book.

Douglas S. Craig of Fellers/Gaddis Craig Lamm and Don Stalinsky of Stalinsky Design masterminded the contents and design of the entire book.

My thanks to GCA Horticulture Judge Edwina H. Winter of Beaumont for correcting plant names, and to The Garden Club of America and ROGC member Ila B. Nunn for fine assistance with PLANT NOMENCLATURE.

My gratitude to Kathryne S. Marr and the late John D. Marr for much of the information in the chapters AZALEAS and CAMELLIAS.

Thanks to Susie K. Bace, Helen E. Bering, Lynne T. Campbell, Elsie L. Layton, Mimi M. McDugald, Janet H. Head, Alice P. Craig, Susan B. Keeton, Jackie C. Magill, Mary B. Smith, Ann S. Thomas, Caro Ivey Walker, Mrs. Blake C. Vaughan, and Ann A. Symonds.

Gratitude to those who allowed photography of their homes: Helen S. Anderson, Laura Lee S. Blanton, Marion M. Britton, Jeaneane B. Duncan, Lucile M. Harris, Ida Jo B. Moran, Blanche H. Strange, Carroll S. Masterson, Carolyn J. Young, and Margaret C. Symonds, Betty F. Doherty, and Martha A. Huge.

Thanks to Betsy C. Reichert and Marion M. Britton for their arrangements.

Special thanks to Alice C. Tillett for laboriously arranging plants in special subjects to aid the reader.

Thanks to Dorothy B. Tasin for her tireless proofreading of countless proofs.

Thanks to C. Love and Associates for word processing and indexing.

The professionals listed below gave unstintingly of their time, experience, and knowledge. *A Garden Book For Houston* is a better garden guide because of their interest and assistance. Ole's and enduring appreciation to each of them.

Bob Ross, administrator of the Bayou Bend Gardens, assisted in numerous ways to improve information; he edited the charts of FERNS, TREES, and SHRUBS, and the chapters AZALEAS and CAMELLIAS, as well as providing lists for those chapters.

The following are Texas Certified Nurserymen with the Cornelius Nurseries:
Ellen Fuller and Margaret Cherry spent countless hours editing and augmenting the charts: ANNUALS AND PERENNIALS, BULBS, FERNS, GROUND COVERS, HERBS, and VINES.
L. P. Kojis, a Master Texas Certified Nurseryman, patiently answered my numerous questions.
Zack Ratliff checked the HINTS FOR LANDSCAPING chapter and introduced me to many new plants now available.

David L. Myers and Kathy Dean Windham of the Soil Conservation Service of the United States Department of Agriculture guided me down the bumpy road of understanding soil and helping me make it understandable to our readers. Mr. Myers also checked the DRAINAGE and WATERING chapters. My many calls to them were always answered correctly and pleasantly. If you have any questions about soil, call them.

Jack G. Swayze, Forester with Davey Tree Co., gave invaluable assistance with the TREES chart and chapter and with several other chapters—plus patient explanations to me.

Dr. Roger Funk, plant physiologist, also with Davey Tree Co., clarified certain physiological changes in soil.

J. M. Stroud and Margaret P. Sharpe, both consulting rosarians of the Houston Rose Society, improved the ROSES chapter, and The Houston Rose Society provided special instructions.

John M. Koros, Director of the Mercer Arboretum and Botanic Gardens, reviewed, edited, and improved the charts of TREES, SHRUBS, VINES, ANNUALS AND PERENNIALS, BULBS, GROUND COVERS, and FERNS, and also donated numerous photographs while boosting my spirits when they faltered.

Doug Williams, Botanist with the Houston Arboretum and Nature Center, edited the charts TREES and SHRUBS, provided slides, and introduced me to Nanci and Gary Freeborg, who typed lengthy lists of special plants onto computer discs. Mr. Freeborg is a Horticulturist with the Armand Bayou Nature Center.

Mary Jo Gussett of the Houston Cactus & Succulent Society graciously compiled the list of plants and their culture appearing in the CACTI & OTHER SUCCULENTS chapter.

Mike McBee and Berdie Deanda of the Grimes Grass Co. and Steve Potter of Lawn & Turf Grass Applicators led me with kindly patience through lawn grasses and their maintenance.

Earl R. Limb, Sr. gave me the benefit of his success in growing vegetables through conversations and in the writing of his own experiences as expressed in the VEGETABLE GARDEN chapter. Dashes of Mr. Limb's philosophy helped me through the rough places.

Don Portie, Harris County Agricultural Extension Service, Houston, for the Spring and Fall Vegetable Planting Guide in the VEGETABLE GARDEN chapter.

David Foresman, ASLA, of Foresman & Co. assisted with the HINTS FOR LANDSCAPING and SOIL chapters.

Sally Bantarri edited and improved the HINTS FOR LANDSCAPING chapter.

Gary Outenreath of McDugald-Steele Landscape Architects is the author of THE TROPICAL GARDEN chapter. His continuing interest in our book and the updating of the plant list are much appreciated.

Richard Eggenberger of Living Earth Technology contributed to the VINES chart.

Dudley Warner, Horticulturist, also of Living Earth Technology, assisted with soil and mulch information.

W. Meade Wheless, Jr. reviewed the CAMELLIAS chapter and added interesting and helpful information.

John Thomas of the WILDSEED Co. graciously read and approved the chapter WILD FLOWERS-NATIVE PLANTS.

The Fountainview Office Supply staff and Dromgoole's Office Supply in the Village have my everlasting appreciation for their cheerful assistance with the reams of photocopies I made along the way.

The Texas Agricultural Extension Service and The Texas A&M University System of the U.S. Department of Agriculture, especially the persons in the Houston office including Bill Adams, Horticulturist. Also Dr. Richard Duble, turf grass specialist, Robert E. Moon, Everett Janne, Director Daniel C. Pfannstiel, and the compilers of the several bulletins from which I garnered important information. To all of them, my appreciation of their work and my thank you's.

Lana Owens, Horticulturist, assisted with annuals, perennials, and herbs.

Frank Willingham, Turtle Pond Nursery, assisted with the AZALEA list.

Carter Taylor, Condon Gardens, Inc.; Eddie Russell, Wolfe Nurseries.

Karen Lehto, Managing Editor Program Guide, Ch.8.

Photographic Contributors

To all we extend sincere appreciation for their excellent work, freely donated. The photographs add immeasurably to the attractiveness and the educational value of this book. Each photographer is identified throughout the book by initials that appear next to the photo.

In alphabetical order:

Richard J. Baldauf, Museum of Natural Science

Harry L. Brister

Buddy Clemons, professional photographer

George Craig, professional photographer

G. E. Davis of the Houston Camellia Society

Tom Fox, photographer with the SWA Group

Mary Jo Gussett of the Houston Cactus & Succulent Society

Jean Hardy of Houston Metropolitan Magazine

Carlos Hernandez

Charlotte W. Horton, member River Oaks Garden Club

John M. Koros, Director Mercer Arborertum & Botanic Gardens

Julie H. Lee, member Garden Club of Houston

Muffy McLanahan, member River Oaks Garden Club

Rob Muir, professional photographer

Plumeria People, Mr. and Mrs. Richard Eggenberger of Living Earth Technology

Bob Ross, Administrator of the Bayou Bend Gardens

F. T. Saadeh, Ph.D.

Louise A. Stevenson, member River Oaks Garden Club

Mary Stewart, vegetable grower par excellence

J. M. Stroud, of the Houston Rose Society

Brenda Beust Smith

Table of Contents

Yellow pansies, stokesia, begonia, geranium and roses beside St. Augustine grass lawn, yaupon tree.

Month By Month In Your Garden

Spring

CWH

Summer

L.A.S

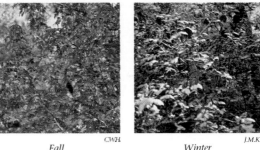

CWH

Fall

J.M.K.

Winter

*I*n reading *A Garden Book for Houston* you are joining many other residents in Houston and the Texas Gulf Coast who have depended on this garden guide since its first edition in 1929. Gardeners, professional and amateur, have contributed to the horticultural information in every edition concentrating on the planting times and the broad selection of plant material particularly suitable to the year-round gardening enjoyed in the hospitable climate of this near tropical zone. The Month by Month calendar offers appropriate suggestions for planting and lists of those plants which bloom each month, together with timely cultural suggestions. The chapters and charts of special plants and important gardening subjects are arranged for easy cross-reference with the calendar to gain even more information to encourage a flourishing garden. The encyclopedic INDEX lists both common and botanical names in a helpful double indexing, a guaranteed quick identification when you have only one name. *A Garden Book for Houston* simplifies the what, when, where, and how of growing numerous varieties of plants, be they trees, shrubs, lawns, bulbs, vegetables, herbs, tropical plants, annuals and perennials. May you and your garden enjoy each other!

1

January

*"Come ye cold winds, at January's call,
On whistling wings, and with white flakes bestrew the earth."*
— Ruskin

B.C.

Seedlings in open ground may not survive a freeze. If they don't, there is time to reseed.

**SEEDS
which may now
be sown in flats (f)
or open ground (o)**

Ageratum, *f*
Alyssum, Sweet, *f* or *o*
Arctotis, *f*
Babysbreath, *f* or *o*
Blanket flower
Browallia, *f*
Calendula, *f*
Candytuft, *o*
Chinese Forget-Me
 -Not, *f*
Cleome, *o*
Coreopsis, *f* or *o*
Cornflower, *f* or *o*
Cosmos, *o*
Feverfew, *f* or *o*
Forget-Me-Not, *f* or *o*
Gayfeather, *o*
Gerbera, *f*
Hollyhock, *f*
Larkspur, *o*
Lobelia, *f*
Lupine, *o*
Mallow, *f*
Marigold, *o*
Nasturtium, *o*

Nicotiana, *f*
Petunia, *f*
Phlox, Drummond, *o*
Pinks (Dianthus), *f*
Poppy, Shirley, *o*
Queen Anne's-lace, *o*
Salpiglossis, *f*
Salvia, *f* or *o*
Scabiosa, *f* or *o*
Snapdragon, *f* or *o*
Stock, *f* or *o*
Strawflower, *f* or *o*
Sweet Pea, *o*
Sweet William, *f* or *o*
Verbena, *f* or *o*

**PLANTS
which may now be
placed in the open
ground**

Arctotis
Bluebonnet
Calendula
Candytuft
Columbine
Coreopsis
Cornflower
Daisy,
 English
 Michaelmas
 Shasta
Delphinium
Forget-Me-Not
Gerbera
Hollyhock

Honeysuckle
Larkspur
Lupine
Nicotiana
Pansy
Petunia
Phlox, Louisiana
Physostegia
Pinks (Dianthus)
Queen Anne's-lace
Salvia
Shrubs
Snapdragon
Stock
Sweet William
Trees
Verbena
Viola
Violet

**BULBS, TUBERS,
RHIZOMES
which may now be
placed in the open
ground**

Agapanthus
Allium
Alpinia (Ginger)
Alstroemeria
Amarcrinum
Amaryllis
Anemone
Blackberry Lily
Canna
Calla
Chlidanthus
Cooperia (Rain Lily)
Crinum
Crocus
Dahlia
Freesia
Gladiolus
Hedychium
 (Butterfly Lily)
Hemerocallis (Daylily)
Hyacinth, Dutch

Iris,
 Bulbous
 Louisiana
Ismene
Kniphofia (Torch Lily)
Liatris
Lily-of-the-Valley
 (pots)
Liriope
Marica (Walking Iris)
Montbretia
Nerine
Ornithogalum
Oxalis
Ranunculus
Scilla
Sprekelia
Tigridia
Tuberose
Tulbaghia
Tulip
Zephyranthes
 (Fairy Lily)

**PLANTS
which bloom in
January**

---

t–Tree   *s*–Shrub   *v*–Vine
b-Bulb, Tuber or Rhizome
e-Evergreen   *d*-Deciduous
p–Perennial   *bn*–Biennial
a–Annual

Alyssum, Sweet, *a*
Arctotis, *a*
Azalea, *s e*
Babysbreath, *p*
Bouvardia, *s e*
Calendula, *a*
Calla Lily, *b*
Camellia, Japonica, *s e*
Candytuft, *a*
Daisy,
 English, *a*
 African Golden, *a*
Forget-Me-Not, *p*

Holly, *s e* and *d*
Honeysuckle,
  fragrantissima, *s d*
Horsechestnut,
  Dwarf, *s d*
Huisache, *t*
Hyacinth, *b*
Iris, unguicularis, *b*
Jasmine,
  nudiflorum, *s d*
  primrose, *s e*
  pubescens, *v e*
Lachenalia, *b*
Lantana, *s d*
Magnolia,
  Pink, *s* or *t d*
Narcissus, *b* spp
Oxalis, *b*, spp
Pansy, *a*
Pear, *t d*
Pentas, *s e*
Pinks, *a* and *bn*
Plum, *t d*
Poinsettia, *s d*
Quince, Japanese
  Flowering, *s d*
Redbud, *t d*
Rice Paper Plant, *s e*
Salvia, *a*
Shrimp Plant, *p*
Spirea, thunbergii, *s d*
Sweet Olive, *s e*
Sweet Pea, *v*
Viola, *a*
Violet, *p*

Soil is the basic element of growing any plant. Study SOIL chapter before beginning any bed preparation.

Arbor Day, the third Friday in January, encourages the planting of trees.

Azaleas: Plants may be moved. Keep moist to lessen cold weather damage. See AZALEAS chapter.

Birds: Provide food and fresh water. More birds die from lack of water than from lack of food.

Cacti: Semi-dormant now. Reduce watering.

Camellias: Plants may be moved. Pick up and discard fallen blooms. See CAMELLIAS chapter.

Cultivation: Changes in design may now be made, new beds dug and old ones rebuilt. Correct defects in drainage. Incorporate gypsum into heavy soils; repeat in three weeks. Dig granite dust, rock phosphate and quantities of organic matter into soil. Allow time for settling before planting.

Fertilize: Daylilies, spuria, Louisiana, and bearded irises with complete fertilizer. Give strawberries 1 teaspoon ammonium sulfate, keeping six inches away from plant. Fertilize pansies with manure tea or blood meal. Water in.

Fruits: Plant fruit trees. Mulch figs with grass or straw to prevent freeze damage to crown.

House Plants: Water when surface soil is crumbly dry. Wash dust off leaves to open pores. Mist often. Inspect for diseases and insects. Reduce water for poinsettias.

Lawns: Remove thatch, aerate, and feed with low nitrogen mixture.

Pests: For petal blight prevention, spray azaleas and camellias as flowers open. Spray for scale with dormant oil solution if temperature will be above 35° and below 85° for next 48 hours. *Always* read and heed manufacturer's directions *before* spraying. See INSECT chapter.

Propagation: Ivy cuttings root easily this month and next. Root cuttings of shrubs in mixture of loam and coarse sand; keep damp and semishaded until rooted.

Prune: Fruit trees in advance of new growth. Prune to groom and shape. Do not remove too much. See TREES. Remove dead wood from trees and shrubs before spring buds swell, but do not prune spring bloomers. Prune crapemyrtles. Prune nandinas and others of similar growth habit by cutting unwanted canes out at base of plant. See PRUNING.

Roses: Annual pruning about the middle of February, just before the spring buds break. To prevent later appearance of disease in the old beds, keep garden clean of debris and weeds. Complete preparation of new beds for roses. See ROSES chapter.

Transplanting: January is one of the best months to transplant woody plants, both evergreen and deciduous, especially trees. Energy will be expended on roots instead of foliage. Learn ultimate size and cultural needs of tree or plant before buying. Consider dwarf varieties to avoid crowding later. Group plants of similar cultural needs. Do not work wet soil. Assure good drainage. Keep plants moist.

Vegetables: Prepare beds, preferably raised for drainage, with about 50% humus, including rotted manure. Refer to VEGETABLE and SOIL chapters.

Winter Protection: Expect freeze any time; plan for protection of tender plants. Water. Remove coverings, particularly plastic, when temperature rises. Protect low plants with dry leaves, pine needles or soil mulch, but remove when weather warms.

February

"A February face, so full of frost, of storm, and cloudiness."
—Shakespeare

J.M.K.

SEEDS
which may now
be sown in flats (f)
or open ground (o)

Alyssum, Sweet, *f* or *o*
Arctotis, *f* or *o*
Babysbreath, *f* or *o*
Blanket flower
   (Gaillardia), *f* or *o*
Browallia, *f*
Calendula, *f*
Calliopsis, *f* or *o*
Candytuft, *o*
Chinese Forget-Me
   -Not, *f*
Cleome, *o*
Coreopsis, *f* or *o*
Cornflower, *f* or *o*
Cosmos, Early, *f* or *o*
Dahlia, Dwarf, *o*
Daisy, in variety, *f* or *o*
Everlasting, *f* or *o*
Feverfew, *f*
Forget-Me-Not, *f* or *o*
Four-o'clock, *o*
Gayfeather, *o*
Globe Amaranth, *f*
Hollyhock, *f*
Larkspur, *o*
Lobelia, *f*
Lupine, *o*
Mallow, *f*
Marigold, *o*
Nasturtium, *o*
Penstemon, *o*

Petunia, *f* or *o*
Phlox, Drummond, *o*
Pinks (Dianthus), *f* or *o*
Salpiglossis, *f* or *o*
Salvia,
   Blue, *f* or *o*
   Scarlet, *f* or *o*
Scabiosa, *f* or *o*
Snapdragon, *f* or *o*
Stock, Dwarf, *f*
Strawflower, *f* or *o*
Sweet Pea,
   Early, *o*
   Late, *o*
Tobacco, Flowering,
   f or *o*
Verbena, *f* or *o*

PLANTS
which may now be
placed in the open
ground

Ageratum
Alyssum, Sweet
Arctotis
Bluebells
Calendula
Chinese Forget-Me-Not
Columbine
Coreopsis
Cornflower
Daisy,
   English
   Michaelmas
   Shasta
Delphinium

Forget-Me-Not
Four-o'clock
Fruit Trees
Gaillardia
Gerbera
Hollyhock
Honeysuckle
Larkspur
Lemon Balm
Lobelia
Lupine
Mint
Nicotiana
Oregano
Pansy
Petunia
Phlox,
   Creeping
   Drummond
   Louisiana
Physostegia
Pinks (Dianthus)
Queen Anne's-lace
Roses
Rosemary
Sage
Salvia, Blue
Scabiosa
Shrimp Plant
Shrubs
Snapdragon
Stock
Sweet William
Trees

Verbena
Viola
Violet
Wallflower

BULBS, TUBERS,
RHIZOMES
which may now be
placed in the open
ground

Agapanthus
Allium
Alpinia (Ginger)
Alstroemeria
Amarcrinum
Amaryllis
Blackberry Lily
Calla
Canna
Chlidanthus
Cooperia
Crinum
Dahlia
Dietes
Gladiolus
Gloriosa (Climbing Lily)
Habranthus
Haemanthus
Hedychium
   (Butterfly Lily)
Hemerocallis
Hymenocallis

Anemones

J.M.K.

4

Iris,
 Bearded
 Dwarf
Ismene
Kniphofia (Torch Lily)
Liriope
Milla
Montbretia
Neomarica
 (Walking Iris)
Oxalis
Ranunculus
Scilla
Sisyrinchium
Sprekelia
Tigridia
Tuberose
Tulbaghia
Zephyranthes

PLANTS which bloom in February

---

t–Tree *s*–Shrub *v*–Vine
b–Bulb, Tuber or Rhizome
e–Evergreen *d*–Deciduous
p–Perennial *hn*–Biennial
a–Annual

Alyssum, Sweet, *a*
Azalea, *s e*
Bougainvilleas, *v e*
Calendula, *a*
Calla Lily, *b*
Calycanthus
 Floridus, *s d*
Camellia, Japonica, *s e*
Candytuft, *a*
Chinese Forget-
 Me-Not, *a*
Cornflower, *a*
Daisy,
 African Golden, *a*
 English, *a*
Daphne, Winter, *s e*
Gerbera, *p*

Heather,
 Mediterranean, *s e*
Honeysuckle, *s d*
 fragrantissima
 Morrowii
 tartarian
Hyacinth, Roman, *b*
Iris, *b*
Jasmine,
 Carolina, *v e*
 nudiflorum, *s d*
 primrose, *s e*
 pubescens, *v* or *s e*
Lantana, Weeping, *s d*
Moss Pink, *p*
Narcissus, *b*
Oxalis, *b*
Pansy, *a*
Parsley Hawthorn, *t d*
Petunia, *a*
Phlox, Drummond, *a*
Pinks, *a* and *bn*
Quince, Japanese
 Flowering, *s d*
Scilla, *b*
Snowdrop, *b*
Snowflake, *b*
Spirea, *s d*
 prunifolia
 thunbergi
Stock, *a* and *bn*
Sweet Olive, *s e*
Sweet Pea, *a*
Verbena, *p*
Viburnum, *s e*
 tinus
 suspensum
 japonicum
Vinca, *v e*
Viola, *a*
Violet, *p*

Azaleas: Plants may be moved. Keep watered. Must have good drainage. See AZALEAS chapter.

Bulbs: Plant summer flowering bulbs now. Gladioli every two weeks from January through May and from July through October for succession of bloom. Divide crowded daylilies; side dress with fertilizer.

Camellias: Pick up, and discard all old blooms. Reproduce plants by grafting.

Cuttings: Most favorable month to set cuttings of hardwood shrubs, trees and vines.

Fertilize: Trees, shrubs (except azaleas, camellias, pink magnolias) with complete fertilizer, watered in, keeping it away from trunks and stems of plants. Fertilize with organic-base product containing trace elements. Many use slow-release fertilizer to save time and effort. Use plant tablets to feed pot plants. Destroy insects as you work. Treat hydrangeas for color. See SHRUBS chart.

Lawns: Treat St. Augustine with fungicide to avoid Brown Patch whenever it appears. Treat and water discolored lawn areas first.

Maidenhair: While dormant and thin, work bone meal into the soil. Divide and reset. Water

well. Will spread quickly.

Perennials: Divide, separate, and transplant.

Pruning: Last chance for figs, other fruit trees and many shrubs to avoid losing summer bloom. Remove diseased, dead or weak wood. See PRUNING.

Roses: Plant bare root not later than February. Check new leaves and buds for aphids. Annual pruning now. Spray rose beds with fungicide to prevent Black Spot. *Do not* fertilize newly planted rose bushes until after first blooming.

Spray: Peach and plum trees when 75% of flowers have fallen to control fruit or brown rot. Spray shrubs for scale. Use soluble iron on acid-loving plants if pH is high. Use high pressure stream of soapy (not detergent) water to remove aphids.

Vegetables: Set out cool-weather varieties. Sow seeds of summer varieties in flats. See VEGETABLE chapter.

Winter Protection: February 10th is average date of last frost, but freezes can come later. Budding pecan trees seem to be reliable sign danger is past.

March

*"Ah, March! we know
thou art kind-hearted,
spite of ugly looks and
threats, and, out of sight,
art nursing April's violets."*
—Helen Hunt Jackson

R.M.

SEEDS
which may now
be sown in flats *(f)*
or open ground *(o)*

Ageratum, *f* or *o*
  after 15th
Alyssum, Sweet, *f* or *o*
Arctotis, *f* or *o*
Bells-of-Ireland, *f* or *o*
Blanket flower
  (Gaillardia), *f* or *o*
Browallia, *o*
Calliopsis, *f* or *o*
Candytuft, *o*
Castor Bean, *o*
Chinese Forget-Me
  -Not, *f* or *o*
Cleome, *o*
Cockscomb, *f* or *o*
Coleus, *f* or *o*
Coral Vine, *f* or *o*
Cosmos, Early, *f* or *o*
Cypressvine, *o*
Dahlia, Dwarf, *o*
Daisy, African Golden, *o*
Impatiens, *f*
Lobelia, *f*
Mallow, *f* or *o*
Marigold, *o*
Moonflower, *o*
Morning-Glory, *o*
Nasturtium, *o*
Periwinkle, *f* or *o*
Petunia, *f* or *o*

Phlox, Drummond, *o*
Portulaca, *o* after 15th
Salpiglossis, *f* or *o*
Salvia,
  Blue, *f* or *o*
  Scarlet, *f* or *o*
Scabiosa, *f* or *o*
Sunflower, *o*
Sweet Pea, Perennial, *o*
Sweet Sultan, *o*
Tithonia, *o*
Tobacco,
  Flowering, *f* or *o*
Torenia, *f*
Verbena, *f* or *o*
Vinca, *o*
Zinnia, *f*

PLANTS
which may now be
placed in the open
ground

Ageratum
Alyssum, Sweet
Arctotis
Azalea
Blanket flower
Bluebells
Browallia
Butterflyweed
Calendula
Calliopsis
Camellia
Candytuft

Carnation
Chinese Forget-Me-Not
Coleus
Coral Vine
Coreopsis
Cornflower
Cosmos, Klondyke
  Late
Dahlia, Dwarf
Daisy,
  Michaelmas
  Shasta
Delphinium
Dusty Miller
Eranthemum
Ferns
Feverfew
Forget-Me-Not
Four-o'clock
Geranium, after 15th
Gerbera
Hibiscus
Honeysuckle
Hydrangea
Jasmine,
  Day-blooming
  Night-blooming
Lantana
Larkspur
Lemon Verbena
Lobelia
Lupine
Lythrum
Mallow
Marigold, after 15th
Mistflower
Moonflower
Periwinkle
Petunia
Physostegia
Phlox,
  Perennial,
  Louisiana
Plumbago
Salvia
Scabiosa
Sedum
Shrimp Plant

Snapdragon
Sweet Sultan
  (Centaurea)
Verbena
Vinca
Wallflower
Zinnia

BULBS, TUBERS,
RHIZOMES
which may now be
placed in the open
ground

Achimenes
Agapanthus
Alstroemeria
Allium
Alpinia
Amarcrinum
Amaryllis
Billbergia
Blackberry Lily
Calla
Canna
Chlidanthus
Crinum
Dahlia
Dietes
Ginger Lily
Gladiolus
Gloriosa (Climbing Lily)
Habranthus
Haemanthus
Hedychium (Butterfly
  Lily)
Hemerocallis
Hosta
Hymenocallis
Iris, Louisiana
Ismene
Kniphofia
Liriope
Montbretia
Neomarica
  (Walking Iris)
Sisyrinchium

Sprekelia
Strelitzia (pot)
Tigridia
Tuberose
Tulbaghia
Water Hyacinth
Water Lily
Watsonia
Zephyranthes

PLANTS
which bloom in
March
(weather permitting)

t–Tree   *s*–Shrub   *v*–Vine
b–Bulb, Tuber or Rhizome
e–Evergreen   *d*–Deciduous
p–Perennial   *bn*–Biennial
a–Annual

Agarita, *s d*
Almond, Flowering, *s d*
Alyssum, Sweet, *a*
Amazon Lily, *b*
Anaqua, *t e*
Andromeda, *s e*
Anemone, *b*
Arctotis, *a*
Ardisia, *s e*
Azalea, *s d* and *e*
Bignonia, *v* and *p e*
Bluebonnet, *a*
Calendula, *a*
Calla *b*
Camellia, Japonica, *s e*
Candytuft, *a*
Cerastium, *p*
Cherry laurel, *t* or *s e*
Chinaberry, *t d*
Chionodoxa, *b*
Clivia, *b*
Cornflower, *a*
Crinum, *b*
Currant, Flowering, *s d*
Daffodil, *b*
Daisy, *p*

Daphne, *s e*
Delphinium, *a*
Dogwood, *t d*
Doxantha, *v d*
Flag, Native Iris, *b*
Fringetree, *t d*
Gerbera, *p*
Godetia, *a*
Grape-hyacinth, *b*
Guava, Pineapple, *s e*
Hawthorn, *t d*
Heather,
   Mediterranean, *s e*
Honeysuckle, *v d* and *s e*
Huisache, *t d*
Hyacinths, *b*
Iris, *b*
Ixia, *b*
Jasmines, *s e*
Jonquil, *b*
Kerria, *s d*
Laceflower, Blue, *a*
Lantana, *s d*
Larkspur, *a*
Laurel, Texas
   Mountain, *s* or *t e*
Magnolia, Star, *t d*
Mahonia, *s e*
Mexican Buckeye, *t d*
Milla, *b*
Moss Pink, *p*
Nandina, *s e*
Narcissus, *b*
Orchid Tree, *t d*
Ornithogalum
Oxalis, *b*
Pansy, *a*
Peach, *t d*
Pear, *t d*
Pearlbush, *s d*
Petunia, *a*
Phlox, *a* and *p*
Photinia, *s e*
Pinks, *a, bn* and *p*
Pittosporum, *s e*
Plums, *t d*
Poppies, *a*
Quince, Flowering, *s e*

Ranunculus, *b*
Redbud, *s* and *t d*
Scabiosa, *a, bn* and *p*
Silverbell Tree, *t d*
Snapdragon, *a*
Snowflake, *b*
Spireas, *s d*
Squill, *b*
Stock, *a* or *bn*
Styrax, native, *s d*
Sweet Olive, *s e*
Sweet Pea, *a s*
Tulip, *b*
Verbena, *p*
Viburnum, *s e*
Vinca, *v e*
Viola, *a*
Violet, *p*
Wallflower, *a*
Watsonia, *c*
Weigela, *s d*
Wild Flowers, *a p*
Wisteria, *v* or *t d*

Azaleas: To avoid azalea petal blight, spray every week as flowers open. Prune immediately after blooming and fertilize. May be sheared to thicken plants for screen or hedge. To keep natural shape cut branches at their origin.

Bulbs: Feed with 5-10-10, 1/2 cup per 10 square feet, keeping away from foliage. Water ground first. Water and rinse foliage after. Do not remove foliage until it is brown.

Camellias: Spray for tea scale. Fertilize lightly.

Color: Plan and plant now for summer blooms. Containers of seasonal color plants need at least 1/2 day sun. Water often.

Cultivation: Systematic surface cultivation of small bedding plants is essential to insure strong and rapid development. Mulch. Pinch chrysanthemums at main stem until fall. Divide and replant winter blooming iris. Sow most seeds now.

Fertilize: Shrubs and plants to stimulate rapid spring growth. Do not allow dry fertilizer to touch stems or leaves of young plants. Follow label directions carefully *when* applying. Never use stronger dilution than recommended. May burn plants, harm wildlife as well as people, and raise cost of gardening. Keep dry fertilizers away from stalks of plants and trunks of trees. *ALWAYS KEEP ALL FERTILIZERS, PESTICIDES AND HERBICIDES OUT OF REACH OF CHILDREN.* Feed flowering shrubs and trees following bloom. Fertilize early blooming bulbs (narcissus) with bone meal after bloom. Use high phosphorus fertilizer for more blooms on annuals and perennials. Exception: Nasturtiums, moonflower and morning glories bloom best in poor, fairly dry soil.

Herbs: Most may be planted now from seeds. Germination is often slow; plants are preferable. If seeds are planted, use flats of loose, well-draining, slightly alkaline soil; protect from full sun until plants are at least 2" tall then move gradually into partial sun. Transplant. Check chart on HERBS.

Hydrangeas: Shady locations—preferably north exposure—perfect drainage, and abundance of rotted compost in soil. Mulch and water copiously after plants are in leaf. Prune only dead wood now. Blooms on last year's branches. Acidify for blue color. See SHRUBS chart.

Lawns: Rake or use thatcher to remove dead growth. Apply complete, controlled-release or organic-base fertilizer, manure or sludge type fertilizer. Raking, or thatching and aerating may be all lawn needs, especially if foundation soil contains quantity of humus and drains well. Application of gypsum may help drainage. Watch for new varieties of pest and disease-resistant grasses. Water lawn night before feeding and again after application. See LAWNS chapter.

Flowering Dogwood   J.M.K.

Maidenhair: Does well on north side of house or in shade under trees. Pieces of well-rotted bark or wood placed under the roots prove helpful. Compost added to sandy loam is ideal for spongy soil, good drainage. Keep beds moist.

Mulch: Freshen compost mulch where necessary.

Palms: Feed with organic based 13-13-13.

Pests: Watch for aphids on new growth; also red spider and cut worm. Hand pick when possible. See DISEASES, INSECTS & WEEDS chapter.

Pruning: Finish pruning roses and dormant shrubs. Branches damaged by freeze should be cut back to green wood. See PRUNING chapter.

Roses: Follow monthly feeding and spraying program. Weekly fungicide spraying for Black Spot is recommended. Organic fertilizers excellent for seasonal balance. A handful of fertilizer high in phosphorus, such as 12-24-12, may be broadcast around each established bush. Water before and after. Liquid and foliar feeding are faster, but do not last as long. A combination of methods, used at different times, is often successful. *Do not* feed new bushes until after first blooming. Water by soaking. Try miniature roses. See ROSES chapter for details.

Tuberose: Remove bulblets from old bulbs and plant separately for future bloom, or plant new bulbs now. Cover with two inches of soil.

Vegetables: Beds prepared at least three weeks earlier may be ready for planting. Weather permitting, transplant seedlings. If soil sticks to trowel, wait for dryer weather. Vegetables should grow quickly to be flavorful. Sun and well-drained, loose, rich soil are essential. If pecan trees have budded out, it should be safe to plant tender vegetables outdoors. Vegetables and herbs may be interplanted with annuals and perennials if their cultural needs are alike and if they have enough space. Peppers, eggplants, asparagus roots, kale, chard, parsley, lettuce, radishes and others may be used successfully with flowers. This diversity may retard insect infestation. A plant of French marigold and sweet basil to every four tomato plants may be an insect repellant. Weed, mulch and water. Hand pick insects early in a.m.. If pesticides or fungicides are needed, *BE SURE BEFORE USING* they are intended for food crops, use exactly according to directions; take note of the waiting date to harvest after spraying or dusting.

Water: Always before and after fertilizing.

April

*"Oh, the lovely fickleness
of an April day!"*
—W. H. Gibson

P.P.

SEEDS
which may now
be sown in flats *(f)*
or open ground *(o)*

Ageratum, *f* or *o*
Alyssum, Sweet, *f* or *o*
Amaranthus, *o*
Balsam, Garden, *f* or *o*
Blanket flower, *f* or *o*
Castor Bean, *o*
Celosia, *o*
Cleome, *o*
Cockscomb, *f* or *o*
Coleus, *o*
Coral Vine, *o*
Cosmos, *o*
Cypressvine, *o*
Dahlia, Dwarf, *o*
Feverfew, *o*
Four-o'clock, *o*
Globe Amaranth, *o*
Gourd, *o*
Impatiens, *f*
Marigold, *o*
Moonflower, *o*
Morning-Glory, *o*
Nasturtium, *o*
Periwinkle, *f* or *o*
Petunia, *f* or *o*
Portulaca, *o*
Queen Anne's-lace, *o*
Salvia, *o*
Scabiosa, *o*
Sunflower, *o*
Sweet Pea, Perennial, *o*

Tithonia, *o*
Torenia, *f*
Vinca, *o*
Zinnia, *f*

PLANTS
which may now be
placed in the open
ground

Acalypha
Ageratum
Alternanthera
Alyssum
Amarantha
Aralia
Balsam, Garden
Banana
Begonia, Bedding
Bluebells
Browallia
Butterflyweed
Calliopsis
Canterbury Bells
Carnation
Chinese Forget-Me-Not
Chrysanthemum
Cleome
Cockscomb
Coral Vine
Cosmos
Croton
Dahlia, Dwarf
Dusty-Miller
Eranthemum
Feverfew

Four-o'clock
Geranium
Gerbera
Hibiscus
Honeysuckle
Jasmine
Lantana
Lemon-grass
Lemon-verbena
Lythrum
Mallow
Marigold
Mistflower
Moonflower
Periwinkle
Petunia
Phlox,
   Louisiana
   Perennial
Physostegia
Plumbago
Potato vine
Queen Anne's-lace
Salpiglossis
Salvia
Sedum
Shrimp Plant
Snapdragon
Sweet Sultan
Tobacco, Flowering
Torenia
Verbena
Vines, Flowering
Violet
Wallflower
Zinnia

BULBS, TUBERS,
RHIZOMES
which may now be
placed in the open
ground

Achimenes
Agapanthus
Alpinia (Ginger)
Amarcrinum

Amaryllis
Calla
Canna
Chlidanthus
Crinum
Dahlia
Dietes
Galtonia
Ginger Lily
Gladiolus
Gloriosa (Climbing Lily)
Haemanthus
Hedychium (Butterfly
   Lily)
Hemerocallis (Daylily)
Hymenocallis (Spider
   Lily)
Lachenalia (Pot)
Liriope
Lycoris
Montbretia
Neomarica
   (Walking Iris)
Sprekelia
Tigridia
Tuberose
Tulbaghia
Water Lily
Zephyranthes

PLANTS
which bloom in
April

---

t–Tree   *s*–Shrub   *v*–Vine
b–Bulb, Tuber or Rhizome
e–Evergreen   *d*–Deciduous
p–Perennial   *bn*–Biennial
a–Annual

Ageratum, *a* or *p*
Almond, Flowering, *t d*
Alyssum, Sweet, *a*
Amaryllis, *b*
Anaqua, *t e*
Anemone, *b*
Aralia, *s d*

9

Arctotis, *a*
Azalea, *s d* and *e*
Babysbreath, *a*
Begonia, Bedding, *a*
Bignonia, *v e p*
Bluebonnet, *a*
Bottlebrush, *s e*
Calendula, *a*
Calla, *b*
Camellia, japonica, *s e*
Candytuft, *a*
Canterbury Bell, *a* or *p*
Catalpa, *t d*
Chinaberry, *t d*
Chinese Forget-Me-
   Not, *a*
Chionodoxa, *b*
Citrus trees and
   shrubs, *e*

Clethra, *s d*
Columbine, *p*
Coralbean, *s d*
Cornflower, *a*
Crabapples, *t d*
Crinum, *b*
Currant, Indian,
   (Coralberry) *s d*
Dahlia, *b*
Daisies, *a*
Daphne, *s e*
Daylily, *t*
Delphinium, *a*
Ebony, Texas, *t e*
Eucharis, *b*
False-Indigo, *s d*
Feverfew, *a* and *p*
Forget-Me-Not, *a* and *p*
Gazania, *p*

Geranium, *p*
Gerbera, *p*
Gladiolus, *b*
Godetia, *a*
Gorse, *s e*
Guava, Pineapple, *s e*
Hawthorne, *t d*
Honeysuckle, *s* and *v*
Horse-Chestnut,
   Dwarf, *s d*
Huckleberry, *s* and *t d*
Hyacinth, *b*
India Hawthorn, *s e*
Indian Paintbrush, *a*
Iris, *b*
Jack-in-the-Pulpit, *b*
Jasmines, *v* and *s e*
Kerria, *s d*
Laceflower, *a*

Lantana, *s d*
Larkspur, *a*
Ligustrum, Privet, *s e*
Lilies, *b*
Lobelia, *a*
Locust, Black, *t d*
Love-in-a-Mist, *a*
Lupine, *a*
Magnolia, *t e*
Magnolia fuscata, *s e*
Milla, *b*
Mimosa, *t d*
Mockorange, *s d*
Narcissus, poeticus, *b*
Nasturtium, *a*
Ornithogalum, *b*
Oxalis, *b*
Pandorea, *v*
Pansy, *a*

J.M.K.

Texas' State Flower: Bluebonnets (Lupinus subcarnosus, L. texensis)

Parkinsonia, *t d*
Pearlbush, *s d*
Penstemon, *p*
Petunia, *a*
Phlox,
   Drummond, *a*
   subulata, *p*
   Louisiana, *p*
Photinia, *s e*
Pinks, *a bn p*
Pittosporum, *s e*
Pomegranate, *s d*
Poppies, *a*
Pyracantha, *s e*
Queen Anne's Lace, *a*
Rocket, *a* or *p*
Roses, *s d*
Salt Cedar, *s d*
Salvia, blue, *p*
Gregg, *s d*
Scabiosa, *a* or *p*
Schizanthus, *a*
Sedum, *p*
Shrimp Plant, *p*
Silver Bell Tree, *t d*
Snapdragon, *a*
Sparaxis, *b*
Spirea, *s d*
Stock, *a* or *bn*
Sweet Olive, *s e*
Sweet Pea, *v a*
Sweetshrub, *s d*
Tulip, *b*
Tulip Tree, *t d*
Verbena, *p*
Viburnum, *s*
Viola, *a*
Violet, *p*
Wallflower, *a*
Watsonia, *c*
Weigela, *s d*
Weaver's-Broom, *s d*
Wild Flowers, *a* and *p*
Wild Olive, *t d*
Wisteria, *v d*

Azaleas: Prune after bloom, now if not pre-viously. Check soil acid-ity. Late April, spray for disease prevention and insect control; fertilize again 4 to 6 weeks after first feeding; work into soil with fingers, not hoe. Water.

Bulbs: Fertilize with bone meal after blooming. Allow foliage of spring bloomers to die on plant to feed bulb. When cut-ting lilies, leave about 1/4 of stem to mature bulb. Leave at least four leaves on lower part of stem when cutting gladioli. Separate water lilies and renew earth in tubs.

Camellias: Check soil acidity. Spray with fun-gicide for dieback control. Prune.

Chrysanthemums: Di-vide last of April or early May. If divided earlier, plants are apt to grow woody and make poor flowers. New shoots make better plants than old central root. Pinch tips for bushier growth and more blooms.

Cutting of Blossoms: Cut flowers freely, espe-cially stock, pinks, arc-totis, coreopsis, snap-dragon, and petunia to prolong blossoming pe-riod. Enjoy the blossoms of spring flowering shrubs, for cutting merely amounts to pruning, which should be done anyway as soon as the flowering season is over. See PRUNING.

Fertilize: See SHRUBS chart. Feed gardenias and magnolias with azalea food (acid) scratched into soil and watered well. Mulch with compost containing manure and pine needles.

Growth: Three main ele-ments for healthy plant growth are: nitrogen for leaf and stem; phospho-rus for fruit, bloom and root; and potash for vigor and winter protection.

Herbs: Set out plants of chamomile, coriander (cilantro), Italian parsley, basils, lemon balm, mints in variety, rosemary, sages, and thymes.

Layering: Many trees and shrubs, including pink magnolia, japonica, viburnum, honeysuckle, and many vines, such as wisteria and jasmine, may be successfully layered this month. Slit bark on underside of a branch, bend and fasten securely to ground and cover with about two inches of earth. Treat verbenas in same manner, except cover with only 1/2" of earth. See PROPAGATION.

Mulch: All flowers, shrubs and trees at time of planting. Replace on established plants. A mulch keeps the soil from caking, promotes healthy growth of plants and de-ters weeds. Mixed mulch materials allow more aeration and better pene-tration of water. Keep mulches 2" to 4" thick.

Mildew: Dust, while the dew is on the plants, with sulphur; or spray with fungicide.

Prune: Flowering quince, bridalwreath, weigela, deutzia, and other flow-ering shrubs and trees af-ter blooming. Prune and repot poinsettias. Shape as you prune. See PRUN-ING.

Roses: Continue fungi-cide spray for Black Spot. For aphids use hard sprays of water or remove by hand, before resorting to pesticide. Healthy plants are resistant to in-sects. See DISEASES chap-ter.

Vegetables: See Mulch above. Check in morn-ing for insects, and hand pick when possible.

Water: Deep watering. See WATER chapter. Or-namentals need one inch per week.

May

*"When Spring unlocks the
flowers to paint the
laughing soil."*
—Bishop Heber

J.M.K.

SEEDS
which may now
be sown in flats *(f)*
or open ground *(o)*

Ageratum, *f* or *o*
Alyssum, Sweet, *f* or *o*
Balsam, Garden, *f* or *o*
Castor Bean, *o*
Cleome, *o*
Cockscomb, *f* or *o*
Coleus, *f* or *o*
Coral Vine, *o*
Cosmos, *o*
Cypressvine, *o*
Dahlia, Dwarf, *o*
Feverfew, *o*
Four-o'clock, *o*
Globe Amaranth, *o*
Gourd, *o*
Impatiens, *f* or *o*
Marigold, *o*
Moonflower, *o*
Periwinkle, *o*
Petunia, *f* or *o*
Pinks, *o*
Portulaca, *o*
Scabiosa, *o*
Sunflower, *o*
Sweet Pea, Perennial, *o*
Tithonia, *o*
Torenia, *o*
Vinca, *o*
Zinnia, *o*

PLANTS
which may now be
placed in the open
ground

Acalypha
Ageratum
Alternanthera
Amarantha
Aralia
Balsam Garden
Banana
Begonia, Bedding
Blanket flower
Browallia
Butterflyweed
Calliopsis
Chrysanthemum
Cleome
Cockscomb
Coleus
Coral Vine
Cosmos
Croton
Dahlia, Dwarf
Eranthemum
Foliage plants
Four-o'clock
Geranium
Gerbera
Godetia
Hibiscus
Impatiens
Jasmine
Lantana
Lythrum

Mallow
Marigold
Mistflower
Moonflower
Morning Glory
Periwinkle
Petunia
Phlox, Louisiana
Physostegia
Plumbago
Portulaca
Potatovine
Purslane
Salvia
Sedum
Shrimp Plant
Sweet Sultan
Tithonia
Torenia
Verbena
Vines, Flowering
Violet
Wallflower
Zinnia

BULBS, TUBERS,
RHIZOMES
which may now be
placed in the open
ground

Achimenes
Alpinia (Ginger-like)
Alstroemeria
Alyssum
Amaryllis
Amarcrinum
Caladium
Canna
Carnation
Cooperia
Dahlia
Daisy
Dietes
Feverfew
Gladiolus
Gloriosa (Climbing Lily)

Habranthus
Hedychium
    (Butterfly Lily)
Hemerocallis
Iris,
    Evansia
    Kaempferi
    Louisiana
Liriope
Lobelia
Lycoris
Montbretia
Neomarica
    (Walking Iris)
Tuberose
Water Hyacinth
Water Lily
Zephyranthes

PLANTS
which bloom in
May

t–Tree   *s*–Shrub   *v*–Vine
b–Bulb, Tuber or Rhizome
e–Evergreen   *d*–Deciduous
p–Perennial   **bn**–Biennial
a–Annual

Abelia, *s e*
Agapanthus, *b*
Ageratum, *a* or *p*
Alyssum, Sweet, *a*
Amaryllis, *b*
Anchusa, *a*
Arctotis, *a*
Azalea, *s e*
Babysbreath, *a*
Balloon-flower, *p*
Balsam, *a*
Barbados Cherry, *s e*
Beargrass, *s e*
Begonia, Bedding, *a*
Bignonia, *v p e*
Blanket flower, *a*
Blue-eyed Grass, *b*
Bluebonnet, *a*

Bottlebrush, *s e*
Bougainvillea, *s e* or *v e*
Browallia, *a*
Bushclover, *s d*
Butterflybush, *s d*
Butterflyweed, *p*
Calendula, *a*
Calla Lily, *b*
Calliopsis, *a*
Candytuft, *a*
Canna, *b*
Canterbury Bell, *bn*
Cape Jasmine, *s e*
Catalpa, *t d*
Chaste Tree, *t d*
China Aster, *a*
Chinese Forget-Me-
   Not, *a*
Citrus shrubs and trees
Clarkia, *a*
Columbine, *p*
Coralbean, *s d*
Coral tree, *t d*
Coreopsis, *a*
Cornflower, *a*
Cosmos, Early, *a*
Crinum, *b*
Dahlia, *b*
Daisies, *a* and *p*
Daylily, *t r*
Delphinium, *a*
Deutzia, *s d*
Duranta, *s d*
Elderberry, *s d*
Evening-primrose, *p*
Feverfew, *a* and *p*
Forget-Me-Not, *p*
Four-o'clock, *a*
Geranium, *p*
Gerbera, *p*
Gladiolus, *b*
Globe Amaranth, *a*
Godetia, *a*
Guava, Pineapple, *s e*
Hibiscus, *s e*
Hollyhock, *a* or *bn*
Honeysuckle,
   Common, *v e*

Hydrangea, *s d*
Impatiens, sultani, *a*
Indian Hawthorn, *s e*
Iris, *b*
Jasmines, *v* and *s*
Kerria, *s d*
Laceflower, Blue, *a*
Lantana, *s d*
Larkspur, *a*
Lavatera, *a*
Lily,
   Ace, *b*
   Easter, *b*
   Estate, *b*
   Madonna, *b*
   Spider, Wild, *b*
   Regal, *b*
   Tiger, *b*
Liriope, *b*
Lobelia, *a*
Lupine, *a*
Lythrum, *p*
Magnolia, *t e*
Mallow, *p*
Mimosa, *t d*
Mock orange, *s d*
Myrtle, Sweet, *s e*
Nasturtium, *a*
Nepeta, mussini, *p*
   (catnip)
Oleander, *s e*
Oxalis, *b*
Pansy, *a*
Parkinsonia, *t d*
Penstemon, *a*
Petunia, *a*
Phlox, Drummond, *a*
Pinks, *a, bn* and *p*
Plumbago, *p*
Poinciana, *s d*
Pomegranates, *s d*
Poppy, *a*
Portulaca, *a*
Potatovine, *v p*
Queen Anne's Lace, *a*
Rose. *s*
St. John's Wort, *s d*
Salt Cedar, *s* or *t d*

Salvia, *s d*
Scabiosa, *a* and *p*
Schizanthus, *a*
Sedum, *p*
Shrimp Plant, *p*
Snapdragon, *a*
Spirea, *s d*
Stock, *a*
Sunflower, *a* and *p*
Sweet Pea, *a*
Sweet Sultan, *a*
Tobacco, Flowering, *a*
Torenia, *a*
Trumpet vine, *v*
Verbena, *p*
Veronica, *p*
Viola, *a*
Vitex, *t*
Water Hyacinth, *b*
Waterlily, *b*
Waterpoppy, *p*
Wild Flowers, *p* and *a*
Zephyr Lily, *b*
Zinnia, *a*

Azaleas: Last chance to prune and fertilize. Keep mulch several inches thick at all times.

Camellias: Fertilize lightly for second time. Spray for tea scale. Keep mulch several inches thick at all times.

Chrysanthemums: Best month to divide. See "April."

Conifers: Water foliage, spray vigorously in late afternoon every two weeks from now on throughout the summer, on inner branches to prevent pests. Late afternoon

spraying avoids scalding. Watch for red spider and bag or basket worm.

Fall Garden: Several varieties in the plant list above will make garden rich in fall bloom. Practice garden cleanliness, removing dead wood and flowers. Pick up debris.

Fertilize: Bearded Iris and Louisiana Iris after blooming.

Gardenias: Drop leaves normally now. If buds drop off check drainage and pH of soil which should be slightly acid.

Hibiscus: Interchange fertilizer every other month: use superphosphate one month, 8-8-8 and copperas the next, until September. Water before and after each feeding.

Mulch: Maintain mulch at least two inches thick to keep roots cool, retain moisture in soil, add humus and deter weeds.

Peppers: Planted in sun or partial shade, they ornament the August garden and supply peppers until frost for the kitchen and the mockingbirds.

Potted Plants: Leach soil of accumulated salts by filling and draining pot with water about ten times. Repot if needed, using just one pot size larger. May be moved outside to shady spot for a vacation, perhaps half burying pot in soil. Plants like the fresh air and additional light outside. Any plant of cascading habit is especially suitable for hanging baskets.

Roses: Water first. Feed 1-2-1 ratio, organic base. Handful per bush, watered in, every 3-4 weeks. Spray for fungus. Cut out blind shoots. See ROSES chapter. 2 inches of water per week.

Pruning: Most spring flowering shrubs may be safely pruned after blooming.

Transplanting: Choose cloudy day. Retain sufficient earth around roots to prevent drying out and injury. Loosen soil in sides of planting hole for easier root penetration. Use transplanting solution, then water. Protect plant from sun, or transplant on cloudy day. Trees and shrubs should be partially defoliated. Keep moist for several days.

June

"It is the month of June,
The month of leaves
and roses,
When pleasant sights
salute the eyes,
And pleasant scents,
the noses"
　　　　—N. P. Willis

J.M.K.

SEEDS
which may now be sown in flats *(f)* or open ground *(o)*

Ageratum, *f*
Alyssum, Sweet, *f* or *o*
Balsam, Garden, *f* or *o*
Blanket flower
  (Gaillardia), *o*
Blue Lace Flower, *o*
Castor-bean, *o*
Cleome, *o*
Cockscomb, *f* or *o*
Coleus, *f* or *o*
Cosmos, *o*
Dahlia, Dwarf, *o*
Feverfew, *o*
Four-o'clock, *o*
Impatiens, *o*
Marigold, *o*
Moonflower, *o*
Morning Glory, *o*
Periwinkle, *f* or *o*
Portulaca, *o*
Sunflower, *o*
Tithonia, *o*
Torenia, *o*
Vinca, *o*
Zinnia, *o*

PLANTS
which may now be placed in the open ground

Acalypha
Ageratum
Alternanthera
Amaranthus
Artemisia
Aspidistra
Balsam
Begonia
Blanket flower
Bloodleaf (Iresine)
Browallia
Chrysanthemum
Cleome
Cockscomb
Coleus
Copperleaf
Coreopsis
Cosmos, Klondyke
Croton
Dahlia, Dwarf
Dusty Miller
Feverfew
Four-o'clock
Geranium
Hollyhock
Impatiens
Marigold
Michaelmas Daisy
Periwinkle

Petunia
Pinks
Plumbago
Portulaca
Purslane
Salvia
Shrimp Plant
Sweet Sultan
Tithonia
Tobacco, Flowering
Torenia
Verbena
Vinca
Wallflower
Zinnia

BULBS, TUBERS, RHIZOMES
which may now be placed in the open ground

Aspidistra
Billbergia (Bromeliad)
Caladium
Canna
Crinum
Dahlia
Daylily
Dietes
Eucharis
Habranthus
Haemanthus
Hemerocallis
Iris,
  Evansia
  Kaempferi
  Louisiana
Lycoris
Neomarica
  (Walking Iris)
Oxalis
Sisyrinchium
Sprekelia
Tulbaghia
Water Lily
Zephyranthes

PLANTS
which bloom in
June

t–Tree *s*–Shrub *v*–Vine
b–Bulb, Tuber or Rhizome
e–Evergreen *d*–Deciduous
p–Perennial *bn*–Biennial
a–Annual

Abelia, *s e*
Achimenes, *b*
Agapanthus, *b*
Ageratum, *a* or *p*
Allamanda, *v p e*
Althaea, *s d*
Alstroemeria, *b*
Alyssum, Sweet, *a*
Balloon-flower, *p*
Balsam, *a*
Barbados Cherry, *s e*
Bean, Scarlet Runner, *v a*
Begonia, Bedding, *a*
Blackberry Lily, *b*
Blanket flower, *a*

Bluebell, Texas,
(Lisianthus), *a*
Blue-Eyed Grass, *b*
Bougainvillea, *v e*
Browallia, *a*
Bushclover, *s d*
Butterflybush, *s d*
Butterflyweed, *p*
Buttonbush, *s d*
Caladium, *b*
Calliopsis, *a*
Canna, *b*
Cape Jasmine, *s e*
Cardinal Climber, *v a*
Catnip, *p*
Chaste Tree, *s* or *t d*
China Aster, *a*
Chinese Forget-Me-
Not, *a*
Clarkia, *a*
Clematis, *v pt*
Cleome, *a*
Clerodendron, *p*
Clitoria, *v a*
Cockscomb, *a*
Coneflower, *p*

Confederate Rose, *s d*
Coral tree, *t d*
Coral Vine, *v p*
Coreopsis, *p*
Cosmos, *a*
Crapemyrtle, *s* or *t d*
Crinum, *b*
Cypressvine, *v a*
Dahlia, *b*
Daisies, *a* or *p*
Datura Metel, *a*
Daylily, *b*
Duranta, *s d*
Elderberry, *s d*
Everlastings, *a*
False-Dragonhead, *p*
Feverfew, *a* and *p*
Forget-Me-Not, *p*
Four o'clock, *p*
Geranium, *p*
Gerbera, *p*
Gladiolus, *b*
Globe Amaranth, *a*
Grand Duke Jasmine, *s e*
Hibiscus, *s e*
Hollyhock, *a* or *bn*

Honeysuckle, *v e*
and *v p d*
Hydrangea, *s d*
Impatiens, sultani, *a*
Iris, *b*
Ismene,(Lily), *b*
Jacobean Lily, *b*
Jacobinia, *s e*
Jasmines, *s*
Kerria, *s d*
Lantana, *s d*
Larkspur, *a*
Lemon Verbena, *h d*
Leucophyllum, *s e*
Lilies, *b*
Liriope, *b*
Lobelia, *a*
Lythrum, *p*
Madeira-vine, *v p*
Marigold, *a*
Magnolia, *t e*
Mallow, *p*
Mimosa, *t d*
Montbretia, *b*
Morning Glory, *v a*
Morning Glory Tree, *s d*

Yellow Daylilies. (Hemerocallis)

J.M.K.

Moss Pink, *p*
Neomarica
   (Walking Iris), *b*
Nasturtium, *a*
Oleander, *s e*
Parkinsonia, *t d*
Passionflower, *v p*
Periwinkle, *a*
Petunia, *a*
Phlox,
   Drummond, *a*
   perennial, *p*
Pinks, *a, bn* and *p*
Plumbago, *p*
Poinciana, *s d*
Pomegranate, *s d*
Portulaca, *a*
Potato Vine, *v p*
Rain Lily, *b*
Roses, *s d*
Rose Acacia, *s d*
Rose Mallow, *p*
Sage, Desert, *s e*
St. John's-Wort, *s d*
Salpiglossis, *a*
Salt Cedar, *s d*
Salvias, *s p* and *a*
Scabiosa, *a* and *p*
Sedum, *p*
Shrimp Plant, *p*
Silver-lace Vine, *v p*
Snapdragon, *a* and *p*
Spirea, *s d*
Stokesia, *a*
Sunflower, *a*
Sweet Sultan, *a*
Thunbergia, *v a*
Tithonia, *a*
Tobacco, Flowering, *a*
Torenia, *a*
Trumpet Vine, *v p*
Tuberose, *b*
Turk's Cap, *s e*
Valeriana, *a*
Verbena, *p*
Veronica, *p*
Water-hyacinth, *b*
Waterlily, *b*

Water poppy, *p*
Willow, Flowering, *s d*
Yucca, *s e*
Zephyr Lily, *b*
Zinnia, *a*

Azaleas and Camellias:
Water by deep soaking once a week or as needed during hot weather.

Chlorosis: If leaves are yellowing with veins remaining green, apply 1 T agricultural sulfur per plant. Scratch into soil, water.

Fertilize: Water annuals with solution of one tbsp. ammonium sulphate (21-0-0) dissolved in three gallons of water for a slow- acting acidifying re-action. Manure, manure tea, and phosphates en-courage blooms. 13-13-13 in solution of one tea-spoon to one gallon wa-ter is good general fertil-izer. Slow release fertiliz-ers are time savers.

Lawns: Brown spots in-dicate chinch bug or fun-gus damage.

Mulch: Keep beds well mulched, except bearded iris. Flowering quince likes a 3"-4" mulch of compost or pine needles; do not disturb shallow root system.

Perennials: To bloom well geraniums like good

garden soil low in nitro-gen, with pH 6.5-7.5, fairly dry soil, sun. In hottest months, full morning sun or bright shade is enough. Dusty Miller (*Centaurea cineraria argentea*) has gray-white leaves which provide a fine color and texture contrast to bright geranium blossoms; same cultural needs. Check pH of soil.

Pests: Busy month for insects. Frequent spraying and dusting may be nec-essary. Take care; use weaker solutions. Do not use sulphur dust when temperature is over 85°. Wear protective clothing and gloves. Do not burn plants. Watch for pow-dery mildew on roses, crape myrtles, zinnias, euonymus and treat. Watch for flying beetles, "June Bugs", and destroy. Their larvae destroy lawn grass. Use insect-repellent light bulbs. Spray cannas with soapy water to deter leaf rollers, or pick them off. See DISEASES, IN-SECTS, WEEDS chapter. Eliminate Poison Oak and Poison Ivy. See POISON-OUS PLANTS. Use herbi-cide as directed.

Roses: After the blossom period of climbing roses, the old and new wood is easily distinguishable. Cut out oldest canes and all dead wood. Feed roses

lightly. They need 2" of water per week. Groom bushes as flowers are cut, keeping center of bush open. Cut just above out-side bud.

Staking: Many tall-grow-ing plants will be less apt to overcrowd and will better attain their proper beauty and strength if not allowed to spread over the beds. Bamboo stakes are good. Tie firmly to the stake, but loosely about the stems of the plant.

Vegetables: Pick okra pods young to avoid sucking insects which cause curling and bumpy pods. Try cherry toma-toes, climbing (Malabar) spinach, Japanese egg-plant and herbs in hang-ing baskets.

Watering: As in April. Bougainvillea, geraniums, ixoras, kalanchoes, moonflowers, morning glories are among plants that like dryish soil. Do not overwater. Potted plants outside may need watering once or more a day. Wilting in noon sun does not signify dryness, but wilting in early morn-ing or late afternoon does. Plants benefit from spraying water on foliage, but not during heat of day. Always water before and after fertilizing, and water deeply.

July

*"The summer looks out
from her brazen tower,
Through the flashing bars
of July."*
—Francis Thompson

C.W.H.

SEEDS
**which may now
be sown in flats (f)
or open ground (o)**

Ageratum, *f*
Alyssum, Sweet, *f* or *o*
Balsam, Garden, *f* or *o*
Blanket flower, *o*
Bluebonnet, *o*
Castor-bean, *o*
Cockscomb, *f* or *o*
Cosmos, Late, *o*
Four-o'clock, *o*
Marigold, *o*
Moonflower, *o*
Morning-Glory, *o*
Pansy, *f*
Petunia, *f* or *o*
Portulaca, *o*
Sunflower, *o*
Tithonia, *o*
Torenia, *o*
Vinca, *f* or *o*
Zinnia, *o*

PLANTS
**which may now be
placed in the open
ground**

Acalypha
Ageratum
Alternanthera
Aspidistra
Begonia
Blanket flower
   (Gaillardia)
Bloodleaf
Calliopsis
Chrysanthemum
Cockscomb
Coleus
Copperleaf
Cosmos, Klondyke
Croton
Dahlia, Dwarf
Feverfew
Foliage Plants
Four-o'clock
Geranium
Gerbera
Impatiens
Marigold
Periwinkle
Petunia
Phlox
Pinks
Portulaca
Salvia
Shrimp Plant
Tithonia
Tobacco, Flowering
Torenia
Vinca
Zinnia

BULBS, TUBERS, RHIZOMES
**which may now be
placed in the open
ground**

Amaryllis
Billbergia
Caladium
Cooperia
Crinum
Dahlia
Gladiolus
Hemerocallis
Iris,
   Evansia
   Kaempferi
   Roof
Liriope
Lycoris
Neomarica
   (Walking Iris)
Oxalis
Tulbaghia
Water Hyancinth
Water Lily

PLANTS
**which bloom in
July**

t–Tree   *s*–Shrub   *v*–Vine
b–Bulb, Tuber or Rhizome
e–Evergreen   *d*–Deciduous
p–Perennial   *bn*–Biennial
a–Annual

Abelia, *s e*
Achimenes, *b*
Ageratum, *a* or *p*
Allamanda, *v p*
Althaea, *s d*
Alyssum, Sweet, *a*
Balloon-flower, *p*
Balsam, *a*
Barbados Cherry, *s e*

Bean, Scarlet Runner, *v a*
Begonia, Bedding, *a*
Bignonia, *v p*
Blackberry Lily, *b*
Bluebell, Texas, *a*
Bougainvillea, *v e*
Browallia, *a*
Bushclover, *s d*
Butterflybush, *s d* or *e*
Butterflyweed, *p*
Buttonbush, *s d*
Caladium, *b*
Calliopsis, *a*
Canna, *b*
Cape Jasmine, *s e*
Cardinal Climber, *v a*
Catnip, *p*
Celosia, *a*
Chaste Tree, *s* or *t d*
Chinese Forget-Me-
   Not, *a*
Clematis, *v p*
Cleome, *a*
Clitoria, *s a*
Cockscomb, *a*
Coleus, *a*
Coneflower, *p*
Confederate Rose, *s d*
Coral tree, *t d*
Coral Vine, *v p*
Coreopsis, *p*
Cosmos, *a*
Crabapple, *t*
Crape myrtle, *s* or *t d*
Crinum, *b*
Cypressvine, *v a*
Dahlia, *b*
Daisies, *p*
Datura Metel, *a*
Daylily, *b*
Duranta, *s d*
Elderberry, *s d*
Everlastings, *a*
False-Dragonhead, *p*
Feverfew, *a* and *p*
Forget-Me-Not, *p*
Four-o'clock, *p*
Gaillardia, *a*

17

Gayfeather, *p*
Geranium, *p*
Gerbera, *p*
Gladiolus, *b*
Globe Amaranth, *a*
Habranthus, *b*
Hibiscus, *p*
Hollyhock, *a* or *bn*
Honeysuckle, *v e*
Impatiens, sultani, *a*
Iris, *b*
Jack bean, *v a*
Jacobinia, *s e*
Jasmines, *s d* and *e*
Kerria, *s d*
Kniphofia, *b*
Lantana, *s d*
Lapeirousia, *c*
Lemon Verbena, *s d*
Leucophyllum, *s e*
Lilies, *b*
Liriope, *b*
Lobelia, *a*
Lythrum, *p*
Madeira-vine, *v p*
Marigold, *a*
Mallow, *p*
Mexican Flame Vine, *a*
Mimosa, *t d*
Montbretia, *b*
Moonflower, *v a*
Morning Glory, *v a*
Morning Glory Tree, *s d*
Moss Pink, *p*
Nasturtium, Climbing, *a*
Oleander, *s e*
Oxalis, *b*
Parkinsonia, *t d*
Passionflower, *v p*
Periwinkle, *a*
Petunia, *a*
Phlox, Drummond, *a*
  perennial, *p*
Plumbago, *p*
Poinciana, *s d*
Pomegranate, *s d*
Portulaca, *a*
Potatovine, *v p*

Rainlily, *b*
Rangoon creeper, *v p e*
Roses, *s d*
St. John's-Wort, *s d*
Salt Cedar, *s d*
Salvias, *s p* and *a*
Sedum, *p*
Shrimp Plant, *p*
Silver-lace Vine, *v p*
Snapdragon, *a* and *p*
Spirea, *s d*
Strawflower, *a*
Sunflower, *a*
Thunbergia, *v a*
Tigridia, *b*
Tithonia, *a*
Tobacco, Flowering, *a*
Torenia, *a*
Trumpet creeper, *v p d*
Tuberose, *b*
Tulbaghia, *b*
Turk's Cap, *s e*
Valeriana, *a*
Verbena, *p*
Veronica, *p*
Water-hyacinth, *b*
Water lily, *b*
Water poppy, *p*
Willow, Flowering, *s d*
Wisteria, *v*
  Flowering, *v e*
Yucca, *s e*
Zephyr Lily, *b*
Zinnia, *a*

Annuals: Apply complete fertilizer such as 8-8-8. Water. To extend color into later summer sow seeds of quick-growing varieties.

Azaleas: If azaleas have failed to bloom well, look overhead in July and August to be certain that the plants are receiving sunlight during these months when they are setting buds. A high canopy of trees usually allows enough sunlight, but low branches may not. Water regularly and well.

Beds: Clean up between seasons and alter design if desired. Make out lists of seeds, bulbs, and plants for next year's garden.

Bluebonnets: Sow now as nature does, with this year's seed. Scatter on ground, rake lightly and allow natural rainfall to germinate seed. May sow from now until January to have flowers next spring, but early sowing brings best results and longer flowering. Bluebonnets prefer gravelly, well-drained, alkaline soil.

Crape Myrtles: Cut off dead seed pods to encourage more bloom.

Disease: Control fire blight in pear trees by cutting off affected limbs. Sterilize shears.

Fertilize: Guernsey lilies, lycoris and other flowering plants with superphosphate worked into soil. Water in.

Herbs: Cut for drying or freezing.

Hollyhocks: Don't water too freely after bloom, as this often destroys the roots.

Lawns: Cut St. Augustine 2-1/2" high, Bermuda and Zoysia 1-1/2", and Tif Bermudas 1" to conserve moisture and prevent burning.

Mulch: Maintain mulches. Allow grass clippings to compost, or dry out, before using as thin mulch. Green plant matter used as mulch takes nitrogen from the soil, and might burn tender plants during the hot decomposition process.

Pests: Sooty mold indicates presence of aphids, scale, or whiteflies. Examine foliage and spray accordingly. Sometimes strong streams of water or soapy (not detergent) water knock the insects off. The mold should disappear when the insects are gone.

Poinsettias: Pinch back until August to make bushy plants. Same for hydrangeas.

Shear: Alyssum and Scarletta begonias when they get scraggly to encourage new bloom.

Vegetables: Plant proven varieties and those recommended by your Agricultural Extension Service. Keep mulched and watered. Prepare soil in new beds for planting late in August and September. Start seeds in flats.

Water: Soak deeply. Leaves appreciate water, too, but not when sun is on them. Drops of water act like prisms, increasing heat of sun's rays. Do not overwater drought-resistant lantana, pampas grass, yucca, vitex, and oleander. Plants in hanging baskets require more water, usually daily.

August

"O for a lodge in a garden of cucumbers!
O for an iceberg or two at control!
O for a vale that at midday the dew cumbers!
O for a pleasure trip up to the Pole!"
—Rossiter Johnson

J.M.K.

SEEDS
which may now
be sown in flats *(f)*
or open ground *(o)*

Ageratum, *f*
Alyssum, Sweet, *f* or *o*
Amaranthus, *f*
Balsam, Garden, *f* or *o*
Bluebonnet, *o*
Calendula, *f* or *o*
Castor-bean, *o*
Cockscomb, *f* or *o*
Cornflower, *o*
Cosmos, Late, *o*
Four-o'clock, *o*
Gerbera, *f*
Hollyhock, *f*
Marigold, French, *o*
Pansy, *f*
Pinks, *f*
Snapdragon, *f*

Tobacco,
  Flowering, *f* or *o*
Tithonia, *o*

PLANTS
which may now be
placed in the open
ground

Acalypha
Aspidistra
Chrysanthemum
Cockscomb
Cosmos, Klondyke
Dahlia, Dwarf
Eranthemum
Four-o'clock
Gerbera
Marigold
Michaelmas Daisy
Periwinkle
Portulaca

Salvia
Shrimp Plant
Tithonia
Torenia
Verbena
Vinca

BULBS, TUBERS,
RHIZOMES
which may now be
placed in the open
ground

Amaryllis
Belladonna Lily
Caladium
Canna
Chlidanthus
Dahlia
Dietes
Habranthus
Haemanthus
Hemerocallis
Iris,
  Evansia
  Kaempferi
Lycoris
Sparaxis
Tulbaghia
Water Hyacinth
Water Lily
Watsonia
Zephyranthes

PLANTS
which bloom in
August

t–Tree   *s*–Shrub   *v*–Vine
b–Bulb, Tuber or Rhizome
e–Evergreen   *d*–Deciduous
p–Perennial   *bn*–Biennial
a–Annual

Abelia, *s e*
Achimenes, *b*

Ageratum, *a* or *p*
Allamanda, *v p*
Althaea, *s d*
Balloon-flower, *p*
Balsam, *a*
Barbados Cherry, *s e*
Bean, Scarlet Runner, *v a*
Begonia, Bedding, *a*
Bignonia, *v p*
Blanket flower, *a*
Bluebell, Texas, *bn*
Bougainvillea, *v e*
Browallia, *a*
Bushclover, *s d*
Butterflybush, *s d*
Butterfly Lily, *b*
Butterflyweed, *p*
Buttonbush, *s d*
Caladium, (foliage), *b*
Calliopsis, *a*
Canna, *b*
Cape Jasmine, *s e*
Cardinal Climber, *v a*
Celosia, *a*
Chinese Forget-Me-
  Not, *a*
Cistus, Rockrose, *s e*
Clematis, *v p*
Cleome, *a*
Cockscomb, *a*
Coleus, *a*
Confederate Rose, *s d*
Coral tree, *t d*
Coral Vine, *v p*
Cosmos, *a*
Crape myrtle, *s* or *t d*
Crinum, *b*
Cypressvine, *v a*
Dahlia, *b*
Daisies, Shasta, *p*
  Gloriosa
Datura, *a*
Daylily, *b*
Duranta, *s d*
Elderberry, *s d*
Everlastings, *a*
False-Dragonhead, *p*
Feverfew, *a* and *p*

Flamevine, *p e*
Forget-Me-Not, *p*
Four o'clock, *p*
Gayfeather, *p*
Geranium, *p*
Gerbera, *p*
Gladiolus, *b*
Globe Amaranth, *a*
Globe thistle, *a*
Goldenrod, *p*
Hibiscus, *s*
Honeysuckle, *v e*
Impatiens, sultani, *a*
Jacobinia, *s e*
Jasmines, *s*
Kerria, *s d*
Kniphofia, *b*
Lantana, *s d*
Lemon Verbena, *s d*

Leucophyllum, *s e*
Lilies, *b*
Liriope, *b*
Lobelia, cardinalis, *p*
Lycoris, *b*
Lythrum, *p*
Madeira-vine, *v p*
Marigold, *a*
Mallow, *p*
Mexican Flame Vine, *a*
Mimosa, *p*
Montbretia, *b*
Moonflower, *v a*
Morning Glory, *v a*
Morning Glory Tree, *s d*
Moss Pink, *p*
Nepeta, mussini, *p*
Oleander, *s e*
Oxalis, *b*

Parkinsonia, *t d*
Passionflower, *v p*
Periwinkle, *a*
Petunia, *a*
Phlox, Drummond, *a*
  perennial, *p*
Plumbago, *p*
Poinciana, *s d*
Pomegranate, *s d*
Portulaca, *a*
Potato vine, *v p*
Rain Lily, *b*
Rose Mallow, *p*
Roses, *s d*
Rudbeckia, *p*
St. John's-Wort, *s*
Salvias, *s p* and *a*
Senna, Cassia, *s d*
Shrimp Plant, *p*

Silver-lace Vine, *v p*
Spirea, *s d*
Strawflower, *a*
Sunflower, *a*
Thunbergia, *v a*
Tigridia, *b*
Tithonia, *a*
Tobacco, Flowering, *a*
Torenia, *a*
Trumpet vine, *v p*
Tuberose, *b*
Tulbaghia, *b*
Turk's Cap, *s e*
Verbena, *p*
Veronica, *p*
Water-hyacinth, *b*
Water lily, *b*
Water poppy, *p*
Willow, *s d*
Wisteria, v *e*
Yucca, *s e*
Zephyr Lily, *b*
Zinnia, *a*

Azaleas: Water regularly and well. Plants are setting buds. See "July."

Camellias: Continue watering. Check soil acidity.

Clean Up: Rose and flower beds of fallen foliage, yellowed leaves and dead wood. Cut off faded blossoms. Light green leaves may signify lack of iron (chlorosis). Correct with iron chelates, applied carefully as manufacturer directs, and water well. Cut leggy annuals back for new growth and bloom.

Cold Frames: Prepare

J.M.K.

White Caladiums in shade of a tree

now for fall planting when seedlings may need protection from rain.

Crape myrtles: Prolong bloom by removing faded flowers and seed pods.

Dahlias: Cut back after first crop, leaving about half the growth.

Fall or Early Spring Garden: Traditional month to sow seed in flats for fall and early spring gardens. Most perennials should be sown early for bloom following season.

Fruits: Prune blackberries after fruiting. Cut out old canes and fertilize with high-phosphate food. Keep watered. Water figs with slow soaking, 1 foot deep, but do not fertilize.

Iris: Cut off and burn old dead foliage, for it has already stored the rhizomes with nourishment and now only harbors disease. Scratch in a little bone meal around the roots.

Maidenhair: This fern is partially dormant now and may look a little rusty. Do not permit it to dry out. Keep moist and well-drained. It will flourish again in the fall.

Pests: Scale insects, resembling small white round scabs often appear on foliage now. Use summer oil spray in dilution suitable for hot weather. Sprays are apt to burn foliage in very hot weather, causing defoliation. Plants need as many leaves as possible now.

Pink Magnolia: Water thoroughly and maintain soil acidity.

Potted Plants: Overwatering is most frequent cause of failure with indoor plants. Use kitchen bulb baster to remove excess water easily from saucer under pot.

Remove: Faded flowers.

Shasta Daisies: Do not water too freely following bloom since this often destroys the plant.

Watering: Water to sustain life, saturating the soil thoroughly each time so the roots will not be drawn too near the surface. Water or mist in late afternoon to avoid danger of scalding.

Vegetables: Keep watered, weeded, and mulched. Plant seed potatoes whole in mid-August. Put collar around tomatoes to protect from cutworms. Collars should extend 1" above ground and 1" below. Work quantity of decomposed organic matter into the soil before planting.

September

*"When bounteous
autumn rears her head,
he joys to pull the
ripened pear."*
—Dryden

SEEDS
which may now
be sown in flats (*f*)
or open ground (*o*)

Alyssum, Sweet, *f* or *o*
Arctotis, *f* or *o*
Babysbreath, *f* or *o*
Balsam, Garden, *f* or *o*
Bells of Ireland, *o*
Bluebell, Texas, *f* or *o*
Bluebonnet, *o*
Calendula, *f*
Candytuft, *o*
Chinese Forget-Me-
    Not, *f* or *o*
Cleome, *o*
Cockscomb, *o*
Columbine, *o*
Coreopsis, *f* or *o*
Cornflower, *f* or *o*
Daisy,
    African, *f* or *o*
    Golden, *f* or *o*
    English, *f* or *o*
    Shasta, *f* or *o*
Delphinium, *f*
Everlasting, *f* or *o*
Four-o'clock, *o*
Gayfeather, *o*
Gerbera, *f*
Hollyhock, *f*
Laceflower, Blue, *f* or *o*
Larkspur, *o*
Lupine, *f*
Mallow, *f* or *o*

Pansy, *f*
Petunia, *f* or *o*
Phlox, Drummond, *o*
Pinks, *f* or *o*
Poppy, *o*
Salpiglossis, *f*
Salvia, Blue, *f* or *o*
Scabiosa, *f* or *o*
Snapdragon, *f* or *o*
Stock, *f* or *o*
Stokesia, *f*
Sweet William, *f* or *o*
Sweet Sultan
    (Centaurea)
Viola, *f*
Wallflower, *f*

PLANTS
which may now be
placed in the open
ground

Ageratum
Alyssum
Aspidistra
Calendula
Chrysanthemum
Cosmos, Klondyke
Dahlia, Dwarf
False-dragonhead
Four-o'clock
Gerbera
Hollyhock
Lantana
Lupine
Marigold

Petunia
Phlox, Louisiana
Verbena
Violet
Zinnia

BULBS, TUBERS, RHIZOMES
which may now be placed in the open ground

Allium
Amaryllis
Anemone
Banana
Calla
Chlidanthus
Cooperia (Rain Lily)
Dahlia
Dietes
Gladiolus tristis
Hemerocallis.
Iris,
  Bearded
  Bulbous
  Evansia
  Kaempferi
  Louisiana
  Siberian
  Spuria
  Unguicularis (Winter Blooming)
Ismene
Ixia
Lachenalia
Lapeirousia
Leucojum
Lilies,
  Centifolium
  Creole
  Croft
  Estate
  Madonna
  Philippine
  Regal
  Speciosum

Sunset
Tiger
Liriope
Muscari
Narcissus
Neomarica
Ornithogalum
Oxalis
Ranunculus
Scilla
Tritonia
Veltheimia (pots)
Watsonia
Zephyranthes

PLANTS
which bloom in September

---

t–Tree   *s*–Shrub   *v*–Vine
b–Bulb, Tuber or Rhizome
e–Evergreen   *d*–Deciduous
p–Perennial   *bn*–Biennial
a–Annual

Abelia, *s e*
Achimenes, *b*
Ageratum, *a* or *p*
Allamanda, *v p*
Althaea, *s d*
Balsam, *a*
Barbados Cherry, *s e*
Begonia, Bedding, *a*
Bignonia, *v p*
Blanket flower, *a*
Boltonia, *p*
Bougainvillea, *v e*
Browallia, *a*
Butterflybush, *s d*
Butterfly Lily, *b*
Butterflyweed, *p*
Buttonbush, *s d*
Canna, *b*
Cardinal Climber, *v a*
Cassia, *s d*
Celosia, *a*
Chinese Forget-Me-Not, *a*

Cistus, Rockrose, *s e*
Clematis, *v p*
Cleome, *a*
Cockscomb, *a*
Coleus, *a*
Confederate Rose, *s d*
Coral Vine, *v p*
Cosmos, *a*
Crapemyrtle, *s* or *t d*
Crinum, *b*
Cypressvine, *v a*
Dahlia, *b*
Datura Metel, *a*
Daylily, *b*
Duranta, *s d*
Feverfew, *a* and *p*
Forget-Me-Not, *p*
Four o'clock, *p*
Geranium, *p*
Gerbera, *p*
Globe Amaranth, *a*
Gloriosa Daisy, *p*
Goldenrod, *p*
Guernsey Lily, *b*
Hibiscus, *s*
Honeysuckle, *v e*
Impatiens, sultani, *a*
Jacobinia, *s e*
Jasmines, *s d* and *e*
Kerria, *s d*
Kniphofia, *b*
Lantana, *s d*
Lemon Verbena, *s d*
Leonotis, *s e*
Leucophyllum, *s e*
Lilies, *b*
Liriope, *b*
Lobelia, cardinalis, *p*
Lycoris, *b*
Lythrum, *p*
Madeira-vine, *v p*
Marigold, *a*
Mallow, *p*
Mexican Flame Vine, *a*
Mistflower, *p*
Moonflower, *v a*
Morning Glory, *v a*
Morning Glory Tree, *s d*

Moss Pink, *p*
Oleander, *s e*
Passion flower, *v p*
Periwinkle, *a*
Petunia, a
Phlox, Perennial, *p*
Plumbago, *p*
Poinciana, *s d*
Pomegranate, Dwarf, *s d*
Portulaca, *a*
Potato vine, *v p*
Rain Lily, *b*
Roses, *s d*
St. John's-Wort, *s d*
Salvias, *s d* and *a*
Shrimp Plant, *p*
Silver-lace Vine, *v p*
Spirea, *s d*
Sunflower, *a*
Thunbergia, *v p*
Tigridia, *b*
Tithonia, *a*
Tobacco, Flowering, *a*
Torenia, *a*
Trumpet creeper, *v p*
Tuberose, *b*
Turk's Cap, *s e*
Verbena, *p*
Veronica, *p*
Water-hyacinth, *b*
Waterlily, *p*
Waterpoppy, *p*
Wisteria, *v e*
Zephyr Lily, *b*
Zinnia, *a*

Azaleas: Check soil acidity and mulch. Keep watered. If foliage is yellowing, spray with one tablespoon copperas diluted in one gallon water.

Camellias: Water by deep soaking. To disbud or gib see CAMELLIAS.

Chrysanthemums: Give liquid manure or commercial fertilizer every two or three weeks until flower buds appear; then weekly until buds show color. Water as necessary. For large flowers, leave center bud in each cluster and pinch off all lateral buds before they start stemming. This applies only to the large flowered and not to pompom, anemone-flowered, or singles. For garden display, pinch out center bud and leave others.

Compost: Arrange for compost pile in hidden area. See "Compost" in SOIL chapter.

Cultivation: After first cool spell, clean up beds, burning old stalks and leaves which may harbor insects. Add fertilizer if needed. Dust lightly with sulphur to combat fungus when temperature is under 90°. Prepare beds or boxes into which pansy and other seedlings move when first pricked out. See PROPAGATION.

Cuttings: Take cuttings of coleus and geraniums and pot for next year.

Ferns: Maidenhair is dormant and brown now. Water well.

Fertilize: Gardenias regularly with acid food. Ger-

Hummingbird and feeder   D.W.

beras like rose food every four to six weeks; plant with crowns high in friable, humusy soil.

Herbs: Plant chives, coriander, dill, garlic, lovage, and winter savory.

Lawns: Feed with low-nitrogen fertilizer, 5-10-10 with organic base. Mulch all beds.

Pests: Spray for scale, red spider on shrubs and plants. Grayish, stippled leaves mean red spider; try strong water spray first and improve air circulation.

Potted Plants: For indoors, select varieties suitable to your light and temperature conditions. Light intensity more than 6 feet from a window is usually not enough for most plants. See CONTAINER GARDENING. Repot if crowded. Leach to wash out collected salt.

Roses: Keep mulched, fed and watered. Collect infected leaves and burn. Cut out blind, dead and weak wood. As cool weather approaches, water in the mornings to discourage black spot and mildew. Black spot must be prevented from entering leaf tissues. May apply fungicide before disease appears. Continue regular dust and spray schedule. See ROSES. Fall roses are often finest of the year. Foliar feed only when temperature drops below 85° to avoid burning. Prepare beds for new roses to be planted in February.

Soil: Unless soil has the texture to allow drainage, aeration, and penetration of food additives, neither seeds nor plants will prosper. See SOIL chapter.

Vegetables: Need sun, excellent drainage and fairly loose, not too acid, soil and at least 6 hours sun, preferably morning. Prepare new beds now. 1 part soil, 1 part sand, and 1 part pine bark mulch or compost, 12" to 18" deep, is good soil mixture for beets, carrots, onions and turnips. Strawberries and parsley like mix of pine bark and manure. Cauliflower, brussel sprouts, Chinese cabbage, and broccoli need cool weather. See VEGETABLES and SOIL chapters. Be aware of safe waiting periods if using pesticides on food crops. Do not use weed killers or herbicides on or near food crops because they last up to 18 months in the soil.

Violets: If not already divided, separate old clumps to single crowns with roots. Reset, fertilize, and reap a wealth of early bloom

October

*"Behold congenial
Autumn comes, the
Sabbath of the year!"*
　　　　　—Logan

J.M.K.

SEEDS
which may now
be sown in flats *(f)*
or open ground *(o)*

Alyssum, Sweet, *f* or *o*
Arctotis, *f* or *o*
Babysbreath, *f* or *o*
Blanket flower, *f* or *o*
Bluebell, Texas, *f* or *o*
Bluebonnet, *o*
Calendula, *f*
Chinese Forget-Me-
　Not, *f* or *o*
Columbine, *o*
Coreopsis, *f* or *o*
Cornflower, *f* or *o*
Daisy,
　Michaelmas (Aster), *o*
　Golden, *f* or *o*
　English, *f* or *o*
　Shasta, *f* or *o*
Delphinium, *f*
Everlasting, *f* or *o*
Forget-Me-Not, *f* or *o*
Gerbera, *f*
Godetia, *f*
Hollyhock, *f* or *o*
Laceflower, Blue, *f* or *o*
Larkspur, *o*
Mallow, *f* or *o*
Nasturtium
Pansy, *f*
Petunia, *f* or *o*
Phlox, Drummond, *o*
Pinks, *f* or *o*

Poppy, California, *o*
Iceland, *o*
Shirley, *o*
Queen Anne's-lace, *f* or *o*
Salpiglossis, *f*
Salvia, Blue, *f* or *o*
Scabiosa, *f* or *o*
Sedum, *f*
Snapdragon, *f* or *o*
Stock, *f* or *o*
Stokesia, *f*
Sweet Pea, *o*
Sweet William, *f* or *o*
Viola, *f*
Wallflower, *f*
Wild Flowers, *o*
　(See chapter)

PLANTS
which may now be
placed in the open
ground

Ageratum
Alyssum, Sweet
Aspidistra
Bluebonnet
Calendula
Candytuft
Carnation
Columbine
Coreopsis
Cornflower
Daisy,
　English
　Shasta

Delphinium
Forget-Me-Not
Four-o'clock
Gerbera
Hollyhock
Pansy
Petunia
Phlox,
　Drummond
　Louisiana
　Perennial
Physostegia
Pinks
Salvia, Blue
Shrimp Plant
Snapdragon
Stock
Sweet William
Verbena
Violet
Wallflower

BULBS, TUBERS,
RHIZOMES
which may now be
placed in the open
ground

Agapanthus
Allium
Alstroemeria
Amarcrinum
Amaryllis
Anemone
Banana
Calla
Chlidanthus
Clivia (pots)
Cooperia
Crinum
Crocus
Dietes
Freesia
Ginger
Gladiolus
Hemerocallis
Iris, all kinds

Ismene
Ixia
Lachenalia
Leucojum
Lilies,
　Centifolium
　Creole
　Croft
　Estate
　Goldband
　Madonna
　Philippine
　Regal
　Speciosum
　Sunset
　Tiger
Liriope
Lycoris
Marica
Milla
Montbretia
Muscari
Narcissus
Ornithogalum
Ranunculus
Scilla
Sparaxis
Spuria
Sprekelia
Strelitzia
Tulbaghia
Veltheimia (pots)
Watsonia
Zephyranthes

PLANTS
which bloom in
October

t–Tree   *s*–Shrub   *v*–Vine
b–Bulb, Tuber or Rhizome
e–Evergreen   *d*–Deciduous
p–Perennial   *bn*–Biennial
a–Annual

Ageratum, *a* or *p*
Alyssum, Sweet, *a*

Amaranthus, *a*
Anemone, Japanese, *a*
Angel's Trumpet, *s d*
Arbutus, *t e*
Azaleas, *s e*
Balsam, *a*
Barbados Cherry, *s e*
Begonia, Bedding, *a*
Bignonia, *v p*
Blanket flower
  (Gaillardia), *a*
Boltonia, *p*
Bougainvillea, *v e*
Bouncing Bet, *p*
Bouvardia, *s e*
Butterflybush, *s d* or *e*
Butterfly Lily, *b*
Canna, *b*
Cardinal Climber, *v a*
Caryopteris, *s d*
Cassia, *s d*
Celosia, *a*
Chrysanthemum, *p*
Clematis, *v p*
Cleome, *a*
Clethra, *s d*
Coleus, *a*
Confederate Rose, *s d*
Coral Vine, *v p*
Cosmos, *a*
Crinum, *b*
Cypressvine, *v a*
Dahlia, *a* or *p*
Daylily, *b*
Elaeagnus, *s e*
Forget-Me-Not, *p*
Four o'clock, *p*
Franklinia, *t d*
Garlic, *b*
Geranium, *p*
Gerbera, *p*
Ginger, Shell, *b*
Gladiolus, *b*
Globe Amaranth, *a*
Hibiscus, *s e*
Honeysuckle, *s* or *v e*
Impatiens, sultani, *p*
Jasmines, *s e*

Lantana, *s d*
Lapeirousia, *b*
Lobelia, cardinalis, *p*
Lycoris, *b*
Mallow, Rose, *p*
Marigold, *a*
Michaelmas Daisy, *p*
Mistflower, *p*
Moonflower, *v a*
Morning Glory, *v a*
Narcissus, *b*
Oxalis, *b*
Periwinkle, *a*
Petunia, *a*
Phlox, Perennial, *p*
Plumbago, *p*
Pomegranate, *s d*
Portulaca, *a*
Potatovine, *v p*
Raintree, Golden, *t d*
Roses, *s d*
Salvias, *a* and *p*
Shrimp Plant, *p*
Silver-lace Vine, *v p*
Tea Plant, *s e*
Thunbergia, *v a*
Tithonia, *a*
Tobacco, Flowering, *a*
Turk's Cap, *s e*
Verbena, *p*
Violet, *p*
Water-hyacinth, *b*
Water lily, *b*
Zinnia, *a*

Azaleas: Check soil pH. If above 5.5, dress with 1 part agricultural sulphur and 2 parts copperas, mixed and sprinkled dry around edges of bushes to maintain acidity. Do not disturb shallow root system. Carefully hand water at once to liquify chemicals. Check for signs of root rot. Prune long unsightly branches near base of bushes to maintain symmetry and promote bushiness. Azaleas bud out where cut.

Bulbs: Plant spring flowering bulbs in rich loam with plenty of humus and good drainage. Mix 1 tbsp. each bone meal and superphosphate in soil at bottom of hole. *DO NOT PLANT TULIPS BEFORE LATE DECEMBER.* Dig caladiums now and store in dry, ventilated place. Bearded and Dutch irises like bone meal; Louisiana irises like cotton seed meal and manure; spurias are gross feeders and want a fertilizer such as 8-8-8 mixed with half as much sheep manure. Feed other bulbs now with bone meal and superphosphate. Fertilize daylilies. They need six hours sun to bloom well.

Camellias: Before October 15th spray for tea scale if necessary. Check undersides of leaves.

Compost: Keep healthy leaves, clippings and small branches in compost pile or containers to decompose. Compost helps the soil and saves money. See SOIL chapter.

Container Gardening: Gradually accustom plants to less light for their winter quarters.

Cultivation: Clean up beds; plan changes. Correct drainage problems, perhaps by raising beds. Check and correct pH factor according to plant needs. Add humus, compost, and manure to beds and work in at least 8", but never work soil unless it is dry enough to crumble in hand. Water.

Fertilize: Withhold nitrogen-high fertilizer to avoid stimulating growth which would be susceptible to freezing. Exception: winter vegetables. Feed spring-blooming shrubs lightly with 4 parts superphosphate mixed with 1 part sulphur of potash. Sprinkle lightly, away from trunk and water in.

Forget-Me-Nots: Clumps may be moved to partially shaded exposure with morning sun. Add quantities of old manure to the soil, for these plants are greedy feeders. They prefer a bed to themselves where they will form a dense mat with tiny blue flowers from spring to fall. Water freely during hot weather and protect from frost.

Frost: Be prepared to protect against frost even though average date of first frost is December 10th.

Fruits: Plant strawberries between October 15 and November 15 in beds with good drainage, slightly acid, rich, loose soil with ample humus. Set crown even with soil level. Mulch with straw, paper or plastic to keep fruit clean.

Herbs: Divide and re-plant: chives, garlic and multiplying onions.

Iris: Fertilize existing beds with well-rotted manure or a balanced fertilizer and water in. Plant all kinds.

Lawns: If necessary, use a fungicide for brown patch and an insecticide for chinch bugs. Fertilize for nutrition. Follow la-bel. Water. See LAWNS chapter.

Perennials: Cut tops af-ter blooming; divide roots and transplant any time from now until March, but the sooner the early-blooming varieties are moved, the earlier and more satisfactory will be their blooms.

Pests: Beware of stinging caterpillars (asps) usually seen on limbs and twigs of oak trees, but may be on other trees or shrubs also; wear gloves as a safe-

guard. Their sting is vi-cious. Watch for bag or web worms. See DIS-EASES, INSECTS AND WEEDS chapter.

Plant: One of best plant-ing months for trees, shrubs and many flowers.

Roses: Soak beds. Groom to cut out dead wood but do not prune heavily until February. Feed lightly with 0-10-10 in solution to harden off for dormancy and improve bloom.

Spray: Dormant oil such as Volck to prevent scale insects on hollies, camel-lias, magnolias, gardenias, euonymus and citrus.

Trees and Evergreens: When selecting trees, consider those with fall color. See TREES chart. Feed and water; remove dead wood.

Watering: Water in the morning to avert fungus disease. Avoid wetting bloom and foliage.

Wisteria: To encourage flowering the following spring, root-prune wis-teria that has failed to bloom. Cut through the roots with a spade in a circle about 30 inches from the stem of the vine, and feed with bone meal through this cut. Water.

November

"Divinest Autumn! Who may paint thee best, Forever changeful o'er the changeful globe."
—R. H. Stoddard

SEEDS
which may now
be sown in flats *(f)*
or open ground *(o)*

Alyssum, Sweet, *f* or *o*
Arctotis, *f* or *o*
Baby's-Breath, *f* or *o*
Blanket flower, *f* or *o*
Bluebell, Texas, *f* or *o*
Bluebonnet, *o*
Calendula, *f*
Candytuft, *o*
Chinese Forget-Me-
Not, *f* or *o*
Cleome, *o*
Coreopsis, *f* or *o*
Cornflower, *f* or *o*
Daisy,
African, *f* or *o*
Golden, *f* or *o*
English, *f* or *o*
Shasta, *f* or *o*
Delphinium, *f*
Everlasting, *f* or *o*
Forget-Me-Not, *o*
Four-o'clock, *o*
Gerbera, *f*
Hollyhock, *f* or *o*
Laceflower, Blue, *f* or *o*
Larkspur, *o*
Lobelia, *f*
Mallow, *f* or *o*
Nasturtium
Pansy, *f*
Petunia, *f* or *o*

Phlox, Drummond, *o*
Pinks, *f* or *o*
Poppy,
California, *o*
Iceland, *o*
Shirley, *o*
Queen Anne's-lace,
f or *o*
Salpiglossis, *f*
Salvia, Blue, *f* or *o*
Scabiosa, *f* or *o*
Snapdragon, *f* or *o*
Stock, *f* or *o*
Sweet Pea, *o*
Sweet William, *f* or *o*
Verbena, *f* or *o*
Viola, *f*
Wallflower, *f*
Wild Flowers, *o*

PLANTS
which may now be
placed in the open
ground

Alyssum, Sweet
Arctotis
Aspidistra
Bluebonnet
Calendula
Candytuft
Canterbury Bell
Columbine
Coreopsis
Cornflower

Daisy,
  English
  Shasta
Forget-Me-Not
Four o'clock
Gerbera
Hollyhock
Honeysuckle
Lupine
Pansy
Penstemon
Petunia
Phlox,
  Louisiana
  Perennial
Pinks
Queen Anne's-lace
Salvia, Blue
Shrimp Plant
Snapdragon
Stock
Sweet William
Verbena
Viola
Violet

BULBS, TUBERS, RHIZOMES
which may now be
placed in the open
ground

Agapanthus
Allium
Alstroemeria
Amarcrinum
Amaryllis
Anemone
Calla
Chlidanthus
Clivia (pots)
Cooperia
Crinum
Crocus
Dietes
Freesia
Gladiolus tristis

Habranthus
Hemerocallis
Hyancinth, Roman
Iris,
  Evansia
  Bearded
  Louisiana
  Unguicularis
Ismene
Ixia
Lachenalia
Leucojum
Lilies, all kinds
Liriope
Lycoris
Milla

Camellia Sasanqua   C.H.

Montbretia
Muscari
Narcissus
Neomarica
  (Walking Iris)
Ornithogalum
Oxalis
Ranunculus
Scilla
Sisyrinchium
  (Blue-eyed Grass)
Sparaxis
Sprekelia
Tulbaghia
Watsonia

Zephyranthes

PLANTS
which bloom in
November

---

t–Tree *s*–Shrub *v*–Vine
b–Bulb, Tuber or Rhizome
e–Evergreen *d*–Deciduous
p–Perennial *bn*–Biennial
a–Annual

Ageratum, *a* or *p*
Alyssum, Sweet, *a*
Balsam, *a*

Bougainvillea, *v e p*
Calendula, *a*
Camellia,
  japonica, *s e*
  sasanqua, *s e*
Canna, *b*
Cardinal Climber, *v a*
Chinese Forget-Me-
  Not, *a*
Chrysanthemum, *p*
Clematis, *v p*
Confederate Rose, *s d*
Crinum, *b*
Dahlborg Daisy, *a*
Dahlia, *b*

Eranthemum, *s*
Geranium, *p*
Gerbera, *p*
Gladiolus, *b*
Hibiscus, *p*
Honeysuckle, *s v e*
Jasmines, *s*, *d* and *e*
Lantana, *s d*
Loquat, *s e*
Marigold, *a*
Michaelmas Daisy, *p*
Pansy, *a*
Periwinkle, *a*
Petunia, *a*
Pinks, *a*, *bn*
Plumbago, *p*
Poinsettia, *s d*
Potato vine, *v p*
Roses, *s d*
Salvias, *p* and *a*
Scabiosa, *a bn* and *p*
Shrimp Plant, *p*
Silver Lace Vine, *v p*
Sweet Olive, *s e*
Turk's cap, *s e*
Verbena, *p*
Violet, *p*
Waterlily, *b*
Zinnia, *a*

Azaleas and Camellia:
May be moved. Keep
moist to lessen cold
weather damage. Main-
tain mulch. See "Octo-
ber."

Bulbs: See "October." Put
tulips in refrigerator now
in old nylon hose to re-
main at least 6 weeks to
induce a strong root sys-
tem which, in turn, pro-
duces better flowers. Keep
bulbs dry.

Cultivation: See "October." Cut back perennial tops. Thin out and transplant volunteer seedlings. Beds made now will profit by weathering before being planted. If soil is heavy, dig six inches deep, leave rough, cover with gypsum, leaves and strawy manure, water and allow to mellow.

Fruit Trees: Plant these and flowering shrubs, deciduous and evergreen, now.

Garden Sanitation: Remove dead foliage to help eradicate insects and disease organisms which can overwinter in debris. Add healthy prunings to compost.

Lilies-of-the-Valley: Force pips to bloom for Christmas by planting in sand or sphagnum moss in a shallow bowl. Keep moist in a dark room. Allow to grow 4 inches high, bring gradually to light. They should bloom about 25 days after planting.

Pansies: Place in the beds after weather has cooled. Use a little blood meal mixed in soil under each plant.

Perennials: As chrysanthemums and other perennials finish blooming, cut flowering stalks to

ground to permit all strength to be used in making root growth. Pinch off the tops of calendula, delphinium, snapdragon, stock and wallflower, to induce bushy growth and prevent flowers from forming so early that they may be destroyed by frost. Cultivate lightly.

Roses: Feed lightly, but avoid nitrogen fertilizers. *Do not* prune now. Keep up spraying program. Water deeply.

Vegetables: See "March" and VEGETABLE chapter with chart.

Violets: Manure heavily any time between now and March 15 for a full harvest of bloom.

Winter Protection: Be prepared from now until April for quick freezes. Plastic coverings should not touch plants. In the southern zones there can be as much damage to covered plants from heat following freeze as from the cold itself, so remove plastic covers as soon as temperature rises. Low plants may be covered with leaves; but remove when weather warms. See WINTER PROTECTION and TROPICAL GARDEN chapters.

December

"See, Winter comes to rule the varied year."
　　　　　—Thomson

J.M.K.

SEEDS
which may now be sown in flats (f) or open ground (o)

Alyssum, Sweet, *f* or *o*
Arctotis, *f* or *o*
Baby's-Breath, *f* or *o*
Blanket flower
　(Gaillardia), *f* or *o*
Bluebell, Texas, *f* or *o*
Bluebonnet, *o*
Calendula, *f*
Candytuft, *o*
Chinese Forget-Me-
　Not, *f* or *o*
Cleome, *o*
Coreopsis, *f* or *o*
Cornflower, *f* or *o*
Daisy,
　African
　Golden, *f* or *o*
　English, *f* or *o*
　Shasta, *f* or *o*
Everlasting, *f* or *o*
Forget-Me-Not, *o*
Four-o'clock, *o*
Gerbera, *f*
Godetia, *f*
Hollyhock, *f*
Larkspur, *o*
Lobelia, *f*
Mallow, *f* or *o*
Petunia, *f* or *o*
Phlox, Drummond, *o*

Pinks, *f* or *o*
Poppy, California, *o*
Shirley, *o*
Salvia, Blue, *f* or *o*
Salpiglossis, *f*
Scabiosa, *f* or *o*
Snapdragon, *f* or *o*
Stock, *f* or *o*
Sweet Pea, *o*
Sweet William, *f* or *o*
Verbena, *f* or *o*
Wallflower, *f*

PLANTS
which may now be placed in the open ground

Alyssum, Sweet
Arctotis
Aspidistra
Bluebonnet
Calendula
Candytuft
Coreopsis
Cornflower
Daisy,
　Bush
　English
Dianthus
Four-O'Clock
Honeysuckle
Larkspur
Pansy
Penstemon

Petunia
Phlox,
  Drummond
  Louisiana
  Perennial
Physostegia
Pinks
Queen Anne's-lace
Salvia, Blue
Snapdragon
Stock
Verbena
Viola
Violet
Wallflower

BULBS, TUBERS, RHIZOMES
which may now be placed in the open ground

Agapanthus
Allium
Alstroemeria
Amarcrinum
Amaryllis
Anemone
Blackberry Lily
Calla
Camassia
Chlidanthus
Clivia (pots)
Cooperia
Crinum
Crocus
Dietes
Freesia
Gloriosa
Hemerocallis
Hyacinth
Hymenocallis
Iris,
  Bulbous
  Spuria
  Louisiana

Ixia
Jack-in-the-Pulpit
Kniphofia
Lachenalia
Leucojum
Lily-of-the-Valley (pots)
Liriope
Milla
Montbretia
Muscari
Lycoris
Narcissus
Neomarica
  (Walking Iris)
Ornithogalum
Oxalis
Ranunculus
Scilla
Sisyrinchium
Sprekelia
Tulbaghia
Tulip
Water Hyacinth
Water Lily
Zephyranthes

PLANTS
which bloom in December

---

t–Tree *s*–Shrub *v*–Vine
b–Bulb, Tuber or Rhizome
e–Evergreen *d*–Deciduous
p–Perennial *bn*–Biennial
a–Annual

Alyssum, *a*
Calendula, *a*
Calla, *b*
Camellia,
  Japonica, *s e*
  Sasanqua, *s e*
Chrysanthemums, *p*
Daisy,
  Bush, *p*
  Golden, *a*

Elaeagnus, *s e*
Eranthemum, *s*
Forget-me-not, *p*
Gerbera, *p*
Honeysuckle, *s d*
Iris,
  unguicularis, *b*
  stylosa, *b*
Jasmine, *v e*
  floridum, *s e*
Loquat, *s e*
Michaelmas Daisy, *p*
Narcissus, *b*
Oxalis, *b*
Pansy, *a*
Pinks, *a, bn*
Plumbago, *s*
Poinsettia, *s d*
Quince, Japanese
  Flowering, *s d*
Roses
Salvia, *p a*
Sweet Olive, *s e*
Sweet Pea, Early, *a*
Turk's Cap, *s e*
Viola, *a*
Violet, *p*

Azaleas and Camellias: Plants may be moved. Keep moist to lessen cold weather damage. May acidify again. See "October."

Bulbs: Last month to plant early blossoming spring bulbs, speciosum and other varieties of lilies. Mulch.

Cultivation: A season of heavy garden work begins this month. Clean up beds where fall flowers have bloomed. Pre-pare soil in new beds now, to allow time for settling before planting. Add leaves to compost heap but discard diseased or bug-infested refuse.

Fertilize: Established trees, spring-blooming shrubs, spurias, and sweet peas (after they are a foot tall) with fertilizer such as 13-13-13; Louisiana iris with cotton seed meal and manure.

Maidenhair: Even if frozen it will come back from roots in the spring. Allow fallen leaves to remain on bed as mulch.

Pansies: If long flowering period is desired, plants should be placed in their permanent beds not later than this month. Fertilize monthly with manure, super-phosphate or a liquid high- phosphate product. Keep flowers picked for more bloom.

Shrubs and Trees: This month and the next two are considered best for planting.

Tulips: Take tulips out of cold storage and plant late this month.

Watering: Water well before a freeze. See WINTER PROTECTION chapter.

Varicolored caladiums among the trees

Hints For Landscaping

"Landscapes are Nature's pictures."
—M. E. Lee

Some inner compulsion leads us outdoors—a yearning to dig in the soil, to nurture growing plants, to be in communion with the earth, the sky, the natural elements. Sooner or later we want to arrange our piece of ground for outside activities. That's when landscaping enters the picture. Landscaping is the arrangement, in a pleasant, orderly way, of our outdoor space for our enjoyment.

The secret to attaining a satisfying plan for your portion of land lies in the cooperation between you and any others who will also be enjoying the garden. Get together. Speak your minds. Discuss exactly how everyone envisions the use of the grounds. Though the many ideas may at first seem disconnected, a workable compromise can usually be achieved through careful thought and discussion.

Be realistic before proceeding with a plan. Decisions made now have long-term implications. Determine how much time and money you can budget to maintain a garden area. Gardens don't stand still. There will be leaves to rake, grass to mow, and shrubs to prune. The plants will need to be planted, watered, and fertilized. In Houston, we garden all year round, and our summers are long and hot. If you enjoy gardening, the chores won't seem burdensome. But if you are short of time and funds to devote to spacious grounds, think small. Plan for a garden area you can easily and happily care for. A small, well-kept garden is much more enjoyable and more attractive than one beyond your available time and money. You want your garden grounds to be a pleasure, not a thorn in the flesh!

Having come to terms with reality, you can turn to developing a plan for *your* family's pleasure. Toward that goal, ponder these basic considerations:

- Is your garden to be a background for entertainment? Relaxation? Or principally for the cultivation of plants? Do you plan to cook and serve meals outside? Play yard games?
- Do you prefer a secluded garden space or do you enjoy keeping an eye on what's going on in the neighborhood?
- If you have dreams of a swimming pool, investigate first. Talk to people who have had one for a year or so. Do you know that pools below ground level are subject to taxes, or that the city requires a pool to have certain safety precautions? Would your pool be for swimming or just sunbathing? The answers to these decisions will determine the size, shape, and therefore, the cost of a pool. A pool requires frequent maintenance. Allow adequate storage space for necessary

31

equipment. Who will clean the pool? Will a fence be needed to protect young children? Check carefully before hiring a pool-building company. Or employ someone whose pools you have admired.

- Will a swing set, jungle gym, or sand box be in your plans? Plan ahead for play areas to be used differently as the children mature. The sand box might become a lily pond; the location for the swing set might be perfect for a greenhouse. Visualize flexibility for the years to come.
- Will pets need a fenced area?
- Who will be mowing the lawn and maintaining the garden? Do you yearn for beds of blooming flowers? A southern exposure allows maximum sunshine, a must for blooms.
- What kind of watering system do you foresee? Refer to WATER AND WATERING chapter.
- Does your community have restrictions to be met?
- What part of the gardening can you handle yourself? Which chores will require a hired person?

When all the ideas and the preceding considerations have been discussed and re-discussed, you have made real progress. Now it's time to determine who will implement your plans—you yourself, a landscape architect, or a garden designer? Select someone who has experience with landscaping in the Houston locale—someone who is familiar with the plant material which thrives here and with the micro-climate typical of Houston.

Consider the possibilities:
- If you are among the lucky few who have a strong sense of design and a broad knowledge of Houston-area soil and plants, then you might take on the planning and execution of the plan yourself for the experience you undoubtedly will acquire. However, if your plan calls for a pool, a terrace, or a deck,

it would be wise to confer with a professional. A pool that leaks or fails to meet the city's safety requirements, a terrace that accumulates surface water, or a deck that leans or is unsteady can be a catastrophic disaster, as well as a financial loss.

- If you are seeking a landscape architect, ask for referrals from friends who have been pleased with a professional whom they employed. Landscape architects must be registered by a state board of examiners. They must pass extensive examinations after meeting educational and experience requirements. Landscape architects can provide valuable assistance by preventing costly mistakes and coordinating the work to minimize time and effort. The local chapter of the American Society of Landscape Architects can assist you in the search for the right person for you.
- On the other hand, you may prefer to consult a garden designer, who can give helpful advice though not usually trained or licensed as is a landscape architect.

Fees vary. Don't hesitate to discuss costs. Having a financial understanding in the beginning is helpful to both parties. You might prefer to implement the plan a few steps at a time, letting the landscape develop gradually to be sure you are satisfied.

Whether or not you decide to hire a professional garden planner, you will probably require contractors for some portions of your plan. Employ only those contractors who come well recommended or who are approved by the Better Business Bureau. *Don't pay fees in advance unless you are positive you are dealing with a reputable company.*

While you are weighing ideas for your garden space, study the following principles of landscaping which have been held in good stead through the years:
- BALANCE of sizes, shapes, masses, and colors of plants.

- PROPORTION and UNITY of all the elements to avoid the helter-skelter look that leaves one feeling vaguely disoriented or uncomfortable.
- CONTRAST of textures in leaves, bark of trees, surfaces of masonry materials, and containers.
- FOCUS on the views of the garden from the house. Will those views be complementary to the interiors? Project the view from each room facing the garden. Compatibility between indoors and outdoors visually enlarges both home and garden.
- PRIVACY to allow relaxation from tension and noise in a pleasing, secluded but not confining environment through appropriate placement of trees, shrubs, and fences.
- BEAUTY in plants and flowers, in balanced and interesting design, in pleasing combinations of color, in views of tree branches against the sky and shadows on the lawn.
- COMFORT at all times of year by placing trees and shrubs to temper the summer's hot sun with cool, leafy shade, and also to allow sun-spots for enjoying the winter's warm sun, and comfortable seating.
- SAFETY and CONVENIENCE, especially with non-slip surfaces on paths and walkways, with steps having properly proportioned treads and risers to prevent falls, and with non-glare night lighting.

- EASE OF MAINTENANCE to allow maximum time for enjoyment of the garden and minimum time for chores.

Drawing a plan of your garden helps you visualize the landscape you have been thinking about. Obtain 24 inch by 36 inch graph paper and tracing paper—and a supply of erasers. On the graph paper, using a convenient scale, such as 1/4 inch equals 1 foot, draw everything that is on the property *now*, including:
- Boundaries of the property indicating easements and power lines.
- Your house properly located, showing doors, windows, and gutter downspouts.
- Indicate directions: north, south, east, and west. Then plot the arc of the sun as it falls on your house, windows, and garden areas at different seasons of the year. Plotting the sun's rays as they touch your property during the different seasons allows you to know how, where, and when to protect your home from summer sun, but also to allow winter rays to benefit your property, where to position trees or shrubs appropriately, and where to plan beds for maximum sun.

Reminders:
1. Blooming plants, vegetables, and herbs require maximum sun, therefore, their beds should run east and west.

Landscape design, or any design for that matter, is for *people* in one way or another. In the home landscape, people are of paramount importance because they are in close contact with outdoor spaces and with the items in those spaces. Houses and furniture are designed with "people dimensions" in mind and landscapes should be too.

Walkway Widths
2' — minimum for garden path
3' — a one person walk
4' — accommodates two people
    uncomfortably
5' — accommodates two people
    comfortably

Step Dimensions
6" riser/14" tread (12" is acceptable)
5" riser/16" tread
4" riser/18" tread
3" riser/20" tread

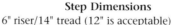

*Spring Landscape: Mexican Plum trees, spiraea, ligustrum, St. Augustine grass,
azaleas, snapdragons, gerberas, monkey grass. Curving walk.*

2. Evergreen trees and shrubs are best for screening purposes, and can be used to block summer sun from windows; but because they remain in leaf all year, they also block the beneficial winter sun.

3. Deciduous trees are in leaf during the summer and block the hot sun; but after they drop their leaves in the fall, they allow warming winter sun in.

4. A frequent mistake is failing to determine the mature size and the growing habits of trees and shrubs *before buying*. Learn their size and allow sufficient space between tree or shrub and the house. The plantings should complement your home, not hide it, nor do you want an invasive root system to invade your water or sewage pipes.

5. Position all existing trees, shrubs, and flower beds.

6. Note dry, wet or sloping areas. The DRAINAGE chapter has suggestions for corrections.

7. Show all structures other than the main house: garage, terrace, deck, walks, driveways, fences, pool, and air-conditioning equipment.

8. Views to retain and those which should be screened from sight.

> HINT: Planning around existing features saves cost of transplanting or replacement later.

Now cover your graph plan with tracing paper and sketch in your ideas for improvement. Try different sketches until you are satisfied with a plan. While sketching, consider pleasing views of your garden from inside the house.

Include in your final plan:
• Storage for car with ample space to back out.

- Driveway with entrance broad enough to avoid driving car onto lawn when entering or leaving. A spacious driveway can be useful as a space for games or skating.
- Parking space for guest cars.
- Convenient, protected entrances to house from street and garage, preferably lighted at night for safety and security.
- Properly drained walkways with a brushed or other non-slip finish, from house to garage, to street, and to garden. People always take shortcuts, so plan walks accordingly. Walks should be a bit higher than lawn because lawns get higher through the years from annual top dressings. Plan for sufficiently sturdy foundations to avoid cracking. A curving walk makes for easier, quicker mowing. *Frequent mistake:* Walks that are too narrow. A 3-foot wide walk accommodates only one person. A 5-foot wide walk accommodates two abreast— a friendlier arrangement. *Happy thought:* Wide curving walkways are good for riding tricycles, skating, hopscotch, and other activities for children; especially useful following a rain shower.
- Fences, trellises, or plantings to screen unsightly areas. Determine necessary height of screening material for effectiveness; check *mature* size of any plantings *before* purchasing to avoid the frequent mistake of buying a small plant only to realize too late that its mature size is greater than the space allowed. See plant charts for information of mature sizes of trees and shrubs.
- Clothesline. Even with a dryer, a clothesline is useful.
- Outdoor play area easily visible from kitchen or other often-used room allows supervision of children from indoors *except* where there is a pool. *Never leave young children unsupervised in the area of or in a pool, even for "a minute."*
- Storage facilities for garbage, trash, garden equipment, outdoor games and toys, bicycles, etc. With careful, imaginative planning, these areas can be attractively hidden from view

and still be conveniently available.
- Night lighting for beauty and security. Require a wiring-piping system which stretches as the tree trunk grows.
- Sufficient exterior electrical plugs.
- Water spigots placed conveniently for watering. *Reminder:* Locate spigots where they will not be blocked in the future by planting beds.
- Plan attractive view from the kitchen sink!

When you have completed your final plan, you are ready to consider the plantings you want to create your landscape. As a rule of thumb, avoid the use of too many types of plants for any one planting, and never buy a plant that is not worthy of being in the spotlight all by itself.

Learn the mature size and cultural requirements of every plant you intend to use before *purchasing and planting.* Select only those whose ultimate size and cultural requirements are appropriate for the space and the sun, soil, and moisture conditions in your garden. There is the possibility of amending the soil and water conditions, but rarely the sun.

Plan sufficient space between plants according to their mature size. Be patient. Don't try for an instant garden by planting twice as many plants as the space can support. Empty space can be well mulched, thus discouraging weeds while the plants are growing to their ultimate size. Enjoy the stages of growth.

Group plants according to their cultural requirements for more convenient and time-saving care when watering, fertilizing, and spraying. Groupings of similar plants convey a calmer, more spacious appearance to the landscape than individual, "dotted" plantings. The same principle applies to groupings of blooming plants, with the exception that color is an important element with the blooming plants. If they are of the same color or pleasantly blending colors, they give a sense of unity.

Color is an extremely important element in landscaping. Think of your favorite colors and of how your garden's colors will look from the house. You can be an artist in your own garden. Annuals, perennials, some bulbs, azaleas, roses, and some shrubs bloom in mass color. Of all of them, the annuals and perennials probably have the longest season of color, though nothing can compare with the blaze of color from massed azaleas. With careful selection of blooming plants, you can have color in your garden at least ten months of the year. The trick is to chart their times of bloom and plan for one type to begin to bloom as another completes its bloom. Be sure to consider the colors of both the incoming and the outgoing bloomers to avoid unfortunate color combinations if the groups overlap each other in bloom time. The plant charts give color and bloom-time information.

The red-orange-yellow range of colors is considered "warm." They call attention to themselves to the extent that they appear to be closer to the viewer than they actually are. Groups of the bright, warm colors are often used for accent. Since they attract attention, be sure the area in which you plant them warrants attention!

The blues, greens, and pastels are considered "cool" colors, and tend to lead the eye into the distance, giving the garden a more spacious appearance. Clumps or ribbons of those colors give a soothing, cooling effect.

White flowers can give either effect, depending on how they are used.

Nature combines colors in every which way, but usually in a wide open expanse. Within the confines of a private garden, a certain control of color seems more appealing. A trick gardeners sometimes employ is placing pots of blooming plants, of single or blending colors, in various parts of the garden, moving them around until the effect is the most attractive. Then they plant according to the arrangement of color...and texture...and height they prefer. One of the nicest aspects of garden plants is that they are easily moved to another location if you don't like the original placement.

HINT: Plants of different heights in tiers give a more interesting appearance than plants of all the same height. Exception: plants in a formal hedge.

Only ground covers and plants using the wall for support should be planted closer to the house than three feet. The mature size of the plants is the final guide. Consider using plants and trees which attract birds. Birds eat millions of pounds of weed seeds and insects each year and benefit the garden while you enjoy their songs, their colors, and the vitality they display.

HINT: Keep fresh, clean water available for the birds, because more birds die of thirst than of hunger. Refer to the various charts of plants to find those which entice not only birds but also bees and butterflies to our gardens. See BIRDS & BUTTERFLIES chapter.

Trees are beautiful when they complement a house at an appropriate distance, but appalling when they appear to engulf a house because too big a tree was planted too close to the house.

Again: Learn the size any plant will be at its maturity before buying or planting.

A group of evergreen shrubs or trees planted a sufficient distance from the north wall of your house can act as an insulator to block cold winds, thus reducing heating costs.

Raised beds built of bricks or garden timbers have several advantages: They are easier to fill with the exact soil mixture desired. They drain more easily and seem to harbor fewer insects, diseases, and weeds. When built to a convenient height, gardening in them is easier on the gardener's back.

The use of long-term, slow-release fertilizers twice a year eliminates more frequent fertilization.

A composted organic mulch of at least a two-inch thickness on garden beds at all times retains moisture, discourages weeds, feeds the soil, and protects plant roots, especially during periods of extreme drought, heat, or cold. Keep mulch damp to prevent it from blowing away.

> HINT: Composting grass clippings, pine needles, chipped leaves (but not leaves from a pecan tree), and any other once-living material gives a steady supply of organic mulch. See Compost in SOIL chapter.

When making your plant selections, look for attractive foliage and/or flowers, a delight to have for arrangements in your home. See ARRANGEMENTS FROM YOUR GARDEN chapter.

To avoid mowing in cramped areas, consider substituting paving, mulch, or ground cover for grass. *Remember:* Lawns, mulch, and plants absorb heat and help the soil to retain moisture. Bricks, stones, and masonry reflect heat into the garden's atmosphere. Light-colored paving materials reflect more light and heat than those darkened with a dye in the mix.

Stepping stones in a lawn should be avoided because grass grows so rapidly in Houston that frequent hand-clipping is required.

There is a trend toward Xeriscaping, a term referring to the use of native and adapted plants in our landscape. Especially when planted in the locale to which they are indigenous (original or native), such plants seem to require less water, fertilization, spraying, and pruning, less attention in general. Xeriscaping is being recommended to those interested in conserving water, protecting our environment from chemical pollution, and reducing maintenance. More frequent use of plants native to our locales also contributes to the preservation of our horticultural heritage, while freeing the gardener to have more time to enjoy the garden. See WILDFLOWERS-

NATIVE PLANTS chapter.

For any garden to flourish there should be:
- Adequate sunshine, preferably at least five hours a day;
- Sufficient water;
- Effective drainage; and
- Properly prepared fertile soil.

Reading the chapters SOIL, WATER AND WATERING, and DRAINAGE is of utmost importance for successful gardening.

After all is said and done, the most important thing to remember about landscaping is that the garden is to be for your pleasure and satisfaction. Keep it within your time, financial, and physical limitations. Plan it to be a joy, a source of pleasure.

When seeking ideas for design and plantings, visit gardens.
- The River Oaks Garden Club's Azalea Trail every March offers a fine opportunity to view gardens at their best.
- The Bayou Bend Gardens, open to the public several days a week.
- The Mercer Arboretum has acres of native and cultivated plantings. It is open to the public.
- The Houston Arboretum, open to the public, allows walks through the acres of native woods and presents frequent special exhibits.
- The gardens in Hermann Park, open to the public, have several different planting areas and are especially noted for their rose plantings.

All these gardens afford opportunities to familiarize yourself with plants and trees which flourish in the Houston area.

HAPPY GARDENING!

Miniature arrangement: roses, pansies, daisies, ligustrum in bud.

Arrangements From Your Garden

"He must have an artist's eye for color and form who can arrange a hundred flowers as tastefully, in any other way, as by strolling through a garden, and picking here one and there one, and adding them to a bouquet."

—Beecher

Among the pleasures of having a garden is the enjoyment of cutting flowers and foliage for arrangements to bring the fragrance and the freshness of the garden into your home. As you select trees, shrubs, bulbs, ferns, annuals, and perennials for your garden, visualize their foliage and colors in your rooms. One of the most essential considerations is the appropriateness of the arranging material to your containers and to the rooms in which they will be placed. Visualize arrangements in your home and select plants accordingly.

Be aware of the colors, textures, and shapes of the leaves and flowers of the plants you are considering. Will your choices complement your decor? Do the flowers and foliage keep well when cut? Included in this chapter is a list of plants known to last well when cut and another list suggesting how to keep cut flowers and foliage looking fresh for a maximum length of time.

Arrangements to welcome each season might include peach blossoms to celebrate spring; lilies for Easter; colorful annuals and aromatic greens to cool the summer; and holly berries and pine boughs for Christmas festivities. You may become interested enough to open a new world for yourself in arranging fresh bouquets for all to enjoy.

Flower Arranging
(by Suzanne Cain)

Before starting any flower arrangement, observe the area where the flower arrangement is to be placed. Observe the room as to color, size, furnishings, and the exact space it will adorn—whether it be console tables, pedestals, or a mantel. Think of flowers that will go nicely with these considerations. Think of containers that harmonize with the objects in the room. Decide on the height, width, and depth of the materials to be used. Pick from your garden flowers that will enhance the room; flowers that will not be too large or too small for the space the arrangement will occupy.

Have on hand:
- sharp clippers and small cutting shears,
- floral tape and wire,
- pin holders or wire holders,
- florist's frog cage for large arrangements and heavy material, and
- materials to anchor the arrangement in the container, such as floral clay and floral foam.

If using floral foam or oasis thoroughly saturate it in water, cut it with a knife to fit the container and anchor it with sticky floral tape across the top of the container, before starting the arrangement. Oasis holds water and flowers very well, but it may shorten the lasting ability of some flowers.

- Always start with a clean, freshly washed container. Add a small amount of commer-

G.C.

Arrangement of aspidistra leaves and podocarpus branches.

cial cleaning bleach to the rinse water to rid it of any bacteria.
- To extend life of an arrangement, add a capful of bleach to each quart of water, stirring well. Do NOT use bleach in silver containers.
- To absorb odors, drop in a piece of charcoal.

Flower arranging is an art unto itself. First and foremost, the material used should be fresh. Carry with you into the garden a pail of water to which has been added a few drops of denatured alcohol to destroy offensive odors and prolong the flowers' life. Cut all stems diagonally. Place stems in deep water as soon as they are cut.

Available to us are multitudinous varieties of plant specimens which flourish in our climate. Have an idea which containers you will use. Look to the flowers and what they tell you. Study their colors and size. Each combination

Arrangement of lilies, ranunculas, tulips, alstroemaria.

J.H.L.

*Arrangement of roses, bluebonnets, ranunculus,
colored foliage, and sprays of berries.*

- Wilting flowers can sometimes be revived and made to last longer if laid in a basin with water completely covering the stems. Hot water will often revive wilting flowers.
- Cut flowers last longer if they are not crowded in the container.
- One teaspoon of sugar in a vase of marigolds will help compensate for their strong odor.
- One or two tiny drops of melted wax dropped into the centers of freshly cut tulips or magnolias will prevent their opening wide.
- Two ounces of glycerin to 1 quart of water in a vase of autumn leaves keep them from drying out.
- Weak tea added to water helps lengthen the life of arrangements.
- One lump of sugar in water will encourage rose buds to open faster.

says something different. Let the vase's color and shape help decide on material: a composition of flowers or fruits, large blooms, feathery tendrils, tiny, fragile flowers, each has its own character.

Wash all foliage. Flowers and other materials such as green foliage should be thoroughly conditioned in water before attempting to arrange them.

Cut all stems under water on a slant to allow the absorption of more water, and put them in deep tap water up to the flower heads. Large or woody stem ends should be crushed with a small hammer, frayed, or peeled to help them take up more water.

All material may be stored in a cold box or refrigerator, in water, until ready to start arranging.

G.C.

Arrangement of shrimp plant and aucuba leaves.

41

Informal arrangement of wild flowers grown at home: bluebonnets, shasta daisies, gaillardia, coreopsis, and primrose.

J.T.

- Aspirin makes water somewhat acid; flowers like an acid condition and it possibly holds down bacterial growth.
- Vinegar in water provides the same acid treatment as aspirin.
- Copper pennies may help keep rose buds from opening.
- Wire caladium stems; use hairspray or clear shellac on front and back of leaves. They should last over a week.
- Remove all leaves below the waterline, as decaying matter adds poisons to the water.
- To make some flowers stand tall and straight in a large vase, place the flowers in a tall glass inside the vase.
- To dress the base of an arrangement and hide the mechanics, use marbles, sand, pebbles, or rocks. Use the appropriate one or two or all, as you like.
- Change container water every other day, or at least add some fresh water each day. Spray a fine mist of water on flower heads every day to add freshness and prevent dehydration. Pick or cut out dead material as needed, to add life to the remaining material.
- Avoid placing arrangements in drafts.
- Compositions of flowers, fruits, and other material form a still-life. Flowers are like an artist's palette. It is up to you to complete the picture.

Tips on preparing cut flowers:

Agapanthus: Cut stems at an angle and soak in tepid water.

Amaryllis: Cut with sharp knife. Will perk up if given 1/2 cup of vinegar to 2 cups of water.

Anemone: Cut under water.

Aspidistra: Cut stem at an angle and wash leaves front and back.

Azalea: Cut at an angle and put in deep, cool water.

Bamboo: Submerge one hour in one quart of water with two tablespoons of salt.

Baby's Breath: Cut under water.

Begonia: Add one teaspoon of salt to one quart of water.

Blueberry: Cut under water.

Bluebonnet: Submerge in cool water.

Broom: Cut under water.

Calla: Cut under water and rub salt into stem.

Canna: Cut in water. Difficult to preserve.

Camellia: Cut under water and allow to soak at least one hour.

Carnation: Under water, snap rather than cut stems.

Clematis: Cut under water.

Chrysanthemum: Burn stem ends and let stand in cold water two hours. Do not wet foliage.

Cosmos: Cut under water and rub salt in stem.

Crocus: Cut under water and rub salt in stem.

Cyclamen: Pull blossoms and leaves from ground, cut under water, and condition overnight.

Daffodil: Cut under water and stand in water at least two hours.

Delphinium: Add one tablespoon of alcohol to one quart of cold water.

Dogwood: Crush stems under water.

Fern: Cut under water only established fronds, as new growth withers quickly. Dip fronds completely in water to clean, then store in cool water.

Flowering Fruit Tree: Cut with sharp knife, crush ends, and soak in cool water.

Forsythia: Cut just below node.

Geranium: Cut under water.

Gerbera Daisy: Cut stem at sharp slant and soak stem in tepid water.

Gladiolus: Condition in five tablespoons of vinegar to one quart of water.

Grass: Dip in vinegar or alcohol.

Hawthorn: Cut under water.

Heliotrope: Add five drops of alcohol to one pint of water.

Holly: Split or crush ends of stems.

Honeysuckle: Burn ends.

Hyacinth: Cut under water and dip in alcohol.

Hydrangea: Dip in alcohol.

Iris: Put in cold water.

Ivy: Soak in cool water.

Jasmine: Cut stem with knife and submerge in cool water.

Lilac: Remove all foliage, split stems, and cut under water.

Magnolia: Hammer stem ends and place in cool water.

Marguerite and Daisy: Dip in hot water for 5 seconds.

Marigold: Cut under water and soak stems one hour.

Maple: Cut in water and dip stems in alcohol.

Nasturtium: Cut under water

Pansy: Cut under water.

Petunia: Cut under water.

Poppy: Place in deep water for two hours.

Ranunculus: Cut under water.

Rose: Cut under water and dip stems in alcohol.

Snapdragon: Strip lower leaves and place stems in two quarts of water with three tablespoons of baking soda.

Spirea: Cut under water.

Stock: Strip lower leaves and condition in cold water.

Sunflower: Dip stem ends in boiling water.

Sweet Pea: Cut under water and condition in alcohol water.

Thistle: Cut under water.

Tulip: Cut under water and condition in water (one part gin to one pint water).

Violet: Submerge in cold water for one hour.

Wisteria: Crush stem ends and condition in cold water two or three hours.

Zinnia: Remove lower leaves, cut under water, and condition in alcohol water.

Cardinal's Guard. (Pachystachys coccineus)

The Tropical Garden

*"My soul can find no staircase to Heaven
unless it be through Earth's loveliness."*
—Michelangelo

*T*here are so many "tropical" plants growing in Houston gardens that we sometimes forget they are natives of a more tropical climate than ours. Even though Houston has a temperate, often tropical temperature much of the year, when November comes give thought to the possibility of frosts and plan accordingly. Before planting tropicals, careful consideration should be given to their placement in the landscape to afford them protection through the winter.

Freezing weather is unpredictable in the Houston area. True, the average dates of the first and last frosts are December 10 and February 10, but many a freeze has come before and after those dates. It is necessary to keep abreast of weather reports beginning in November and at least through March, particularly with tropical plantings in the garden. If a freeze is predicted, water your garden *before* the temperature drops to freezing. (Please refer to the WINTER PROTECTION chapter.)

Plant the more tender vegetation in protected locations such as south or southeast exposures near a building, near a protected swimming pool, especially a heated one, or next to doors or windows, which readily transmit heat from a home.

Of greatest importance is the necessity to keep all plants in a healthy condition by careful fertilization, thorough watering, cleanliness in the garden, and appropriate pruning, especially the removal of dead wood.

For maximum growth apply three times yearly either granular fertilizer or slow-release fertilizers less often, each according to the directions on the package. In March a 15-5-10 ratio is indicated and in June a balanced ratio of 12-12-12. Fertilize no later than mid-September with a low nitrogen feeding. Nitrogen encourages rapid growth which is subject to frostbite, but potash helps harden the plants for winter cold. The use of organic fertilizers containing trace elements is usually advisable. *Never fertilize a dry plant.* Always water before and after applying fertilizers on the soil.

Keep plants evenly moist through the spring and summer to avoid the stress of their being too dry during the hot weather. In September and October gradually decrease the amount of water. Rainfall usually provides sufficient moisture during the fall season, but if there is no rain, then water, but not as much. Dryness in plants induces dormancy, making them resistant to winter frosts. (This does not mean the plants should be allowed to dry out completely, but reduce the amount of moisture.)

All good gardens start with good soil. Unless you are lucky enough to have fast-draining, sandy loam or can amend your soil to be well drained, raised beds are the best means of assuring drainage and aeration. (See SOIL and DRAINAGE chapters.) The most economical way to modify the black gumbo clay frequently found in Houston is to add to it sand and generous quantities of organic matter.

Part of the fascination of gardening is the continual change in the evolving landscape. To create a tropical garden, begin by planting hardy shrubs and trees. Tender plants may also be interplanted with hardier ones. For the desired effect shrubs should be planted in masses and bed outlines should have gradual contours. A cross section of a typical bed would show the hardy material in the center with perennial-type tropicals, such as bananas, gingers, and rice paper plants, to the back. This way when the tender tropicals freeze in the winter, you can trim them below the line of vision, hidden by sheltering evergreens. Allow enough space in front of the shrubs for masses of seasonal color with copper plants, lantana, caladiums, coleus, impatiens, and similar dependable summer plants.

There are numerous plants which are effective in the tropical garden. The following list includes only some that are usually available, dependable, and require a minimum of special attention. You can observe many of the plants listed at Houston's Hermann Park Zoo and the Mercer Arboretum.

Shrubs for Background

CLEYERA *(Cleyera japonica)*: Culture similar to camellia. Slow growth; may be pruned tree-like. New growth reddish. Hardy. Fertile, slightly acid loam. Scale-resistant. Semi-shade.

LEUCOTHOE, DROOPING *(Leucothoe catesbaei)*: Beautiful broad-leafed evergreen. To 5', with arching branches of large shining leaves, bronze autumn color on new growth. White flowers in clusters along stem, resembling Lilies-of-the-Valley. Protect. Moist, acid sandy loam. Will not tolerate winter drying. Full sun to semi-shade.

LILY OF THE VALLEY BUSH *(Pieris japonica)*: 6'. Fast growing. Handsome form, lustrous leaves delicately tinted when young. Upright panicles of white flowers. Sheltered position in sandy loam with dampened peat or organic compost. Requires good drainage and acid soil.

LOQUAT, BRONZE *(Eriobotrya deflexa)*: 5-8'. Asiatic. Beautiful, bushy, small shrub. Ideal for small gardens. Sun or semi-shade. Hardy. Well-drained loam. Excellent in pots.

MAHONIA,CHINESE *(Mahonia fortunei)*: 5-6', erect, woody, bamboo-like stems. Rosettes of long pinnate leaves. Clusters of yellow flowers, blue berries. Shady north exposure. Sandy, well-drained, rich, acid loam.

> LEATHERLEAF *(M. bealei)* and BURMESE *(M. lomarifolia)*: Orange flowers, powdery blue berries. Partial shade, rich soil.

OLEANDER *(Nerium oleander)*: Medium to large shrub, dark green, lance-shaped leaves. Flowers from white to dark red with many intermediate shades. Full sun is best for flower production. Drought tolerant. Endures heat, any soil, and seashore conditions.

PAPER PLANT, GLOSSY-LEAVED *(Fatsia japonica)*: Native of Southern Asia, grows more slowly and finer quality than *Aralia papyrifera*. Hardy to 15°. Palmate leaves, white flower panicles, black berries. Decorative in pots. Shade and good drainage.

PAWPAW TREE (NATAL PALM) *(Carica papaya)*: South Africa. Very branched, spiny. Fragrant, large, white, star-shaped flowers; plum-like red fruit. Tolerates pruning. Sandy, well-drained soil, sun. Tender. Best treated as an annual.

PEPPER TREE, BRAZILIAN *(Schinus terebinthifolius)*: Bushy, 5-15' high. Freezes but comes back more shrub-like. Striking in shrub borders. Bright red fruit. Sun.

RICE PAPER PLANT *(Tetrapanax papyriferus)*:

Sago Palms in containers. (Cycas revoluta)

Leaves toothed lobes, 1' across. Tall stalks of creamy flowers. Semi-sun to shade. Tolerates various soils. Prefers to be moist.

SWEET BOX *(Sarcococca humilis)*: 3-5'. Good drainage; tolerates shade and drip of trees. Glossy green leaves. Clusters of small white flowers April until June.

Smaller Shrubs for Foreground Planting and Accent Plants

ALGERIAN IVY *(Hedera canariensis)*: Hardy to 17°. Leaves 5-8" wide. Lobes more widely spaced than English Ivy. Moisture and semi-shade. Deep organic soil. Fine wall or ground cover.

AUCUBA, JAPANESE *(Aucuba japonica, nana)*: Asiatic. 18"-2' high. Hardy, dwarf evergreen; waxy, dark green leaves. Clusters of bright red berries fall and winter. Must have male and female plants to produce berries. Shady, moist, humus soil with good drainage.

GOLD-DUST BUSH *(A. japonica, variegata)*: 3-5'. Form and culture similar to above, leaves larger, longer, with gold yellow spots.

BEAR'S-BREECH *(Acanthus mollis)*: Perennial old world, thistle-like shrub; decorative leaves provided pattern for capitals of Corinthian columns. Semi-hardy, full sun in rich, well-drained soils, not too wet. 2' tall with large spineless leaves. Protect.

CARISSA, 'BOXWOOD BEAUTY' or NATAL PLUM *(Carissa grandiflora, dwarf)*: To 2'. Compact, upright growth. No thorns; tolerates pruning. White star-like flowers, red fruit. Loose rich soil. Drainage.

COPPERLEAF *(Acalypha Wilkesiana)*: Ornamental foliage and showy bracts, 3-5'. Needs sun for vivid leaf color, variegated copper, bronze, red, and purple. Well drained fertile soil.

IXORA or JUNGLEFLAME *(Ixora coccinea)*: Tropical

47

evergreen. Handsome woody plant, bushy growth. Tender. Fibrous loam with peat and sharp sand. Good drainage. Prune after flowering. Light shade. Flowers.

> *I. acuminata*: white.
>
> *I. chinensis*: red to orange.
>
> *I. fulgens*: scarlet.

PLUME FLOWER *(Jacobinia carnea)*: 2-3'. American shrubby plant of Acanthus family. Rosy-pink flowers most of the year if in protected sunny location; good loamy soil. Excellent for color.

SAGO CYCAS or COONTIE *(Zamia integrifolia)*: In species. Dwarf, 2-3' wide leaflets, stiff and leathery. Palm-like. Sandy, moist loam, well drained. Shade or semi-shade. Hardy. Very good for pots. Tolerates cold weather, attractive on terrace for winter. Organic matter in soil, regular watering key to success here. Prune in spring. Remove dead leaves.

Tropical and Semi-Tropical Plants for Pots, Tubs, and Planting Areas

AFRICAN IRIS *(Dietes vegeta)*: Clumping, iris-like, narrow foliage and white waxy flowers with brown and orange markings. Ultimately to 4', usually less. Drought resistant and needs good drainage. Moist, fertile soil. Cut back if damaged by cold weather.

ARALIA IVY *(Fatshedera Lizei)*: A true hybrid between *Fatsia japonica* and English Ivy. Leaves dark green 3-5" lobes like large ivy. Needs support. Shape by pinching and pruning. See VINES chart.

BIRD-OF-PARADISE FLOWER *(Strelitzia reginae)*: South Africa, 3-4'. Banana-like foliage. Blooms bright orange and blue. Good drainage, rich, sandy loam. Plenty of moisture as growth starts, but keep fairly dry during dormancy. Sun, southern exposure. Semi-hardy.

> *S. nicolai*, giant variety: Rapid growth. White flowers, large banana-like leaves. Tender below 22°.

CARISSA or DWARF NATAL PLUM *(Carissa*, var. 'Minima' *)*: 1 to 1-1/2'. Full sun. Superior foliage. Loose rich soil.

CARNATION OF INDIA *(Tabernaemontana grandiflora)*: Asiatic. 4-5'. Foliage similar to gardenia, but resistant to white fly. Flowers small, double, white, fragrant. Acid soil, some sun, much water. Tender.

> *T. coronaria*: Small leaves, more compact.

CROSSANDRA *(Crossandra infundibuliformis)*: India-Malaya. Deep green, waxy leaves. Dense terminal spikes of salmon-colored, funnel-shaped flowers. Protect. Best variety is "Florida Sun."

CROTON *(Codiaeum variegatum)*: Extensively grown in warm or protected regions. Ornamental foliage varies in form and color. Mass in sunny place for tropical summer effect. Rich, fibrous loam with leaf mold and sand. Some shade in heat of day to prevent leaf burning. Gradually move indoors for winter; feed monthly, bright light, keep moist. Dwarf varieties also.

DIOON, CHESTNUT *(Dioon edule)*: 2-5'. Graceful, gray fern-like leaves from a pineapple-like trunk. Leaves rigid, leaflets sharp-pointed. Light shade, well-drained soil. Plant away from passing traffic to prevent bruising leaf points. Hardy to 15°.

> MEXICAN CYCAD *(D. spinulosum)*: Slimmer, taller trunk and longer leaves than *D. edule*. To 5' indoors, generally below 10'. Less hardy but same culture as *D. edule*. Protect below 26°.

FRANGIPANI *(Plumeria)*: Shrub or small tree, deciduous. Long, pointed, wide leaves. Fragrant 2" waxy flowers. Sun. Fine in large heavy tubs. Garden soil with 50% rotted cow manure, handful of bone meal per 12" pot, leaf mold or moistened peat moss. Tender.

> *P. alba*: Yellow to white flowers.
>
> *P.r. acutifolia*: White or pink flowers.
>
> *P. rubra*: Pink to bright red flowers.

MANDEVILLA 'Alice du Pont' *(Mandevilla x amabilis)*: Twining tropical vine with large oval, dark green leaves and bright pink, trumpet-shaped flowers which are produced abun-

A tropical scene.

CWH.

dantly. Full sun to light shade. Rapid grower. One of the best annual vines. See VINES chart.

PAMPAS GRASS *(Cortaderia sellowiana)*: Low maintenance, 3-5', excellent for noise abatement. Showy fall plume. Drought resistant. Sun. See SHRUB chart.

PHILODENDRON TREE *(Philodendron Selloum)*: Large leaves. Interesting trunk pattern, unusual roots; primeval. Tender under 20°. Semi-shade, very moist soil mixture of loam, leaf mold, and sharp sand. Very tropical effect.

    P. selloum juvenile: Same as above but small growth pattern.

    P. 'Evansii': Giant, wavy-edged leaves to 6'. Rapid growth with ample water. Also dwarf form.

PRICKLY SHIELD FERN *(Polystichum aculeatum)*: Feathery fern; new fronds develop from crown. Rich, moist loam in shade. Tender under 30°.

Palms

CANARY DATE PALM *(Phoenix canariensis)*: Large, fast growth to 75'. Dark green, feathery leaves. Huge trunk. Good drainage. Sun, sandy soil.

    SENEGAL DATE PALM *(P. reclinata)*: Picturesque leaning trunks. Semi-hardy, any good soil, requires good drainage.

CHINESE FAN PALM *(Livistona chinensis)*: Shade. Weeping effect. Medium size. Very hardy. Needs good drainage, moist fertile soil, and protection.

DESERT FAN PALM *(Washingtonia filifera)*: Very hardy. Trunk to 3' diameter, 60' tall. Common, easy. Plant in clumps of assorted heights.

EVERGLADES FAN PALM *(Acoelorrhaphe Wrightii)*: U. S. Native. Clustering form with slender 4-6' trunk up to 30' tall. Slow growing and tender.

MEDITERRANEAN FAN PALM *(Chamaerops humilis)*: North Africa. Dwarf. Hardy, satisfac-

J.M.K.

Chinese Hibiscus. *(H. Rosa sinensis)*

49

tory low-growing palm. All fronds come from base of plant, giving desirable shape for container or ground planting. Sun or part shade. Fibrous loam with well-mixed leaf mold and sand. Palms must be watered freely in summer, not allowed to dry in winter. Tolerant of seashore.

MEXICAN BLUE PALM (Brahea armata): Beautiful, powder blue fan leaves. Arching flower stalk. Slow growth to 25'. Very hardy. Best with green background.

SAGO PALM (Cycas revoluta): Ancient, primitive plant. Good outdoor specimen. In tubs, thrives in good, sandy loam, with drainage and abundant moisture in the growing season. Stiff, evergreen leaves in rosette form on strong trunk. Protect from freeze.

SLENDER LADYPALM (Rhapis humilis): 4-6' clustering stems. A reed-like oriental palm of ancient genus. Excellent in tubs or protected areas in beds. Well-drained, rich, sandy loam. Protect.

WINDMILL PALM (Trachycarpus martianus): To 50'. Slim trunk, devoid of fibers; more graceful than T. fortunei. Slow growing, hardy, desirable. Soil as for Sabal, below. Sun.
> T. takil: Neat dwarf. Slow growing, to 6'. Hardy, rare.

SAW PALMETTO (Serenoa repens): A dwarf palm with silvery foliage forming clumps. Good for shade. Very hardy. Keep moist. Rare in nurseries. Soil with organic matter, moist, well-drained.

TEXAS PALMETTO (Sabal texana or mexicana): Attractive trunk and leaves, to 50'. Hardy and robust. One of the best sabals. Soil with organic matter, moist, well-drained.

Miscellaneous Tropical Plants

CENTURY PLANT (Agave americana): Long, stiff leaves forming rosettes from which rise tall, bare flower stems. Native of semi-arid regions of America. Porous soil, good drainage. Many varieties.

NEW ZEALAND FLAX (Phormium tenax): Makes

striking groups. To 15', with long, narrow leaves and numerous dark red flowers clustered on long stems. Showy color forms, variegated reddish-purple foliage. Tolerant of any soil, wet or dry, and seashore.

UMBRELLA PLANT (Cyperus alternifolius): Cultivated Sedge, long stems with large palm-like heads. Very good for patios and in pots. Grows in water or in dry places. Any soil. Semi-shade.

Bamboos (See SHRUBS chart.)

BLACK-JOINTED BAMBOO (Phyllostachys nigra): 8-10'. Black cane, sparse, medium-sized leaves, delicate growth pattern. Hardy to 15°, moist soil.

HEDGE BAMBOO (Bambusa multiplex): Fern-like leaves, long, glabrous, deep green, silver cast beneath; forms clumps to 10' in height.
> DWARF BAMBOO (B. multiplex, nana): 3-4'. Woody, hollow, green purplish grass-like canes.

PYGMAEA BAMBOO (Sasa pygmaea): Rarely over 8", creeping rootstock, dense clumps. Small, leathery leaves, deep green. Excellent ground cover; moisture.

Bananas*

ABYSSINIAN BANANA (Musa ensete): Very large ornamental; leaves originating from base of trunk. Dark red veins on mature leaves. 12-15'. Semi-shade and moisture. Any good soil.

PLANTAIN or COMMON BANANA (M. paradisiaca sapientum): India. Tree-like; to 25'. Spiralling leaves, yellow flowers, purplish bracts. Edible fruit; the stem dies after fruiting but is replaced by new suckers. Fairly rich soil with moisture.

SUMATRA BANANA (M. Sumatrana): Semi-dwarf. Leaves long and narrow, reddish-brown underneath, green and brown spots on top. Well-moistened, fibrous soil, semi-shade, 4-6'.

*All members of the banana family may be damaged by freezing but put on new growth next spring.

Hardy Trees for Sun

CAMPHOR TREE *(Cinnamomum Camphora)*: Beautiful, slow-growing evergreen with bright green leaves, fragrant foliage and flowers. Best as multi-trunked specimen. Do not plant near paved area. See TREES chart.

TRINIDAD FLAME BUSH *(Calliandra Guildingii)*: Small tree related to mimosa. Bright red flowers cover entire plant in spring and fall; scattered bloom in summer. Sun. Fertile porous soil. Also FLAME BUSH *(C. Tweedii)*.

VIBURNUM *(Viburnum japonicum)*: Large bright green leaves and clusters of small white flowers. Fast growing. Excellent small, multi-trunked tree. Many other viburnums available. See SHRUBS chart.

WHITE ORCHID TREE *(Bauhinia forficata)*: Small tree with bloom summer to late August. Protect when young. Any soil. Grows in shade or sun. See TREES chart.

XYLOSMA *(Xylosma congestum)*: Excellent small tree. To 20'. Shiny, bright green leaves. Spines on branches make it good barrier plant. See TREES chart.

Semi-Hardy Trees

CARROTWOOD TREE *(Cupaniopsis anacardioides)*: Fast growing, to 40'. Pinnate-leaved tree, tolerant of wet soils, poor drainage and coastal conditions. Very attractive foliage.

FIREWHEEL TREE *(Stenocarpus sinuatus)*: Large, shiny, dark green, oak-like foliage. Circular, bright red-orange flowers.

GRECIAN BAY TREE *(Laurus nobilis)*: The bay leaves for cookery come from this tree. Aromatic, light green, magnolia-like foliage. Requires excellent drainage in any soil. Needs afternoon shade. Little water after established. Yellow flowers.

SILK OAK *(Grevillea robusta)*: Fern-like, dark green foliage. Fast growing. Orange flowers. Hardiness increases with age. Sun; likes heat, well-drained soil.

Plants for the Shade

AUSTRALIAN TREE FERN *(Sphaeropteris Cooperi)*: Rapid growing; 20-30'. Hardy to 32°. Good organic soil and even moisture. Excellent in container.

BRAZILIAN SPIDER FLOWER *(Tibouchina semidecandra)*: Large shrub or small tree with velvety leaves and purple flowers. Spectacular. Almost evergreen; rapid growing. If frozen, will sprout from base. Excellent as single-trunk standard in container. Slightly acid, well-drained soil with roots in shade, top in sun. Pinch for bushiness.

TASMANIAN TREE FERN *(Dicksonia antarctica)*: Slower than above, but much hardier. Protect under 20°. Good organic soil and even moisture. Fine in containers.

CWH

Various plants in containers enhance a patio.

Container Gardening

"Plants bear witness to the reality of roots."
—Maimonides

*I*n the natural world of horticulture, there is no such thing as a "container plant." Was it *Homo sapiens* who tired of roaming the land in search of plants to eat? Or was it *Homo erectus* who decided to grow plants close by his shelter? It may have been the more modern man *Homo sapiens sapiens* who had the bright idea of putting some dirt in one of his crude vessels, a cracked one, no doubt, for drainage, and planting a pretty flowering plant from the woods to embellish his humble abode.

Today every type and size of plant is planted in containers. Even large trees are placed in huge containers in the vast lobbies of buildings to introduce warmth and human scale to the steel architecture. Whatever the decor, there are plants to bring the natural world indoors. Careful thought should be given to the containers for they play a large part in the effect and in the plant's well being.

A container is any vessel in which a plant will grow. Because of the repeated waterings, a container should be made of a material which holds moisture as well as soil. It should drain satisfactorily. If you already have a container you want to use, select a plant for it whose root system will be accommodated properly. A plant like an azalea, which has a shallow but broad root system, should be planted in a pot which is shallow and broad. There are clay pots called "azalea pots" designed for just such plants. Naturally, a tall plant requires a deep container to support the root system and to be in scale with the plant.

There are numerous decorated containers. Consider the texture and overall shape of the plant and its leaves, its texture, and shades of green when placing a plant in a decorated container. And vice versa, if the room has much design in floral fabrics, perhaps a simple container is the best choice as long as it is also chosen to be a happy home for the plant itself. Clay pots "breathe" because clay is a porous material. Plastic pots do not breathe. There are differences of opinion which is the better material for plants. Clay can be made impervious to water by painting it with several coats of vegetable oil or a special sealing product. A suitable saucer deep enough to hold a layer of attractive pebbles is often employed to hold the pot and the roots of the plant above the moisture which accumulates in the saucer after watering. When roots are in constant touch with water they usually die. For larger plants, especially outdoors, there are various kinds of wood containers. Some gardeners use half wooden barrels to plant minigardens. Whatever type of container you select, consider the relationship between plant and container. The container should not detract from the plant.

True, there are plants suitable for every situation whether they be in dish gardens, terrariums, hanging baskets, or pots, but the basic requirements of the plants must be respected if they are to grow in beauty. Remember, the plants have been removed from their natural habitat. Different species and varieties of plants have somewhat different requirements for growth, but all need a growing medium for their roots to grow into. Though a few are content to grow in water alone, the great majority demand soil or a soil-like substitute. For years it has been thought that each plant required its own specially mixed soil, but today the trend is that one carefully formulated planting medium will give sustenance to any potted plant. Many of these formulations do not contain soil as we are accustomed to think of soil. Instead, the mixtures are composed of organic matter or compost and mineral elements. Compost is composed of any material which was once living. It becomes a part of the soil as it decomposes, but until decomposition is complete compost is spoken of as "organic matter." Minerals eventually break into miniscule pieces and gradually become integrated into the soil. With that knowledge in mind, we can think of the soil-less mixture as being, in effect, soil's cousin. Some of the formulas include not the usual fertilizers, but those adapted for slow release of food into the soil, thereby reducing the frequency for fertilization. Little by little horticulturists are making all types of gardening easier. By reducing the time spent on maintenance, they allow the gardeners more time to smell the flowers.

Plants need more than soil alone. Success in growing potted plants depends on several factors which must be adjusted to work in harmony with each other. There must be proper temperature, light, air, and moisture as well as a fertile growing medium. All should be combined to create the atmosphere suitable to plants.

72° F. is considered the best temperature for plants in containers, but indoor plants must become accustomed to living in the normal temperature of the house and its "other" occupants, whatever the plants' native preferences. Plants can readily adapt to a temperature which remains between 50° and 100° F. Photosynthesis is the ability of plants to manufacture starch and sugar, but there must be light for the process to take place. Photosynthesis is recognized as the most important function leaves have, an ability not yet achieved by chemists. It is obvious, therefore, that the placement of potted plants in the maximum amount of light is of primary importance. This is not to say that every plant should be in full sunlight coming through a glass pane. The glass intensifies the heat of the sunlight. If your hand, placed between the light source and the plant, casts a shadow on the plant, the darkness of the shadow indicates the amount of light striking the plant.

Flowering plants and cacti need the maximum amount of light to thrive, at least 3 hours of sunlight each day in a sunny east or south window. Foliage plants, like philodendrons, dieffenbachias, and draceanas, prefer bright light or partial sunlight of north or west exposures. There are also other plants, such as ferns, bromeliads, and spathiphyllum, which are pleased with a diffused interior light. Most of the tropical plants ask for 50% to 90% direct sun filtered through sheer curtains. Because plants grow toward the available sunlight, all container plants should be turned a quarter circle every week to keep their growth straight and balanced. Artificial light, as from a fluorescent tube or a 110-watt bulb, usually gives enough light to make up for the lack of real sunlight. When plants are leaning to one side or have become spindly and lusterless, they are probably indicating the need for more light. Place them in the garden for the summer for a miraculous rejuvenation, being careful to give them a chance to adjust gradually to the extra sunlight. Place them first in a shady area and

Grouped containers of sweet alyssum and primulas.

gradually move them into more light, but rarely the full hot sunshine of our summers. If the leaves become too much lighter, move them back into a little less light once again, but gradually.

The air or atmosphere in which plants are placed obviously reflects the temperature of the room. Air suitable for human beings is appropriate for potted plants—not too dry, not too humid. Like people, plants have differing preferences about humidity, but since it is not easy to change the home environment for each plant, the selection of species of plants which can prosper in your home conditions is one of the keys to success.

Watering container plants is a sensitive skill to be acquired by experience. More questions are asked about this subject than any other. The trick is to moisten the growing medium thoroughly without letting the water drain out the drainage hole carrying valuable nutrients with it. Potted plants, captive in their container, are dependent on their owner to provide them water, their life-giving liquid. Setting the pot in a vessel of water with the level reaching no higher than 3/4 up the sides of the pot allows the soil to enter the drain and water the soil by osmosis, particle by particle, until the potting medium is completely and evenly soaked. When bubbles no longer appear on the surface of the medium, it is an indication that the watering has been completed. Immediately remove the pot from the water and allow it to drain well before replacing it in its accustomed location. Watering in this way reduces the frequency of watering. Avoid allowing a plant's soil to become entirely dry, a condition which puts the plant in stress. The condition is easily recognized by the shrinking away of the growing medium from the inner sides of the container. If water is poured onto the dry soil, the water will follow the easiest route downward, along the vacant spaces left by the shrinkage of the soil, and out the drain. Because the surface appears to be wet, it might be assumed that the soil is thoroughly wet. Not so. The soil allowed to become that dry needs a soaking as described above. During the process of soaking, soluble fertilizer may be added to the water as specified on the label, thereby accomplishing both watering and fertilizing simultaneously. Learn to feel or scratch the soil for moisture. If it is dry, it is time to water; if it is still moist, wait a few more days—except for pots outdoors for the summer. They require watering thoroughly at least every other day, preferably with a slow dripping of a hose on the soil's surface or the soaking method described above. You will soon notice that some, and eventually probably all, pots get a white crusty matter on the lower outside portion of the pot. That crust is an indication of salt accumulation in the growth medium carried down by water as it filters through the soil. The deposit on the outside should be removed with a cloth or a non-metallic scouring pad and a solution of vinegar and water. The soil should be flushed by repeated waterings, perhaps even 6 or 7 times, to wash out the salt accumulation in the soil. This flushing should be practiced every 3 to 6 months. Strangely enough, both too little water and too much water often cause the leaves to turn yellow, but the leaves of a plant which lacks water usually have a dry look and often a browning of the tips. Some plants may be watered by the use of wicks, a practice often followed with African Violets. For plants known to appreciate it, misting of the foliage occasionally is suggested. Remember to protect any nearby wood furniture surfaces. The use of tepid water is appreciated by most plants, as is rain water caught in tubs placed outside during a heavy rain. Cleaning the leaves of accumulated dust is also helpful, using a soft paint brush. Never apply an oil substance to the leaves; it clogs their pores.

Feeding

Do not feed newly purchased plants for about a month because they were probably fertilized at the nursery. Inquire if the plant has a slow-release fertilizer in the soil medium and ask when it should be fed. Acquaint yourself with the slow-release fertilizers and how to apply them. Fish-meal liquid fertilizer is popular because it has a high nitrogen ratio and it does not burn the roots. Use as directed. Plants appreciate regularly spaced feedings—just as people do, and they prefer a lighter concentration on a schedule than one whopping feeding when the owner happens to remember it. Plants grown entirely under artificial light need only about 1/3 as much fertilizer as those growing outdoors. Those in the natural light grow faster. Potted plants are often moved outside for warm spring and summer into fall. When moved from indoors they must have time to become accustomed to the greater amount of light, air, and wind. Move them first to a shaded and protected area for about a week. Then gradually move them into more light until they are in a place which gives them their maximum amount. Indoor plants can seldom stand our hot strong sunshine. Protect them from sun at noon and on into the afternoon. Potted plants may also be placed in the garden beds under trees or wherever they can receive proper conditions. They can be sunk into the soil if they are not in decorative containers. The interior of the house may take on a barren appearance, but think about how happy the plants are outdoors. In the fall follow the same gentle procedure in reverse, accustoming the plants to less light indoors. That may be an appropriate time to repot them.

Repotting

Even with adequate food, the medium's fertility diminishes, partially because the nutrients are washed out of the soil by the waterings. When the plant looks a bit lusterless or appears to be crowded in its pot, investigate. Moisten the soil first. Tap the pot in several places and, holding the pot upside down in your hand, or tilting it as it lies on the ground, gently slide the plant out. If the roots are a solid mass, it is time to repot, but if you prefer to leave it in that particular pot for decorative reasons, gently spread the roots out and clip them off with sharp scissors. Have on hand a mixture of soil or soil-less growth medium and mix some of the pot's soil into the new soil. Place a square of screening over the drainage hole to prevent slugs from entering the hole, cover with a layer of crocking (small chips of broken pots or rough gravel), and then with some of the growing medium to the thickness which allows the plant to rest at its original depth. Place the plant on the soil and gently put in more soil until the pot is about 2/3 filled. Water with a very soft flow of water and allow it to drain. Fill with soil and water again. As the soil settles, you may need to add more soil to the previous planting depth. A line showing a difference in color indicates the previous level. Firm the soil to dispel air pockets. A thin mulch or some attractive pebbles or a layer of sphaghnum moss may be used to cover the soil itself.

There are ready-mixed potting soils available at garden nurseries. One called Fortified Potting Soil contains compost, sand, enriched mulch, and additional composted organics with the addition of a time-release fertilizer and a high micro-nutrient content. There are those called soil-less and some with soil. Read the labels on the packages. There are also ingredients available for you to mix your own. The basic contents of a soil mix are: 2 parts loam, 1 part compost, 1 part coarse sand, and 1/2 part each of well-rotted manure and bone meal. Beware of using peat moss because it is very difficult to re-wet after it has once dried, and when it dries it becomes as hard as concrete.

A soil-less container mixture with a 1-2-1 nitrogen-phosphorus-potash ratio, recommended by the Texas Agricultural Extension Service includes:

1/2 bushel compost
   (1 bushel = 8 gallons)
1/2 bushel horticultural perlite

2 ounces 20% superphosphate
2 ounces limestone, ground
2 ounces agricultural gypsum
4 ounces slow release complete fertilizer.

To be satisfactory, a potting medium must support the plant mechanically, allow circulation of air throughout the medium, and retain adequate moisture. The mixture weighs about 50% less than most soil-containing mixtures. The ingredients are easily obtained, uniform in grade, inexpensive, and sterile. It is disease resistant, drains well, and neither shrinks nor expands with continuous watering. The mixture can be prepared and kept available until needed.

To keep plants shapely practice pinch-pruning of the new growth tips, removal of all dead or withered parts, and turning of the pot a quarter turn every week to allow all sides to have light. Plants lean toward the light source in their effort to receive the light they must have.

Hanging Baskets

If you are considering planting or buying some hanging baskets, remember they usually need daily watering. However, they are attractive hanging on a tree limb or on a hook and chain from the ceiling. Every breeze sets them in motion giving an interesting feature to the garden and a vertical accent. Useful particularly in small spaces, baskets can be planted with a wide assortment of plants. In fact, any plant whose root system is compatible with the small area allowed in the container for roots may be used. Look through the lists in the charts of ANNUALS AND PERENNIALS, GROUND COVERS, HERBS, SHRUBS, FERNS, and VINES for suggestions. Those whose water demands are not heavy are better choices. As you peruse the charts, think about the texture of the leaves, the overall shape of the plants and the color they provide to find those compatible with your landscape. If you plan to plant the basket with different species of plants, be sure they all have the same cultural needs for soil, light, and water. Do not fertilize a newly planted basket, but do soak it well after planting. Suggested soil mixes are those listed previously for other containers, or 2 parts organic matter (compost, finely shredded pine bark) and 1 part mineral matter (soil, sand, perlite, vermiculite). The perlite and vermiculite are much lighter in weight than the soil and sand, which makes a big difference when you are handling a wet basket. To this mixture add a small amount of slow-release fertilizer.

The moss and wire baskets lined with damp sphaghnum moss, green side facing outward and thick enough that no light shines through, are very attractive and can be planted on all sides. The plants eventually form almost a ball. Dwarf Wandering Jew is stunning in such a planting. However, this type of basket requires more frequent watering. A wire basket may also be lined with plastic, planted, then poked with holes through the plastic for drainage. Clay baskets are porous, therefore requiring daily watering. They are also heavier. Plastic baskets do not require as much watering, are lighter weight, allow more space for the root systems, but are not as attractive unless planted in something like ferns which hide the plastic. Take your choice, and be prepared to water every day and fertilize with a weak soluble fertilizer about once or twice a month.

Line the basket if necessary, soak the root systems of the chosen plants, and gently arrange them in the basket on a layer of soil-mix. Continue adding the mixture until the roots are well covered and protected. Firm the soil to remove harmful air pockets, water to settle the roots and place the newly planted baskets away from sun and wind for several days to give them a chance to start growing. The soil should never be allowed to dry out. Always water before feeding and keep the baskets lush and symmetrical by periodically pinching off the tips of each lateral branch and turning them.

Though hanging baskets require more care, the unusual effect they offer in the garden seems worth the extra effort. Few hanging baskets can survive winter cold. Be prepared to protect them.

Terrariums

Terrariums are planted in transparent containers with a removable top. They require very small rooted plants in a container with 1/2 inch of gravel in the bottom, and activated charcoal over that (*not* the cooking charcoal). Mix 9 parts of container mixture, add 1 part of activated charcoal, and use as a layer over the gravel. Water the plants you are using, and gently remove the soil from the roots, disturbing them as little as possible. Using a small spoon or pencil, make an opening in the soil for each plant, arranging them attractively as you plant, and covering the roots firmly but carefully with the mix.

Water just to moisten the roots. Water can be added, but not subtracted so go easy on the water.

Add any decorative pebbles or figures you choose, keeping the composition in scale. Replace the cover or top on the terrarium. The little grouping will recycle the moisture inside the container.

Afterthought

Plants which bloom require much stronger light, preferably sunshine, than those which do not bloom, with a few exceptions, like spathiphyllum. With adequate sunlight, annuals and perennials will bloom in the house. A plant brought into bloom outside may be enjoyed inside for a few days but will probably not flower again until placed in the sunlight outside. What do you suppose *Homo sapiens sapiens* would think of container gardening as practiced today?

Some Plants for Containers

AFRICAN VIOLET, in variety (*Saintpaulia*): Small gesneriad, 4-6" tall, with rosettes of hairy, green-to-bronze leaves, forming plant about 10" broad; flowers in single or double forms, from white through pinks to purples. Bright,

African Violets (Saintpaulia) bloom in the light of a glazed porch.

indirect or filtered light. Water just enough to keep evenly moist, not wet. Misting cleans leaves. Feed monthly. Pot in equal parts loam, peat moss, sand.

AIRPLANE PLANT (*Chlorophytum*): Long thin green or variegated leaves on plant with drooping racemes which produce plantlets at ends after blooming. Medium to strong light. Moist but not wet. Feed monthly. Easy.

ALUMINUM PLANT (*Pilea Cadierei*): Small plant to 12", leaves with puffy design of metallic-gray color, resembling watermelon markings. Average light. Keep barely moist. Feed half-strength every two months. Normal potting soil. Dwarf form *P. Cadierei minima* and *P. crassifolia*; *P. involucrata*; *P. pubescens*; *P.* 'SILVER TREE.'

ARALIA ELEGANTISSIMA (*Dizygotheca*) or FALSE ARALIA: 3-5' plant of upright growth with leaflets of long, thin, jagged leaves like fingers of a hand. Foliage begins coppery, turning black-green as it unfolds. Bright to medium light, average humidity; keep soil barely moist. Propagate from stem cuttings spring or summer.

BROMELIADS, in variety: All bromeliads grow outside in Houston in warm weather, but it is essential to accustom them to sunshine gradually or their foliage will burn. Bromeliads grown as house plants should be kept in bright light. Any well-draining growing medium which anchors the roots, such as osmunda, fern bark, or a mixture of equal parts of peat moss, perlite, and sand is recommended for bromeliad culture. Some bromeliads can be attractively attached to a tree trunk, a wood slab, or a piece of driftwood by tying with strips of nylon hose or by gluing. Used this way, they need frequent misting. Water in cup of plant until it overflows around roots. Do not overwater. Feed with 1/4 strength balanced, water-soluble fertilizer; pour around root system, not in cup. There are about 40 genera and hundreds of species of bromeliads, each with its own stylistic form and fascinating coloring of leaves, bracts, and flowers. Though each plant blooms only once, it will remain attractive for years if given proper care. Bromeliads form pups which can be removed from the mother plant and potted when at least half the size of the mother. Need winter protection.

BULBS, in variety:

AMAZON LILY *(Eucharis grandiflora)*: Fragrant, waxy white flowers 2" across, in clusters on stalks 1' tall, several times a year. Shade outside; low bright light inside. Potting soil with sharp sand or perlite, kept very moist; withhold water for few weeks in winter to force bloom. Feed balanced fertilizer during growing season.

CALADIUM: Variegated, colorful foliage, moderately rich, loose soil with good drainage; shade or part shade; moist, but not soggy. Water every day in summer heat. Plant 2" deep. Pinch off blooms; they rob plants of food needed to produce leaves. Very colorful summer patio or garden plant until cool fall nights.

CLIVIA: See BULBS, TUBERS, RHIZOMES, CORMS AND TUBEROUS ROOTS chart. *C. cyrtanthiflora* and *C. miniata*, both called KAFFIR LILY: Waxy, strap-like, dark green leaves arching from bulb; clusters of flowers on single tall 14" stalk; lily-like flowers orange to red with yellow throats. Allow to become crowded before repotting. Feed liquid manure.

CAST IRON PLANT *(Aspidistra elatior or A. Lurida)*: Leathery, dark green, shiny, long leaves arching from base. Survives with neglect, but thrives with care. Likes shadowless north window light, with soil barely moist at all times. Feed monthly, spring through early fall. *A. elatior variegata* has white stripes on leaves that disappear if plant is fed too much. Sunlight burns leaves.

CACTUS, in variety: See CACTI AND OTHER SUCCULENTS chapter.

CHINESE EVERGREEN *(Aglaonema commutatum)*: Large, dark green lanceolate leaves emerging closely from stalk to 24" tall. No direct sun, but bright light. Good soil kept evenly moist. *A. treubi* is variegated form with arrow-shaped leaves; needs medium to bright light. Both grow in water also.

CHRISTMAS CACTUS *(Schlumbergera Bridgesii)*: Epiphyte to 2' across; branches arching; red flowers at joint ends. Needs 6-8 weeks of short days, as in a closet without water. Potting soil with sand and moist peat moss.

CLOSET PLANT or SPATHE FLOWER *(Spathiphyllum)*: Glossy green, elliptical and pointed erect leaves rising direct from soil. Compact habit. Low to medium light, but sun burns leaves. Feed lightly when indoors. Likes to be potbound. Puts up white spathe flower resembling calla lily, slightly fragrant. Pot in equal parts potting soil and sharp sand or perlite.

CRAB or THANKSGIVING CACTUS *(S. truncata)*: Smaller plant with varying color flowers. Medium to bright light; 6-8 weeks of lower light and short days to bloom. When buds form, move plant gradually into brighter light. Keep evenly moist. Potting soil. High-phosphate food monthly.

CREEPING CHARLIE *(Pilea nummularifolia)*: Shade. Any fertile soil, ample water. A trailing species of Pilea.

CROWN OF THORNS *(Euphorbia Milii)*: Orange-red blooms on spiny gray-green stalks to 12". Bright light, average potting soil. Regular water, but small amount; dryish in winter. Likes low humidity. Succulent.

FALSE CACTUS *(E. Lactea 'CRISTATA')*:

Distorted spiny growth of compact form, 2-3' tall.

PENCIL TREE or PENCIL CACTUS (*E. Tirucalli*): Succulent.

DEVIL'S IVY, POTHOS (*Epipremnum aureum*): Tropical vine adapting well to low light and humidity. Green and white heart-shaped leaves. Any soil or in water. Easy, attractive.

DRACAENA, in variety: Bright indirect light, 65°-85°. Keep soil moist but never allow to stand in water. Average potting soil. Do not fertilize recently purchased or potted plants. Feed at six-month intervals. Varieties differ in appearance.

CORN STALK PLANT (*D. Fragrans massangeana*): To 6' with leaves almost 30" long and 3" wide, having yellow strip down middle.

'JANET CRAIG' (*D. deremensis*): Strap-like, shiny, long dark green leaves.

D. Marginata: To 8' tall. Looks like Spanish dagger with clusters of 14" thin, pointed leaves.

D. d. 'WARNECKI': Sword-like stiff leaves 7-12" long, white stripes on gray-green leaves.

DUMB CANE (*Dieffenbachia*): Upright growth of large 14" leaves, variegated, emerging from stalk. Leaves arch gracefully as plant grows, but lower leaves finally drop off leaving tall, snake-like stalk. Adapts to medium-low light. Don't water until soil is dry. Feed monthly. Dieffenbachias are poisonous when eaten and can paralyze vocal cords. Protect children.

EASTER CACTUS (*Rhipsalidopsis Gaertneri*):Potting mixture kept moist. Light shade. Curving stems easily broken. Scarlet flowers.

FERNS, in variety: One of the oldest plant forms with a multitude of species, most of similar culture: rich, loose, organic soil, lots of peat moss, kept evenly moist with high humidity and part to full shade. Lower temperature than most plants. Keep dead fronds cut off and protect from injury. Feed lightly. Sun bleaches and burns ferns. Springeri (Asparagus), in variety, is kept moist to dry, and is exception because it will take sun, though it bleaches. Light green, needle-like leaves on vining or branching thin stalks. Develops little tubers on top of soil when potbound; repot. Cascading habit. See FERNS chapter and chart.

BIRD'S NEST FERN (*Asplenium nidus*): Attractive rosette of broad upright leaves, to 30"; reduce humidity during winter.

BOSTON FERN (*Nephrolepis exaltata 'BOSTONIENSIS'*): Classic parlor plant. Graceful, arching fronds. *Whitmannii* and *Rooseveltii* are more feathery and finely cut. Cool north light. Water when dry.

ELK or STAGHORN FERN (*Platycerium bifurcatum*): Epiphyte; grows attached to another object, but is not a parasite. Native to rain forest in Asia. Fairly bright light. Fibrous moss to which plant is attached must be kept moist. Water twice weekly. Feed fish oil monthly, after watering; can be hung on wall in winter, or on tree in summer.

FICUS:

WEEPING or BENJAMIN FIG (*Ficus benjamina*): Tree with branches weeping from dense head on trunk, dark green, small, shiny, laurel-like leaves. To 15'. Bright light but no direct sun. Evenly moist. Rich garden loam with compost or potting soil. Condition to any change gradually. Will drop leaves if moved too suddenly, in too dark an area, or in draft as from air conditioner vent. Mist. In proper location, very attractive small tree for house.

INDIA RUBBER TREE (*F. elastica*): Grows to 15' in sprawling habit; very large, dark-green, oval, long leaves from stalk. Good filtered light half day at least. Keep evenly moist in average, well-drained soil. Wipe off leaves and mist. Sudden temperature change may cause leaf drop.

FIDDLE-LEAF RUBBER PLANT *(F. Lyrata)*: Large oblong, dark green, prominently veined leaves from upright trunk. Good in dark corners; burns in sun. Wants high humidity, but do not water until completely dry. Sponge leaves for humidity. Needs good drainage. Overwatering signified by large black spots on leaves.

FITTONIA ARGYRONEURA: Silver-veined, strong mosaic pattern; *F. Verschaffeltii* has red veining. Creeping plants for very warm, humid area. 2-4" leaves are unusual in patterning. Low light of north window or in terrarium. Placing pot on pebbles in water-filled saucer keeps humidity high. Average potting soil. Keep soil moist and feed monthly with half-strength fertilizer, very lightly.

GRAPE IVY *(Cissus rhombifolia)*: Shiny green leaves in threes. Filtered sun for medium light. Standard potting soil. Keep moist. Roots in water. Good for hanging baskets. Ivy does not grow very well in house unless it is placed outside in shade frequently, but grows well in containers in shade. English Ivy *(Hedera Helix)*, Hahn's Ivy are good varieties.

HEN-AND-CHICKENS *(Echeveria*, in variety): American succulents with rosettes of fleshy leaves which retain water. Flowers in panicles, spikes, or racemes. Good light. Easy on water; allow to dry thoroughly. Soil of 1/2 sand, 1/2 compost, and a little bone meal. Easy to propagate.

IXORA or JUNGLEFLAME *(Ixora)*.: To 3' tall. Tropical with clusters of red, orange, white, or pink flowers. Requires rich, fertile soil. Excellent drainage. Protect from cold. Bright light, but not strong sun.

JADE TREE *(Crassula argentea)*: Many species, native of South Africa. Long-lived. Medium to bright filtered light. Do not overwater.

Tree form to 3' with small fleshy leaves on branches. Leaves store water and show need for it with wrinkled look. Water only when necessary. Pinkish-white bloom about Christmas. Feed lightly each month with complete house plant fertilizer. Can stand heat and drought. Pot in very well-drained mixture of 2 parts loam, 1 part sand and charcoal or wood ashes with a little ground limestone.

KALANCHOE: Succulent. Small flowers in flower heads red, yellow, orange-red, orange. Leaves fleshy, to 3", oval. Dwarf form available. Needs good, airy light but no noonday sun. Likes short days to bloom. Keep out of drafts. Don't stand in water, but keep evenly moist. Allow to dry out. Average potting soil on gritty side with good drainage. Feed monthly when growing and blooming.

LEOPARD PLANT (*Ligularia tussilaginea Aureomaculata)*: Large, rounded leaves, blotched cream and yellow; yellow daisy-type flowers. Any garden soil. Bright light but not full sun. Outside in shade.

NEPHTHYTIS *(Syngonium podophyllum)*: Arrow-shaped leaves, very dark green on vining-type plant. Adapts well to low light and low humidity of house. Grows in water and is good for totem pole. Average soil. Tough and easy. Many species have colored leaves.

NORFOLK ISLAND PINE *(Araucaria* in variety *A. excelsa)*: Symmetrical tree with branches of evenly whorled, dark green leaves of fine texture. Beautiful Christmas tree (without lights); good patio tree. Long-lived. Bright indirect or filtered light. Place near window for it to receive 1/2 day light, not direct sun. Keep soil on dry side or barely moist. Mist foliage. Fertile, sandy soil with organic matter, well-drained. Fertilize rich, sandy soil every 3 months. Feed twice during growing season.
    BUNYA-BUNYA *(A. Bidwilli)*: Glossy, green-

Tulips bloom in grouped pots.

B.C.

leaved Australian tree; sharp pointed leaves.

MONKEY PUZZLE TREE (*A. Imbricata*): Hardy outdoors; prickly branches twist and turn in tortuous fashion.

ORCHIDS: Thousands of species, some from hot jungles, others from cool mountains, not easily grown in Houston except in greenhouse. The terrestrial varieties grow in loose, moist soil rich in organic matter like humus; require continuing supply of water and moisture as well as sun; do not allow to sit in water. Cymbidiums, their hybrids and dwarf forms, are in this category. The epiphytics grow perched on tree branches, getting their food from air, rain, and any decaying organic matter they can reach with their roots; Cattleyas, their hybrids and dwarf forms, belong in this category. Phalaenopsis and Vanda are among most tolerant of house conditions. Orchids must have ample circulation of humid air, temperature from 60° to 80°, no direct noon sun, but good light. Experiment to find proper location in your home for these beautifully flowering plants.

PALMS: A large diversified family with some producing foliage at top of bare trunk while others put out fronds in clusters. Most come from tropical or subtropical areas. Some of the hardier types are listed in the TROPICAL GARDEN chapter. Indoors, palms like to be in good average potting soil, very well drained, in a not too big container in bright indirect light.

ARECA PALM (*Chrysalidocarpus lutescens*): Feathery, yellow-green, arching fronds with yellow stems; needs light (6-8 hours). Potting soil. Keep evenly moist and mist foliage. Fertilize monthly with organic food. Prefers to be outside in light, but not sun. Iron and nitrogen feeding and outdoor light may revive it after a stint indoors.

63

BAMBOO PALM *(Rhapis humilis)*: Tall to 15', bamboo-like stalks of grace and charm; likes east window filtered light. Feed lightly to retard rapid growth. Water weekly or bi-weekly.

FISHTAIL PALM *(Caryota)*: Name reflects shape of leaves on stems rising upwards before branching from center; likes small pot with bright light, wet soil, and monthly feeding spring until fall. Potting soil.

HOWEA, in variety: SENTRY OR CURLY PALM *H. Belmoreana (Kentia belmoreana); H. forsterana (K. forsterana)*, flat, thatch-leaf or paradise palm. Both are fine for indoors. Slow growth, graceful, feathery, arching leaves with slender leaflets. Sentry spreads in habit; Paradise attains vase shape; both have single trunks, but 2 or 3 may be placed in same pot for effect of multiple trunks. Potting soil, well-drained.

PARLOR PALM *(Chamaedorea elegans)*: Dwarf form, growing in clusters of dark green fronds to about 2' tall. Fine table plant with medium light; also outdoors in part shade in summer. Potting soil with peat and vermiculite. Good drainage. Frequent watering.

PONY TAIL or ELEPHANT-FOOT PALM *(Beaucarnea recurvata* or *Nolina recurvata* or *N. tuberculata)*: Tall-growing, with slender, drooping leaves at top of bare stalk emerging from huge bulbous swelling of trunk at soil level which serves as water reservoir; direct sunlight at least 4 hours daily or very bright indirect light. Allow soil to dry out between waterings. General purpose potting soil. Feed established plants only once annually.

SLENDER LADYPALM *(Rhapis excelsa)*: 5-12' tall, slow growth, tolerant of poor light and drought, responds to good light and feeding; hardy to 22°.

WINE PALM *(Caryota urens)*: Tall with solitary trunk, broad, dark green leaves, very long. Warm, moist air. Not too wet during winter.

PALM GRASS *(Curculigo capitulata, C. recurvata)*: Stemless plant from Java, of Amaryllis family, with cluster of attractive foliage almost hiding yellow flowers. Leaves have ribbed or plaited look. Medium light, warm humid atmosphere, about 75°. Soil: good drainage in mixture of sand, loam, peat moss with a little limestone and bone meal.

PEPEROMIA, in variety: Low-growing table plants with foliage of varying designs. WATERMELON PLANT *(P. arifolia, P. argyreia)*. 'EMERALD RIPPLE' *(P. caperata)* with dark green, very wrinkled leaves on red stems. Average to bright light. Allow potting soil to dry out between waterings. Feed every 3-4 months with half-strength house plant food.

PRAYER PLANT *(Maranta leuconeura)*: Name derives from fact leaves move upward at dark as though in prayer. Table plant; grows well under lamp. Light makes leaves move back into normal position. To 9" tall. *M.l. kerchoveana* has grayish green leaves that have, when young, reddish spots resembling animal tracks. *M.l. Massangeana's* leaves have fishbone patterned veins and purple undersides. Potting mix. Good drainage. Water often during growing season.

PHILODENDRON, in variety:

P. pertusum: Sold as Split-Leaf Philodendron, is actually *Monstera deliciosa,* an evergreen, vining plant with very large leaves needing filtered shade outdoors, rich soil, ample water, and a stout support. Must have good drainage. Protect from freeze. Indoors same culture; keep leaves clean. Not in sun.

HEARTLEAF *(P. scandens)*: Name describes leaves which are small, medium green and vining, usually grown on a support.

P. 'SAO PAULO': Vigorous with deeply frilled leaves.

P. Eichleri: Very large, hardy, self-heading hybrid, resistant to sun.

P. gloriosum: Rosette form with ivory ribs.

P. Imbe: Vine with dark red spots.

P. ornatum: Vine with silvery gray spots, red stems.

P. Selloum: Hardy, bold, to 4' tall, spreading to 6', with short trunk and handsome leaves, long and wide, deeply cut. The *P.s.* 'LUNDII' is more compact. Excellent plant.

REDBIRD CACTUS, *Pedilanthus tithymaloides variegatus (Euphorbia T.V.):* To 3'. Stems have zig-zag effect bending slightly at each leaf; pointed leaves variegated green and white with pink edge; flowers small, red, appearing at tips of stems. Bright indirect light, average potting soil kept barely moist. Feed only spring through summer at 2 or 3-month intervals. CAUTION: Milky juice in stems is caustic and irritant.

SCHEFFLERA (*Brassaia actinophylla*): Large, glossy green leaves in bushy form to 12' tall. Good, filtered light most of day. Avoid air vents. Sandy, fertile potting soil, well drained. Feed once or twice monthly when growing. Medium moisture and misting but leaves turn yellow with overwatering.

SNAKE PLANT or AFRICAN BOWSTRING HEMP, *Sansevieria (S. hyacinthoides):* Tropical succulent of lily family; erect stiff, pointed, basal leaves, variegated or mottled in green, and yellow or white. Very easy. Low sunlight. General potting soil kept moderately dry. Feed every 3 or 4 months while growing.

SUCCULENTS, in variety: Fleshy stems which retain water, as cacti do, making them drought resistant. Leathery, coarse or spiny foliage that suspends growth like yuccas do. Least demanding of all container plants. Give them sun, dry air, minimum water, and quick-draining, gritty soil. Propagated by seeds, cuttings, or graftings. See CACTI & OTHER SUCCULENTS chapter.

SWEDISH IVY (*Plectranthus Oertandahlii*): Sun or partial shade. Rich soil, good drainage. Roots easily. Many species.

TI PLANT (*Cordyline terminalis,* or *C. minima* 'BABY TI'): Long narrow stems arising from single trunk, to 3-6'. *C.t. bicolor* has red-edged leaves; *C.t. tricolor* has green, pink, red, and white variegated leaves. Needs good bright light, good potting soil, and even moisture.

YUCCA *(Y. filamentosa and flaccida):* Bluish sword leaves in bold rosette. To 2-1/2'. Sandy loam; good drainage; open exposure.

ZEBRA PLANT (*Aphelandra squarrosa*), in variety: Favorites in Victorian times. Leaves heavily veined in white. Flowers yellow to scarlet. High intensity light makes white stripes wider. Needs bright light and high humidity, but must not be over-watered. Never stand in saucer with water. Allow to dry out, but not to wilting point, before watering thoroughly. Feed balanced food, such as 20-20-20 or 20-10-10. After bloom, cut to one or two pairs leaves for bushiness. Loose, well-drained potting soil.

ZEBRA PLANT *(Calathea Zebrina):* Bold vigorous plant to 3', with magnificent deep, velvety leaves, having mid-rib and lateral veins yellow, palish green above, purple beneath. Good medium light. Keep evenly moist, but very well drained. Rich soil. Grouping around larger plants increases needed humidity.

Some Fragrant Plants For Containers
CAPE JASMINE
CONFEDERATE JASMINE
GARDENIA
'GRAND DUKE' and 'MAID OF ORLEANS'
MEYER LEMON, citrus.
SWEET OLIVE (*Osmanthus fragrans*)

Close-up of a Golden Barrel cactus shows interesting details.

Cacti & Other Succulents

*"Full many a flower is born to blush unseen,
and waste its sweetness on the desert air."*

—Gray

*T*he definition of cacti and succulents is a riddle in itself. "Every cactus is a succulent, but not every succulent is a cactus." Though there are definite differences, the principal similarity is the ability of all succulents to store water within themselves.

The natural habitats of these plants are dry regions. Most found in the United States are natives of the Southwest, a region of minimal rainfall. Through the thousands of years, succulents adapted themselves to the arid climate.

These stubborn plants gradually dropped their leaves and developed thick fleshy stems to act as water reservoirs. In addition, the roots became unusually long in proportion to the plant. These far reaching roots, growing just under the surface of the soil, are able to absorb every raindrop that falls and store it for the plant's future use.

To protect themselves from predators, cacti developed sharp bristles and spines. The plants thus became unpalatable to the ranging animals looking for food. What wonders Nature hath wrought!

One of the characteristics which differentiate cacti from other succulents is that cacti have spine cushions or areoles which other succulents lack, even though they are spiny.

Their successful adaptation to drought has made cacti and succulents popular for house plants in the artificially air-conditioned, often dry atmosphere of our homes.

The cactus and succulent families include species ranging from virtually thimble-size to 20-foot trees. There are all types of shapes and many different shades of green, gray, and yellow. No wonder they are fascinating subjects to many gardeners.

Mary Jo Gussett of the Houston Cacti and Succulent Society has kindly prepared the following list and cultural information to assist gardeners who choose to grow these beguiling plants.

When to Water

During the growing season, March 1 to November 10, water once a week. Beginning in March, gradually start increasing the water. On cold, rainy days refrain from watering. It is always best to water on warm, sunny days early in the day.

During the dormant season, you can water plants in very small pots more often, but usually once a month is all that is necessary to keep succulents from shriveling and some need no water at all (see list).

How to Water

Your own experience ultimately will acquaint you with the best way to water each type of plant. Generally, thoroughly wet soil. The water must be able to drain through the pot in just a few minutes. Therefore, it is necessary to have a hole in the bottom of the pot and porous soil. Water should not be poured on the plant but into the pot.

Soil Requirements

Soil must be porous and must drain freely. It should be nutritious, repotted at least every two years. The soil should provide support, not over or under potted, too much soil holds too much water and may rot roots.

Components of soil
  1/3 soil
  1/3 peat
  1/3 sand (coarse builders sand) or perlite or
      vermiculite.

Some commercial potting soils contain a rich peat. If you are using this soil, you need to use 2/3 potting soil and 1/3 perlite or sand. Cacti usually need more drainage, so the mix could be 1/2 potting soil and 1/2 sand or perlite.

Fertilizing

As the weather starts warming in the spring, it is a good idea to encourage strong healthy growth by using a 1/2-strength balanced fertilizer such as Peters 20-20-20 or even BR-61. You can fertilize each time you water or just once a month. By fall all fertilizing should be stopped.

Light Requirements

Plants can be damaged by too much or too little light. East light (morning sun) is perfect for most succulents. Southern exposure is best for cacti. Most all succulents, including cacti, need bright light. Only epiphytic cacti, such as the Orchid Cactus or Christmas Cactus, can take a moderate amount of light. Sanseverias can stand moderate to low amounts of light.

In nature, the majority of cacti are found on the east side of hills or under scrub brush. Therefore, a filtered sun should be provided. Rotate shelf plants so growth is even.

Minimum Temperature

Cool winter temperatures are necessary to aid in setting buds (as is dormancy).

Dependent upon country of origin, the general minimum is:

South American Cacti	40-50 degrees
North American Cacti	35-45 degrees
African Succulents	50-60 degrees
Other Succulents	40-50 degrees

Growing plants freeze easier than dormant ones so this is why it is necessary to keep them dry in winter.

Outdoor Beds

The major problems in growing cacti in an outdoor bed in Houston are the rain and humidity. Most successful beds are located under a covered bright area, such as the eaves of the house, a greenhouse glass, or fiberglass-type roof or a patio cover with light fiberglass roof. Very few cacti or other succulents can stand sitting in damp soil or being constantly exposed to rains. Even if there is the recommended 2 or 3-foot drainage under the plants, when a winter front comes through Houston preceded by rain and followed by cold temperatures, an unprotected plant will rot because the moisture content of the plant is too high. Temporary covers of heavy plastic over a wood frame can be used to protect the bed in winter. Or, special plants that you are worried about can be removed from the bed,

Agave Victoria Regina compacta.

wrapped in newspapers and stored for the winter with no bad effects on the plants (must be dry).

Insecticides

Malathion or Diazinon can be used to treat a large infestation of mealy bugs or scale insect. Alcohol can be used for a few bugs. Do not spray when plants are exposed to bright sun. Sensitive plants, such as Echeverias or Jade Plant, should be sprayed carefully and rinsed with water 20 minutes after spraying. Be sure to mix 2 or 3 drops of a wetting agent with the spray to enable spray to stick to waxy leaves or plant body. Root mealy can be treated by immersing the plant for 20 or 30 minutes in a solution of insecticide. Throw away badly infected plants or remove from rest of plants as bugs travel.

Culture of Cacti

BALL CACTUS *(Notocactus)*: Sun to light shade; 2/3 potting soil and 1/3 perlite. Average water during the growing season. Dry in winter. Flower easily at different times during spring and summer.

BARREL CACTUS *(Ferocactus)*: Full sun when mature, light shade for young plants; 1/2 potting soil and 1/2 perlite. Water well in hot weather and always let soil dry out between waterings. Keep dry in winter. Daisy-like flowers form on new growth in summer. Takes many years to reach blooming size.

BISHOP'S CAP *(Astrophytum myriostigma)*: Full sun to light shade; 1/2 potting soil and 1/2 perlite. Will take plenty of water in hot sunny weather only. Keep dry in winter. Blooms in summer and early fall.

CHIN CACTUS *(Gymnocalcium)*: Partial shade or morning sun; 2/3 potting soil and 1/3 perlite. Can give plenty of water during the growing season. They are hardy if dry in winter. Bloom

69

when 2 years old, flowering freely with flowers lasting several days.

CROWN CACTUS (Rebutia): Partial shade with protection from sun; 2/3 potting soil and 1/3 perlite. Average water during the growing season. Keep dry in winter. Bears flowers in a circle around the base of plant in spring and summer.

EASTER LILY CACTUS (Echinopsis): Light shade or morning sun, east exposure; 2/3 potting soil and 1/3 perlite. Watering should not be too heavy as sides of plant may split or root rot. Humidity tends to cork plant from base. Keep dry in winter. Beautiful 3 to 5-inch blooms appear in summertime. They have a heavy scent and last about 24 hours.

GOLDEN BARREL (Echinocactus grusonii): Full sun with good overhead light; 1/2 potting soil and 1/2 perlite. Very sensitive to moisture and should be watered infrequently and only if roots are established. Keep dry in winter. Sun not strong enough in Houston so even the largest most mature plants are difficult to bloom.

OLD MAN CACTUS (Cephalocereus senilis): Light shade to full sun (if mature); needs good overhead light or will elongate; 1/2 potting soil and 1/2 perlite. Water lightly on warm sunny days only and dry out between watering. Keep dry in all cool weather. Blooms in spring after reaching 3 feet in height.

ORCHID CACTUS or NIGHT-BLOOMING CEREUS (Epiphyllum): Partial sun; 2/3 humus-rich potting soil and 1/3 perlite. Keep plants moist but not wet. In winter, water only after soil dries out. 5 to 7-inch blooms appear from May to November.

PERUVIAN TORCH (Cereus peruvianus): Light shade with good overhead light; 2/3 potting soil and 1/3 perlite. Give plenty of water from spring to fall. Keep dry in winter. 7-inch white blooms appear in June.

PINCUSHION CACTUS (Mammillaria): Full sun to light shade; 1/2 potting soil and 1/2 perlite. Will take average watering during spring and summer. Water wooly and feathery-spined varieties in soil only. Dry in winter. Blooms appear anywhere from March to October on last year's growth.

PRICKLY PEAR (Opuntia): Full sun; 1/2 potting soil and 1/2 perlite. Give plenty of water during summer and keep dry in winter. Blooms appear during spring and summer forming prickly pears in late summer.

Culture of the Other Succulents

AGAVE (Century Plant): 300 plus different species. Full sun; 2/3 potting soil and 1/3 perlite. Give plenty of water during the growing season. Blooms once in a lifetime after 10 plus years.

ALOE (Lily Family): 300 plus species. Full sun to partial shade; 2/3 potting soil and 1/3 perlite. Plenty of water during the growing season which may be fall and winter. Of the many varieties, there is one that will bloom in each month of the year.

CRASSULA (Bead Plant): 300 plus species. Full sun to light shade; 2/3 potting soil and 1/3 perlite. Water moderately and dry out between waterings. Small blooms on a bloom stalk of many flowers appear in spring and summer.

ECHEVERIA (Hens and Chicks): 130 plus species. Sun to partial shade; 2/3 potting soil and 1/3 perlite. Ample water when growing. Blooms appear on a stem above the plant usually in late fall and winter.

EUPHORBIA (The Spurge Family): 1,000 plus species. Sun to partial shade with good overhead light; 2/3 potting soil and 1/3 perlite. Average watering from spring to fall and keep dry in winter. Very small flowers appear in late fall and winter.

GASTERIA (Lily Family): 80 plus species. Shady to light shade; 2/3 potting soil and 1/3 perlite. Plenty of water from spring to autumn and keep on dry side in winter. Blooms appear on a long flower stem in spring.

HAWORTHIA (Lily Family): 160 plus species.

MJ.G.

Native Texas Mammilaria cactus.

MJ.G.

From the left: Agave V. R., Opuntia, Purple Sage, Hamatacactus, Sotol. The last four are Texas natives.

Prefer shade; 1/2 potting soil and 1/2 perlite. Plenty of water in hot weather and keep on dry side in winter. Blooms appear on long flower stem in summer and fall.

HOYA (Wax Plant): 10 plus species that are succulent. Partial shade to shade, will take morning sun; 1/2 potting soil and 1/2 perlite. Water generously during spring and summer. Water only if shriveling in winter. Most are summer bloomers forming round clusters of flowers that arise from spurs. Do not cut spurs as flowers are produced again and again from these spurs.

KALANCHOE (Stonecrop and Houseleek Family): 120 plus species. Partial shade but will tolerate full sun; 2/3 potting soil and 1/3 perlite. Water freely from spring to autumn and water sparingly in winter. Flowers appear in winter in clusters and a long stem.

PACHYPODIUM (Madagasgar Palm): 20 plus species. Need bright light from above or will elongate—morning sun; 1/2 potting soil and 1/2 perlite. Give plenty of water during warm weather. Stop watering when leaves begin to fall and begin to water again in spring when new growth of leaves appears. Blooms appear at beginning of growing season on top of stem.

SANSEVIERIA (Century Plant Family): 50 plus species. East morning sun to shade. Grow well inside in moderate light; 1/2 potting soil and 1/2 perlite. Prefer low humidity and less than average water, very little in winter. Never let water sit in center of plant, will rot. Blooms appear on a spike from soil in fall and winter.

SEDUM (Stonecrop and Houseleek Family): 600 plus species. Full bright light; 2/3 potting soil and 1/3 perlite. Plenty of water in warm weather. Flowers appear throughout the year as small star-like blooms and in clusters.

STAPELIA (Milkweed Family): 110 plus species. Sun to partial shade; 2/3 potting soil and 1/3 perlite. Water moderately in warm weather and keep on dry side in winter. Star-shaped flowers bloom in late summer and through fall.

Broccoli from the garden.

The Vegetable Garden

*"To own a bit of ground, to scratch it with a hoe,
to plant seeds and watch the renewal of life
—this is the commonest delight of the race, the
most satisfactory thing a man can do."*
—My Summer in a Garden
Charles Dudley Warner, 1870

More than a hundred years ago the above quotation was written, yet today many feel just as Mr. Warner did. Through the centuries the growing of vegetables and herbs has enriched not only Man's physical body but also his inner being. A strong feeling of gratification, even of reward, comes with working the soil and growing food necessary for our sustenance.

There are two open secrets to growing vegetables: grow only those you know are going to be relished, and plant varieties which bear the largest quantity per plant. One green pepper bush bears enough peppers for weeks of eating, whereas it takes several long rows of spinach to make a meal. That is not to say you should eat pepper instead of spinach. The idea is to decide what you and your family enjoy eating and concentrate on those vegetables and herbs. (Refer to the HERBS chart.)

The most common mistake beginning vegetable gardeners make is to prepare too large a garden area. The first year try a garden no larger than 100 square feet. It can always be enlarged next year, but it is much more satisfying to keep a small garden in clean, proper condition, allowing the plants to grow to their full potential, than to stare at an untended large garden you wish you had never begun.

As for timing, allow a minimum of 4 weeks to prepare the soil. Locate the garden where it can receive maximum sunshine, 6 hours a day being the minimum number of hours to grow vegetables successfully. Place the bed away from trees and shrubs to avoid shade as well as the competition from their root systems for food and water. Be sure there is a water faucet within easy distance from the bed. Vegetables need water. Determine the type of drainage in the proposed area by digging a hole 10" to 12" deep. Fill it with water and check the time taken to drain completely out of the hole. If it drains in 20 or 30 minutes, the drainage is sufficient. If it drains even more quickly, you are in luck. If it drains almost immediately, the soil is probably predominantly sand and will require the addition of a large quantity of organic matter and some loam to help the soil retain water long enough for the plants' roots to benefit. But if the water does not drain in an hour, the drainage must be improved.

The addition of compost, probably accompanied with sharp sand, is in order. Even if the decision is made to use raised beds, the general drainage on the property should be corrected to avoid flooding from our heavy rainstorms. Refer to SOIL and DRAINAGE chapters.

It is now time to call the nearest Agricultural Extension Service Office to request information on how to obtain a soil test. It is very important to determine the type of soil in your garden, which, if any, amendments it needs, and its pH rating. This may seem time-consuming but it will save not only time spent in incorrectly preparing the soil, but also money spent on unnecessary additives, and definitely will guide you in the preparation of a fertile, productive vegetable bed. To grow to their potential, vegetables require a fertile soil of the proper texture, loose enough to allow seeds to grow yet heavy enough to support the plants. With the guidance of the soil test results that should be a simple matter. "Don't guess; have a soil test."

There are several other things to do while awaiting an answer on the soil test. Determine which vegetables, herbs, or fruits you want to grow. Let this be a decision in cooperation with everyone who will be enjoying the harvest. Make a list of the choices and check the accompanying charts to learn when each should be planted, and whether they will be planted from seed or transplants. Take care to select the varieties known to grow and produce well in Houston.

Much up-to-date information on vegetable and fruit selection and growing is available from local sources: the Office of the Agricultural Extension Service, nurseries, and newspaper and magazine articles *if* their information is intended to be used in our climate. Hybridizers are continually striving to develop varieties more disease and insect resistant, more tolerant of extremes of weather, stronger, more flavorsome, and more prolific. However, a beginner would do well to plant tried and true varieties.

Reading a personal account of a successful Houston gardener will give you some helpful and interesting hints:

Gardening
By Earl R. Limb, Sr.,
Houston, Texas

"There is probably no better way to enter the subject of Houston area gardening than to recognize that Mother Nature has given us two distinctly separate growing seasons, Spring and Fall.

The Spring season may be considered to begin February 15, the average date for the last freeze of Winter. Similarly, the Fall season ends on the average date, December 10, marking the expected first freeze of Winter. The Seasons are separated by the interval of hot dry summer. With these dates in mind, charts have been prepared for the optimum planting dates for the entire list of common vegetables. See attached charts.

These guides make it a fairly simple matter to select dates for planting and crop succession based on vegetables' temperature tolerance. Whereas most vegetables may be grown equally well in either season, experience has shown that the Fall is preferred for leaf crops because most are hardy enough to remain viable after Winter's first light freezes.

Typically, the Houston average garden is relatively small which fact presents a challenge to gain maximum yield out of minimum space. Nature cooperates by providing a comprehensive time schedule.

The preparation of the garden is almost a year-round activity. When summer ends, most of the spring plants have run their course and the garden is a near-jungle of dead vines, stalks, weeds, and grass. Clearing these away may be a sizeable job but it should be done with dispatch to ready the plot for reuse. At this point a thorough work-up with the rototiller is timely, including the addition of compost and other organic matter for soil improvement.

The Fall garden usually includes: beets, cabbage, chard, collards, green beans, lettuce (loose

Cornucopia of homegrown vegetables.

and Bibb lettuce), mustard, onion sets, parsley, purple hull peas, spinach, and tomatoes. Tomatoes, collards, and cabbage are purchased from a local nursery for transplanting.

All these vegetables are planted with due allowance for maturity before winter freezes. However, the leaf crops are hardy enough to withstand light freezes.

The first Spring planting in early January is Snow Peas. These are quite hardy. Also in mid-January, indoor sowing of tomato seed is done in flats. The seedlings are ready for garden planting by the time the soil warms in early March. Enough seedlings are thus available to have 100 or more transplants.

The Spring garden includes: beets, bell peppers, corn, eggplant, green beans, lettuce, okra, onion sets, purple hull peas, summer squash, and zucchini. The bell peppers (12) and eggplant (6) are purchased as nursery seedlings.

This is not intended to reflect an ideal garden selection but is merely one gardener's options based on space limitations and dietary preferences."

In a small garden, avoid space-taking plants and those which grow very slowly, such as corn, cantaloupe, watermelon, and pumpkin.

Intercropping, the practice of planting small varieties like radishes, green onions, and lettuce, all of which mature quickly, between medium sized plants which take longer to mature, like tomatoes, allows the planting of more varieties in less space.

Crop rotation and plant diversity are both helpful in controlling disease which can spread rapidly through a large number of plants of the same variety. Rotation of crops prevents soil insects and disease which have a penchant for a particular plant, waiting quietly for the same plant to appear in the same location.

Plant in rows running east and west to

allow all plants equal sunshine rights. If the rows run north and south, place taller plants on the north side to prevent them from shading smaller plants.

Draw a plan on paper of where you will plant each variety and how much row space they will take. While planning consider the characteristics of each plant at its maturity and allow the proper amount of space for each. With those decisions on paper, the actual planting will be speeded up.

Even if you have not yet received the results of the soil test, you can begin to prepare the proposed bed, assuming the drainage is correct.

Clear the area of all grass, weeds (roots and all), rocks, and any other debris. Break up the soil with a spade, a fork, or a rototiller. If it is very difficult to break, it is probably the black gumbo soil common in much of Houston. In that case, sprinkle the surface with a coating of agricultural gypsum. Water as directed and wait a week or so. Try again to break it up. It should be easier this time. See SOIL chapter.

For every 100 square feet apply:
  organic compost and sharp sand in a 2 to 4-inch covering
  5 lbs. of superphosphate
  5 to 10 lbs. each of bone meal, blood meal, and potash
  100 lbs. of sheep or steer manure.

Spade or rototill several times until the texture of the soil is homogenous. The texture should be loose and fine enough to allow the roots to grow through it. Add to or subtract from the above materials according to the recommendations of the soil test. In 2 weeks cultivate and water the bed again, removing first any weeds which have come up. In another 2 weeks, the soil should be tilled or worked again to ready it for planting. The day before planting, water the soil enough for it to be just moist or damp for planting. Some gardeners prefer to add into the soil a chemical fertilizer such as 13-13-13. Most

authorities agree that compost is the single most important additive to soil for it encourages the growth of the all-important micro-organisms in the soil, enhances water retention, improves the tilth, fertilizes and promotes hormones which in turn promote growth. It also improves aeration of the soil and returns rich nutrients to the soil. Compost is Nature's miracle worker. Whatever kind of soil you have, properly prepared compost such as Organic Compost will improve it. See SOIL chapter.

Vegetables have better flavor and less time to be attacked by insects if they grow rapidly. Side-dressing with composted manure hastens the growth of plants after they are established and growing. The ground should always be moist before applying any fertilizer and should be watered again after an application. Chemical or commercial fertilizers especially are apt to burn plants if not used according to directions and watered properly. Some growers believe in an application of a root stimulant such as 1 tablespoon of 12-24-12 to a gallon of water, poured around the roots.

Sowing seeds is explained in detail in the ANNUALS AND PERENNIALS chapter and there are usually specific directions on the seed packets. Plant enough to be sure there are plenty for a good harvest but not enough to crowd the bed. The soil must be kept moist from the time of sowing until after the seedlings have been thinned, that is pulling or clipping out the excessive number of sprouts or seedlings, leaving the strongest seedlings at the proper distance apart for that particular variety of vegetable or fruit or herb. Soon after the seeds sprout is a critical time to watch for die-back, an untreatable fungus disease which makes the little plants turn black at the soil line and die. It is thought that keeping the soil too wet or allowing the leaves to be wet helps promote the disease. Keep a close eye on the seedlings and remove any infected ones and discard in a bag. Wash your hands to avoid spreading the disease. The soil must be damp or moist, but not really wet.

Cinnamon basil (Ocimum Basilicum) in bloom. J.M.K.

When the seedlings come up, try to protect them the first day or so from the hottest sun if it is summer time. Use small branches or twigs broken off of shrubs or trees and stick them in the ground by the plants for a bit of shade.

Some vegetables seem to prefer being sown in a flat or other container first and transplanted to the garden when they have several leaves. Tomatoes is one of those. When handling a transplant, try to avoid touching its roots. Hold the little plant gently by the base of the stem and tuck it carefully into the damp loose soil. Transplanting is most successful on a cloudy day when the sun cannot burn them. Otherwise, protect them with make-shift parasols of small branches.

Mulching is of real importance to the vegetable bed because it protects the soil from extremes of temperature, summer and winter. It also discourages weeds and makes it easier to pull those which venture through. As an organic mulch deteriorates, it adds nutrients to the top soil, improves the soil's texture, allows more water penetration, reduces moisture evaporation, and improves aeration in the soil. Of particular importance to the cook, a mulch keeps the produce clean. To avoid compaction, use a mixture of mulching materials like shredded pine bark, old hay, pine needles, and manure. There is a newly developed mulch called Composted Bark Mulch which does not "wash away" as many others tend to do.

Staggering the planting time of a vegetable prevents its ripening all at the same time. The time to plant is in the charts in this chapter.

Many vegetables and herbs lend themselves to growing in containers. Place a piece of wire screen over the drainage hole to prevent slugs from entering, and add pieces of broken pots over the wire to allow proper drainage. Fill the container with your favorite mix or with the newly developed Fortified Potting Soil. The soil should be of a quicker draining nature than that in the ground. Before planting, water the soil in

Fragrant lemon grass (Cymbopogon citratus) and 'Spicy Globe' Basil with other herbs. J.M.K.

the pot thoroughly and allow it to drain. The soil should be moist, but not soggy when planting. Proceed with directions on the seed packet or for planting seeds in the ground. Remember that containers should be watered every day during hot weather. Pots are adaptable for small areas, for moving around to catch the most sun, and for attractive display for porch or patio...or a balcony. Scented mint plants are delightful placed close to a summertime sitting area. The fragrance is cooling and delightful.

Gardeners who enjoy the scent as well as the flavor of herbs revel in a nose-tingling herb collection, in the ground or in containers. The HERBS chart lists many with the cultural requirements of each. It is said that some herbs have insect-repellent qualities, so why not border your vegetable bed with herbs? Indulge in a bit of nostalgia.

VARIETIES OF VEGETABLES FOR HARRIS COUNTY, TEXAS

BEANS (Bush): Contender, Tender Crop, Strike, Topcrop, Greencrop, Blue Lake, Jumbo

BEANS (Pinto): Pinto 111, Luna

BEANS (Pole): Stringless, Blue Lake, Kentucky Wonder, Dade, Romano

BEANS (Lima) - Bush Type: Jackson Wonder, Henderson bush, Fordhook 242

BEANS (Lima) - Pole Type: Florida Butter, Sieva (Carolina)

BEETS: Detroit Red, Green Top Bunching, Pacemaker

BROCCOLI: Green Comet, Emperor, Premium Crop

BRUSSEL SPROUTS: Jade Cross, Catskill

CABBAGE: Early Round or Flat Dutch, Early Jersey Wakefield, Savoy Hybrids - Golden Acre, Rio Verde, Ruby Ball (Red), Greenboy

CABBAGE (Chinese): Michihli

CARROTS: Imperator, Danvers 126, Nates, Red Core Chantenay, Spartan Winner

CAULIFLOWER: Snowball, Snow Crown Hybrid

COLLARDS: Georgia

CORN(Sweet): Merit, Calumet, Florida Staysweet, Guardian, Buttersweet, Funk's G90

CORN (White): Silver Queen

CUCUMBER (Pickling): Victory, Liberty, National Pickling, Ohio MR17, SMR 58

CUCUMBER (Slicers): Slice Master, Poinsett, Sweet Slice, Ashley, Straight 8, Burpless

EGGPLANT: Florida Market, Black Beauty, Ichiban

GARLIC: Texas White

KOHLRABI: Grand Duke Hybrid, Early White Vienna

LETTUCE (Butterhead): Summer Bibb, Tender Crisp, Butter Crunch

LETTUCE (Leaf): Black Seeded Simpson, Salad Bowl, Ruby, Oakleaf

LETTUCE (Romaine): Valmaine

MUSTARD: Tender Green, Florida Broadleaf

OKRA: Clemson Spineless, Louisiana Green Velvet, Dwarf Green, Emerald, Lee

ONIONS (Green): Beltsville Bunching, Crystal Wax, South Port White

ONIONS (Plants) - Bulbing: Burgandy, Granex (white, yellow, and red), Supersweet (1015Y), Eclipse, Grano 502

PEAS(English): Sugar Snap, Little Marvel, Laxton, Alaska, Cleo, Wando, Premium Gem

PEAS(Southern): Mississippi Silver, Blackeye No. 5, Purple Hull, Queen Ann, Brown Sugar Crowser, Cream 40, Champion

PEPPER (Hot): Cayenne, Tobasco, Fresno Chile, Serrano Chile, Hungarian Wax, Jalapeno, TAM Mild Chile 2

PEPPER (Sweet) (Bell Type): Tambel 2, Shamrock, Gypsy, Belltower

PEPPER (Other Type): Yellow Banana

POTATOES (Irish) (Red): Red Lasoa, Pontiac

POTATOES (Irish) (White): Kennebec (Russett) Norgold

POTATOES (Sweet): Centennial, Rose Centennial, Jewel, Jasper

RADISH: Cherry Belle, Early Scarlet Globe, White Icicle

RADISH (Winter): Black Spanish, White Chinese

SPINACH: Early Hybrid 7, Melody

SPINACH (Summer Production): New Zealand, Malabar

SQUASH (Summer): Dixie, Multipik, Hyrific, Hybrid Crookneck, White Bush Scallop, Zucchini, Butterbar

SQUASH (Winter): Acorn, Butternut

TOMATOES (Large Fruited): Spring Giant, Better Boy, Big Set, Floramerica, Freedom, Traveler, Terrific, Homestead 24, Walter

TOMATOES (Small Fruited): Small Fry, Patio, Sweet 100 Hybrid, (Heat Setting) TAMU Chico 111, Improved Sumemrtime, Hot Set

TOMATOES (Nematode Resistant): Big Set, Jackpot, Better Boy, Terrific, Nematex

TURNIPS (Root & Tops): Purple Top White Globe, Just Right, Tokyo Market

TURNIPS (Greens): Seven Top, Crawford, Shogoin

SPRING AND FALL VEGETABLE PLANTING GUIDE

Name of Crop	Inches Between Rows	Inches Between Plants	Spring Planting Dates	Fall Planting Date	Approximate Days to Maturity
Beans (Bush)	18-30	3-4	Mar. 5-Apr. 30	Aug.1-Sep. 20	50-70
Beans (Pole)	24-30	12-18	Mar. 1-Apr. 15		50-90
Beets	12-24	2-3	Feb. 1-Mar.1	Sep. 15-Nov.1	60-70
Broccoli	24-30	12-20	Feb. 1-Feb. 15	Aug. 15-Sep. 10	70-100
Brussel Sprouts	24-30	12-20	Sep. 1-Sep. 10		70-100
Cabbage	24-30	12-20	Jan. 15-Feb. 15	Sep. 1-Sep. 10	70-100
Carrots	12-24	2	Jan. 15-Feb. 15	Oct. 1-Nov. 1	80-90
Cauliflower	24-30	12-20	Feb. 1-Feb. 15	Aug. 15-Sep. 10	80-100
Collards	12-24	6-12	Feb. 1-Feb. 28	Sep. 1-Oct. 1	60-90
Corn (Sweet)	24-36	8-12	Mar. 5-Apr. 15	Aug. 1-Aug. 15	80-100
Cucumber	36-48	18-36	Mar. 15- May 1	Aug. 15-Sep. 20	60-80
Eggplant	18-30	18-24	Mar. 15-Apr. 15		90-100
Garlic	12-24	2-4		Sep. 25-Oct. 15	150-160
Kohlrabi	12-24	3-5	Jan. 15-Mar. 1	Sep. 15-Oct. 20	65-85
Lettuce (Leaf)	12-24	2-3	Feb. 1-Apr. 1	Sep. 25-Oct. 15	50-90
Mustard	12-24	4-8	Feb. 15-Apr. 1	Sep. 1-Nov. 1	40-50
Okra	30-40	18-24	Apr. 1-July 15		65-75
Onion (Seeds)	12-24	2-3		Sep. 1-Oct. 15	100-130
Onion (Plants)	12-24	2-3	Jan. 15-Feb. 15	Oct. 15 Nov. 10	90-130
Peas (English)	18-30	1	Oct.1-Oct. 10		65-105
Peas (Southern)	24-36	3-5	Apr. 1-May 20	Aug. 1-Sep. 1	70-90
Pepper (Trans.)	24-36	18-24	Mar. 1-Apr. 10	July 20-Aug. 1	70-100
Potatoes (Irish)	24-36	8-12	Jan. 15-Feb. 10	Aug. 15-Sep. 1	90-110
Potatoes (Sweet)	30-36	10-14	Apr. 1-May 20		110-140
Radish	12-24	1	Feb. 1-Apr. 15	Sep. 1-Nov. 15	35-50
Spinach	12-24	3-4	Jan. 1-Feb. 15	Sep. 1-Nov. 1	50-70
Squash (Summer)	30-40	14-30	Mar. 10-Apr. 15	Aug. 1-Sep. 1	60-70
Tomatoes	24-40	18-30	Mar. 1-Mar. 30	July 15-Aug. 1	80-100
Turnips (Greens or Roots)	12-24	2-3	Jan. 15-Mar. 15	Sep. 1-Nov. 15	40-70

HERBS

CULTURAL REQUIREMENTS: Sun, preferably morning, to bring out fragrance of their oils. Afternoon summer sun can burn. Excellent rapid drainage. Soggy wet soil kills them. Beds raised 10", or containers, filled with light, fine (preferably screened) soil mixture of garden loam, coarse sand, small amount of wood ashes or small amount of lime for alkalinity, potassium, composted leaves, rice hulls, manure, and bone meal for phosphorus should satisfy any herb. Water when dry. Fertilize periodically with weak solution of manure tea or organic fertilizer such as fish emulsion, 1/2 strength. Keep flowers cut off for improved flavor. Pinch-prune to shape, to control, and to enjoy the prunings. Most herb seeds are very slow to propagate. Better to obtain plants. Container planting encourages rapid draining and allows protection from heat or cold, but increases maintenance with frequent watering.

A = Annual	E = Evergreen	P = Perennial	B = Biennial	spp. = Species	Cv = Cultivar
Common Name *Botanical Name*	**Height**	**Time To Plant**	**Comments**		
ALOE VERA P E *A.v. barbadensis*	3'	Spring	While *A.v. barbadensis* is a succulent and not really an herb, it is here because the gel from its leaves is excellent for burns, sunburn, and minor abrasions. Partial shade, protection from hot summer P.M. sun and from freezes. Minimum water. Well-drained, sandy soil. Spiny gray-green leaves. Yellow-orange flowers in clusters. Every garden should have Aloe vera. Properly wrapped leaf keeps well in freezer for easy use.		
BASIL, SWEET A *Ocimum basilicum*	10" - 3'	Seed or Plant after Frost	Sun to part sun, fertile soil. Average water. Pinch-prune leaf tips for shaping and for use. Small white flowers. Keep flowers picked off for better flavor. Many varieties: 'Dark Opal' and 'Purple Ruffles' have purple leaves. 'Minimum' has smaller leaves. 'Spicy Globe' retains 18" globular shape. Dry leaves between paper towels. May freeze. Lemon, cinnamon, and licorice are among other scents. Leaves add spicy taste to vinegars, salads, sauces, and vegetables (especially tomatoes). Basil 'Picollo' is good in containers in warm season.		
BEE BALM (OSWEGO TEA, BERGAMOT) P E *Monarda didyma*	to 5'	Any time	Sun to shade. Slightly acid soil. Average water. Many varieties, some leaves to 6"; flowers red, purple, white, pink. May become invasive. If it freezes back, cut to ground; it will return. Hardy. Use for tea, potpourri, in jellies, and with fruit. Attracts bees. *M.d.* 'Panorama' especially attracts hummingbirds.		
BORAGE A *Borago officinalis*	1-1/2' - 2'	Early Spring Seed/Plant	Sun. Soil on the poor side. Not too much water. Likes to be cool. Allow space for sprawling habit. Beautiful small, blue star-shaped flowers. Hardy. Reseeds. Wear gloves to handle hairy, cucumber-flavored leaves. Use young leaves in salads and flowers in arrangements or to be candied.		

HERBS

Common Name *Botanical Name*	Height	Time To Plant	Comments
BURNET P E *Sanguisorba minor*	2'	Mar.-Apr.	Sun to part sun. Sandy soil, not too rich. Must be well-drained. Water when dry. Evergreen winter border. Dark green leaves in rosettes. Insignificant rose-colored flowers. Good in container. Use young cucumber-flavored leaves in salads, butters, and vinegars.
CATNIP (CATMINT) P *Nepeta Cataria*	2'	Mar.-Apr.	Sun to part sun. Light, sandy, fertile soil. Water when dry. Gray, 3" heart-shaped leaves; lavender or white flowers. Use leaves in hot tea to ease cold. Some cats are attracted to this plant. Prune to shape. Several other varieties.
CHERVIL A *Anthriscus* *Cerefolium*	18"	Seed Fall	Prefers some afternoon shade. Well-drained soil. Leaves used in soups, salads. New leaves similar to parsley with anise flavor. White flowers in flat heads.
CHIVES P *Allium schoenoprasum*	1' - 2'	Apr. and Oct.	Any garden soil in partial shade.Water when dry. Can't stand summer heat or freezes. Move container inside in good light. Lavender flowers. Chop into salads, soups. Garlic Chives (*A. tuberosum*) similar.
COMFREY P *Symphytum officinale*	3'	Mar. and Oct.	Average soil with fertilizer from time to time. Hardy. Allow space. Leaves rich in potassium, calcium, Vitamins A, B, and C, and phosphorus. Cook as greens in soup or tea, or in salads.
CORIANDER A *Coriander sativum*	2'	Seed Sept.-Oct.	Sun to semi-shade. Light, fertile soil. Good drainage. Hardy. Use seeds in Latin-American dishes.
DILL A *Anethum graveolens*	3'	Sept.-Oct.	Sun. Any well-drained soil. Average water. Hardy. If seeds are not collected or cut off when brown, they will seed everywhere they fall. Ferny fragrant leaves used in sauces, salads, on vegetables, with cucumbers, and in bread.
FENNEL P *Foeniculum vulgare*	4'	April	Bright green, feathery leaves. Yellow flowers. Usually grown as annual. Also bronze or red-leaved variety. For garnishes and salads. Used in Italian dishes.
GERANIUM, SCENTED P *Pelargonium* spp.	1-1/2'	Root Cuttings Plant Spring	Sandy soil. Summer shade, fall sun. Water when dry. Many species: rose, coconut, lemon, nutmeg, peppermint, and apple-scented. Trailing habit. Flavor for custards, jellies; large leaf under dessert very attractive. Leaf in bottom of custard dish before cooking is wonderful. Cooling effect in arrangements for house during summer. Roots easily in water.

HERBS

Common Name Botanical Name	Height	Time To Plant	Comments
GERMANDER P *Teucrium Chamaedrys* *Cv. 'Prostratum'*	6" - 1'	Feb.-Mar.	Sun. Poor soil; good drainage. Low but spreading. Hardy. Gray wrinkled leaves are aromatic.
T. lucidum	1'		Upright growth, white or purple flowers. May keep clipped into low hedge. Takes heat. Knot-garden plant.
LAVENDER, FRENCH A *Lavendula dentata* Several other spp	3'	April Seeds in Fall	Requires excellent drainage. Try in pot. Partial shade in summer. Green and gray-leaved, blue or lavender fragrant flowers. Oils used in toilet water, soap, and perfume. Leaves and flowers in potpourri. Plant in raised bed or in container.
LEMON BALM (MINT) P *Melissa officinalis*	2'	April	Likes partial shade, especially during summer afternoons. Fertile, moist soil. Light green, fragrant leaves fine in tea or as garnish. Prune when straggly. If it freezes, cut back at end of winter. Protect from afternoon summer sun. Nice in sachet bags.
LEMON GRASS P *Cymbopogon citratus*	3'	Mar.-Apr.	Partial sun in summer. Well-drained, garden soil. Water when dry. Forms clumps of long, gray-green, scratchy-surfaced leaves, looking a bit like Johnson Grass but larger and grayer. Makes delightful tea. Attractive in garden. To propagate, cut back to 4-5", divide into small clumps, each with roots. May have to cut apart. Wear gloves when working with Lemon Grass. Edges of leaves are sharp-edged.
LEMON VERBENA P *Aloysia triphylla*	2' - 5'	Mar.-Apr. Cuttings	Sun. Average garden soil; good drainage. Deciduous. May grow to 6'. Best in container to allow bringing in for protection. May sink pot in summer garden in sunny area. Even if leaves fall during winter inside they will probably return when placed outside in warm weather. 5" slightly rough leaves shiny light green with lemon fragrance. Purple, white flowers. Prune when leggy. Use leaves to flavor tea and jellies, and in finger bowls for delightful fragrance. Do not overwater while dormant.
MARJORAM, SWEET P *Origanum Majorana*	1' - 2'	Seed - Apr. Plant - Apr.	Sun. Well-draining, loose soil. Water as needed. Grow as annual. Low and wide plant. Tender. Protect. Woody stems, small oval gray-green leaves, grayish underneath. White flowers. Grows in containers. Sweet, spicy herb complements cooked mushrooms. Used in vinegars, wine marinades, sauces, butters, and on meats.

HERBS

Common Name *Botanical Name*	Height	Time To Plant	Comments
MEXICAN MINT MARIGOLD P *Tagetes lucida*	2'	Mar.-Apr.	Sun. Average fertile soil. Water well. Hardy bush, nice in low hedge. Small licorice-fragrant leaves. Lack of sun makes it scraggly. Yellow flowers. Leaves make good tea and are fine in potpourri. Flavor similar to French Tarragon, licorice flavor.
MINT P *Mentha* spp	12" - 2'	Mar.-Apr.	Partial shade to filtered sun. It burns in hot summer afternoon sun. Light, loose, fertile soil. Very good drainage. Hardy. Grows from plants, cuttings, and root divisions. All mints (*Menthas*) have square stems and opposite, aromatic leaves which differ in appearance and scent/flavor according to species. Mint becomes invasive with spreading of underground roots and overground stems, but is definitely worth having for enjoyment. Sinking tiles or boards into the ground may prevent the spread. Why not give the mint a bed to itself? Some of the 500 plus species in the *Mentha* genus are: Peppermint (*M. piperita*), Orange (*M. citrata*), Spearmint (*M. spicata*) fine for iced tea, Pineapple (*M. suaveolens variegata*), Golden (*M. spicata*) variegated leaves, Corsican (*M. requienii*) makes a fragrant 1" high ground cover, especially between flagstones, sending out a minty fragrance with every footstep. Use mint in teas, with green peas, and as fragrant garnish. Add crushed leaves to coleslaw, vegetables, as well as teas. Fine in sauces for lamb and veal. Prune often, especially flowers.
OREGANO (WILD MARJORAM) P *Origanum vulgare*	1' - 3'	Mar.-Apr.	Sun to part shade. Loose garden soil. Keep purple-pink flowers cut. Shrub-like. Many varieties. Leaves from green to white. Some are wooly. Fresh or dried leaves good on vegetables and meats, tomato sauce, salads, pizza, or Mexican-type dishes. Pick leaves just before needed.
CURLY PARSLEY A or B *Petroselinum* *crispum* ITALIAN PARSLEY (FLAT LEAF) *P.c.* var. *neapolitanum*	6" - 12"	Apr.-June September	Sun to light shade, especially summer afternoon. Moist garden soil. Soak or freeze seeds before planting or buy plants. Makes nice low border. Best in cool weather. Dies after flowering in second year. Has long tap root. Curly prettier, but flat-leaved species are more flavorful. Use as garnish, chopped into soups, in salads, on new potatoes, meats, with chives, onions, and garlic.

HERBS

E = Evergreen   P = Perennial   B = Biennial   spp. = Species   Cv = Cultivar

Common Name *Botanical Name*	Height	Time To Plant	Comments
ROSEMARY, UPRIGHT P E *Rosemarinus* *officinalis* ROSEMARY, PROSTRATE *R.o.* 'Prostratus'	4' 1'	Spring Seeds in Fall	Likes sun, but protect from hot summer sun. Soil not too rich; crushed eggshells add lime it likes; minimum water. Likes heavy mulch over root area. Fine roots grow close to surface. Don't disturb them. Many varieties and cultivars. Appearance varies from grayish to dark green leaves; from blue to pinkish flowers. Very attractive plant. Said to repel bean beetles, carrot flies, and cabbage moths. Sprinkle chopped rosemary on chicken, lamb, and roasts for spicy flavor. Similar to mint.
RUGULA (ARUGULA or ROCKET-SALAD) A *Eruca versicaria* *sativa*	18"	Mar.-Apr.	Sun to filtered sun. Medium rich soil. Easy on the water. Hardy. Sprout seeds in 90-degree oven or buy plants. Plant no deeper than it was in original pot. Strong flavored salad green. Cut often for tenderness. Best in spring and late fall.
SAGE, GARDEN P *Salvia officinalis* PINEAPPLE SAGE P *S. elegans* PURPLE SAGE P *S.o.* var. 'Purpurea' (rare)	to 3' 3' 3' 2'	Mar.-Apr.	Plant in sunny spot with sandy, well-draining soil in raised bed. Numerous species and varieties. Drought tolerant. Red flowering sage, such as Pineapple Sage, Scarlet Sage (*S. coccinea*), and Salvia Greggi (Autumn Sage) are hardy, easy to grow and attract hummingbirds to the garden. *Salvia officinalis* must not be heavily pruned. Instead, pinch-prune tips. There are dwarf varieties also. Sage is slightly bitter. Use leaves in stuffings, cheese, and herb breads as well as with turkey, chicken, and baked fish.
SAVORY, SUMMER A *Satureja hortensia*	18"	Apr.-May	Sun. Prefers light, well-drained soil. Drought tolerant. Sun. Pinch-prune tips for bushiness. Lance-shaped, medium-sized leaves. Small lilac flowers. Pleasant spicy scent.
SAVORY, WINTER P *Satureja montana*	6" - 18"		Sun. Well-drained, sandy soil. Hardy. Spreading shape. Attracts bees. Use both savorys to flavor meats, beans, salads, and anything else you want to put it on.
TARRAGON, FRENCH P *Artemisia* *Dracunculus*	18"	March October	Doesn't like our climate. Poor sandy soil results in best flavor. Tender. Protect from cold and freeze. Used often in French recipes. Also to flavor salads, spinach, cauliflower, roast, turkey, fish, and egg dishes. Excellent for vinegars. See Mexican Mint Marigold.

HERBS

Common Name Botanical Name	Height	Time To Plant	Comments
THYME, GARDEN P *Thymus vulgaris* Many varieties	12" - 16"	Mar.-Apr.	Hardy. Minimum water. Sun but protect from P.M.-summer sun. Very well-drained, loose soil. Prune flowers off for best flavor. Tiny lavender flowers. Do not fertilize. Creeping Thyme or Mother of Time (*T. sergyllum*) is interesting ground cover. Lemon Thyme (*T. citriodorus*) is lemon-scented. Clove-like flavor enhances gumbos, stews, and cooked vegetables. Makes stimulating tea.

G.C.

The fall splendor of an oak tree.

Trees

*"He that plants a tree
loves others besides himself."*
—Thomas Fuller

F rom trees, the largest members of the plant world, come some of our prime necessities—houses, food, shade, furniture, rubber, the paper this book is printed on, and, vitally important, the oxygen we breathe. Year by year there are more people, more machines, and more factories, each releasing carbon dioxide into the atmosphere. Trees and their foliage absorb this noxious gas and convert it into oxygen. One person's breathing equals the carbon dioxide absorbed by one tree. It takes numerous trees, per person, to maintain carbon dioxide in atmospheric balance. Just one more way in which trees help people. It behooves us, therefore, to give particular consideration to these long-lived and beneficial plants.

Like all other plants, trees grow to their inbred height, spread, and shape, though climatic conditions have some effect on them. The live oak may well be the most favorite tree in Houston, but it grows to a height of 75 feet and has a spread of at least 50 feet. It is, indeed, a majestic tree—but few homesites can accommodate such a size and a house and garden as well. The most frequent mistake made by homeowners is to plant too large a tree, or too many trees, in too small a space. It is imperative to ascertain the *mature* size of trees you are considering for your home space.

Begin your search well before the usual planting time (December-April) to allow ample time to make this long-range decision. Many trees live for 50 years or more.

There are at least 175 trees listed in the TREES chart—evergreen and deciduous, tall and short, wide and slender. Their leaves are of various shapes, sizes, and textures. Some offer bright yellow-to-red fall foliage. Some display attractive flowers. Some bear colorful fruit. In some cases, only the female trees bear berries. So if you are interested in berrying trees, choose them while they are actually berrying. In any event, it is helpful to see trees while they have their foliage.

Don't buy trees off a truck by the side of the road! There is no way of knowing how healthy they are, or even what species they are. It is worthwhile to deal with a respected tree company and with registered Texas nurserymen who know their business. Ask questions about the mature size, the shape, and any particular characteristics of different trees. Avoid those with messy, high-maintenance habits. If you study the TREES chart before you begin your search, you can narrow down the list of those you want to consider. It is essential to determine the type of root system. Some trees put out surface roots which are inconvenient, to say the least. Others, like the picturesque but short-lived

G.C.

The white bark of a sycamore tree accented against the blue sky. (Plantanus occidentalis)

on those areas, then consider a deciduous tree which drops its leaves in the fall; some have the extra benefit of colorful fall foliage. You must determine the tree's mature size to know how far away from the house to plant it.

- If you prefer screening your windows, and perhaps also screening an unattractive area, select evergreen trees which retain their leaves all year, though some drop leaves periodically. The beautiful and evergreen magnolia tree, for example, drops leaves much of the year, so it would not be advisable near a terrace, pool, or paved area.
- If the sounds and sights of birds please you, select trees and shrubs which attract them. Remember to give birds access to fresh water every day. Trees and shrubs which attract birds are so designated in the charts.
- If fragrant flowers or aromatic foliage appeal to you, those characteristics are also noted in the charts.

silver maple, have roots which invade any sewer or water pipe they can reach.

It is advisable to measure the entire space you have for a tree. Take the measurements along with you and show them to the nurseryman. Compare the available space with the mature height and spread of the trees you are considering. There are numerous interesting trees of reasonable size. There are also large, attractive shrubs which can easily be pruned into tree form, perfect for a patio or other small garden. Check the SHRUBS chart. Hybridizers have developed smaller-sized trees from some of the larger favorites. For example, there are some especially beautiful small magnolias.

As you consider your choice, decide also what purpose you want the tree or trees to fill.
- Do you want to block the summer sun from windows and terrace?
- If you want to allow winter sun for warmth

J.M.K.

Houston's summer beauty: Crape Myrtle.

88

- For attractive foliage and flowers for arrangements, perhaps holly and pine branches for Christmas, look for those trees. Also refer to the ARRANGEMENTS FROM YOUR GARDEN chapter.

As you become acquainted with the different kinds and types of trees, visualize the possible selections for your garden. Are the drainage conditions, soil, and sunshine culturally appropriate for your garden? Exactly where would you place the trees? Look from inside your house to the garden: which placements would be beneficial and attractive? The SOIL, DRAINAGE, and WATER AND WATERING chapters offer suggestions for improving the cultural conditions in your homescape, and the HINTS FOR LANDSCAPING chapter offers ideas for tree placement. Among the principal goals are the selecting and planting of trees which will complement, not overwhelm your home.

A Drummond's red maple in fall dress. (Acer rubrum Drummondii)

A redbud tree's color signals spring. (Cercis canadensis)

Many homesites have power lines stretching across the boundary lines. If a tree interferes with the lines, the power company will probably "top" the tree, that is, cut the limbs straight across to correct the interference. That type of pruning, of course, ruins the shape of the tree. If you are not yet faced with that problem, avoid it by proper placement. If you already have the problem, consider thinning limbs to form a "hole" in the foliage, *around* the wires. That is not an ideal solution, but it's better than the alternative. Employ a professional tree surgeon who is trained to work around power lines. See PRUNING chapter for details.

If you are planning to add camellias or azaleas to your landscape, consider planting pine trees. They have a deep root system which does not interfere with plantings; they allow just the right kind of filtered sun to reach the shrubs; and their leaf-needles fall gently, forming a very helpful, acid-maintaining mulch. The spread or width of pines is usually narrower than many other trees. See the CAMELLIAS chapter.

Reminders

- When building a house, protect the trees on your lot by encircling them with barricades to prevent injury to the bark and root system.
- Do not pile soil or sand or anything else over the root area of trees. The tree roots can suffocate over time.
- The use of strong herbicides or pesticides can cause the death of a tree even 50 feet away.
- Dense shade on terraces, particularly in the winter, promotes the growth of mildew.
- A smaller tree may outgrow a larger tree of the same species because it recovers more quickly from transplanting shock.
- The fastest growing trees are often structurally weak and short lived.
- If you want to have a planting bed under a tree, select a deciduous tree or one which allows ample sunlight through its branches. Few plants can grow without sunlight. Consider the tree's type of root system. Is it invasive to water and sewer pipes? Does it continually send up volunteers?
- Allow enough space between trees and house for natural growth and for air circulation.
- When a shade tree is placed on the *west* side of the house, the shade *lengthens* as the sun sets. If the tree is *too close* to the house, the slanting rays of the sun will come *under* the tree and onto the house.
- Planted on the east side of the house, the tree may be placed a bit closer to the house; distance depends on the mature size of the tree.
- *The area for the tree must first be checked for proper drainage. Refer to the DRAINAGE chapter, and correct, if necessary,* before *planting anything.* Also be sure there is adequate space for growth.

Transplanting Trees in the Houston Area

These directions are intended for trees small enough to be handled easily by the homeowner.

Trees which do not require large moving equipment are sometimes planted by nurseries.

Trees may be balled and burlapped (B&B) or containerized. When a tree is in a container, inquire if it was grown in the container. If it was, then the roots have probably not been cut. However, if it was transplanted into the container, the roots probably were cut or else may be circling in the pot. It is important to find out. Trees whose roots have been cut should be pruned at transplanting. Roots which are circling in the pot must be trimmed or spread out into the hole, thereby requiring a transplanting hole large enough to accommodate the roots in spread-out fashion. Otherwise, the roots may continue to circle or girdle and choke the tree.

Transplanting bare-root trees, usually fruit trees, follows the same procedure as for other trees. The hole must be dug wide enough to accommodate the spreading out of the roots as described above. Pruning bare-root trees may be recommended to lessen stress on the root-system. Especially when it has been cut or damaged, the root system must be relieved of providing sustenance for the mass of tree and leaves. Following transplanting, the leaves require more water than the root system can supply; the leaves wilt and the tree may die for lack of sufficient water. Removal of 1/2 or 1/3 of the leaves and limbs relieves the roots. They can re-establish themselves and will soon be able to do their job again. See PRUNING chapter.

If pruning of a transplanted tree becomes necessary, corrective pruning may be accomplished at the same time. Damaged, weak, or undesirable limbs may be removed—within reason. Do not remove more than, at the most, one-half of the limbs. Other than putting root system and tree tops and leaves back in proportion to each other, the goal in pruning now is to develop a good arrangement of scaffold branches, the "skeleton" of the tree.

Back to Transplanting:

- Dig a hole the same depth of the tree's root-ball or of the soil in the container. In Houston, the top surface of the tree's root-ball should be at the same level, or 2 or 3 inches *above*, never below, the level of the surrounding ground. The line on the trunk of the bare-root tree showing a difference in color usually indicates the depth to which the tree has been planted.

- Widen the hole to be 6 inches to 8 inches wider than the root-ball or wide enough to accommodate comfortably the spread of the bare roots.
- Remove the root-ball from the container and inspect the roots as well as you can without breaking the soil ball. If they are damaged, prune them. If they are girdling or circling the tree, either cut them away (unless that would include too much of the root) or spread them out.
- For a container-grown tree, combine:
    1/2 part soil from the planting hole, and
    1/2 part soil similar to that in the container.
- Lower the root-ball into the hole. The top surface of the root-ball should be just a little above the surrounding soil, as described above. Add native soil to half fill the hole. If planting a bare-root tree, add enough native soil which was removed from the hole to keep the tree erect.
- Water gently but thoroughly to wet the entire root-ball and to push the air pockets out of the soil. Stirring a bit with a stick helps break up the air pockets which could cause the later death of the tree if left in the soil.
- Mix the remaining native soil with an equal quantity of a combination of rotted organic material, such as manure, pine bark, pine needles, and compost and fill in the rest of the hole with the mixture; follow with water.
- Pour a root stimulant, mixed according to directions, into the water and stir a bit. Repeat this root-stimulant treatment every 2 weeks for several months. Root-stimulant is optional, but better than over-fertilizing with a high salt index fertilizer.
- Spread a combination of organic materials over the root area in a 3-foot diameter, 2-inches thick, to conserve moisture and discourage weeds.
- The soil must be kept moist, but not soggy-wet, until the tree shows growth; thereafter, be sure the soil is watered thoroughly whenever it feels dry. There is a fine line—soil too wet or soil too dry, either can damage or kill a recently transplanted tree.
- Though root stimulant is suggested for a newly planted tree, general fertilization is not usually recommended until the year following planting.
- Bare-rooted trees are planted according to the directions listed above: the hole should be wide enough to allow the roots to be spread out in an uncrowded way. The roots should *not* be coiled around in the hole, for they will continue coiling and eventually choke the tree. The roots must be encouraged to grow *out into* the surrounding soil.

To remain healthy, trees need:
- Watering to reach down to the roots; usually requiring long, slow dripping.
- Adequate drainage.
- A 2-inch to 3-inch thick mulch of decomposed organic material around it, never thicker than the trunk itself.
- Removal of Spanish Moss and mistletoe if they appear to be growing out of control.
- Frequent inspection for signs of insect or disease damage. Refer to PRUNING and DISEASES, INSECTS, AND WEEDS chapters. If in doubt, consult a professional tree person.
- Fertilization in early spring.

TREES

Before buying or planting, know characteristics and ultimate size of each tree. Beware of planting large-growing trees too close to the foundation of your home. That spells future trouble. Determine if trees you like have root system which invades sewers and pipes.

General Directions Unless individually noted, the following suggestions are recommended:

Safest Buy: (1) Container grown or (2) burlap-wrapped trees with trunk diameter no larger than 2", purchased from Certified Texas Nursery. B&B should meet minimum nursery standards.

Best Planting Time: December through April. If planted later, will require close attention to watering deeply. EXCEPTION: Plant bare-rooted trees only in their dormancy.

Location: Appropriate amount of sun for the species. Sufficient space all around tree for proper development.

Soil: Loose, fertile soil. See SOIL chapter.

Good drainage: This is a MUST. See DRAINAGE chapter.

Deep watering: Shallow watering brings roots to surface. See WATERING chapter.

Fertilizing: Generally in early spring using a fertilizer such as 13-13-13 with iron and sulphur as well as other nutritional trace elements. A 12-24-12 ratio is recommended for flowering trees. *Follow manufacturer's directions*. NO STRONGER. Water first, then mix fertilizer with peat moss or sand and spread around tree inside drip-line, but at least one foot away from trunk, or put fertilizer in holes along drip line. Water. Organic slow-release fertilizers are safer, less burn potential.

Pruning: October - March (dormant season) considered best time. Try to retain natural growth pattern.

Likes: Tender loving care from owner.

See more listings in TROPICAL GARDEN chapter

	E = Evergreen D = Deciduous	
Common Name *Botanical Name*	**Average Height X Width**	**Comments**
ACACIA (GUAJILLO) D *Acacia berlandieri* Several species	12' x 8'	Requires full sun, loose, fertile soil, good drainage. Makes attractive background tree as a change from shrubs. Ferny leaves. Low-branching. Yellow flowers. Uncommon.
AILANTHUS (TREE OF HEAVEN) D *Ailanthus altissima*	65' x 40'	Sun or part shade. Any soil. Tolerant of city conditions like pollution and drought. Adapted to Texas. Spreads readily by seeds and suckers; can become pest. Weedy. Leaves 24-48" long.
AMERICAN (EASTERN) HOP HORNBEAM D *Ostrya virginiana*	30' x 15'	Filtered shade from larger trees it likes to grow under in its native habitats. Found usually in acid, loose, dry soil. Uncommon in nurseries; difficult to transplant but worthy if available. Leaves to 5" long. Produces catkins, green fruit. Yellow, red in fall. NATIVE in East Texas. Beautiful form.
AMERICAN HORNBEAM (BLUE BEECH) IRONWOOD D *Carpinus caroliniana*	30' x 18'	Prefers wet, swampy area, light shade. Deep, rich, soil. Yellow in fall. NATIVE in Texas. Wildlife food. Naturalistic. Slow growing.

TREES

Common Name *Botanical Name*	Average Height X Width	Comments
AMERICAN YELLOW WOOD D *Cladrastis lutea*	40' x 15'	10" racemes of small, white, fragrant flowers in spring. U.S. NATIVE. Hardy. Slender head. Occurs naturally in rich limestone soils of stream banks or cliffs.
ANACAHUITA (TEXAS WILD OLIVE) *Cordia Boissieri*	15' x 8'	Sun. Fertile, sandy soil. Requires good drainage and protection from freezes. White, trumpet-shaped flowers bloom from Apr.-Oct. Greenish, edible fruit follows flowers. Not pretty. Holds yellow leaves.
ANAQUA D *Ehretia anacua*	40' x 35'	Sun to part shade. Likes fertile soil and ample water. Requires good drainage. Mulch. White flowers in Mar., Apr. Edible, yellowish-orange berries June-July. Drought resistant. Almost disease free. Medium growth rate. Rough, olive green leaves. Shade tree. Texas NATIVE. Sprouts from roots should be cut or mowed off.
ARBORVITAE, AMERICAN E *Thuja occidentalis*	12' x 7'	Prefers full sun, fertile soil. Requires very good drainage as all conifers do. Tolerates other soil conditions. Fast growth. Conical form. Allow space for width. Pruning is difficult without destroying shape. The dominant form is difficult to combine with other plants. Some cultivars have foliage variegated with gold. Subject to insect damage: bagworms, spider mites, blight. Dwarf forms also available.
ASH, ARIZONA D *Fraxinus velutina*	35' x 30'	Sun to semi-shade. Moist, fertile soil. Tolerant of others. Fast growth. Very brittle. Pretty shape, but prone to damage from disease and insects. Short-lived: 5 to 12 years. Yellow fall color. NATIVE of Southwest U.S.
ASH, GREEN D *Fraxinus pennsylvanica*	80' x 40'	Sun to semi-shade. Grows in moist, organic soils. Likes water. Tall, narrow spread. Medium-fast growth. Good shade tree. Fall yellow to purple. Clean. NATIVE of U.S. Seedless cultivars available.
ASH, WHITE D *Fraxinus americana*	75' x 40'	Needs like Green Ash above but likes well-drained soil. Leaves more oval. Excellent shade tree. Yellow fall color. Long-lived. Needs water. NATIVE in Louisiana, Georgia, and Texas. Better tree than Arizona Ash.
TEXAS ASH *F. texensis*	50' x 35'	Similar to White Ash. Grows in any soil. Beautiful salmon fall color. Fast growth. Long-lived. Drought resistant. Hard, strong wood.

TREES

Common Name *Botanical Name*	E = Evergreen D = Deciduous	
	Average Height X Width	Comments
BALD CYPRESS D *Taxodium distichum*	45' x 20'	Needs full sun. Average soil with ample water. Prefers wet site. Conifer. Medium growth rate. Conical form. Long-lived. Feathery foliage bright green in spring, coppery-red/brown in fall. Seeds attract birds. Accepts very wet soil, even being in water. Knee-like stumps when growing in wet area. Rough cones. NATIVE of East Texas swamps. Massive to 130' x 70' when older.
'Montezuma' *T. mucronatum*		Requires moist soil.
BAUHINIA (ORCHID TREE) (ANACACHO) D *Bauhinia* spp. *B. alba 'Congesta'* *B. forficata*	12' x 12'	Sun to filtered shade. Acidic, fertile soil with plenty of humus kept evenly moist. Requires good drainage. Small, fast growing tree. Tender to cold, but usually root hardy. Protect root zone with thick mulch in winter cold. Shrubby habit. Orchid-like flowers, lilac or white, according to species. Blooms May till winter. Mexican species has red-orange flowers. NATIVE of Texas.
BEECH, AMERICAN D *Fagus grandifolia*	65' x 45'	Sun. Tolerates shade, but not urban stresses. Acid, fertile, sandy, well-draining soil. Oval with wide branches; smooth, gray bark. Bright, yellow-green leaves in spring, yellow in fall. Common in East Texas.
BLACK CHERRY D *Prunus serotina*	40' x 20'	Sun to semi-shade. Acid, moist, rich soil. Fast, shrubby growth. Attractive bark. Coppery fall color. Fragrant white flowers in spring with leaves. Volunteers readily. Edible purplish fruit. Bird food. NATIVE in Texas.
BLACK GUM D *Nyssa sylvatica*	55' x 35'	Full sun. Prefers moist, fertile, sandy, acid soil; similar to Cypress. Narrow, pyramidal with long shiny leaves turning red early fall. Several varieties. East Texas NATIVE. Wildlife eat blue fruit. Shade tree, resistant to breakage. For cleaner fruit-less tree, plant male tree.
BLACKHAW, SOUTHERN or RUSTY D *Viburnum rufidulum*	20' x 15'	Sun or part shade. Rich, humusy, loose soil. Requires good drainage. Shiny, leathery leaves. White flowers in beautiful, showy clusters in spring. Dark blue fruit. Red fall color. Brilliant. Good size for small areas.

TREES

Common Name *Botanical Name*	Average Height X Width	Comments
BOIS D'ARC (OSAGE ORANGE) D *Maclura pomifera*	25' x 40'	Sun to partial shade. Tolerates alkaline soils, drought, and city conditions. Fast growth. Round, green fruit turns orange, causes clean-up problem. Male trees have clusters of creamy flowers, no fruit. Roots exposed on surface. Difficult to grow plants under. Fruit said to repel roaches. New cultivar is thornless and fruitless. NATIVE in Central and East Texas. Hard wood. Thorny.
BOXELDER D *Acer negundo*	40' x 20'	Sun to part shade. Most soils, but likes swampy conditions. NATIVE to East Texas. Compound leaves distinguish it from other Texas Maples. Short-lived, weak, brittle wood, subject to disease, but tolerant of city conditions. Other trees make better choice. Also variegated variety.
BUCKEYE, MEXICANA D *Ungnadia speciosa*	15' x 10'	Sun to semi-shade. NATIVE in Texas. Prefers moist, mildly alkaline soil, but will grow in clay or sandy soil. Showy pink flower clusters in Mar.-Apr. are fragrant. Leathery dark green leaves turn golden yellow in late fall. Drought resistant. Beautiful small tree.
BUCKEYE, RED (HORSE CHESTNUT) D *Aesculus pavia*	15' x 10'	Sun to part shade. Moist, fertile soil, mulched. Red flowers in spikes, coppery new growth in spring. Good for small spaces. Yellow fall color. Not often available but worth looking for. Also pink-flowered variety. *FRUIT AND NEW GROWTH ARE POISONOUS.* NATIVE in Texas.
YELLOW BUCKEYE *A. octandra*	60' x 20'	Panicles of yellow flowers. Culture as above.
CAMPHOR TREE E *Cinnamomum camphora*	40' x 30'	Sun to part shade. Fertile, moist loam, not alkaline. Needs good drainage. Drought tolerant. Rounded head. Medium growth rate. Freezes back in harsh winters, usually root hardy. Glossy foliage. Aromatic leaves said to repel mosquitos. Fruit too messy to plant near paved area. Volunteers readily. Adapted to Houston. Shallow-rooted. Difficult to grow grass under.
CAROLINA BUCKTHORN D *Rhamnus caroliniana*	10' x 15'	Full to semi-shade. Moist, fertile, acid soil. Tolerates wet soil. Medium growth rate. Yellow in fall. Red berries in Aug., black in Sept. Bird food. Shrub or small tree. NATIVE in Texas.

TREES

Common Name *Botanical Name*	E = Evergreen D = Deciduous	
	Average Height X Width	Comments
CATALPA (CIGAR TREE CATAWBA) D *Catalpa bignonioides* *C.b.* 'Nana,' dwarf	40' x 30' 20' x 10'	Sun to semi-shade. Any soil. Good drainage. Ample water. Fast growth. Broad crown. Heart-shape, 12" long, rough leaves. White blooms spring and summer give tropical effect. Hanging bean pods. Yellow fall color. Subject to catalpa worms which strip leaves. Not long lived. Messy on ground.
C. speciosa		Very similar to above; naturalized in East Texas.
C. chilopsis	30'	Recent cross of great merit. Vigorous, drought tolerant, free blooming. Color ranges white to orchid.
CEDAR, BURK RED E *Juniperus virginiana* 'Burkii'	20' x 10'	Sun or part shade. Almost any soil that is quick draining. Water in spring and summer. Columnar type, pyramid shape. Dense foliage, steel blue turning purplish-red in winter.
CEDAR, DEODAR E *Cedrus Deodara*	50' x 25'	Full sun. Requires well-drained soil. Drought resistant. Tolerates various soils. Grows well in the limestone soils of the Edwards Plateau. Conifer. Pyramidal form. Blue-green needles. 2" cones. Aromatic foliage. Subject to borers. Allow for wide spread.
CHERRY LAUREL (WILD PEACH) E *Prunus caroliniana*	25' x 15'	Sun to part shade. Must have loose, well-drained soil. May require chelated iron to acidify soil. Average watering. Eastern U.S. NATIVE. Fast growth. Spreading, upright, dense shape; glossy dark green leaves have cherry odor when crushed. Small creamy flowers in spring. Birds like black fruit. *P. serotina* and *P. compacta* also good varieties. Best to buy container-grown.
CHINA FIR E *Cunninghamia lanceolata*	25' x 15'	Must have full sun. Loose soil, excellent drainage. Conifer. Conical form. Spiny, needle-like foliage. Brown cones. Benefits from pruning. Subject to red spider.
CHINABERRY TREE D *Melia azedarach* Cv. *M. umbraculifera* (TEXAS UMBRELLA TREE)	30' x 20'	Sun. Fertile, sandy soil. Fast growth. Umbrella-like crown. Quick shade. Fragrant, lilac-like spring flowers. Attracts hummingbirds. Birds like yellow berries. Self-seeding. Adapted to Houston. Weedy. Berries and twigs cause maintenance problem. Structurally weak wood.

TREES

Common Name *Botanical Name*	Average Height X Width	Comments
CHINESE PARASOL D *Firmiana simplex* (JAPANESE VARNISH TREE) *F.s.* Cv. 'Variegata'	35' x 15'	Sun to semi-shade. Average soil. Requires drainage. Fast growth. Tall. Unique triangular form. Bright green trunk, orange and green flowers late spring. Green pods in summer. Good for narrow spaces. Yellow fall color. Volunteers readily. Subject to white fly; otherwise recommended.
CHINQUAPIN D *Castanea pumila*	30' x 25'	Sun. Acid, sandy (not clay), well-drained soil. Short-lived...20 years. Wildlife like fruit. Fall color. Several varieties. NATIVE to East Texas.
CORAL TREE (FIREMAN'S CAP) D *Erythrina* *crista-galli*	17' x 13'	Prefers full sun, well-drained soil, but is tolerant of different conditions. Heat and drought tolerant. Often freezes back. Untidy plant with pretty, red-coral racemes of waxy flowers spring and summer, bright green leaves. Rapid growth. May use as tree or shrub.
COTTONWOOD D *Populus deltoides*	60' x 30'	Sun. Fertile, moist soil. Prefers wet site. Fast growth. Pyramidal. Largest of the Poplars. Leaves quake in breeze. Hairs from seeds blow off, forming "cotton." Male trees are cottonless. Quick shade. Fall color. Texas NATIVE; grows along streams. Roots may invade water and drain pipes. Generally very messy tree. Structurally weak wood. Trunk bark is gray. Male cultivar 'Siouxland' is neater.
CRABAPPLE, SOUTHERN FLOWERING D *Malus angustifolia*	25' x 18'	Sun. Fertile, moist soil. Spring flowering pink, rose, or white. Fall fruit. Sends up sucker growth from roots. For Houston area select cultivars that bloom with fewer than usual chilling hours required. 'Teas Crab' cultivar developed by Teas Nursery, Houston, worth looking for. Lovely. *M. ioensis* 'Bechtel's Crab' has double flowers. Crabapples attract hummingbirds. Sucker profusely.
WILD (TEXAS) CRABAPPLE *M. ioensis* *var. texana*	15' x 8'	Sun. Deep clay and manure soil, well drained. Clusters of fragrant pink flowers in April. Small fruit. Texas NATIVE. Plant Nov.-Mar. Fine tree for small landscapes.

TREES

Common Name *Botanical Name*	E = Evergreen D = Deciduous Average Height X Width	Comments
CRAPE MYRTLE D *Lagerstroemia* *indica* Numerous varieties in all sizes allow selection of appropriate size to avoid heavy pruning which destroys natural shape; most hybrids are mildew-and- aphid resistant Dwarf cultivars	20' x 15' 3'	Needs at least 6 hours of sun, well-drained, moist soil with humus. Good air circulation to resist mildew and to bloom better. Removal of seed pods prolongs blooming. Excellent summer and early fall bloomer. Pink, lilac, red, or white flowers. Best to select when in bloom. Fall foliage color. Small tree or large shrub. In late winter or early spring feed and prune to maintain attractive form and to stimulate bloom. For maximum bloom, keep seed pods cut off. Bark and trunk become more picturesque with age. 'Near East' is pink-flowered, weeping form, to 15'. If mildew appears, spray with Benlate. There are new mildew resistant varieties. May be pruned into single or multi-trunked tree.
CRAPE MYRTLE, **HYBRID D** *Lagerstroemia* *indica x Fauriei* Hybrid 'Basham's Party Pink' 'Natchez,' white 'Muscogee,' pink	30' x 15' to 35' x 12'	Needs same as *L. indica* above. More upright, faster growing than the *L. indica*. Resistant to mildew. Flowers: pink, lilac, not as large as *L. indica*. More vigorous, growing 6' in one summer. Red, orange, yellow fall color. Numerous cultivars, all sizes.
CRAPE MYRTLE, **JAPANESE D** *Lagerstroemia* *Fauriei*	30' x 28'	Same culture as *L. indica* above. Larger, more vigorous growth. Mildew resistant. White flowers smaller but in profusion all summer. Cinnamon-red, peeling bark of larger trunk and limbs very attractive. Fine small tree.
CYPRESS, ARIZONA E *Cupressus* *arizonica*	30' x 15'	Conifer with bluish-green needles. All conifers benefit from fertile, well-drained soil and full sun. Grows throughout Texas. May reach 60' height.
CYPRESS, FALSE **HINOKI E** *Chamaecyparis obtusa*	60' x 20'	Conifer. Needs full sun, excellent drainage, fertile, moist soil. Pyramidal, upright. Protect from hot, dry wind. Other species also.
CYPRESS, ITALIAN E *Cupressus semper-* *virens* 'Glauca'	60' x 25'	Cypress and Junipers, both conifers, share same culture: tolerate full sun or semi-shade in almost any soil but require excellent drainage. Blue-green, needle-like foliage in dense, narrow column. Subject to bagworms, blight, fungus, aphids, and spider mites in our climate. Control with appropriate spray.

TREES

Common Name *Botanical Name*	Average Height X Width	Comments
DAWN REDWOOD D *Metasequoia glypto-* *stroboides*	55' x 25'	Conifer. Filtered sun. Excellent drainage. Slightly acid, moist, high-organic soil. Fairly fast growth. Bronze fall color. Clean. Conical form. No major insects or diseases. Good for parks, screening. Fine tree for Houston if enough space.
DOGWOOD D *Cornus florida*	25' x 20'	Semi-shade to shade. Best in South exposure protected from winds. Sandy, well drained, slightly acid soil with rotted manure. Best here in raised areas for the good drainage it requires. Thrives under high trees, with mulch—but no commercial fertilizer. Horizontal branches, oval canopy. White flowers early spring, red fall color. Red fruit is bird food. NATIVE in East Texas. *C.f.* 'Cherokee Chief,' smaller tree, dark pink blossoms; *C.f.* 'Cloud,' very large leaves; 'Bay Beauty,' double-flowering cultiver. May prune immediately after bloom before new flower buds form but red seed pods will be sacrificed.
DOGWOOD, GIANT *Cornus controversa*	40' x 20'	Filtered sun to shade. Fertile, loose, acidic soil with quick drainage. White blooms in spring. Blue-black fruit.
DWARF POINCIANA D *Caesalpinia pulcherrima*	10' x 10'	Hot sun. Light, porous soil. Good drainage. Fast growing. Water deeply and infrequently. Orange to red clusters of flowers all summer. Good for quick screening, but tender to cold.
EBONY, TEXAS E *Pithecellobium* *flexicaule*	30' x 20'	Sun to semi-shade. Protected location in well-drained soil. Small specimen shade tree. Spiny. Cream-colored, fragrant flowers in early spring. Rounded form. Long-lived. Texas NATIVE.
ELM, AMERICAN D *Ulmus americana*	75' x 45'	Sun. Moist, fertile soil. Volunteers. Texas NATIVE. Fine in Houston. Attractive, vase-form shade tree. Long-lived. Copper-yellow fall color. Very large. May need cabling when mature; structurally weak.
ELM, CEDAR D *Ulmus crassifolia*	75' x 35'	Sun. Loamy, moist soil. Drought resistant. Tough. Especially good for Houston area. Flaking bark attractive. Texas NATIVE. Clean, neat shade tree. Upright form. Tolerant of wet clay soils and of urban stress. Yellow fall color. Good in Houston. Desirable.

TREES

	E = Evergreen D = Deciduous	
Common Name *Botanical Name*	**Average** **Height X Width**	**Comments**
ELM, CHINESE (EVERGREEN) D *Ulmus parvifolia* *var. sempervirens*	40' x 30'	Sun. Loamy soil, fertile and moist. Dark green, shiny leaves, yellow or red-purple in fall. Fairly drought tolerant. Good city tree. A cultivar: 'Drake,' nearly evergreen, small durable shade tree. Broad sweeping branches.
ELM, SIBERIAN D *Ulmus pumila*	40' x 25'	Weak and brittle; short-lived. Undesirable. Bloom, fruit in spring. Same culture as Chinese Elm. Elm leaf beetle attacks it.
ELM, SLIPPERY D *Ulmus rubra*	40' x 25'	Yellow fall foliage; shape similar to Live Oak. Culture same as Chinese Elm.
ELM, WINGED D *Ulmus alata*	45' x 30'	Likes full sun, fertile, moist soil, but grows in other conditions. Fast growth. Yellow fall color. Develops interesting corky wings on branches. Good for Houston. NATIVE of East Texas.
EUCALYPTUS (SILVER DOLLAR TREE) E *Eucalyptus cinerea* *E. tereticornus* *E. pulverulenta*	25' x 15' 40' x 20' 16' x 7'	Sun. Good drainage, fertile, not alkaline soil. Position so as to protect from cold winds. Quick growth. Upright, irregular, open shape. Handsome bark. Silver-green aromatic leaves. Cut foliage is long-lasting with spicy smell. Cut branches remain pliable several weeks when kept in solution of 1 part glycerine to 3 parts water. Freezes back in severe winters. Other varieties, including *E. viminalis* 'Manna Gum.' Many species, some cold resistant. May need guy wiring.
E. camaldulensis (RIVER RED GUM)	Medium	One of best. Spectacular bark. Hardy.
E. Gunnii (CIDER GUM)		Silver foliage. Small. Sculptural form. Needs good drainage. Hardy.
E. leucoxylon (BLUE GUM)		Very showy coral to magenta flowers.
FARKLEBERRY, HUCKLE-BERRY Semi-E *Vaccinium arboreum*	15' x 10'	Full sun to semi-shade. Prefers peaty, sandy soil. Moist. NATIVE of East U.S. Upright, slow crooked growth habit. Can be pruned into beautiful sculptural small tree for a patio. Open form. White, fragrant flowers like Lily-of-the-Valley in spring. Good red foliage and black edible fruit in fall. Wildlife food. Bark turns reddish with maturity. Fine under-story. Difficult to transplant. NATIVE tree in Houston.

100

TREES

Common Name *Botanical Name*	Average Height X Width	Comments
FLORIDA ANISE TREE E *Illicium floridanum*	6' x 3'	Prefers filtered shade, sandy, acid soil with good drainage. Tolerates poor drainage. Long, dark green, aromatic leaves. Mahogany-red small flowers in spring. NATIVE to Coastal Plains.
I. parviflorum		Larger leaves, smaller flowers. Excellent.
FRINGE TREE (GRANCY GRAYBEARD) D *Chionanthus* *virginicus* *C. retusa* (CHINESE FRINGE TREE)	20' x 13'	Sun to part shade. Moist, loose, sandy, acid soil. Good drainage. NATIVE of Eastern U.S. Small, upright. Long 4" leaves. Oval form. Clusters white, fragrant, pendant flowers in March; blue, inedible fruit on female tree in fall with yellow leaves. Wildlife food. *C. retusa*, smaller. Both species should be used more.
GINGKO (MAIDENHAIR) D *Gingko biloba*	30' x 20'	Sun. Any soil with good drainage. Very slow growth. Pyramidal form. Fan-shaped, fern-like foliage. Hardy. Drought resistant. Tolerates environmental stress. Plant only male trees. Fruit on females has foul odor. Yellow in fall. Insect and disease resistant. Distinctive form of branches in winter. 'Autumn Gold' especially good fall color.
GORDONIA (FRANKLINIA) E *Gordonia alatamaha*	20' x 15'	Sun or light shade. Moist, peaty or sandy soil, slightly acid. Good drainage. Medium growth rate. Rounded head, small. Fall red and yellow color best in sun. 5" long bright shiny green leaves. 3" fragrant white flowers in spring.
HACKBERRY, SUGAR D *Celtis laevigata* COMMON HACKBERRY *C. occidentalis*	75' x 40'	Sun to part shade. Any soil, even alkaline. Drought tolerant. Reseeds and volunteers easily to being a pest. Attractive shape. Birds like berries. Subject to disease and insects. NATIVE in Texas. Yellow fall color. Long-lived but trashy. Many other trees preferable.
C. l. smallii		Smaller variety.
HAW, RED D *Crataegus mollis*	20' x 17'	Sun or part shade. Rich, well- drained soil. NATIVE. Red fall foliage and fruit. Wildlife food. All Hawthorns attract birds. Also may carry rust disease.
HAWTHORN, 'MAJOR' D *Crataegus pinnatifida* 'Major'	15' x 10'	Sun to part shade. Rich, loamy soil. Keep on dry side. Double rose-to-red flowers. Red berries and red foliage in fall, especially when grown in sun. Haws are subject to fire-blight. Spray and prune affected branches. Disinfect pruning tools to avoid spread of disease.

TREES

Common Name *Botanical Name*	E = Evergreen D = Deciduous	
	Average Height X Width	Comments

HAWTHORN, contd.

Common Name *Botanical Name*	Average Height X Width	Comments
'PAUL'S SCARLET' HAWTHORN D *C. coccinoides*		Small rounded form. Reddish flowers. Red berries. Red fall color. Multiplies.
HAWTHORN, MAY (MAY HAW) D *Crataegus opaca*	20' x 18'	Sun to semi-shade. Rich loamy soil, moderately wet. East Texas NATIVE. Medium growth rate. Mound form. Tolerant of growing conditions. Clean, small tree. 1" white flowers late winter. Red fruit makes good jelly. Large fruited, heavy bearing selections now available.
C. spathulata 'Little Hip Hawthorn'		Convoluted bark and trunks. Bark exfoliates to reveal rusty-red. Sculptural form. Adapted to Texas.
HAWTHORN, PARSLEY D *Crataegus marshallii*	24' x 15'	Part sun to high shade. Good drainage. Tolerates range of soils. Slow growth rate. Leaves have parsley-like appearance, yellow in fall. Small, white, spring flowers, red fall fruit. Thorny. Naturalistic. NATIVE of Texas.
HICKORY, BITTERNUT D *Carya cordiformis*	55' x 40'	Full sun. Deep, moist soil. Has long, deep taproot. Long-lived. Long, shiny leaves. Good fall color. NATIVE of East Texas. Slow growing. Several species.
HICKORY, BLACK D *Carya texana*	50' x 40'	Large shade tree. Slow-growing, long-lived. Sun to part shade. Fertile, deep, loose soil. Other species: *C. ovata*, *C. glabra*. None easy to find, but worthwhile looking for.
HOLLY, AMERICAN E *Ilex opaca*	35' x 20'	Sun best. Tolerates semi-shade but does not berry as well. Rich, slightly acid, moist, loamy soil. Good drainage. *Berries form on female tree only when male holly tree is nearby for pollination.* Slow growth. Long-lived. Red berries. Wildlife food. Columnar form. NATIVE of East Texas.
Cv. *I.o. xanthocarpa* E		Yellow berries.
I.o. 'Savannah' E	30'	Excellent in Houston. Fine shape. Female trees heavy bearing, upright pyramidal or columnar form. Needs sun and a male holly nearby to have abundant red berries. Small, semi-glossy, dark green leaves.

TREES

Common Name *Botanical Name*	Average Height X Width	Comments
HOLLY, contd.		
I.o. 'East Palatka' E	to 30'	Medium growth rate. Tall, pyramidal form. Medium green foliage. Red berries on female trees.
I.o. 'Hume #2'	to 20'	Informal pyramidal form. Heavy bearer of red berries. Dark green leaves. Cut for Christmas.
HOLLY, BURFORD E *Ilex cornuta* 'Burfordii'	10' x 7'	Full sun, fertile soil with moisture. Good drainage. Glossy leaves. Red berries. *I.c.* 'Burfordii Nana' is dwarf form, 5' x 3'.
HOLLY, CHINESE (HORNED) E *Ilex cornuta*	9' x 7'	Likes sun, fertile, well-drained soil with some clay. Oval form. Glossy, dark green, leathery 2" leaves. Scarlet berries on female trees. Spray for scale insects. Feed late winter. Small tree. Male holly trees must be nearby for female tree to bear berries, which are produced on old (last year's) growth.
HOLLY, DAHOON E *Ilex cassine*	30' x 15'	Shrub or small tree. Sun. Well-drained, acid soil. Gray bark, multiple trunks, narrow leaves. Bright, orange-red berries on females Nov. to Mar. when birds eat all berries. Bee and bird food. U. S. NATIVE. Fertilize late winter or early spring.
I.c. myrtifolia 'Lowei'		Yellow berries.
HOLLY, FOSTER'S E *Ilex attenuata* 'Fosteri'	20' x 10'	Sun. Fertile, moist soil. Good drainage. Medium growth rate. Pyramidal form. Dense. Long, pointed, dark green leaves. Large red berries on female trees. Cuts well. Wildlife food. Spray for mildew, scale, and insects when necessary to keep foliage clean. May use as large shrub.
HOLLY, INTEGRA (MOCHI TREE) E *Ilex integra*	20' x 20'	Sun. Fertile, loose, slightly acid soil with very good drainage. Compact branching, dark green, glossy leaves, 1-3" long. Red berries.
I.i. 'Xanthocarpa'		Yellow berries.

TREES

	E = Evergreen D = Deciduous	
Common Name *Botanical Name*	**Average** **Height X Width**	**Comments**
HOLLY, JAPANESE E *Ilex crenata* *microphylla*	5' x 3'	Sun to semi-shade. Slightly acid, sandy, loamy soil. Water. Requires good drainage. Black berries. Good hedge plant. Dwarf forms: 'Compacta' and 'Helleri,' 3' x 3'.
HOLLY, LUSTERLEAF (TARAJO) E *Ilex latifolia*	25' x 17'	Part shade. Moist, loose,fertile soil with very good drainage. Cannot tolerate hot, direct sun or compacted soil. Conical shape. Silver-gray branches, dark green, leathery, glossy, aromatic leaves, 4-6" long and 3" wide. Female trees, with male Holly nearby, produces large red berries. Medium growth rate. Fairly new to our area. Worth looking for.
HOLLY, POSSUM HAW D *Ilex decidua*	15' x 10'	Full sun to part shade. Moist, fertile, loamy soil. Tolerant of poor drainage. Small, multi-trunked tree. Red berries only on female trees show up best against gray branches after leaves fall. Berries turn red only after frost. Striking effect. Birds love berries. NATIVE here. Best to buy in berry from nursery. Red or yellow berries.
HONEY LOCUST D *Gleditsia triacanthos* *G.t. inermis,* thornless *G. texana,* Hybrid	35' x 25'	Full sun to semi-shade. Any soil, kept evenly moist. Good drainage. Said to be salt-tolerant. Trouble-free, graceful shade tree; good for street planting. Use only thornless varieties. Hardy. Several cultivars. Lacy foliage allows sunlight to reach ground below. Amber summer flowers attract bees. Wildlife eat pods which are messy on lawn. Roots enrich their soil.
HUISACHE D *Acacia farnesiana*	28' x 22'	Sun. Loose, well-drained, alkaline soil. Intolerant of wet soil. Thorny. Fern-like leaves. Fuzzy, yellow, ball flowers in spring, fragrant. South Texas NATIVE. Gives filtered shade.
A. Baileyana		Australian NATIVE has blue-gray foliage. Excellent and highly ornamental. Should use more often in Houston. *A.B. var. purpurea* has purple seed pods, very showy.
JAPANESE RAISIN TREE D *Hovenia dulcis*	30' x 15'	Part shade. Sandy loam. Good drainage. Very attractive foliage. Greenish flowers. Reddish fruit stalks considered edible in Japan.

TREES

Common Name *Botanical Name*	Average Height X Width	Comments
JUJUBE (CHINESE DATE) D *Ziziphus jujuba*	22' x 15'	Sun. Prefers alkaline soils, but requires good drainage. Medium growth rate. Thorny. Dark green, glossy leaves quake in breeze. Edible, mahogany-colored fruit; messy on ground.
JUNIPER (BLUE OR SILVER CEDAR) E *Juniperus virginiana* 'Glauca'	30' x 15'	Full sun. Prefers poor, alkaline soil, very well-drained. Slow growth. Columnar form. Aromatic, needle-like, gray or blue-gray foliage. Bluish berries on female trees. Wildlife food. Attains picturesque, silvery bark and form in 25 years or more. Subject to bagworm, rust, canker, spider mites. Transplanting more successful with small specimens. This cultivar preferable to the native Eastern Red Cedar (*J. virginiana*), which is subject to insect and disease problems.
JUNIPER, CAENART E *Juniperus virgin-iana canaertii*	25' x 16'	Sun. Like most conifers it requires good drainage. Tolerates alkaline soil. Small, dark green leaves, yellow-green in spring. Some cultivars have blue-green foliage. Pyramidal form. Susceptible to cedar blight, bagworms, and rust. Feed annually.
JUNIPER, CHINESE (BLUE VASE) E *Juniperus chinensis* 'Glauca'	7' x 5'	Full sun. Any very well-draining soil. Fast growth. Vase form. Blue-green foliage. Good for screen. Very large. Difficult to prune. Water to discourage bagworms and spider mites. Dwarf cultivar: *J.c. viridifolia*, but very few "dwarfs" stay small.
J.c. 'Tortulosa' E	20' x 12'	Has twisted branches.
JUNIPER, HOLLYWOOD E *Juniperus chinensis* 'Torulosa' (tree type)	15'	Same culture as Red Cedar Juniper. Irregular, twisted, upright branches with rich green foliage. Requires effective rapid drainage. Allow ample space for growth.
VARIEGATED HOLLYWOOD JUNIPER E *Juniperus chinensis* 'Torulosa' (tree type)	10'	Conical, irregular form.

TREES

Common Name *Botanical Name*	E = Evergreen D = Deciduous	
	Average Height X Width	Comments
JUNIPER, RED CEDAR E *Juniperus virginiana* (tree type) *J. chinensis* Cv. 'Blue Point' (tree type)	35' x 15' 15'	Tolerates full sun or part shade. *Must* have excellent drainage. Any well-draining soil. Heat, humidity, and poor drainage cause serious problems with blight, fungus, spider mites, and aphids. Use appropriate spray. Dark green, needle-like foliage, reddish in winter. Columnar shape.
J.v. 'Skyrocket' (tree type)		Silver-blue foliage.
HILLSPIRE JUNIPER E *J.v.* 'Cupressifolia' (columnar form)	20' x 7'	Dark green, needle-like foliage. Compact, pyramid shape.
LEATHERWOOD (TITI) Semi-E *Cyrilla racemiflora*	12' x 9'	Sun to bright shade. Woodsy soil with humus. Tolerates well or pooly drained soil. NATIVE of Gulf Coast. Leathery, light green leaves turn yellow in fall, dark red in winter. Fragrant, large, white flowers in racemes in late spring attract bees. With age trunks turn reddish. Small attractive tree, fine for small areas. Good for bonsai, too. May be difficult to find, but keep trying.
LIGUSTRUM		Used as small tree. See SHRUBS chart.
LIGUSTRUM, TREE E *Ligustrum lucidum* 'Glossy Privet'	20' x 10'	Shrub or small tree. Sun or part shade. Tolerates most any soil but appreciates organic content and fertilizing. Edges of leaves are translucent. Blue berries on orange stems in winter. Subject to white fly. Also yellow variegated form.
LIME PRICKLY-ASH E *Zanthoxylum fagara*	15' x 10'	Sun. Light, sandy, well-drained soil. Small, thorny, fine texture. Adapted to Houston. Foliage lime green.
Z. clava Herculis	30' x 20'	Texas NATIVE.
LINDEN, AMERICAN (AMERICAN BASSWOOD) D *Tilia Americana*	50' x 30'	Sun. Fertile, moist soil with humus. Large shade tree with broad crown, drooping branches. Plant species NATIVE to Northeast Texas. Heart-shaped leaves. Fast growth. Good for parks. Fragrant, yellowish flowers, May-June, attract bees. Yellow fall color. Wildlife food.
T. Caroliniana and *T. Floridiana*		NATIVE to Houston area.

TREES

Common Name *Botanical Name*	Average Height X Width	Comments
LOBLOLLY BAY (GORDONIA) E *Gordonia lasianthus* *G. axillaris*	30' x 20'	Sun to semi-shade. Morning sun; summer afternoon shade. Takes hot sun if kept watered. Moist, acid, sandy, peaty, humusy soil. Good drainage. Slow growth rate. Similar to single rose, 2-3" white blooms early summer. Delicate fragrance. Red fall foliage. NATIVE in Southeastern U.S. Does not require fertilizing if soil is properly prepared. Enjoys same culture as Azaleas and Camellias. Attractive planted with Azaleas.
LOBLOLLY SWEET BAY (POET'S LAUREL) E *Laurus nobilis*	30' x 20'	Sun. Slightly acidic, peaty, rich soil. Ample moisture. Aromatic foliage. Glossy, dark green, 4" long leaves used of old in victory garlands. Protect from sudden freezes.
LOCUST, BLACK D *Robinia pseudoacacia*	60' x 25'	Any soil with good drainage. Prefers full sun. Open, upright form. Spiny, wisteria-like, white flowers in racemes. Fragrant. Attracts hummingbirds. Good for stabilizing soil. Adapted to Texas. Too large for home gardens. Cold hardy. Colonizes (multiplies) rapidly from stolons that root. Subject to locust borers.
LOQUAT (JAPANESE PLUM) E *Eriobotrya japonica*	20' x 20'	Full sun. Fertile, loose, draining soil. Large, coarse leaves, rusty-bronze undersides. White, fragrant flowers in fall. Edible orange fruit. Wildlife food. Forms dense mass. Reseeds. Subject to fire-blight. Tender. Espaliers nicely.
MAGNOLIA, PINK, ORIENTAL, or SAUCER D *Magnolia soulangeana*	20' x 15'	Full sun with protection from summer's hot afternoon sun and winter's cold winds and freezes. Loose, sandy, acidic, moist loam. Requires good drainage. Very large white, light pink, or mauve fragrant flowers, early spring before large 5" to 6" leaves come out. Apply complete fertilizer late winter. Many varieties. Striking accent. Needs careful watering in spring and summer. Allow for natural spreading shape. Do not crowd.
MAGNOLIA, SOUTHERN E *Magnolia grandiflora*	60' x 35'	Sun to semi-shade. Blooms better in sun. Loose, acid, fertile soil with plenty of organic matter. Water. Careful not to plant too deep or in compacted soil. To accelerate growth, feed with fertilizer high in nitrogen annually. Long lived. Very large. Allow 35-50' between trees or from a structure. Dense spreading, pyramidal form. Sheds leaves all year. If lower limbs are allowed to remain, they hide leaf-litter. The result-

TREES

Common Name *Botanical Name*	E = Evergreen D = Deciduous Average Height X Width	Comments
MAGNOLIA, SOUTHERN, contd.		ing leaf mulch protects the shallow roots. Large, glossy, dark green leaves. Large 6", creamy white, waxy, fragrant flowers. Leaves turning light green may indicate lack of acidity in soil. Work sulphur or iron sulphate into soil at base of tree, but away from trunk, and water well. Not suited to patios or small gardens. East Texas NATIVE. Almost impossible to garden under. Several cultivars, including 'Samuel Sommer's,' 'Majestic Beauty,' and the smaller, more compact 'Russet Beauty.' 'Little Gem' cultivar, 25' x 10', for small gardens.
MAGNOLIA, STAR D *Magnolia stellata*	9' x 6'	Full sun or semi-shade. Well-drained, fertile soil. Water when dry. Oval form. Long leaves. Fragrant, white flowers Jan., before foliage. Locate to protect from cold north winds and freeze.
MAGNOLIA, SWEET BAY E *Magnolia virginiana*	40' x 25'	Sun or part shade. Moist, loose, acidic soil with ample organic matter. Likes being wet but also grows in well-drained soil. Leaves silver-white underneath. Large, fragrant, white flowers Apr.-May. May plant in tub. Wildlife food. Feed after bloom. Semi-evergreen. Specimen tree. NATIVE to East Texas. Pruning seldom needed. Pest free.
MAPLE, CHALK *Acer leucoderme*	20' x 15'	Grows well beneath other larger trees. Brilliant red fall foliage. NATIVE of Southeastern U.S. Hardy. Culture like Drummond's Red, below.
MAPLE, DRUMMOND'S (SOUTHERN) RED D *Acer rubrum drummondii*	65' x 35'	Sun or semi-shade. Prefers low, moist, sandy, acid soil, but tolerates others. Soak well when dry. Small, rounded form. Fast growth. Colorful. Small red flowers in spring, leaf stems red in summer, red or yellow foliage in fall. Good in Houston. Clean tree with attractive gray bark. East Texas NATIVE. Tolerant of seashore conditions. 'Scarlet Swamp' *(Acer rubrum)* also excellent fall red color, but roots more aggressive than the Drummond's.
MAPLE, JAPANESE D *Acer palmatum*	10' x 14'	Sun to semi-shade. Light soil. Needs good drainage and ample water. Slow growth. Protect from hottest sun, but color is best in sun and wind. Small, almost miniature, interesting tree. Fall color, red to gold. Cultivars have different color foliage. Distinctive leaf color.

TREES

Common Name *Botanical Name*	Average Height X Width	Comments
MAPLE, SABINAL BIG TOOTH *Acer saccharum grandidentatum*	30' x 50'	Tolerates alkaline soils. NATIVE of Edwards Plateau and mountains in Trans Pecos, Texas. Red branchlets. Fall color best in Southwest.
MAPLE, SILVER D *Acer saccharinum*	80' x 40'	Requires excellent drainage. Ordinary soil. Sun. Weak wood, silvery on underside of leaves. Shallow roots interfere with nearby plants. Vigorous root system invades drainlines, breaks (buckles) pavement. Yellow in fall. Fall color good after very cold winter. Prone to diseases and insects. Messy. Fast growing but short-lived. Not recommended. Other Maples preferable.
MAPLE, SOUTHERN SUGAR CADDO D *Acer saccharum floridanum*	to 70'	Sun. Moist, well-drained, sandy loam. Brilliant red-orange-yellow fall color. Texas NATIVE. Tolerates tight clay soils of Houston. Dense shade tree. Plant only trees from local sources.
Var. FLORIDA SUGAR MAPLE D *A. barbatum* 'Michx'	45' x 60'	Shade or semi-shade. Moist, well-drained loam. Young leaves hairy underneath.
MESQUITE D *Prosopis glandulosa or juliflora*	30' x 35'	Sun. Any soil. Drought tolerant. Very long taproot. Ferny foliage. Fragrant small flowers attract bees. Crooked branches, multi-trunk. Thorny. Problem free. Wildlife food. NATIVE of South and West Texas. Can become a pest.
MIMOSA (SILK TREE) D *Albizia Julibrissin*	30' x 30'	Sun. Good drainage. Any soil. Tolerates coastal location. Brittle. Puffs of pink or yellow-pink blooms in May-June. Attracts hummingbirds. Fast growth, quick shade. Fern-like foliage. Graceful umbrella shape. Self-seeds. Subject to damage from twig girdler beetle. Short-lived.
MULBERRY, RUSSIAN D *Morus alba* var. *tatarica*	50' x 40'	Sun to semi-shade. Fertile soil, moist. Hardy. Fast growth but shallow root system. Black berries very messy, but good bird food. Fallen fruit stains brick, pavement, etc. There is a fruitless variety. Naturalized in Texas.
TEXAS or RED MULBERRY D *M. rubra*		Sweeter berries. U. S. NATIVE. Attracts unusual birds during spring migration: late April, early May. Problems with woody aphids. Messy.

TREES

Common Name *Botanical Name*	E = Evergreen D = Deciduous Average Height X Width	Comments
MULBERRY, TEAS WEEPING D *Morus alba* 'Teas Weeping'	10' x 4'	Sun to semi-shade. Fast growth. Large, medium-green leaves. Black berries, edible. (Developed by John Teas, Houston, in 1888.) Good specimen in tub or for open hedge. 'Chaparral Weeping' (*M.a.* 'Chaparral') is berry-less.
OAK, BUR E *Quercus macrocarpa*	80' x 50'	Sun. Prefers rich, well-drained soil. Tolerant of drought, cold, alkaline soil, and urban stresses. Heavy, spreading limbs, very large acorns. Rapid growth rate. Yellow and crimson fall foliage. Too large for most yards. Texas NATIVE. Trouble free.
OAK, CHINQUAPIN (YELLOW CHESTNUT OAK) D *Quercus muhlenbergii*	40' x 25'	Sun. Good drainage. Tolerates all soils except swampy. Straight, shapely trunk, round form. Shade tree. Copperish fall color. Notched, dark green leaves to 6" long x 3" wide. Drought resistant. Texas NATIVE.
OAK, ESCARPMENT LIVE (PETITE LIVE) E *Querqus fusiformis*	36' x 20'	Sun. Any soil including lime-stone. Drought tolerant. Hardy. Sends up many suckers. Forms groves. Texas NATIVE.
OAK, JAPANESE E *Quercus myrsinifolia*	35' x 25'	Full sun to high shade. Rich, moist soil. Good drainage. Medium growth rate. Pyramidal form. Long, narrow, glossy, yellow-green leaves. Wildlife food.
OAK, LIVE (SOUTHERN) E *Quercus virginiana*	50' x 75'	Tolerates variety of local soil conditions. Best in moist, fertile, sandy soil and sun. Strong wood, resistant to breakage. Few diseases or insects. Very long-lived. Broad spreading form. Allow space. Dependable. Hardy. Annual feeding with 10-10-10 is beneficial. NATIVE in deep South. Majestic tree. Allow space. Leaves fall Dec. to Mar.
OAK, NUTTALL *Quercus nuttallii*	75' x 45'	Adapts to heavy clay soils. Sun. Good for this area. Fine red-yellow fall foliage. May be hard to find. A Red Oak.
OAK, OVERCUP (SWAMP POST) D *Quercus lyrata*	75' x 85'	Sun to part shade. Tolerates wet sites. Moist, rich, peaty soil. Found in East Texas. 8" long leaves turn to scarlet and orange in fall. Rough, gray bark tinged with red. Slow growing, long-lived. Insect and disease resistant.

TREES

Common Name *Botanical Name*	Average Height X Width	Comments
OAK, PIN D *Quercus* *palustris*	80' x 50'	Sun. Slightly acid soil. Good drainage. Allow space for width of branches which tend to droop slightly. Dark green foliage turns yellow and red in fall. Good lawn tree. NATIVE to Eastern U.S. Not as good an Oak for Houston as Shumard Oak.
OAK, POST D *Quercus stellata*	90' x 55'	Sun. Moist, fertile soil with good drainage. Valuable to landscape design. Protect from fill dirt and root system damage during construction. Other Oaks more desirable here.
OAK, RED D *Quercus rubra*	40' x 25'	Fast growth. Large leaves turn reddish in fall and stay on tree. Leaves of Shumard Red Oak do not cling through winter as do those of Red Oak. Durable tree. Tolerant of dry soil.
OAK, SAWTOOTH D *Quercus* *acutissima*	55' x 40'	Sun. Moist, rich soil, but tolerates wide range of conditions. Medium to fast growth. Clean, pest-free shade tree. Wildlife food. Hard to find but worth the try. Good for this area. Shiny green leaves.
OAK, SHUMARD D *Quercus* *Shumardii*	60' x 40'	Sun. Moist soil. Good drainage. Very good for Houston area. Medium growth rate. Durable. Tolerant of mildly alkaline soil. Reddish bronze foliage in fall. Select tree in fall while it is in color to assure getting one that turns bright red. When planting, allow space for the 40'-plus spread of branches. NATIVE of Southern U.S.
OAK, SOUTHERN RED D *Quercus* *falcata*	75' x 50'	Sun. Dry, sandy soil with good drainage. Dense shade tree. Oval, upright form. Long-lived. Wildlife food. Reddish brown in fall. Small acorns. Adapted to eastern half of Texas. Large percentage of the trees that toppled over in Houston during Hurricane Alicia were Southern Red Oaks, *Q. falcata.* It has a weak root system. Also easily damaged during construction.
RED OAK D *Q.f.* var. 'Pagodifolia	70' x 45'	Similar to *Q. falcata* above. Prefers growing along streams. Small acorns. Red foliage in fall. Gray-black trunk tolerates poor drainage.
OAK, SWAMP CHESTNUT D *Quercus prinus* 'Michauxii'	65' x 45'	Best in sun and loose, fertile, draining soil. Tolerates moist and gumbo soil. Leaves 6" to 9". Texas NATIVE. Fine fall red foliage. A White Oak.

TREES

Common Name *Botanical Name*	E = Evergreen D = Deciduous	
	Average Height X Width	Comments
OAK, TEXAS RED D *Quercus shumardii* var. *texana*	45' x 35'	Sun. Tolerant of soils, even alkaline. Slow growth rate. Good red fall color. Insect resistant. Shumard and Nuttall Oaks fine here. Texas NATIVE. Excellent tree.
OAK, WATER D *Quercus nigra*	55' x 35'	Sun. Clayey soil. Moisture. Likes wet sites. Not as desirable as some other varieties, subject to iron chlorosis in alkaline soil and insects, but tolerant of poor drainage. Not good fall color. Fast growth. Accepts moist soil. A Red Oak.
OAK, WHITE D *Quercus alba*	75' x 70'	Best in full sun, well-drained, deep, fertile, moist soil. Not too wet but not too dry either. Some years has good fall color. Long-lived, good upright shade tree. Annual fertilization speeds normally slow growth. Resistant to oak wilt.
OAK, WILLOW (PIN) D *Quercus phellos*	75' x 45'	Best in full sun, moist or wet but well-drained soil. Medium to fast growth. Narrower leaf than other oaks. Sun filters through leaves. Wildlife food. Long lived shade tree. Yellow fall foliage. A Red Oak. Distinctive form. Insect resistant, but subject to leaf spot fungus and chlorosis.
OLIVE E *Olea europaea* *O.e.* 'Little Ollie,' dwarf	15' x 10'	Requires full sun, dry, sandy soil, and excellent drainage. Fine for hot, dry areas. Prune to shape. Small tree or shrub. Narrow, gray-green leaves. Feed twice yearly.
PARKINSONIA (JERUSALEM THORN) D *Parkinsonia* *aculeata*	30' x 25'	Sun, fertile soil, good drainage. Tolerant of heat and drought but not wet soil. Fragrant yellow flowers in summer. Thorny. In early spring prune to shape and to increase bloom. Container-grown best.
PAW PAW D *Asimina triloba*	25' x 15'	Partial shade. Rich, moist soil. Little known but attractive as tree or shrub. Unusual greenish, yellow, purple flowers. Edible fruit, 2-7" long.
PEACH, FLOWERING D *Prunus persica*	17' x 8'	Full sun. Very well-draining, fertile soil. Several varieties available, both single and double flowering, with white, red, or pink flowers. Enjoyed for the bloom in early spring, not for the fruit. Variety 'Peppermint' has variegated flowers. Charming in garden, though not long-lived. Subject to borers and chlorosis.

112

TREES

Common Name *Botanical Name*	Average Height X Width	Comments
PEAR, BRADFORD FLOWERING D *Pyrus calleryana* 'Bradford'	25' x 15'	Full sun. Very good drainage, fertile soil. Less susceptible to fire-blight disease than other Pears. Upright, pyramidal form, later oval. Plant only fire-blight resistant varieties; hybrids most resistant. New leaves coppery, purple in fall. Profusion of white flowers in very early spring. Wildlife food. Street tree. *P.c.* 'Aristocrat' is smaller, wider, more nearly oval. When buying, inquire if it is blooming cultivar.
PEAR, EVERGREEN Semi-E *Pyrus kawakami*	25' x 20'	Sun. Fertile soil. Drainage. Medium-fast growth. Espaliers well. White flowers in very early spring (Jan.-Feb.).
PECAN D *Carya illinoinensis*	80' x 65'	Best in sun in fertile, deep, and moist soil. Medium-slow growth. Broad shape. Dropping leaves and fruit require maintenance. Texas NATIVE. Texas State Tree. For fruit production, regular spraying against pests is required. Numerous varieties. Do not add Pecan leaves to compost pile or mulch. Long-lived. Very subject to limb breakage. Many improved species. Allow at least 35' from any structure when positioning.
PERSIMMON, JAPANESE D *Diospyrus kaki*	17' x 10'	Sun. Loose, well-drained, fertile soil. White flowers in spring, yellow fall leaves. Large, edible, orange fruit in fall. Umbrella form. Sprouts from roots. Male trees cleaner. For fruit production, plant two varieties for pollination. Subject to scale and other insects.
BLACK PERSIMMON *D. texana*	30' x 15'	Southwest Texas NATIVE species. Very sculptural. Shape and bark like Crape Myrtle.
D. virginiana	30' x 18'	Sun. Rich soil on dry side. Good drainage. Small, orange-brown fruit, sweet when completely ripe.
PHOTINIA, RED-TIP		Pruned into small tree form. See SHRUBS chart.
PINE, JAPANESE BLACK E *Pinus Thunbergiana* Cv. 'Variegata'	22' x 10' in 10-12 yrs.	Sun. Good drainage. Slow growth rate. Conifer. Tolerant of coastal conditions, urban stresses. Picturesque form for accent.

TREES

Common Name *Botanical Name*	E = Evergreen D = Deciduous	
	Average Height X Width	Comments
PINE, LOBLOLLY E *Pinus taeda*	80' x 35'	Full sun and good drainage. Prefers fertile, sandy, acid loam, tolerates others. Fast growing. Southeast Texas NATIVE yellow pine. Fusiform rust and pine insects can disfigure it. Fine, high shade for Camellias and Azaleas. Conifer. All Pines have needle-like leaves.
PINE, LONGLEAF E *Pinus palustris*	55' x 25'	Full sun, deep, sandy, acid soil. Good drainage. Open, upright form. Tall straight trunk. Long-lived. 20" needles, large cones, good for decorating use. NATIVE of East Texas. Wildlife food. Conifer. Not good for most locations in Houston.
PINE, SHORTLEAF E *Pinus echinata*	50' x 25'	Full sun, well-drained, sandy, acid soil. 4" needles, bluish green. Texas NATIVE. Good survival rate from diseases and insects. Oval form. Wildlife food. Conifer.
PINE, SLASH E *Pinus Elliottii*	60' x 30'	Sun. Moist, acid soil, but requires good drainage. Grows rapidly. Upright form. Conifer. Allow minimum 25' between for spread of canopy. Attractive in groups. Fusiform rust, pine tip moths, and pine beetles cause damage. Adapted to East Texas. Others better choice.
CUBAN PINE *P. caribaea* may be same as *P. Elliottii*		Needles to 12" long; cones to 6" long.
PINE, SPRUCE E *Pinus glabra*	25' x 18'	Sun. Tolerates some shade. Likes rich, fertile soil and good drainage, but tolerates heavy and moist soils. Medium growth rate. Casts heavy shade. Smaller than native Pines.
PINEAPPLE GUAVA E		Used as small tree. See SHRUBS chart.
PISTACHIO, CHINESE D *Pistacia chinensis*	40' x 30'	Full sun, fairly dry soil. Requires excellent drainage. Fast growth. Tolerates alkaline soil. Good red-salmon-yellow fall color. Rounded form. Plant only male trees to avoid messy fruit. No insect or disease problems. Long-lived. Self-pruning. Drought resistant. Fir.
PISTACHIO, TEXAS D *Pistacia texana*	20' x 15'	Adapted to alkaline soil, smaller, excellent, red-purple fall color. Well adapted to Houston area. Reddish-yellow flowers. Multiple trunks.

TREES

Common Name *Botanical Name*	Average Height X Width	Comments
PLUM, FLOWERING, PURPLE LEAF D *Prunus cerasifera* 'Atropurpurea'	14' x 10'	Prefers full sun, fertile soil good drainage. Foliage rich purple in sun. Loses color in dense shade. Flowers pinkish white in spring. Use for accent, especially in groups. Protect from P.M. sun.
'Krauter's Vesuvius'		Holds dark, reddish purple foliage throughout season. Whitish spring flowers. Good small tree. Other cultivars also.
PLUM, MEXICAN or WILD D *Prunus mexicana*	25' x 18'	Best in sun, fertile soil, drainage. Attractive form. White, fragrant, early spring flowers stunning against dark branches. Wildlife food. August fruit purplish red, for jelly. Texas NATIVE. Spray in winter, very early spring with oil emulsion to protect from scale. Feed after bloom.
POPLAR, WHITE D *Populus alba*	60' x 40'	Sun. Any soil. Quick growth. Short-lived. Under side of leaves is white. Oval shaped. Tolerant of pollution and city stress. May invade sewer lines. Volunteers readily. Plant away from structures.
QUINCE, CHINESE D *Cydonia sinensis*	20' x 12'	Full sun to shade. Fertile soil. Requires good drainage. Pink flowers in early spring. Yellow fruit. Fall color. Hard to find.
RAIN TREE, SOUTHERN GOLDEN D *Koelreuteria* *bipinnata* *K. b. 'formosana'*	30' x 25'	Full sun. Fertile soil. Good drainage. Fast growth. Abundant seedlings. Broad, irregular shape. Yellow flowers in panicles, October, turning into pinkish, papery sacs which dry well for cutting. Yellow fall foliage. Place to protect from hard freeze.
REDBAY E *Persea borbonia*	30' x 20'	Sun to semi-shade. Moist, rich, sandy soil. Upright form, slender. Semi-glossy, willow-like, aromatic foliage. Subject to leaf-gall and wax scale. Choice bay leaf for Cajun cookery.
SILK BAY E *P. humilis*	8' x 5'	NATIVE to Gulf Coast. Yellow-white flowers in clusters.
REDBUD D *Cercis canadensis*	25' x 15'	Sun to part shade. Fertile, moist, acid soil, good drainage. Lilac pink, small, pea-like flowers early spring, often with Azaleas. Irregular form. Yellow fall color. Several cultivars: *C.c. alba* has white flowers; *C.c. reni-formis* is 'Texas Redbud;' *C.c. var. texensis*, NATIVE of Texas. *C.c. 'Oklahoma'* blooms better, foliage more

TREES

E = Evergreen	D = Deciduous	
Common Name *Botanical Name*	**Average** **Height X Width**	**Comments**
REDBUD, contd.		resistant to pests and disease; *C.c.* 'Forest Pansy' is smaller with wine red foliage. Prune following bloom. Feed annually early spring. Water when dry. Avoid injury to bark because of heart rot.
RIVER BIRCH D *Betula nigra*	50' x 20'	Sun. Likes very well-drained, but moist, even wet, sandy, acid soil. Fast growing. One of best for erosion control. Interesting peeling bark. Pyramidal. Casts light shade. Yellow fall color. Often multi-trunk. Look for varieties with larger leaves and borer and chlorosis resistance.
SALT CEDAR D *Tamarix gallica*	45' x 25'	Requires full sun and good drainage with any soil. Sparse, feathery foliage. Pink flowers in summer. Thrives on seashore. Good wind-break.
SASSAFRAS D *Sassafras albidum*	40' x 20'	Full sun. Requires sandy, acid soil. Tolerates drought. Upright, oval form. Aromatic lime-green foliage. Greenish-yellow flower cluster, spring. Long-lived. Pest-free. Tea made from roots. Wildlife food. Beautiful yellow, orange, red fall color. Difficult to transplant.
SERVICE BERRY (SHAD BUSH) D *Amelanchier* *arborea*	15' x 8'	Part shade. Sandy, acid soil. Moisture but good drainage. Culture similar to Dogwood. Small tree. Racemes of fragrant white flowers in March. Reddish purple, edible fruit follows in May. Prefers banks of rivers or ponds. Not common.
SILVER-BELL TREE, TWO-WINGED D *Halesia diptera*	30' x 18'	Likes part shade in acid soil on slopes. Tolerates less than good drainage. White, bell-shaped, spring flower. Seed pod has two broad wings. Yellow fall color. Clean. Good patio tree. Use balanced fertilizer in late winter before bloom. NATIVE of Gulf Region. Culture similar to Dogwood.
SOAPBERRY D *Sapindus saponaria* *var. drummondii*	45' x 25'	Full sun. Medium growth rate. 8" leaves, usually turn golden yellow in fall. Desirable. Tolerates dry, rocky soil. Large clusters of white flowers. Yellow fruit.
SOPHORA (TEXAS MOUNTAIN LAUREL) E *Sophora* *secundiflora*	15' x 8'	Best in sun to part-sun. Almost any soil, but requires *excellent* drainage. Dark green foliage. Good mass. Lavender flowers in spring in wisteria-like clusters, fragrant. *SEEDS IN PODS ARE POISONOUS.* Very slow growth. Shrub-like. NATIVE in Texas. Easily trained as a standard.

116

TREES

Common Name *Botanical Name*	Average Height X Width	Comments
SOPHORA, TEXAS (EVE'S NECKLACE) E *Sophora affinis*	20' x 16'	Sun to semi-sun. Prefers mildly alkaline soil, good drainage. Open form. Finely textured. NATIVE in Texas. Fruit-beans form in curious necklace-like string. Pink-tinged white spring flowers. Excellent accent tree. Casts light shade.
SOUTHERN WAX MYRTLE E *Myrica cerifera*	12' x 14'	Sun. Moist, peaty soil. Aromatic foliage. Tolerant of wet or mildly alkaline soils or coastal conditions. Multi-trunked. Whitish waxy berries attract birds. NATIVE in Texas. Shrub or small tree.
M. pusila	5'	Dwarf form. May be a separate species.
STEWARTIA, VIRGINIA D *Stewartia malacodendron*	6' x 5'	Part shade. Deep, fertile, acid soil containing humus. Good drainage. Flowers similar to Camellia, white, Apr.-May. *S. malacodendron* very rare. Found in Newton County near Toledo Bend Reservoir.
ORIENTAL STEWARTIA D *S. pseudocamellia*		Worth trying.
SUMAC, SMOOTH D *Rhus glabra* 'Wing Rib' *R. copallina* 'Prairie Flame' *R. lanceolata* *R. aromatica*	16' x 10'	Best in sun, sandy garden soil, but tolerant of imperfect conditions. Fast growth. Birds feed on clusters of red fall fruit. Forms clumps. Sumacs are the most dependable for bright red fall color. *BEWARE OF POISON SUMAC GROWING NEAR BEAUMONT.*
SWEET GUM, AMERICAN D *Liquidamber styraciflua*	65' x 35'	Full sun. Moist, loose, fertile soil. Does not tolerate limey soil. Likes ample water. Good drainage. Fast erect growth. Large leaves like maples. Fruits are woody, spiny balls, nuisance on lawn. Almost pest-free. Early fall color: reds and yellows. Various cultivars and clones. Different cultivars have different fall colors. Safer to buy while in color. *L.s.* 'Burgundy,' wine; *L.s.* 'Festival,' yellow and peach; *L.s.* 'Palo Alto,' yellow and red. Forest tree in East Texas. Fine in Houston. Fruit attracts many species of birds.

TREES

Common Name *Botanical Name*	E = Evergreen D = Deciduous Average Height X Width	Comments
SYCAMORE, AMERICAN PLANE TREE D *Platanus occi-* *dentalis*	75' x 40'	Full sun with good air circulation. Fertile, moist soil. Requires lots of water and excellent drainage. Very large leaves, yellowish-green; yellow-amber fall color. Leaves shed periodically. Interesting, greenish-white, peeling bark. Varieties differ in fall color. Susceptible to diseases anthracnose and bacterial leaf scorch. Grows throughout East Texas. Roots may invade water and sewer pipes. Needs space. Litter from twigs, leaves, fruit.
TALLOW, CHINESE D *Sapium sebiferum*	35' x 30'	Sun. Any soil, wet to dry, except alkaline. Fast growth. Brittle wood messy, shallow roots, but fine fall color: red, yellow, orange, even purplish. White berries in clusters. Volunteers readily. Well adapted to Houston.
TAPIOCA TREE *Manihot esculenta*	10' x 4'	Shrub or small tree rich, sandy soil. Water. Sun to semi-shade. Very fast growth. Brittle. Palmately lobed leaves flutter attractively in breeze. Has a very tropical appearance. Roots yield tapioca. Tender.
TULIP TREE OR YELLOW POPLAR D *Liriodendron* *Tulipifera*	60' x 20'	Prefers sun, rich, deep, moist, well-drained soil. Once established does well. Spring flowers greenish-yellow, tulip shape. Yellow fall color. Clean shade tree. Has deep roots. Attracts hummingbirds.
TUNG OIL TREE D *Aleurites fordii*	20' x 25'	Sun. Likes dry, sandy loam. Fast growth. Broad crown. *FRUIT IS POISONOUS.* White spring flowers. Fall bright red-orange color. Tender.
VITEX (CHASTE TREE) D *Vitex agnus castus* *V. Negundo var.* *heterophylla*	12' x 8'	Sun. Sandy, well-draining loam. Average water. Medium to fast growth. Long-lived. Easy. Aromatic, gray-green, lacy foliage. Flowers on terminal spikes: color: lavender, white, or pink in summer. May prune and feed early spring. Adapted to Houston.
WALNUT, EASTERN BLACK D *Juglans nigra*	80' x 45'	Sun. Good loamy soil with excellent drainage. Straight trunk with interesting fissured bark. Large, yellow-green leaves. Rapid growth. Allow ample space. Root-prune to 10" for good root system. Bears large edible nuts. Specimen tree for park-like areas; should be used more often even though litter is a nuisance. Adapted to Texas.

118

TREES

Common Name *Botanical Name*	Average Height X Width	Comments
WILLOW, CORKSCREW (DRAGON-CLAW) E *Salix Matsudana* 'Tortuosa' GOLDEN WILLOW *S. alba tristis*	25' x 8' 80'	Sun to semi-shade. Any soil. Ample water. Spirally twisting branches are main attraction. Slightly weeping, narrow leaves, small catkins. Interesting in arrangements. Branches root in water.
WILLOW, WEEPING D *Salix babylonica*	35' x 25'	Full sun. Any soil, especially wet or near water. Arching, weeping branches. Graceful. Weak, brittle, shallow roots invade sewer lines. Prune to keep shape.
WITCH HAZEL D *Hamamelis* *virginiana*	12' x 8'	Filtered sun. Moist to wet soil. Yellow flowers in fall. Yellow fall color. High maintenance. Small tree or large shrub. NATIVE in Texas.
XYLOSMA E *Xylosma congestum* *X.c.* 'Compacta,' smaller	20' x 15'	Full sun to semi-shade. Requires good drainage. Likes fertile soil, but tolerates others. Glossy, medium green, small leaves, coppery when new. Small but profuse, yellowish flowers. Same uses as Ligustrum, but daintier appearance. Fine patio shade tree.
YAUPON D *Ilex decidua*		See POSSUM HAW HOLLY in SHRUBS chart.
YAUPON E *Ilex vomitoria* *I.v.* 'Saratoga,' yellow berries *I.v.* 'Nana,' dwarf *I.v.* 'Pendula,' weeping form	20' x 15'	Tolerant of various soil and light conditions, but not standing water. Medium growth rate. Fruiting best in sun. Only female trees have red berries. Best to buy when in berry. Shrub or multi-trunked tree. Smooth gray bark sometimes with white splashes, attractive. Trouble free; hardy. In early spring cut off inside branches to retain shape. Pruning outside branches will cut away next season's berries. Weeping and dwarf cultivars available. NATIVE in East Texas.
ZELKOVA, JAPANESE D *Zelkova serrata*	70' x 65'	Sun. Moist, fertile soil. Considered possible substitute for the American Elm. Long, sharp-toothed leaves. Insignificant flowers. Attractive shape for shade tree. 'Village Green' more cold hardy. Growth slower than American Elm.

To obtain the radius of a tree's trunk, measure the circumference 4 feet from the ground. Use the formula:

$$2 \text{ Pi } R = C$$

(Pi = 3.1416; C = circumference; R = radius)

P.P.

A Bradford pear tree in spring glory.

120

Fruit Trees & Fruits

*"If you tell me that you desire a fig,
I answer you there must be time.
Let it first bloom, then bear fruit,
then ripen."*

—Epictetus

*T*he exhilarating blossoms of pear and plum trees proclaim that Spring is just around the corner. The pink haze of peach trees will soon follow. What a fine gift...beautiful flowers and tasty fruit from the same trees!

There are, of course, trees which bear fruit that don't put on a show of colorful bloom. Figs, for example, are the standby fruit-bearers. Mulberries are much maligned because their fruit is messy on the ground, but oh, how the birds enjoy those berries! And how the children love to climb the sturdy branches and munch on the berries.

Although Houston is not a natural mecca for many species of fruiting trees because of our warm-ish winters and clayey, not too well-drained soils, skillful hybridizers and expert grafters have developed trees which can and do bear fruit in Houston, especially when planted in amended soil as in raised beds or in containers.

Chilling hours are those below 45 degrees Fahrenheit. On the average, fruit trees require between 800 to 1,000 chilling hours. Houston's number of chilling hours is between 400 and 600. Quite a discrepancy! The trick, then, is to select species which tolerate Houston's generally warm but also fickle weather. Our warm days in the middle of the supposed winter throw the fruit trees into a spurt of growth and budding, only to be caught by another freeze.

To compound the situation, fruit trees react differently in different soils and different climates.

Houston's knowledgeable Texas-certified nurserymen are well aware of the usual cold weather needs of most fruiting trees and will assist you in selecting those which have a good chance to fruit in this area.

Fruit trees and fruits must have sun, preferably 6 hours daily, and a loose, fertile soil with exceptionally good drainage and air circulation. Though the blooms are beautiful and the fruits delicious, fruiting is always an uncertainty in Houston, particularly for fruit trees. Neither our climate nor our soil is hospitable to the fruits which like good drainage and cold weather. True we may have freezing weather, but it is usually of short duration.

Think before you buy fruit trees; they need special care. You might be willing to give that, but there is not much to do about the weather. Even frost protection may not be enough.

Specialists are in the process of developing dwarf trees for Houston which can be grown in

121

containers, but so far only very careful gardeners have succeeded in reaping many fruits from them. In time we can all benefit from fruit trees developed especially for Houston.

The best chance with fruit trees is to plant those native to this area, such as the Mexican plum. It puts on a stunning show of white blossoms on almost black branches and trunk but not necessarily an edible fruit crop. Again, it depends on the weather.

Upon request, your County Extension Horticultural agents will supply you with a list of the kinds of fruit which may grow well in the Houston area and detailed suggestions for the cultural requirements, plus approved sprays for the various diseases and insects which attack fruits here. Ask for spraying and pruning advice also. (The United States Department of Agriculture publishes changes in approved chemical aids periodically.)

Fruit trees are usually planted bare-rooted during January and February when the trees are still dormant. Growers prefer to see the roots to determine their condition, though many good trees are in containers. Fruit trees should be planted early in the year to allow them to get some growth before our summer heat sets in. *Admonition:* Do *not* buy from the backs of trucks or temporary stands by the side of the road. The salespeople may well be fleeing as well as fleeting. Buy from established, reputable sources who stand behind what they sell.

Raised beds are helpful for the good drainage they afford. Refer to the SOIL chapter for suggestions about soil mixtures and to the DRAINAGE chapter to achieve correct drainage, for without those two elements and 6 hours of sun a day, there is no use planting fruiting trees. A root stimulant at planting time is recommended, unless a heavy rainfall pours down just after planting. In such a case, delay.

Pecan trees are rarely included in the term "fruit trees." Pecans are, after all, nuts. Once again you should carefully consider the space available on your home property. How much of it do you want to give up to a pecan tree? If you live on a farm or ranch, you will have plenty of space. Pecan trees grow to the height of 100 feet with a spread of 65 feet by 75 feet. That is big enough to cover an entire lot and house. However, smaller-sized pecan trees have been developed. Talk to your nurseryman about the dwarf pecans. Though the pecan tree is the State Tree of Texas and is of majestic size, it also is a messy tree on a home lot, dropping leaves and limbs periodically. It also is subject to damage from a long list of insects and diseases. Their nuts quickly grow wherever they drop, or wherever a squirrel plants them, and puts down a deep root so rapidly that even a seedling one foot high is difficult to pull out of a flower bed. The production of pecans is dependent on the species of pecan tree, the weather, and the health of the tree. A schedule of spraying pecan trees can be obtained from your County Extension Agent or from your nurseryman.

Citrus fruits can be grown successfully in Houston if they are provided with full sunshine, well-drained, fertile, acidic soil, and protection from winter cold. Planting them in containers allows all three conditions to be met more easily. Ask your nurseryman about fertilizing because it differs with the fruits. Citrus prefers a higher ratio of nitrogen than most fruits do.

Soil for citrus fruits should contain:
   2 parts loam
   2 parts peat moss (wet)
   2 parts sand
   1-1/2 cup aluminum sulphate per bushel
     of mix.

The Meyer Lemon, one of the most satisfactory citrus fruits for Houston, is an attractive, glossy, dark green-leaved plant. The lemons are large, very juicy, and tasty. They are less acid than commercial lemons. Sun, good circulation of air, fertile, loose, well-drained soil, judicious watering, and cold protection keep them growing and happy.

Kumquats grow on small shrubby trees. The orange fruits are quite pretty against the dark green foliage and have a nice flavor. Their culture is similar to that of the Meyer Lemon and both fruits make interesting container plants on a sunny porch.

When purchasing fruiting plants, take the time to investigate the different varieties of each, learn their cultural requirements, the care they need, and decide if you have an appropriate location for those in which you are interested. Yes, they will take care, but doesn't every living thing? It's a question of whether or not you have the time to give and whether or not you will enjoy that care.

If your answer is a resounding "yes," then look for the varieties which grow well in Houston, plant them as directed, delight in their appearance, and relish their fruit.

FRUIT TREES AND FRUITS

Self-pollinator = does not require a pollinating tree close by to produce fruit.   spp. = Species

Fruit *Botanical Name*	Variety	Ripens	Comments and Description
Apple	Granny Smith (grafted)	June	Takes 180 days to mature. Crisp tart flesh flavor. Several varieties, including dwarf 'Reverend Morgan.'
	Anna		Large. Mild, sweet flavor. Use Golden Dorsett or Ein Shermer as pollinator.
	Golden Dorsett		Sweet, mild flavor. Good storing apple.
	Ein Shermer		Good, crisp cooking apple. Yellow. Self-pollinator.
Apricot	Dwarf varieties best		Not as fruitful as other fruit trees. Beautiful for flowers. Self-fruitful.
Blackberry *Rubus* spp.			Blackberries like slightly acid soil (pH about 6.5). Sulfur worked into alkaline soil helps. Plant in hills and mulch to prevent weeds. Prune fruiting branches after harvest.
	Brazos	May	Thorny, prolific bushes. Old recommended variety. Tart, large berries. Upright canes. Self-fruitful. Good for jams, jellies, and freezing. Self-pollinator
	Brison		Sweeter.
	Rosborough		Good for Gulf Coast growing. Fewer seeds, better flavor.
	Humble		Cooking variety.

FRUIT TREES AND FRUITS

Self-pollinator = does not require a pollinating tree close by to produce fruit.   spp. = Species

Fruit *Botanical Name*	Variety	Ripens	Comments and Description
Dewberries	Boysen	May	Good quality, large wine-red fruit. Self-pollinator. Vining.
	Young	May	Good quality, large size.
Fig			Well-drained soil with organic matter. Likes manure, not chemical fertilizers.
	Celeste	June	Small, blue, sweet. Good preserves. Self-pollinator.
	Texas Ever-Bearing	June-July	Medium to large. Brown color. Good quality. Needs water.
Grape	Muscadine (NATIVE)	July	Wild in Gulf Coast area. Fine on arbor. Makes good jelly. Several new varieties. Likes acid, sandy loam.
Kumquat	Nagami Marumi Meiwa	Oct.-Apr.	Cold hardy. Shrubby, small tree. Bright orange fruit. Fragrant flowers. To be safe, plant in protected place.
Lemon	Meyer	Sept.-Oct.	Large, flavorful, very juicy. Attractive plant, best in container for winter protection. Tender. Self-pollinator. Flowers very fragrant.
Loquat	*Eriobotrya japonica*	Mar.	Prolific yellow, firm fruit. Stunning on trees. See TREES chart.
Peach	Mid Pride, dwarf	May-June	Beautiful flowers.Dwarf type good in large pots or barrels. Subject to damage from many pests.
	Sam Houston		Requires at least 500 chilling hours. Large freestone.
Pear			Suffers from fireblight.
	Garber	August	Fireblight resistant. Small, yellow. Check with your nurseryman for varieties which are resistant to fireblight. Makes clouds of white flowers in very early spring.
	Keiffer	August	Bears at early age. Very productive. Fair quality.
	Orient	August	Spreading, decorative tree. Shade and fireblight resistant. Good quality.

FRUIT TREES AND FRUITS

Self-pollinator = does not require a pollinating tree close by to produce fruit.   spp. = Species

Fruit *Botanical Name*	Variety	Ripens	Comments and Description
Pecan *Carya illinoisensis*			Texas State Tree. The Agricultural Extension Service sends detailed maintenance instructions upon written request.
	Desirable	October	Old standby. Disease resistant. Good producer. High quality nuts. Self-pollinator; its early shedding of pollen makes it good pollinator. Allow at least 50' to 60' space from house or other trees.
	Mahan	Oct.-Nov.	Old favorite in Houston. Sheds pollen late. Large, thin paper shell. Good flavor.
	Stuart	November	Fine landscape tree. Large/medium soft-shell. Paper shell nuts. Sheds pollen early.
	Success	November	Large soft shell. Sheds pollen early.
Plum	Methley	June	Requires pollinator. Tasty flavor. Purple with amber flesh. Needs frequent spraying from bloom time to harvest.
Plumco		June	Hybrid of plum and apricot. Beautiful decorative tree. Must have pollinator.
Pomegranate *Punica granatum*	Mexican 'Wonderful'	Fall	Tolerates alkaline soil and summer heat. Deep watering. Shrub or pruned tree. Dark green, glossy foliage, ruffled orange-red flowers in summer. Grows to 12' height.
Strawberry *Fragaria* spp.		Spring	Requires excellent drainage, slightly acid, very sandy soil and sun. See SOIL and DRAINAGE chapters. Best in raised beds or strawberry jars. If planted in fall, plants will bear better. Mulch with straw to protect berries from rotting and from getting dirty.
	Florida 90	May	Soft fruit; good flavor. Large. Old favorite.
	Sequoia	Apr.-May	Good at-home variety. Sweet. Large.

Other fruiting plants designated in charts.

Bridalwreath in high shade, (Spiraea) in bloom.

Shrubs

"In arches weighed by fragile suds,
the bridal wreath looks drenched."
—John Updike,
Styles of Bloom, 1985

Whatever you envision for your Houston area garden, there are shrubs suitable for your plan. A shrub is loosely defined as a woody plant which produces branches or stalks from its base. These multi-branched mainstays of our gardens range from one to twenty feet in height and from one to twelve feet in spread. They may be evergreen (retaining their leaves all year) or deciduous (dropping their leaves in the fall). The many shrubs which are native or adapted to our region are often the most tolerant of drought, heat, and cold. (See NATIVE in charts.) Exotic shrubs from the tropics, when given the proper soil, moisture, and the protected exposure which they require, are quite at home in our near-tropic climate while adding spectacular beauty to our gardens. Hybrid shrubs, the products of a cross of two shrubs of different species, usually exhibit the best qualities of each parent and are now more numerous in our nurseries. Dwarf forms of old favorites are excellent choices for smaller gardens or for containers on patios or balconies. (*Hint:* If you want to keep them dwarf, feed only sparingly, if at all.) With discerning selection, the air can be filled with the fragrance of flowers or aromatic leaves of shrubs. There also are those which produce berries. Many shrubs attract bees, butterflies, and birds, bringing song and flashes of color and motion to your garden. Watching a pair of birds build their nest and following the growth of the nestlings is a heart-warming experience. It is said that having a bird's nest in your garden will bring good luck. See BIRDS & BUTTERFLIES chapter.

The varying habits of growth and the diversity of size, shape, color, and texture of leaves make shrub selection even more intriguing. Take time to observe the extensive selection of shrubs which thrive here. Visit gardens, arboretums, and nurseries, asking questions as you go. Gardeners, professional and amateur alike, enjoy talking about their gardens.

Few shrubs are very particular about soil, though all develop better in a fertile, easily cultivated, well-draining soil. Most need sunlight, but many grow in part shade. The majority demand effective drainage because they don't like wet feet. (Excessive water in the soil suffocates plants. Their roots need oxygen, and standing water pushes the oxygen out.) All plants want sufficient water and space to grow to their inbred size. Provide these conditions and you will be well rewarded with a flourishing garden.

Before going any further in the search for the perfect shrubs for your garden, read the HINTS FOR

Native Texas shrub, Agarito. (Mahonia trifoliata)

J.M.K.

the window sill, thus avoiding a battle of pruning to allow light to come in the window. The same principle applies when planting shrubs close to the house. The mature size of the shrub should be considerably lower than the eave-line of the roof to avoid having a huge shrub leaning out from the house seeking space and light.

There are more than 150 shrubs listed with a brief description and cultural requirements for each in the SHRUBS chart in this book. More shrubs are listed in THE TROPICAL GARDEN, with ways to use them. The ROSES, CAMELLIAS, and AZALEAS chapters discuss in detail the care of those beautiful shrubs. Studying those chapters will be helpful in your selection.

Suggestions for choosing plants to buy:
- Look at the plant carefully. If it has a lusterless, wilted appearance, don't buy it. Look for another.

LANDSCAPING chapter, which will help you to see your landscape as a whole. There are helpful suggestions to follow and some common mistakes to avoid. View your garden from inside your house as well as outside. When garden and house are in harmony, the garden visually extends the living space.

This is an appropriate time to observe whether your windows would benefit from protection from our hot summer sun. Shade will keep your house cooler. Think about placement of shrubs according to the sun's arc, in winter as well as in summer. A grouping of evergreen shrubs planted at least three or four feet from an outside north wall of the house acts as an insulator, keeping the house cooler in summer and warmer in winter, reducing energy use and cost.

When planting shrubs under a window, select those whose full-grown height is lower than

J.M.K.

Yaupon in berry.

128

Aralia, tropical look but hardy, and variegated pittosporum.

- Lift the shrub gently by the stem or trunk. You can tell by its "solid" feel whether it has been in the container long enough to become adjusted. If it feels loose and wobbly, move on.
- Generally speaking, all things equal, it's better to buy shrubs in 2 or 5 gallon cans because of the larger root systems. A well-grown, healthy-looking small plant will outgrow a larger, weak, spindly plant.
- Check the branch pattern of the plant. Limbs should take a pleasing form. They are the skeleton of the future shrub.

Shrubs are often planted together to form hedges that provide seclusion and privacy, outline boundaries, screen unsightly service areas, absorb urban noises, or form a background for smaller plantings.

When hedges are to serve as a background, they may be composed of various species of shrubs. This type of hedge is usually allowed to grow naturally with only occasional shaping. Evergreen shrubs would naturally be the choice if they are to screen an unattractive area, but evergreen and deciduous shrubs can be combined if the planting is to be a background. In such a situation consider the time of blooming or fruiting, the similarity of their cultural needs, the shape, the foliage, and the size of each of the shrubs in relation to the others. Information in the SHRUBS chart will be helpful.

When a hedge is to be kept clipped at a certain height, in a formal manner, then all the plants should be of the same species. The *mature* height of the chosen species should be as close as possible to the desired height of the hedge. Don't fight a naturally large-growing plant by pruning

129

to the height you want. The plant will win, and too much time and effort will have been spent in maintenance. Use the SHRUBS chart to check the heights of plants or go to your local nursery. Select shrubs to meet your particular purpose.

Whatever your purpose, the cultural conditions—soil, light, drainage, and water needs—should be met. Read the SOIL, DRAINAGE, and WATER AND WATERING chapters for suggestions to determine if you should amend conditions in your garden, and if so, how. When the location of the planting bed has been determined, the soil should be prepared at least three weeks before you actually start planting. The various amendments to the soil: sand, rotted manure, bone meal, gypsum, and perhaps copperus or sulphur if the soil needs some acidifying (and most Houston soil does)—require time to settle and meld into a harmonious whole. (Read details in the SOIL chapter.)

When the plants are all the same species, the trench type of planting is feasible. Locate the hedge-bed well away from any driveway or walk so the plants do not encroach on these often-used traffic areas. Determine the mature spread of the selected shrub and plant more than half of that measurement away from the drive or walk. Before purchasing the plants, measure the space in your garden where the hedge is to be placed, compare that to the mature spread of the plants, and determine how many plants you need. Don't picture the plants remaining the size they are in the 2 or 5-gallon cans. They will inevitably grow to their predestined size. Plan for *that* mature size, thereby using fewer plants. It will take longer to achieve a look of fullness but the plants will be healthier and happier in the long run and you will have saved money. To speed up growth and assure thickness of the hedge, pinch off the center tip of each branch as you are planting and continue to do so for two or three months. Such tip-pruning will multiply the number of growth-tips on each plant and encourage a thick, lush hedge.

Begin early in the plants' growth to shape the hedge with the top surface being kept narrower than the lower hedge, in a trapezoidal shape. This allows sunshine to reach the lower portion of the plants, keeping them growing as full at the bottom as at the top. Failure to follow this type of clipping will lead to legginess in the lower portion of each plant and a much less attractive hedge. Sunshine must reach the entire plant for a beautiful hedge.

When you buy the plants, have the nursery slit the sides of the cans. This will greatly facilitate slipping the plants out of each container and will avoid injury to their root system. *Hint:* Wear protective gloves; edges of metal cans are sharp.

Water the plants as soon as you get them home and again a while before planting time. They should be kept moist.

Planting

The soil has been prepared, the plants purchased, and now it is time to plant. For a hedge, dig a trench in the prepared bed 2" to 3" shallower than the depth of the soil in the cans. Loosen the soil at the bottom of the trench, if necessary, and add about two inches of prepared soil in the bottom. The top surface of the root ball of each plant should be positioned 2" to 4" *above* the level of the surrounding ground to allow for the inevitable settling of the soil in the trench. Positioning the plants a bit above soil level will help drain away any excess water, especially during our typically heavy rainstorms. Space the plants as already determined, turning them to find the most effective position. Now, gently replace the loose soil until the trench is half-filled, enough to hold the plants erect. To avoid air pockets in the soil, fill the trench with a gentle flow of water and allow it to drain. Replace the remainder of the soil. Press the surface of the soil just enough to stabilize the plants and fill the trench. The root ball of each plant should be covered with soil to the same level as it was in the cans and should be at least an inch or more above the level of the surrounding soil. With

Coral Bean. (Erythrina herbacea)

J.M.K.

careful to protect the bark. *Hint:* Run the support wire through a piece of garden hose that is long enough to surround and protect the bush.

Water the plants thoroughly before a predicted freeze. If the freeze is to be severe, mulch the ground around the plants with 4 or 5 inches of leaves or moss, being sure to remove the extra mulch when the sun comes out and it is hot again. Shrubs tender to cold should be planted in a protected location, for example: on the south side of the house, away from cold winds.

When planting shrubs individually or in groupings, a hole for each plant will probably be more feasible, but the procedure should be the same.

Follow-up Care

Newly planted shrubs should be kept moist, not soggy-wet, for at least several weeks. Thereafter, water whenever the soil feels dry. Water thoroughly each time; do not sprinkle. No fertilizing is advisable for another several months, not until the plants show real growth. In the fall, use a low nitrogen, high potash fertilizer to increase cold protection. In the spring, use a higher nitrogen and higher phosphorus mixture to encourage growth and flowering, always according to the label directions. See Fertilizing in the SOIL chapter and PRUNING chapter.

Choose shrubs whose qualities appeal to you and whose cultural needs are appropriate for your garden, your lifestyle, and the time you have for gardening. It's your garden and it is for your pleasure. Don't allow it to be a burden. Plant just what you can take care of easily and enjoyably.

Houston's climate and its flat terrain, the root ball surface should always be planted above ground level, never below. Water the plant using a root-stimulant solution prepared exactly according to the manufacturer's instructions to give the root system a nice boost. Apply 2" to 3" of rotted pine bark or a mixture of mulching materials around the plants. Refer to Mulches in SOIL chapter. If the shrubs are tall or in a windy location, they should be securely staked, being

SHRUBS

BEFORE BUYING OR PLANTING, learn *mature* height and spread, and cultural needs of each shrub. Unless individually noted otherwise in the chart, the following procedures are recommended:

Best Planting Time: December through March. Container-grown shrubs may be planted any time with deep watering and protection from extreme heat and cold.

Culture: At least 4 hours of sun, preferably morning. Fertile, loose soil with about 1/3 decomposed organic matter. (Details in SHRUBS and SOIL chapters.) Excellent drainage and deep watering to encourage deep rooting.

Fertitlize: Early spring (Feb.-Mar.) with balanced fertilizer with organic base and trace elements. Again in fall (Nov.-Dec.) with high phosphorus and potash ratio. *Always water* both before and after feeding. Slow-release fertilizers available. Follow label directions.

Pruning: Pinch-prune new growth for bushiness. Detailed pruning in PRUNING chapter.

	D = Deciduous	E = Evergreen	spp. = Species	
Common Name *Botanical Name*	**Color**	**Approximate** **Height X Spread**	**Time of** **Blooming**	**Comments**
ABELIA GLOSSY E *Abelia grandiflora*	Pinkish White	5' x 5'	May-Sept.	Sun to part shade. Protect from winds and summer afternoon sun. Fertile, well-drained soil. Drought resistant but water when dry. For hedge, plant 1' apart. Fertilize with 8-8-8 or 12-24-12 ratio. Fragrant, glossy-bronze foliage in fall. Mulch. Prune early spring to control legginess. Also dwarf and prostrate forms and a pink-flowering variety.
AGARITO E *Berberis (Mahonia)* *trifoliolata*	Yellow	7' x 6'	March	Full sun. Sandy, well-drained, alkaline soil. Water as needed.. Red fruit makes good jelly and attracts birds. Dense foliage. Drought resistant. Flowers slightly fragrant. Leaves spiny and sharp.
ALMOND, FLOWERING D *Prunus glandulosa*	White, Pink	4' x 3'	Mar.-Apr.	Full sun. Sandy, fertile, well-drained soil. Ample water. Prune after bloom to revitalize. Soil should contain minerals and rotted manure.
ALTHAEA (ROSE OF SHARON) D *Hibiscus syriacus*	Lavender, Rose, White, Pink, Single and Double	12' x 4'	June-Sept.	Sun to part shade. Moist garden soil. Good drainage. Water regularly until well established.

SHRUBS

Common Name *Botanical Name*	Color	Approximate Height X Spread	Time of Blooming	Comments
ALTHAEA, contd.				Prune very early spring. Upright. Free blooming. Hardy. Drought tolerant. Reseeds. 'Blue Bird,' 'Helene,' 'Diana' have larger flowers. Easily trained to tree form. Does not send up suckers. Single and double carnation-like flowering types. Blooms last one day but others open daily. Cuttings root well in spring or early summer. Feed in early spring. Very easy and satisfactory.
ANDROMEDA (LILY-OF-THE-VALLEY BUSH) E *Pieris japonica*	White	15' x 7'	Feb.-Mar.	Semi-shade. Acid, sandy soil with humus. Good drainage. Dainty flowers, beautiful foliage. Keep mulched. Flower buds develop in fall. Prune only for symmetry.
ANGEL'S TRUMPET (DATURA) D *Brugmansia* *suaveolens*	White	10' x 6'	June-Oct.	Full sun. Fertile, moist soil. Good drainage. Easily grown from divisions. Best used as a small specimen tree. Drought resistant. Root hardy with protection but freezes easily. Fragrant, prominent 7" bloom. Flowers and seeds are *POISONOUS*.
B. 'Charles Grimaldi' *B. versicolor*	Salmon Yellow			
ANISACANTHUS *Anisacanthus* *wrightii*	Orange	3' x 3'	June-Oct.	Full sun, rich soil, good drainage. Free blooming. Cut back hard to revitalize. Drought tolerant. Attracts hummingbirds and butterflies. Also gold form.
ARALIA JAPONICA (SIEBOLDI) E *Fatsia japonica*	White	5' x 4'	Sept.	Shade or part shade. Moist, loose, well-drained soil with organic matter. Root hardy. Large tropical leaves.
ARDISIA, CORAL E *Ardisia crispa*	White	18" x 18"	April	Part shade, no direct sun. Fertile, moist soil, draining well. Flowers fragrant but not showy. Coral-red berries form in fall, remain through winter. May become invasive.

133

SHRUBS

Common Name *Botanical Name*	Color	Approximate Height X Spread	Time of Blooming	Comments
	D = Deciduous	E = Evergreen	spp. = Species	
AUCUBA D and E *Aucuba japonica* *A.j. variegata* 'Gold Dust Plant' *A.j.* 'nana'	Red Berries Yellow-Spotted Foliage	4' x 3' Dwarf 3' x 2'		Partial shade with no direct sun. Blackening of tips and margins of leaves may signal sunburn. Move to shadier spot. Loose garden soil, not too acid. Use light application of lime to neutralize acidity. Ample water with excellent drainage. Blackening of stems and leaves may be from fungal disease or too much moisture. (Cleyera, nandina, mahonia, or leucothoe better choices for semi-sun where direct sun hits leaves.)
AZALEA D and E *Azalea* spp.	Yellow, Lavender, Pink, White, Red, Purple	From 12" x 10" To 8' x 7' To 4' x 3' To 18" x 18"	Oct.-May	Best in A.M. or filtered sun or partial shade. Plant high for good drainage. Sandy, acid soil with high organic matter. Ample water. Do not disturb roots with cultivation. Heavy mulch. Prune and feed following bloom. Scatter Azalea food over mulch and water in well. See AZALEAS chapter.
BAMBOO *Bambusa vulgaris*	Yellow-Green Woody Grass	25' Tall		Sun to semi-shade. Any dry or moist soil. 10" narrow leaves on tall stalks. Green unless frozen. Tender, but almost always comes back from roots. Extremely difficult to control. Sinking 3' metal sheets around roots when planted might contain them. Easily becomes a pest unless there is lots of room. Graceful screen. To propagate, lift and divide clumps in early spring and plant right away. *B. glaucescens* (Multiplex) is smaller, 8' tall.

SHRUBS

Common Name *Botanical Name*	Color	Approximate Height X Spread	Time of Blooming	Comments
BAMBOO, BLACK E *Phyllostachys* *nigra*	Purple-Black Canes	26' x 6'		Sun. Fertile, well-drained soil. Tender below 0 degrees. Needs sun to turn canes to purple-black. Leaves dark green. Fine accent. Allow space for spreading form. Rhizomes underground spread rapidly; must contain as above. Also other desirable varieties.
BANANA SHRUB E *Michelia Figo*	Cream	15' x 6'	Mar.-May	Sun to part shade. Sandy, moist, acid soil with humus. Drainage. Small, fragrant, waxy blossoms. Shiny medium green leaves. May be pruned after bloom. Makes nice small tree, usually multi-trunked.
BARBADOS CHERRY D *Malpighia glabra*	Pink	3' x 3'	May-Oct.	Sun. Well-draining garden soil. Beautiful red berries while blooming. Effective in groups or foundation planting. Good in Houston. NATIVE to southwest U.S. Berries good for jelly. Many stolons from which stems sprout.
BARBADOS, WINTER- GREEN E *Berberis Juliana*	Yellow	6' x 4'	March	Same culture as B. Cherry above. Glowing red winter foliage on about half the leaves makes interesting red and green mix.
BARBERRY, JAPANESE D *Berberis* *Thunbergii* B.T. 'Crimson Pygmy,' dwarf	Yellow	6' x 4' 20" x 26"	March	Sun. Soil with humus, not rich. Very good drainage. Tolerates dry soil but do not overdo it. Prune in dormant season, cutting oldest stems to ground. Oval shape. Red berries. In spring, prune old canes. Some varieties have yellow or red-purple foliage which need sun to color. Also dwarf.
BAY, LOBLOLLY or GORDONIA E *Gordonia lasianthus*	White	20' x 15'	May-Fall	Full sun. Moist, acid, rich, loose soil. Good drainage. 2-6" leaves, pale beneath, dark green above. Gray to reddish-brown bark. Upright.

135

SHRUBS

D = Deciduous　　E = Evergreen　　spp. = Species

Common Name *Botanical Name*	Color	Approximate Height X Spread	Time of Blooming	Comments
BAY, SWEET E *Laurus nobilis*	Yellow	15' x 10'		Semi-shade. Don't allow to dry out completely. Rich, peaty soil. The true laurel of antiquity. Garlands represented victory. Slow growing. Good in container or as a standard. Leaves used in cooking.
BEAR GRASS E (TEXAS SOTOL) *Dasylirion texanum*	White	3' x 3'		Open sun. Dry, sandy, alkaline soil with good drainage. Sparse water. Yucca-like. Texas NATIVE. Long narrow leaves. Blooms once when about 10 years old. Accent plant. Grows in pots.
BEAUTYBERRY D *Callicarpa americana*	Pink, Lilac, Red, White	5' x 5'	Summer	Sun to semi-sun. Moist garden soil. Loose form. Rose-purple berries attract 10 species of birds. *C. lactea* has white berries. U.S. NATIVE. Prune early spring.
BOTTLEBRUSH E *Callistemon* spp.	Red	10' x 7'	May-Oct.	Full sun. Soil with organic matter. Needs excellent drainage. Stop water in late summer. Tender. For winter protection, plant on south side of house. Attracts hummingbirds. Drought tolerant.
BOUVARDIA E *Bouvardia*	White	3' x 3'	Sept.-Jan.	Shade. Loamy soil. Water well during growing season. Tender. Often grown in pots. Fragrant. Waxy flowers. Winter blooming. Prune hard in spring.
BOXWOOD E *Buxus microphylla japonica* (JAPANESE) *B.m. Koreana* (KOREAN) *B.m.* 'Compacta'		6' x 4' 3' x 3' 2' x 18"		Full sun, part shade. Water when dry. Garden soil, very well drained. Raised bed helpful. Prune well. Trim narrower at top than bottom to keep full growth and shape. Excellent low hedge or shaped accent plant. If needed, prune very early spring.

SHRUBS

Common Name *Botanical Name*	Color	Approximate Height X Spread	Time of Blooming	Comments
BOXWOOD, contd.				Fertilize with bonemeal scratched in soil at base and water in.
BOXWOOD, AFRICAN (CAPE MYRTLE) E *Myrsine africana*		3' x 6'		Full sun or partial shade. Well-drained garden soil. Water when dry. Rounded form. Nice for narrow beds or hedges. Excellent cut foliage. Susceptible to red spiders.
BRIDAL WREATH (See SPIREA, REEVE'S)				
BRUNFELSIA E (LADY-OF-THE-NIGHT) *Brunfelsia americana*	White	10' x 5'	Apr.-Oct.	Several hours A.M. sun. Fertile, loose soil with compost. Uniform moisture. Needs protection from winter cold. Plant on south side of house. Just before new growth begins, prune if necessary. Feed in early spring with fertilizer such as 8-8-8 or 12-24-12 ratio and water in. Feed periodically during growing season with high phosphorus food. Espaliers nicely. *B. americana* best in pot to move for cold protection.
(YESTERDAY-TODAY-AND-TOMORROW) *B. australis*	Dark Purple Fading to White	5' x 5'	April	
BUSH CLOVER D *Lespedeza formosa*	Purple	5' x 3'	May-Aug.	Sun. Open, sandy soil. Water sparingly. Delicate foliage and sprays of blossom. Contrasts well with other shrubs. Tender. Root hardy.
BUTTERFLY BUSH D *Buddleia alternifolia* *B. davidii*	Lilac, Purple, Blue, White	8' x 6'	May-Oct.	Sun. Rich soil with organic matter. Water. Needs good drainage. Graceful gray-green foliage. Spreading form requires ample space. Spikes of fragrant blooms attract butterflies, cut well. Remove nonproductive canes, prune severely in very early spring to avoid scraggliness, and feed for more bloom. Root hardy.

SHRUBS

Common Name *Botanical Name*	Color	Approximate Height X Spread	Time of Blooming	Comments
	D = Deciduous	E = Evergreen	spp. = Species	
BUTTONBUSH D *Cephalanthus occidentalis*	White	8' x 10'	June-Sept.	Sun or part shade. Very moist, good soil. U.S. NATIVE. Hardy. Handsome foliage and flowers. Prune in very early winter and feed. Susceptible to some insects.
CALYCANTHUS (See SWEET SHRUB)				
CAMELLIA E *Camellia japonica* *C. sasanqua*	White thru Red	10' x 5' 14' x 8'	Feb.-Mar. Dec.-Jan.	Best in semi-shade. Both varieties do best in acid soil. Plant high. Requires good drainage. See CAMELLIAS chapter.
CARNATION OF INDIA *Tabernaemontana grandiflora*	White	4' x 2'	May-Aug.	Likes sun to filtered sun. Loose, rich, acid soil. Ample water. Small, double, fragrant flowers. Glossy, dark green, gardenia-like leaves. Resistant to whitefly. South or other protected exposure. Tender foliage. Root hardy. Grows well in pots. *T. Coronaria*: smaller leaves, more compact shape. Protect from freeze.
CARYOPTERIS D (BLUE SPIRAEA) *Caryopteris incana* *C. clandonensis*	Pale Blue	4' x 2'	July to Frost	Full sun. Humusy, well-drained loam. Minimum water. Attracts bees and butterflies. Powder-blue fringed flowers, grown in clusters. Dense rounded form. Freezes to ground. After mild winter cut it back to ground.
CASSIA D *Cassia alata* (CANDLESTICK) *C. corymbosa* (SENNA) *C. splendida* (GOLDEN WONDER)	Yellow Clusters	8' x 6' 10' x 7' 10-12' x 10-12'	Aug.-Oct. Spring-Fall Sept.-Nov.	Sun and water. Light, sandy loam. Protect from cold. If killed by freeze, worth replanting. If not frozen back, prune hard in spring. Fast growing. Free flowering. Fertilize every three weeks during summer.
CHAENOMELES (See JAPANESE FLOWERING QUINCE)				

SHRUBS

Common Name *Botanical Name*	Color	Approximate Height X Spread	Time of Blooming	Comments
CHENILLE PLANT E *Acalypha hispida*	Red-Purple	3' x 3'	July-Sept.	Strong light, but not sun. Rich, humusy, loose soil. Keep moist, not wet. Good in pots. Tender. Unusual drooping blooms.
CHINESE LANTERN E *Abutilon hybridum*	Orange, Red, Yellow, White	4' x 4'	Aug.-Oct.	Sun to semi-shade. Requires strong light to bloom. Likes deep, rich topsoil or loam. Good drainage. A herbaceous shrub. Keep soil moist. Rapid growth. Pinch out branch tips to keep good form. Makes nice, loose espalier. Protect from freeze. May plant in container to allow easy move during cold weather. Subject to white fly and scale.
CIGAR PLANT E *Cuphea micropetala*	Red and Yellow	5' x 3'	Apr.-Oct.	Sun. Garden soil. Water. Prune after blooming. Freezes back every winter.
CLETHRA D *Clethra alnifolia*	White, Pink	8' x 6'	Aug.-Oct.	Part shade or sun. Moist, acid soil. Neat growing. Fragrant. Eastern U.S. NATIVE.
CLEYERA JAPONICA E *Ternstroemia gymnanthera*	Cream	15' x 6'	April	Light, filtered sun to part shade. Moist, fertile, slightly acid soil of loam, sand, and humus. Requires good drainage. Glossy foliage. Requirements similar to camellias. New foliage reddish. Slow growth. Hardy. Prunes easily into small tree.
CONFEDERATE ROSE D *Hibiscus mutabilis*	Pink	8' x 5'	June-Oct.	Sun. Acid, fertile soil. Average water. Good drainage. Flowers white at morning, pink at noon, crimson at night, then fall. New flowers each day. Large 7" leaves. Rare.
CORAL BEAN D *Erythrina herbacea*	Scarlet	9' x 6'	April	Sun. Fertile, sandy, moist soil. Effective. Long, handsome sprays of slender flowers. Showy red seeds in dark brown pods. Rangy shape. Do not prune.

SHRUBS

D = Deciduous   E = Evergreen   spp. = Species

Common Name *Botanical Name*	Color	Approximate Height X Spread	Time of Blooming	Comments
CRAPE MYRTLE *Lagerstroemia* spp. Many varieties. All sizes. Buy the right size for your garden to avoid heavy pruning and to retain a natural shape.	White, Pink, Red, Lilac	18' x 12'	June-Nov.	Full sun. Fertile, well-draining soil and moisture. Requires fine air circulation to discourage mildew. If necessary, spray with Funginex or other benlate product. Keep seed pods clipped off for more blooms, and right after bloom season. Prune for shape and better bloom in very early spring. Scratch 12-24-12 fertilizer into soil at base of plant in spring and again in June. Best summer/fall blooming shrub/tree here. Foliage turns red in fall. Shrub or multi-trunked tree.
CRAPE MYRTLE, DWARF D *Lagerstroemia indica* Cv.	White, Pink, Purple	4' x 4'	June-Oct.	Full sun. Best bloom with fertile, well-draining soil and moisture. Needs air circulation to discourage mildew.
CUPHEA E (FALSE HEATHER) *Cuphea hyssopi- folia*	Lavender	2' x 1'	May-Aug.	Sun to part shade. Fertile, moist, well-drained loam. Tender. Requires excellent drainage and warm soil. Feed during growing season.
CURRANT, INDIAN D (CORALBERRY) *Symphoricarpos orbiculatus*	White	6' x 4'	May-Aug.	Partial shade. Poor soil. Water when dry. Red berries. U.S. NATIVE. Carefree. Red fall foliage. Good erosion control. Gets powdery mildew.
DAPHNE, ROSE E *Daphne cneorum* WINTER DAPHNE *D. odora*	Pink Rose-Purple	1' x 1'	Mar.-Apr.	Part shade. Moist soil. Mulch with peat moss and sand, mixed. Fragrant. Feed once after bloom. No pruning necessary. Difficult in Houston.
DEUTZIA D *Deutzia gracilis* *D. rosea*	 White Pink	4' x 3'	May	Requires sun and good drainage. Water freely. Garden soil. Prune after bloom. Resistant to pests. Likes cold winters. Not reliable here.

SHRUBS

Common Name *Botanical Name*	Color	Approximate Height X Spread	Time of Blooming	Comments
DURANTA E (GOLDEN DEWDROP) *Duranta repens*	Blue Flowers, Yellow Berries	7' x 5'	May	Sun. Fertile soil. Good drainage. Water when dry. Light green foliage, arching branches. Espaliers easily but tender to cold. Protect. Prune dead wood just before new growth, then feed.
ELAEAGNUS E *Elaeagnus pungens*	Silver-White Leaves Orange-Red Fruit	8' x 7'	Fall	Sun or semi-shade. Any soil. Good drainage. Feed annually. Large. Hardy. Foliage silver underneath. Thorny, fast growing. Allow space; loose spreading habit. Several varieties. Fragrant. Drought resistant. Grows at seashore. Several cultivars including 'Variegata' with yellow-white leaf margins, and a compact form *E. macrophylla* 'Ebbengi.'
ELDERBERRY D *Sambucus canadensis*	White	12' x 5'	May-Aug.	Sun or part shade. Rich soil, wet to dry. Multiple-stemmed shrub or small tree. Berries are wildlife food. Fast growth. U.S. NATIVE. Spreads by underground stems. Fragrant flowers. May be pruned in early spring.
ERANTHEMUM (BLUE SAGE) *Eranthemum pulchellum nervosum*	Blue	3' x 2'	Nov.-Dec.	Filtered shade. Loose, rich soil. Ample water. Good in pots. Very tender.
ESCALLONIA E *Escallonia* spp.	White, Pink, Red	5' x 4'	July	Sun or semi-shade. Light, sandy soil with excellent drainage. Likes seaside conditions but not summer heat. Similar to bridalwreath. Graceful, arching branches. Clusters of fragrant flowers. Plant Nov.-Mar. Several fine cultivars. Also dwarf variety. Thrives in ground or containers. Prune after bloom-time to maintain compact shape.

SHRUBS

D = Deciduous	E = Evergreen	spp. = Species		
Common Name *Botanical Name*	**Color**	**Approximate** **Height X Spread**	**Time of** **Blooming**	**Comments**
EUONYMUS E spp. *Euonymus japonica* 'microphylla' (BOXLEAF EUONYMUS) *E. alata* 'compacta'	White	To 7' x 4' 20" x 25" 3' x 6'	Nov.-Mar.	Sun to shade depending on species. Loose, rich soil. Needs good drainage. Stiff upright form. Some species have yellow-margined leaves, red fruit. Trim outer tips often to maintain form. Subject to pests.
EUONYMUS (STRAWBERRY BUSH) D *Euonymus americana*		6' x 3'		Same culture as Euonymus above, but tolerates wet soils. Leaves persistent. Very showy pink, warty fruit. Good in flower arrangements. Nice fall foliage color. U.S. and Texas NATIVE.
FALSE HOLLY E H *Osmanthus hetero-* *phyllus* *(illicifolius)* 'Variegatus'	Cream	4' x 3'	May	Sun to part shade. Slightly acid, moist, fertile soil. Requires excellent drainage. Plant in raised bed or in container. Slow growing. Protect from summer sun. Small green and white leaves, attractive in arrangements. To direct growth and shape, tip prune branches early spring.
FALSE INDIGO D *Amorpha texana*	Purple	8' x 3'	Apr.-May	Sun to semi-sun. Any soil. Likes moist soil. Texas NATIVE. Prunes well into small tree. Reseeds readily, but cutting off flower heads before seeds form can control that problem.
FLORIDA (PURPLE) ANISE E *Illicium flori-* *danum*	Purplish-Red	10' x 8'	March	Light shade. Sandy, acid, humusy, moist soil. Good drainage. Southern U.S. NATIVE. Other varieties.
FOUNTAIN (CORAL) PLANT E *Russelia equi-* *setiformis*	Red	3' x 3'	May-Nov.	Sun. Tolerates any soil. Good drainage. Drought tolerant. Fine coastal plant. Slender, rush-like branches weep gracefully. Free blooming. Usually root hardy.

GALPHIMIA (See THRYALLIS)

SHRUBS

Common Name *Botanical Name*	Color	Approximate Height X Spread	Time of Blooming	Comments
GARDENIA (CAPE JASMINE) E *Gardenia jasminoides*	White	6' x 5'	May-June	Sun or evenly filtered sun. Well-drained, moist, acid-rich soil of manure, pine bark, and loam. 'Mystery' and 'August Beauty' fine varieties. *G. thunbergia* coarser but resistant to nematodes. Dark glossy foliage. Fragrant. Good in tubs. Tender. Fertilize.

JASMINE, DWARF E
    G. radicans
    jasminoides
    'Prostrata'
	White	2' x 2'	May-June
			Partial
			flower
				Partial shade. Loose acidic soil kept moist. Fragrant 2" flowers.

GARDENIA, FORTUNE E *Gardenia* *jasminoides* *fortuniana*	White	3' x 2-1/2'	May-June	Culture same as above. 3" flowers are fragrant and waxy. 4", thick, large, glossy leaves. Mulch. Protect from cold. High phosphorus fertilizer for bloom; apply when buds begin to swell. Water in. If leaves yellow, apply iron sulphate and water. Do not prune in late summer; new buds are forming.
G.j.f. 'Veitchli'		4' x 3'	Summer	Prolific 1" - 1-1/2" blooms.
G.j.f. 'August Beauty'	Double Cream	4' x 3'	Off and On All Summer	Prune very early spring for neatness.
G.j.f. 'Mystery'	White, Double	7' x 5'		

GOLD DUST PLANT (See AUCUBA)

GORDONIA (See LOBLOLLY BAY)

GUAVA, PINEAPPLE E *Feijoa sellowiana*	White, Red Stamens	12' x 10'	Mar.-Apr.	Sun. Sandy loam, rich in humus. Requires good drainage. Interesting flower. Prune after fruiting. Easily pruned to small, multi-trunk tree for small gardens. Interesting red-white flowers. Fruit makes fine jelly. Leaves gray underneath.
STRAWBERRY GUAVA *Psidium littorale* var. *longipes*	White	3' x 4'		

HAMELIA E (See HUMMINGBIRD BUSH)

SHRUBS

D = Deciduous		E = Evergreen	spp. = Species	
Common Name *Botanical Name*	**Color**	**Approximate** **Height X Spread**	**Time of** **Blooming**	**Comments**

HAWTHORN (See TREES CHART)

| HIBISCUS E
Hibiscus
rosa-sinensis | White, Red, Pink,
Yellow, Orange | 5' x 4' | Apr.-Oct. | Prefers sun with afternoon shade. Sandy, slightly acid, loose soil with manure. Good drainage. Ample water. Feed monthly |
| TEXAS STAR
HIBISCUS E
H. coccineus | Red | 6' x 4' | Summer-
Fall | during bloom time. 8-8-8 fertilizer is effective. Also high potassium fertilizer. Grows well in tubs. Fine on coast. Very tender. Many cultivars including 'Cooperi' with foliage variegated in green, red, rose, and cream. Flowers last only one day, closing in evening, but proper feeding keeps several buds waiting to open. Bloom period can be extended by picking off developing seed. May prune early spring. H. *cardiophyllus* and *H. militaris* are NATIVE Texans. Hardy. Water every day during summer heat. |

HIBISCUS MOSCHEUTOS (See ROSE MALLOW)

| HOLLY
Ilex decidua D
(POSSUM HAW)
I. crenata
'Convexa' or
'Bullata' E
(JAPANESE HOLLY) | Greenish
Red Berries

Black Berries | 15' x 10'

3' x 3' | April | Sun, part shade. Acid, sandy, draining soil with humus. Male with female plants needed for berry production. Birds love the berries. 'Hume,' 'Fosteri' and other varieties good in this area. Prune while cutting for Christmas decoration. Dormant oil spray for scale. Several dwarf forms. See TREES chart. |
| HOLLY, BURFORD E
Ilex cornuta
'Burfordii' | White | 10' x 6' | April | Sun or part shade. Fertile, well-drained soil with some clay. Dense, long, spiny, glossy leaves. Prune while cutting for Christmas decoration. Red berries. Subject to whitefly. 'Burfordii Nana' is dwarf form, 3' x 3'. See TREES chart. |

SHRUBS

Common Name *Botanical Name*	Color	Approximate Height X Spread	Time of Blooming	Comments
HOLLY, CHINESE E *Ilex cornuta*	Red Berries	8' x 5'		Sun. Fertile soil with some clay. Good drainage. Red berries. Glossy foliage. Prune while cutting for Christmas decoration. Subject to whitefly. Dwarf forms: 2' x 3' are fine.
HOLLY, JAPANESE E *Ilex crenata* *microphylla*	Black Berries	5' x 3'		Sun to semi-shade. Slightly acid, sandy, loamy soil. Water. Requires good drainage. Fine hedge plant. 'Compacta' and 'Helleri' are dwarf forms, 3' x 3'.
HONEYSUCKLE, HALL'S E *Lonicera japonica* cv. *Halliana*	Yellow and White	5' x 5'	May-Frost	Sun or shade. Any soil. Very vigorous growth. Although it is a vine, may use as a shrub only with frequent pruning. Flowers very fragrant. Becomes invasive. Best as ground cover or vine when there is plenty of space. Hardy and pest free. Hall's is somewhat less vigorous but still very invasive. Think twice before you plant in your garden.
HONEYSUCKLE, WINTER D *Lonicera fragran-* *tissima*	Cream	6' x 5'	Nov.-Feb.	Sun. Any good soil. Very fragrant. Winter bloom. Western White Honeysuckle (*Lonicera albiflora*), 5-9', drought tolerant. Many species.
HORSE CHESTNUT, RED (RED BUCKEYE) D *Aesculus Pavia*		9' x 7'	April	Sun to semi-sun. Garden soil. Water. Handsome foliage. Long spikes of showy flowers. Minimum reseeding makes it good choice as ground cover or in flower bed. Shrub or small tree. U.S. and Texas NATIVE. Grows well under larger trees.
HUCKLEBERRY, EVERGREEN E *Vaccinium ovatum*	White	10' x 7'	April	Part shade. Acid soil. Moisture. Mulch. U.S. NATIVE. Clusters of flowers like Lilies-of-the-Valley. May use as small tree. *FRUIT IS POISONOUS.*

SHRUBS

D = Deciduous	E = Evergreen	spp. = Species		
Common Name *Botanical Name*	**Color**	**Approximate Height X Spread**	**Time of Blooming**	**Comments**
HUMMINGBIRD BUSH *Hamelia patens*	Red-Orange	to 12'	July-Oct.	Full sun brightens bronze-red foliage. Any soil. Average water. Tolerates drought. Root hardy. Attracts butterflies and hummingbirds. Shrub or small tree.
HYDRANGEA, FRENCH D *Hydrangea macro-phylla* 'Hortensia'	Blue, Pink, White	3' x 3'	May-June	For best bloom, needs sun to part sun. Likes north exposure. Moist, fertile, loose soil with humus (organic matter). To promote blue flowers, increase acidity in soil by sprinkling 2 tablespoons aluminum phosphate or sulphur around each plant in early fall. For pink blooms, sprinkle one cup dolomitic lime around each plant. Either way, water in well; wash leaves clean. Protect flower buds from freeze. Roots are usually hardy through normal freezes. Even though plant may look scraggly and leafless in Jan. and Feb., do not prune until after bloomtime. Earlier pruning will sacrifice flower buds. *POISONOUS* if eaten.
VARIEGATED HYDRANGEA D *H.m. 'variegata'*	Lavender	4' x 4'	Spring	Unusual flower form referred to as "Lace cap." Best variegation in shade. Excellent specimen.
OAKLEAF HYDRANGEA *H. quercifolia*	White	6' x 4'	May-June	Tolerates more sun than other Hydrangeas. Requires excellent drainage. Conical spikes of blooms dry well for fall arrangements. Fine fall foliage.
INDIAN HAWTHORN E *Raphiolepis indica*	Pink, White	3' x 4'	Feb.-May	Sun with ample air circulation. Fertile, moist soil. Good drainage. Leathery green leaves. Blue berries in summer. Hardy. Also a dwarf variety, 2' x 2', pinkish flowers. Foliage may turn red in winter.

146

SHRUBS

Common Name *Botanical Name*	Color	Approximate Height X Spread	Time of Blooming	Comments
ITEA (See SWEETSPIRE)				
JACARANDA D *Jacaranda mimosi- folia*	Blue	20' x 15'	May-June	Sun. Sandy loam. Mimosa-type foliage. A sheltered south location may reward with fragrant blue blossoms. Tender.
JAPANESE YEW E *Podocarpus macrophyllus*	Inconspicuous Yellow-Green	20' x 7'	Dec.-Mar.	Sun or filtered shade. Loose, fertile, acid soil with organic matter. Mulch. Requires good drainage. Dense foliage. For screen, plant 3' apart. Upright columnar form. *P.m.* 'Maki' excellent variety, is shrubbier. Clip as needed for form. May be pruned to tree form. Feed lightly early spring.
JASMINE E *Jasminum floridum*	Yellow	4' x 5'	Mar.-Nov.	Sun or part shade. Water freely. Garden soil. Pendulous foliage. Mulch thickly. Good for slope stabilization. Feed 12-24-12 or 8-8-8 early spring. Also thin out old wood. Similar to Pink Jasmine.
JASMINE, CAPE (See GARDENIA)				
JASMINE, ITALIAN E *Jasminum humile*	Yellow	6' x 5'	May-Aug.	Sun. Moist, loamy soil with good drainage. Thick, long, dark green leaves. Fragrant. Can be espaliered.
JASMINE, PINK D or E *Jasminum polyanthum*	White Inside, Pink Outside	13' to 20'	Summer	A scrambling shrub. Open sun. Fertile, loose, humusy soil. Water regularly. Tender. Likes organic mineral fertilizer. Usually trouble free.
JASMINE, PRIMROSE E *Jasminum Mesnyi*	Yellow	12' x 12'	Jan.-Feb.	Sun. Rich, well-drained soil. Moisture. Fertilize. Drooping, attractive foliage. Allow ample space for arching branches. Hardy.

SHRUBS

	D = Deciduous	E = Evergreen	spp. = Species	
Common Name *Botanical Name*	**Color**	**Approximate** **Height X Spread**	**Time of** **Blooming**	**Comments**
JESSAMINE, DAYBLOOMING D *Cestrum diurnum*	Cream	6' x 6'	July-Oct.	Sun. Fertile, draining soil. Beautiful fall berries, shades lavender to purple. Root hardy.
JESSAMINE, NIGHT BLOOMING E *Cestrum nocturnum*	Greenish White	7' x 6'	July-Oct.	Sun. Well-drained, fertile garden loam with organic material. Tiny flowers very fragrant at night. White berries in fall. Tender. Mulch heavily for cold protection. Irregular form with arching branches. Feed in late winter.
JUNIPER E *Juniperus* *chinensis*	Wide Range Tree/ Ground Cover			Must have full sun and excellent drainage. Do not attempt to plant without. Plant high in loose, draining soil. Scale-like foliage from dark green to gray to blue. Watering well discourages bagworms and spider mites, their ever-ready enemies. Pyramidal or creeping form depending on cultivar. One variety has variegated foliage with yellow. Stiff, dense mass. Allow ample space for spreading habit. Numerous species. *J.c.* 'Torulosa' is tree with twisted branches.
JUNIPER, CREEPING E *Juniperus hori-* *zontalis*		3' x 5'		Full sun. Any soil but must drain well. May use as ground cover. Forms dense mat close to ground. Foliage is blue-green in winter, emerald other times. Tolerant of drought, wind, and cold. Many cultivars. *J. conferta* is tolerant of seashore conditions.
KERRIA D *Kerria japonica* 'Pleniflora'	Yellow	6' x 4'	Mar.-Sept.	Shade from hot sun. Well-drained, humusy garden soil. Requires good drainage. Double 1" flowers, open graceful rose shape. Allow space for arching form. Cut out suckers and dead wood. Prune heavily after bloom.

148

SHRUBS

Common Name *Botanical Name*	Color	Approximate Height X Spread	Time of Blooming	Comments
LANTANA D *Lantana Camara*	Orange-Yellow to Red, White	3' x 5'	Apr.-Nov.	Likes sunny, dry exposure. Good drainage. Any soil. Easily grown. Rank grower, profuse bloomer, flowers in small clusters. Dwarf forms. Drought tolerant. May be pruned into a standard. Prune all lower side growth, leaving top growth to form head. Stake. Keep pruned as desired. Butterflies and hummingbirds love Lantana blossoms.
LAVENDER COTTON E *Santolina* *Chamaecyparis*	Yellow	2' x 2'	June	Sun or partial shade. Requires well-drained, sandy soil. *S.C.* Cv. 'Plumosus' has aromatic silver-gray foliage. Cut back after blooming for compactness.
LEUCOPHYLLUM (See TEXAS SAGE)				
LEUCOTHOE E *Leucothoe Fonta-* *nesiana or* *Catesbaei* *L. populifolia* *L.F.* 'Rainbow'	White Yellow, Green, Pink Foliage	4' x 3' 8' x 6'	May	Sun or part shade. Moist, acid, sandy soil with peat moss. Hardy. Arching branches. Fall color. Also other species. Fragrant. Attractive in arrangements.
LIGUSTRUM, CALIFORNIA PRIVET E *Ligustrum* *ovalifolium*	White	20' x 13'	April	Sun. Rich, well-drained soil. Pollution tolerant. Bird food. Subject to whitefly. Hardy. Tolerates poor soil. Light gray bark.
L.o. 'Aureo- marginatum'	Yellow-Margined	10' x 5'		Sun brightens foliage. Fertile, well-drained soil. Water. Rapid, graceful growth. Prune branches inside bush to different lengths for graceful shape. Attractive accent in front of dark foliage or wall, but do not overuse. Pest resistant.
LIGUSTRUM, CURLY E *Ligustrum coriaceum*	White	8' x 3'	April	Culture same as Wax Leaf Ligustrum. Upright. Curly, dark green, rounded leaves. Dark blue berries. Found wild here.

149

SHRUBS

Common Name *Botanical Name*	Color	Approximate Height X Spread	Time of Blooming	Comments
D = Deciduous		**E = Evergreen**	**spp. = Species**	
LIGUSTRUM, GOLDEN VICARY E *Ligustrum 'vicary'*	White	4' x 3'	April	Same culture as Curly Ligustrum. Best yellow leaf color on un-sheared plants. Use as a specimen.
LIGUSTRUM, TREE (WHITE WAX TREE) (GLOSSY PRIVET) E *Ligustrum lucidum*	White	25' x 15'	May	Shrub or small tree. Sun or part shade. Tolerates most any soil but appreciates organic content and fertilizing. Edges of leaves are translucent. Blue berries on orange stems in winter. Subject to white fly. Competitive root system. Also yellow variegated form.
LIGUSTRUM, WAX LEAF or JAPANESE (WAX-LEAF PRIVET) E *Ligustrum japonicum*	White	12' x 7'	Apr.-May	Sun to part shade. Good, loose soil. Needs drainage. Dark green foliage, dark berries, blooms well. Considered best of Ligustrums. Often pruned into tree form for patios or other small areas. Also variegated cultivars. Water when dry.
LILY OF THE VALLEY BUSH E *Pieris japonica*	White	6' x 4'	Spring	Filtered sun. Moist, acid soil. Flowers in pendulous clusters. Many other species; several varieties are dwarf.
MAHONIA, CHINESE E *Mahonia Fortunei*	Yellow	4' x 4'	Feb.-Mar.	Shade or filtered sun. Soil with bonemeal and manure, fertile, moist, and well-drained. Very few pests. Needs time to become attractive clump. Fertilize late winter. Protect from harsh winds. Blue berries attract birds.
MAHONIA, LEATHERLEAF E *Mahonia Bealei*	Yellow	8' x 4'	Spring	Filtered sun to shade. Moist, fertile, loose soil. Good drainage. Erect form. Interesting, stiff, bold leaves. Grape-like clusters of dusty blue berries. In spring cut some of tallest canes at ground level to keep low mass. Do not trim top of bush. Grows well in

150

SHRUBS

Common Name *Botanical Name*	Color	Approximate Height X Spread	Time of Blooming	Comments
MAHONIA, LEATHERLEAF, contd. OREGON GRAPE MAHONIA *M. aquifolium*	 Yellow	 6' x 3'		pots. Also compact form: 2-1/2 - 3'. Dark green, large holly-like leaves turn purplish to bronze in fall. Very prickly.
CREEPING MAHONIA *M. repens*	Yellow	3'		Keep low by removing tallest canes at ground. Do not shear.
MOCK ORANGE D *Philadelphus* spp.	White	9' x 6'	Apr.-May	Full sun to light shade. Moist, fertile loam. Requires good drainage. Prune non-flowering canes right after bloom, cutting canes to ground to encourage growth and bloom. Flower buds form on previous year's lateral growth. Some varieties fragrant. Long sprays of white blossoms for 2 weeks. Excellent new hybrids.
MORNING GLORY BUSH P E *Ipomoea* *fistulosa*	Pale Pink, White	8' x 4'	May-Sept.	Sun for more flowers and compact growth. Light, very well-draining soil. Keep silver gray foliage dry. Prune to avoid legginess. Subject to spider mites.
C. tricolor 'Dwarf Royal Ensign'	Blue			Very blue. Attractive in tub with Dusty Miller or Creeping Zinnia.
MYRTLE, SOUTHERN WAX E *Myrica cerifera*	Brownish (Insignificant)	15' x 12'	Spring	Sun to part shade. Almost any soil, but prefers fertile, acid, moist soil. Aromatic, small leaves. Forms large, mounding, dense mass. May be sheared in dormant season to control size. Numerous species of birds feed on grayish-green, waxy berries which may be boiled with the leaves to extract wax for bayberry candles. Only female plants produce berries. May prune to small tree. Hardier than True Myrtle. Texas NATIVE. Tolerant of seashore conditions. Compact form to 18" is *M. pusilla*.

SHRUBS

D = Deciduous	E = Evergreen	spp. = Species		
Common Name *Botanical Name*	**Color**	**Approximate** **Height X Spread**	**Time of** **Blooming**	**Comments**
MYRTLE, TRUE E *Myrtus communis*	White	6' x 5'	May-June	Sun to partial shade. Sandy, well-draining loam. Small, dark green, aromatic leaves. Blue winter berries. Tender. Dwarf forms. Must have good drainage. Raised bed or containers. Thin by cutting longest shoots out well below surface. Water when dry.
M.c. 'Compacta'				Low; similar to Boxwood. Shear or keep natural growth.
NANDINA E (HEAVENLY BAMBOO) *Nandina domestica*	White	6' x 3'	April	Needs full sun to form red berries and reddish foliage, but will grow in part shade. Fertile, well-draining soil, but tolerates any soil. Ample water. Upright, vertical, graceful growth. New foliage copper colored. In late winter cut out at ground of tallest canes for fullness and growth control. Drought tolerant and versatile. Feed lightly in early spring with balanced fertilizer; scratch into soil at base of plant and water. Flower arranger's delight. *N.d.* 'compacta,' to 4' high, and *N.d.* 'purpurea', 1' high with purple, red, and orange foliage. 'Nana' grows 12-18"; 'Pygmaea' to 15". New varieties and cultivars coming in.
OLEANDER E *Nerium oleander*	White thru Red Yellow thru Orange	10' x 8' 4' x 3'	Apr.-Sept.	Needs full sun to bloom well. Sandy soil low in nitrogen. Fragrant. Good at seashore. Dwarf forms about 4' high. *ALL PARTS ARE POISONOUS AND NOXIOUS IF EATEN. DO NOT USE CANES EVEN FOR FIREWOOD OR SKEWERS.* May prune very early spring. Cut down on water in August for more hardiness. Drought tolerant.

SHRUBS

Common Name *Botanical Name*	Color	Approximate Height X Spread	Time of Blooming	Comments
ORANGE, WILD D *Poncirus* *trifoliata*	White	8' x 6'	April	Sun or part shade. Likes good soil but grows in poor. Very thorny, almost impenetrable hedge. Fragrant. Dull yellow fruit inedible. Used as rootstock for commercial citrus. Water.
OREGON GRAPE (See LEATHERLEAF MAHONIA)				
OSMANTHUS (See SWEET OLIVE)				
PAMPAS GRASS E *Cortaderia* spp.	Silver-White	10' x 10'	Fall	Prefers full sun, any soil that is well-drained. Very dense, mounding clumps of light green, sharp-edged, narrow leaves to 6' or 8' long. Very difficult to contain spreading. Best for highway or other spacious areas. Use for roadside plantings, slope stabilizer, or almost impenetrable barrier. *C.s.* 'Rubra' has pink inflorescence above foliage. When frozen, cut back to ground in late winter. Drought tolerant.
PAVONIA (ROCK ROSE) D *Pavonia lasiopetala*	Rose-Pink	2' x 2'	May-Oct.	Full to part sun. Any soil with good drainage. Very drought tolerant. Showy hibiscus-like flowers every day. Cut back hard in spring. Texas NATIVE.
PEARLBUSH D *Exochorda racemosa*	White	10' x 5'	Mar.-Apr.	Sun. Sandy, moist, fertile soil with clay. Good drainage. One of the showiest of the early spring flowering, Spiraea-like shrubs. Prune after bloom.
PHILADELPHUS (See MOCK ORANGE)				
PHILODENDRON (See TROPICAL GARDEN CHART)				
PHOTINIA, JAPANESE (RED LEAF) E *Photinia Fraseri* *glabra*	White	12' x 8'	April	Sun. Loose loam. Water when dry. Requires good drainage. New leaves are bronzy-red. May be pruned to tree form. Shearing encourages red tips. May prune

SHRUBS

	D = Deciduous	E = Evergreen	spp. = Species	
Common Name *Botanical Name*	**Color**	**Approximate Height X Spread**	**Time of Blooming**	**Comments**
PHOTINIA, contd. CHINESE PHOTINIA *P.F. serrulata*				to contain and shape after bloom. May feed lightly late winter.
P.F. 'Indian Princess'		3' x 4'		Dwarf, globular form.
PITTOSPORUM E *Pittosporum Tobira* *P.T.* 'Variegata'	Cream	20' x 12'	Mar.-Apr.	Sun, part shade. Rich, draining soil with sand and peat. Water. Feed. Excellent dense shrub, either green or variegated. Prune and feed lightly throughout year. Prune for shape after bloom. Spreading mound. Allow ample space. Fragrant. Good coastal plant. *P.T.* 'Wheeleri' is dwarf, to 2-1/2'. *P.T.* 'Variegata': grayish-green leaves edged with white give nice contrast.
P.T. nana 'Wheeler' E		3' x 3'		Attractive. Useful in large and small areas. Nice potted.
PLUMBAGO (See ANNUALS AND PERENNIALS CHART)				
PODOCARPUS (See JAPANESE YEW)				
POMEGRANATE, DWARF D *Punica granatum* 'Nana' and 'Chico'	Orange-Scarlet	5' x 4' (18" when pruned)	Summer	Sun. Well-drained, fertile, moist loam. Grows well in containers. Usually deciduous.
POMEGRANATE, FRUITING D *Punica granatum*	Orange-Scarlet Double Flowers	12' x 10'	Apr.-Sept.	Sun. Deep, heavy, fertile loam with good drainage. Dense, shiny foliage. Edible fruit. Many varieties. New foliage is coppery. Yellow fall color. No fruit on double-flowered cultivars. May prune very early spring.
PRIVET (See LIGUSTRUM)				
PYRACANTHA E (FIRE THORN) *Pyracantha coccinea*	White, Yellow to Red Berries	16' x 10'	April	Needs sun to flower. Fertile soil. Water when dry. Red berries produced on older (2 years plus)

SHRUBS

Common Name *Botanical Name*	Color	Approximate Height X Spread	Time of Blooming	Comments
PYRACANTHA , contd.				wood. Very thorny. Upright growth, horizontal branches. Tip prune to encourage branching. Espaliers well. Wildlife food. Some cultivars have orange berries. Spray when insects attack. Also dwarf forms: 3-4', and a variegated form.
QUINCE, JAPANESE FLOWERING D *Chaenomeles* *japonica*	Crimson, Pink, White	4' x 3'	Dec.-Mar.	Likes full sun. Tolerates part shade. Loose garden loam. Water. Good drainage. Stiff, twiggy branches. Needs careful winter pruning to maintain attractive shape. Branches with flower buds may be cut to force bloom indoors. Many hybrids. Virtually pest free. Appreciates mulch.
RAPHIOLEPIS (See INDIAN HAWTHORN)				
RHUS (See SUMAC)				
RICE PAPER PLANT E *Tetrapanax papyri-* *ferus* (See ARALIA also)	Greenish-White	3' x 3'	Dec.-Jan.	Sun or partial shade. Hardy. Flowers excellent for cutting. Dark green foliage resembles Castor Bean. Tender. Cut back if frozen. Powdery substance on stalks may cause allergy.
ROCK ROSE E *Cistus* spp.	White, Rose	?2-1/2' x 2'	Aug.-Sept.	Sun. Dry, light, limestone soil, well-drained. Water often. Grown from seeds, cuttings, and layers.
ROSE (See ROSE CHAPTER)				
ROSE ACACIA D *Robinia hispida*	Rose	6' x 5'	May-June	Sun. Any moist soil. Drainage. When planting seeds, soak overnight. Hardy. Clusters of wisteria-like flowers. A handsome Locust. U.S. NATIVE.
ROSE MALLOW P D *Hibiscus* *moscheutos*	Rose, White, Pink, Burgundy	7' x 5'	June-Frost	Sun. Fertile, moist soil. Ample water. Pruning will keep it bushy and blooming. Remove faded

SHRUBS

D = Deciduous	E = Evergreen	spp. = Species		
Common Name *Botanical Name*	**Color**	**Approximate Height X Spread**	**Time of Blooming**	**Comments**
ROSE MALLOW, contd.				flowers for more bloom. Tender, but root hardy if protected. 6" flowers, heart-shaped, dark green leaves. Many varieties including dwarfs.
ROSE OF SHARON (See ALTHAEA)				
ROSEMARY (See HERBS CHART)				
SAGE, TEXAS OR PURPLE (CENIZA) E *Leucophyllum frutescens*	Orchid	5' x 3'	June-Sept.	Requires full sun, excellent drainage. Neutral dry soil. Best in raised, free-standing bed for drainage and air circulation. Gray leaves. Texas NATIVE. Carefree. Blooms after rain. Drought tolerant. Good coastal plant. *L.f.* 'Green Cloud,' a hybrid, best for Houston. Compact form: 'Compacta.'
ST. ANDREW'S CROSS *Hypericum hypericoides*	Yellow	3' x 2'	June-Sept.	Full sun to semi-shade. Sandy, loose soil. Bright green leaves. Petals in shape of cross. Does not take pruning very well.
SALVIA (See ANNUALS AND PERENNIALS CHART)				
SANTOLINA (See LAVENDER COTTON)				
SHRIMP PLANT (See ANNUALS AND PERENNIALS CHART)				
SOPHORA (See TEXAS MOUNTAIN LAUREL)				
SPIREA, ANTHONY WATERER D *Spiraea Bumalda*	Rosy Pink	3' x 2'	May-Sept.	Filtered sun to sun. Garden soil. Water when dry. Spreading form.
SPIREA, REEVE'S D (BRIDAL WREATH) *Spiraea cantoniensis*	White	5' x 5'	March	Prefers full sun, but grows in part shade. Rich, loose, fertile, well-draining soil. Ample water. Mulch to retain moisture. Prune and feed after bloom, retaining natural, arching form. Bluish-green leaves. Usually blooms

SHRUBS

Common Name *Botanical Name*	Color	Approximate Height X Spread	Time of Blooming	Comments
SPIREA, REEVE'S, contd.				with Azaleas. *S.c.* 'Lanceata' has white double flowers.
SPIREA, VANHOUTTE D White *Spiraea Vanhouttei*	White	6' x 5'	Feb.-Mar.	Needs full sun to bloom well. Tolerates most soils with drainage. Bluish-green leaves, orangy-red in fall. Blooms later than Reeve's Spirea. Prune and feed right after bloom, but never shear. Retain natural grace of form, allowing light to reach center of plant. Several other cultivars.
SPIREA 'Little Princess' Pink *S. japonica*	Pink	24" x 36"	Off and On All Summer	Culture as above. Dwarf form.
STROBILANTHUS (See PERSIAN SHIELD)				
SUMAC, FLAMELEAF D Greenish-Yellow *Rhus copallina*	Greenish-Yellow	10' x 7'	June-July	Best in full sun, dry sandy soil, and good drainage. Bright red fall foliage. Glossy leaves. Crimson fruit. Bird food. U.S. NATIVE. Spreads underground.
SWEET OLIVE E *Osmanthus fragrans*	White	14' x 6'	Jan.-Apr.	Sun to partial shade. Well-drained, fertile, moist soil. Upright, loose habit. Tiny fragrant flowers appear often and perfume the area. Long-lived. Few pests. Cultivar *O.f. aurantiacus* has yellowish-orange bloom. If necessary, prune and feed in early spring. Tip prune all year to direct growth.
SWEET SHRUB D *Calycanthus floridus*	Reddish Brown	6' x 4'	April	Sun or part shade. Rich, acid, humusy soil, well-drained. Ample water. Yellow fall foliage. Fragrant. U.S. NATIVE.
SWEETSPIRE Semi-E *Itea virginica*	White	10' x 6'	Apr.-May	Sun or part shade. Moist garden soil. Tolerant of excess water. Texas NATIVE. Fragrant white flowers in racemes. Red fall foliage. Sensitive to iron chlorosis.

SHRUBS

Common Name *Botanical Name*	Color	Approximate Height X Spread	Time of Blooming	Comments
D = Deciduous		**E = Evergreen**	**spp. = Species**	
SWEETSPIRE, contd.				Feed early spring with acid-type fertilizer.
TEXAS MOUNTAIN LAUREL (MESCAL-BEAN SOPHORA) E *Sophora secundflora*	Blue	30' x 12'	Mar.-Apr.	Sun. Slightly alkaline soil. Requires excellent drainage. Thick, dark green foliage. Slow growth. Violet flowers fragrant. Ornamental. *BRIGHT RED SEEDS POISONOUS.* Shrub or small tree. Texas NATIVE. Also *S. affinis* (Necklace Tree), pink to white flowers.
THRYALLIS (GALPHIMIA) E *Galphimia glauca*	Yellow	7' x 4'	July	Full sun. Fertile loam. Good drainage. Yellowish-green leaves. Freeze tender. Good for mass or foundation planting. Stands pruning well. 'Yellow Plumbago.' May use as small tree.
TURK'S-CAP E P *Malvaviscus arboreus* var. 'Drummondii'	Red	To 6' x 5'	May-Dec.	Sun to semi-shade. Garden soil. Good drainage. Fast growth. Root hardy. Likes exposure with morning sun, protection from cold. Heart-shaped leaves. Bird food. Hummingbirds like it. Tolerant of city stressful conditions, but susceptible to insects. If frozen, cut off old stalks when freezes are past. NATIVE.
VIBURNUM, D and E *Viburnum* spp.	White to Pink	40' x 8'	Feb.-Mar.	Sun or partial shade. Fertile, moist soil, must be well-drained. Position to protect from cold north winds. Fertilize in early spring after bloom with balanced fertilizer. Prune to thin or shorten only as needed. Foliage is bird refuge. Birds feed on berries.
Some VIBURNUM Species: *V. acerifolium* E	White	12' x 6'		Fragrant blooms. Foliage similar to maple. Fall red color.

SHRUBS

Common Name *Botanical Name*	Color	Approximate Height X Spread	Time of Blooming	Comments
VIBURNUM, contd. *V. dentatum* D (ARROWWOOD)	White	12' x 6'		Open habit. Informal hedge.2-3" leaves, blue-black berries.
V. japonicum E	White	9' x 5'		Large, glossy, bluish-green leaves. Upright habit. Makes fine screening hedge, but allow ample space. Pest resistant. Severe damage when temperature falls to 20°s or lower. Heavy mulching and watering might protect.
V. luzonicum E	White	12' x 6'	Spring	Good fall color. Excellent bloom. Not picky about soil or location.
V. macrophyllum E (LEATHERLEAF VIBURNUM)	White	10' x 5'		Waxy, shiny, medium green, 2-4"leaves. Pest and cold resistant. Foliage fine in arrangements.
V. nudum D (POSSUMHAW VIBURNUM) (BLACK ALDER)	Whitish	10' x 6'		Likes boggy soils but grows in others. Plant in sandy, acid soil. Water. Forms spreading canopy over oval form. Shiny leaves, red fall color.
V. odoratissimum E (SWEET VIBURNUM)	White	10' x 16'		Large shrub or small tree. 5"leaves, shiny, leathery. Subject to sooty mold and whitefly. Dwarf form is *V.o. nanum*; *V.o. variegatum* has variegated foliage.
V. rufidulum D (RUSTY BLACKHAW VIBURNUM)	Pinkish	To 25' x 12'		Tree or shrub. Dark, glossy, 4", finely toothed leaves, rusty beneath. April bloom, colors to orangy gold in fall. Flower clusters very showy. Velvety-blue berries. Texas NATIVE. Excellent.
V. suspensum E (SANDANKWA VIBURNUM)	Pinkish	7' x 5'		Dark green, thick leaves. Fragrant flowers. For a hedge plant 3' apart in soil with organic matter. Damaged by temperature mid-20°s or less.

159

SHRUBS

	D = Deciduous	E = Evergreen	spp. = Species	
Common Name *Botanical Name*	**Color**	**Approximate Height X Spread**	**Time of Blooming**	**Comments**
VIBURNUM, contd. *V. Tinus* E (VIBURNUM LAURUSTINUS)	White, Pinkish	8' x 5'		Leaves rough to the touch. Black berries. Some cultivars dwarf; 'Variegatum' has variegated foliage. Doesn't stand summers as well as others do.
VITEX (CHASTE TREE) (See TREES CHART)				
WEAVERS (SPANISH) BROOM D *Spartium junceum*	Yellow	8' x 5'	April	Sun. Light, fast-draining soil. A glorious sight in bloom. Water when dry.
WEIGELA D *Weigela florida*	Pink, Red, White	4' x 3'	Mar.-Apr.	Sun to part shade. Loose garden soil. Good drainage. Likes cold winters. Several cultivars. Prune after bloom. Fertilize late winter.
WITCH HAZEL (See TREES CHART) *Hamamelis*				
XYLOSMA, SHINY E *Xylosma congestum* or (*senticosum*)		20' x 15'		Full sun to part shade. Requires good drainage. Prefers fertile soil. Spiny. Bright shiny foliage with bronzy new growth. Feed balanced fertilizer (8-8-8) in late winter. Prunes easily to small tree. Small cream flowers.
YAUPON, DWARF E *Ilex vomitoria* 'Nana'		3' x 2'		Full sun to semi-shade. Tolerant of many soils, but appreciates garden soil and water when dry. Fertilizing in late winter with balanced fertilizer makes for a healthier, bushier plant. Makes fine low hedge. Mounding, dense form. No berries. Grows well in containers. 'Strawn's Yaupon,' dwarf with soft foliage.
I.v. 'Pendula'		10' x 5'		Weeping form. Produces small flowers and red berries. Good in narrow spaces. Gray branches. Also in pots. Tolerant of seashore conditions.

SHRUBS

Common Name *Botanical Name*	Color	Approximate Height X Spread	Time of Blooming	Comments
YAUPON HOLLY E *Ilex vomitoria*	White	17' x 8'	Spring	Open sunny location encourages berrying. Best in fertile, moist soil, with good drainage. Red berries in time for Christmas decorating. Small, dark green leaves. When pruning, cut out inside branches, keeping natural shape. Prunes easily into tree form. Sends up suckers from roots. Select plant with berries; only female shrubs produce them. NATIVE in Texas. Very satisfactory plant.
YUCCA (SPANISH BAYONET) E *Yucca aloifolia*	Cream	5' x 3'	Spring	Hot sun. Sandy moist loam. Excellent drainage. Showy 4' spikes of bell-shaped flowers. Gray-green leaves. Cold hardy. Plant in small groups for bold effect. Upright, pointed, stiff leaves are dangerous, especially to children. U.S. NATIVE.
YUCCA, ADAM'S NEEDLE E *Yucca filamentosa*	White	5' x 3'	Summer	Hot sun. Sandy loam. Good drainage. Sparse water. Dark blue-green leaves in rosettes.
YUCCA, RED E *Yucca hesperaloe*	Coral-Pink	6' x 3'	Summer and Fall	Sun. Sandy loam. Drainage. Similar appearance to Yucca, not as sharp-pointed. Tolerant. Good rock garden plant. Flower spikes to 6'. Small blooms along spikes for 6 or so months. In pot use 1/3 each topsoil, sharp sand, and peat moss or perlite, making a light but still moisture-retaining soil.
YUCCA, SOFT LEAF *Yucca recurvifolia*	White	5' x 3'	Summer	Sun. Sandy loam, very well drained. Shrubby clumps of soft, harmless, dagger-shaped leaves, 2" wide.

St. Augustine grass.

Lawns

*"I believe a leaf of grass is no less
the journey-work of the stars."*
—Walt Whitman

*L*awns, whether large or small, provide the visitor with a gracious welcome. The aesthetic appearance of lawns suggests the feeling of hospitality. Besides offering visual pleasure, grass lawns serve several other essential functions. Lawns, the most popular and probably the most usable ground cover for large expanses, prevent soil erosion and lessen water run-off. They offer a soft, inviting playground surface for somersaults and cartwheels, badminton and volleyball. Lawns muffle disturbing urban noises and diminish the sun's glare. Moreover, grass improves the quality of the air we breathe by absorbing air pollutants and adding refreshing oxygen.

Some say too much water and fuel and too many chemical products are used for the maintenance of lawns. When properly applied, the water is not lost. It filters through the lawn, seeping into the water table to be used again. Those who care for lawns can reduce the use of chemical substances, and of expense as well. The following suggestions are made with that goal in mind.

Location
Consider the proposed location for your lawn:
- Does it receive at least four to six hours of sunshine a day? No known grass suitable for Houston's climate grows in dense shade.
- Is the soil fertile and loose enough to sustain grass? A soil test by your County Extension Agent is the only way to get a definite answer. (See listing in telephone book under County Extension, Texas Agricultural Extension Service.) Soil can usually be amended to become fertile enough to support plants. Refer to SOIL chapter for details.
- Grass demands excellent drainage. The DRAINAGE chapter describes ways to test for drainage and methods of attaining suitable drainage. The lawn area should be graded so the water drains *away* from your house. Do not even consider planting grass until the drainage is appropriate. Insufficient drainage suffocates and weakens grass, encouraging insect and disease damage.

Selection
After assuring that the necessary conditions for growing healthy grass have been met, study the

list of the types of grass in the next listing. Consider how you want your lawn to look and how you plan to use it. Each type of grass has a different appearance. Some grasses tolerate foot traffic more than others. Some require more maintenance than others. Notice the cultural needs of each grass and the height to which it should be mowed.

Soil Preparation

The only opportunity to prepare the soil for growing a healthy lawn is *before* the grass is planted. A lawn is too important in the landscape and too expensive a planting not to have the soil properly prepared. Grass plants are virtually permanent, not seasonal. To reduce future maintenance, give these lawn plants a soil in which they can thrive. You will never regret it. Refer to SOIL chapter.

To prepare the soil for a lawn, begin by removing all debris: stones, rocks, rubble, and weeds *and* their roots. Then break up the soil. Depending on the area's size, use a sharp shooter, a fork, and a hoe, or even better, rent a power-tiller. Dig and turn the soil to a minimum depth of 6 inches, breaking up clods as you go. If the soil is a gumbo clay which is very difficult to break up, sprinkle a layer of agricultural gypsum over the broken soil, wet it well, and allow the soil to sit for several days. The gypsum's interaction with the soil helps break up the clods by rearranging the platelets in the clay, creating larger air spaces and helping to break the clods.

Till and work the soil until it is plantable. You may have to spread sharp sand and loam over the area and till or work it in to achieve the right soil condition. Never work wet soil.

If the soil has been tested, as suggested earlier, you will know what soil additives are indicated. Soil for a lawn should have a relatively large quantity of organic matter incorporated into it, approximately 10 cubic yards of rotted or composted organic matter per 1,000 square feet. As used here, organic matter refers to anything which was once living and is now decomposed, such as: rotted manure, shredded pine bark, rice hulls, compost, decayed leaves, and well-dampened peat moss. Combining different types and textures of organic matter prevents the soil from packing.

Spread organic matter in a 4" layer over the entire area. Over this spread gypsum, bonemeal, cottonseed meal, agricultural sulphur, loam, and sharp sand. On top of that layer sprinkle, or spread with a fertilizer spreader a fertilizer with a 1-1-1 ratio, such as 15-15-15 (15% nitrogen, 15% phosphorus, and 15% potash) with trace elements in the amount of 2 to 2-1/2 pounds per 1,000 square feet with watering, or 1 pound per 1,000 square feet if watering is not possible. Repeat in 45 days with 1 pound per 1,000 square feet.

Till and mix the fertility-increasing additives into the soil. Let the soil settle, preferably 2 to 4 weeks. (Remove any new weeds before planting.)

- The organic matter and the loam in the soil encourage the growth of essential soil organisms, and improve the soil's fertility, texture, and moisture retention.
- Sand creates a more porous soil.
- Chemical additives to the soil, watered in, impart quick food to the plants.

Buying

When buying the grass, ask if it has been fertilized recently. If it has been, then wait until later to begin fertilization, to avoid burning the grass.

Quantity

Divide the square footage of the lawn-to-be area by 9 to determine how many square yards of grass are needed. Add 5% more for a circular lawn and 10% more for an irregularly shaped lawn. The distance between plants is given in the preceding Types of Grass section.

Planting

Water the soil a day or two before planting so

it will be damp for planting. Just before planting loosen the top 3 inches of soil, rake and smooth or roll the surface. Be sure to firm the soil around the plugs and press the sod firmly against the soil and water thoroughly to avoid harmful air pockets and to wet the roots. Without sufficient water, the plants will dry out and die.

Solid sodding, placed in a staggered pattern, covers immediately. A plugged lawn will naturally take longer to cover the ground. Weeds will grow in between the plugs. Remove them as they appear; it's easier sooner than later.

When the grass has covered, is growing vigorously, and has reached a height of 2 inches, mow off 1/2".

Reduce waterings but don't allow the soil or grass to dry out. Push a trowel or a stick into the ground to measure the depth of the moisture. It should be wet down to 3 or 4 inches.

Mowing

All lawns must be mowed, some more frequently than others. A man-powered mower uses no gas and just a little oil, and it gets you out into the open air for healthy exercise. There are various other types of mowers, powered by gas and oil. Reel-type mowers cut the grass blades whereas the rotary-type mowers tear the grass blades. Understandably, reel mowers leave the grass looking much neater, but the rotary mowers have more power to mow the thick, tough St. Augustine grass.

Whatever kind of mower you use, keep the cutting blades very sharp. Dull blades chew the grass blades instead of cutting them cleanly. The sharper the mower blades, the more attractive and healthy the lawn will be. On the reel-type mowers, both the cutting edge of the bedknife and the reel should be kept sharp. Blades of the rotary-type mowers must be sharpened often or replaced to give the cleanest possible cut. Blades of edging machines should also be kept sharp. All mowers should be kept properly adjusted, preferably by a professional. Some gardeners use a Weed-eater to edge and trim their lawns. It,

too, should be kept in good condition.

Improper mowing is often responsible for the deterioration of lawns. Torn grass blades are sensitive to disease. Never cut off more than 1" of the grass blade at a time. There is only one exception to the "never mow close" rule: when the lawn must be "scalped" and de-thatched. Read on for further information.

Mow your lawn only when necessary. Different types of grass grow at different rates of speed according to their own vigor and the weather. Mow to the height recommended for the type of grass. Mow higher during the summer. Cutting it lower than recommended shocks and weakens the plants. Waiting too long between mowings and then cutting the grass blades lower than they should be is an incorrect way to reduce the number of mowings.

Now available is a mulching-type rotary mower developed to prevent the build-up of thatch, a problem discussed later in this chapter.

The person who is using the mower or edger should be careful to avoid allowing the blades or the Weed-eater's cord to scar the trunks of trees. If the grass grows right up to the tree trunk, clip it by hand; or, keep the area around trees covered with a porous mulch so the mower need not come close to the trunk. Open wounds in a tree's bark make easy access for harmful insects and diseases. Care should also be taken to avoid hitting the sprinkler-heads of a sprinkler system. The mower blades easily shear off the heads, requiring their replacement.

There are differences of opinion as to allowing the grass clippings to remain on the lawn. However, there is agreement that the clippings add to the organic matter that grass likes. Allowing the clippings to fall on the ground every other mowing may be the answer or perhaps the new mulching-type rotary mowers will solve the problem.

If there is a thatch build-up over the grass roots, it can weaken the grass, attracting insects and fungal diseases.

Thatch refers to the accumulation of debris

which settles among the grass blades, choking the soil and the grass roots. If the clippings are raked into the grass, and if a top dressing of gypsum, cottonseed meal, rotted manure, and fine loam are applied to the grass, spring and fall, a thatch build-up will probably be avoided. However, if you discover that your lawn does have a thick build-up, it can be de-thatched. First "scalp" the grass; that is, mow it to one or one half an inch and remove all the clippings. (Toss them in the compost pile.) Rent a de-thatching machine and proceed according to directions. This procedure is best done in the early spring, just after the grass begins to grow again. Immediately following the scalping and/or de-thatching is an opportune time to spread the top dressing described above. Water carefully and deeply to wash the dressing down into the soil.

Aeration

The soil surface is apt to become tight and compacted because of both foot traffic and the quality of the water. The most successful way to correct this condition is to use a coring-type aerator. The aerator, which can be rented, is about the size of a lawn mower and usually comes with adjustable weights for different kinds of conditions. The aerator removes plugs or cores of soil, allowing the soil particles to expand. This makes it easier for air, water, and nutrients to get down into the soil, thus improving the soil's fertility condition and health. Immediately following de-thatching, when the grass is growing, is a beneficial time to aerate. The soil should be damp for better penetration, but *not wet*. Run the aerator over the lawn several times for best results. The soil cores may be raked and incorporated into the soil in a flower bed.

Watering

Water your lawn deeply, to 6 inches, and only when necessary. Shallow watering is harmful. The WATER AND WATERING chapter gives suggestions for deep watering and for water conservation.

The grass itself indicates when it needs water:
- Its appearance takes on a grayish color with a definite sheen.
- The grass blades curl and wilt.
- Grass blades fail to spring erect again after being walked on.

Become familiar with the symptoms which indicate that the grass needs water. Avoid light sprinklings which do more harm than good by forcing the roots to grow toward the surface as they seek moisture. The shallow roots become weakened and are easy prey for insect and disease invasion.

Grass abutting concrete usually dries out more quickly than the remainder of the lawn. With the hose, water slowly and deeply. It is just such dry, weakened areas which attract chinch bugs, another good reason for keeping the lawn evenly and deeply moist.

Fertilization

Reading the Fertilizers section of the SOIL chapter will be helpful for the explanations of the benefits various fertilizing elements give.

Most grasses require two or three feedings annually to produce the luxuriant growth expected of a lawn. The repeated mowings stimulate the grass plants into continuous growth, so they need extra sustenance.

A soil test is the only accurate way to determine what the lawn's soil is lacking. However, vigilant gardeners learn through experience to recognize soil deficiencies by observing the grass.

- Slow growth may indicate a lack of nitrogen.
- A general yellowing of the lawn, particularly green/yellow stripes on the leaves, usually indicates chlorosis, a condition signaling lack of iron in the soil, or the inability of the roots to absorb iron. Six ounces of iron sulfate or iron chelate per 1,000 square feet applied to the lawn, followed by a thorough watering to wash the iron off the grass blades and into the soil, should remedy the deficiency.

- A chlorotic mottling of the leaf blades is probably a symptom of St. Augustine Decline (SAD), for which there is no cure at this time.
- Yellowing or paleness of the entire leaf may indicate a lack of nitrogen. Application of a soluble nitrogen, following the manufacturer's directions, about 2 pounds per 1,000 square feet, may correct the deficiency.
- Susceptibility to insects and diseases sometimes suggests a general debility of the grass, resulting in the inability to withstand the invaders. Possible causes for the debility:
  - deficiency in balanced fertilization of the soil;
  - application of nitrogen in mid-summer or too early in the fall; and/or
  - too strong an application of nitrogen, encouraging soft, tender growth, thus inviting attack from insects and fungal diseases like Brown Patch.

When nitrogen is applied properly in the recommended dosage, never more, at the right time, and watered in thoroughly, it is beneficial to lawns in several ways by encouraging:
- darker green color;
- increased density;
- better resistance to drought;
- quicker recovery in the spring; and
- greater tolerance to foot traffic.

For spring fertilizing, preferably after the 2nd or 3rd mowing when the grass has resumed vigorous growth, use a fertilizer such as 10-5-5 in the amount to supply 1 pound of nitrogen per 1,000 square feet. The usual spring fertilizing should be between February 1st and May 30th, using a 3-1-2 ratio (1st number = nitrogen; 2nd number = phosphorus; and 3rd number = potassium or potash). For the summer feeding between June 1st and August 30th, use a 4-0-1 ratio.

For fall fertilizing, September 1st to November 30th, depending on the weather, use a 3-1-2 ratio to give grass the best winter-survival rate and the fastest spring-recovery rate.

For general fertilization, a sulfur-coated 21-7-14 fertilizer with 50% Urea and 2% iron is recommended because it lasts longer in the soil.

Some gardeners fertilize grass immediately after it is planted, but if it has been fertilized recently, don't feed again for several weeks.

A light fertilizer, such as 1/2 pound per 1,000 square feet of a 15-5-10 ratio, or an application of a liquid root stimulant or grass starter, applied according to directions, is recommended for newly planted grass (which has not recently been fertilized by the grass company).

If your lawn appears to need fertilizing during the summer, be very careful to avoid using an excessive amount of nitrogen. Reasons for this caution are listed earlier in this chapter. Instead of chemical nitrogen, consider using organic sources. They are explained and listed in the SOIL chapter.

Insects

Insects are more fully discussed in the DISEASES, INSECTS, AND WEEDS chapter.

Chinch bugs often attack areas which are too dry in a nitrogen-deficient soil. Their summer damage becomes noticeable as discolored, irregular patches in the grass, often where concrete borders the lawn (areas often missed when the lawn is watered, especially with a sprinkler system). Sprinklers putting water out in a square pattern are helpful, but be aware of such problem areas and their needs. Flood the affected area and fertilize *very* lightly with a higher phosphorus ratio fertilizer to strengthen the roots. Water. Diazinon and Dursban are two of the insecticides which can be useful to stop chinch bugs, but conscientious watering may prevent the problem. Follow manufacturer's directions carefully.

Grubs or White Grubs are the larvae of June Bugs, the brown or black, 1/2 to 1-inch beetles appearing in May and June. The best way to prevent grubs is to use yellow or insect-repellent light bulbs instead of the usual bulbs to which the beetles are attracted at night, or by spraying the beetles with an insecticide. During the day the June Bugs hide in debris. They lay their eggs in the soil. When the grubworms hatch out, they feed on the grasses' roots. Begin in late June to check for grubs by trying gently to pull up a handful of grass. If there is a grub infestation, the grass pulls up easily. In that case, cut three sides of the suspected area and roll it back. If you see as many as 4 of the repulsive, fat, white, wormlike insects, there is an infestation. Leaving the underside of the grass patch open, you may entice the birds to eat the invaders. Treat with Dursban liquid or granules during first two weeks of July. You may have to repeat for 2 years if infestation is severe. Follow manufacturer's directions. An insecticide potent enough to kill the grubs may be poisonous to birds and pets, as well as to earthworms and other beneficial soil insects. It's better to discourage the beetles from coming around than to have to use strong insecticides.

Mites may infest several different types of grass causing abnormal growth. Eventually the grass turns brown. Hosing the grass periodically with a strong thrust of water may disrupt the mites' reproduction cycle. There are miticides such as Kelthane, but try water first.

Diseases
See chapter on DISEASES, INSECTS, AND WEEDS.

Brown Patch is a fungal disease which attacks all parts of the grass plants. It seems to be encouraged by mild, moist weather and poor drainage. In Houston it usually appears in early fall as circular patches outlined by a yellowish-brown ring. Inside the ring the grass turns brown. The grass stolons (the shoots that run along the ground and take root) do not die, but the leaf blades do. If the dead blades are carefully removed, the stolons may green again. To avoid an unsightly spot in the lawn, remove the damaged grass, correct the drainage if necessary, and replant with fresh soil and grass. A fungicide like Terraclor is a suggested one. Use as directed. However, unless there is sufficient drainage in the affected area,

the Brown Patch will appear again the next year. Avoid late evening watering. The use of a fertilizer with a ratio too high in nitrogen, applied during mid-spring and summer, is thought to encourage Brown Patch.

Fungal Leaf Spot disease may strike both St. Augustine and Bermuda grass as well. Small brown spots on the leaf blades gradually enlarge to form large blotches on the stems and blades of the grass. As the disease spreads, the leaves die. Moist cool weather seems to encourage leaf spot. Control with a fungicide such as Benomyl or Captan, following directions.

St. Augustine Decline, a viral disease known as SAD is one of St. Augustine grass's most formidable enemies. At this time, there is no known cure. An appearance of general decline may be the first indication of the disease. Examination of the leaf blades will show a grayish or yellowish mottling on the blades.

'Raleigh' and 'Seville' are two St. Augustine hybrids which are resistant to SAD.

Ways to alleviate the possibility of fungal diseases:
- Be sure you are applying the correct ratio of nitrogen, no more.
- Do not apply fertilizer with a high ratio of nitrogen during mid-spring or summer.
- Avoid light watering at any time, but especially in the evening. Leaf blades that stay wet all night seem to weaken the grass and invite fungus.
- Water deeply and only when necessary.
- Allowing an accumulation of debris (prunings, dead flowers, pulled weeds, leaves, etc.) attracts insects and disease.
- Grass cannot tolerate dense shade. Provide for more light or remove the grass. Prune to thin the foliage of the trees or replace the grass with a suitable ground cover or a porous mulch.
- Keep your lawn turf healthy.

Weeds

There are numerous weeds which invade our lawns. Refer to DISEASES, INSECTS AND WEEDS chapter .

If you dig the weeds out, roots included, as they appear, you will be ahead of the game. If the weeds are allowed to multiply, they are more difficult to eradicate. You may have to resort to herbicides.

If Poison Ivy or Poison Oak appear, an unusual occurrence in lawn grasses though you might encounter them when the planting area is being cleared, be very careful you do not allow any exposed area of your body to touch the poisonous plants. Refer to POISONOUS PLANTS. Familiarize yourself with the appearance of the poisonous weeds.

Conclusion

To keep a lawn healthy and, therefore, resistant to unwelcome invaders, *provide*:
- sunshine at least half a day, preferably 6 hours;
- sufficient organic matter in the soil;
- adequate fertilization, including appropriate top dressings;
- thatch removal when necessary;
- aeration when needed;
- deep watering;
- proper mowing with sharp blades on the mower; and
- an alert gardener.

Be Careful

As desirable as it is to maintain an attractive lawn, there are hazards in the operation of mowing machines. Even though many mowers have built-in safety devices, there is an alarming rise in the number of accidents. For your own protection and that of others follow these rules:
- Wear long pants, a long-sleeved shirt, and sturdy shoes while mowing to protect you from sun, insect bites, and mower accidents.
- Never mow barefooted.
- Wear gloves, but even then *never* put your hands or feet under a mower while it is run-

ning. *Always* turn the mower off and wait until the blade stops turning before trying to make an adjustment.
- Attach a grass catcher when there are any people nearby, and certainly when near a children's playground.
- Keep other people out of the area while mowing.
- Rocks or nails etc. thrown by a mower can reach a velocity of 300 feet per second.
- Inspect and clear the area of debris before mowing.
- Don't leave the mower running and unattended, even for a few minutes.
- Never allow anyone to ride a mower "for fun." It is not designed to be a recreational vehicle.
- Never handle electrical equipment with wet hands or when the lawn is very wet. Keep cords in good condition, repairing breaks and taping exposed wire immediately.
- When working under a hot sun, protect yourself from sunburn, heat stroke, or heat exhaustion. Take breaks, sit in the shade, and drink water, not iced.

Home Lawns Help the Environment

Mowing, watering, fertilizing, edging, spraying...a home lawn requires a lot of time and attention, but take heart, it also serves you well and improves your environment.

The next time you're mowing on a hot day, thinking that green concrete may really be the answer, consider all of the ways your lawn returns your favor of good care:

1. The front lawns of a block of eight average houses have the cooling effect of about 70 tons of air conditioning. The average home central air conditioning unit has about 3-4 ton capacity. Consider how much energy is saved by those lawns!
2. On a hot summer day, grass can be 10 to 14 degrees cooler than exposed soil and as much as 30 degrees cooler than concrete or asphalt.
3. A 50-by-50-foot well maintained grass area

169

will create enough oxygen to meet the needs of a family of four every day.

4. Acting like a gigantic sponge, lawns absorb all types of airborne pollutants such as soot, dust, and carbon dioxide, as well as noise.

5. Recent studies show healthy lawns absorb rainfall six times more effectively than a wheat field and four times better than a hay field, being exceeded only by virgin forest. Lawns filter the moisture to the water table where it can again be used by everyone.

6. A recent study showed "thick lawns slow the velocity of runoff and allow the water to infiltrate." Differences of the magnitude of 15 times between runoff from a high quality lawn and that from a patchy lawn with a lot of weeds have been documented.

7. A turfgrass-sodded test plot, without soil patches showing, scientifically registered a runoff rate of about half gallon a minute during peak rainfall. By comparison, 7.5 gallons a minute of runoff water occurred on a neighboring plot that was thinly seeded and had bare areas.

8. While a quality turf grass reduces runoff water, it also prevents erosion by water or wind and the loss of valuable topsoil.

9. Homes, sports fields, and parks with healthy lawns provide safe recreation areas when grass acts as a cushion to reduce shock and potential injury.

10. Aethestically, there can be no argument that a beautiful lawn is immediately pleasing to the eye and relaxing in its appearance.

11. While some may scorn its needs, others find lawn maintenance requirements an excellent opportunity to enjoy reasonable exercise and a diversion.

12. An average 2,500-square-foot lawn contains approximately 482 million separate grass plants.

13. While your lawn is busily performing all of these functions, you may not have noticed...it's very quiet and has no moving parts.

14. Carl Sandburg may have said it best..."I am the grass. Let me work."

Courtesy of Grimes Grass Co., Houston, Texas.

PRINCIPAL GRASSES FOR HOUSTON LAWNS

Name	Light Needs	Color Texture	Mowing Height Frequency	When/ How to Plant	Maintenance	Rate Per 1,000 Sq. Ft.
COMMON BERMUDA *Cynodon dactylon*	Full Sun	Med. Green Medium	1 to 1-1/2" Weekly	Spring Seed	Low to Medium	3 to 5 lbs.
BERMUDA HYBRIDS	Full Sun	Dark Green Fine to Very Fine	1/2" - 1" Twice Weekly	Spring Sprigs & Stolons	High	4-6 sq. ft. on 12" centers
RYE *Lolium multiflorum*	Sun	Bright Green Soft, Fine	1-1/2" - 2" Weekly or as Desired	October Seed	Medium	6-8 lbs.

COMMENT: Annual winter grass. Freeze browns but does not kill it.

Name	Light Needs	Color Texture	Mowing Height Frequency	When/ How to Plant	Maintenance	Rate Per 1,000 Sq. Ft.
ST. AUGUSTINE (COMMON) *Stenotaphrum secundatum*	Full Sun to Semi-Sun 4-6 hours	Med. Green Coarse	1-1/2" - 3" 7-10 days	Mar.-Sept. Solid Sod Sprigs/Plugs	Medium to High	1,000 sq. ft. 20 sq. ft. on 12" centers
ST. AUGUSTINE HYBRID 'Raleigh'	Full Sun to Part Shade	Green Finer	1-1/2" - 3" 7-days	Mar.-Sept. Solid Sod Sprigs/Plugs	Low to Medium	1,000 sq. ft. 20 sq' ft. on 12" centers

COMMENT: St. Augustine Decline (SAD) resistant.

Name	Light Needs	Color Texture	Mowing Height Frequency	When/ How to Plant	Maintenance	Rate Per 1,000 Sq. Ft.
'Pursley Seville'	Sun to Shade	Dark Green Semi-Dwarf	1-1/2" - 2" 8-10 days	Mar.-Sept.	Low	20 sq. ft. on 12" centers

COMMENT: St. Augustine Decline (SAD) and chinch bug resistant; brown in winter.

Monkey grass (Ophiopogon japonicus) in bright shade.

Ground Covers

"All sorts are here that all the earth yields."
—Milton

*B*e it large or small, every plant covers ground. When allowed to follow its natural growth, a magnolia tree will cover a circle with a diameter of 35 feet and a height of 70 feet. Shrubs, planted in groups, cover the ground attractively (though, unfortunately, leaving space for weeds), but the term "ground cover," as customarily used, refers to low growing, spreading plants massed to cover the soil. Pine straw, gravel, mulch, and stones can also be used to cover ground, but here we are considering living plants.

Ground covers are available in numerous sizes and shapes with varying leaf textures, colors, and shapes. Generally speaking, unless kept well trimmed, ground covers present a looser and somewhat taller appearance than the closely cut, manicured look of a grass lawn.

Gardens sometimes develop areas which do not support the growth of grass, the most often used ground cover. Whether because of excessive foot traffic, insufficient sunlight, interference from tree roots, or poor drainage, some situations call for a ground covering plant other than grass. Or perhaps there is simply a desire to introduce a different effect in color, texture, or height in the landscape, thereby increasing the garden's interest and attractiveness.

There is no known plant which will survive heavy foot traffic. If that is the problem, the answer lies in a path of gravel, mulch, pine needles, brick, stepping stones, or concrete. People are going to take short cuts no matter what, so you might as well plan paths accordingly.

Although ground covers are sometimes referred to as being trouble-free, that is a wishful statement. No living organism can truly live up to that term. However, with careful consideration given to selecting plants most appropriate for your situation, proper preparation of the soil, sufficient drainage, and a suitable amount of water, the plants should flourish.

When planting ground covers, it is quite appropriate to consider using larger plants, such as those in 10-inch cans. The larger plants have a stronger, more developed root system and should begin growth more quickly after transplanting than smaller, less-developed plants. The more rapidly the plants produce new growth, the less time there is for weeds to grow into the empty spaces, obviously reducing the amount of time and effort expended on removing weeds.

The GROUND COVERS chart includes more than thirty different varieties of plants with their cultural preferences. Some cover the ground by sending out stems which root upon touching the soil, some by underground roots, and some by simple multiplication of plants.

Before buying any plants, consider the sunlight available to the area to be covered. Is it in the morning? Or in the afternoon? What time of year? For how many hours? The amount of sun the bed receives is a determining factor in plant selection. The majority of plants require 4 to 6 hours of sun, preferably morning sun. However, there are many plants which not only tolerate but prefer shade, and those are identified in the GROUND COVERS chart and in the plant charts.

To check the drainage, dig a hole 10 inches deep in the proposed bed. Fill it with water and wait. If the water seeps out in 20 minutes, the drainage is adequate. If it doesn't, study the DRAINAGE chapter for methods to correct the problem. Plants don't like wet feet.

If a handful of soil in the bed-to-be crumbles through your fingers, the texture is satisfactory. But if the area has not been a planting bed before, you will probably have to prepare the soil. The roots of plants need a fertile, fairly loose, well-drained soil. For details to prepare a bed, see SOIL chapter.

Dig, spade, or better yet, till the soil to a depth of at least 10 inches. Power tillers can be rented and they are time and back savers. Cover the bed with a 2-inch thick layer of 1/3 part each of loam, sharp builders' sand, and organic matter such as compost, well-rotted manure, pine bark mulch, rice hulls, and pre-dampened peat moss. Sprinkle gypsum heavily and a balanced fertilizer lightly over the bed. Work all the additives in until the soil is loose and loamy. Allow at least three weeks for the soil to settle, watering it to help the gypsum break up the dirt clods.

When making your plant selection, consider the size and shape the bed will have as well as its color and texture. Will its appearance be compatible with the rest of your landscape?

The frequency of trimming depends on the effect you want. Keeping ground covers clipped gives a formal appearance and increases maintenance. Depending on the style of the remainder of your garden, a loose look may well be your choice. Select the ground covering plants accordingly.

Spacing distances are included with each list-ing in the GROUND COVERS chart. The method of estimating the number of plants required is at the end of this chapter.

After planting, water the bed gently but thoroughly. There must be sufficient moisture in the soil to reach the roots, but the force of the water should not wash away the soil from the roots. Keep the bed moist but not soggy until growth is obvious. Weeds should be kept pulled so they cannot steal soil nutritives. A 2-inch thick mulch of rotted organic matter around the plants is advised to deter weeds and retain moisture. (See Mulches in SOIL chapter.)

Once the new plants cover the soil, there should be regular watering to keep the soil moist but only occasional weeding and fertilizing will be required to maintain the bed attractively.

Creeping plants are also excellent to control soil erosion, especially on a slope or steep bank. Knotweed (*Polygonum capitatum*), holly fern, asparagus fern, liriope, aspidistra (for shade only), and monkey grass (if the sun is not too strong and hot) are suggestions for such a location.

A bed of ground covering plants often provides just the right height and mass along the foundation of a house, particularly if the bed is interspersed with higher plants, such as loosely growing shrubs or small trees. Take into consideration, however, whether the taller plants will cause too much shade on the ground cover.

As with all landscaping, keep firmly in mind their proportion, in mass, to the landscape when selecting your plants.

Spacing for Ground Covers

Inches between plants	Sq. Ft. 64 plants will cover	Sq. Ft. 100 plants will cover
4	7	11
6	16	25
8	28	44
10	45	70
12	64	100
15	100	156
18	144	225
24	256	400

GROUND COVERS

| B = Bulb | P = Perennial | S = Shrub | V = Vine | spp. = Species |

Common Name *Botanical Name*	Height	Space Apart	Comments
ABELIA, GLOSSY S PROSTRATE *Abelia x grandiflora* Cv. 'Prostrata'	2'	2-3'	Sun. Fertile soil with plenty of humus. Requires good drainage. Enjoys ample water. Small pink-white flowers May-Oct. Shrubby, small leaves, cascading habit. Not often used but has possibilities, especially used alone. 3-4" mulch should discourage weeds and the plant is not susceptible to pests. Feedings in late winter are advised. Shrub.
AJUGA (BUGLEWEED) P *Ajuga reptans*	3-4"	6"	Semi-sun to light shade. Protect from afternoon summer sun. Slightly acid, fertile soil. Regular watering. Must have good drainage and air circulation to help avoid fungus diseases to which it is prone. Nice interplanted with bulbs to hide browning bulb leaves. Attractive between stepping stones or other small areas. Plant forms flat rosette of leaves under which runners creep and root. Differing varieties have green, bronze, or rose leaves. White, blue, or cream flowers.
ALSTROEMERIA B (PERUVIAN LILY) *Alstroemeria* *psittacina*	18"-2'	12-14"	Sun or shade. Any soil. Light green, whorled foliage. Excellent ground cover if invasiveness doesn't bother you. It takes over the garden if allowed to. Attractive foliage and form. Interesting flowers, red and green. Very easy to grow, though it has a slow start. May become invasive. Dormant in winter.
ASPARAGUS FERN P *Asparagus* 'Sprengeri'	2-3'	18"	Part sun to filtered shade. Fertile, moist soil with humus. Needs good drainage. Prickly arching light green fronds. Insignificant white flowers followed by red berries. Turns yellow if too dry or sun too hot. Root hardy.
ASPIDISTRA (CAST IRON PLANT) B *Aspidistra* *elatior*	18"	6-10"	Shade to filtered shade. Direct sun burns leaves making them unsightly. Very erect growth. Multiplies quickly. Porous, well-draining, fertile soil. Regular watering. Requires cutting out of leaves periodically to keep attractive. Tall, broad leaves nice in arrangements.
CAROLINA JESSAMINE V *Gelsemium sempervirens* *G.s.* 'Plena,' double flowers	1'	6'	Sun-part shade. Any well-drained, acid garden soil. Usually trained upright but can be informal ground cover, too. Fragrant yellow flowers bloom profusely in early spring; sometimes sporadically through year. Rapid growth. Prune to control during growth season. Hummingbirds love it.

GROUND COVERS

B = Bulb   P = Perennial   S = Shrub   V = Vine   spp. = Species

Common Name *Botanical Name*	Height	Space Apart	Comments
CEDAR, DEODAR S 'Prostrata' *Cedrus Deodara*	6"		Sun. Excellent drainage is mandatory. Loose, fertile soil with pine bark and sand. Water in dry spells. Coniferous.
CREEPING JENNY P *Lysimachia* *Nummularia*	4"	10"	Sun to full shade. Sandy garden soil with leafmold. Likes moist, even boggy conditions. Roots at nodes as it creeps across ground. Yellow flowers summer and fall. Cv. 'Aurea' has yellow leaves, lemon-yellow flowers. Small rounded, light green leaves. Used also to climb shady walls, on slopes, in hanging baskets. Several cultivars, some taller. Creeper.
HOLLY, DWARF S or T *Ilex cornuta* 'Burfordii Nana' *I.c.* 'Rotunda' (DWARF CHINESE) *I.c.* 'Helleri' (DWARF JAPANESE) *I. vomitoria* 'Nana' (DWARF YAUPON)	4'	12"	Full sun or light shade. Fertile, slightly acid, loose, soil. Needs good drainage but wants some watering. Many varieties which share same culture but differ in shape of bush and leaf; some bear berries. Size varies from 2' to 4'. Study plants at nursery to make your selection.
HOLLY FERN *Cyrtomium falcatum*	3'	18"	Shade (sun burns fronds). Prefers light, loose, fertile, moist soil, with good drainage. Ample water. Prepare soil with plenty of organic matter and sand. Stiff, leathery, dark green, 2' long fronds form rosettes. Attractive cover along paths or under large shrubs. Root hardy in most winters. Their seeds cling to backs of fronds.
HONEYSUCKLE (See VINES chart)			
IVY V *Hedera* spp.	8-12"	12-18"	Shade or filtered A.M. sun. (Sometimes found in almost full sun but is fickle about that.) Loose soil with plenty of organic matter. Requires excellent drainage. Water when dry but avoid over watering which encourages the fungus diseases to which it is sometimes susceptible. Trailing stems take root where they contact the soil. Pinning stems down to ground encourages rooting. Will grow up trees.

GROUND COVERS

Common Name *Botanical Name*	Height	Space Apart	Comments

IVY, contd.
  ALGERIAN IVY
   Hedera
    canariensis
			Larger, shinier leaves with stems dark red. Tolerates more sun but requires more water.

ENGLISH IVY *Hedera helix*			Dull dark green 2-4" leaves, lobed similar to a maple leaf.

JASMINE ASIATIC V
  Trachelospermum
   asiaticum
	8-10"	16-24"	Sun or filtered shade. Fertile, well-draining soil. Small, glossy, dark green leaves on runners. No flowers. Excellent ground cover. Winter hardy. Benefits from mowing or trimming every 2 or so years. Shrubby.

JASMINE CONFEDERATE V
  Trachelospermum
   jasminoides
	14-18"	6-14"	Sun or part shade. Fertile, sandy, acid soil, with excellent drainage.Water when dry. Vining runners. As ground cover, it looks neater and covers better when kept clipped, but then leaves become smaller and flowers fewer. Cream flowers very fragrant. Will run up trees. Shrubby.

JUNIPER S
  Juniperus
   horizontalis
   (*J. prostrata*)
	8-18"	3-4'	Prefers full sun. Requires excellent drainage. Tolerates almost any soil, but prefers light, sandy soil, not too fertile. Rainfall usually enough water. Easy on the fertilizer. Weeding is problem until plants reach mature size, but must be planted wide apart as suggested Difficult to prune without ruining shape. Subject to insects.

LAMIUM (DEAD or SILVER NETTLE) V *Lamium* spp.	6-8"	10"	Shade or filtered shade. Garden soil with good drainage. Different species have different leaf colorings. *L. galeobdolon* has silvery leaf markings and yellow spike flowers. *L. maculatum* 'Beacon Silver,' green-edged silver leaves turn to purple and pink in the fall and have purple flowers. Hardy except in coldest winters. Protect from summer sun.
LANTANA S *Lantana montevidensis*			Sun or bright shade. Fertile, well-draining soil with manure for best growth. Pruning in early spring stimulates bloom. Dwarf types and other varieties also. Dwarf, bright rose, orange or yellow flowers bloom well even in summer sun. Fertilize in early spring. Water in summer. Semi-evergreen.

GROUND COVERS

B = Bulb	P = Perennial	S = Shrub	V = Vine	spp. = Species

Common Name *Botanical Name*	Height	Space Apart	Comments
LILY TURF B *Liriope muscari*	12-16"	12'-16'	Sun or filtered shade. Protect from hottest P.M. sun. Water when dry. Tuberous root. Garden soil with good drainage. Blue or white blooms in summer and fall. In early spring prune back almost to ground for cleaner growth. Feed and water. Divide when crowded. Tough plant. Also variegated varieties.
L. spicata	12"	8"	Narrower leaves. Cream flowers.
MAIDENHAIR FERN *Adiantum pedatum*	14"	8-10"	Shade to partial or filtered A.M. sun. Peaty soil, rich in humus. Moist in winter, water often in summer. Airy, dainty fronds give light effect. Fine under trees or shrubs. Likes stones in bed.
MONKEY GRASS B (MONDO GRASS) *Ophiopogon japonicus*	6-10"	4"	Shade to filtered sun. Full, all day sun tends to burn tips and bleach foliage. Prefers moist, rich loam with organic content. Tolerates poor drainage. Grasslike leaves, very dark green. Spread by underground runners. For best final appearance, plant very small clumps, just one or two tuberous roots, 3-4" apart. Forms dense mass of thin fine leaves which billow in a breeze. There are also variegated forms as well as a fine dwarf form to 3" high. Pest-free. May be mowed when too thick or may be divided. Effective standby. Also variegated forms.
PACHYSANDRA (JAPANESE SPURGE) P *Pachysandra terminalis*		5-7"	Shade to filtered morning sun. (Hot sun turns leaves yellow.) Slightly acid, fertile soil. Ample water. (Culture similar to that of Azaleas; therefore, Pachysandra grows well in front of Azaleas.) Stems erect with rosettes of leaves at top, medium green. Scattered small white flowers in summer. For bushiness, pinch or prune tops in early spring. Unusual in Houston; begin with small area. Very attractive. Hardy. Tendency toward chlorosis. If leaves show yellow between veins, acidify soil with sulphur or copperas, taking care to water in and to wash off leaves. If used in solution, follow with water.
PARTRIDGE BERRY P *Mitchella repens*	14"	4"	Shade. Acid, loose soil. Normal water. Variable; some forms stringy but others mat well. Red berries after white flowers pretty and attract birds. Good in woodland plantings and in terrariums. Texas NATIVE.

GROUND COVERS

Common Name *Botanical Name*	Height	Space Apart	Comments
PHLOX SUBULATA P (MOSS PINK) *Phlox subulata*	7-8"	12-14"	Sun. Light, loose, fertile soil. Needs good drainage. Do not allow to dry out in summer heat. Needle-like, dark green 1/2" leaves on creeping, prostrate stems which root when in contact with soil. Profuse bloom Feb.-Apr.: pink, blue, white, dark reddish pink, according to variety. Good bulb cover or informal border. Nice cascading on slope or over rocks. Root hardy. Best to protect from freeze with mulch of leaves or grass, removing when cold is over. Reapply when necessary. Winter bloom is very welcome.
PITTOSPORUM, WHEELER'S DWARF S *Pittosporum tobira* 'Wheeler's Dwarf'	2-3'	2'	Sun to semi-shade. Prefers heavy, well-drained soils with regular watering. Neat mound of dark green glossy leaves, similar to orange tree in look and fragrance. White flowers in early spring. Use in small or large areas. Keep weeds pulled.
POLYGONUM (KNOTWEED) P *Polygonum capitatum*	7"	10"	Full sun or light filtered shade. Any soil, with ample water. Low mat of trailing stems which root in soil. Small oval-pointed leaves turn from bronzy-green to shades of red, yellow, orange in fall. Makes attractive ground cover or cascading basket but is invasive. Plant where it can be contained. Pink clover-like flowers almost all the time. Usually root hardy. Protect from hard freeze with mulch of leaves, moss, grass which must be removed each time warm weather returns. Best in small sunny areas.
SEDUM (STONECROP) P *Sedum* spp.	2-8"	6"	Sun. Prefers loose, loamy soil. Must have excellent drainage. Likes to be moist, but tolerates drought. Foliage color varies from yellow-green to gray-green depending on variety. Succulent leaves creep across soil forming a mat. Best in fairly small areas or between stones. Tiny, star-shaped yellow or white flowers in spring. May be clipped, especially after bloom. Hardy. Numerous varieties.
GOLDMOSS STONECROP	4"		Full sun and good drainage.
WHITE STONECROP	7"		Sun; sandy, well-drained soil. Fast and easy; cascades. Intolerant of walking. Cover short cuttings with sandy, loose soil; keep moist.

GROUND COVERS

B = Bulb	P = Perennial	S = Shrub	V = Vine	spp. = Species

Common Name *Botanical Name*	Height	Space Apart	Comments
STRAWBERRY (or GERANIUM) BEGONIA P *Saxifraga stolonifera*	3-4"	8"	Shade. Prefers cool, rich, loose soil and ample moisture. Variegated leaf similar to a Begonia but small, 2". Because of hot summers, use in small areas where shade can keep plants relatively cool. Accommodates itself well with Ajuga. Racemes of small white flowers in spring. Trailing habit. Variegated leaves.
STRAWBERRY, WILD P *Fragaria virginiana*	4"	6-8"	Shade. Slightly acid, loose soil containing ample humus. Requires good drainage and ample water. Surface runners, rosettes of typical strawberry leaves. Tiny red berries.
THYME, MOTHER OF P *Thymus* spp.	2-6"	4-8"	Full sun. Light, loose soil. Requires dry conditions with good drainage. Water when dry. Creeping stems root and form dense mat giving out fragrance when stepped on. Tolerates light traffic. Fine between stepping stones. Varieties with different color leaves and flowers.
VINCA (DWARF PERIWINKLE) V *Vinca minor*	6-8"	12-16"	Semi-to-full shade. Rich, loose soil with humus. Requires regular watering and fertilizing. Light blue flowers. Leaves smaller than *V. major*. Not as successful in Houston area as *V. major*.
VINCA (PERIWINKLE) V *Vinca major*	20-24"	14-24"	Part sun, preferably morning. Loose, fertile soil with humus. Ample water. Long trailing stems root when in contact with soil, forming mounds. Violet blue flowers, spring and summer, amid dark green leaves. Attractive. Also cultivars with white flowers and with variegated leaves. Loose ground cover, nice for bulb cover. Feed late winter with balanced fertilizer but wash off leaves.
VIOLET P *Viola odorata* *V.o. 'alba'*	6-10"	6"	Bright shade. Soil of sand, humus, rotted manure 6-8" deep. Water if rainfall is infrequent. Fragrant flowers. Low border or ground cover. Loose mat. Dark green, heart-shaped leaves. Nice in small areas, especially in natural areas. Small fragrant blue flowers.
WANDERING JEW, INCH PLANT V P *Tradescantia* spp.	4-6"	6"	Sun or shade. Likes fertile soil but grows almost anywhere. May become a pest. Nice in hanging baskets. Trailing habit. For rapid growth, keep soil moist and feed every month. There are variegated and purple-leaved varieties. Flowers small, usually white.

GROUND COVERS

Common Name _Botanical Name_	Height	Space Apart	Comments
WANDERING JEW, contd.			
T. bicolor or Rhoeo spathacea (THREE MEN IN A BOAT)			Large purple leaves.
WEDELIA P _Wedlia trilobata_	12-22"	18-22"	Flowers best in full sun. Tolerates part shade. Garden soil. Prefers ample water, but tolerates neglect. Fast growth. Best in contained area to avoid invasiveness. Very dark green leaves on bushy plant which sends out rooting runners. 1" bright yellow, daisy-like flowers much of year. Root hardy. Best for informal garden. Use in large areas. Trim occasionally. May become invasive.
WINTERCREEPER S _Euonymous Fortunei_ 'Colorata'	7-10"	18"	Full sun to semi-shade. Fertile, humusy, moist soil hastens coverage. Requires good drainage and good water supply. Shrublike, creeping branches in mounds will climb up trees, shrubs, walls, adhering by aerial rootlets. A slow start becomes a rapid growth. This one needs room. Leaves purple in fall. Prune runners annually or as needed.
WOODFERN _Dryopteris_ spp.	20-24"	12-18"	Semi-shade; wooded areas. Rich, humusy, light, moist soil. Erect, bright green, leathery fronds, about 18" long. Grows in wet soils. Spreads quickly by underground runners. Numerous varieties. Since it can be invasive, use either in large informal areas or small contained ones. Root hardy, but fronds do freeze. Plants comes back in early spring in a beautiful light green.
YARROW, WOOLY P _Achillea tomentosa_	12-16"	8"	Prefers sun. Will grow in semi-shade. Grows in most soils if watered and well-drained. Multiplies rapidly. Invasive. Root hardy. Tops freeze but grow back multifold. Ferny appearance. Leaves aromatic when crushed. Summer flowers, yellow, pink, or white, keep well when cut. Good for erosion control.

Close-up of azalea indica flower showing darker blotch some indicas have.

Azaleas

"The flowers that bloom in the spring..."
—Gilbert

By Sadie Gwin Blackburn

*A*zaleas became a popular plant for landscaping in Houston in the early 1930's. Their evergreen foliage, spectacular spring bloom, and relatively trouble-free cultivation has placed them among the most widely used landscape plants in this area. The River Oaks Garden Club's first Azalea Trail in 1933 featured these beautiful plants, and the annual spring event has become a community tradition. The Houston climate is so hospitable to the azaleas that all Houstonians can enjoy them in their gardens with minimal effort if attention is given in a careful and timely manner.

All the deciduous varieties of azaleas are native to the United States. They were discovered in Virginia in 1690 and in Florida and the Carolinas in 1730. In the first book classifying the plants of the world, *Species Plantarum* by Carolus Linnaeus, published in 1753, these azaleas were classified as a separate genus. Later in the century, when evergreen Asian azaleas were imported into Europe by the East India companies, it became obvious to botanists that azaleas, both evergreen and deciduous, were a species of the genus Rhododendron. In 1834 azaleas officially became a subgenus of Rhododendrons.

It is much too warm in Houston to grow rhododendrons, but azaleas enjoy the climate. The semitropical moist air is similar to that of their native habitat, rain forests. Our soil, however, must be prepared in a specific way to make azaleas feel completely at home; it should be acidified to a pH ratio of 4.5 to 5.5 for azalea culture. (Refer to SOIL chapter for pH.) Beds for azaleas should be raised above ground level to provide sufficient drainage. (It is wise to establish good drainage in the ground soil under the raised bed also. See DRAINAGE chapter.) Decomposed organic material and perlite should be incorporated into the soil for the raised bed to improve the drainage even more. Azaleas require watering at regular intervals because of their shallow roots, but they do not appreciate being kept soggy; in fact, standing water will suffocate the roots and kill the plants. Since most soils in the Houston area are alkaline and the city water is also alkaline with a pH of 7.0, it is obvious that periodic checking and acidifying the soil is necessary to maintain the health of azaleas.

Location

In landscaping, azaleas may be used in mass plantings, as hedges, as specimen plants, as elements in a mixed planting, or in large containers for accent. Azaleas were understory plants in the ancient rain forests, enjoying partial sunlight under tall trees whose falling leaves provided an acidic mulch. That is still a favored situation for them. However, certain azaleas, particularly the Indica azaleas in the Formosa group of varieties, seem to thrive in direct sun in sunny portions of a garden. Other less heat-hardy varieties do best planted in filtered sunlight under tall trees. No variety of azalea has been found which will bloom when planted in deep shade. Azaleas must have sunshine, especially from June to September, to be able to form buds for spring bloom. Pine trees are excellent in azalea beds because their lower limbs fall off naturally, the trees cast filtered sunlight, and their needles (leaves) fall gradually forming a loose mulch which, in time, acidifies the soil. The leaves of oak trees also acidify the soil but they compact as they pile one on another. Oak trees and pine trees together make a good combination if the oak trees' foliage is kept thinned to allow sunlight through the branches to the azaleas.

If azaleas are combined with other plants in a large bed, the companion plants should be those which have the same culture requirements as azaleas. All plants in the bed should relish a loose, well-draining, acidic soil, usually filtered sun, and abundant water. Avoid plants with creeping or invasive roots and tendrils which would disturb the shallow roots of the azaleas. Though they are effective, be especially careful when planting small bordering plants such as bulbs or pansies not to cultivate the soil close to the azaleas' roots growing just beneath the soil's surface. Instead plant them beyond the branches of the azalea plants. If ivy is planted, it must be kept cut back from the azaleas' root system. Such trees as pecans, live oaks, and others which create dense dark shade and have surface roots which would compete with the azaleas' roots for nutrition and water should not be planted close to azaleas. Camellias, fruit trees, dogwood, crabapple, hollies, cherry laurel, and others are com-patible with azaleas in cultural requirements. When selecting plants to grow alongside azaleas, consider their textures and leaf shapes, as well as the colors of their flowers so the bed as a whole will be attractive. The more tender varieties of azaleas, such as the Belgian hybrids and the Pericats, may be planted in sheltered areas under trees or in courtyards or other locations protected from winter cold and summer hot sun, though they should receive enough sunlight between June and September to encourage flower buds. When planted in containers, the acidity of the soil, appropriate light exposure, and watering requirements must be checked frequently. Potted plants can be conveniently moved for winter and summer protection, but they should be watered daily during the summer. Water until air bubbles no longer appear on the surface of the soil. Azaleas properly planted in the ground under the circumstances described above, that is, in a duplication of their natural habitat, require relatively little attention.

Planting

Clear the native soil of all debris within the outline of the desired bed. Loosen the soil to a

J.M.K.

Kurume Coral Bells. Hinode-giri

Bright red 'Hershey' azaleas.
J.M.K.

depth of about 12 inches. Do not remove the soil. Add prepared soil (see formula below) to a height of 8 or 10 inches into the loosened native soil and incorporate the two thoroughly with a roto-tiller or fork. The two different textures of soil must be completely mixed into a homogenous whole.

A mixture proven to be successful is:
   1/3 top soil
   1/3 well-rotted humus (compost, leafmold,
      shredded pine bark, or a mixture of these)
   1/6 coarse construction sand
   1/6 perlite.

An easy method of making this soil mixture is to put proportionate bucketfuls of the ingredients into a wheelbarrow until it is full, then add two handfuls of copperas (ferrous sulphate) and one handful of powdered acidifier to the wheelbarrow mix. Meanwhile if the plant is in a ball of peat moss, the peat must be removed.

If the plants are field-grown, it is simple to remove some of the soil with a stream of water from a nozzled hose, but unfortunately most azaleas are now planted in peat moss, which must be removed before planting. If the roots

are not freed from the peat moss, the plants will surely die. There is the method of slashing deeply into the ball of peat moss with a sharp knife on the theory that the water can then reach the roots, but many azaleas thus treated die during their first hot summer because water cannot penetrate through the peat moss to the roots.

Soak the peat moss root-ball in water for at least 30 minutes; then remove the peat with your gloved fingers or a clawed handtool until at least 2 inches of roots are freed. A strong stream of water will help. It is essential for the health of the azalea plant that most of the peat be removed.

After the prepared soil is well worked into the bed up to the indicated height, a hole should be dug for the azalea plant with a diameter one foot beyond the root-ball. If the plant is bare-rooted, the hole should be large enough to accommodate a cone of soil in the middle to support the crown of the plant and to allow the roots to fall down naturally into the surrounding trough. The roots of the plant should be soaked in Transplantone or an equivalent root stimulator while the hole is being dug. After the plant is in place

J.M.K.
Native American shrub, Florida Azalea.
(Rhododendron austrinum)

185

in the hole, pack prepared soil firmly around the roots to prevent the formation of air pockets. The plant should be 4 to 6 inches higher than the surrounding native soil level. Air pockets allow the roots to dry out and die. Pour the root stimulator mixture around the newly planted azalea, thoroughly wetting the soil. Mulch the bed with shredded pine bark, pine needles, cane, rotted leaves, or compost to a depth of about two inches. Do not fertilize azaleas until one year after planting. Keep them well watered but not soaking wet.

Yearly Care

Azaleas should be pruned and fertilized immediately after blooming. Young plants may be lightly pruned, older plants may be more heavily pruned to keep the shrub full-leaved, avoiding a leggy look. Plants can be safely pruned as much as one-third of their height. Most azaleas bloom in the spring in Houston and should be fertilized with any good azalea plant food according to the directions on the package. Fertilizing may be repeated after several weeks but *not* after June 1 when the heat in Houston becomes intense.

Periodic acidifying is advisable because of the naturally alkaline soil and water in Houston. (A meter for measuring soil acidity may be purchased at the hardware or garden supply store or ordered through gardening magazines. The soil should be wet when the test is made.) A good rule of thumb is to acidify azaleas with powdered acidifier once in the spring and once in the fall. If, in the interval, leaves become yellow, the plant should be acidified again. Sequestrene of iron or chelated iron may be sprayed on the plant and used to wet the surrounding soil; this method usually gets quick results but does not provide the long lasting effects of a powdered acidifier. In extreme cases of yellowing leaves, known as chlorosis, the remedies may be combined. An application of iron chelate compound followed in two weeks by an application of a mixture of one part powdered acidifier to two parts ferrous sulphate usually restores the leaves

to a healthy green.

Watering is important. Azaleas should be thoroughly watered and then left to drain and dry until another deep watering. In extremely hot or dry weather, azalea leaves will wilt and droop—a clear call for water. A deep watering two or three times a week during the summer and once a week during the winter is usually sufficient. When freezing weather is expected, a good soaking before the temperature drops will protect the plant from freezing and prevent the splitting of branches. Do not listen to the old wives' tale of watering *during* a freeze; ice does not protect a plant; it kills it.

Weeding around azaleas should be done carefully because their shallow roots may be damaged by vigorous or deep digging. Azaleas should be mulched twice a year, once at the beginning of cold weather to protect the roots and once at the beginning of summer to retard weed growth and retain moisture. A well-mulched bed will discourage the growth of weeds and make possible their removal by gentle hand pulling rather than by digging. Azaleas should not be underplanted with ground covers or with other plants which would compete with the delicate roots for sustenance.

Diseases

One of the advantages of using azaleas as a landscape plant in Houston is their relative freedom from disease. They are susceptible to some, however, and gardeners should check for symptoms and treat diseases promptly.

Chlorosis, a yellowing of the leaves, is the most common problem with azaleas for the reasons discussed previously in connection with soil acidity. Acid soil is necessary for the azalea to assimilate the iron it needs to remain a healthy growing plant. It should be noted, additionally, that chlorosis may also occur when the azalea is planted too deeply. Even if properly planted in the beginning, the bed may build up around azaleas because of repeated mulchings. Check the depth of planting when pruning each year

White indica azaleas blooming along a woodsy path.

and raise the plant if necessary. Dig a trench around the outer branches and loosen the plant in the soil. By pulling the plant up a little, it is usually easy to find the right spot to slip the spade under the shallow root system. If the soil has been prepared previously to raise the bed and the azalea is replanted immediately and watered well, the plant usually re-establishes itself rapidly.

Petal blight is probably the next most frequent disease of azaleas in Houston. The flowers of the plants are attacked by fungal spores, and the disease spreads rapidly. Two varieties of petal blight have now been identified, *ovulinia* and *botrytis*.

The first symptom of *ovulinia* is small whitish spots on colored flowers or rust-colored spots on white flowers. From that point, the disease progresses at a rapid pace, quickly reducing the flowers to a slimy mass, often spreading throughout the garden in a day or two. Diseased flowers dry and remain on the plant, while healthy azalea flowers fall to the ground, still in full color. The spores of the fungus are airborne, and, when the

disease is first detected, the only protection is to spray the flowers, plants, and soil with a mixture of materials such as Diathane Z-78 or Bayleton, according to directions. If the disease is widespread in a garden one year, it is advisable in the following year to spray azalea buds when their color first appears. The spray may leave small white spots on the flowers, but the alternative is to lose all blooms for that year while leaving the spores in the soil to attack again the following year.

The *botrytis* fungus manifests itself as a gray mold on the flowers, which spreads to other flowers and leaves causing brown spots. If detected early, removing affected flowers and leaves may control this disease; if not, use a spray such as Benlate or Zyban. It is always advisable to remove fallen flowers and leaves of azaleas from the soil underneath the shrubs. Lingering spores of various disease fungi may cause reinfestation the following year. Disinfect tools and wash hands after working with infected plants.

Leaf gall occurs when leaves are attacked by the fungus *Exobasidium vaccinii*. The leaves become fleshy and sometimes twisted out of shape. If only a few are present, it is usually sufficient to pinch them off and destroy them; if large numbers develop, use a spray such as Zyban, according to label directions.

Dieback describes the dying back of one or more branches of an azalea; the whole plant may eventually die. This condition is caused by the fungus *Phomopsis*. A cut stem of the plant will show brown streaks. Dieback is usually the result of some form of stress, such as drought in summer, freezing in winter, or pruning damage. Good consistent care and protection is the best prevention. There is not yet a fungicide which has proved effective against this disease. If trimming of the affected branches does not stop the spread of the infection, the best thing to do is to dig up and discard the plant and a goodly amount of soil around it, leaving the spot exposed to sunlight for a time before replanting.

Root rot is a serious disease of azaleas that occurs as a result of poor drainage. The fungus *Phytophthera cinnamomi* may not be apparent in a plant kept in cool, dry conditions, but it will develop when the azalea is planted in a warmer, wetter environment. Application of a good systemic fungicide, such as Banrot, has been found to be effective in controlling this disease.

Powdery mildew, *web blight* and *leaf rust* are less frequent problems with azaleas in the Houston area. All of these diseases respond to applications of materials such as Benlate or Zyban. Follow label directions.

The above discussion reveals that most diseases of azaleas are caused by fungi and can be controlled by applications of appropriate fungicides. It is important to use such applications only when specifically needed, not as a routine treatment, because there are beneficial fungi in the soil necessary to the growth of the azalea.

Selection of Plants

The first step toward acquiring a good azalea plant is to find a reliable nursery. Houston has a number of good nurseries with long standing reputations for good plant material. They provide healthy plants of good quality, accurately labeled, and some offer horticultural advice and landscaping services as well. Unless one is an experienced gardener or horticulturist, it is best to rely on the advice of these reputable nurserymen. The next step is to decide what role azaleas are to play in the garden: a mass of color in a hedge or a corner, a succession of bloom over a period of time, or a particular effect in a formal planting in a courtyard or pool garden. Each situation suggests different varieties of azaleas.

The Southern Indian or Indica azaleas are the easiest to grow in Houston and, therefore, are good varieties for beginning azalea culture. These plants came from the Belgian Indian hybrids developed in Belgium from evergreen azaleas imported from Asia; they were imported into the United States in the early part of the nineteenth century as greenhouse plants for Boston, New York, and Philadelphia. When it was discovered that they were hardy as outdoor plants in the South, they became known as Southern Indian azaleas. The hybrids of the Formosa group: the purple Formosa, pink Southern Charm and Judge Solomon, pale lavender George L. Tabor, and white Mrs. G. G. Gerbing are the hardiest. They grow into very large plants, however, unless they are fairly heavily pruned, so mature size should be kept in mind when they are planted. Generally speaking, they grow well in sunny locations, although Mrs. G. G. Gerbing also seems to thrive in partial shade. Other Indicas which bloom well in Houston are Daphne Salmon, Kate Arendall, and Fisher Pink.

The Kurume azaleas are very satisfactory in more formal plantings because they are smaller plants at maturity than the Indicas. Kurumes are Japanese azaleas found growing on three volcanic mountains in the southern part of the island of Kyushu near the village of Kurume. Kurumes were available in Japan at the Yokohama Nursery Company for some years before they were introduced in this country at the 1915 Pacific Exposition in San Francisco. The enthusiasm with which they were received led to the importation of other varieties by the Domoto Brothers of California and by Ernest Wilson of the Arnold Arboretum in Boston. After 1920, however, only bare-rooted plants were permitted to enter the United States, so Americans have been essentially limited to those varieties and their hybrids which were introduced into this country between 1915 and 1920. Hinodigiri, Christmas Cheer, Coral Bells, Apple Blossom, and Snow are some of the varieties which do well in Houston.

The Pericat hybrids are less well known than the Kurumes, but they also grow quite well in the Houston area. Alphonse Pericat of Pennsylvania developed and introduced them at the Philadelphia Flower Show in 1931. He developed them as greenhouse-forcing plants, probably by crossing Kurumes and Belgian hybrids. Like the Indicas, they were found to do well when planted outdoors in the South. Some of the proven Pericats are: Hampton Beauty, Pericat Pink, and Sweetheart Supreme. They need a bit more protection than the Kurumes, but their lovely pastel colors and rose-shaped blossoms are worth the care.

The Glenn Dale hybrids are a result of hybridizing begun in 1935 at the Plant Introduction Station of the U. S. Department of Agriculture at Glenn Dale, Maryland. They were bred to produce large flowers and to be cold hardy. They bloom in April and May in the Washington, D.C., area, but in Houston they provide bloom from December to March, sometimes blooming briefly again in early fall. The Glenn Dale 'Fashion' azalea is probably the most widely used azalea in Houston because of its bright coral color in the gray winter landscape. Other very satisfactory Glenn Dales are Glacier, Gypsy, Pippin, and Sagittarius. Those with the Mucronatum parentage tend to bloom at the same times as 'Fashion'; others bloom early to midseason in Houston.

A number of hybridizers in the South have been working in recent years, and it is likely that their new varieties will do well in Houston. A few early-blooming varieties have been grown extensively and are well proven: 'Hershey's Red' and the Rutherford 'Pink Ruffles' and 'Red Ruffles.' Newer varieties now being tried include the Carla hybrid 'Pink Cloud' and the Kurume hybrids 'Apple Blossom' and 'Betsy.' Some varieties that bloom later than the Houston midseason in March are being planted to extend the blooming season for azaleas in this city. Some of them from the Robin Hill group bed in New Jersey are doing well: 'Lady Robin,' 'Nancy Robin Hill,' and 'Peter Pooker.' The wonderful azalea 'Amy,' developed by Tom Dodd of Mobile, Alabama, blooms in early April with lovely blossoms of the palest pink. 'Margaret Douglas' and 'Marian Lee' are Back Acre hybrids developed by Ben Morrison on the back acre of his farm in Mississippi after his retirement from the Department of Agriculture. These late-blooming azaleas are growing in popularity with Houstonians.

The Satsuki azaleas bloom in May in Houston, as they apparently also do in their native Japan. The literal translation of Satsuki is "fifth month." Earlier blooming varieties within this time frame are: 'Amagasa' (red orange), 'Wakaebisu' (pale salmon pink), 'Orange Macrantha' and 'Pink Macrantha.' Somewhat later, the Gumpos come into bloom: 'Fancy Pink Gumpo' and 'Fancy White Gumpo.'

Ground cover and cascading azalea plants are also being developed and are beginning to appear in Houston in hanging baskets. The variety 'Pink Cascade' has been developed by James Harris in Lawrenceville, Georgia.

The azalea world is expanding with explosive speed as many new hybrids become available. The Houston climate is so hospitable to these beautiful plants that gardeners may participate not only in the excitement of growing many varieties previously unavailable but also may enjoy the luxury of selecting from a wide variety of colors and growth habits exactly suited to the gardens they envision for their homes.

AZALEAS

Type of Azalea: Indica = Southern Indian Hybrid R. = Rhododendron

Bloom Time: E = early season M = mid-season L = late season

Height: S = small T = tall

WHITE

BETH BALLARD - Pennington (Satsuki X Glenn Dale)

BRIDE'S BOUQUET - Kerrigan Hybrid - M - gardenia-like

DELAWARE VALLEY WHITE - *R. mucronatum* - E - 3" single - medium height

FIELDER'S WHITE - Indica - E - M - hose-in-hose - T - sun tolerant

GARDENIA SUPREME - Pericat Hybrid - E - hose-in-hose

GLACIER - Glenn Dale - M - 2-1/2" single white, green throat - M

GUMPO WHITE - *R. eriocarpum* - L through summer - large flower

H. H. HUME (Yerkes-Pryor Hybrid) - Kurume Hybrid - E - pale yellow throat - 2-3'

KATE ARENDALL - Indica - M - pure white, hose-in-hose - medium T - sun

KING'S WHITE - Indica - E - M - chartreuse throat - T 4-6' - needs sun

MRS. G. G. GERBING - Indica - M - large flowers - T 4-6' - shade

SNOW - Kurume Hybrid - E - 1-3/4" hose, pure white

TREASURE - Glenn Dale - E - single white, pink blotch, 3"

PINK

AMY - Kurume - M - S - pink

APPLE BLOSSOM - Kurume - M - white, flushed pink, 1-1/2" single

CORAL BELLS - Kurume - E - bright shell pink, double in miniature - 2-3'

DESERT ROSE - Mossholder-Bristow Hybrid (Gold Cup) - pink-salmon, semidouble

DOUBLE PINK MACRANTHA - Indica - M - large, hose-in-hose - compact

ELEGANS - Indica - E - M - lilac-pink, 2" single - T - sun

EROS - Glenn Dale - L - 3" pink, low spreading

FISHER PINK - Indica - M - light pink - medium height

GLORY - Kurume - hose-in-hose - peach-pink - M - T

HAMPTON BEAUTY - Pericat Hybrid - M - blush pink, carmine tips, 2" single

JUDGE SOLOMON - Indica - M - pink, violet-red blotch - T - sun tolerant

LADY LOUISE - Robin Hill - L - rose-pink, 3", semi-double, hose-in-hose

LADY ROBIN - Robin Hill - early April - pink - 3-4'

LORNA - Gable - M - 1-1/2" double hose-in-hose pastel pink

LAVENDER BEAUTY - Kurume - double pink-lavender

MADAME PERICAT - Pericat - M - 2" hose-in-hose

PEARL BRADFORD - Glenn Dale - L - deep rose pink, 3" single

PERICAT - E - true pink double - 3-4" - sun tolerant

PERICAT PINK - Pericat - M - 2" hose-in-hose

PINK GUMPO - *R. eriocarpum* - L - delicate pink - to 16"

PINK PEARL - Kurume - E - phlox-pink, 2" hose-in-hose single - sun or shade

PINK RUFFLES - Rutherford - E - rose-pink, 2-3" hose-in-hose

PRIDE OF MOBILE - Indica - M - deep rose, 3" single - medium - shade

PRUDENCE - Glenn Dale - M - deep rose pink, 2" single, low spreading

REFRAIN - Glenn Dale - E - rose pink, white margin, hose-in-hose, 2" - medium T

ROSE QUEEN - Rutherford - M - rose with white throat

SEBASTIAN - Glenn Dale - M - pink

SOUTHERN CHARM - Indica - M - sport of Formosa - T - sun

SWEETHEART SUPREME - Pericat - E - blush pink, double, hose-in-hose

SHINNYO-NO-TSUKI - Satsuki - L - white with rose margin single

WAKA-BISU - Satsuki - L - single rich pink, 2" - upright - small-medium

ORANGE SALMON

CALIFORNIA SUNSET - Belgian Indica - best in greenhouse - double salmon pink, white feathered edge

AZALEAS

Type of Azalea: Indica = Southern Indian Hybrid R. = Rhododendron

Bloom Time: E = early season M = mid-season L = late season

Height: S = small T - tall

DAPHNE SALMON (LAWSAL) - Indica - L - M - salmon pink 2-1/2" - medium height 4', sun

DUC DE ROHAN - Indica - E - M - pinkish blotch on salmon red - medium size, spreading - needs some sun, good on north side

FASHION - Glenn Dale - blooms sporadically fall through spring - deep orange - medium

MARGARET DOUGLAS - Back Acre - M - L - pale salmon, white throat, single - medium size - needs some sun

ORANGE CUP - Kurume - E - salmon-orange-red, hose-in-hose 1-1/2" - medium size

PRESIDENT CLAEYS (PRESIDENT CLAY) - M - orange red, 2-1/2" - tall - shade

PRINCE OF ORANGE - Indica - L - orange-red - medium size - sun

SAINT JAMES - Back Acre - M - salmon-pink with white blotch

SALMON BEAUTY - Kurume - M - salmon pink, hose-in-hose - medium size

SALMON SOLOMON - Indica - E - M - large deep salmon - T 4-6'

SALMON SPRAY - Rutherford - M - deep salmon pink - medium size

STEWARTSTONIAN - Gable - E - M - 2" double, hose-in-hose, bright orange/red

RED

AMAGHASA - Satsuki Hybrid - L - orange-red single 3-1/2" - 3-4' high

CHRISTMAS CHEER - Kurume - E - brilliant red, 1-1/4" hose-in-hose - small

DIXIE BEAUTY (RED FORMOSA) - Indica - M - L - ruby red with violet tinge

FLANDER'S FIELD - Pericat - M - 2-1/4" single/semi-double, rich orange red

HERSHEY'S RED - Hershey - Kurume - E - double bright red - medium size

HEXE - Kurume - M - crimson-red, hose-in-hose, small

HINODE-GIRI - Kurume - E - single rose-red 1-1/2" - L

JENNIFER - Indica - E - red - 4' high

MASSASOIT - Allan - E - bright red single 1-1/4"

MOSS POINT RED (TRIOMPHE DE LEDEBERG) - L - 3" orange-red - spreading bush - moderate to full sun

RED RUFFLES - Rutherford - cerise red hose-in-hose, blooms in late fall and into spring

REDWING - Brooks Hybrid - E - M - deep blood red, 3" hose-in-hose

VUYK'S SCARLET - Vuyk Hybrid - E - single vivid scarlet red 2-3/4"

VUYK'S ROSY RED - Vuyk Hybrid - rose red

LAVENDER-PURPLE

FORMOSA - Indica - M - magenta-lavender - T - very hardy, needs sun

GEORGE L. TABOR - Indica - M - large, pale lavender-pink flowers - T - shade

HERBERT - Gable - E - deep mauve - medium size

MAY BLAINE - Back Acre - L - double 3" light purple - medium size

MERLIN - Glenn Dale - M - 3" rosy lavender single

MILDRED MAE - Gable - E - orchid purple single 1-1/2" - small bush - some sun

PURPLE SPLENDOR - Gable - M - orchid purple, hose-in-hose - medium size

SHERWOOD ORCHID - Sherwood-Kurume - E - orchid lavender, single 2-1/4" - M

NATIVE AMERICAN AZALEAS - deciduous, long bloom season, fragrant. Difficult though possible to grow in Houston

Rhododendron alabamese (Alabama Azalea) - white with yellow blotch

R. austrinum (Florida Azalea) - cream yellow to orange to red - adaptable here

R. canescens (Florida Pinxter Azalea) - near white - medium pink

R. oblongifolium (Texas Azalea) - white or pale pink - on open wooded hillsides and along streams - clove scent - blooms July - discovered 1850

Camellia japonica

Camellias

"And the spring arose on the garden fair
like the spirit of love felt everywhere."
—Shelley

One of the most aristocratic shrubs in the plant world, camellias travelled from their native southeast Asia to Europe, and eventually to the United States. About 150 years ago camellias charmed South Carolinians, but another 100 years were to pass before camellias found their way to Houston.

In 1927, Miss Ima Hogg planted camellias in her Bayou Bend Gardens. These are thought to have been the first in Houston.

In February 1938, the River Oaks Garden Club presented the first flower show featuring camellias in Houston.

Soon after their appearance, the fame of the handsome shrub and its beautiful flowers spread among gardeners here.

Of the 200 known species of the genus camellias, at least three are grown in Houston: *Camellia japonica, Camellia sasanqua,* and *Camellia reticulata.* The first two species are the ones most popular. But when you hear gardeners speaking of "camellias," they are ordinarily referring to the *C. japonica,* the impressive shrub with leathery, slightly glossy, dark green foliage, perfect for providing a fine mass in the landscape. Camellias are actually trees with varying growth habits, but they grow so slowly that they are considered shrubs. However, some grow to a 20-foot height in time. Others have a slightly weeping form. These elegant plants have single or double flowers of fascinating loveliness. Usually non-scented, the full petaled blooms range in color from pristine white through pinks into reds with some being variegated. In one of Nature's quirks, a fungus infection of the root stock is usually the cause of the variegations. The fungus does not harm the plant but sometimes produces a new variety of the *C. japonica.* Many of the single flowers have long, numerous, yellow stamens which contrast with the flower colors, increasing the effect of the bloom. The flowers keep well when cut and are striking in arrangements and corsages. With careful attention to the bloom-time of each variety, there can be camellia blossoms in the garden from October to April.

The *C. sasanqua* is a beauty in its own right. The plant is of a loose, informal, graceful habit with fairly small but attractive dark green leathery leaves. The unscented or faintly scented blossoms are single or double in shades of white, pink, and red, quite pretty in their simplicity. Unfortunately, they do not keep well when cut, but the shrubs are cold-hardy and do give the garden an effective flowering shrub with bloom beginning in October. Their blossoming season is usually over by mid-December but, depending on the weather, there is a lovely red variety, 'YULETIDE,' which appropriately blooms at Christmas time. The sasanquas are versatile shrubs, attractive in groups, espaliered on a cool wall, or as stunning, flowering hedges. A *C. sasanqua* hedge is most effective when composed of plants of the same variety. The *C. sasanqua* has excellent root stock value for grafting.

The *C. reticulata* and the reticulata hybrids are handsome shrubs with some varieties producing very large (from 4 to 7-inch), semi-double flowers with a special sheen to their rich colors. The serrated or notched leaves have veins arranged like a net, "reticulated," hence the name "reticulata." Regrettably, the reticulatas are the least cold hardy of the three camellia species which are grown in the Houston area. If provisions can be made to protect them from our unpredictable winter cold, they will enrich your garden.

When they are grown in the soil and climate they prefer, camellias live to a ripe old age, even to 300 or 400 years. Houston's climate, terrain, soil, and water are far from ideal for camellias; most of the Houston area is flat and poorly drained, the soil is often a heavy, dark gumbo or clay, and the city water is alkaline. Therefore, special preparation is necessary to attain a slightly acid soil with good drainage. The grower must work around these limitations. Certain precautions in placement and culture which should be observed for success in growing camellias will be covered later. In spite of the difficulties involved in growing camellias, many gardeners will attest that the rewards are well worth the effort.

If you have become charmed by camellias, walk into your garden and look first for an area under tall pine trees protected from the north winds. The soil can be amended, the drainage corrected, but the location under a canopy of high trees and the protection from winds must already exist. Protection from strong winds and filtered shade are intrinsic to the health and vigor of camellias when grown outdoors.

Pine trees are especially healthful for camellias not only because they provide a high canopy of bright filtered shade, but also because camellias like a slightly acid soil. The pine needles falling gently to form a loose mulch around the shrubs' roots help retain the acidic pH of the soil. The pine's roots grow deep enough not to disturb the camellias' shallow, very tender root system.

Camellias are grown successfully under other trees also, for example, oaks. The leaves of the oak trees also help retain acidity in the soil, but oak leaves, used alone as a mulch, tend to become compacted, forming a mat which sheds water. Oak leaves should be incorporated with pine needles or shredded pine bark, or other mulch material which would prevent compaction. A loose combination of leaves allows water to percolate into the all-important mulch and the soil it protects. Oak trees also have thicker foliage which often casts too deep a shade on the camellias, necessitating thinning out of the oak trees' foliage and/or branches. Camellias must have some sunlight, preferably filtered.

Plant Selection

Camellias may be planted any time during their long flowering period from October to April. However, early planting, before February, allows them time to produce new root growth and to become established before our hot weather begins. Good medium-size plants, which are 2 or 3 year old grafts on strong root stock, will bloom the first year. Select healthy, fresh looking plants with clean, dark green foliage and no evidence of dead twigs or the cottony scale. Be sure to inspect the back sides of the leaves.

Examine the balls of canned or burlapped plants. Many canned plants are dug from the field and stuck in containers carelessly. They may have defective root systems and poor planting mediums. The soil or planting medium should be loose, friable, sandy loam, or a mixture containing that plus sharp sand and humus similar

'Anita', Camellia japonica, variegated. B.R.

counteract Houston's water. A light sprinkling of 16-mesh agricultural sulfur over the bed will probably be adequate when the soil tests pH 5.5 to 6.5. If the soil tests pH 6.8 or higher, use a quick-acting chemical, such as iron sulfate (technically copperas) or iron chelate. In large doses, these strong chemicals can easily burn the feeder roots. *Use cautiously.* One tablespoonful in one gallon of water sprinkled over the foliage and bed of a 5-foot plant is adequate. This treatment may be repeated in 2 weeks. If the soil in the bed tested pH 4.5 to 5.0, do not add acid. If the soil tested very acid, pH 4.0 or lower, add bone meal or a little agricultural lime, worked into the soil to raise the pH. Water after treatment. Sickly, chlorotic, yellow plants may be the result of soil

G.E.D.

'Charlie Bettes', Camellia japonica, showing long yellow stamens.

to the medium in which you intend to place the plant. If there is heavy soil, a clay ball, or over one inch of soil above the first roots, bare-root the plant before planting or look for another plant.

If you have found the perfect location in your garden with high filtered shade and protection from winds, the next step is to test the drainage. Dig a hole about 12 inches deep and fill it with water. If the water drains out in 30 minutes, the drainage is adequate; if not, the drainage must be corrected. Refer to the DRAINAGE chapter for suggestions to accomplish this goal. Even if you plan to plant in a raised bed, it is also important for the soil under the raised bed to drain well.

Soil and Bed Preparation

Camellias must have a slightly acid soil, but too acid (low pH) is just as bad as too alkaline (high pH). See the SOIL chapter. A small simple soil test kit takes the guesswork out of maintaining the proper pH. Test the soil twice each year if Houston's alkaline city water is being used. It is usually necessary to add acid to the soil to

that is poorly drained, or too acid, or too alkaline. Check the soil periodically.

Some growers find that a successful way to maintain sufficient drainage and the soil pH requirements for camellias is to plant the bushes in raised beds. A bed is best raised by building a little retaining wall of bricks, landscape timbers,

195

or large stones at least 1 foot high and preferably 2 feet high. Remember to leave sufficient drainage holes and to strengthen the wall with retaining rods. The extra support will be needed because of the normal shifting of soil which could cause the wall to collapse.

A bed can be raised to 8" or 10" in height by forming a dirt "rise" or low wall of soil planted thickly in liriope, ophiopogon (Monkey or mondo grass), or other similar border plant. Choose the type of soil-retaining method which would be the most compatible with your landscape.

Since the planting time for camellias is between October and April, with February being the recommended time, the bed and soil preparation should begin at least 4 weeks before the planned planting time. It takes that long, or longer, for the soil to settle and for any additions to the soil to mellow.

Planting

Wherever you choose to plant, the area first should be lined out for shape and size. A water hose is convenient for that purpose because it is flexible and easy to shape. When the bed's shape is established, follow this procedure:

- Mark the outline of the bed with a sharp spade or a hose. Sprinkling gypsum along the outline is also helpful.
- Remove any grass, weeds, rocks, or other debris from the location.
- Break up the soil with a spade or fork down to a depth of 12 inches. *Do not work the soil while it is wet.*
- If the soil is difficult to break up, sprinkle the area with a coating of agricultural gypsum, wet it well, and allow to settle for several days. If the soil had a high pH, the gypsum will rearrange the clay platelets. The soil will then have larger air spaces for better aeration and percolation of water. (See SOIL chapter.)
- If you are planting in an area already having friable, workable soil, skip the gypsum treatment, but be very sure that the soil is well

draining.
- Work the soil well after breaking it up and level the surface.
- Select *one* of these two mixtures:
  1/3 part fertile sandy loam
  1/3 part humus, ground or shredded rotted pine bark, compost containing rice hulls, barnyard manure, sawdust, oak leaves— all well-rotted
  1/6 part sharp or torpedo sand
  1/6 part agricultural perlite
  Mix well. When ready to use, add 1 cup agricultural sulfur per builder's size wheelbarrow and mix thoroughly.
  Or
  2/5 fertile sandy loam
  1/5 leaf mold, humus, or organic compost (available at garden supply places)
  1/5 well-rotted barnyard manure
  1/5 sharp sand.
  When mixed thoroughly and ready to use, add 1 cup agricultural sulfur to each builder's size (large) wheelbarrow and combine thoroughly with the soil mixture.

If you are planting in a raised bed, and if the drainage is good, fill the bed with the soil you have prepared. In about 10 to 12 days the soil will be settled. You will probably have to add more prepared soil to bring the level of the bed high enough.

If you are planting a bed raised by a border of plants, be sure that the native soil drains well *before* adding the prepared soil. Spread a layer of the prepared soil mix, 4 inches thick, over the native soil and level. The soil should be well above the bordering plants or the retaining wall.

Set the camellia ball in the bed in a scooped out, saucer-like depression but *not* in "a hole."

At least 1/3, preferably 1/2 of the root-ball should be above the surface of the soil when planting is finished. Camellias' roots require a lot of air. When planted too deep, the roots smother.

'Tom Eagleson', a many-petalled Camellia japonica.

With the camellia ball sitting on the soil, begin to add more of the prepared soil around the ball, enough to cover lightly the top feeder roots. *Do not* put any pressure on top of the ball. Camellias have numerous very small but very important surface feeder roots which are easily damaged.

Settle the soil carefully around the soil ball. Be sure the ball is properly balanced. Water gently but thoroughly to rid the soil of any air pockets. (Roots cannot grow into air; they need soil.)

Cut the burlap of the ball, if any, only from the top of the ball, making sure there is no *excess* soil left on top of the feeder roots.

Water the plants gently but thoroughly.

Finally, add a 4-inch thick mulch composed of a combination of well-rotted organic materials, such as listed earlier, with the soil mix directions. The combination of different textures of organic material prevents compaction of the mulch and allows water to percolate through the mulch and into the soil. The use of peat moss alone is not recommended because it packs and, therefore, sheds water rather than absorbing it. If allowed to dry out, peat moss is very difficult to re-wet. Refer to Mulches in the SOIL chapter.

Keep the soil moistened—not soggy—for several weeks. For the camellia's sake, keep the mulch damp all the time to prevent the wind from blowing it away. Replenish the mulch as needed to maintain a 4-inch thickness.

If the camellia you are planting is in a container, cut the sides of the pot away to allow easy removal of the plant, retaining as much soil on the roots as possible. Dampening the soil of the plant before planting tends to hold the soil together.

If the dirt of the balled or canned plant is not similar in texture and content to the soil in which the camellia must now grow, plant it bare-rooted. Wash all the soil from the roots and treat the roots with a plant hormone, such as Transplantone or OD4, according to label directions. Keep roots wet. Container-grown plants, which have complete root systems, may now be planted in the prepared bed. Field-grown plants which have lost some roots during the digging and burlapping process should be heeled-in in sawdust for several months to allow new root growth prior to bare-rooting.

To plant a bare-rooted camellia, follow above directions for mixing soil and plant in a bed raised at least 1 foot above soil surface, as described previously, allowing at least 2-1/4 feet diameter of bed area for each inch of the plant's trunk diameter. In this well-drained bed, you may now dig a hole and form a cone of soil on which to set the bare roots of the bush. Complete the planting procedure with soil around the roots. Water well. Later add just enough soil to cover the top feeder roots. Do not fertilize for one year. Support the plant with a strong stake one foot taller than the camellia. Bare-rooted camellias must be protected from damage by sun, wind, and dehydration. To accomplish that purpose, envelope the entire plant in a plastic bag, sealed at the top, and supported by the stake to hold the bag off the plant. Pile dirt around bottom edges and hold and seal securely. Protect the plant with a sun shade, such as burlap on a chicken wire frame. Water as needed to keep the plant moist. After one month, loosen the bag and gradually remove it. If the plant begins to wilt, replace the bag.

Buying

Most members of the Houston Camellia Society stay away from California-grown camellias. Unfortunately, the majority of nurseries here have been stocking California grown plants, although there is at least one nursery in Houston which often carries balled and burlapped camellias. *C. japonicas* and *C. reticulatas* which have been grafted onto *C. sasanqua* root stock grow much better in our climate and soil conditions than do the California camellias. However, if you decide to buy California plants, leave them in the container until cool weather has arrived. Then bare-root them completely before planting.

Some camellia growers in this area buy plants from the nurseries in Louisiana, Mississippi, and Alabama which specialize in grafted plants. Many Texas camellia enthusiasts buy sasanqua understock and graft scions of show-winning varieties onto *C. sasanqua* understock. Scions or cions are detached shoots containing 2 or more buds used for grafting. The scions are mailed to the buyers, but the grafted plants must be picked up by the purchasers at the nurseries. The visits to camellia nurseries allow the enthusiasts to keep abreast with the latest advances in the camellia world.

Insects and Diseases

Healthy, robust plants which have been properly planted in a suitable bed mixture, adequately watered, and kept slightly acid will not be particularly subject to disease.

Tea scale infestation is the most common problem in this area. In the dormant stage, it appears as small brown specks, considerably longer than wide. In the active stage, tea scale appears as cotton-like matter on the bottom of the leaves; when the infestation is severe, the tops of the leaves become yellow and mottled. The scale is actually a sucking insect which attaches itself to the leaf of the plant and sucks out plant food and fluids.

Aphids are also troublesome to new growth. Chewing insects and bugs which inhabit the mulch around the beds may come up at night to feed on the new foliage. These do not injure the plant, but they chew holes in the foliage, making it unsightly.

To treat all these problems, use a combination spray of an insecticide, such as Malathion or equivalent, and an oil spray. The insecticide will control the aphids, the oil spray will control the scale infestation, and spraying the bed in the vicinity of the plant helps control other bugs and chewing insects. It is usually necessary to spray twice in the spring after all danger of frost is past, and again in the early fall. Do not use an oil spray when temperatures get above 90° or later than October 15, as an oil-sprayed plant is particularly vulnerable to an early freeze. In addition to spraying, sprinkle an ant-killing material on the camellia beds.

Research on the commercial application of systemic insecticides has been extensive during the past few years. These chemicals, applied to the surface of a plant, either to the root system or above ground, are absorbed into the plant's circulation system and transmitted to all parts of the plant, rendering it repellent to certain insects for a period of time. CYGON 2E has proven effective for camellias. CYGON can be used as a soil drench over the area of the root system, in accordance with the manufacturer's instructions. It can also be applied full strength with a 2-inch paint brush, painting a narrow stripe around the trunk of the plant just above the soil line. It is effective against tea scale.

Dieback, a disease caused by the fungus *Glomerella cingulata*, frequently infects camellias grown in the Gulf Coast area. The first symptom usually noticed is wilting and death of small new growth, with the leaves falling off and the dead twigs remaining for a few days. Older twigs may be involved and killed, but the leaves turn brown and do not fall off. The fungus spores also enter and infect the plant through breaks in the bark caused by wounds, insect punctures, and normal leaf fall. At the base of an infected twig, leaf, or in a wound, fungus invades and kills the wood cells and spreads up and down the stem. The surrounding healthy wood continues to grow, thus enlarging the stem diameter. The infected area of dead cells appears sunken and is called a canker. The canker provides the food base for the fungus and produces millions of spores each year. The spores are distributed by rain splashing to nearby plants and to other parts of the same plant. Crawling and flying insects may also distribute the spores. Severe infection may kill large branches or even the entire plant. There is no known cure for an infected area or canker except to cut it out down to healthy green wood and immediately disinfect the wound with a mixture of the fungicides Benlate and 50 W Captan in water. Both chemicals are effective protectants but will not

R.M.

Bush of 'Pink Perfection', smaller type Camellia japonica.

cure after infection has occurred. They should be used to disinfect pruning and grafting tools, to disinfect scions and stocks during grafting, and can be used as a plant disinfectant by spraying after pruning or at normal leaf fall. All the usual garden species and hybrids of camellias are susceptible to the fungus, but *C. sasanqua* is much more sensitive. Certain cultivars in each species are also much more sensitive than others. Excess high nitrogen fertilizer and too much acid contribute to the disease and overhead sprinkling spreads it. Camellias should be sprayed at least once in March, April, and May with a Benlate-Captan mixture as a preventive for dieback.

Camellia flower blight, a disease caused by the fungus *Sclerotinia camellia* Hara, infects camellia flowers grown in many parts of the Gulf Coast area. It attacks only petals of camellia flowers during the spring flowering season. Therefore, any fall flowers resulting from early-blooming varieties of any species or hybrid, or those stimulated to flower early by gibberellic acid applications, will escape infection. The fungus does not cause disease on leaf, stem, or root tissue, and in no way impairs the health of the plant. The fungus invades camellia flower tissue and its symptoms are brown specks or blotches which spread to invade most of the flower tissue. The brown diseased flower finally falls to the ground where it eventually forms sclerotia, small hard fibrous bodies which are the dormant form of the fungus. The fungus remains dormant until the next winter, when it becomes active and spores are ejected from January to April and are disseminated by air currents to infect the new crop of camellia flowers and thus start a new life cycle. There is no positve chemical cure for the disease. The spores can be carried at least one mile by air currents; so if infection is in the area, it is difficult to avoid. There are contact fungicides which will kill the spores but discolor the flowers. The fungicide PCNB (trade name Terrachlor) used as a ground spray in December prevents the activation of the fungus but gives no off-premises control. The best control procedures are to exclude it if possible by planting only bare-rooted plants, spray the bed areas early in December with PCNB at 2 lbs./1,000 sq. ft., and pick up from the ground all infected or spent camellia blooms.

Systemic fungicides are available for some non-woody plants, but so far none are systemic in camellias in the United States. It is possible that research may develop them for camellias in the future.

Pruning

Camellias are frequently pruned to control the shape and size. Sometimes the pruning is severe, but it is usually done the way trees are pruned. The weak interior twigs and branches should be removed along with all dead wood to provide air circulation and reduce insect and disease susceptibility. When pruning to shape a plant, care should be taken to prune down to a growth bud which is pointing in the direction you want a branch to take. Some pruning can be done when you cut flowers.

Fertilization

Fertilization is probably the least important aspect of camellia culture. A little fertilizer goes a long way, so be sure not to over-fertilize. Avoid high nitrogen fertilizers. A 5-10-10 acid fertilizer, balanced especially for camellias and azaleas, is available under several brand names. Use according to directions. The amount and frequency of fertilization depends on conditions in your garden and what you are trying to accomplish. It is best to start with two light applications in the spring—the first shortly after the plants have finished blooming, and the second about a month or six weeks later. Ordinarily, this is sufficient; but if the plants are competing with large tree roots or are growing in sandy, porous soil which has a tendency to leach out, give them a little foliar feeding as a small additional boost in the early summer. At this time, as soon as flower buds can be distinguished from growth buds, twist off all of the twin buds except one pointing outward, not upward, on each stem to produce a larger, more perfect flower. If a mass effect or longer flowering period with small blossoms is desired, do not disbud. If you want specimen flowers for a special occasion, a light fertilization about one month prior to the expected date will help the plant mature ripening buds to blossoms of maximum size and vitality. Be extremely cautious with any of these experimental procedures; be moderate with your fertilizer.

One grower's suggestion for fertilization is to fertilize each plant the first year with one handful of 13-13-13 commercial fertilizer. The second year fertilize with 2 handfuls per plant, the third year with three handfuls per plant, and the fourth year with four handfuls of 13-13-13 per plant. Then stop fertilizing. Meanwhile, during those 4 years, gradually add enough pine needles around each plant to maintain a 4-inch or thicker layer of needles as a mulch. The pine mulch will become humus as it rots and will acidify the soil. That is Nature's way in the forest, the camellias' native habitat. About 2 or 3 years after planting, a network of white roots can be seen in the humus on top of the ground. These are feeder roots. Do not ever disturb these life-giving roots, either by cultivation or by stepping on them or by planting bulbs or other small plants too close to the feeder roots. Water. The above-ground plantings will dry out, and the soil will require thorough watering for the first few years. Always water gently and deeply to allow the camellia's roots to grow deeper into the soil as they seek water. It is much better for the plant and the gardener for deep root growth to be encouraged. Water deeply when the lack-luster appearance of the leaves indicates that the plant needs moisture. However, be alert for signs of their need for water, especially during times of drought. The retention of 4 inches of mulch, at all times, around the plants is necessary.

Figure 1.(A) Single mature flower bud on a strong twig, with adjacent mature growth bud.

Figure 1.(B) Growth bud broken off, leaving vegetative basal cup. Drops of GIB placed in cup and increase size and quality of blooms.

Chemical Bloom Stimulation

Chemical treatment of camellias with a natural plant hormone, gibberellin (GIB), to accelerate the normal blooming cycle and increase the size of the blooms, has been widely adopted by the camellia flower show group. The same hormone is used more commonly in commercial agriculture to accelerate the normal maturation cycle and increase the crop yeild. For camellias, GIB can be used in the acid or potassium salt form in a 10,000 ppm solution. It is usually applied by removing a growth bud adjacent to a mature flower bud and placing one drop of the solution in the vegetative cup at the base of the growth bud, as illustrated by Figure 1. This supplies the flower bud with an excessive amount of the same growth hormone that produces the normal flower. The effect of the treatment varies with species, variety, and bud. It speeds up blooming time in varying degrees, increases the bloom size, improves the quality of many blooms, damages others, does not damage mature plants if used in moderation, damages small plants if used to excess, and may kill very small plants.

GIB is useful to the camellia show hobbyists because it gives larger flowers early in the year so shows can be held before the flowers can be damaged by freezing weather and fungus diseases. Home gardeners are eligible to participate in all American Camellia Society shows, and some may desire to practice the GIB treatment for their own home enjoyment.

Propagation

Camellias can be reproduced by the conventional propagation methods: cuttings, layerings, or grafts. Seeds will not reproduce true to the parent plant. Rare varieties are propagated by grafting scions, using the cleft graft method, on large *C. sasanqua* or *C. japonica* root stock (see PROPAGATION chapter).

It is possible to have a good specimen blooming plant after about three years; but it is usually cheaper and more satisfactory to buy well-established, two or three-year-old grafted plants from a reputable nursery.

The summer and winter care of camellias, as well as watering, is similar to that for azaleas.

CAMELLIAS

BBG = growing at Bayou Bend Gardens   E = early blooming   M = mid-season blooming
L = late blooming   1800 = date of introduction.

CAMELLIA SASANQUA
Blooms Mid-October to Mid-December.
APPLE BLOSSOM: white blushed pink; single, BBG.
BONANZA: deep red; large, semi-peony form.
CHANSONETTE (species *Hiemalis*): first Peer award winner; brilliant pink; large, formal double with ruffled petals.
CLEOPATRA: rose pink; semi-double, BBG.
DAYDREAM: white edged deep rose pink; large, single, BBG.
JEAN MAY: shell pink; large, double.
HARRIETTE RUSTER: white-tipped pink; large, anemone form with undulating outer petals.
LESLIE ANNE: white-tipped reddish lavender; large, semi-double with irregular petals to peony form.
MINE-NO-YUKI (SNOW, WHITE DOVES): white; large, peony form, BBG.
MISS ED: light pink with lavender and deeper pink tints; medium, peony form with wavy and notched petals.
NARUMI-GATA (OLEIFERA): white shaded pink; large, single of cupped form, BBG.
SHISHI-GASHIRA (species *Hiemalis*): red; medium, semi-double to double, BBG.
SHOWA-NO-SAKAE (species *Hiemalis*): soft pink; occasionally marbled white; medium, semi-double to rose form double.
SPARKLING BURGUNDY: ruby rose with sheen of lavender; small to medium, peony form with intermingled stamens and petaloids.
STAR ABOVE STAR (species *Vernalis*): white shading to lavender pink at edge; medium, semi-double.
YULETIDE: orange red; small, single, compact upright.

CAMELLIA JAPONICA
Blooms October to April.
ALBA PLENA: white; medium to large, formal double, BBG-E-M-1792; Fimbriata, formal double mutant with fringed petals, 1816; Mrs. Hooper Connell, peony form mutant, 1950.
ADOLPHE AUDUSSON: dark red; large, semi-double, BBG-M-1877; Variegated, dark red, spotted white, 1920's; Special, predominantly white with some red, 1942.

BETTY SHEFFIELD: white, faintly striped red and pink; medium to large, semi-double to loose peony. This is a beautiful bloom, but its claim to fame is that it has produced 12 outstanding mutants which have been named and registered but have not received awards to date, M-1949.
BETTY SHEFFIELD SUPREME: mutant; white with deep pink to red border on each petal, M-1960.
BOULE DE NEIGE: white; medium, peony form, BBG-M-1935.
CAMEO PINK: light pink sport of Lilyi; medium, BBG-1938.
CARTER'S SUNBURST: pale pink, striped deeper pink; large to very large; semi-double to peony form, M-1958.
CARTER'S SUNBURST PINK: mutant; deep pink. The variegated form is often considered the finest bloom, M-1964.
CHARLIE BETTES: white with deep yellow stamens; large to very large, semi-double, E-M-1960.
CLARK HUBBS: brilliant dark red; full to loose peony form with fimbriated petals, M-1960.
CORONATION: white; very large, semi-double, vigorous, open, spreading growth, BBG-M-1954.
DAIKAGURA: bright rose pink splotched white; large, loose peony form, BBG-E-1891; Daikagura Pink, mutant, 1936; High Hat, blush pink mutant, 1945; Conrad Hilton, white mutant, 1955.
DON MAC: deep red; semi-double to loose peony form with curled and creped petals around a large mass of white stamens. An excellent garden variety, M-1956.
DONCKELARII: red marbled white in varying degrees; large, semi-double, slow, bush growth, BBG-M-1834.
DRAMA GIRL: deep salmon rose pink; very large, semi-double, vigorous, open, pendulous growth, BBG-M-1950.
DUCHESSE DE CASE (OPELOUSAS PEONY): flesh pink veined pink and edged white; medium, full peony form, vigorous, upright, compact growth, BBG-M-1908.
EARLY WOODVILLE RED: full peony; light red mutant of Woodville Red, E-1822.

CAMELLIAS

ELEGANS (CHANDLER): rose pink with center petaloids often spotted white; large, anemone form. Produces outstanding mutants, M-1831.

ELEGANS SPLENDOR: mutant; light pink-edged white with deep petal serrations, M-1969.

ELEGANS SUPREME: mutant of Elegans; rose pink with very deep petal serrations; anemone form, M-1960.

ELISABETH (ELIZABETH, TEUTONIA WHITE): white, sometimes striped light pink; medium, formal double, vigorous, upright, spreading growth, BBG-L-1851.

FAITH: rose pink; large, semi-double with irregular petals to anemone form with slightly variegated white petaloids, vigorous, sturdy upright growth, BBG-M-1956.

GOVERNOR MOUTON: Oriental red, sometimes splotched white; medium, semi-double to loose peony form, vigorous, upright growth, BBG-M-early 1900's.

GRAND SLAM: brilliant dark red; large to very large, semi-double to anemone form, M-1962.

GUILIO NUCCIO: coral rose pink; large to very large, semi-double with some upright petals. The variegated bloom is frequently the most beautiful, M-1956.

GUS MENARD: white with canary yellow petaloids; large anemone form with center petals divided by petaloids, M-1962.

HELEN BOWER (Chimera of Dr. Knapp grafted on Mathotiana Var.): bloom very similar to Mathotiana, BBG-M-1964.

HERME (JORDAN'S PRIDE): pink petals with irregular white border and streaked deep pink; medium, semi-double, vigorous, upright growth, BBG-M-1875.

IMPERATOR-FRANCE: dark red; full peony form, M-1908.

JULIA FRANCE: very light pink; large, semi-double with fluted petals, M-1958.

KRAMER'S SUPREME: turkey red; large to very large, full peony form. An excellent garden variety, M-1957.

LADY CLARE (EMPRESS): deep pink; large, semi-double, vigorous, bush growth, BBG-E-M-1887.

LADY VANSITTART: white striped, rose pink; medium, semi-double with broad, wavy-edged petals, slow, bush growth with holly-like foliage, BBG-M-L-1887.

LEUCANTHA: white form of Tricolor (Siebold); BBG-M-1937.

LITTLE BABE: dark red; small, rose form double, vigorous, compact growth, BBG-E-L-1974.

MAGNOLIAEFLORA: blush pink; medium, semi-double hose-in-hose type bloom, M-1886.

MATHOTIANA (PURPLE DAWN): crimson sometimes with purple cast; large to very large, rose form to formal double, BBG-M-1840's; there are many mutants of this variety, such as Flowerwood, Sultana, Red Wonder, Rosea Superba, etc.

MAMAM CACHET: white; medium, peony form, vigorous, upright growth, BBG-M-early 1900's.

MARGARET DAVIS: mutant; white to cream white with a few rose red lines and dashed and edged bright vermillion; medium, full peony form, M-1961.

MARIE BRACEY: coral rose; large semi-double to peony form. The variegated form is frequently the best bloom, BBG-E-M-1953.

MATHOTIANA SUPREME: mutant; crimson sometimes with purple cast; very large semi-double with loose irregular petals sometimes interspersed with stamens. An outstanding garden variety, M-1951.

MATHOTIANA, VAR. (JULIA DRAYTON): variegated form of Mathotiana; scarlet blotched white; large to very large, BBG.

MRS. D. W. DAVIS: blush pink; very large semi-double with large petals; also a peony form, M-1954.

PINK PERFECTION: shell pink; small, formal double, BBG-M-1875.

PRINCE EUGENE NAPOLEON (POPE PIUS IX): cherry red; medium, formal double with many small, rounded petals which are progressively smaller toward center, medium, compact, upright growth, BBG-M-1859.

PROFESSOR CHARLES S. SARGENT: dark red; medium, full peony form, vigorous, compact, upright growth, BBG-M-1925.

ROSE DAWN (DAVIS): deep rose pink; medium, formal to rose form double, vigorous, spreading

CAMELLIAS

BBG = growing at Bayou Bend Gardens   E = early blooming   M = mid-season blooming
L = late blooming   1800 = date of introduction.

growth, BBG-M-1944.

RUTLEDGE MINNIX: bright red; medium, semi-double, BBG-E-L-1959.

SARAH FROST: crimson, varying to deep rose pink; medium, formal double, vigorous, compact, upright growth, BBG-M-L-1841.

SNOWMAN: white; large, deep semi-double with curled and notched petals, M-1964.

TEUTONIA PINK: shell pink; medium, formal double with incurved petals, slow, compact growth, BBG-M-1937.

TOMORROW: strawberry red; large to very large, semi-double with irregular petals and large petaloids; to full peony form. A tremendous parent plant with 8 outstanding mutants, M-1953.

TOMORROW PARK HILL: mutant of Tomorrow Var.; light soft pink generally deepening toward edge and variegated white. Another mutant without the white variegation has now developed, M-1964.

TOMORROW'S DAWN: mutant; deep soft pink to light pink, shading to white at edge, with some white petaloids, M-1960.

TRICOLOR SUPERBA: variable colors from nearly white to solid red, but majority white-striped red or light pink margined white; large, semi-double, BBG-1944.

VILLE DE NANTES: dark red, blotched white; medium to large, semi-double with upright fimbriated petals, M-1910. Mutant of Donckelarii, 1834.

WHITE BY THE GATE: white, medium, formal double, vigorous, upright growth, BBG-M-1955.

CAMELLIA HYBRIDS
Species Reticulata and Hybrids with Reticulata Parentage

Reticulata 'Captain Rawes' and Reticulata 'Crimson Robe,' whether true reticulatas or hybrids, produce magnificent carmine and crimson flowers on strong-growing rangy plants outdoors in Houston. The following reticulata hybrids may be cold hardy and are worth a try outdoors, as well as protected, because of their parentage.

AZTEC: deep rose red; very large semi-double to loose peony form, M-1971; reticulata 'Crimson Robe' x japonica 'Lotus.'

DR. CLIFFORD PARKS: red with orange cast; very large anemone form, M-1971; reticulata 'Crimson Robe' x japonica 'Kramer's Supreme.'

DREAM CASTLE: silver pink; very large semi-double with fluted upright petals, M-1972; reticulata 'Crimson Rose' x japonica 'Coronation.'

FRANCIS L: rose pink; very large, semi-double with irregular, upright, wavy petals, M-1964; reticulata 'Buddha' x saluenensis 'Apple Blossom.'

LILA NAFF: a proven cold hardy variety; silver pink; semi-double with wide petals, often upright, M-1969; reticulata 'Butterfly Wings' x japonica.

MILO ROWELL: deep rich pink; very large, semi-double with irregular petals to loose peony form, M-1968; reticulata 'Crimson Robe' x japonica 'Tiffany.'

Hybrids with Other than Reticulate Parentage

The following group, except El Dorado, are saluenensis x japonica hybrids and bloom outdoors unprotected in Houston.

ANGEL WINGS: white washed and shaded orchid pink; semi-double with narrow upright petals, medium size, M-1970.

ANTICIPATION: deep rose; large peony form, M-1962.

CHARLEAN: medium pink with faint orchid overtone; large, semi-double, M-1963.

EL DORADO: light pink with lavender overtone; large full peony form; M-1967, petardii x japonica 'Tiffany.'

ELSIE JURY: clear medium pink; large, full peony form, M-L-1964.

JULIA HAMITER: delicate blush pink to white; medium, semi-double to rose form double, M-1964.

Species Hiemalis

SHISHI-GASHIRA: red; medium, semi-double to double, BBG.

Species Sinensis

C. SINENSIS: flowers, white; leaves elliptic with rounded apex, size quite variable according to the variety, maximum reported 5-3/4" x 2". The leaves constituted the tea of commerce; a shrub growing to a

CAMELLIAS

BBG = growing at Bayou Bend Gardens   E = early blooming   M = mid-season blooming
L = late blooming   1800 = date of introduction.

tree up to 53'. China, Tibet, Taiwan, Japan, Laos, Viet Nam, Siam, Burma, BBG.

CAMELLIA JAPONICA MINIATURES
FIRCONE: blood red; similar in shape to a fir cone; semi-double, M-1950.
LITTLE RED RIDING HOOD: crimson; formal double to peony form, M-L-1965.

LITTLE SLAM: rich red; full peony form, E-M-1969.
PEARL'S PET: rose red; anemone form, E-M-1959.
PINK SMOKE: light lavender pink; anemone form, M-1965.
TAMMIA: white with pink center and border; formal double with incurved petals in a geometric design, M-L-1971.

'Christian Dior' Hybrid Tea rose.

J.M.S.

Roses

"Oh, no man knows,
Through what wild centuries
Roves back the Rose."
—Walter de la Mare[1]

*C*onsidered "the oldest and most decorative of horticultural plants,"[1] the rose is now, by Congressional vote, the national flower of these United States. How appropriate that decision is, for the rose is surely nearly everyone's favorite flower. It is beautiful, elegant, romantic, colorful, fragrant, long-lasting, and grows in each of our 50 states.

Houston is indeed fortunate to have not only the American Rose Society's headquarters in nearby Shreveport, Louisiana, but also the largest rose society in the world, the Houston Rose Society, whose members receive the Rosette, a monthly informative bulletin covering all facets of rose growing in Houston.

Many of our local nurseries handle fresh #1 quality plants, particularly during January and February when gardeners' minds are on rose planting. Many other rose nurseries in Texas and in other states are happy to send a catalogue upon request.

There are several different types of roses which thrive in our temperate climate, although the humidity does attract fungus diseases. But there are remedies for those, and once you have enjoyed roses blooming 9 months of the year in your garden, the pleasure overshadows the extra attention.

If there is an area in your garden which benefits from at least 6 hours of sunshine daily, preferably morning, you can grow roses. Poor drainage can be corrected easily with raised beds, and the necessary formula for soil, provided in this chapter, is very simple. Locate the rose bed or planting site an adequate distance from large trees or shrubs to prevent their greedy roots from competing with those of the thirsty and hungry roses. Sunshine, good drainage, and fertile soil are the principal requisites for contented roses, adding, of course, an attentive gardener.

With so many types, forms, and colors of roses from which to choose, it is wise to plan, before buying, how you want to use them in your landscape. Are you anticipating long-stemmed beauties to cut for arrangements? Or lavish color in the garden from spring until Christmas? Do you favor a somewhat formal or a natural landscape? Do you envision a colorful climber on a wall or fence? Wouldn't roses be attractive on the terrace or balcony of your townhouse or apartment? Or do you prefer roses in containers to move as you please for maximum effect, for seasonal sunshine, and for convenient winter protection? There are roses to satisfy every situation.

[1]Dr. William C. Steere, *The Dictionary of Roses in Color*, Madison Square Press, Grosset & Dunlap, New York, New York.

'Sunbonnet' Hybrid Tea rose.

'Sarabande', beautiful contrast of yellow stamens with orange-red rose petals.

Classifications of Roses

Hybrid Teas: To 8 feet tall, elegantly formed flowers with high centers and usually long pointed buds. A wide range of colors and blends, some fragrant, fine for floral designs, and most long lasting when conditioned properly. Bloom 9 to 10 months a year when faded blooms are kept cut off to the second set of 5 leaflet leaves above the base of the bloom stem. Plant 3 to 4 feet apart in beds raised 8 to 12 inches above the surrounding ground level, usually in beds to themselves.

Polyanthas: To 4 feet tall, usually bushy, low plants bearing small roses in clusters. Perpetual bloomers in full sun when twiggy and dead growth are kept pruned away. Plant 1 to 1-1/2 feet apart in beds, hedges, or borders.

Floribundas or Hybrid Polyanthas: To 6 feet, a cross of hybrid teas and polyanthas, they usually bloom in clusters, seldom singly. Everblooming when spent blooms are pinched off. Usually planted 2 to 4 feet apart, depending on variety, for mass landscape effect in beds,

hedges, borders, or containers like half-barrels.

Grandifloras: To 9 feet tall. A cross between hybrid teas and floribundas. Produce "grand" roses blooming in long-stemmed clusters of hybrid tea-type roses. A wide choice of colors and bush sizes. Plant 4 to 6 feet apart depending on variety, usually in beds interspersed with hybrid teas, or in containers. Queen Elizabeth was the first grandiflora developed and still is the most popular.

Climbers: Many hybrid teas, floribundas, polyanthas, and miniature bush roses have climbing counterparts. Some roses are in climbing form only. They are the true climbing roses, not a climbing sport of a bush rose. Some climbing roses which may be trained to lean on a pole or post have long canes but the bush does not grow large; these are called pillar roses and may reach an 8-foot height. Climbers have long arching canes (branches) which produce flower stems at each leaf joint exposed to the sunshine. Secured in a horizontal position on a fence, wall, trellis, or arbor, these

'Dainty Bess' single, soft rose-pink,
charming, repeat bloomer. 1925

'Fragrant Cloud', a rose true to its name.

canes bloom heavily. Cut the spent blossoms to the second leaf from the stem source to encourage production of continuing bloom through the year. Climbers' canes allowed to grow upright produce blooms only near the tips. Some climbers bloom only in the spring, and many of the older types do not begin to bloom until the third year after planting, though they put out profuse growth. Some bloom in the spring; others are repeat bloomers. Some large climbers, like Mermaid, may be used as ground covers, especially on slopes, or to cover unsightly structures.

All roses bloom on new wood. Prune to remove dead wood, twiggy growth, spent blooms, and undesired lateral canes from the base of the plant or source. Climbers need space to grow in sunlight: miniatures, polyanthas and floribundas need 20 feet, and the large growers, like climbers Peace, Cecile Brunner, Don Juan, etc., at least 40 feet. Consider carefully the space available when selecting a climber and determine its mature size before buying.

Old Garden Roses: All types of roses in existence before 1867, the year the first hybrid tea rose was introduced. They include: Specie roses, Gallicas, Damasks, Centifolias, Mosses, Albas, Chinas, Noisettes, Portlands, Bourbons, Tea Roses, and Hybrid Perpetuals. The "Shrub Roses" are modern classes of hybrid musks, rugosas, kordesii, wichurianas (ramblers), and many others. These old roses are used primarily for landscape purposes, such as the cottage gardening type of design.

"Victorian Roses" is an arbitrary term some commercial sources apply to roses grown between 1867 and 1930 at the turn of the century, and refers to roses grown within the last 50 years. Paul Neyron and the climber Red Radiance are examples.

Tree Roses: The name describes the form of the plant, a rose bush budded to a strong 1 to 4-foot tall rose cane. Tree standards budded to floribunda or polyantha roses are shorter and easier to care for than those budded to hybrid tea roses. Short survival rate. For strength, plant a retaining rod (inserted into a length of old water hose) along with the tree rose bush, placing the supporting rod on the sunny

209

side of the bush to protect the cane from sunscald and wind as well as for support. Use heavy insulated electrical wire firmly secured around the support and rather loosely around the standard. As it appears on the standard, remove all growth from the ground at the base to the bud union atop the standard. Care for tree rose as for any other rose bush. Types are: Standard - 4 feet tall; Patio - 2 feet tall; Miniature - 1 and 1-1/2 feet tall. Tree roses grown in containers should have heavy weights in the bottom of the containers to avoid being blown over.

The term Patented or Patent Pending means the hybridizer has obtained a copyright on the introduction and no one else may legally propagate it for resale without permission from the hybridizer. Patents remain in effect for 17 years. Many excellent roses with expired patents are available at less cost than those with current patents, and are often excellent roses to buy.

Seeing roses growing in gardens is the best way to decide which roses you want. Visit rose gardens of friends and visit public plantings.

For example:
- The rose garden in Hermann Park is an All-American Rose Selection Display Garden of the American Rose Society. Open without charge.
- Old Rose plantings in Sam Houston Park in gardens of historic houses maintained by the Harris County Heritage Society: Old Garden Roses in the garden of the Nichols-Rice-Cherry house and Victorian Roses at the Staiti House. No cost.
- Civic rose plantings over the city include those at 700 Bagby Street and in a park at 600 Texas Avenue.
- The American Rose Center near Shreveport, Louisiana, displays numerous varieties of roses, and different ways of planting and growing roses. Entrance is free; parking is not.

Consult books about roses at the branches of the Houston Public Library. For a reference guide, the Houston Rose Society recommends the Ortho paperback, "All About Roses."

Rose Beds

Prepare the rose bed at least 8 weeks before planting time to allow for the settling and mellowing of the soil. The recommended planting time for Houston is the last 2 weeks of February. Roses planted in a newly prepared soil medium will settle too deeply into the ground, frequently causing the bushes to lean as the soil settles.

If this is your first rose bed, start small. Give yourself a chance to get acquainted with roses and their needs. For example, a bed 5 feet by 20 feet comprises 100 square feet with ample room. Various types of roses, some tall and slender, others short and wide, have their own space requirements. Placed away from trees and other plantings, the bed has enough space for a service walk around it and ample space to tend each rose bush without stepping in the bed, a practice which compacts the soil of the bed and also breaks the important feeder roots growing just beneath the soil's surface. Try to locate the bed away from prevailing winds, but if that is impossible, plant the bushes a bit closer together than usually recommended to lend each other support. However, it is best to allow ample space between bushes for good circulation of air to discourage fungus diseases and insect damage. Our temperate climate encourages rose bushes to grow larger than stated in the catalogue. Well-tended roses bring the reward of more blossoms. Keeping spent blooms cut is one of the open secrets for getting lots of rose blooms, requiring "servicing" each bush each week.

Site of Planting Bed
Requirements for growing healthy blooming roses are:
- At least 6 hours sunshine each day, preferably in the morning. The more sun the better.

A garden landscaped in roses.

- Excellent drainage. Before planting, follow suggestions in the DRAINAGE chapter to determine if drainage in your garden needs improvement. Without proper drainage, roses will die. Correcting the overall drainage in your garden is recommended. Establishing appropriate drainage in the rose planting bed is imperative. Beds raised at least 8 to 12 inches above native ground level is usually accomplished by using landscape timbers, railroad ties, or bricks to form a low wall to hold the prepared soil. Allow for drainage through the sides of whatever materials are used for the wall. If using brick, include retaining rods; otherwise, the bricks may pull apart because of the subsidence of the soil. A border of thickly planted liriope or monkey grass will hold the soil approximately 8 inches above native ground level, but the plants may become host to harmful spider mites.

The higher the bed, the better probability for good drainage and for circulation of air and water through the soil and around the roots.
- Fertile, friable (tillable), slightly acid soil with a pH of 6 to 6.5. An explanation of pH of soil is in the SOIL chapter. Test the soil annually.

Soil Preparation

Preparing the planting site in time to allow the soil to settle and mellow pays big dividends in future enjoyment. For the recommended mid-February planting, prepare the planting site in the fall before cold weather arrives, a better working time for the gardener, too. Preparing the soil properly allows roses to grow successfully.

Most soils in Houston are a heavy clay "gumbo," difficult to till and slightly alkaline. Roses need slightly acid soil, though some seem to like clay mixed with organic matter. Clay soils are easily recognized by their thick stickiness

211

when wet, but clay itself is fertile and its texture can be amended with incorporation of gypsum to rearrange the platelets in clay, thus making it of a more open texture and allowing air and water to circulate through it. The addition of quantities of decomposed organic matter and sharp sand and/or perlite improves its texture and fertility. Refer to the SOIL chapter for details in preparing the soil for planting. There is a difference of opinion about the incorporation and use of peat moss. Some growers consider peat moss a very unsatisfactory organic matter around roses. It is true that peat moss dries out easily and is difficult to moisten again.

For the raised planting bed, prepare the soil following the formula recommended by the Houston Rose Society for a 100 sq. ft. bed:

1/2 yard of fine ground pine bark mulch (not Deco bark)
1/2 yard builder's or sharp sand or 4 large sacks of Perlite
1/2 yard manure, preferably well-rotted barnyard
1/2 yard compost (refer to SOIL chapter)
25 lbs. agricultural gypsum
10 lbs. superphosphate or bone meal
5 lbs. complete commercial rose food.

Mix all ingredients thoroughly and shovel into a prepared planting site. This makes 4 cubic yards of soil and the mixing is best done on the apron of a concrete driveway using a scoop shovel.

Buying

It is best to buy bare-root #1 grade roses from sources which guarantee them to live and bloom the first season and to be true to name. When purchasing from mail-order growers, send your order in the fall to assure obtaining your particular choices. They will be shipped to you at the time you specify—mid-February for Houston. The rose bushes will be ready for planting and growing when you receive them. If you must delay in

planting, follow the directions on the package label; or if the planting bed is ready, proceed as follows: Upon receipt, submerge the roses in a large container of water (perhaps a bath tub) for 12 to 18 hours. Clip any restraining ties, and cut off any broken canes or roots.

- A #1 hybrid tea or grandiflora should have 3 or more strong canes. Light growing varieties may have 2 canes, but all types of roses should be branched no higher than 3 inches above the bud union.
- #1 floribundas need 3 or more strong canes, with small-growing varieties having 2 or more canes.
- #1 polyanthas need 4 or more strong canes.
- #1 climbers must have 3 or more strong canes.

At planting time remove one bush at a time and inspect it. Prune any spindly canes (branches) and top growth, and also remove damaged roots.

Dig a planting hole wide enough and deep enough to accomodate the bush, being sure the bud union (the swelling at the base of the main stem or trunk) will be above the soil level. Spread the roots in a natural, uncrowded manner. Gently work soil into the hole, around and over the roots to stabilize the bush, until the hole is about 2/3 filled. Pack soil firmly and fill hole with a slow flow of water. Allow to drain. Repeat the filling and draining to dispel harmful air pockets and to settle the soil. Check again that the bud union is above ground level. Fill the hole with soil and press soil firmly. Mulch plant with organic material for protection (See SOIL chapter for mulch). As the weather warms, remove the mulch gradually to expose the bud union and the canes to the sunshine encouraging them to leaf out. (If the mulch covering is left too long, roots instead of leaves may sprout from the canes)

At any time of year plant Old Garden own-root roses from containers or bare-rooted directly into the ground and water thoroughly. Plant them a little deeper than they were planted before they were dug. The soil line on the base

Yellow Lady Banksia climbing rose. Small roses in abundance in the spring. Old rose ca. 1800.

CWH

above the roots will guide you as to the depth. These roses grow quite rapidly. Don't let their small size discourage you.

When planting potted roses with blooms or new growth, wet the pot's soil thoroughly 24 hours before. Cut the bottom out of the pot and place pot in the hole. Slash the sides of the pot and remove, leaving the rose bush with its soil undisturbed. Cover ball with soil and proceed as directed previously. Do not wait until after March 1st to plant any roses for they will not have time to establish a root system to carry them successfully through a hot, dry summer, unless you have a method of careful and regular watering.

It is well to use a mixture of mulching materials to keep the mulch from getting packed together and shedding water like a thatched roof. Pine needles and oak leaves are the favorite mulch with most Houston rose growers; however, pine bark mulch, rotted manures, and garden compost from grass clippings, in combination, make fine mulch. Even old hay is acceptable as a mulch, despite its seeds and briars. When growing roses, mulching is truly necessary to conserve moisture, insulate the soil from summer heat as well as from sudden winter cold, retard weed growth, and to protect the vital feeder roots which lie close under the soil's surface. In the gradual decomposition of the mulch the soil and therefore the rose bushes are fed. The surface protection with mulch allows rose foods to be broadcast over the root areas and watered into the soil through the mulch materials. As water is so important to roses, so is the mulch which encourages growth in the soil of the micro-organisms which, when suspended in water, convert plant foods into a form the roots can absorb. Maintain about a 4-inch mulch over the entire planting site, but do not allow it to cover the bud union. The exception is when a freeze is predicted, which calls for covering the bud union and part of the cane for protection from the cold.

The mulch must be removed upon the return of warm weather, which might be the next day.

Allow the bush to bloom the first time and then sprinkle fertilizer lightly around the base of each bush, about 8 inches from the shank. Water in well and rinse off the foliage for safety's sake.

Miniature roses grow on their own roots and may be planted at any time as long as the plants will be kept watered and the foliage misted daily until they are well established. By fall they will be blooming. Treat miniatures the same way as their larger cousins, including mulching. Do not feed the miniatures much because they have small appetites. Overfeeding causes an excessive growth of the bushes themselves and also their blooms and petals. At regular intervals clip spent blooms and undesirable tall canes. Prune to force side growth for bushiness. About 3 times a year cutting some of the canes close to the ground forces new growth from the roots and controls their size; otherwise, the bushes grow rank and large, an appearance unbecoming to miniatures.

Suggested soil mixture for miniature roses[2]:

    1 bale (6 cu. ft.) Canadian (acid) peat moss *or*
        fine milled and screened pine bark mulch
    8 cu. ft. #6 Perlite
    6 cu. ft. fine pine bark mulch screened through
        1/4-inch mesh
    1 large wheelbarrow of washed sand
    2 cups 48% Superphosphate
    1 cup time-release rose food (13-13-13 Osmo-
        cote)
    3 lbs. cottonseed meal
    20 lbs. kiln run steer manure
    1 cup Sulfasoil
    1 qt. Carl Pool Root Activator.

    Mix well. Should be light, friable, and full of
        tiny air spaces for fine roots to develop
        and spread easily.

[2]Courtesy of Mrs. Margaret P. Sharpe, Consulting Rosarian, the Houston Rose Society.

214

Feed miniature roses about once a month with a soluble fertilizer reduced to half or less of the recommended strength for pot plants. Keep soil moist and mist as frequently as possible. Spray for blackspot and mildew control as for larger roses. Use Funginex in a small sprayer and drench each plant about every 7 to 10 days to cover the new growth. For an extremely severe blackspot infestation, use Triforene, the chief ingredient in Funginex, but stronger. One tablespoon of Funginex to the gallon of water. One teaspoon of Triforene to the gallon of water. Do not combine with any other materials. Both are systemic but of extremely low toxicity. They do not travel through the plant, remaining systemic where sprayed on the plant. Very effective for both blackspot and mildew fungus control, not an insecticide. Use regularly for control of fungus problems. This method makes rose growing a pleasure and works for all roses susceptible to fungus.

It is important that miniature rose bushes be protected from spider mite infestation. Spray with a strong stream of water daily until the mites disappear, usually about a week. Spider mites can destroy a miniature rose in 3 hours. Cold does not seem to hurt miniature roses, but it is wise to mulch and water them before freezes arrive.

Fertilizers

Rose bushes want to bloom, grow, and bloom. Consequently, they appreciate regular feedings of effective fertilizers such as natural organic fertilizers, including well-rotted manures and composts, but they need even more food to support the frequent blooming. Dry fertilizers, preferably those with an organic base, and many lawn fertilizers are appropriate for roses if used with care. Overfeeding is harmful and allowing dry fertilizer to touch the foliage can be disastrous. Always water copiously before and after fertilizing and rinse off the foliage after feeding. A rose fertilizer with a high phosphorus ratio (the middle number on the package) is the best to use; the phosphates encourage blooms. Nitrogen, the first number, stimulates foliage growth, and potash, the third number, encourages strong growth of stems and roots. See SOIL chapter. An effective rose food includes trace elements of the minerals which help the plant to utilize the soil nutrients. Broadcast the fertilizer over the mulch around the bushes in a thin coating. The amount depends on the size of the bush. One teaspoon per inch of bush height is safe. Water the fertilizer through the mulch. Some growers feed lightly every 2 weeks while others feed once a month. The 2-week intervals of light feeding seem to produce more bloom. Other growers fertilize every 2 weeks, alternating with dry food and liquid fertilizer sprayed on the plants. Liquid fertilizers are of short effectiveness. When poured on the soil, liquid fertilizers must be absorbed by the roots within 24 hours or the nutrients leach from the soil. Dry fertilizers have the advantage of breaking down slowly and helping neutralize the high sodium content in our treated city water.

Modern roses used for color in the landscape and for cut blooms benefit greatly from continuous fertilization. This is not as true of the old garden roses. The old timers respond somewhat but do not appreciate heavy fertilization. They have their own times to bloom. The age and size of the plants and the weather control their amount of bloom. Old garden roses cannot be forced and are rather easily killed with too much fertilizer. They respond to some fertilization and especially to the natural organic fertilizers: the manures, compost, and others. Soil bacteria and weather affect them even more.

A beneficial practice to follow is to stop fertilizing on the 1st of September. By the time the fertilizer is available to the plants' use, the weather is getting cool and frosts may occur. New growth on plants is susceptible to being severely nipped by frost or freeze and the plant may be severely damaged. As a rule, there are enough nutrients in the soil to sustain the rose bushes through the winter provided they receive plenty of water. Roses do not need as much water during the fall and winter as they do in spring and fall, but keep

a constant vigil to prevent the soil from becoming too dry during cool weather. The soil should be moist all the time.

Pruning Practices for Houston[3]

This is a condensation of the "Thompson" school of rose pruning considered best for our area. Some rosarians prune high, others prune low. High or low is largely a matter of personal preference and growing requirement. A pruning height of 24 to 30 inches is most common for hybrid tea and grandiflora roses.

Prune all roses about February 15, weather permitting. Use well-sharpened shears of the scissors type.

Steps to follow (in this order):
- Clean the dirt and mulch from the bud union.
- Stand off and examine the bush, observing where canes originate.
- Remove:
  1. any growth which originates from below the bud union; it is a sucker; and
  2. all dead, diseased, and deformed canes.
- Use these guidelines to determine which canes should be retained:
  1. A well-pruned rose bush should follow the variety's own growth habit.
  2. Prune a first-year bush for pattern formation.
  3. Retain three to six new canes.
  4. Do not rely on soft, green canes which have not had time to harden. If a late freeze occurs, they may not survive.
  5. Remove cross canes.
  6. Remove old canes if there are enough new or replacement canes for the desired vase-shaped bush pattern. Replacement canes should originate from the bud union or not more than eight inches above it.
- Cutting the canes, keep the following points in mind:
  1. Cut top canes at 20 to 30 inches from the

[3]Courtesy of the Houston Rose Society and J. M. Stroud

bud union. Prune on a slant 1/4 inch above a bud.

2. A mature rose bush should not have a jointed or forked terminal. However, a jointed or forked cane may be retained on a first-year bush to complete the desired shape.

3. Do not leave stubs at bud union. Clean corky and dead tissue from bud union. (This is very important. "Basal breaks" or replacement canes renew the life of the bush. Their development is stimulated by sunlight on the bud union but is discouraged by stubs, old canes, and corky tissue on the bud union or low on old canes.)

- Remove all twiggy growth and all leaves to force dormancy.
- Sealing cuts is no longer recommended.
- Water ground thoroughly.
- Use a cleanup spray. A fungicide mixture used according to label directions will control over-wintering problems. Spray bed area *immediately* after pruning and mulch thoroughly. Do not wait for leaves to appear.
- Spray again with fungicide in about 10 days. Drench canes and bud union. Also spray any other host plants for fungus diseases.

All roses require pruning to keep them within bounds. Climbing roses bloom on mature wood, on canes at least 2 years old. Cut out the very oldest canes, all dead and weak wood, and all twiggy growth to keep climbers shaped. When in doubt, leave an old cane until after the first spring bloom. If it does not produce blooms, cut it out at the juncture with another cane or at the trunk or base.

For pruning miniature roses, use small pruning shears, like the Corona Mini-Shear #6. Prune to the best eyes on the most productive new canes. Cut back all canes and growth to 6 or 8 inches, depending on the vigor of the variety. New growth keeps miniatures young. After pruning, water and feed with 1/2 strength mixture of Carl Pool Instant Rose Food or Terra Tonic. Spray with a fungicide.

Prune your bushes to shape the way you like them, but follow the basics of pruning. Pruning too early, before mid-February, puts the new growth at risk of damage from a late freeze. Water thoroughly and spray with a fungicide.

Tree roses are pruned the same way that hybrid teas and floribundas are pruned. No growth should be permitted below the bud union of the rose bush atop the standard.

Old garden roses do not appreciate much, if any, pruning of live wood. Cut dead wood and twiggy growth as they appear, but otherwise prune very little.

Watering

Generally speaking roses need 2 inches of water per week to thrive and bloom well. Water soil before and after fertilizing. See WATER chapter for methods.

Allow the first blooms on new bushes to remain until they have faded. Thereafter you may cut them for arrangements, just don't cut the stems too long until the bushes develop. Reading the ARRANGEMENTS FROM YOUR GARDEN chapter will be helpful for suggestions to cut and condition roses.

The best defense against pests is a steady program of sensible gardening practices: prune dead wood regularly, remove debris to keep the garden clean, and give the plants the sunshine, fertile soil, and water they like. Healthy bushes are more resistant to attack. Practice keen observation in your daily visits to your garden and read the DISEASES, INSECTS & WEEDS chapter for common sense management. The WATER chapter describes various watering methods and ways to conserve water.

ROSES

HYBRID TEAS

BRANDY - apricot blend, fragrant
CHABLIS - white
CENTURY TWO - pink, fragrant
DOUBLE DELIGHT - red blend, fragrant
FIRST PRIZE - pink blend, fragrant
FOLKLORE - orange blend, fragrant
FRAGRANT CLOUD - orange-red, fragrant
LEMON SPICE - yellow, fragrant
OREGOLD - yellow, fragrant
PEACE - yellow blend
PERFUME DELIGHT - pink, fragrant
SWARTHMORE - pink blend, fragrant
UNCLE JOE (TORO) - dark red
VOODOO - orange blend, disease resistant

GRANDIFLORA

ARIZONA - orange blend
CAMELOT - medium pink
MOUNT SHASTA - white, fragrant
QUEEN ELIZABETH - medium pink, fragrant
SONIA - pink blend

CLIMBERS

BLAZE - red, vigorous
AMERICA - orange blend
DON JUAN - dark red
GOLDEN SHOWERS - yellow
RHONDA - pink
(Many other roses in climbing form)

MINIATURES

BEAUTY SECRET - red
ETHEL ORR - rose-red
JEAN KENNEALLY - apricot blend
MILLIE WALTERS - dark pink
MINNIE PEARL - pink blend
OLYMPIC GOLD - medium yellow
PEACHES 'N CREAM - pink blend
RAINBOW'S END - yellow blend
SNOW BRIDE - white

FLORIBUNDAS

ANGEL FACE - lavender, fragrant, medium
APRICOT NECTAR - apricot blend, fragrant, medium
CHARISMA - red blend, small
CIRCUS - yellow blend, medium
CHERISH - medium pink, tall
EUROPEANA - dark red, wide
FIRST EDITION - orange blend, medium
GRUSS AN AACHEN - 1909, pink, fragrant, 3-4', reblooms
IVORY FASHION - cream-white, fragrant, tall
PINK ROSETTE - light pink, medium
PLAYBOY - orange blend, tall
SUNSPRITE - deep yellow, fragrant, medium

POLYANTHAS

CECILE BRUNNER - light pink, medium, 1881
CHINA DOLL - pink, small
MARGO KOSTER - coral, medium
THE FAIRY - pink, tall, 1932

OLD GARDEN ROSES

CHEROKEE ROSE - Species, 1540, single white, fragrant, 10-12'
DUCHESSE DE BRABANT - Tea, 1857, white, fragrant, 3-5', reblooms
GRUSS AN TEPLITZ - China, 1894, double red, fragrant, 4-6', reblooms, shrub
LOUIS PHILIPPE - China, 1834, double crimson, fragrant, 3-5', reblooms
MERMAID - Species Hyb., 1918, single yellow, fragrant, 15-30', reblooms
PAUL NEYRON - Hybrid Perpetual, 1869, lavender-pink, fragrant, 5-6', reblooms
PRAIRIE FIRE - medium red
SOUVENIR DE LA MALMAISON - Bourbon, 1843, double pink, fragrant, 3-4', reblooms
YELLOW LADY BANKS - Species, 1815, double, 5-7', reblooms

Beds of larkspur, alyssum, pansies, calendulas, and ornamental cabbage.

Annuals & Perennials

"The Earth laughs in flowers."
— Denham

*F*or a garden full of vitality and color...plant annuals and perennials. For a garden of seasonal changes...enjoy annuals and perennials. For a garden of fragrances...select annuals and perennials. For a delightful but inexpensive garden...grow annuals from seed and perennials from friends' divisions.

Chinese proverb: "All the flowers of all the tomorrows are in the seeds of today."

Annuals are flowering plants which complete their life span in one season, from seed to plant to flower to seed. They may be planted from seed or small plants. Sow annuals any month you choose and marvel at the eternal miracle of the seed. During the cold months, the seeding can be done in the greenhouse or a cold frame or even on a bright window sill because annuals are not "hardy," meaning they are not tolerant of very cold weather. Plants of annuals should not be placed outside until the freezes are definitely past. However, annual seeds often lie dormant in the cold soil waiting for the sun's warmth to sprout again. That process is called "reseeding." Seed can be harvested from non-hybrid plants for sowing the next year.

There are annuals suitable for numerous landscaping purposes, all easily grown from seed. For example: amaranthus tricolor (one of two annuals nicknamed "Joseph's Coat") makes a stunning 4-foot hedge, as does castorbean. For a tropical effect, coleus offers its bright-hued foliage. Low, ground-covering sweet alyssum cloaks itself with white or purple blossoms. From tiny seeds, impatiens plants fill our shady summer-to-fall gardens with color.

In common usage and in this book, perennials are defined as flowering plants with herbaceous (fleshy) stems and a life span of at least three years. Many other plants live that long or longer but they differ from perennials in other ways: Trees have woody or wood-producing stems. Bulbs have the ability to store food for next year's growth, an ability perennials don't have.

Perennials prepare for next year's growth through a strong root system, which usually survives freezes, thus allowing the plant to rejuvenate itself the following spring. The fleshy-stemmed foliage may collapse down to the ground in a cold winter, but don't despair. New growth will probably sprout with the return of warm weather. The ability of perennials to renew themselves from their roots classifies them as being "root-hardy."

Although Houston's climate seldom meets the usual requirement of most perennials, that is, a well-defined dormancy period brought about by sustained cold weather, there are numerous perennials which thrive here. Some of these are considered "natives"; others have been "adapted" to our particular micro-climate.

Many perennials bloom the first year from seed, but they are usually planted from divisions of the multi-rooted plants. The roots multiply rapidly, becoming too crowded for their own good. Every three or four years the crowded plants should be dug up. Separate the roots carefully and replant, leaving sufficient space between them for their future growth. If you don't have space elsewhere in the garden to plant the leftovers, exchange them with gardener friends. That's why perennials are called "friendship plants."

Perennials range in height from 4 inches to 3 feet and vary widely in foliage and flower. Some of the familiar perennials which grow in our Houston gardens are: ajuga, the 5-inch high border plant which forms rosettes of leaves low to the ground and puts out blue or white flowers; the bright-flowered, evergreen coreopsis with its 2-foot high lacy foliage, native to much of our state of Texas; the straight-stemmed shasta daisy whose single or double white flowers are prized for arrangements; that summer favorite lantana which tolerates our summer heat and keeps smiling; and the native Louisiana phlox with its flowers of blue, the rarest color in the garden.

There is another type of plant in the same category with annuals and perennials—the biennials—which live two years, usually developing their vegetative growth (roots, stems, and leaves) the first year and blooming, setting seed, and dying the second year. They, too, prefer climates with defined seasons. Sweet William and pinks (both dianthus) and hollyhock are three of the few biennials planted here. However, one-year-old plants of biennials can be purchased and enjoyed in our gardens during their second or blooming year. In effect, they are treated as annuals and seldom referred to as biennials.

Reading the HINTS FOR LANDSCAPING chapter will assist you in the effective placement of annuals and perennials.

As you ponder which varieties to choose, think about the color of their flowers and when they bloom. The very bright colors—yellow, orange, and red—are considered hot or warm. They attract the eye immediately. The cool colors—blue, green, and violet hues—along with all pastels are tranquil colors which tend to fade into the distance, making their location seem farther away than it really is. White blossoms seem to cool the garden and are particularly effective at night. Think also what color of flowers you like to use in your house and and if the garden's colors complement those in the house.

Annuals and perennials combine easily and attractively in the same bed—as long as they share similar growing requirements. A constant rule in all planting: Before buying any plant or seed, familiarize yourself with the sun, shade, soil, drainage, and space conditions in your own garden. Then, select plants whose cultural needs can be met in your garden. When grouping the plants, combine those which share the same needs, taking care not to crowd them. Studying the charts for blooming time will allow you to select varieties to provide a succession of bloom. Remember to consider fragrance also.

With careful placement, perennials can effectively screen the unattractive but necessary dying foliage of bulbs. Keep in mind Nature's way—no polka-dotted single plantings. Instead, group three or more of the same variety and color together, or place them in broad ribbons of color. Planted with shrubs as their background, annuals and perennials show off their color. Consider the foliage color and texture when grouping differing varieties. Another thought: Plant annuals and perennials in containers to use as accents. Just move them into a protected area during cold spells. Fragrant ones are delightful up close.

If you enjoy cutting flowers and foliage for arrangements in your home, refer to the ARRANGEMENTS FROM YOUR GARDEN chapter for suggestions for plants with suitable

Bright red plumes of celosia.

perennials. If your garden has drainage problems, read the DRAINAGE chapter. If you are beginning your first garden, the SOIL and WATERING chapters offer suggestions which may save you many a future headache.

Summary

Success and pleasure in gardening can be better assured by planning ahead. Visiting gardens and nurseries and studying appropriate information are the background. Preparing the soil several weeks before planting time will allow your plants a healthy start. If you have determined the mature size of each variety, you can judge how far apart to place the plants. The chart ANNUALS AND PERENNIALS suggests distance for many. Allow enough space for natural growth, but close enough so the mature plants will cover the ground, thus discouraging weed growth. The bed should appear comfortably filled with

arrangement material. Studying the chart ANNUALS AND PERENNIALS in this book will give you the information you need to make decisions for plants you will enjoy in your garden. The chart gives the cultural requirements, size, color, and time of blooming for each plant. Such knowledge enables you to select those plants which will thrive in your garden.

Visits to homes and gardens during the River Oaks Garden Club's Azalea Trail every March, as well as to the Mercer Arboretum gardens, Bayou Bend Gardens, and nurseries, will allow you to see annuals and perennials growing.

Though some annuals and perennials tolerate or even prefer shade, the majority needs sun, lots of it, 4 to 6 hours a day, though shade from the hottest summer afternoon sun is welcomed by plants and gardeners alike. Loose, fertile soil, excellent drainage, and sufficient water are the remaining requirements for most annuals and

Coleus leaves of many different patterns of color.

221

blooming plants, but not overcrowded.

The following formula for planting seeds is also appropriate for plants. The only exception is that the soil need not be as fine for plants as it must be for seeds, but should be deeper for perennials' long roots.

To prepare a seeding bed:
- Select an area which receives at least four hours of sun, preferably six hours.
- With shovel or fork break up the soil, removing weeds and their roots as you go. NEVER work, till, hoe, or use heavy machinery on wet soil. The resulting compaction is very difficult to correct.
- Till or hoe the soil until the clods are broken up. If the soil is very dry, moistening it a little may help. If the soil is typical "gumbo" clay found in Houston, wet it, then cover it with gypsum and let it set for several days. Gypsum helps break up the clods. Otherwise, add loam to your soil.
- Even with the addition of loam, the soil will benefit from a layer, 2 to 4 inches thick, of a combination of:
  1. Well-rotted compost with aged manure and pre-dampened peat moss to make the soil more hospitable to the all-important soil micro-organisms, to improve aeration and moisture retention, and to increase the friability (the ability of soil to crumble). See SOIL chapter.
  2. Bonemeal, cottonseed meal, blood meal, and phosphorus for nutrition.
  3. Gypsum to loosen the soil.
  4. Sulphur to acidify the usually alkaline soils in Houston (a test of your garden soil by the nearest County Extension office is the only sure way to know the composition and needs of your garden soil).
  5. Sand for improved texture and porosity.
  6. Balanced fertilizer (2 pounds to 100 square feet of area) to feed the plants.
- Work or till the soil to mix it thoroughly into a homogenous whole.

- Water the bed thoroughly to help the additives meld.
- Covering the bed with plastic discourages weeds.

Several days before planting, remove plastic, work the soil again, rake, and moisten it. Plants should thrive in such soil.

When ready to plant, loosen top 2 or 3 inches, rake smooth again, and with your finger form drills (little ditches) to the depth suggested on the seed packet. If the seed is very fine, you may mix it in a salt shaker with sand and shake seed into the drills. Cover seeds with the loose soil. Press soil firmly and water with fine spray, enough to get the moisture down to the seeds. Mark the rows with the name of the annuals you planted. You think you'll remember, but you won't. All you do now is watch for the sprouts, the cotyledons, to push up through the soil, followed by the first two "true" or typical leaves. Until you gain experience in identifying the leaves, don't pull up anything green. Wait until you're sure which is a weed and which is an annual. Keep the soil damp.

In a few weeks the little plants may be transplanted to the location you had planned and prepared, with soil similar to that of the seeding bed to lessen the shock of transplanting. With a trowel, remove each plant along with a goodly amount of soil around its roots, and, wasting as little time as possible, get it into place in a suitably sized hole. The roots should, of course, be covered, but take care not to set the plant too deep. The transplant should be at the same depth in which it was growing originally—no deeper. Push the soil carefully around the seedling, press gently but firmly, and water carefully. After watering, you may need to add a little more soil. Now mix a transplanting solution with water according to directions on the container, and pour or sprinkle it gently to soak the plants.

Plan to transplant on a cloudy day or in late afternoon; but if you must plant in the sun, protect the seedlings with a branch from a shrub

The brilliance of Louisiana phlox emphasized by the white of Sweet Alyssum.

P.P.

as a tent. They will surely wilt without protection from the sun.

If you buy plants, still follow the procedure described above for seedlings. Tap the little pot against a hard surface to loosen the soil and gently shake the plant out. Loosen the soil around the roots a bit and position the seedling in a hole. Proceed as above. If the little plants are in bloom, steel yourself and pinch off the blooms and the tip of the branch, thus encouraging the plant to branch out. The tip of each increased number of branches will produce flowers. Presto! More flowers in your garden.

Keep transplants damp but not soaking wet until you see they are putting out new growth; then water regularly to prevent the soil from drying out, harming the roots.

When planting or transplanting divisions or containers of perennials, prepare the soil to the depth of the length of the roots, probably down to 8 or 10 inches, if not more. Care for the perennials just as you do the annuals. Since they have more mature roots, you may add a teaspoon of fertilizer in each hole and stir it into the soil at the bottom, adding a little soil to cover the fertilizer so as not to burn the tender roots.

Bonemeal is a safe fertilizer for this purpose. Whatever kind of plant you are putting in the ground, BE CERTAIN that it sits in the ground at the same level it was before or a little higher than soil level for it will inevitably sink down a bit. In Houston climate, drainage is of great importance. Planting high helps assure drainage.

Also allow sufficient room for the plant to grow to its innate size. Fewer plants with ample room will out-flower more plants too crowded. When the plants have attained more height and strength, spread a mulch of compost, or rotted manure mixed with pine bark, around them to retain moisture. Using a mixture of organic materials in a mulch prevents compaction. Keeping the mulch damp prevents it from blowing away.

Plants have an inner compulsion to propagate their kind. Annuals accomplish their purpose by producing flowers which go to seed and lie dormant until their appointed season. Then, the seeds germinate and begin the reproductive process all over again. Since we gardeners are interested in having as many flowers as possible, we must trick the plants by cutting the blossoms, either fresh ones for use in arrangements or those which have faded, to encourage the plant to

223

bloom again in its desire to reproduce its species. Pinching off flowers at their base is called "deadheading" and is one effective way to increase flowering. The other is to fertilize the plants each month through their season, especially with a fertilizer high in phosphorus content. There are liquid fertilizers to mix in solution with water and pour around the plants, and there are dry, granular fertilizers to scratch in gently around the base of the plants. Water both before and after using a dry fertilizer to prevent burning the plants and to liquify the fertilizer to activate it. Always follow the manufacturer's directions. More than the recommended dosage can burn or over-stimulate the plant.

However, each kind of plant has its season to bloom. When its time in the sun is over, it will go to seed and die. *Interesting project:* When you see seed pods on your plants, take the time to sit quietly to witness a thrilling event. Pansies' seed pods pop open and bluebonnets' green-bean-like seed pods twist in a quicker-than-the-eye corkscrew way. Seeds from both flowers are cast several feet away onto the ground. Dandelions and Mexican Love Vine have seeds attached to an airy substance acting as wings. When the seeds are at the exact ripeness, a kindly wind lifts them up into the air and carries them to land who knows where. What a sight!

Houston's near tropical climate not only permits gardening but encourages it at least ten months a year. With their habit of blooming brilliantly and bounteously, annuals and perennials are a delight. Share your garden. Plant a bed of these colorful beauties and enjoy the expressions of pleasure on the faces of passersby. Brighten the corner where you are.

Guidelines for selecting bedding plants:
- The tallest are not necessarily the best. Short, bushy plants are better.
- Dark green stems and leaves are a sign of good health. Bare stems, whose lower leaves have fallen off, and yellow-green foliage indicate trouble.

- Check carefully for insects on the top and bottom sides of leaves. Some bugs are very tiny, like aphids and red spiders, which often hide where the leaf and stem join. Don't take home any more insects to add to those you probably already have.
- Look at the growing medium. Many growers now use a soil-less mix which dries out quickly and is often difficult to moisten even when the plants are planted and watered. Peat moss is notorious that way.
- Even though they seem cheaper at the time, don't buy plants growing together in a small box. Their roots will suffer when the plants are pulled apart to plant. Buy plants in separate containers, even 2-inch ones.
- Inquire when the plants were fertilized or sprayed. Don't feed if the plants have recently been fed, unless perhaps to use a *weak* solution of root stimulant.
- Apply these guidelines to larger plants also.

Annuals and perennials also bloom very well when planted in containers. With careful selection there can be garden flowers virtually all year, and the containers are easy to move into the appropriate light as the sunlight varies. The movable bouquets are especially appreciated during the cooler months when there may not be as much color in the garden. Plants in containers need more frequent watering, but using the following method of double-potting can reduce that necessity. Place the planted container into another 3 or 4-inch larger container which has gravel in the bottom. Fill the space between the two pots with gravel, sand, or mulch to protect the plants not only from drying out, but also from cold winds. Of course, these double pots—as all pots—must be protected from really cold or freezing weather. Move them into the house, garage, or greenhouse until the cold spell has passed. Bulbs may be interspersed with lower growing annuals or perennials. For example, tulips or Dutch Iris overplanted with pansies or pinks.

GARDEN COLOR WITH ANNUALS AND PERENNIALS

Basic needs for a blooming garden: At least 5 hours of sunshine, morning best, preferably raised beds for good drainage. Fertile soil with 1/3 organic matter. Deep watering as needed. Good drainage. Monthly feeding with complete high phosphorus fertilizer and trace elements, with an organic base. Mulch around all plants all year for temperature protection. Quality seeds and plants. Caring gardeners who learn the mature size, shape, color, and cultural needs of each plant BEFORE BUYING. Dead twigs and faded flowers removed.

| A = Annual   B = Biennial   P = Perennial   spp. = more than one species   H = Hardy |||||||
| HH = Half-hardy; freezes   T = Tender; killed by freeze   E = Evergreen |||||||
Common Name *Botanical Name*	Height	Space Apart	Time To Plant	Color	Time of Blooming	Comments
AGERATUM A T HH *Ageratum Houstonianum*	6-18"	8-12"	Mar.-Aug.	Blue, White, Pink	Apr.-Nov.	Sun to light shade. Loose, moist garden soil. Do not allow to dry out completely. Dwarf variety also. Grows also from divisions and cuttings.
AGERATUM, WILD (MISTFLOWER) P *Eupatorium coelestinum*	24"	18"	Sept.-May	Blue, White	July-Oct.	Sun. Any moist garden soil, 3" flower heads. Use coarse mulch to conserve moisture. Also from divisions. Texas NATIVE. Drought tolerant.
AJUGA (BUGLEWEED) P E *Ajuga reptans* *A. reptans* 'Alba' and 'Tricolor'	5"	6"	Apr.-Nov.	Blue White Rose-Pink	Apr.-Sept.	Filtered sun, shade. No hot summer sun. Loose, sandy, fertile, slightly acid soil. Requires excellent drainage to protect from fungal disease. Likes to be damp but not wet. Water especially in hot summers. Forms flat rosette of leaves. Foliage may be dark green, bronze or purple depending on variety. Ground cover for small areas, as between stepping stones or in narrow spaces.
ALTERNANTHERA (JOSEPH'S COAT) A T *Alternanthera* spp.	6-12"	10"	May (Plants)	Colored Foliage Yellow, Orange, Red, Green	Summer	Sun or part shade. Garden soil. Water when dry. Feed. Colorful as border or ground cover in small area.

GARDEN COLOR WITH ANNUALS AND PERENNIALS

A = Annual   B = Biennial   P = Perennial   spp. = more than one species   H = Hardy
HH = Half-hardy; freezes   T = Tender; killed by freeze   E = Evergreen

Common Name *Botanical Name*	Height	Space Apart	Time To Plant	Color	Time of Blooming	Comments
ALYSSUM, SWEET A HH *Lobularia Maritima*	2-6"	6"	Oct.-Mar.	White, Lavender, Rose	Feb.-Frost	Sun, light shade. Any well-drained soil, not too wet. Cut back after bloom or frost damage for renewed growth and bloom. New heat resistant varieties.
AMARANTHUS (JOSEPH'S COAT) A T *Amaranthus tricolor*	3-4'	18-36"	Mar.-Apr.	Red- Yellow- Green Foliage	June-Oct.	Sun. Garden soil, not too rich. Half-hardy. Coarse, colorful. Keep blooms pinched off for better foliage.
ANCHUSA (SUMMER FORGET- ME-NOT) A or P HH *Anchusa azurea* (*A. italica*) *A. capensis*	3-5' 18"	2'	Feb.-Mar.	Blue Pink	May-July	Full sun. Moist, not too fertile soil. Good drainage. Water sparingly. Good for cutting. Dwarf variety also. Best in masses. Reseeds. Tiny flowers in loose clusters. Propagate from cuttings.
ARCTOTIS (AFRICAN DAISY) A T *Arctotis stoechadifolia*	1-2'	12"	Sept.-Mar. (Seeds) Nov.-Mar. (Plants)	White and Lavender	Nov.-May	Best in sun. Light, dry, sandy soil. Likes cool weather. Flowers close late afternoon. Excellent for cutting.
ASTER, ALPINE P *Aster alpinus*	15"	12"	Mar., July, Sept.	Lavender, Pink, Blue	Fall	Sun. Garden soil. Good drainage. Keep faded flowers picked off.
ASTER, CHINA A T *Callistephus chinensis*	6-18"	8"	Feb.-Mar. (Seeds)	Various	May-June	Sun or light shade. Rich soil. Little water. Fine for cutting.
FRIKARTII P	12-18"	12"	Apr. or Oct.	Blue	Oct.-Nov.	Same as China Aster above.
BALLOON-FLOWER P H *Platycodon* spp.	24"	12"	Feb.-Mar.	Blue, White, Red	May-July	Sun or partial shade. Light, sandy, well-drained soil. Water. Fine for cutting. Hates wet soil in winter.
BALSAM, GARDEN A H *Impatiens balsamina*	12-18"	6-8"	Mar.-Sept.	Pink, White, Red	May-Nov.	Sun or filtered shade. Fertile, sandy, moist soil. Good drainage. Most are double, rose-flowered, clinging along stem.

GARDEN COLOR WITH ANNUALS AND PERENNIALS

Common Name *Botanical Name*	Height	Space Apart	Time To Plant	Color	Time of Blooming	Comments
BALSAM, SULTAN (SULTANA) A T *Impatiens Wallerana* *I. Sultanii*	18"	12"	Mar.-May	Rose, Salmon, White, Red, Bicolors, Purple, Lavender	May-Oct.	Partial shade. Rich, moist soil. Dwarf and midget forms. Accepts seashore conditions. Profuse bloomer.
BEGONIA, REIGER, P T *Begonia x hiemalis* 'Rieger's Schwabenland'	18-20"	10-12"	Mar.-Apr.	Red		Sun, but not full hot sun. Keep moist in loose fertile soil with some pre-dampened peat moss. Protect. Good house plant if enough light.
BEGONIA, *Richmondensis* A	24"	12"	Mar., July, Sept.	Pink	Spring, Fall	Semi-shade or sun. Garden soil. Likes good drainage. In sun pink of flowers intensifies and leaves get reddish cast, like Begonia Scarletta.
BEGONIA, WAX A or P T *Begonia semperflorens-* *cultorum Hybrids*	8-18"	1'	Apr.-Sept.	White, Pink, Red, Orange-Red	May-Frost	Needs cool shade to germinate, then light sun or filtered shade in moist, humusy soil. Many varieties. 'Scarletta,' red, and others tolerate sun. 'Charm' has variegated foliage. Single and double flower forms. Remove faded flowers to avoid spread of disease.
BELLS-OF-IRELAND A H *Moluccella laevis*	24"	12"	Early Spring	Green Bracts	Spring- Summer	Sun. Well-drained soil. Water when dry. Prized for arrangements. Flowers dry well. Best grown from plants.
BLUE DAZE A T *Evolvulus* *nuttaliana*	12"		Mar.-Aug.	Blue	May-Frost	Sun. Garden soil. Water. Sprawling habit. Flowers close after noon.
BLUE CARDINAL FLOWER P *Lobelia x Gerardii*	36"	12"	Mar.-Apr.	Violet-Blue	July-Oct.	Sun to part shade. Moist loose fertile soil. Large spikes of dramatic flowers. Vigorous and easy.

GARDEN COLOR WITH ANNUALS AND PERENNIALS

Common Name *Botanical Name*	Height	Space Apart	Time To Plant	Color	Time of Blooming	Comments
BLUEBONNET A H *Lupinus subcarnosus* *L. texensis*	12"	8-12"	Aug. or Jan. (Seeds) Fall and Spring (Plants)	Blue	Apr.-May	Full sun. Light, well-drained soil. Water when dry. Good for cutting. Naturalizes. Mass rural planting suggested. Texas NATIVE.
BOLTONIA P *Boltonia asteroides*	2-3'	30"	Mar.-Sept.	White, Pink, Lilac	Aug.-Sept.	Sun or shade. Any soil; divisions or seeds. Average water. Star-like flowers. B. *Latisquama nana* multiplies. Roots become invasive. Divisions root easily.
BOUVARDIA, SCARLET P *Bouvardia ternifolia*	2'	12"	Mar.-Apr.	Scarlet	Summer	Full sun. Garden soil. Good drainage. Hardy. Attracts butterflies and hummingbirds. West Texas NATIVE.
BROWALLIA A T *Browallia Americana,* *B. speciosa*	12-18"	6-10"	March	Blue, White, Purple	May-Aug.	Filtered shade. Rich, well-drained soil. Water when dry. Reseeds. Pinch plants back for more compact growth. Nice in hanging baskets. Also grown from cuttings. Tender.
BUTTERFLY FLOWER (POOR MAN'S ORCHID) A HH *Schizanthus* *pinnatus*	12-18"	6"	Sept.-Mar.	Pink, Yellow, Violet,Red, Gold, Magenta	Apr.-May	Partial shade. Likes rich,moist, sandy soil with compost. Fine for cutting. Requires perfect drainage. Subject to aphids. Difficult to grow. Protect from cold.
BUTTERFLY WEED (MILKWEED) P *Asclepias tuberosa*	10"-3'	14"	Sept.-Feb. (Tuberous Root)	Yellow, Orange, Red, Purple	Mar.-Oct.	Full sun to part shade. Any well-drained, sandy soil. Water regularly. Very drought resistant but needs watering. Daisy-like flowers on flat mat-rosette of foliage. Tiny flowers in large heads. Bush, shrub-like. Best in narrow spaces as bulb cover. Texas NATIVE. Keeping spent flowers picked encourages bloom. Attracts bees, hummingbirds and butterflies.

GARDEN COLOR WITH ANNUALS AND PERENNIALS

Common Name *Botanical Name*	Height	Space Apart	Time To Plant	Color	Time of Blooming	Comments
CALENDULA (POT MARIGOLD) A H *Calendula officinalis*	8-20"	12"	Sept.-Feb.	Lemon thru Orange	Nov.-May	Full sun. Fertile soil. Feed with superphosphate. Likes cool weather but needs protection in freeze. Nice for cutting beds or containers. Reseeds. Subject to mildew. Keep foliage dry.
CALICO PLANT A *Alternanthera ficoidea* cv. 'Bettzickiana'	24-30"	12"	Apr. and Sept.			Semi-shade or A.M. sun. Known for its variegated foliage: cream, salmon, and green. Rare purple-leaved form, too. Growth similar to Coleus.
CALLIOPSIS *C. tinctoria* A H	Dwarf: 8-12" Regular: To 36"	12"	March	Crimson, Yellow, Orange, Bicolors	All Summer	Sun. Any garden soil. Good drainage especially during winter. Cuts well.
CANDYTUFT A or P HH *Iberis* spp.	10-18"	6"	Sept.-Mar.	White thru Red, Lavender	Nov.-May	A.M. sun to light shade. Light, fertile soil. Useful for border and cutting. Hyacinth-flowered type best. *I. sempervirens* good for ground cover. Free bloomer.
CAPE JEWELS A or P *Nemesia*	12"	10"	Oct.-Jan.	Bright Colors	Mar.-May	Full to part sun. Rich garden soil with good drainage. Very showy flowers in wide range of colors, resembling penstemons.
CAPE MARIGOLD A HH *Dimorphotheca sinuata*	12-18"	6-12"	Mar.-Apr. (Seeds)	Cream, Orange, Salmon, Rose	Apr.-June	Best in sun. Well-drained, sandy loam with humus. Beautiful for display and cutting. Flowers close at night. Subject to fungus.
CARNATION (CLOVE PINK) P HH *Dianthus caryophyllus*	20"	8"	Oct.-Nov.	White, Yellow, Pink, Red	May	Sun. Soil with clay, well-rotted manure and leaf mold with sand. Liquid fertilizer during growth period. Water often. Fragrant. Not easy. Cuts well.
CASTOR BEAN A T *Ricinus communis*	5-10'	60"	Apr.	Bronze Foliage		Sun. Any soil, moisture. *SEEDS POISONOUS. WARN CHILDREN.* Very rapid growth. Colorful foliage. Grows from cuttings also.

GARDEN COLOR WITH ANNUALS AND PERENNIALS

A = Annual   B = Biennial   P = Perennial   spp. = more than one species   H = Hardy
HH = Half-hardy; freezes   T = Tender; killed by freeze   E = Evergreen

Common Name *Botanical Name*	Height	Space Apart	Time To Plant	Color	Time of Blooming	Comments
CHINESE FORGET-ME-NOT A or B H *Cynoglossum amabile*	18"	8"	Sept.-Nov.	Blue, White, Pink	Apr.-Aug.	Sun or light shade. Garden soil. Tolerates drought. Reseeds. Wonderful blue in the garden.
CHINESE LANTERN PLANT P H *Physalis Alkekengi* *Abutilon hybridum*	12-18"		Sept.-Mar.	Whitish	June-Sept.	Partial shade. Light, well-drained soil. Start seeds indoors. Grown for ornamental orange seed pods, which may be dried. Invasive. Give it room.
CHOCOLATE PLANT A HH *Pseuderanthemum* *alatum*	18"	16"	Mar.-June	Lavender	June-Oct.	Sun to light shade. Light, rich soil. Ample water. Often returns from roots. Brown, silver-splotched leaves, gray underneath. Flowers in racemes. Reseeds.
CHRYSANTHEMUM P H *Chrysanthemum* spp.	2-4'	12-20"	Feb.-Mar. June	White, , Pink Lavender, Maroon, Yellow, Bronze	Oct.-Dec.	Full sun. Rich, fertile, sandy soil. Drainage. Best grown from cuttings, divisions and plants. Numerous varieties and forms. After bloom, keep trimmed back until Aug. Adequate fertilizer. Water when dry, trying to keep water off foliage to avoid mildew.
CIGAR or FIRECRACKER PLANT A T *Cuphea ignea* (*C. platycentra*)	12'	8-10"	Mar.-Apr.	Red, Scarlet with Black and White Tips	June-Frost	Full sun or light shade. Light, loose, fertile soil. Good drainage. Planted in mass shows up color of blossom and shiny green leaves. Wild flower. Mounded plant covered with flowers.
CLARKIA A HH *Godetia* spp.	12"	6"	Oct.	White thru Red	Mar.-May	Sun with part P.M.. Shade in summer. Sandy, light loam, low in nitrogen. Keep soil moist.
COCKSCOMB A T *Celosia argentea* *cristata* *C.a. plumosa*	1-3'	8-12"	Mar.-Sept.	Red, Yellow	June-Dec.	Full sun. Deep, fertile soil. Coarse texture. Dwarf forms also. Water when dry. Drought tolerant. *C.a. cristata* has crested flower heads. *C.a. plumosa* is plume type. Dries well.

GARDEN COLOR WITH ANNUALS AND PERENNIALS

Common Name *Botanical Name*	Height	Space Apart	Time To Plant	Color	Time of Blooming	Comments
COLEUS A T *Coleus*	12-24"	12"	Feb.-May	Variegated Foliage in Yellow, , Red, Green	Contin- uous	Sun or partial shade. Drainage. Rich soil. Keep flowers cut off for better foliage. Tolerates seashore. Cuttings and divisions root easily.
COLUMBINE P H *Aquilegia* spp. and hybrids *A. hinckleyi* (NATIVE species)	18-24"	10-20"	Spring	White, Pink, Blue, Red, Orange, Lavender Yellow Yellow	June-Oct.	Light shade. Well-drained, moist soil with organic matter. Must have excellent drainage. Plant in raised bed with sand in soil. Buy two-year plants for first season bloom. Airy foliage. Buy species suitable to our southern location. Feed often after spring growth begins. Protect from summer heat.
COPPERLEAF (COPPER PLANT) A T *Acalypha* *wilkesiana*	2-1/2'	16"	Mar.-June	Copper- Gold-Red Foliage		Full sun for brightest colored foliage. Garden soil. May over-winter in greenhouse or if well mulched. Accepts seashore planting. Shrubby. Other varieties also.
COREOPSIS (TICKSEED) P HH *Coreopsis grandiflora* *C.g.* 'Sun Ray' *C. auriculata* 'Nana' P E *C. verticillata*	2' To 8" 2"	12-18" 8"	Sept.-Feb. (Seeds) Spring (Plants) March	Yellow- Orange Yellow- Orange Yellow	May-Sept. Apr.-Dec. All Summer	Sun. Soil not too rich. Water when dry. Also from divisions. Tolerant of heat and drought. Texas NATIVE. Full sun or part shade. Garden soil. Demands good drainage. Drought tolerant, but water when dry. Foliage rosette sends out runners, forms flat mat. Good bulb cover, between stepping stones. Keep faded flowers cut.
CORNFLOWER (BACHELOR'S BUTTON) A H *Centaurea cyanus*	3'	8-12"	Sept.-Feb.	Pink, Blue, Purple, White	Feb.-May	Full sun. Loose, light, fertile soil. Drainage. Water when dry. Good for cutting. *C. americana* (Basket Flower) is lilac to purple.

GARDEN COLOR WITH ANNUALS AND PERENNIALS

A = Annual   B = Biennial   P = Perennial   spp. = more than one species   H = Hardy
HH = Half-hardy; freezes   T = Tender; killed by freeze   E = Evergreen

Common Name *Botanical Name*	Height	Space Apart	Time To Plant	Color	Time of Blooming	Comments
COSMOS, EARLY A HH *Cosmos bipinnatus*	4-5'	6-10"	Feb.-Mar. (Seeds)	Crimson, Lavender, Pink, White	Apr.-July	Full sun. Light, sandy soil, not too rich. Good drainage. Water when dry. Pinch young plants for bushiness, more blooms. Tall and airy. May need staking. Long bloom time. Scatter seed on bed and rake in. Water gently.
COSMOS, KLONDYKE A HH *Cosmos sulphureus*	4-6'	6-10"	Apr.-June	Orange, Red, Yellow	July-Nov.	Sun. Light, moist soil, but not too wet. Water when dry. Stake or plant against fence. Dwarf and double-flowered varieties. Keep flowers picked. Cuts well.
CUP FLOWER A *Nierembergia hippomanica*	8"	10"	Spring	Purple	All Summer	Sun or part shade. Any soil. Normal water. Easy. Masses well for blooming ground cover.
DAHLIA, BEDDING A *Dahlia x hybridus*	1-4'	18"	Jan.-Feb. (Seeds Indoors) Mar.-Apr. (Plants Outdoors After Frost-Time)	Every Color Except Blue	June-Nov.	Sun. Rich, sandy loam, with compost and manure, slightly acid. Water freely and thoroughly, but don't wet foliage to avoid mildew. Requires excellent drainage and air circulation. Feed often. Dwarf varieties recommended. Pinch tips for bushiness, more bloom. Good for cutting. Pruning back after first bloom encourages second bloom.
DAISY, BLUE or BLUE MARGUERITE P *Felicia amelloides*	18-24"		Spring	Blue	Summer	Full sun. Fertile, humusy soil, well aerated. Water often. Trim plant in fall. Trouble-free but tender to frost. Protect. Propagate from spring cuttings. Semi-prostrate, shrubby. Nice in pots on terrace or balcony.
DAISY, BUSH P E *Euryops* spp.	14"	12"	Sept.-Oct.	Yellow	Fall, Winter, Spring	Sun. Garden soil. Water when dry. Requires excellent drainage. Once established needs little water. Finely divided leaves.

GARDEN COLOR WITH ANNUALS AND PERENNIALS

Common Name *Botanical Name*	Height	Space Apart	Time To Plant	Color	Time of Blooming	Comments
DAISY, ENGLISH A *Bellis perennis*	4-6"	6-8"	Sept.-Dec.	White, Pink, Red	Jan.-Apr.	Partial shade. Garden soil kept moist in blooming season. Small dainty flower. Fine winter annual. Cuts well.
DAISY, GLORIOSA (BLACK-EYED SUSAN) T *Rudbeckia hirta* cultivar 'Gloriosa'	2-3'	14"	Apr.-Aug.	Yellow, Gold, Mahogany	May-Aug.	Sun, light shade. Any well-drained soil. Drought tolerant. Cut to encourage bloom. Water as needed, especially at planting time. Dwarf cultivars. 'Gold Sturm' good. Hybrids excellent. Also Texas NATIVE double forms.
DAISY, LAZY A *Aphanostephus* *skirrhobasis*	6-12"	8"	Spring	White	Mar.-Dec.	Sun to part shade. Garden soil. Water when dry. Good on the coast. Tidy border plants bloom non-stop, profusion of flowers open late morning. Reseeds. Drought tolerant. Trouble free. Texas NATIVE.
DAISY, MICHAELMAS P *Aster* spp.	3-5'	12-18"	Jan.-Mar.	Lavender, White, Yellow, Blue, Pink, Red	Sept.-Dec.	Sunny, open location in light fertile, well-drained soil. Water well when dry. Stake. Cut to ground in fall. Numerous species. Grows well from divisions.
DAISY, PAINTED P *Chrysanthemum* *coccineum*	10-30"	12"	Sept.-Mar.	Pink, Red, White	Apr.-June	Sun or partial shade. Rich, clayey, fertile soil with organic content, such as manure, humus. Protected location. Winter mulch. Excellent for cutting.
DAISY, SHASTA P *Chrysanthemum* *x superbum*	10-24"	12-18"	Aug.-Sept. Mar.-Apr.	White; Single and Double	May-Nov.	Sun or partial shade. Well-drained, rich, moist soil. Water when dry. Also from divisions. Good for cutting. Flowers on sturdy stems. Hybrid variety 3-4' available. Many varieties.
DAISY, SWAN RIVER A HH *Brachycome* *iberidifolia*	12"	6"	Sept.-Mar. (Seeds)	Blue, White, Pink	Apr.-June	Full sun. Rich soil. Water when dry. Good in borders and pots. Fragrant 1-1/2" flowers.

GARDEN COLOR WITH ANNUALS AND PERENNIALS

A = Annual   B = Biennial   P = Perennial   spp. = more than one species   H = Hardy
HH = Half-hardy; freezes   T = Tender; killed by freeze   E = Evergreen

Common Name *Botanical Name*	Height	Space Apart	Time To Plant	Color	Time of Blooming	Comments
DELPHINIUM A *Delphinium*	2-4'	16-30"	Feb.-Mar. (Plants)	Blue, Pink, White, Red, Violet	Mar.-June	Full sun. Good drainage. Keep soil damp. Rich, sandy, humusy soil, not acid. Mulch in summer. Stake. Protect from wind and freeze. Cuts wells. Gives fine vertical accent in flower bed. Difficult in Houston.
DIANTHUS (PINKS) B H *Dianthus*	8-12"	12"	Sept.-Feb.	Rose, Pink, White, Red	Nov.-June	Sun with protection from P.M. summer sun. Fertile, slightly alkaline, sandy soil. Water as needed. Good drainage. Fragrant. Many species. Drought tolerant. See 'Sweet William.'
D. chinensis 'Magic Charms'	7-10"	7"	Feb.-June	Pink, Red, White	Mar.-Oct.	Forms tidy 10-12" clumps. Flowers slightly fragrant. Also 'Snow Fire,' 'Telstar,' 'Princess' series. Heat tolerant.
DUSTY MILLER A *Centaurea cineraria* *Senecio cineraria*	8-16"	10"	Mar.-Apr.	Yellow	Summer	At least 5 hours sun. Shade during summer afternoon. Sandy, loose soil. Requires excellent drainage. Generous water in summer. Raised beds best. Desirable for its thick whitish-gray/green lobed leaves. Very effective. Many kinds, each with different leaf pattern. Stunning with red geraniums.
FEVERFEW P *Chrysanthemum* *Parthenium*	18"	12"	Feb.-Apr.	White, Yellow	Apr.-Sept.	Partial shade. Sandy, well-drained garden soil. Easy on the water. Good for bedding, borders, and cutting. Naturalizes.
FORGET-ME-NOT A *Myosotis palustris* *semperflorens*	6-8"	10"	Oct.-Nov.	Blue	Apr.-Dec.	Filtered shade. Rich, sandy, loose, well-drained soil. Water and feed freely. Grows in moist areas. Reseeds. Also from divisions.

GARDEN COLOR WITH ANNUALS AND PERENNIALS

Common Name *Botanical Name*	Height	Space Apart	Time To Plant	Color	Time of Blooming	Comments
FOUR-O'CLOCK P H *Mirabilis jalapa*	3'	18-24"	Jan.-Dec.	White, Red, Yellow	May-Oct.	Sun. Garden soil. Water when dry. Self sowing. Opens in P.M. Fragrant.
FOXGLOVE, WILD or COMMON P *Penstemon Cobaea*	2'	12"	Jan.-Feb. (Seeds)	Rose, White, Lavender	May	Sun to part shade. Loose, light soil with a little lime. Add sand for good drainage. Keep soil damp. May propagate from divisions.
GAILLARDIA - See INDIAN BLANKET						
GAZANIA P *Gazania* spp.	1'	12"	Oct.-Nov.	White, Orange, Yellow, Bicolors	May-July	Sun. Loose, sandy soil. Good drainage. Do not overwater. Drought resistant. Gray-green leaves. Daisy-like flowers close at night. Propagated from divisions and cuttings.
GERANIUM A T *Pelargonium x hortorum*	14-26"	10-20"	Mar.-May (Plants)	Red, Salmon, White, Pink, Orange	Mar.-Frost	Sun to part shade, especially during summer heat. Well-drained, rich, loose soil with ample organic matter. Water freely and feed monthly. Pinch-prune for shape and bloom. May be planted in pots, but grows well in ground, if very well drained.
GERBERA (TRANSVAAL DAISY) P T *Gerbera jamesoni hybrida*	1-1/2'	12-15"	Feb. and Aug. (Divisions or Plants)	White, Red, Pink, Yellow, Orange	All Year	Sun to light shade. Deep, rich, humusy soil, excellent drainage. Divisions best. Water often but not so soil is soggy. Keep crown above soil level. Feed 5-10-5 often. Protect from freeze and summer p.m. sun. 'Happipot' is more compact with shorter stems.
GLOBE, AMARANTH A T *Gomphrena globosa*	24"	12"	Feb.-May	White, Pink, Red, Purple, Yellow	May-Oct.	Sun. Loose, fertile soil. Requires good drainage. Clover-like flowers dry well. Dwarf forms also.

GARDEN COLOR WITH ANNUALS AND PERENNIALS

A = Annual   B = Biennial   P = Perennial   spp. = more than one species   H = Hardy
HH = Half-hardy; freezes   T = Tender; killed by freeze   E = Evergreen

Common Name *Botanical Name*	Height	Space Apart	Time To Plant	Color	Time of Blooming	Comments
GODETIA A H *Clarkia* spp.	12"	6"	Sept.-Nov.	Red, Pink, White	Mar.-May	Sun to partial shade. Light, sandy soil with well-rotted manure and leaf mold. Needs good aeration. Water well. Likes liquid fertilizer during growth period. Excellent for cutting. Blooms best in crowded plantings.
GOLDENROD P *Solidago* spp.	2-4'	15-18"	Sept.-Mar.	Yellow	July-Sept.	Best in sun. Also from divisions. Hybrids advisable. Any soil. Water as needed. Drought tolerant. Texas NATIVE. Stake tall varieties. Ragweed (Ambrosia) is the plant that causes hay fever, not Goldenrod, though they bloom the same time.
HERBS - See HERB CHART						
HOLLYHOCK A *Alcea rosea*	4-6'	1-2'	Mar.-Apr. (Plants)	Yellow, White thru Red	July-Nov.	Sun or partial shade. Deep fertile, well-drained soil. Ample water. Lovely against wall or fence. Buy annual types.
HONESTY (SILVER DOLLAR PLANT) A *Lunaria annua*	18-30"	12"	July	Purple, White	April	Start seed in damp peat moss in shade. Transplant to rich soil in full sun. Keep moist. Shelter from north wind. Grown for silvery-white partitions of seed pods; keeps well in arrangements. Fragrant.
HOSTA - See BULBS CHART						
IMMORTELLE A *Xeranthemum annuum*	3'	1'	March (Seeds)	All Colors, Mixed	May-July	Sun. Sandy, light soil. Water as needed. Bright double flowers dry well hung upside down in airy location. Sow seeds in garden bed.

GARDEN COLOR WITH ANNUALS AND PERENNIALS

Common Name *Botanical Name*	Height	Space Apart	Time To Plant	Color	Time of Blooming	Comments
IMPATIENS (SULTANA) (TOUCH-ME-NOT) A H *Impatiens Wallerana*	To 24" and 8"	10-16" 6"	Mar.-May (After Ground Warms to 65°)	Rose, White, Bicolor, Red, Orange,, Yellow Purple, Salmon	May-Oct.	Partial shade. Rich soil with ample organic matter, kept moist. Profuse bloomer. Dwarf forms. Also 'New Guinea' and other hybrids. Fine all summer bloomer. Pinch and feed to encourage blooms. Remove old blooms to prevent disease. Curling of leaves even when soil is moist indicates cyclamen mites. Treat with miticide. Reseeds from cuttings when winters are mild.
INDIAN BLANKET (BLANKET FLOWER) HH *Gaillardia* *pulchella* A	12-18"	12"	Oct.-Apr. (Seeds) Feb.-Apr. (Divisions or Plants)	Yellow thru Red	May-Oct.	Sun. Well-drained soil. Not too wet. Heat and drought tolerant. Reseeds. Texas NATIVE. Excellent for cutting. *G. x grandiflora* not so tolerant.
JACOBINIA CARNEA P *Justicia carnea*	to 3'	24"	Mar.-Apr.	Red, Pink, Orange, Yellow	June-Nov.	Part shade. Sun burns foliage. Fertile soil with sand and humus. Water freely. Root hardy. Feed with 12-24-12 ratio. Protect from freeze.
KNOTWEED (FLEECE FLOWER) P *Polygonum capitatum*	8"	8"	Feb.-Nov.	Pink	May-Frost	Sun. Fertile soil. Water when dry. Forms mats of small leaves which turn red and yellow in fall. Spreads by runners. Pink clover-like small flowers. Nice ground cover in fairly small space. May be invasive. Root hardy; protect roots with leaves or moss during freeze; remove when it warms again. Attractive in pots or baskets. Flowers well.
LACE FLOWER, BLUE A HH *Trachymene coerulea*	18"	12"	Sept.-Nov. (Seeds)	Blue, White	Mar.-May	Full sun. Light, sandy soil with humus. Sparse water. Fine for cutting. Grayish leaves. Requires good drainage. Sow seeds where to remain.

GARDEN COLOR WITH ANNUALS AND PERENNIALS

A = Annual   B = Biennial   P = Perennial   spp. = more than one species   H = Hardy
HH = Half-hardy; freezes   T = Tender; killed by freeze   E = Evergreen

Common Name *Botanical Name*	Height	Space Apart	Time To Plant	Color	Time of Blooming	Comments
LAMB'S EARS P *Stachys byzantina*	6-8"	18"	Apr., June, Sept.	Pink, Purple	Fall	Sun, garden soil with excellent drainage. Stems, leaves covered with silver fuzz. Makes dense mat of fuzzy, silvery foliage.
LAMIUM (DEAD NETTLE) P *Lamiastrum Galeobdolon*	10"	8"	Mar.-May	Yellow, White	May-July	Needs shade for protection from Houston's heat. Fertile, well-draining soil. Water when dry. Good under trees as ground cover. When interplanted with bulbs, Lamium hides the browning bulb leaves. Vining habit. Nice in containers. Many varieties with differing variegation.
LANTANA, TRAILING P E HH *Lantana* spp. *L. montevidensis (sellowiana)*	3'	2'	Spring	Rosy-Lilac	May-Frost	Full sun. Prefers sandy, well-draining soil with manure or other humus. Water when dry, though it is salt and drought tolerant. Root hardy. Trailing habit. Nice tall ground cover.
LARKSPUR A H *Consolida ambigua*	2-3'	6"	Sept. and Feb.	White, Shades of Blue, Purple, Pink	Mar.-June	Full sun. Good for bedding and cutting. Rich, loose soil. Water when dry. Feed often. Reseeds.
LIATRIS (GAY FEATHER) P *Liatris* spp.	2-3'	12"	Sept.-Mar.	Lavender, Purple, Rose	Aug.-Oct.	Sun or light shade. Good sandy, moist garden soil. Good drainage. Vertical accent. Dry for winter bouquets. NATIVE wildflower in Texas and Houston.
LOBELIA (CARDINAL FLOWER) P *Lobelia cardinalis* Cv. 'Alba' Cv. 'Rosea'	2-3'	12"	Feb. Sept.	Red White Pink	Oct.-Nov.	May be grown from seeds or root divisions. Grows best in semi-shade. Moist soil with sharp sand for drainage, half each, peat and compost. Likes to be cool. Texas NATIVE. Attracts hummingbirds.

GARDEN COLOR WITH ANNUALS AND PERENNIALS

Common Name *Botanical Name*	Height	Space Apart	Time To Plant	Color	Time of Blooming	Comments
LOBELIA, EDGING A HH *Lobelia Erinus*	4-10"	6-12"	Fall (Seeds) Jan.-Mar. (Plants)	Blue, White	Mar.-May	Filtered sun. Protect from afternoon sun. Sandy loam. Ample water. Good drainage. Fine for bedding, edging. Tolerates wet places. Nice in containers.
LOVE-IN-A-MIST A H *Nigella damascena*	12-24"	6-12"	Jan. (Seeds)	Blue, White, Pink	Apr.-July	Sun. Garden soil. Requires excellent drainage. Water when dry. Lace-like flower and foliage. Good for cutting. Pods dry well. Reseeds. Feed monthly. Very invasive.
LYTHRUM (LOOSESTRIFE) P *Lythrum salicaria*	12-15"	12-16"	Mar.-May (Seeds)	Shades of Purple and Pink	May-Oct.	Sun or shade. Garden soil to boggy soil. Water. No pests. Keep faded flowers picked off. Wildflower.
MARIGOLD, AFRICAN A T HH *Tagetes erecta*	3-4'	12"	Apr.-May (Plants)	Lemon, Cream, Orange, White	June-Frost	Full sun. Rich garden soil. Water when dry. Pungent fragrance. Deadhead for more bloom and larger flowers. *T.e. x patula* very good.
MARIGOLD, FRENCH A T *Tagetes patula*	12-18"	12"	Apr.-May (Plants)	Yellow, Mahogany, Bicolors, Maroon	June-Nov.	Sun. Rich, garden soil. Said to discourage nematodes. Dwarf forms also. *T. lucida*, Mexican Marigold Mint (Sweet Scented Marigold) for tea and to flavor vinegar. Easy on the water for Marigolds, only when dry.
MONKEY FLOWER A *Mimulus hybrids*	8"	6"	Feb.	Yellows, Reds, Bronze with Speckled Throats	Feb.-Apr.	Shade. Moist soil. Showy flowers in profusion. Calypso hybrids best.
NASTURTIUM A *Tropaeolum majus*	2-3'	10"	Oct.-Apr.	Yellow to Mahogany, White	Apr.-June	Full sun. Moist but not soggy. Drought tolerant. Flowers well in poor soil. Trailing variety left on ground produces long stems and more flowers. Dwarf and double varieties available. Edible. Do not feed. Good in containers. Attracts butterflies.

GARDEN COLOR WITH ANNUALS AND PERENNIALS

A = Annual   B = Biennial   P = Perennial   spp. = more than one species   H = Hardy
HH = Half-hardy; freezes   T = Tender; killed by freeze   E = Evergreen

Common Name *Botanical Name*	Height	Space Apart	Time To Plant	Color	Time of Blooming	Comments
NICOTIANA (FLOWERING TOBACCO) A T *Nicotiana alata* *grandiflora* *N. sanderae* *N. sylvestris*	12-36"	6-12"	Sept.-Mar.	White, Violet, Mauve, Red, Yellow-Green, White, Pink, Yellow	May-Oct.	A.M. sun or partial shade. Sandy loam with some lime and potash. Water freely, especially in hot weather. Fertilize for continuous bloom. Very fragrant. Likes to be on north side of house.
ORNAMENTAL CABBAGE and KALE (WILD CABBAGE) A T *Brassica fimbriata* *B. oleracea* *var. acephala*	7-14"	12"	Winter	Cream, Pink, Red, Green, Purple Foliage	Nov.-Feb. (Colorful Foliage)	Sun. Deep, rich, well-worked soil with a little lime. Soil should be able to hold water. Set plants out after cool weather comes. Cold resistant, but protect from freeze. Frilled, colorful leaves attractive in arrangements. Edible. Showy in mass. Good with Parsley border.
PAINTED TONGUE A *Salpiglossus* *sinuata*	12-18"	8"	Sept.-Mar.	Wide Range	May-June	Part shade. Light soil. Water before it gets dry. Flowers have velvety texture, throats marbled and veined.
PANSY A H *Viola x* *Wittrockiana*	6"	6-8"	Aug.-Nov.	Purple, Lavender, Pink, White, Gold, Blue, Rose, Mixed, Orange, Red, Black, Yellow, Rust	Nov.-May	Sun. Rich, sandy soil with humus. Blood meal worked into soil when planting encourages bloom. Water when dry. Feed monthly. Cuts well. *V. tricolor*, 'Johnny-Jump-Up', reseeds. Keep flowers picked for more bloom. Nice bulb cover. Tolerates moist soil. F2 hybrids "Crystal Bowl" and "Universal" are more heat tolerant, better for Houston.
PENSTEMON (BEARD-TONGUE) P *Penstemon spp.* *P. tenuis* *P. laxiflorus* (NATIVE spp.)	18"-2'	1'	Oct.-Dec. (Seeds) Spring or Fall (Plants)	White, Pink, Lavender, Rose Pink White	Apr.-May	Sun. Requires good drainage. Light, acid, sandy, moist soil. Hardy. Suitable for our mild climate. Some have tinted foliage.

240

GARDEN COLOR WITH ANNUALS AND PERENNIALS

Common Name *Botanical Name*	Height	Space Apart	Time To Plant	Color	Time of Blooming	Comments
PENTAS (EGYPTIAN STAR-CLUSTER) A *Pentas lanceolata*	To 2'	18"	Spring	Red, Pink, Lilac, White, Magenta	Summer	Part to full sun. Sandy loam with humus. Water as needed to keep from drying out. Large dark green leaves. Small flowers in clusters. Attracts butterflies and hummingbirds.
PERIWINKLE MADAGASCAR (VINCA) A T *Catharanthus roseus*	15"	8-12"	Mar.-June	Pink, White, Lavender	June-Nov.	Full sun. Excellent for mass planting and borders. Garden soil. Drought tolerant. Water when dry. Requires good drainage. Likes heat. Reseeds. Pinch tips of plants for bushiness. 'Carpet Series,' 6" tall, spreading.
PERSIAN SHIELD P (MEXICAN PETUNIA) *Strobilanthes* *Dyeranus*	5'			Violet	June	Best in shade. Loose, well-draining soil. Water. 8"leaves, purple beneath. Attractive foliage. Tends to become weedy. Pinching promotes full growth. Good with Ginger.
PETUNIA A HH *Petunia x hybrida*	12-18"	12"	Sept.-Mar.	White, Pink, Rose, Yellow, Purple, Salmon, Lavender, Red, Bicolors	Apr.-Nov.	Sun or part shade. Light, rich, drained soil. Water to keep moist. Many varieties. Fragrant. Feed monthly. Fine for massing and cutting. Blooms well in fall. Protect from freeze by covering with boxes, cloth, or leaves. Remove on warm days. Trim to prevent legginess.
PHLOX, BLUE LOUISIANA (WILD SWEET WILLIAM) P E HH *Phlox divaricata*	18"	6"	Sept.-Oct.	Blue to Mauve to White	Feb.-Apr.	Sun or semi-shade. Loose, rich soil with manure. Keep soil moist. When planting, cover entire plant with soil, leaving only tip exposed, in order to make joints take root. Protect from frosts. Makes nice cover for bulbs.

GARDEN COLOR WITH ANNUALS AND PERENNIALS

A = Annual   B = Biennial   P = Perennial   spp. = more than one species   H = Hardy
HH = Half-hardy; freezes   T = Tender; killed by freeze   E = Evergreen

Common Name / Botanical Name	Height	Space Apart	Time To Plant	Color	Time of Blooming	Comments
PHLOX, DRUMMOND (ANNUAL PHLOX) A HH *Phlox Drummondii*	12"	4-6"	Feb.-Apr.	White, Red, Pink, Mauve, Salmon	Mar.-June	Full sun. Light, fertile, sandy loam, kept moist. Good drainage. Cut back when leggy. Naturalizes. Flowers cut well. Slightly fragrant. Feed often.
PHLOX, MOSS PINK (THRIFT) P E H *Phlox subulata*	4-6"	24"	Mar.-June	Blue, Pink, White	Feb.-May	Sun. Likes manure in fertile soil. Good drainage. Water to avoid dryness, especially in summer. Spreading habit; forms low dense mass. Hardy. Feed often with organic fertilizer or very weak chemical fertilizer, especially in spring. NATIVE of U.S. Trim after blooming season. Good bulb cover.
PHLOX, PERENNIAL (SUMMER) P *Phlox paniculata*	18-30"	12-15"	Sept.-Feb. (Divisions or Roots)	Salmon, Red, White, Pink, Purple, Magenta	May-Oct.	Sun. Ample organic matter deeply worked into soil. Mulch. Requires good drainage. Keep mulch moist. Water often, but do not drown plants. Stake. Fragrant. Stately when well grown and cared for. Feed monthly. Protection from afternoon summer sun is helpful. To avoid mildew, provide air circulation and do not wet foliage. Flowers cut well.
PHLOX, PRAIRIE (PINK LOUISIANA) P E HH *Phlox pilosa ozarkana*	12"	10"	Mar.-Apr.	Lilac-Pink	May	A.M. sun and afternoon shade. Fertile, loose garden soil. Likes to be moist or wet, but not soggy. Good drainage. Feed following bloom in spring. Multiplies. Protect clumps from frost with pine straw and leaves piled around clumps; remove when weather warms. When dividing and transplanting clumps, try to keep some soil on roots. Requires good air circulation to avoid

GARDEN COLOR WITH ANNUALS AND PERENNIALS

Common Name *Botanical Name*	Height	Space Apart	Time To Plant	Color	Time of Blooming	Comments
PHLOX, PRAIRIE, contd.						powdery mildew. Spray when necessary. U.S. and Texas NATIVE.
PHYSOSTEGIA (FALSE-DRAGONHEAD) (OBEDIENT PLANT) P *Physostegia* spp.	1-3'	12"	Sept.-Dec.	Lavender, Pink, White	June-Aug.	Sun or partial shade. Best in sandy soil. Water to keep damp. Also from divisions. Good for cutting. Also Texas NATIVE varieties. Reseeds. Invasive. Allow room; remove dead flowers.
PLUMBAGO P T *Plumbago auriculata (capensis)*	5' x 3'	3'	Feb.-Apr.	White, Blue	May-Nov.	Full sun best. Fertile, moist, loose soil. Water when dry. Good drainage. Fertilize periodically, making sure there is manganese in fertilizer. Prune old foliage and to shape in late winter. Tender. Plant in protected location on south with morning sun. Root hardy. In hard freeze, cover roots with leaves. Will vine up walls on a support or cascade to form mound.
POPPY, CALIFORNIA A *Eschscholzia californica*	To 2'	4"	Oct. (Seeds)	White, Pink, Salmon, Orange	May June	Sun. Poor soil. Moderate water with good drainage. California wild flower.
POPPY, ICELAND A *Papaver nudicaule*	14-16"	6"	Aug.-Sept. (Seeds in Garden Bed)	Yellow, Red, White, Purple, Salmon, Pink	Apr.-May	Sun or partial shade. Well-drained, sandy loam. Water moderately. Best in border. Fern-like foliage. Exquisitely dainty blossoms. To cut, sear stems in hot water. Likes cool weather. Plant later blooming perennials in front of Oriental Poppy to hide after it has bloomed.
POPPY, ORIENTAL P *P. orientale*	12-14"	6"	Mar.-Apr.	Rose-Pink, White, Orange, Crimson, Maroon	May-June	

GARDEN COLOR WITH ANNUALS AND PERENNIALS

A = Annual   B = Biennial   P = Perennial   spp. = more than one species   H = Hardy
HH = Half-hardy; freezes   T = Tender; killed by freeze   E = Evergreen

Common Name *Botanical Name*	Height	Space Apart	Time To Plant	Color	Time of Blooming	Comments
POPPY, SHIRLEY (FIELD) A H *Papaver Rhoeas*		4"	Oct.-Nov. (Seeds)	White, Pink, Rose, Salmon	May-July	Sun. Loose, fertile soil. Good drainage. Gather pods of seeds when dry and store until next fall to plant. A strain of European field poppy. Sprinkle seeds on fine loose loam. Likes cool weather.
PORTULACA (MOSS ROSE) A T *Portulaca grandiflora*	4-6"	4-6"	Mar.-July	All Colors Except Blue; Single and Double	May-Oct.	Full sun. Best in sandy soil. Brilliant in borders and beds. Flowers close in afternoon. Drought tolerant. Water especially in summer; do not drown plants.
PURSLANE *P. oleracea hybrid* (also perennial cultivars)	4-6"	4-6"	Mar.-July		May-Oct.	Purslane grows in seashore area. Same culture as Portulaca. Sometimes reverts to insidious weed.
PRIMROSE A HH *Primula malacoides* (best for Houston)	12"	6"	Nov.-Feb.	Pink, Lavender, White	Feb.-May	Protected semi-shaded area. Soil of equal parts sand, loam, leafmold, or compost. Keep moist but not saturated. Plants spread 6-8", close to ground. Be prepared to spray for leaf disease or insects. Flowers in cluster-heads. Attractive foliage. Nice in mass or in containers. Several varieties.
P. obconica	12"	6-8"	Nov.-Feb.	Peach, Rose, Blue	Jan.-May	
PRIMROSE P *Oenothera* spp.	1-3'	18"	May	Yellow, Pink	Summer	Sun to partial sun. Poor soil, as in cracks in concrete. Drought tolerant. Rangy plants for informal garden. Some open A.M., others P.M. Texas NATIVE.
PRIMULAS A *Primula polyanthus* hybrids	8-12"	8"	Nov. (Plants)	Pastels	Nov.-May	Shade. Loose, rich soil. Excellent drainage. Giant Pacific and Magnus varieties more vigorous than *acaulis* or *obconica*. Great impact in winter landscape. Flowers rise 6" from rosettes of leaves. Susceptible to snails.

GARDEN COLOR WITH ANNUALS AND PERENNIALS

Common Name *Botanical Name*	Height	Space Apart	Time To Plant	Color	Time of Blooming	Comments
PURPLE CONEFLOWER (RUDBECKIA) P *Echinacea purpurea* *E. sanguinea* H	3-5'	12-18"	Apr.-May Sept.-Oct. (Seeds)	Rosy- Purple, White Lavender	Spring- Fall	Full sun to semi-shade. Rich, moist, sandy, well-drained soil with humus. Easy on water. Re-seeds. Forms clumps. Drought tolerant. Texas NATIVE. Old-time favorite. New cultivars better; in many colors. May divide clumps. Very prickly seed heads.
QUEEN ANNE'S LACE A *Daucus Carota*	3-4'	12"	Nov.-Sept.	White	Apr.-May	Sun. Deep, rich, friable soil. Good for cutting. Texas NATIVE. Fern-like foliage, large heads of flowers. Attracts Black Swallow-tail Butterflies.
ROSE MALLOW P HH *Hibiscus moscheutos* (NATIVE) *H. coccineus* 'Texas Star' *H. cardiophyllus* *H. militaris*	4-8' 6' 3'	3-4'	Sept.-Mar.	White thru Red Red (Single) Red Pink, White	June-Frost	Sun, semi-shade. Fertile, moist soil. Water often, daily in summer heat. 5" flowers, large leaves. Pinch prune. Vigorous. Good for seashore planting. Feed regularly. Winter hardy. Cover roots with mulch of leaves.
SAGE, PINEAPPLE P *Salvia elegans*	2-3'	12"	Apr.-June	Red	Fall	Sun to semi-shade. Rich sandy soil with manure. Requires good drainage. Herb. Fragrant leaves. Attracts hummingbirds.
SALVIA (AUTUMN SAGE) P HH *Salvia Greggii*	2-3'	2'	Nov.-Apr.	Crimson, White, Peach	Apr.-Oct.	Open, sunny location. Rich, sandy soil, manure dressing. Must have well-drained soil. Water when dry. Texas NATIVE. Feed monthly. Dwarf variety 'Salmon Pygmy.' *C.G.* 'Alba' is white. *C.G.* 'Rosea' is pale red. Flowers fine for cutting or air-drying.

GARDEN COLOR WITH ANNUALS AND PERENNIALS

A = Annual   B = Biennial   P = Perennial   spp. = more than one species   H = Hardy
HH = Half-hardy; freezes   T = Tender; killed by freeze   E = Evergreen

Common Name *Botanical Name*	Height	Space Apart	Time To Plant	Color	Time of Blooming	Comments
SALVIA (MEXICAN BUSH) P *Salvia leucantha*	3-4'	2'	Mar.-Sept.	Lavender	Fall	Sun or bright shade. Rich,sandy soil with well-rotted manure. Good aeration. Water regularly. Branches which have flowered benefit by being cut back to main stalk or stem. Gray-green foliage. Fine background plant. Flowers good cut or dried. Cut back following bloom. Texas NATIVE.
SALVIA (SCARLET SAGE) A HH *Salvia splendens* *S.s.* 'Compacta,' dwarf	2-3' 12-15"	1'	Feb.-May	Red, White, Pink, Blue Purple, Rose, Salmon	May-Dec.	Morning sun or bright shade. Requires well-drained garden soil. Water when dry. Attracts hummingbirds. 'Salmon Pygmy' dwarf. Moisture. Fertilize. Red flowering 'Rodeo' and 'Blaze of Fire' attract butterflies and hummingbirds.
SALVIA, BLUE (MEALY-CUP SAGE) P HH *Salvia farinacea* *S.f.* cv. 'Alba'	2-3'	1'	Sept.-Mar.	Blue, White	Apr.-Dec.	Sun. Sandy garden soil with manure. Requires good drainage. Easy on water; moist, not wet. Airy, silvery foliage. Texas NATIVE. Feed. Good bloomer. Root hardy. Attracts hummingbirds. Salvias' square stems indicate their membership in the Mint Family.
SCABIOSA (PINCUSHION FLOWER) A *Scabiosa atropurpurea*	2-3'	1'	Feb.-Mar.	Pink, (Seeds) Purple	Apr.-June White,	Protect from afternoon sun. Fertile, well-drained soil, slightly alkaline, with humus. Moderate watering.

GARDEN COLOR WITH ANNUALS AND PERENNIALS

Common Name *Botanical Name*	Height	Space Apart	Time To Plant	Color	Time of Blooming	Comments
SEDUM (STONECROP) P E *Sedum* spp.	5-12"	6"	Mar.-Nov.	Yellow, White, Pinkish	Spring (Ground Cover Types) Fall (Large Leaf Types)	Prefers sun. Not particular about type of soil, but requires good drainage. Needle-like foliage. Good ground cover in not too large expanses. Many varieties, some cascading. *S. spectabile* tolerates wet soil. Color of stems and leaves differs with varieties.
SHRIMP PLANT P *Justicia Brandegeana*	2-3'	24"	From Divisions and Cuttings	Red or Chartreuse Bracts	Apr.-Nov.	Sun-part shade. Rich, humusy soil, moist but drained. Pinch to shape. Good for cutting and in pots.
SILK FLOWER P T *Abelmoschus moschatus*	16"	18"	Apr.-Aug.	Red, Pink	Summer	Full sun to part shade. Fertile, loose garden loam. Flowers 3" x 3" wide. New plant kin to hibiscus. Very pretty.
SNAPDRAGON A HH *Antirrhinum* spp.	1-3'	6"	Sept.-Feb. (Seeds)	White, Red, Yellow, Bronze, Pink, Orange, Bicolors	Mar.-June	Sun, semi-shade. Rich, well-drained, slightly alkaline soil. When watering, avoid wetting leaves. Use rust-resistant varieties. Plant with other plants to avoid root rot. Likes cool season. Also dwarf forms to 10".
SPIDER FLOWER A HH *Cleome spinosa*	3-5'	1'	March	White, Pink with Crimson Stamens	June-Oct.	Sun. Garden soil. Drought tolerant but likes moist soil. Reseeds readily.
STATICE A HH *Limonium*	1-1/2-2'	12"	March	Pink, Blue, White	June-Aug.	Sun. Fertile, well-drained soil. Water when dry. To dry, cut when fully open; hang upside down in shady, airy place. Cut on clear day before completely open. Tolerates both drought and seashore planting.

GARDEN COLOR WITH ANNUALS AND PERENNIALS

A = Annual   B = Biennial   P = Perennial   spp. = more than one species   H = Hardy
HH = Half-hardy; freezes   T = Tender; killed by freeze   E = Evergreen

Common Name *Botanical Name*	Height	Space Apart	Time To Plant	Color	Time of Blooming	Comments
STOCK A H *Matthiola incana*	1-2'	1'	Sept.-Jan.	Pink, Red, White, Cream, Lavender, Purple	Feb.-May	Sun or light shade. Well-drained, rich soil. Water as needed. Bedding and border plant. Night-scented good variety. Fine for cutting. Apply liquid fertilizer during growth period.
STOKES' ASTER P *Stokesia laevis* *S. caerulea rosea*	12-18"		March (Seeds) Mar.-Sept. (Divisions or Plants) Pink	Lavender, Blue, White	May-June	Sun. Light, acid, well-drained soil. Water when dry. Grown also from divisions. Good for cutting. Blooms with Daylilies. Requires excellent drainage.
STRAWFLOWER A HH *Helichrysum bracteatum*	2-3'	1'	Jan.-Mar.	Yellow White thru Deep Red	June-Aug.	Full sun. Well-drained soil with sand, manure and humus. Flowers excellent for drying. One of the everlastings.
SUNFLOWER A or P H *Helianthus* spp.	6-8'	2'	Mar.-May	Yellow	May-Sept.	Full sun. Seeds attract birds. Drought tolerant but enjoys water. Fertile soil for large flowers. Texas NATIVE.
SWEET SULTAN A *Centaurea moschata*	3'	1'	Sept.-Oct. March	Lavender, Purple, Rose, White	May-July	Sun. Fertile, moist, light soil. Water regularly. Excellent for cutting. Hardy. Likes crowding. Fragrant.
SWEET WILLIAM A (B) HH *Dianthus barbatus* *D.b.* 'Wee Willie,' dwarf A (best in containers)	5-18" 4"	6" 4-6"	Jan.-Apr. (Plants or Divisions best) Feb.-June	White, Red, Pink, Purple, Lavender, Salmon	Apr.-May Following Year Mar.-June	Sun with afternoon shade from hot sun. Well-drained, light, alkaline, sandy soil with manure. Water moderately. Protect from freeze. Cuts well. Fragrant. Use liquid fertilizer. Subject to rust and fusarium wilt. Keep old blooms picked. If necessary, may spray with zineb or equivalent.

GARDEN COLOR WITH ANNUALS AND PERENNIALS

Common Name *Botanical Name*	Height	Space Apart	Time To Plant	Color	Time of Blooming	Comments
TEXAS BLUEBELL (PRAIRIE GENTIAN) A T *Eustoma grandiflorum*	1-3'	12-24"	April (Plants) Sept. (Seeds) (6 months)	Blue, Pink, White, Purple, Yellow	May-Sept.	Sun/semi-shade. Well-drained garden soil. Ample water. Texas NATIVE. Sometimes referred to as Lisianthus. Long-lasting as cut flowers.
TITHONIA (MEXICAN SUNFLOWER) A HH *Tithonia rotundifolia*	4-6'	3'	Feb.-Apr.	Reddish- Orange	July-Oct.	Sun. Average loam soil. Good drainage. Do not overwater. Robust grower. Excellent for cutting if stem ends are seared. Flowers resemble single Dahlias.
TOAD FLAX *Linaria maroccana* 'FAIRY LIGHTS' A *L. reticulata* A 'CROWN JEWELS'	12"	6"	Jan.	Pink, Lavender, Magenta with Yellow Lip	Mar.-Apr.	Full sun to part shade. Tolerates any soil. Good drainage. Water when drying. Flowers like baby snapdragons in profusion.
TORENIA (WISHBONE FLOWER) A HH *Torenia Fournieri*	8-12"	8"	Mar.-June	Combina- tion of Violet, Yellow, White	May-Nov.	A.M. sun or partial shade. Light, fertile, moist garden soil with humus. Reseeds easily. Forms loose clumps. Plant where color and shape can be enjoyed close up. One of few blue flowers in summer. Cuts well; buds open in vase.
UMBRELLA PLANT P T *Cyperus alternifolia*	14-30"	18"	Mar.-Sept. (Cuttings or Divisions)	Cream		Filtered sun or light shade. Soil with peat moss for good drainage. Water often. Looks like miniature palm. Attractive in clumps or containers. Multiplies. Cuts well. May use in house if enough light, air circulation, and water. Tropical effect. Insignificant flowers. Root hardy. Several types.

GARDEN COLOR WITH ANNUALS AND PERENNIALS

A = Annual   B = Biennial   P = Perennial   spp. = more than one species   H = Hardy
HH = Half-hardy; freezes   T = Tender; killed by freeze   E = Evergreen

Common Name *Botanical Name*	Height	Space Apart	Time To Plant	Color	Time of Blooming	Comments
VERBENA P and A HH *Verbena x hybrida*	8-12"	12"	Anytime (Plants, Divisions, Cuttings)	Yellow, Red, White, Purple, Lavender, Blue, Pink, Rose	Jan.-Dec.	Sun. Light, sandy, fertile soil. Good drainage. Water especially in summer. Forms low growing, spreading mats. Perennials trouble-free. Several varieties. 'St. Paul' has deeply toothed leaves. Naturalizes. Profuse bloomer.
VERONICA (SPEEDWELL) P *Veronica* spp.	15-30"	8-16"	March	Blue, White, Pink, Purple	May-Nov.	Sun. Well-drained and well-aerated, moist garden soil. From divisions also. Reseeds. Remove faded blooms and pinch prune for bushiness and bloom. Blooms along tall spikes. Grayish light green leaves.
VIOLA (JOHNNY JUMP-UP) A *Viola cornuta*	6"	6"	Sept.-Jan.	Blue, White, Yellow, Purple	Jan.-May	Full sun. Light, rich soil. Excellent for bedding, cutting, and edging. Keep faded blossoms picked. Reseeds. Nice bulb cover.
VIOLET (SWEET VIOLET) P *Viola odorata*	6"	8"	Anytime	Purple, White	Oct.-May	A.M. sun or semi-shade. Rich, loamy, well-draining soil with manure and organic matter. Keep soil moist but not soggy. Fertilize with bonemeal. Fragrant flowers. Usually grown from divisions.
WALLFLOWER B or A H *Cheiranthus cheiri*	8-12"	6"	Sept.-Dec.	Yellow, Orange	Feb.-Apr.	Sun or partial shade. Light, rich soil with a bit of lime, well-drained. Ample water. Plant in the border. Fragrant. Fine for cutting. Buy "early flowering" annual varieties.

GARDEN COLOR WITH ANNUALS AND PERENNIALS

Common Name *Botanical Name*	Height	Space Apart	Time To Plant	Color	Time of Blooming	Comments
WEDELIA P E H *Wedelia trilobata*	15-20"	16"	Mar.-May	Yellow-Orange	May-Dec.	Sun to light shade. Loose, fertile, moist soil. Good drainage. Unless rainfall is frequent, water often. Intolerant of long drought. Stems creep along ground, rooting in soil. Root hardy. Feed periodically for rapid growth, more bloom. Prune tops back when growth becomes straggly. Often used as ground cover. Invasive.
YARROW (MILFOIL) P *Achillea* spp.	2'	12"	April	White, Yellow	Summer	Sun. Garden soil, not too rich. Drought tolerant. Water when dry. Texas NATIVE. Reseeds. Root hardy. Invasive. Ferny appearance. Aromatic gray-green leaves. Cuts well.
ZINNIA A T *Zinnia*	1-3'	1'	May-Aug.	White, Red, Pink, Yellow, Chartreuse, Orange, Bicolors	May-Dec.	Sun. Any good, deep, rich soil. Drought tolerant. Water freely, but keep water off foliage to prevent mildew. Needs good drainage. Many varieties and types of blossoms. Easy from seed. Cuts well.

Fancy leaved caladium 'Carolyn Whorton'.

Bulbs

"The daffodil is our door-side queen;
she pushes up the sward already,
to spot with sunshine the early green."
—Bryant

*B*ulbs are unique in that they store their own food. That does not mean they don't ever have to be fed; but when fertilizer is scarce, they can keep themselves alive—for a while, at least, until some more fertilizer comes their way. There are several classifications of bulbs, but in general gardening conversation they are all spoken of as "bulbs." For example: caladiums are actually "tubers" and gladioli are "corms," but they are usually referred to as "bulbs."

The five classifications of bulbs are:
- True bulb: just one type, an almost round form composed of fleshy leaves or scales which protect the embryo plant inside. Example: Tulip.
- Corm: a swollen short bulb which stores its food in its fat center, instead of in scales, and has a bud on top. Example: Gladiolus.
- Rhizome: has its bud on the end (apex) with roots below a long and slender, or fleshy and thick, underground stem of creeping habit. Example: Iris.
- Tuber: an underground stem thicker and shorter than a rhizome; it bears buds (eyes) on its mass of food storage tissue. Example: Caladium.
- Tuberous root: thick, underground, food-storing roots with buds at the base of the plant's stem. Example: Daylily.

Most bulbs thrive in a sunny location in a neutral to slightly acid (pH 6-7), porous, crumbly, well-drained soil with *well-rotted* manure incorporated into it. Bulbs need only two feedings a year: at planting time when they should have a mixture of just a teaspoon or two of bone meal, phosphorus and potash in the bottom of the planting hole, being careful to cover the fertilizer with sand and soil to avoid burning the roots; and again following bloom-time when a balanced fertilizer is appropriate, preferably with an organic base and trace elements. The second feeding refers to those bulbs which can be left in our often damp soil. Too much moisture and not enough really extended cold weather in our Houston climate is not to the liking of many bulbs. One of the definite rules in bulb culture is to allow the leaves to remain on the bulb until they are entirely dry. It is through these drying leaves that bulbs restore their food bank. Planting full but low evergreen plants in front of bulbs can hide the drying foliage.

The generally accepted planting depth for most bulbs planted in Houston is three times the diameter of the bulb measuring from the shoulder of the bulb to the soil's surface. Exceptions are lilies, whose stemroots require deep planting to achieve anchorage, and iris rhizomes, which should be planted just below the soil's surface. The spacing of bulbs depends on their size and habit of growth: small bulbs—4 to 5 inches apart; those of spreading habit—farther apart.

Place the bulb securely on its cushion of fertilizer under sand and cover it with soil, firming the soil well to displace harmful air pockets. Water gently but thoroughly. After the bulbs bloom, remove the faded flowers—but NOT the foliage.

Many bulbs adapt themselves to a location and become naturalized; that is, they return year after year in ever greater numbers. When the clumps become crowded and the flowers are few and small, the bulbs should be lifted and divided by breaking or cutting the bulbs apart from each other. Depending on the kind of bulb, some may be replanted. Others may be dried, dusted with sulphur, and stored in a dry, cool place until their planting time the next season.

When bulbs are to stay in the ground, feed them with a mixture of bone meal and super-phosphate scratched into the soil around, *not on* the bulbs, and watered to encourage fine bloom potential. Never use fresh manure around bulbs.

Because most bulbs last a long time when well cared for, it is worthwhile to buy good quality bulbs. Small, low-grade bulbs usually give low-quality flowers. Always be sure that the bulbs you buy are suitable to our climate. Refer to the BULBS chart for descriptions of numerous bulbs which will undoubtedly catch your fancy.

Amaryllis Family (*Amaryllidaceae*)

This large group includes some of the handsomest plants grown in this area. Hybrid Ama-

ryllis, Amarcrinum, Alstroemeria, Chlidanthus, Clivia, Crinum, Cooperia, Eucharis, Habranthus, Haemanthus, Hymenocallis, Ismene, Leucojum, Lycoris, Narcissus, Sprekelia, Tuberose, Tulbaghia, and Zephyranthes are spectacular-blossoming representatives of this family.

Among the many Amaryllis are traditional favorites and modern hybrids, providing picturesque shapes and exquisite colors for your garden. The Dutch, Sequoia, and Houdyshel hybrids are especially lovely. Amaryllis should be planted with the neck and upper portion of the bulb above the surface of the soil. If in time the bulbs settle, they may be carefully raised and reset on a handful of sand. Amaryllis will bloom well in semi-shade, and they lend themselves to planting alone, in groups, or among the shrubbery.

Crinums are an excellent choice because of their fragrant, long-blooming flowers and attractive foliage. The type commonly known as the Milk-and-Wine Lily is a delightful survivor of old gardens. Improved hybrid varieties, such as the choice early-blooming white *Powellii*, St. Christopher, Ellen Bosanquet, Cecil Houdyshel, *Rattrayi*, and the late-blooming *giganteum*, which thrives in deep shade, provide a succession of bloom from spring through autumn.

Amarcrinum Howardii, an outstanding hybrid of *Amaryllis Belladonna* and *Crinum Moorei,* has especially lovely clusters of shell-pink flowers and prospers in semi-shade, blooming periodically during the summer.

Tuberoses, Ismene (Peruvian Daffodil), and Hymenocallis (Spider Lily) are dependable favorites, bearing fragrant white blossoms in the summer. Tuberoses, single and double, produce fragrant, wax-like flowers. Ismene boast exotic lily-shaped flowers, with segments extending beyond the petals like small horns faintly veined with green. Hymenocallis take their common name from the spidery appearance of their narrow, fragile petals and long stamens.

Clivia, Eucharis, and Haemanthus are tropical plants usually grown in pots or tubs in a

Louisiana Iris in moist bed.

shady garden or patio for the summer and in a protected location for winter. They require a potting mixture of sandy loam, bone meal, and humus with some charcoal to insure good drainage.

Lycoris have strap-shaped leaves and clusters of funnel-shaped flowers in many colors. There are summer and autumn blooms. In addition to those listed in the BULBS, TUBERS, RHIZOMES, CORMS AND TUBEROUS ROOTS chart, the lilac rose *L. squamigera*, the red *L. sanguinea*, and the blush pink *L. incarnata* are beautiful species. The Lycoris and the Guernsey Lily (*Nerine sarniensis*) are similar in appearance. Most of these bulbs naturalize well, but they should not be disturbed unless absolutely necessary because they often fail to bloom for two or more seasons after being moved.

Zephyranthes, Cooperia, and Habranthus are somewhat alike, having grass-like foliage and the habit of blooming intermittently throughout the summer. *Tulbaghia violacea*, with its small orchid clusters, is an almost constant summer bloomer. All these little bulbs are lovely tucked into corners or used as borders.

Other amaryllids providing splashes of brilliant color are the showy *Alstroemeria aurantiaca* (Peruvian Lily), the gorgeous Sprekelia, and the fragrant Chlidanthus, resembling the Amaryllis in miniature.

Narcissi or Daffodils

Narcissus is the botanical name of the genus encompassing all species and varieties of daffodils and jonquils. The name daffodil is used loosely, referring both to narcissi with large trumpets and to others. Jonquil is the term commonly used for the rush-leaved *Narcissus Jonquilla*, *odorus*, and their hybrids. Narcissi are hardy, dependable, and adaptable bulbs, unsurpassed

255

for informal plantings. Since winter in the South is comparable to spring in the North, the early varieties are more satisfactory for the upper Gulf Coast area, giving repeated seasons of bloom. Some, especially the polyanthus or bunch-flowered *N. Tazetta*, will naturalize. The new hybrids are larger and often more beautiful than the older favorites. To increase the blooms in your winter garden, add a few new varieties each year. The following are types of narcissi: Trumpet Narcissi, Large-Cupped Narcissi, Small-Cupped Narcissi, Double Narcissi, Triandrus Narcissi, Cyclamineous Narcissi, Jonquilla Narcissi, Tazetta (Poetax or Bunch-Flowered) Narcissi, and Poeticus (Poet's) Narcissi.

Many of the unclassified varieties produced throughout the South were named to suit their owners. The survivors have become part of the garden heritage in their locale.

Narcissi accept various soils, but they demand adequate drainage and surface fertilization following their spring bloom and again in the fall. About 1/2 pound of mixed bone meal and superphosphate for every ten square feet of clumps should be worked lightly around the bulbs and watered in.

Varieties that naturalize may remain undisturbed until overcrowding is evidenced by smaller and fewer flowers; then lift and divide. The early spring blossoms of narcissi make beautiful and fragrant arrangements. They are best cut as opening buds, taking very few of the leaves through which the bulbs attain food for future growth.

Lily Family (*Liliaceae*)

The lily family is noteworthy for the showy blooms of its numerous genera: true Lilium, Agapanthus, Allium, Camassia, Chionodoxa, Galtonia, Gloriosa, Hemerocallis, Hyacinth, Kniphofia, Lachenalia, Leucojum, Liriope, Milla, Muscari, Ornithogalum, Scilla, and Tulip.

The term "lily" is often used in conjunction with common names of many bulbous plants and is more descriptive than accurate. The number of true lilies which thrive in this climate is somewhat limited, but careful planning and planting will provide a succession of bloom in a wide range of color and variety. The Creole, Regal, and Phillippine lilies are special favorites in this area, as they are easily grown and naturalized. Other lilies raised successfully are the Speciosums, Croft, Estate, Tiger, Goldband, Centifoliums, Turk's-Cap, Coral, Madonna, and the Bellingham and Green Mountain hybrids.

Good drainage is rudimentary in lily culture. A sandy loam with leafmold or organic compost added suits most species. All lilies send out roots from the base of their bulbs, but some also develop roots on the stem above the bulbs. True lilies have loose, fleshy scales that hold water and decay easily. They must be planted in well-drained soil. Companion plants are beneficial to lilies, as they absorb surplus water in the soil and shade the area adjacent to the lilies, but the lilies should not be crowded. A loose mulch helps keep the soil and stems cool and moist, makes cultivation unnecessary, and discourages weeds. The flowers of all lilies are excellent for cutting, but only the top part of the stem should be cut off so the bulb can complete its growth.

Hemerocallis (Daylilies) are unexcelled for colorful, long-lasting bloom. Daylilies thrive in full sun or partial shade. They require only average soil and, once established, demand little care; however, they respond with continued and better bloom if watered liberally and fed with a complete fertilizer. A careful selection of varieties, including dwarf types, will provide a sequence of bloom from early spring until fall. New varieties are introduced continually.

Hyacinths, especially the Dutch and Roman varieties in delightful shades, are most attractive in groups. Store bulbs in a refrigerator and plant after weather cools. Hyacinths may also be grown indoors in hyacinth glasses. The Multiflora and Borah, in blue or white, naturalize.

In this climate, tulips must be refrigerated (not frozen) for at least three to six weeks before planting. Bulbs are usually discarded at the end of the blooming season, except *Tulipa clusiana* and some other species, which may be left in the ground to naturalize. The Cottage and Darwin hybrids, noteworthy for their flower size, length and strength of stem, and beautiful color, do well in this area but do not naturalize.

Called the "harbingers of spring" bulbs, the Muscari (Grape Hyacinth), Scilla (Squill), Leucojum (Snowflake), Ornithogalum (Star of Bethlehem), Chionodoxa, and Milla are hardy, dependable, and indispensable for brightening spring gardens. A light mulch should be used as a winter protection.

Kniphofia (Torch Lily or Red Hot Poker) and Yucca are generally used to add a touch of novelty and give bold accent to summer gardens. They do well in hot sun and require little water. Some smaller hybrids of Kniphofia have more beautiful coloring than the older types, formerly listed as Tritomas. There are a few other summer-blooming bulbs, such as the white-spike Galtonia, Allium, Liriope, Camassia, and the decorative-flowered Lachenalia.

Gloriosa (Climbing Lily) is an unusual and spectacular plant, bearing brilliant yellow and red flowers with tendrils on the tips of its leaves. Given necessary support, the climbing plant reaches a height of five or six feet. To grow, each tuberous root must have an eye. It should be watered freely during the growing season and fed generously with applications of liquid manure every two weeks until the buds begin to form.

Iris Family (*Iridaceae*)

The *Iridaceae* family contains over 60 genera and perhaps 1,000 species. They are generally described as herbs having sword-shaped leaves, rhizomes, bulbs or bulb-like rootstocks, and handsome, six-segmented flowers. Southern garden favorites include: Iris, Blackberry Lily, Dietes, Gladiolus, Ixia, Marica, Montbretia, Sisyrinchium, Sparaxis, Tigridia, and Watsonia.

The genus Iris boasts one of the world's most famous flower forms. Different species of iris grow in sundry climates, from cold mountain regions to swamps, sea coasts, and temperate plains. If their needs are met, some will flourish and naturalize. Irises are divided into two main root classifications: bulbous and rhizomatous; and the rhizomatous classification is in turn subdivided into: Bearded, Beardless, and Crested, according to their petal forms. The bulbous group includes the Dutch, Algerian (*Iris tingitana*), and the small winter-blooming *I. reticulata*. They are most effective in the garden when planted in clumps and may be interspersed with other spring bulbs. Plant three inches deep on a cushion of sand underlain with bone meal and phosphate. Avoid planting them in a bed which requires summer watering as they are subject to rotting. They are excellent for cutting.

Bearded Iris

The beautiful rainbow-hued Bearded Irises do not adapt easily to our scorching summers and mild wet winters but if their basic requirements are met and if the varieties have been tested in mild climates, they may thrive. Varieties "too tender" for northern growers are often just right for us.

Proper varietal selection, plenty of sun, good drainage, and slightly alkaline soil are the keys to good iris culture. Bearded irises cannot share beds with plants needing heavy watering in the summer because the rhizomes' natural cycle demands dormancy and fairly dry soil in the summer. The rebloomers are an exception to this, if you want fall or winter bloom. Early autumn planting in raised beds of sandy loam sweetened with lime and enriched with bone meal and superphosphate is recommended. Rotted manure or commercial fertilizers may be turned deep into the bed where the feeder roots will reach, but must never touch the rhizomes. Each rhizome, with its roots trailing downward, should be placed on a small mound and barely covered with soil. After blooming and in the fall, fertilize with bone meal, either alone or in combination with an inorganic formula. Remember that too much nitrogen in any form produces fine foliage

Louisiana Iris.

Landscape combination of tulips, hyacinths, pansies.

but few flowers. At the first sign of rot, or of growing tips melting away after a prolonged rainy spell, the rhizomes may be lifted and the soft parts cut off. Treat with sulphur, full strength clorox, or Terraclor before replanting, or on noticing the first mustard seed-like particles of the fungus at ground level, douse the entire area with a mild solution of Terraclor. This treatment is also good for Spurias and other irises which have contracted bacterial soft rot.

A few vigorous Bearded Irises have been developed which will give both spring and autumn or winter bloom if continuously fertilized and kept moist all summer. These are called "remontant," or reblooming, and are recommended for this climate; however, they may bloom in only one of those seasons in this area. Few Dwarf, Intermediate or Miniature Tall Bearded Irises have thrived here, but older Intermediates sometimes bloom after a period of years. In selecting Bearded Irises, choose those listed as rebloomers or mild climate irises.

Beardless Iris

The Beardless types which may be grown in this area include the Japanese, Siberian, Spuria,

Algerian (*I. unguicularis*), and the Louisiana natives and hybrids. The spectacular Japanese *I. kaempferi* and its hybrids prefer very rich, lime-free soil and must be kept very wet before early summer blooming and quite dry while dormant in autumn and winter. They may be planted in redwood boxes or tubs, sunk in ponds for flowering, and then removed to a dry situation for their dormant season. The dainty Siberian Iris is an early bloomer which may adapt itself to southern gardens if given a rich soil and plenty of sun and moisture. They are most effective in clumps and do not like to be disturbed. *I. unguicularis*, also called *I. stylosa*, is valuable for its long period of winter bloom. The flowers, which have no real stems, should be gathered in bud and will open in water the next day.

Spuria Iris

Highly recommended are the stately Spuria Irises, which have handsome, sword-like leaves and erect stalks crowned with six or eight blooms in spike formation. They are long-lived as cut flowers and resistant to wind, rain, heat, and cold. The older species *I. ochroleuca* is a favorite for flower arranging because its blooms spiral

258

Tulips en masse.

Dutch Iris with nicotiana, hyacinths, and daffodils.

close around the unbranched stalk in an unusual manner. Plant only in the fall in sunny, well-drained beds, into which any balanced fertilizer or rotted manure supplemented with bone meal has been mixed. Set the rhizome on a mound of soil with roots spread beneath it. The roots must not be allowed to dry out during the purchasing and transplanting process. Barely cover the top of the rhizome with soil and level the bed. Add a little mulch to prevent sunburn. Fertilize in the early fall and again in the late winter. Spurias should not be moved often, so allow a three-foot area for the mother rhizome to spread into a large clump. They like wet winters and dry summers but will tolerate more extremes than the Bearded varieties. Should fungus appear, treatment is the same as for Bearded Irises.

Lousiana Swamp Iris

The slender swamp irises of Louisiana are the most indigenous of their family to our area. With a wonderful range of colors, the new hybrid varieties rival in beauty and gràce the more difficult Japanese. They will adapt easily to most gardens here, whether sunny or semi-shaded. However, an ideal situation for them is a low bed or pond edge where they may occasionally have standing water in their winter growing season and dry out in summer. Rotted barnyard manure and leafmold or organic compost are preferred soil conditioners, but others may be used. The rhizomes should be barely covered with soil, and mulched quite heavily in the hot months with any handy dressing. As with other irises, feed generously after blooming and in early autumn with well-rotted manure or a balanced fertilizer. Never put fertilizer directly on a rhizome; scratch it lightly into the surrounding soil and water.

Evansia Iris

The Crested or Evansia Irises are very useful in Houston gardens. They make good companion plants for azaleas, as they bloom about the same time and have the same acid soil and shade preferences. *Iris cristata*, with lovely little blue flowers, is a miniature variety of Evansia. It prefers year-round moisture and soil with much humus, but will adapt to other conditions. Transplanting is best done immediately after flowering when new roots are produced. Another Evansia iris which has been proven here is the widely branched *I. japonica*, which bears numerous pale lavender flowers with orange crests on a single stem. It does better in considerable shade than in sunlight and, like *I. cristata*, needs humus and leafmold. Two beautiful hybrids, Nada and Darjeeling, have frilled white flowers.

The Beardless Irises in the following list offer a wide color range and have been grown successfully in this area:

LOUISIANA IRIS
Barbara Elaine Taylor (Levingston) - tall white
Bayou Sunset (MacMillian) - soft rose and gold
Chuck (Arny) - wine red
Charlie's Michelle (Arny) - frilled rosy pink
Dean Lee (Arny) - small bright brown
Dixie Deb (Chowning) - yellow, good garden iris
Eolian (Arny) - light blue
F. A. C. McCulla (Arny) - fine red
Faenelia Hicks (Arny) - large pink
G. W. Holleyman (R. Holleyman) - tall yellow
Ila Nunn (Arny) - tall cream
Katherine Cornay (Arny) - mineral violet
Marie Caillet (Conger) - red purple
Mrs. Ira Nelson (Arny) - large lavender
New Offering (Davis) - blue purple
Queen of Queens (Holleyman) - creamy white
The Kahn (Dormon) - black purple, yellow signal
Violet Ray (Dormon) - purple, white ray
Wheelhorse (Dormon) - bright rose
Wood Violet (Dormon) - low, bright blue

SPURIA IRIS
Arbitrator (Ferguson) - purple and yellow
Archie Owen (Hager) - deep yellow
Baritone (Ferguson) - large brown
Driftwood (Walker) - brown
Elixir (Hager) - orange yellow
Fort Ridge (Ferguson) - good blue
Golden Lady (Combs) - good yellow
Good Thunder (Ferguson) - large yellow

Marilyn Holloway (Hager) - blue lavender
Frost (Ferguson) - ruffled white
Minneopa (Ferguson) - pale blue and yellow
Proverb (Ferguson) - dark blue purple
Wakerobin (Ferguson) - white
Windfall (Ferguson) - cream and yellow
Wadi Zem Zem - pale Yellow
I. ochroleuca - white and yellow

DUTCH IRIS
Wedgewood - medium blue, early
Imperator - dark blue, late
Blue Ribbon - vivid blue
White Perfection - white
Golden Emperor - yellow
Le Mogul - bronze
Princess Irene - white and orange

Gladiolus
Gladiolus, another major member of the *Iridaceae* family, is available in a dazzling range of colors, although form varies little. They are easy to grow in good garden soil and will provide succession bloom if planted at two-week intervals in the early spring and late summer and staked. Gladioli give most satisfactory results in garden display and for cutting when selected color blends are planted rather than packaged mixtures, which are usually disappointing and often inferior. For maximum bloom, gladioli should be fed with a liquid fertilizer once a week from the time the stalk begins to lengthen until the first color shows. This is particularly important when growing flowers for exhibition. Flower spikes should be cut when the two lowest florets open, and not more than one leaf should be cut from each plant. Thrips, gladiolus' worst pest, are easily controlled if a recommended soil and bulb dust or spray is applied weekly from the time foliage is six inches high to flowering. Some gardeners let bulbs stay in the ground, but flowering diminishes each year. Bulbs may be lifted and stored for the winter after foliage has dried. Before storage, remove old foliage and treat corms with an insecticide. The *Primulinus* type, the *Gladi-*

olus tristis, and the dainty hybrids known as Baby Gladioli are smaller, more graceful plants popularly grown in this area.

South African Dietes

The South African Dietes, though not a true iris, has iris-like foliage and blooms on and off all summer. Each flower lasts only a day but is rapidly followed by another. The Oakhurst and *Johnsoni* hybrids are particularly adaptable to this climate. Marica, or the so-called "Walking Iris," naturalizes easily. The weight of young plants formed on the ends of old flower stalks pulls the old stems down and the proliferations take root.

Montbretias and Watsonias

Montbretias and Watsonias make a brilliant, colorful, and decorative display in summer gardens and are desirable acquisitions for the border or for cutting. Their culture is similar to that of gladioli, but they may be left undisturbed for several years. The Earlham hybrids of Montbretias are very lovely and excellent for cutting. These bulbs may be left in the ground but will be improved by lifting, separating, and replanting every alternate autumn.

Blackberry Lily

The Blackberry Lily, or Belamcanda, is adaptable to any soil, thriving in full sun or semishade. The yellow flowers brighten summer gardens and keep well when cut. The seed formation, which resembles a blackberry, may be dried and used for winter arrangements.

Ixia and Sparaxis

Ixia and Sparaxis, both originating in South Africa, have similar small, star-shaped flowers borne on long slender stems above grass-like foliage. Lovely for cutting, the colors run the gamut of the golden tones from cream to scarlet.

Tigridias

Tigridias (Shell Flowers) thrive in southern gardens because they can withstand intense heat.

Natives of Mexico, their large, triangular-shaped flowers are brilliantly colored and have a long blooming season. The smallest member of the iris family is the *Sisyrinchium*, or Blue-Eyed Grass. Its small, dainty blossoms open one at a time, keeping up a long succession of bloom.

Arum Family (*Araceae*)

In the South, Callas do best in a light soil to which well-rotted manure, sand, and humus have been added. If desired, the roots may be started early indoors in pots and later transferred to the garden when all danger of frost is past. After blooming, when the foliage has dried, the roots should be dug and stored in dry sand or peat moss to give them a few months rest. The hardy White Callas may be left in the ground for the summer in order to increase, but they, too, will benefit by digging in the fall. The yellow variety, *Elliotiana*, with its interesting spotted foliage, is less hardy and requires semi-shade and a slightly acid soil. The shade-loving evergreen Baby Calla and the Pink Calla, usually grown in pots, are becoming more popular. Rot sometimes occurs in callas and is usually caused by a high soil pH (too alkaline) or by using green manure. Refer to SOIL chapter for pH.

Anthuriums

Anthuriums are highly prized as pot plants for their beautiful exotic flowers. *A. scherzerianum* (Flamingo Flower) and *Spathiphyllum clevelandi* will bloom in high garden shade or in the house. The shade and moisture-loving *Arisaema triphyllum* (Jack-in-the-Pulpit), with its calla-like flowers of mottled green and brown, is most effective when planted among ferns or wild flowers.

Caladiums

Caladiums, related to callas, are highly esteemed as bedding plants for their ornamental veined and marbled foliage and brilliant coloring. They like a well-drained, friable, somewhat acid soil, semi-shade and moisture. They may be used among azalea plantings to provide color during the summer. Tubers may be planted as soon as the ground has warmed. Caladium leaves die back naturally in the fall, when the bulbs should be dug, dusted with sulphur, and stored in dry sand.

Ginger Family (*Zingiberaceae*)

Several varieties of the tropical Ginger family are grown successfully in this area. Butterfly Lilies (*Hedychium coronarium*) bloom in summer and are prized for their pure white, fragrant flowers which resemble large butterflies. Ginger Lilies (*H. gardnerianum*), a more tender variety, have yellow flowers tipped with scarlet and bright green canna-like foliage. After blooming, each *Hedychium* stalk should be cut off near the ground to promote new growth. Pink Shell Ginger (*Alpinia speciosa* or *nutans*) has handsome clusters of pink buds opening into striped yellowish flowers. Hidden Ginger (*Curcuma petiolata*) flowers in a compact spike of pink, yellow, and lavender bracts.

Canna Family (*Cannaceae*)

There are many beautiful Canna hybrids. The two main groups are the orchid-flowered type and the more popular gladiolus-flowered type, which is of dwarf habit and free-blooming. Cannas may be selected according to color and are most effective when planted as bold accents in borders or in large masses. Grand Opera varieties include colors of old rose, salmon, peach-pink, yellowish-pink, and canary yellow. The bronze-leaved varieties are especially desirable for their foliage as well as for their flowers.

Dahlias

Dahlias may be grown successfully in any well-drained soil, but a good garden loam rich in humus is best. They should have an open sunny situation with free air circulation at all times. The tuberous roots should be planted horizontally with the sprout pointing upwards, and they need to be staked at planting time to give support to the plants as they grow. Cultivation should be shallow to avoid damaging the root system. When plants are about a foot high, the top should be pinched out to develop a sturdier, more branching plant. Tall dahlias benefit from disbudding, leaving only the largest and best bud on each branch. The smaller varieties need no disbudding, may be planted closer together, and are more adaptable in landscaping than the larger varieties, especially for the Houston vicinity. They come in a wide range of colors and provide a lavish supply of blossoms, which are long-lasting if cut in early morning or late afternoon and immediately immersed in water to cover most of the stems. The plants should be fed as soon as the flower buds form, using a small amount of commercial fertilizer lightly worked into the soil, but not within several inches of the stem. Feedings may be repeated every ten days during the blooming season. The soil should be well watered after planting; but during early growth, watering should be just sufficient to keep the plants growing well. The plants require more water after feeding begins. A light mulch of leaves or dried grass cuttings will conserve moisture, keep the roots cool, and make cultivation unnecessary.

Waterlilies

Waterlilies bloom in this area from May until frost. They may be grown in tubs or pools, but they must have full sun to bloom freely. When planted in submerged boxes, the soil should be very rich, containing a generous amount of manure or bone meal, renewed every second year. Lilies growing in a natural pool may be fertilized by spreading bone meal on the water surface in March. Roots should be divided in April while the plants are dormant. The roots will not freeze in this climate if they are covered with a foot of water. Among the varieties which are successful here are the Blue Beauty, the Pink Houston Lily, the white, yellow-centered Georgia Prince, and the Pink Zanzibar. Lavender Water Hyacinths and yellow Waterpoppies add interest and color to pools. For large pools or small lakes, the native Chinquapin is ideal, as it has huge pale yellow, lotus-like flowers.

Pot-Grown Bulbs

Most bulbs may be grown successfully in pots. Many gardeners prefer pot culture, even for hardy bulbs, because potted plants may be conveniently moved and easily protected from sudden drops of temperature. Pots and other containers are used for year-round growing as well as for "forcing," that is, grown out of the normal season for flowering.

There are three methods commonly used for growing bulbs in pots; the first and easiest is using fiber, pebbles, or water as the growing medium. Paperwhite Narcissus, Lilies-of-the-Valley, Ismene, and others are grown in this manner. When first planted, the bulbs should be kept in a dark cool place until the root system is developed. When growing bulbs in water and pebbles, keep the level of water just below the bases of the bulbs. Moisten fiber thoroughly before placing bulbs in it, then drain off excess water. The bulbs must be firmly placed with fiber closely packed around them. Never permit fiber to become dry. Bulbs grown by this method exhaust themselves in one season and should be discarded after blooming.

The second method, generally used for hardy bulbs such as Ixia and Sparaxis, is that of forcing in soil with preliminary root growth. While some bulbs require special soil formulas, a light, rich, well-drained soil of an equal mixture of loam, sand, and leafmold or compost suffices for the majority. Two tablespoonfuls of bone meal may be mixed in to each 8-inch pot for nourishment. The potted bulbs should be stored outside in a cold place and covered with leaves and peat moss for six or seven weeks. Clay pots should be well-watered before storing. Slightly dampened sawdust may be used if pots are stored under cover. Bulbs which are grown carefully in this manner may usually be saved for another season's bloom. Bulbs should be ripened properly after flowering by lessening water gradually until leaves turn brown. Leave in pots until fall, then plant in the garden.

The third method, generally used for tender bulbs such as Eucharis and Anthurium, is to plant in a sufficient enriched soil in which the bulbs can make normal growth and development without relying upon the food supply stored within the bulb itself. Many bulbs grown by this method will need replanting only every two to four years.

BULBS, TUBERS, RHIZOMES, CORMS AND TUBEROUS ROOTS

To bloom well most bulbs need sun and fast-draining soil of equal parts rich loam, sand, and humus. The usual planting depth is *twice* the bulb's diameter. A pinch, each, of bonemeal and superphosphate *under* the soil in the bottom of the hole helps. Careful selection from the different categories can bring the pleasure of monthly bloom. See BULBS chapter.

B = Bulbs	T = Tubers	R = Rhizomes	C = Corms	TR = Tuberous Roots	spp. = Species
Common Name *Botanical Name*	**Color**	**Time To Plant**	**Bloom Time**		**Comments**
ACHIMENES R (STAR OF INDIA) *Achimenes*	White, Pink, Blue, Lavender, Magenta	Nov.-Dec. Feb.-Apr.	June-Sept.		Light shade. Fibrous loam, 1/3 each sand, peat, loam. Cover 1". No fertilizer at planting. Uniform watering. Shallow rooting. Thrives in sphagnum moss baskets. Naturalizes. To 8" high, sprawling over ground.
ACIDANTHERA, BICOLOR C	Creamy White	Feb.-Apr.	Aug.-Sept.		Sun. Well-drained soil. Plant 3" deep. Water as needed. Fertilize. To 3' tall. Cuts well. Fragrant. Similar to Gladiolus. Naturalizes.
ACORUS (SWEET FLAG) R *Acorus gramineus variegatus*		Apr.-Aug.			Partial shade. Very moist, fertile, loose soil with rotted manure, humus, and sharp sand. May spread rapidly as ground cover in small area if soil is fertile, loose, and wet enough. Fertilize with 8-8-8 or similar. Cut back old brown leaves in late winter. In pots allow to become rootbound before dividing. 'Variegata' is variegated, green/yellow variety. Multiplies. To 8" high.
AGAPANTHUS R (LILY-OF-THE-NILE) *Agapanthus orientalis* *A. 'Albidus'*	Blue White	Oct.-Feb.	May-June		Sun or partial shade. Good drainage. Half loam and half peat. Cover 2". Water freely in spring. Excellent near edge of pool. Naturalizes. Root hardy. Plant high. Fertilize after blooming and again in the early spring. To 4'. Dwarf form, 'Peter Pan'.

BULBS, TUBERS, RHIZOMES, CORMS AND TUBEROUS ROOTS

Common Name *Botanical Name*	Color	Time To Plant	Bloom Time	Comments
ALLIUM B *Allium Neapolitanum* *Cv. grandiflorum*	White, Pink, Blue, Yellow	Sept.-Mar.	Jan.-Sept.	Sun. Sandy loam. Plant 2-6" deep. Good drainage. Other species. Naturalizes. Long-lasting cut flowers. To 18" tall.
ALSTROEMERIA T (PERUVIAN LILY) *Alstroemeria,* in spp.	Orange, Yellow, Pink, White, Lavender, Red	Oct.-May	May-June	Sun in A.M. Half-hardy, semi-tropical. Must have well-drained, light soil with manure. Excellent for cutting. Requires winter mulch. Azalea-like blossoms. Naturalizes. Multiplies. Plant 6" deep with tuber horizontal. To 26" tall.
AMARCRINUM B *Amarcrinum Howardii*	Shell Pink, White	Oct.-May	Summer	Sun or part shade. Light soil with good drainage. Blooms periodically during summer. 3' tall. Naturalizes. *A.* 'Delkins Find' is smaller. Water freely.
AMARYLLIS B *Amaryllis*	White, Red, Pink, Orange, Two-Tone	Nov.-Feb.	Spring	Sun or semi-sun. Rich, sandy, loose garden soil. Requires good drainage. Plant high, 1/2 of bulb above soil. Feed after blooming and again in the fall. Keep mulched. California and Dutch hybrids. Grows well in pots. Can be timed to bloom for Christmas. Multiplies. Usually needs staking; to 30" tall.
ANEMONE T *Anemone* spp.	Blue, Scarlet, White, Lavender	Sept.-Dec.	Feb.-Mar.	Sun. Good drainage. Light, sandy loam with peat. Requires moisture. Parsley-like foliage. 'De-Caen,' 'Tecolete,' and 'St. Brigid' strains good. Soak tubers 2 hours before planting. Plant 2" deep. Grows to 15" tall. 2" to 3" flowers keep well when cut.
ARUM *Italicum*	Red Seed Pods	Spring	Late Summer	Semi-shade. Calla-like foliage and flowers.

BULBS, TUBERS, RHIZOMES, CORMS AND TUBEROUS ROOTS

B = Bulbs	T = Tubers	R = Rhizomes	C = Corms	TR = Tuberous Roots	spp. = Species

Common Name *Botanical Name*	Color	Time To Plant	Bloom Time	Comments
ASPIDISTRA T E (CAST IRON PLANT) *Aspidistra elatior*	Dark Green or Variegated Foliage	Anytime		Semi-shade or shade. Tolerates heat and poor soil. Acid tolerant. Evergreen. Multiplies. Plant just covering tubers. Cuts well. Good container plant. Direct sun burns leaves. Water when dry. 18" tall. Divide when crowded.
BLACKBERRY LILY TR *Belamcanda* spp.	Yellow-Orange with Black Spots	Aug.-Mar.	June-Aug.	Sun or semi-shade. Any garden soil. Plant 2" deep. Naturalizes easily. Flowers followed by ornamental black seed clusters; nice in arrangements. 2-3' tall. Tolerates heat and drought. 2" flowers. Iris-type leaves. Reseeds.
BLUE-EYED GRASS B *Sisyrinchium iridifolium*	Blue, Yellow, White	Anytime	Mar.-June	Sun. Sandy loam. Barely cover. Succession of tiny blooms during spring and early summer. Clusters of 1/2" flowers. Texas NATIVE. Naturalizes. 12" tall.
BUTTERFLY or GINGER LILY R *Hedychium coronarium* *H. Gardneranum* (KAHILI GINGER)	White Yellow, Scarlet Filaments	Feb.-Mar.	July-Nov.	Part shade; likes A.M. sun. Fertile soil with drainage. Give generous amount of fertilizer. Stalks 4-7' tall with clusters of fragrant, butterfly-like 2" flowers. Root hardy when mulched. Divide when crowded. Many species with different color flowers. Multiplies.
CALADIUM T *Caladium bicolor*	Variegated Foliage Red, White, Pink, Green	May, after soil warms to 70°; planting in cold soil promotes decay and stunts growth	June-Sept. Color	Semi-shade. Mildly acid, loose, well-draining soil with cow manure or other organic matter. Keep soil moist. Lift and store in the fall in dry peat moss. Good summer-long mass display. Cut unattractive flowers to encourage better leaf growth. There are two types: fancy leaved and small strap leaved. Most strap-leaved varieites tolerate sun well. Many varieties. Plant with smooth side of tuber down; cover 1". From 12"

BULBS, TUBERS, RHIZOMES, CORMS AND TUBEROUS ROOTS

Common Name *Botanical Name*	Color	Time To Plant	Bloom Time	Comments
CALADIUM, contd.				to 30" tall. Removing the "eye" in the central point of the bulb increases the number of leaves.
CALLA LILLY R *Zantedeschia* *aethiopica* Var. ELLIOTTIANA C *Z. a. 'Childseana'* *Z. a. Godefreyana* *Z. Rehmanni*	White Yellow with Spotted Foliage White, dwarf White, dwarf Pink, tall	Sept.-Oct.	Feb.-May	Sun or part shade. Loose, rich soil with humus and manure. Water freely. Feed regularly with fertilizer mix high in phosphate. Protect from cold with thick mulch but remove when sun is hot. May leave rhizome in ground. Multiplies.
CANNA R or T *Canna x generalis*	Red, Yellow, White, Salmon, Pink, Some Mottled	May-Dec.	May-Frost	Sun. Rich, 12" deep, organic soil. Good drainage. Water freely. Plant 18" apart. Good for color masses. Feed often during bloom season, 1/2 strength liquid fertilizer, high in phosphorus. Cutting back to ground in winter helps eliminate Leaf Rollers; use thuricide to control. Varieties vary from 5' tall to 18" dwarfs. May divide in spring. Multiplies rapidly.
CAPE IRIS B *Homeria* spp	Various	Oct.-Dec.	March	Sun. Sandy loam with peat moss. Good drainage as in raised bed. Sword-like leaves to 2'. Flowers, in clusters to 18" tall, longlasting. Likes to be dry. Plant in masses or clumps, or along border, but not singly. Multiplies.
CHIONODOXA B (GLORY-OF-THE-SNOW)	Blue, White, Pink	Sept.	Mar.-Apr.	Sun or partial shade. Rich, deep, organic soil. Naturalizes. Star-shaped flowers. Most effective when planted in large clumps. Cover 2-3". 6-10" tall.

267

BULBS, TUBERS, RHIZOMES, CORMS AND TUBEROUS ROOTS

B = Bulbs   T = Tubers   R = Rhizomes   C = Corms   TR = Tuberous Roots   spp. = Species

Common Name *Botanical Name*	Color	Time To Plant	Bloom Time	Comments
CHLIDANTHUS B *Chlidanthus fragrans*	Yellow	Aug.-Apr.	Mar.-Apr.	Sun. Plant in pots with neck above well-draining soil with sand and humus. Cover 3". Flowers resemble miniature Amaryllis. Bulbs should be lifted and stored. Tender. 12" tall.
CLIVIA B or TR (KAFFIR LILY) *Clivia*	Yellow, Apricot, Orange	Anytime	Feb.-Apr.	Shade, in pots, staked, 2" deep. Potting mixture of loam, sand, humus, and bonemeal with charcoal for drainage. Occasional feedings of liquid manure. Evergreen. Outdoors in summer in shady location, then brought to cool but protected porch. Needs to be brought in during very cold weather. Blooms in indirect light for several weeks. 18-24" tall. Multiplies. Likes to be potbound. Do not allow to dry out completely. Uniform water.
COLCHICUM C (AUTUMN CROCUS)	Lavender, Purple, White	Sept.-Oct.	Aug.-Sept.	Sun to part shade. Loose, loamy soil with humus. Needs drainage. Blooms without foliage. Corms bloom even without soil and water. Low growing, 6-8" high. Multiplies.
CRINUM (SPIDER LILY) B *Crinum* Many good species and hybrids	Pink, White, Wine	Anytime	Mar.-Dec.	Sun with partial shade in summer. Moist, rich, organic, sandy soil. Plant high with neck 1-2" above soil. Water freely. Feed early spring with bonemeal after blooming and again in the fall with mixture of old manure and superphosphate. 2-4' tall. Broad, glossy, evergreen leaves. Allow 2-3' between bulbs. Naturalizes. Keep roots moist when dividing and transplanting. *C. americana* (SWAMP CRINUM) will grow in standing water. *C.* 'Ellen Bosanquet,' strong, fragrant, wine-colored blooms cut well; one of best for Houston.

268

BULBS, TUBERS, RHIZOMES, CORMS AND TUBEROUS ROOTS

Common Name Botanical Name	Color	Time To Plant	Bloom Time	Comments
CROCUS C *Crocus*	White, Yellow, Blue, Purple	Sept.-Dec.	Jan.-Mar.	Winter sun. Light, sandy soil. Good drainage. 4-6" tall. 1 T. bonemeal, covered with 1-2" soil, in planting hole. Early spring bloom. Grassy leaves. Houston winters often too warm for Crocus. For improved bloom, refrigerate 6 weeks before planting. Best in clumps or drifts. Meager flowering may indicate poor drainage or crowding of bulbs.
CYCLAMEN T	White, Pink, Mauve, Rose, Lavender	Nov.-Feb.	Nov.-Apr.	Semi-sun. Loamy, sandy soil with good drainage. Tolerates cold but not summer heat. Hardy wild Cyclamen has 1" flowers. Persian Cyclamen, florist type, 2-3" flowers. Both grow in pots. 6-10" tall.
DÁFFODIL B *Narcissus Pseudo-Narcissus*	White, Yellow	Oct.-Jan.	Jan.-Mar.	Sun or semi-shade. Rich, sandy garden soil. Some varieties naturalize. See BULBS chapter. Select varieties known to prosper in Houston's climate. Good in clumps and drifts. 1-3" flowers, 16-24" tall. Slender leaves. Hardy. Following bloom of naturalizing varieties, allow foliage to yellow. Feed until foliage dies down.
DAHLIA T *Dahlia*	Red, Yellow, White, Lilac, Purple	Mar.-May (Plants)	June-Nov.	A.M. sun. Good drainage as in raised beds of rich, porous, fertile soil. Single varieties valuable for cutting. Miniature hybrid types excellent for bedding. To 2'. Stake. Cut back to ground after initial bloom. Will rebloom in fall. When in bud, feed with 5-10-5 fertilizer every 2 weeks. In planting hole, 8-10" deep, add bonemeal or superphosphate and cover with 3" to 4" soil, topped with sand. With the eye up, place tuber on sand and

BULBS, TUBERS, RHIZOMES, CORMS AND TUBEROUS ROOTS

B = Bulbs	T = Tubers	R = Rhizomes	C = Corms	TR = Tuberous Roots	spp. = Species

Common Name *Botanical Name*	Color	Time To Plant	Bloom Time	Comments
DAHLIA, contd.				cover with about 3" of porous soil.
DAYLILY TR *Hemerocallis*	Shades of Orange, Lemon, Red, Pink, Yellow	Anytime	Apr.-July	At least 6 hours sun. Fertile, slightly acid soil best. Water moderately. Good drainage. Free bloomer. Hardy. To 36" tall. Many varieties. Space 1-1/2' to 2' apart. Several buds to each stem. Flowers close at night, lasting only one day, but new buds continue to open each day. Best in groups. More blooms with regular fertilizing from spring to fall. Don't fertilize until 4-6 weeks after planting or during June, July, or August. Use 1/2 recommended amount of a fertilizer low in nitrogen (12-24-12 or 5-10-5) in early spring and fall. Daylilies respond to additional phosphorus in early spring and cottonseed or bonemeal after they're growing well. Multiplies. Thin crowded plants. Do not overwater. In fall cut foliage to 6".
DIETES R (AFRICAN IRID) *Moraea iridoides*	White with Orange or Yellow Throat	Anytime	Summer	Morning sun. Tender. Sandy soil with peat moss. Cover 1". Reflowers on same bloom stalk. Other species also desirable. Evergreen. To 3' tall.
ELEPHANT'S EAR T *Colocasia antiquorum*		Mar.-Oct.		Part sun to shade. Rich, well-drained soil. Abundant water. Root hardy; protect with leaf mulch. To 5' tall. Leaves 2' x 18". Cover 5". *AVOID CONTACT WITH EYES. DO NOT INGEST.* Multiplies.

BULBS, TUBERS, RHIZOMES, CORMS AND TUBEROUS ROOTS

Common Name *Botanical Name*	Color	Time To Plant	Bloom Time	Comments
EUCHARIS B (AMAZON LILY) *Eucharis grandiflora*	White	Nov.-Jan.	Dec.-Feb.	Filtered shade. Plant in pots in rich, coarse, draining soil with humus. Needs drainage. Large clusters of exquisite, fragrant, star-shaped flowers. Plant with neck of bulb above soil. Tender. Evergreen. Feeding during growth stimulates blooming. To 20" tall.
FREESIA C *Freesia*	Blue, Red, Orange, Yellow, White	Sept.-Dec.	Jan.-Mar.	Sun to semi-shade. Sandy loam with peat moss. Fragrant. Water moderately. Feed regularly. About 12" tall. In clumps or borders. Cover 1". White best to naturalize.
GALTONIA B (SUMMER HYACINTH) *Galtonia candicans*	White	Feb.-May	Apr.-June	Sun to part shade. Rich, sandy soil. Water freely. Hardy. Fragrant. Will produce a succession of blooms if flowers are kept cut as they fade. Beautiful bloom spikes 3-4'. Cover 5". To 3' tall.
GINGER LILY R (HIDDEN) *Zingeber* spp. *Cucurma* spp.	Pink, Yellow, Red, Green Bracts, Variegated	Mar.-Sept.	May-Sept.	Partial shade. Loose, rich soil. Drainage. Keep moist year round. Feed in growing season. 2-3' high. Some have variegated foliage. Protect bulb from freeze with mulch of leaves, grass, moss, etc.
GINGER, SHELL R *Alpinia Zerumbet*	Pinkish White	Feb.-Sept.	May-June	A.M. sun. Rich, loamy soil. Abundant water. Pink buds opening to white flowers with yellow lip, red-striped. Won't bloom well if allowed to freeze. Protect. Fragrant. Large tropical plants. Forms clumps. 5-6' tall.

BULBS, TUBERS, RHIZOMES, CORMS AND TUBEROUS ROOTS

B = Bulbs   T = Tubers   R = Rhizomes   C = Corms   TR = Tuberous Roots   spp. = Species

Common Name *Botanical Name*	Color	Time To Plant	Bloom Time	Comments
GLADIOLUS C *Gladiolus Hortulanus*	Various	Feb.-Sept. July-Sept.	Apr.-June Oct.-Nov.	Sun or partial shade. Rich, sandy garden soil. Water freely. To 5' tall. Cover 5". Stake. 'Tiny Tot' series are miniatures to 3' tall. *G. tristis* is fragrant. Each plant blooms 7-10 days. Staggered plantings every 2 weeks allow continuous blooming. Lift and dry corms. Sprinkle with sulphur and store in old nylon hose in dry, airy place till next year.
G. byzantinus	Magenta		May	Plant with other Gladioli. Shorter, 18". Do not require staking. Excellent as cut flowers. Showy. Reliable naturalizers.
GLORIOSA T (CLIMBING LILY) *Gloriosa rothschildiana* (best) *G. superba*	Scarlet Margined with Yellow	Feb.-May	June-Aug.	Full sun. Rich, moist soil. Drainage. Plant horizontally 1' apart, 2" deep. Point tuber in direction to grow. Exotic blooms excellent for cutting. Climbs to 6' on support. Overwinters in ground. Likes shade on roots. Manure in soil and feeding increase bloom. Root hardy.
GRAPE HYACINTH B *Muscari*	Blue, White	Oct.-Jan.	Feb.-Mar.	Sun or partial shade. Good garden soil. Cover 2". Naturalizes. Useful for edging and for ground cover. Fragrant. 6" tall. Several varieties grow well in Houston.
GUERNSEY LILY B *Nerine samiensis*	Coral, Red, Yellow	Feb.-Apr.	September	Sun or shade. Garden soil. Barely cover. Divide every 2 or 3 years. Naturalizes. Fertilize with superphosphate worked in and watered in July or August. To 20" tall.
HABRANTHUS B (RAIN LILIES) *Habranthus brachyandrus* *H. robustus*	Pink to Maroon, Shell Pink	Sept.-Dec. (Bulbs) Anytime (Plants)	May-Aug.	Sun or partial shade. Loose, rich, sandy soil. Good drainage. 7-9" tall. Plant in groups. Winter dormant and hardy. Naturalizes. Best behind small evergreens

BULBS, TUBERS, RHIZOMES, CORMS AND TUBEROUS ROOTS

Common Name *Botanical Name*	Color	Time To Plant	Bloom Time	Comments
HABRANTHUS, contd.				such as Zephyranthes or Liriope. 1-3" flowers. *H. Texanus* 'Copper Lily,' yellow, Texas NATIVE.
HAEMANTHUS B (BLOOD LILY) *Haemanthus katharinae* *H. coccineus*	Red	Jan.-Mar.	Aug.-Oct.	Partial shade. Slightly acid soil containing leafmold. Plant bulb high, just out of soil. Tops die down in winter. Bulbs need winter rest without water. Good in pots. Tender. To 20" tall.
HOSTA TR (PLANTAIN LILY) *Hosta* spp.	White, Lavender	Feb.-Nov.	May July	Semi-shade to shade. Fertile, porous, sand, and humus soil with good drainage. Ample water. Withhold water during dormancy. In garden or pots. Known principally for its clumps of green or variegated strap-like leaves. Flowers on long stems. Good outdoor container plant in shade. Subject to snails and slugs. Root hardy; tops freeze. Plant in cool place. Good for shady, moist areas. Takes several years to get big. Many selections. Grows 1-3' tall.
HYACINTH B *Hyacinthus*	Pink, Blue, White, Yellow	Nov.-Dec.	Feb.-Apr.	Sun. Rich soil, preferably sandy. Plant 2-3" deep. Water freely after leaves come, withhold while blooming. Several varieties. Roman Hyacinths precede Dutch varieties. For water culture, keep in cool, dark place until growth starts, then expose to light. Several types: Dutch, Roman, and multiflora. Best in groups. Some naturalize. May be planted in garden or in pots. Refrigerate 6-8 weeks before planting. To 8" tall.
IPHEION C (STAR FLOWER) *Ipheion uniflorum*	White, Blue	Oct.-Dec.	Mar.-May	Sun to part sun. Light, sandy soil. Requires good drainage. Fragrant. Star-shaped, 1" to 1-1/2", fragrant flowers on 6" stems. Feed for better blooming. Cover

273

BULBS, TUBERS, RHIZOMES, CORMS AND TUBEROUS ROOTS

B = Bulbs	T = Tubers	R = Rhizomes	C = Corms	TR = Tuberous Roots	spp. = Species

Common Name *Botanical Name*	Color	Time To Plant	Bloom Time	Comments
IPHEION, contd.				bulb with 1" soil. Reliable naturalizer.
IRIS R (YELLOW FLAG) *Iris pseudacorus*	Yellow	Sept.-Nov. Anytime (Plants)	Mar.-Apr.	Sun or shade. Fertile, moist soil. Cover with 1" soil. 3-4' tall. Nearly evergreen. Erect growth. Grows well around pools. Multiplies rapidly.
IRIS, ALGERIAN R (WINTER) *Iris unguicularis* *(stylosa)*	White, Lavender thru Purple	March	Nov.-Feb.	Sun or semi-sun. Good garden soil. Drainage. Once growing does not appreciate being disturbed. Blooms on short 6" stems. Multiplies slowly.
IRIS, BEARDED R *Iris setosa* *I. germanica,* hybrid	Wide Color Range White, Yellow, Blue, Purple, Peach	Sept.-Dec.	Feb.-Apr.	Sun. Soil rich with compost, well-rotted manure. Requires very good drainage as in elevated beds. Plant rhizomes high with roots spread evenly and downward. Cover with only 1" of soil. Keep watered until growth starts. Uncertain in Houston though some gardeners have lovely beds of them. Worth trying. Fertilize several times in growing season. To 3' tall. Dwarf type also.
IRIS, DUTCH B *Iris Xiphium*	Blue, Yellow, White Wine-Red, Purple	Sept-Nov.	Feb.-May	Sun. Light, well-drained soil with manure and compost. Excellent for cutting. Cut when color shows at tip; stand in water until open. Water amply except during summer dormant season. 18" stems. Fertilize during growing season.
IRIS, EVANSIA R (CRESTED IRIS) *Iris cristata* *I. japonica* *I. tectorum* (ROOF IRIS)	Blue, White Lavender, Blue	May October September	Feb.-Apr.	Part shade. Acid tolerant. Plant barely covered in Azalea soil mixture. Good for bordering Azaleas. Resembles miniature spray orchids. 6" high. Hardy. Dwarf. Linear crested. Good hybrid, 'Nada.' Tender. Mulch deeply for freeze protection.

274

BULBS, TUBERS, RHIZOMES, CORMS AND TUBEROUS ROOTS

Common Name *Botanical Name*	Color	Time To Plant	Bloom Time	Comments
IRIS, JAPANESE R *Iris kaempferi*	White, Blue, Lavender	Sept.-Oct.	May-June	Sun or shade. Cover 1" with lime-free soil rich in humus. Keep wet before bloom time; dry later.
IRIS, LOUISIANA R *Iris kaempferi*	White, Pink, Red, Purple, Yellow, Blue	Sept.-Nov. Anytime (Plants)	Apr.-May	Sun with protection from afternoon sun. Cover 1-2" with very rich soil with leafmold. Best in moist, swampy area. Keep mulched during summer. Water freely. Use manure or balanced fertilizer like 8-8-8 *around* not *on* rhizome. To 4' high. Many hybrids. Among those named for Houstonians are: 'Ila Nunn,' tall cream; 'F.A.C. McCulla,' fine red; 'Marie Caillet,' red-purple; 'Dean Lee,' small bright brown; 'Laurel Bridgeman,' medium pale yellow. Other varieties: 'Bayou Sunset,' rose and gold; 'Dixie Deb,' yellow; 'Violet Ray,' purple, white ray.
IRIS, NATIVE R (FLAG) *Iris hexagona*	White, Purple	May-Nov.	Mar.-Apr.	Sun or part shade. Any moist soil. Good in rock gardens and around pools.
IRIS, RETICULATA B *Iris reticulata*	Violet, Purple	Oct.-Jan.	Feb.	Sun, good drainage. Rich, sandy soil. Naturalizes. Fragrant. Good companion planting for Narcissus. Dwarf variety about 8" high.
IRIS, SIBERIAN R *Iris sibirica*	Blue, Purple, White	Sept.-Nov. Anytime (Plants)	Mar.-May	Sun. Cover 2" with friable, moist soil. Good drainage. Water freely. Fertilize. Leave in clumps undisturbed. To 24" high.
IRIS, SPURIA R *Iris spuria*	White, Yellow, Blue, Lavender, Bronze, Purple, Bicolors	Oct.-Nov.	Apr.-June	Sun. Very good drainage. Cover 1-2" with moist, friable, neutral soil. Fertilize. When transplanting or dividing do not allow rhizomes to dry out. Long-lasting as cut flower, to 28". Naturalizes. Erect foliage is sword-like, to 3' tall.

BULBS, TUBERS, RHIZOMES, CORMS AND TUBEROUS ROOTS

B = Bulbs	T = Tubers	R = Rhizomes	C = Corms	TR = Tuberous Roots	spp. = Species
Common Name *Botanical Name*	**Color**	**Time To Plant**	**Bloom Time**	**Comments**	

Common Name *Botanical Name*	**Color**	**Time To Plant**	**Bloom Time**	**Comments**
IRIS, WALKING R (MARICA) *Neomarica gracilis*	White, Yellow, Blue	Anytime	June	Filtered sun. Cover 1" with garden loam. Drainage. Acid tolerant. Naturalizes. To 16" tall. Also, *N. longifolia,* variegated flowers. Good in containers. 2" flowers in June.
ISMENE B (PERUVIAN DAFFODIL) *Hymenocallis calathina*	White	Feb.-Apr.	May-June	Sun or partial shade. Cover 4" with garden loam. Water freely. Very fragrant. 2' tall.
IXIA C (CORN LILY) *Ixia* spp.	Various	Oct.-Dec.		Sun. Requires drainage as in raised bed. Peat, loam, sandy soil. Blooms early spring. Small 1-2" flowers. Water sparingly. Likes dry bed to naturalize. To 18" tall.
JACK-IN-THE-PULPIT B *Arisaema triphyllum*	Mottled, Brown, Green	Oct.-Dec.	Feb.-Mar.	Shade. Cover 2" with soil rich in humus. Water freely. Blooms early spring.
JACOBEAN LILY B *Sprekelia formosissima*	Scarlet	Sept.-Dec.	June	Sun. Sandy loam. Good drainage. Water during growing season. Same culture as Amaryllis. Flowers resemble butterflies, 6" across. Plant shallow. Fertilize with bonemeal and superphosphate. May be grown in pots. 12-16" tall.
JONQUIL B *Narcissus jonquilla*	Yellow	Oct.-Jan.	March	Sun (at least 4 hours) or partial shade. Cover 3" with light, sandy soil. Good drainage. To 10" tall. Naturalizes easily. Also *N. odorus.*
KNIPHOFIA R (RED HOT POKER PLANT or TRITOMA) *Kniphofia* spp.	Red, Yellow	Jan.-Mar. Anytime (Plants)	Summer	Full sun. Just cover with light garden soil. Plant in clumps. 4-6' tall.

BULBS, TUBERS, RHIZOMES, CORMS AND TUBEROUS ROOTS

Common Name *Botanical Name*	Color	Time To Plant	Bloom Time	Comments
LACHENALIA B (CAPE COWSLIP) *Lachenalia* spp.	Red, Yellow, Blue	October	Dec.-Jan.	Sun or part shade. Cover 1" with loose, sandy soil with peat moss. Same culture as Clivia. Needs moisture while growing, but keep on dry side during summer months. Will grow in same pots for years. Use liquid manure to feed. Pendulous 1" flowers on 10" stems. After planting keep pot in dark until November; then move into light and feed 1/2 strength. Bulbs not easy to find.
LAPEIROUSIA C *Lapeirousia* spp.	Rose, White	Jan.-Mar.	Summer- Fall	Sun or light shade. Dwarf plants, flowers resemble Freesias. Naturalizes. Sheltered position. Mulch in winter. Cover 2" with light, porous soil. Blooms summer and fall; to 12". In the Iris family.
LEOPARD PLANT TR *Ligularia* *tussilaginea*				Bright shade; no direct sun. Fertile, loose, moist soil. Good drainage. Dense mass of leaves in rounded form. Coarse, shiny, dark 10" green with yellow-cream mottling leaves. Yellow 1" flowers on 2' stems. Accent detail design. Striking. Nice in pots. *L.t. dentata* 'Desdemona' has purple leaves.
LILY, CENTIFOLIUM B *Lilium centifolium*	White	September	May	Semi-shade. Plant in clumps of 3 or 5 covered 6" with light, sandy soil enriched with humus. Hybrid of Regal Lily. Olympic hybrids popular.
LILY, GOLDBANDED B *Lilium auratum*	White with Gold Band	Oct.-Feb.	May-June	Semi-sun. Cover with 6" of well-drained soil, rich in humus. Best in raised bed. Water freely. Stem rooting. Also in pots. True species of Lily.

BULBS, TUBERS, RHIZOMES, CORMS AND TUBEROUS ROOTS

B = Bulbs	T = Tubers	R = Rhizomes	C = Corms	TR = Tuberous Roots	spp. = Species
Common Name *Botanical Name*	**Color**	**Time To Plant**	**Bloom Time**	**Comments**	

Common Name / Botanical Name	Color	Time To Plant	Bloom Time	Comments
LILY, LONGIFLORUM B var. ACE var. EASTER var. CREOLE var. CROFT var. ESTATE	White	October Oct.-Feb. September September September	Apr.-May	Sunny location. Cover 4-6" with well-drained, light, sandy soil, rich in humus. Use sand and bonemeal under bulbs when planting. When growth begins, water freely. Bulbs multiply readily. Bulblets may be removed from mother bulb; reset immediately. Some bloom in clusters, some along stem. 2-4' tall.
LILY, MADONNA B *Lilium candidum*	White	October	April	Sun to part shade. Cover 6" with loose, rich, well-drained soil. Plenty of moisture. Basal rooting. Slight alkalinity good.
LILY, PHILIPPINE B *Lilium philippinense formosanum*	White with Rose Tint	Sept.-Oct.	Aug.-Sept.	Plant in sun with ground cover, away from other Lilies. Cover 8" with mix 1/3 compost, 2/3 loam. Mulch during summer. Wilson hybrid strain most satisfactory. Protect from afternoon sun. Requires excellent drainage. Best in raised beds.
LILY, REGAL B *Lilium regale,* (Aurelian hybrid)	Ivory-White Shaded Pink, Gold White with Yellow Throat	October	Apr.-May	Requires bright, filtered light. Good, well-drained soil, rich in humus. Cover 6". Stem rooting. Grows to 4'.
LILY, SPECIOSUM B *Lilium speciosum* Var. RUBRUM Var. ALBUM	Pale Pink with Crimson Spots White	October	June-July	Sun or partial shade. Plant 6" deep. Soil rich in humus, well-drained. Water freely. Stem rooting.
LILY, TIGER B *Lilium tigrinum splendens*	Orange-Brown Spotted	October	May-June	A.M. sun or partial shade. Plant 6" deep in good garden soil. Water sparingly. Showy. Stem-rooting. Requires excellent drainage.

BULBS, TUBERS, RHIZOMES, CORMS AND TUBEROUS ROOTS

Common Name *Botanical Name*	Color	Time To Plant	Bloom Time	Comments
LILY, TURK'S-CAP B *Lilium superbum*	Yellow to Scarlet Spotted	October	Summer	Partial shade. Fertile soil, rich in humus. Keep moist. U.S. NATIVE wildflower. Basal rooting. 4-7' tall.
LILY, UMBELLATUM B (GOLDEN CHALICE) *Lilium umbellatum*	Yellow, Red, Deep Copper	October	April	Sun. Soil as above. Stem-rooting. Free flowering.
LIRIOPE (Root) (LILYTURF) *Liriope Muscari* *L. spicata*	Purple, White Pale Lilac	Anytime	July-Oct.	Sun or shade. Any garden soil with drainage. Acid tolerant. Ideal as border plant or ground cover. 'Monroe White,' giant 'Majestic,' and variegated forms. Evergreen. Tough. In early spring cut back to 2-3", feed, and water for better foliage and bloom. Divide when too crowded for your purpose.
L. gigantea 'Majestic' *L.m.* 'Silver Dragon' *L.m.* 'Variegata'	Lavender			To 28" high, lavender flowers, black berries. To 8" high, green and white striped leaves. Green and yellow striped leaves, lavender flowers.
LYCORIS B *Lycoris aurea* *L. radiata* (RED SPIDER LILY)	White, Yellow, Rose Orange-Red	Sept. Fall	Sept.-Oct.	Full or 1/2 day sun. Any well-drained soil fortified with bonemeal. Bulbs multiply if not disturbed. 3" blooms appear without foliage. When growth appears, feed and water. Does well in pots. Plant close together, almost touching, with neck of bulb just above soil. Rarely blooms first year because bulbs are not available until September.
MONKEY GRASS (MONDO GRASS) *Ophiopogon*		Anytime		Sun or shade. Any soil with adequate water. Divide when crowded, planting each bulblet separately, 2" apart. Protect from summer afternoon sun to prevent burning of leaves.

B = Bulbs	T = Tubers	R = Rhizomes	C = Corms	TR = Tuberous Roots	spp. = Species

Common Name *Botanical Name*	Color	Time To Plant	Bloom Time	Comments
MONKEY GRASS, contd.				
O. 'Silvery Sunproof' *O. japonicum* 'Nana'				Leaves striped green and white. To 4" high.
O. planiscapus var. Arabicus 'Black Dragon'				4-6" high, clustering growth habit. Leaves purple-black.
MONTBRETIA C *Tritonia uniflorum*	Orange-Red, White, Yellow, Salmon	Oct.-Feb.	May-July	Sun. Fertile garden soil. Good drainage. Water. Naturalizes. Fine for cutting. Feed. Can become invasive; thin when necessary. Plants fall over at bloom time unless staked. Sword-like foliage. To 30" tall. Plant 4" deep. Hardy. Watch for Red Spider.
NARCISSUS B *Narcissus*	White, Yellow	Oct.-Jan.	Dec.-Apr.	Sun or partial shade. Any rich garden soil, sandy best. Water freely. Blooms about 70 days after planting. Jonquils and Daffodils are of *Narcissus* family, but flowers differ in shape or size. Culture is same. Not all varieties naturalize. See BULBS chapter.
ORCHID, GROUND TR *Bletilla striata*	Lilac, White	Oct.-Nov.	Mar.-May	Semi-sun A.M., shade P.M.. Loose, humusy, moist soil. Terrestrial orchid. Good with Azaleas. Cover with 1" soil. Best massed. Light green, plaited foliage. Multiplies. Root hardy. Feed when leaves come up. 15" high.
ORCHID, NUN'S TR *Phaius Tankervilliae*	White with Brown Lip	October	Apr.-May	Same culture as *Bletilla striata*. Showier flower. Naturalizes.
OXALIS B *Oxalis*	Pink, White, Yellow	Anytime	Jan.-Dec.	Sun or shade. Any soil. Naturalizes but *very* invasive. Host plant for Red Spider and Rust. Blooms often.

BULBS, TUBERS, RHIZOMES, CORMS AND TUBEROUS ROOTS

Common Name Botanical Name	Color	Time To Plant	Bloom Time	Comments
RAIN LILY B *Cooperia* spp. Also see: *Habranthus* spp. *Zephyranthes* spp.	White, Yellow	Nov.-Feb. (Bulbs) Anytime (Plants)	July-Sept. (after rain)	Sun to half sun. Light, fertile soil. Plant 2" deep. Water freely. Naturalizes easily. Opens after dusk. Hardy. NATIVE to Texas.
RANUNCULUS TR *Ranunculus asiaticus*	Red, Pink, White, Yellow, Orange	Sept.-Dec.	Feb.-Apr.	Sun. Sandy loam with humus. Water when dry. Well-drained soil. Plant prongs down, 1-1/2" deep, 5-6" apart; water thoroughly with gentle spray after planting. Excellent for cutting. Plant for succession of bloom. Annual. Tecolote strains best for Houston.
SNOWDROPS B *Galanthus nivalis*	White	Oct.-Dec.	Winter	Partial shade. Well-drained garden loam. Likes cold winter. Plant 2" deep. Grows to 8" tall.
SNOWFLAKE B *Leucojum aestivum L. vernum*	White with Green Dot	Oct.-Dec.	Feb.-Apr.	Sun or partial shade. Plant 2" deep in sandy garden loam. Free bloomer on 10" stems. Naturalizes easily. Good for Houston. Allow to grow undisturbed several years before dividing.
SOCIETY GARLIC C *Tulbaghia violacea*	Rose	Nov.-Mar. (Bulbs) Anytime (Plants)	Apr.-July	Sun. Loose, rich, sandy soil. Well-draining. 1" flowers on 16" leafless stems. Naturalizes. Excellent for cutting. Plant 1/2" deep.
SWEET GARLIC or PINK AGAPANTHUS *T. fragrans*	Lavender			Most vigorous.
SPARAXIS C (WAND FLOWER) *Sparaxis grandiflora*	Yellow, Flame, Pink, White	Nov.-Dec.	Mar.-Apr.	Sun. Plant 2" deep in well-drained, sandy, fertile loam. Water until dormant. Excellent for cutting. Spring blooming. To 15" tall with 2" flowers. Naturalizes. Requires sun and excellent drainage to flourish.

BULBS, TUBERS, RHIZOMES, CORMS AND TUBEROUS ROOTS

B = Bulbs   T = Tubers   R = Rhizomes   C = Corms   TR = Tuberous Roots   spp. = Species

Common Name *Botanical Name*	Color	Time To Plant	Bloom Time	Comments
SPATHIPHYLLUM (SPATHE FLOWER) R *Spathiphyllum* spp. *S. Clevelandii* cv. also dwarf var.	White	Anytime (Indoors) Spring (Outdoors)	Periodic- ally	Partial shade outdoors in summer. Never direct sun. Indoors: tolerates low light. Good garden soil with 1/3 peat or humus and sharp sand for drainage. Keep quite moist. Best in pots to move for winter protection.
SPIDER LILY B *Hymenocallis* *Galvestonensis*	White	Oct.-Mar.	June-Aug.	Sun or shade. Plant 3" deep in any well-drained soil. Water freely. The wild lily of this region. Allow ample space, 2-3', between bulbs. Multiplies. Grows to 2' tall. Strong plant. Texas NATIVE
SQUILL B *Scilla* spp.	Blue, Pink, White	Nov.-Dec.	March	Sun to filtered sun. Plant 2" deep in sandy, humus loam. Plant in masses. *S. Siberica* and *S. campanulata* will naturalize. To 10" high.
STAR-OF-BETHLEHEM B *Ornithogalum umbellatum*	White	Sept.-Dec.	Mar.-Apr.	Sun. Plant 3" deep in sandy, well-drained soil. Fertilize moderately. To 18" tall. Good for cutting. *O. arabicum* has dark center, fragrant.
TIGRIDIA B (SHELL FLOWER) *Tigridia Pavonia*	Variegated Scarlet, Yellow, Orange, Rose, White	Feb.-Apr.	June-July	Full sun. Plant 3" deep in garden soil. Requires good drainage. Ample water at blooming time. 5-6", iris-like flowers, beautiful, but last only one day. To 2-1/2' tall.
TUBEROSE T *Polianthes tuberosa*	White	Mar.-Apr.	Summer	Requires sun and excellent drainage. Humus soil. Water freely. Very fragrant. Plant 3" deep. Single and double flowers.
TULIP B *Tulipa*	White, Red, Yellow, Purple, Salmon, Bicolors	Dec. 26- Jan.	Mar.-Apr.	Best in sun. Plant 5" deep or twice the diameter of bulb in friable, sandy soil, plenty of humus. Pinch of bonemeal and superphosphate covered with

BULBS, TUBERS, RHIZOMES, CORMS AND TUBEROUS ROOTS

Common Name *Botanical Name*	Color	Time To Plant	Bloom Time	Comments
TULIP, *contd.*				some soil under bulb when planting. 'Cottage,' 'Darwin,' and 'Breeder' types do best in this area. Refrigerate 6-8 weeks before planting. They do not naturalize. Recent experiments show Tulips need nitrogen and the best sources are cow manure or slow-release nitrogen fertilizer and matter.
T. clusiana	Peppermint: Red and White			Species Tulip. Smaller flowers but more of them. Close in evening. Naturalizes.
WATER HYACINTH R *Eichhornia crassipes*	Lavender	Anytime	May-Oct.	Grown in garden ponds no more than 1' deep, but easily becomes an invasive weed if not controlled. Multiplies rapidly. Beautiful. See BULBS chapter.
WATER LILY T *Nymphaea*	Blue, Pink, White, Yellow, Red	Anytime	May-Nov.	Full sun. Rich, fertile soil. Plant in pool or tub 6-18" under water, 2-3' apart. To 12" tall. Fragrant. Day and night-blooming varieties.
WATER POPPY (Root) *Hydrocleys nymphoides*	Yellow	Anytime	May-Aug.	Tolerates part shade. For ponds, pools, and aquariums. Grown from divisions. Resembles California Poppies. Excellent.
WATSONIA C (BUGLE LILY) *Watsonia*	Lavender, Pink, Orange, Red, White	Sept.-Nov.	Spring	Sun. Plant 3" deep in fertile, sandy, garden soil with humus. Water often. Good drainage. Fertilize with bonemeal. Naturalizes. Excellent for cutting. To 6' tall. Plant behind smaller, lower plants.
ZEPHYR LILY B (FAIRY or RAIN LILY) *Zephyranthes ajax* *Z. candida* *Z. citrina* *Z. grandiflora*	 Yellow White Gold Pink	Nov.-Feb. (Bulbs) Anytime (Plants)	May-Sept. off and on	Sun or part shade. Plant 2" deep in rich garden soil. Water freely. Naturalizes. Effective for massed planting. 6-8" tall.

Oleanders and lantana under the palm trees alongside a lawn, beside the sea.

Gardening
By The Sea

*"We all live under the same sky, but
we don't all have the same horizon."*

—K. Adenauer

What a fascination Man has with the Sea! Is it the enchantment of the tumbling waves? Or the salty scent of the air? Perhaps the wonderment of the limitless horizon! For countless reasons Man feels called to the sea and to living on its shores.

How surprising that sand is the soil found in the arid desert and also on the water-laden shores of the sea. Unexpectedly from a horticultural viewpoint, palm trees are also found in those almost opposite locations. Besides the difference in the amount of moisture in the two, there is the salt content in the soil and in the air to be considered. Salt in quantity is rarely helpful in gardening. Too much water and strong winds are also damaging to plants. At the seashore all three conditions are present. But where there is a will there is a way.

Several significant factors have to be considered. How far from the actual shore will the garden be? If it is back far enough to be away from the strong winds, the salt spray, and the tides, the gardening situation may be similar to that in Houston, except that it may be cooler in the summer and warmer in the winter if the garden site is in close proximity to the warm Gulf sea.

If the garden is far enough from the sea not to be touched by a salt spray or the strong prevailing winds, then the chances are the soil is not predominantly sand; in fact, if the soil has a sandy content, it may not need more than additions of organic matter, including rotted manure and perhaps some clay-loam. The SOIL chapter explains the contents and texture a fertile, plant-supporting soil should have. A soil test is always recommended before beginning to plant a garden. Your nearest Agricultural Extension Office will give you instructions on getting a soil sample from your garden and sending it for testing. The test will give you the pH ratio, that is, how acidic or alkaline it is. This information is very helpful because plants have certain favorite ratios they need to prosper. If there is a heavy salt content, the test will reflect it.

If the soil in your garden-to-be is similar to that in Houston, follow the instructions in the SOIL chapter for its preparation, following also the suggestions in the soil test. There are also detailed directions in the ANNUALS AND PERENNIALS chapter for preparing a seed bed.

However, if the soil is very sandy and close enough to the sea to receive salt spray and strong winds, the situation is a bit more complicated. Barriers of timbers or a masonry wall will be required to retain the soil which will have to be brought in. In effect, it will be a large raised bed filled with

Little-leaf sensitive Briar

B.B.S.

fertile, well-drained soil, following one of the formulas in the SOIL chapter, according to what will be planted.

Groupings of trees and shrubs are very effective as buffers from the winds and as attractive mainstays in the garden landscape. The trick in seashore gardening is to position the house, trees or other screens, and the garden for maximum protection from the natural elements as well as for the most attractive appearance.

> Consult a Water Authority in your area *before* using any chemical substance in or near a body of water near a public watershed.

Following is a list of plants known to be tolerant of seashore conditions.

SOME PLANTS FOR THE SEASHORE

A = Annual   E = Evergreen   H = Herb   P = Perennial   S = Shrub   T = Tree

BALSAM, SULTAN A
(SULTANA)
 Impatiens wallerana

COLEUS A
 Coleus

COPPERLEAF A
(COPPER PLANT)
 Acalypha wilkesiana

ELEAGNUS S E
 Eleagnus pungens

HIBISCUS S E
 Hibiscus Rosa-sinensis

HONEY LOCUST T
 Gleditsia tricanthos
 G. texana

IMPATIENS A
 Impatiens sultanii

JUNIPER, SHORE S E
 Juniper conferta

MAPLE, DRUMMOND'S
RED T
 Acer rubrum

MIMOSA T
 Albizia julibrissin

MUGO PINE S E
 Pinus mugo

OLEANDER S E
 Nerium oleander

PINE, JAPANESE
BLACK T
 Pinus thunbergiana

PITTOSPORUM S E
 Pittosporum tobira

PURSLANE P
 Portulaca oleacea

SALT CEDAR T
 Tamarix gallica

STATICE A
 Statice limonium

TEXAS STAR S E
 Hibiscus coccineus

WAX-MYRTLE,
SOUTHERN S E
 Myrica cerifera

YAUPON S
 Ilex vomitoria

286

P.P.

Vines

*"Where twisted round the barren oak,
The summer vine in beauty clung."*
—Longfellow

*T*he versatility of vines is a boon to gardens and to gardeners. With supervision and judicious pinch-pruning, vines can turn a chain-link fence into a boundary of soft green leaves and flowers. They can climb a tree and give the surprising pleasure of flowers in a non-blooming tree. Vines make excellent screens of unsightly areas—all in the shallowest space of any plant. With just six inches of space, a vine can cover a wall, providing solid green or a tracery of leaves.

There are blooming and non-blooming vines; perennial and annual; flowering and non-flowering. Some have large tropical leaves, others small dainty ones. No other plant gives a garden the vertical interest and the charm that vines can provide.

Proper selection of vines and appropriate location are the key to success. Decide what final result you want and then study the list of vines.

To answer a question frequently asked: vines do not harm adult trees when their growth is confined to the trunk and main branches. Just do not allow the vine to cover the tree's foliage because the tree gets its sustenance from the food manufactured in its leaves which require light.

General Culture

Most vines require rich, deep, well drained soil. To support the extensive growth put out by evergreen vines, their roots must be in soil deep enough to allow full growth. Prepare a hole 2 feet deep and 1-1/2 to 2 feet wide. Fill it with rich, friable soil such as a mixture of loam, sharp sand, and compost including rotted manure, gypsum, and agricultural sulphur. (See SOIL chapter.) Blooming vines require sun and all must have good drainage. Provide the type of support the particular vine needs.

Not all vines appreciate or need frequent fertilization. Some, like morning glories and moon vines, give better bloom when soil is not too rich. Perennial vines, once established, thrive for years with only occasional cultivation, an annual top dressing of manure or other food, judicious watering, and pruning to keep them under control. Guide the growth as you want it to go, particularly with frequent pinch-pruning of new, soft growth.

Vines embellish gardens with their casual, graceful way of growth. Select carefully and appreciate their beauty.

VINES

Flowering vines require sun, especially on their foliage, deep fertile soil, and very good drainage. Water as needed to avoid wilting. The majority must have a support such as a trellis, wire, or stout cord to grow on, and guidance from the gardener. Pinch-prune new tips for fullness and blossoms. Requirements are given for each vine in the following chart.

A = Annual P = Perennial D = Deciduous E = Evergreen Cv. = Cultivar spp. = Species					
Common Name *Botanical Name*	Best From	Time To Plant	Time Of Blooming	Color	Comments
ALLAMANDA (GOLDEN TRUMPET) P E *Allamanda Cv. hendersoni A. cathartica Cv. 'Williamsii' A.c. Cv. 'Stansills Double'*	Plant	Anytime	Spring-Summer	Yellow	Sun. Rich with humus, moist loam. Tender; mulch before a freeze. Fragrant. Long season of bloom. Large 3" flowers. Protect and reduce water during cold weather months. Good in coastal regions. Feed monthly in summer with liquid fertilizer and water. *ALL PARTS ARE POISONOUS.* Non-clinging. Tie to support. Fine on fences. May prune into shrub.
BEAN, SCARLET RUNNER A *Phaseolus coccineus*	Seed	Mar.-Apr.	June-Aug.	Scarlet	Likes sun. Loose, fertile soil. Water when dry. Rapid growing. Flowers ornamental. Pods are edible. *P. caracalla* (Snail Vine), odd and pretty. Twiner on wire or tied to trellis. Fine on chain link fence. May have to order seeds.
BIGNONIA (CROSSVINE) P E *Bignonia capreolata B.c. Cv.* 'Atrosanguinea'	Seed or Cutting	Mar.-Apr.	Apr.-June	Yellowish-Red Darker Flowers	Sun or bright shade. Moist, rich, acid soil. U.S. NATIVE. Vigorous. Large flowers. Prolific bloomer. Fragrant. Bees like it. Tendrils climb on fences, tree trunks, and wire. Not dense. Often mistaken for poison ivy. *B. (Anemopaegna) chamberlayni*, yellow flowers striped purple. Fast grower. Bloom Aug.-Sept. Prune after frosts are over.
BLACK-EYED SUSAN P *Thunbergia alata*	Seed or Plant	Spring	June-Oct.	Yellow with dark centers	Sun to part shade. Rich, fertile, draining soil. Water. Leathery leaves. Erect. Climbs on support. Also blue and white varieties.

VINES

Common Name *Botanical Name*	Best From	Time To Plant	Time Of Blooming	Color	Comments
BLACK-EYED SUSAN, contd. *T. fragrans*	Plant	Spring	May-Oct.	White	Free flowering. Fragrant. Good for small areas and hanging baskets.
T. grandiflora *T.g. 'Alba'*				Blue White	Large vine. Rapid growth. Easy to bloom. Frost tender.
BLEEDING HEART (GLORY BOWER) E *Clerodendrum Thomsoniae* *C. X speciosum*	Plant	Mar.-Apr.	September	White Bracts, Red Center Red Corolla and Red Bracts	Sun to part shade. Loose, fertile, well-drained soil, with ample humus. Water well while blooming. Tender. Protect. Needs support. Rampant growth. Climbing shrub.
BOUGAINVILLEA P E *Bougainvillea*	Plant or Cutting	Mar.-Apr.	May-Dec.	Magenta, White, Crimson, Orange	Sun. Garden soil. Feed with high potash fertilizer May and July. Tender. Prune and pinch for bloom. Do not overwater. May be kept pruned in bush form. If frozen, cut back to live wood when freezes are over. Provide support.
BUTTERFLY VINE P D *Stigmaphyllon ciliatum*	Stem cuttings rooted in fall	April	July-Sept.	Yellow	A.M. sun to part shade. South and southeast exposures best. Needs good drainage. Loose, organic, fertile, soil. Water when dry. Feed during growth period. Tender, but root hardy. Cut to ground after first freeze. Unique, vigorous, fringed vine. Rare. Worth looking for. To 18'. Fruit is butterfly shaped. Covers chain link fence rapidly if protected from north winds.
CARDINAL CLIMBER A *Ipomoea multifida*	Seed	Mar.-May	June-Nov.	Red with White Throat	Sun. Garden soil. Requires little water. Narrow leaves. Showy blossoms. Vigorous. Twiner on fence, trellis.

VINES

| A = Annual | P = Perennial | D = Deciduous | E = Evergreen | Cv. = Cultivar | spp. = Species |

Common Name *Botanical Name*	Best From	Time To Plant	Time Of Blooming	Color	Comments
CAT'S CLAW (YELLOW TRUMPET) E T *Macfadyena (Doxanthus)* *Unguis-cati* *(Bignonia tweediana)*	Plant	Nov.-Mar.	Mar.-Apr.	Yellow	Full sun or part shade, protected position on south side of house or high wall. Tolerates most soils. Water when dry. Tendrils cling to wall and stain it. Very vigorous. Plant only in adequately large space. Can become a pest.
CINNAMON VINE P D *Dioscorea Batatas*	Root Seed Cutting	Mar.-May	July-Aug.	White	Sun to semi-shade. Deep garden soil. Good drainage Water when dry. Fragrant flowers. Large, shiny, ribbed leaves. Rapid growth.
CLEMATIS P E *Clematis* spp.	Plant	Nov.-Apr.	July-Aug.	White, Blue, Pink, Red, Purple	Likes deep planting with roots shaded and tops in sun. Rich, fast-draining, slightly alkaline soil. Water when dry. Mulch. 2-year-old plant best. Climber on string, wire, trellis. Fragrant. Fall pruning.
C. paniculata				White	Masses of starry clusters. Moderate growth. U.S. NATIVE.
CLEMATIS, TEXAS D *Clematis texensis*				Red	Sun. South or southeastern exposures best. Likes some lime in fertile, sandy soil, heavy summer mulch, and water. Small trumpet flowers. Dainty, airy foliage. Texas NATIVE. Hybrids more difficult to grow here. Climber on support. Blooms on growth of current year. Prune before new growth begins.
CLITORIA (BUTTERFLY PEA) A *Clitoria mariana*	Seed or Cutting	Mar.-May	June	Blue	Sun. Sandy soil. Hardy. Attractive twiner on support, such as trellis. *C. ternatea*, blue, is showier. Water when dry.
C. Ternatea	Seed			Sea-Blue, White	Reseeds.

CLOCK VINE (See THUNBERGIA)

VINES

Common Name *Botanical Name*	Best From	Time To Plant	Time Of Blooming	Color	Comments
CLYTOSTOMA E *Clytostoma calli-* *stegioides* *(Bignonia speciosa)*	Plant Layers	Nov.-Mar.	May	Lavender	Sun or partial shade. Rich soil. Water as needed. Subject to freeze. Clings to support by tendrils. Climbing shrub.
CORAL VINE P D *Antigonon leptopus*	Root	Mar.-May	June-Oct.	Pink, White	Sun best. Tolerates partial shade. Cover with two inches of garden soil. Water sparingly. Top growth freezes, but roots remain. Easily grown. Hardy and luxuriant. Clings to wire or cord by tiny tendrils.
CYPRESS VINE A *Ipomoea quamoclit*	Seed	Mar.-May	May-Oct.	Red, White	Best in sun. Any soil, not too rich. Rapid growing. Water in summer. Dense, fernlike foliage. Twiner on support. Although it is a Morning Glory, flowers stay open all day. Reseeds.
DUTCHMAN'S PIPE P D *Aristolochia durior*	Seed Layers	Mar.-May	June	Yellowish- Brown- Purple	Semi-shade. Moist, good, alkaline soil. Hardy. Thrives when lime is added to soil. Exotic flowers. Heart-shaped foliage. Rapid growth. Good to screen porches or cover buildings. U.S. NATIVE.
A. elegans (CALICO FLOWER)				Yellow/ Green with Purple Markings	Easy here. Root hardy.
EASTER LILY VINE (HERALD'S TRUMPET) *Beaumontia grandi-* *flora*	Seed or stem cutting	March	Mar.-Sept.	White	Sun to part shade. Rich, loamy soil. Water when dry. To 10'. Fragrant. Does not thrive in pots. Woody vine.
FATSHEDERA E *Fatshedera Lizei*	Plant	Mar.-Apr.			Filtered sun or part shade. Well-drained, moist garden soil. Semi-erect climbing or trailing shrub. Dark green, leathery, ivy-shaped leaves to 8" wide. To 6' high. Tropical effect. Tie to support on wall. Stains a painted wall. No

VINES

| A = Annual | P = Perennial | D = Deciduous | E = Evergreen | Cv. = Cultivar | spp. = Species |

Common Name *Botanical Name*	Best From	Time To Plant	Time Of Blooming	Color	Comments
FATSHEDERA, contd.					bloom. Protect from freeze. Best in sheltered location. Grows indoors also with at least 4 hours strong sunlight. Regular pruning encourages bushiness. Few pests.
FIG VINE P E *Ficus pumila (repens)*	Plant Layers Root Cutting	Anytime			Sun or shade. Garden soil. Water when dry. Small, glossy, dark green leaves. Roots are invasive. Keep pruned. Good for wall cover. Clings to masonry by tiny adhesive discs. If frozen, cut back to green wood after danger of freeze is past.
FIRECRACKER A *Manettia cordifolia*	Root Divsion or Cutting	May	June-Aug.	Red	Full sun or some shade. Loose, fertile, well-draining soil. Water when dry. 1-1/2" waxy, tubular flower. Hummingbirds love it. Delicate. Tender. After bloom, cut to ground and mulch. Twiner. Grows well on trellis.
FLAMEVINE OF BRAZIL P E *Pyrostegia venusta*	Plant or Cutting	Anytime	Midwinter -Summer	Orange-Red	Hot sun. Rich, moist, well-drained soil with leafmold. Quick growing. Tendrils cling to stone or wood. Tender. Prune heavily after winter bloom.
GARLIC VINE *Pseudocallima alliaceum*	Plant	May	Aug.-Oct.	Purple, Lavender	Sun. Rich soil. Water as needed. Tender tropical vine, but worth protecting.
GLORY LILY *Gloriosa roths-childiana* *G. superba*	Tuber	Feb.-Mar.	Summer	Red and Yellow Yellow to Red	Sun. Very rich mix of loam, peat, and some sand. Water in summer as needed. In pots, needs some shade. To 6'. In winter dig up tubers, lay on sides. Store until spring. Climbs on trees, railings, or trellises. Root hardy.
GOLDEN VINE *Mascagnia macroptera*	Plant		Summer	Yellow	Sun to part shade. Garden soil. Average water. NATIVE of Texas. Leathery leaves.

VINES

Common Name *Botanical Name*	Best From	Time To Plant	Time Of Blooming	Color	Comments
GOURD A *Cucurbita* spp.	Seed	Apr.-May	June-Sept.	Cream, Yellow, Green	Full sun. Garden soil. Water when dry. Very rapid, coarse growth. Fruits unique in shape. Other ornamental gourds in variety. Needs support.
GRAPE, MUSCADINE D *Vitis rotundifolia*	Plant	Feb.-Mar.			Sun. Any well-drained soil. Water as needed. Ornamental. Covers trellis easily. Large leaves turn rich mahogany tint in fall. Edible fruit.
GUINEA GOLD PLANT (BUTTON FLOWER) *Hibbertia scandens*	Stem cutting	May	Summer	Yellow	Part shade in sheltered spot. Well-draining soil with peat moss or compost, kept moist. Large flowers, like single roses. To 15'. Also in large pots with branches tied to trellis. Protect from cold. Prune in early spring to control. Twining shrub.
HAWAIIAN WOOD ROSE E *Merremia tuberosa*	Plant or Seed	Spring	Summer	Yellow	Full sun. Fertile soil. Average water. Seed pods shaped like rose. Protect from cold winds. "Yellow Morning Glory." Twines on support.
HONEYSUCKLE, BELGIAN (WOODBINE) P E *Lonicera periclymenum (belgica)*	Plant	Nov.-Apr.	Apr.-Nov.	Buff and Pink	Likes sun. Rich, moist soil, with humus; good drainage. Very fragrant. Can be grown as bush or vine. Twiner. Birds eat berries. May use as ground cover or erosion control.
HONEYSUCKLE, CORAL (TRUMPET) P E *Lonicera sempervirens*	Plant, Cutting or Layering	Nov.-Apr.	Mar.-Nov.	Red-Orange, Red Berries in fall	Sun to part shade in summer. Well-draining porous, fertile soil, rich in organic matter. Not as rampant as other varieties. Attracts hummingbirds and deer. U.S., Texas NATIVE. Water to establish, but later don't feed or water too much. Protect in winter. In late winter, prune to train on a support. Twines on wire or fences. Cascading flowers. 15-20' growth.

VINES

A = Annual	P = Perennial	D = Deciduous	E = Evergreen	Cv. = Cultivar	spp. = Species

Common Name *Botanical Name*	Best From	Time To Plant	Time Of Blooming	Color	Comments
HONEYSUCKLE, CORAL, contd. *L. X Heckrottii*				Gold/White	Similar growth habit. Easily grown.
HONEYSUCKLE, HALL'S JAPANESE P E *Lonicera japonica var. Halliana*	Plant	Nov.-Apr.	Apr.-Nov.	White Turning Yellow	Sun or part shade. Best in rich garden soil but tolerant of any. Likes to be moist but drought tolerant. Becomes a pest if not controlled. Fragrant, hardy, and beautiful. Prune for ground cover, or as shrub, or provide support to vine. Rampant grower. May use for erosion control. *L.j.* 'Purpurea,' foliage purple tint, vigorous growth; *L.j.* 'Aureo-reticulata,' yellow netting on leaves; *L.* 'flavasims,' yellow-orange blooms, in Apr.-May, leaves bluish-green underneath; *L.j. var. H. repens*, flower white or tinged purple, leaves have purplish veins.
HYACINTH BEAN (JACK BEAN) A *Dolichos lablab*	Seed	Mar.-Apr.	May-Aug.	White and Purple	Likes sun, well-draining garden soil. Water when dry. Rapid growing, 10' to 30'. Flower and fruit clusters ornamental. 6" leaves. Needs trellis, cord, or wire to twine on.
HYDRANGEA, CLIMBING D *Hydrangea anomala petiolaris*	Seed	Nov.-Apr.	May-June	White	Sun or partial shade. Rich, loose, organic soil, kept moist especially first year. Needs good drainage. Clings to stone or stucco by aerial roots which can injure wood. Fragrant. 3-4" oval leaves on very large vine. Hardy, but mulch young plants in fall.
IVY, BOSTON P D *Parthenocissus tricuspidata*	Plant	Nov.-Apr.			Sun or part shade. Deep, fertile soil, with humus. Water. Self-clinging by discs. Light green, quick-growing wall cover. Handsome autumn foliage.

VINES

Common Name *Botanical Name*	Best From	Time To Plant	Time Of Blooming	Color	Comments
IVY, ENGLISH P E *Hedera helix*	Plant	Dec.-Feb.			Shade to filtered sun. Fertile, soil with humus kept moist but not wet, at least to establish. Plant high. Requires good drainage. Dark green 2-3" leaves. Grows up trees.
ALGERIAN IVY P E *H.h. Cv. canariensis*					4-6" dark green leaves; also variegated cultivars. Intolerant of hot P.M. sun.Hardy.
IVY, GERANIUM E *Pelargonium peltatum*	Plant	Apr.-June	May-Sept.	Pink, Lavender, Red, White	Sun. Organic matter in well-drained soil. Keep moderately dry for more bloom. Trailing stems to 4' will root in ground as ground cover or grow up a support. Pinch and prune to prevent legginess. Ivy-shaped, shiny leaves. Flowers in clusters. Fragrant. Grows indoors, too, with 4 hours sunlight a day, in potting soil kept fairly dry. Feed with 1/2 strength houseplant fertilizer.
JASMINE, CONFEDERATE P E *Trachelospermum jasminoides* *T.* 'Mandianum'	Plant	Nov.-Apr.	Apr.-May	White Cream/ Yellow	Sun or part shade. Loose soil with humus and complete fertilizer. Average water. Small clusters of fragrant flowers. Grows on any support it can find. Provide wire or trellis. May be used as ground cover, but blooms sparsely when kept pruned as ground cover.
JASMINE, PINK E *Jasminum polyanthum*	Seed or Cutting	April	July-Oct.	Pink	Full sun to part shade. Light, well-drained soil with peat or compost. Keep moist. Tie stems to a support. Feed monthly during growing season. Prune after bloom.
JESSAMINE, CAROLINA YELLOW P E *Gelsemium sempervirens*	Seed or Cutting	Nov.-Mar.	Jan.-Apr.	Yellow	Sun or part shade. Acid, fertile, sandy soil best. Average water. Requires good drainage. Fragrant. Needs support to twine on. Foliage thinner in summer.

A = Annual	P = Perennial	D = Deciduous	E = Evergreen	Cv. = Cultivar	spp. = Species

Common Name *Botanical Name*	Best From	Time To Plant	Time Of Blooming	Color	Comments
JESSAMINE, CAROLINA, contd.					Among first to bloom in spring. E. Texas NATIVE. *ALL PARTS ARE POISONOUS*. Attracts hummingbirds. Keep suckers cut off. Very drought resistant. Tolerates almost any soil. Also a double form.
KUDZU VINE *Pueraria lobata*					NOT RECOMMENDED FOR THIS PART OF THE COUNTRY. Known as "the vine that ate the South." Virtually impossible to control. Grows very rapidly, covering everything in its path: trees, forests, buildings, everything. An unfortunate import from S.E. Asia. Extremely difficult to eradicate. If it is already in your yard, might be eradicated by Roundup or 2,4-D. DO NOT PLANT.
MADEIRA VINE (MIGNONETTE) P D *Anredera cordifolia*	Tuber, Seed or Division	Mar.-May	May-Sept.	White	Sun. Garden soil. Average watering. Multiplies rapidly. Old garden favorite. Fragrant. Hardy. Rapid twiner to 20'.
MANDEVILLA *Mandevilla X amabilis* *M. splendens*	Plant	Feb.-Apr.	July-Sept.	Pink, White, Deep Pink, Yellow	Part shade. Add humus and sand to rich soil. Water as needed. Requires good drainage. Train on trellis or similar support. Foliage is sparse. Fragrant. Open A.M., close P.M. Mulch roots. Cv. 'Alice DuPont' best. Flowers larger, profuse, and stay open.
M. boliviensis					Leathery leaves. White flowers. Free blooming.
MEXICAN FLAME (LOVE) VINE A *Senecio confusus*	Seed	Nov.-Apr.	June-till. Frost	Orange	Sun. Average soil with good drainage. Water as needed. Rapid grower. Daisy-like flowers bloom all summer. Excellent colorful vine. Fine on chain link fence. 2' to 3' apart. Tender.

VINES

Common Name *Botanical Name*	Best From	Time To Plant	Time Of Blooming	Color	Comments
MOONFLOWER A *Ipomoea alba* *(Calonyction* *aculeatum)*	Seed	Mar.-May	July-Sept.	White	Sun or semi-sun. Fertile soil. Too rich soil encourages foliage at the expense of flowers. Water as needed. Good drainage. 7" white, fragrant flowers, open slowly at dusk; close at sunrise. Fascinating to watch. Rapid coarse growth on wire or cord.
MORNING GLORY A *Ipomoea* spp.	Seed or Cuttings	Mar.-Apr.	May-Sept.	Blue, Red, White, Purple	Sun. Fertile soil, low in nitrogen. Soak seed before planting. Rapid growing. Hot, dry spot. Provide support: fence, trellis, cord. Open at sunrise, close about noon. Beautiful with Moon Vine and/or Coral Vine. Hummingbirds attracted to red and purple flowers.
NASTURTIUM, CLIMBING A *Tropaeolum majus*	Seed	Early Spring	Summer	Yellow, Orange, Red	Sun. Blooms best in poor soil. Water if needed to keep soil moist. Climbing or trailing to 5' on support.
PANDOREA (BOWER PLANT) E *Pandorea jasminoides* *P.j. 'Alba'* *P. pandorana* (WONGA-WONGA V.)	Seed or Cutting	Nov.-Mar.	April	Pink White Yellow/ White	Sun. Rich, organic soil. Keep soil moist. Good drainage. Slow to establish growth. Good for trellises and arbors. Protect from wind. Prune in early spring to shape; remove dead branches. Twiner to 30'. Trumpet flowers. Also other cultivars.
PASSIONFLOWER, WILD (MAY POP) P E *Passiflora* spp.	Root	Mar.-Apr.	August	Lavender, Blue, Red	Full sun. Well-drained, deep, moist, sandy loam with compost. Provide support fence, wire, trellis. Prune heavily in early spring. Interesting flower formation. Prune late winter. Root hardy. Mulch roots for freeze protection. *P. caerulea*, from Brazil, is very similar. *P. fordtii* is pink. Drought tolerant. Many colors.

VINES

| A = Annual | P = Perennial | D = Deciduous | E = Evergreen | Cv. = Cultivar | spp. = Species |

Common Name *Botanical Name*	Best From	Time To Plant	Time Of Blooming	Color	Comments
POTATO VINE P E *Solanum jasminoides*	Plant	Mar.-May	May-Oct.	Lavender, White	Full sun. West or south exposure. Well-drained garden soil. Water as needed. Place close to support. Climbs to 15'. Prune in spring when new growth appears. Star-shaped flowers. Half hardy.
S. Seaforthianum	Seed Reseeds			Blue/Purple	Almost everblooming. Plants quicker than seeds.
RANGOON CREEPER P E *Quisqualis indica*	Seed or Cutting	Mar.-May	Summer	Pink to Red	Sun. Not north exposure. Garden soil. Average water. Tender but root hardy. Fragrant. Flowers in clusters. Prune after blooming to induce new growth. Allow at least 10' width on fence, wall, or trellis; tie branches to support. Extensive roots send up shoots along their length. Can become pest, but stunning show in bloom.
ROSE, CLIMBER P E *Rosa*, in variety	Plant	February	Mar.-Dec.	Various	Sun. Well-drained, rich soil. Regular watering. Numerous types and sizes. Some everblooming. Support. Prune after blooming. See ROSES chapter. For best bloom, train branches horizontally on support. 'Lady Banksia' and 'Blaze' among best.
SILVER LACE VINE P E *Polygonum Auberti*	Seed, Cutting or Division	Mar.-May	Midsummer	Whitish Green	Sun. Any garden soil. Drought tolerant but water as needed. Hardy. Fragrant. Rapid grower. Excellent for screening. Twiner. Flowers in 3" long, erect racemes on new growth. Tie branches to strong support. For bushiness, pinch prune tips during growing season. Prune way back in winter to thin and shape.

VINES

Common Name *Botanical Name*	Best From	Time To Plant	Time Of Blooming	Color	Comments
SNAPDRAGON VINE P A *Asarina (Maurandya)* *antirrhinifolia*	Seed	Feb.-Mar.	May-Nov.	Blue	Sun to part shade. Moist garden soil. Good drainage. Dainty ivy-leaf twiner. Grows on other plants or on cord. Fine in hanging basket. Roots like to be crowded.
STEPHANOTIS (WEDDING FLOWER) *Stephanotis floribunda*	Plant	Spring	Spring- Summer	White	A.M. sun to part shade. Fertile soil. May not be available in Houston. Very fragrant.
SWEET PEA A *Lathyrus odoratus*	Seed	October	Mar.-May	Pink, Red, White, Purple, Lavender	Sun. Sow seeds 2" deep in 6" trench of loose, rich, manured, well-drained soil. Water as needed. As plants grow, add soil. Train on support. Fragrant. Perennial Sweet Pea (*L. latifolius*) to 6', clusters of pink, red, and white flowers.
THUNBERGIA (SKY FLOWER or CLOCK VINE) P D *Thunbergia grandiflora* *T.g. 'Alba'*	Seed or Cutting	Feb.-June	July-Oct.	Blue White	Sun or filtered sun. Rich, humusy soil. Water when dry. Rapid grower. Tender. Protect from strong and cold winds. Tie branches to trellis or other similar support. Mulch plants during freeze. Prune after bloom. 6-7" leaves. Drooping racemes of blue flowers.
T. mysorensis					Sienna red/yellow blooms. Fine in greenhouse.
TRUMPET CREEPER P D *Campsis radicans*	Plant or Seed	Nov.-Mar.	Apr.-Oct.	Orange-Red, Yellow	Full sun. Any soil. Rampant grower. Texas NATIVE. *C. tagliabuana*, var. 'Mme. Galen,' not so rampant. Becomes invasive. Plant away from house, roofs, and garden beds. Sprouts along extensive roots. Root very hardy. Many varieties. Provide support. Hummingbirds like it. Prune while dormant. Drought tolerant. *C.t.* 'Flava' is yellow.

VINES

A = Annual		P = Perennial	D = Deciduous	E = Evergreen	Cv. = Cultivar	spp. = Species
Common Name *Botanical Name*	**Best** **From**	**Time To** **Plant**	**Time Of** **Blooming**	**Color**	**Comments**	
VIRGINIA CREEPER P D *Parthenocissus* *quinquefolia*	Plant, Seed or Cutting	Nov.-Apr.			Sun or semi-shade. Prefers rich, moist soil. Good drainage. Excellent wall cover. Self-clinging by adhesive discs. Prune when leaves drop. Rapid growing. 5-leaved. Scarlet fall color. Texas NATIVE. Blue fruit clusters. *POISONOUS.*	
WISTERIA P D spp. *W. floribunda* *W. sinensis, alba* *W. marcrostachys* NATIVE	Plant	Nov.-Mar. May Apr.-May		Violet-Blue Blue, White	Requires sun to bloom well. Good drainage. Rich, deep soil. Fragrant. Prune severely after blooming to control. Needs very firm support. May be several years before young plants bloom. Don't overwater or overfeed. If not blooming properly root prune in Dec.-Jan. about 2' from trunk. Sets flower buds in fall and winter. Branch prune only immediately after bloom. Excessive nitrogen fertilizer promotes growth but inhibits bloom. See PRUNING chapter.	
WISTERIA, EVERGREEN P E *Millettia reticulata*	Plant or Layering	Nov.	July-Sept.	Purple	Sun. Rich, loamy soil, humus. Drought resistant, disease free. Provide support for twining growth. Semi-evergreen. Dark, glossy green leaves. Not so rampant as other Wisterias.	

G.C.

Ferns For Indoors & Outdoors

"I make a sudden sally and sparkle out among the ferns."

—Tennyson

Some of the 12,000 species of ferns were living even before the dinosaur age. The different cut-leaf designs and varying tones of green of the fern fronds add an airy and intriguing dimension to our homes as well as to our gardens.

Indoors

Ferns growing indoors need strong light but not direct sunlight. Your hand, held between the fern and the source of light, should cast a strong shadow on the plant.

Our homes lack the humidity ferns need to thrive. Either mist frequently or set the pots on trays of gravel or pebbles and water, holding the pot above the water. Evaporation increases the humidity.

Outdoors

Ferns in the garden like partial shade or filtered *morning* sun and soil kept moist. Sprinkle in the early morning before the sun is hot.

During drought periods, extra moisture will be required, as well as foliar spritzing, to raise the humidity level. Heavy mulching with a light, porous combination of well-rotted manure and shredded pine bark or compost helps retain soil moisture and helps provide humidity around the plants.

Other suggestions for growing healthy ferns:
- Keep dead fronds cut off.
- Protect plants from injury.
- Protect ferns from winter cold with extra mulch and by keeping the soil wet, especially before a predicted freeze. New fronds usually grow with the return of warm weather.
- Protect ferns from direct sunlight.
- Give your ferns attention. They will show you if something is amiss.

FERNS FOR INDOORS AND OUTDOORS

Basic requirements for growing most ferns: Shade or filtered shade. No direct sun. Rich soil such as mixture of 1/4 part peat moss, 1/4 part sharp sand, plus 1/2 part garden loam. Addition of leaf mold and some granulated charcoal improves richness and porosity of the soil. Keep soil moist but not saturated. Prune for shapeliness and strength, removing dead fronds. When crowding occurs, divide roots or cut off plantlets to plant elsewhere for new plants. In containers, cover bottom with thick layer of broken crockery or pebbles to improve drainage. Feed regularly with organic fertilizer of 1/2 strength fish emulsion or blood meal. Mist for humidity. Protect from cold.

A = Annual	P = Perennial	D = Deciduous	E = Evergreen	Cv. = Cultivar	spp. = Species

Common Name *Botanical Name*	Height	Comments
ASPARAGUS SPRENGERI FERN E *Asparagus 'Sprengeri'*	2-3'	Excellent indoor fern in filtered sunlight. Moist, fibrous, well-drained soil. Grows well outside in sun to part shade, in ground or containers, in fertile, moist soil. Apple-green. Multiple long, arching fronds with short needle-like leaves. Divide when crowded in pot. Hardy. Other varieties available. Not a true fern; belongs to Lily Family.
BIRD'S NEST FERN *Asplenium nidus-avis*	2-3'	Fine indoors. Requires moist, fibrous, well-drained soil with humus; filtered sunlight. Upright growing green fronds, leathery texture with black mid-rib, forms nest-shaped plant. Epiphytic (grows on trees).
BLUNT-LOBED WOODSIA FERN *Woodsia obtusa*	15" x 4"	Shade to filtered sun. Light, loose, draining soil. Likes to be near rocks. Oblong, lance-shaped, feather-like leaves.
BOSTON FERN *Nephrolepis exal- tata Bostoniensis*	2-3'	Best in part shade, but tolerates some sunlight if soil is moist. Protect from winds. Fertilize monthly with 1/2 strength fish emulsion in water. Indoor growing requires strong light. Clusters of clear, medium-green pinnate fronds, long and arching.
DALLAS or JEWEL FERN *N. e. Dallasii*		More compact than Boston Fern with shorter fronds, not so much shedding of leaves. Better size to place on tables in house.
BRACKEN FERN D *Pteridium aquilinum*	4' x 3'	Shade to filtered sun, protection from wind. Loose, fibrous, sandy, spongy soil which will retain moisture but allow air to come into roots. Combination of sphagnum moss and perlite or sand-peat mix is good. Large, making good background. Protect from cold.

FERNS FOR INDOORS AND OUTDOORS

Common Name Botanical Name	Height	Comments
CHRISTMAS FERN (DAGGER) E *Polystichum acrostichoides*	18"-3'	Open shade or filtered sunlight. Equal parts garden loam, leafmold, peat moss, and sharp sand, with a little charcoal and bone meal. Keep evenly moist. Leathery leaves. Border or foundation fern. NATIVE.
CINNAMON FERN D *Osmunda cinnamomea*	3-5'	Shade to filtered sunlight. Acid, well-draining soil. Pale green. Bronze fronds when new, like candles. Accent plant or background for smaller plants. Similar to ROYAL FERN. NATIVE.
Osmunda regina		Vase-shape tree fern, soft foliage, unique trunks.
EBONY SPLEENWORT FERN E *Asplenium platyneuron*	15"	Shade, filtered sun. Fibrous, organic, spongy soil. Do not allow roots to sit in water. Petioles (stalks) purplish-brown. Alternate narrow leaflets. Effective silhouetted against rocks and roots. Hardy. Feed 1/2 strength fish emulsion in water, monthly. NATIVE.
MOTHER SPLEENWORT *Asplenium bulbiferum*		Good indoors. Divided fronds.
FISHTAIL (SWORD) FERN *Nephrolepis biserrata furcans*	18"	Deep to open shade outdoors, but protect from freeze or bring inside. Soil mix of 1/3 loam, 1/3 builder's sand, and 1/3 leaf mold or peat moss. Moist, well-drained, but slightly dry. Indirect or filtered light indoors. Tips of leaves are split, like fishtails. Needs good air circulation.
FLUFFY RUFFLES FERN *Nephrolepis exalluta*	2-4'	Culture same as FISHTAIL FERN above. No frequent misting. Mutant of the well-known BOSTON FERN. Ruffly arching fronds give fluffy look. Thick, upright. Hardy. Good in baskets, in or out. Also in garden. Light green. Dwarf: 'Mini' Ruffle. Many varieties, including *Nephrolepis exaltata Whitmanii* 'Lace Fern'. Same culture as above.
HARE'S-FOOT FERN (RABBIT'S FOOT or GOLDEN POLYPODY) *Polypodium aureum*	2-4'	Good house plant because it accepts medium light. Plant in 2 parts each of sharp sand, garden loam, and peat moss, 1 part leaf mold or humus, 1/3 part dried cow manure. Keep moist but not soggy. Long-stalked fronds 12-18", deeply cut margins, green or deep bluish-green. Creeping rhizome (root stock). Spores (seeds) on back of fronds. *P. Mandaianum* has blue, wavy-leaved fronds.

FERNS FOR INDOORS AND OUTDOORS

A = Annual	P = Perennial	D = Deciduous	E = Evergreen	Cv. = Cultivar	spp. = Species

Common Name *Botanical Name*	Height	Comments
HAY-SCENTED FERN D *Dennstaedtia puncti- lobula*	30"	Best in open shade, moist, acid soil, well-drained, but tolerates less than perfect conditions with deep shade or full sun. Forms dense mat from rapidly spreading underground creeping stems. When crushed, foliage smells of new-mown hay. Do not remove brown leaves until just before new growth fiddleheads come up .
HOLLY FERN E (POLYSTICHUM) *Cyrtomium falcatum*	3-5'	Light shade or partial sun in moist soil of 1/3 each: peat moss or leaf mold, builder's sand, and loam. Feed with 1/2 minimum strength fish emulsion in water, waiting at least 6 months after planting. Leathery, holly-like leaves about 20" long and broader than most ferns. Tiny black spores (seeds) on back of leaves often mistaken by the novice grower for insects. Hardy. If fronds freeze, plants come back from roots. Mulch for winter protection.
JAPANESE CLIMBING FERN E *Lygodium japonicum*	10-15'	Light shade. Soil of builder's sand, loam, and peat moss to give good drainage so soil can be moist but not soggy. Tolerates other conditions. Fine texture. Easy. Pale green. Usually evergreen. Climbs on trellis or other plants. Root hardy. Can become a pest.
LADY FERN D NATIVE *Athyrium Filix-femina*	3'	Shade, but tolerates early or late afternoon sun if kept moist. Loose, moist, rich soil. Good basic fern. Slow to spread. Yellow-green to darker. Dryness of soil may turn foliage brownish. Easy to grow. Many varieties. Versatile and variable. Delicate, lacy look.
LEATHERLEAF FERN E *Rumohra adiantiformis* (Polystichum)	2'	Light shade. Loose, fertile, moist soil mix of 1/4 builder's sand, 1/4 loam, and 1/2 peat moss. Evenly moist but not soggy. Do not overwater. Heavy texture. Dark green. Bushy. Fertilize monthly with 1/4 recommended strength of fish emulsion. Hardy.
MAIDENHAIR FERN or NORTHERN MAIDENHAIR E *Adiantum pedatum*	10-15"	Shady or filtered A.M. sun. Rich, humusy, moist but not soggy soil with about 2 tablespoons ground limestone to 1 cubic foot of soil. Good drainage and air circulation. Likes moist, rocky areas. Rounded flat fronds on black erect stalks. Delicate, airy appearance. Bluish-green leaves. Hardy. Cut off dead fronds in early spring just before new growth shows. Protect from wind. Slow growing. Don't mist.

FERNS FOR INDOORS AND OUTDOORS

Common Name *Botanical Name*	Height	Comments
MAIDENHAIR FERN, contd. SOUTHERN MAIDENHAIR (VENUS HAIR) E *Adiantum Capillus-Veneris*	 18"	Same culture as above. Not too wet. Light green. Dainty effect. Spreads by under-ground rhizomes. Best outdoors. Likes to be near stones or walkways. Feed with 1/2 strength fish emulsion in solution. Several other varieties. Good in terrariums. When cut for arrangements, lay stalks flat in shallow pan of water for several hours before using.
MICROLEPIA STRIGOSA E spp.	3'	Open shade. Tolerates even clayey soil but prefers a mix of loam, sand, and peat moss, slightly moist to dryish. Graceful, vigorous ferns, nice as background plant in woodland garden. Good cold tolerance. Greener and denser than common native wood fern *Dryopteris*.
MOTHER FERN E *Woodwardia orientalis*		Shade to part shade. Loose, fertile, sandy soil, kept moist but not soggy. Protected place outdoors. Mulch before freezes. Large. Reddish bronze. Baby ferns appear on leaf fronds. Plant entire frond.
NETTED or NARROW LEAF CHAIN FERN D *Woodwardia* *areolata*	1'-18"	Shade in swampy, wet areas. Soil mix of loam, builder's sand, and peat moss. Best outdoors because of rapidly spreading rhizomes and coarse foliage. Can be invasive. *Lorinseria areolata* has narrower leaflets.
POLYSTICHUM SETOSUM E (*P. aculeatum*)	12-15"	Shade. Requires rich loam, kept moist. Hardy to 30°. Low, spreading. 1 1/2' dark green, glossy, feathery new fronds develop from crown.
RESURRECTION FERN E *Polypodium poly-* *podioides*	18"	Light shade. Soil mix of peat moss, loam, and builder's sand kept moist but not soggy-wet. Small fern with coarse fronds. Creeping epiphytic fern, growing on horizontal branches of trees. Even when fronds are brown and look dead, rain revives them. U.S. NATIVE.
ROYAL FERN D *Osmunda regalis* *spectabilis*	4-6'	Prefers deep shade, but tolerates sun if kept evenly moist. Soil mix (acidic) of loam, builder's sand, and peat moss. One of largest native ferns. 4" leaflets. Fronds 2 to 6 feet long. Good background or accent plant. A clump fern. NATIVE.
SENSITIVE FERN D *Onoclea sensibilis*	2-4'	Open shade; tolerates sun, given enough water. Soil mix of 1 part loam, 1 part builder's sand, and 2 parts peat moss. Sturdy. Root hardy to cold. Coarse, thin

FERNS FOR INDOORS AND OUTDOORS

A = Annual	P = Perennial	D = Deciduous	E = Evergreen	Cv. = Cultivar	spp. = Species

Common Name *Botanical Name*	Height	Comments
SENSITIVE FERN, contd.		but broad light green leaves turn to tawny brown with maturity. In early spring red crosiers (new growth) unfurl to become large fronds. Too large to be a house plant. Dry "pods" on stalks attractive in arrangements. Is sometimes invasive. U.S. NATIVE.
SOUTHERN SHIELD FERN D *Dryopteris ludoviciana* *(Kunze)* *(Thelypteris KUNTHII)*	25–40" 3-5'	Dense to light shade. Soil mix of builder's sand, peat moss, and loam, preferably soggy-wet. Leathery, narrow fronds turn parallel to ground. The tips of this fern divide into several small leaflets giving an unusual effect. BROAD BEECH FERN (*Thelypteris hexagonoptera*) grown in sunny, moist to dry woodland soils.
STAGHORN (ELKS-HORN) FERN E *Platycerium alcicorne* *Platycerium bifurcatum*	Hangs down 1-10'	An epiphytic plant, growing attached to another object such as a tree or a piece of bark which is then hung up. Medium light. The long-fibered sphagnum fibrous moss to which the plant is attached (tied with nylon fishing line) must be kept moist. Leathery, gray-green fronds dangle. Water often. Feed with fish emulsion after watering, monthly. Slow growth. Clusters of brown spores (seeds) appear on underside of leaves. Relatively resistant to insects.
TREE FERN, HAWAIIAN E *Cibotium chamissoi*	4-6'	Open shade, filtered sun, if not too hot. Moist, porous soil. Protect from strong winds. Palm-like. Lacy fronds develop pinnately (similar to a feather) from golden-haired trunks. Prefers warm, humid areas. Best in greenhouse.
WOOD FERN (SHIELD) E *Dryopteris spp.*	2'	Semi-shade as in wooded areas. Any rich, humusy, light, moist soil. Erect, bright green, leathery, shiny fronds Hardy. AUTUMN FERN (*Dryopteris erythrosora*) is one of numerous varieties of *Dryopteris* Wood Fern. Grows from a crown instead of spreading rootstock. Tops die back in winter but return in spring. Good ground cover, especially with bulbs. U.S. NATIVE.

T.F.

Wild Flowers, Native Plants

*"To see a world in a grain of sand
and a heaven in a wild flower."*
—William Blake

*E*ach spring brings the anticipated ritual of driving along highways and country roads to admire the colorful blaze of wild flowers in bloom. As far as the eye can see, there are fields of our state flower, the bluebonnet, peppered with the orange brilliance of the Indian paint brush The pale yellow of buttercups and the magenta of wine cups provide a softening contrast. In the past we have enjoyed our wild flowers from afar, but now seeds are available to grow them in our gardens. The trend toward planting our native wild flower plants was undoubtedly engendered by the Bicentennial of our country and encouraged by the founding of the National Wildflower Research Center near Austin, Texas.

Throughout the year of our 200th anniversary celebration, we looked back and realized we were not fully appreciating one of our principal treasures, our horticultural heritage. The celebration was followed quickly by a fuel crisis, an increasing anxiety about the poisoning of our environment, and a concern for the possible scarcity of water. This combination of problems has lead us to concentrate on how we are using or abusing our resources. An almost worldwide drought has further complicated our situation.

The circumstances alerted us to the fact that there has been an excessive use of chemical herbicides and pesticides with little regard for their effect on our environment. The next obvious step was to plan for the reduction of chemical use. But how?

One suggestion for a solution is to change our ways of landscaping. Xeriscaping is a term which refers to the expanded use in our gardens of plants native and adapted to our location. Plants which are native, adapted, naturalized, or indigenous to the area in which they are found growing are virtually self-reliant, requiring less fertilization, less watering, less spraying for pests, in toto, less attention, thereby reducing the use of water and chemical substances.

"Native" plants are not "native" everywhere—a fact that anyone considering growing native plants should understand. Most native plants must be grown in the area to which they have become adapted, or they may require as much care as non-native plants. A plant native to Ohio probably is not native to Houston, Texas. Our state is so large and encompasses so many different soils and climates that we cannot even assume that all native Texas plants are native to all of Texas. Far from it. If Houstonians want to grow wild flowers and native plants in their gardens, it is necessary to learn

Lemon Mint. (Monarda citriodora)

J.M.K.

Native plants are practically self-maintaining and seldom need much pruning—if allowed to follow their inherent growth pattern. Growing native plants teaches us the matter of "not doing." Faded flowers are left on the wild flower plants at the end of their season of bloom so seed pods can form. In their own time the seeds either drop to the ground, are thrown out naturally or blown away by the wind. The seeds fall helter skelter and remain on the ground until it is their season to germinate and rejuvenate themselves. Gardeners have become accustomed to feeding, pruning, and tidying up. If you are of a "tidy" nature, native plants may not be for you. Think about it.

Reputable nurseries in the Houston vicinity are happy to acquaint you with plants native or adapted to this area. Seeds for wild flowers are obtainable at nurseries and garden supply stores.

Perennial Phlox. (Phlox paniculata)

J.M.K.

which plants are considered native, adapted, naturalized, or indigenous to the Houston soil and micro-climate. Though Houston is in the U.S. Horticultural Zone IX, our growing conditions, especially planting *times*, differ from many other portions of Zone IX. Plants should always have their growing requirements matched with those of the planting site.

Consider also that the majority of native plants and wild flowers have a loose and informal growth habit. They do not present a formal or tidy appearance but, instead, accentuate nature rather than improve nature. To place them indiscriminately among plants in a formal landscape would give the garden a feeling of disarray. To be attractive, native plants should be incorporated perceptively with an eye to their natural growth habit and their compatibility to the other plants already in the landscape.

Field of spring primroses with majestic oak trees.

R.J.B.

Many of the wild flower seeds sold in Houston come from WILDSEED, an Eagle Lake, Texas, company which pioneered the art of planting wild flowers in large spaces. They have made many beautiful plantings at business locations and in esplanades. The plantings have added to the beauty of our city while reducing the expense of continuous gardening care. The seed packets usually contain a mixture of annuals and perennials known to thrive here. There are mixtures for shady locations as well as for sunny ones.

Most wild flowers require lots of sun, at least 6 hours daily, and prefer to be planted in the early fall—late August through November. After the plants are established, they will need little watering—none, in fact, if the usual fall showers come. However, the seed bed should be moist or damp when the seeds are planted and must be

**Stop - Look - Enjoy
But Don't Pick the Flowers**

That is the sign whose image should be held in everyone's mind when wild flowers are in bloom. For wild flowers to reseed themselves, their flowers must be allowed to remain on the plants to form seeds. In their own sweet time, the seeds will either drop to the soil or be carried by the wind to another spot. Next year there will be more beautiful flowers. BUT, no flowers = no seeds = no flowers next year. Therefore, do not pick the flowers, and do not dig up the plants in the fields.

If each person removed a few flowers or a plant or two, there would soon be empty fields. Conserve beauty while enjoying it!

kept moist through germination. If showers are non-existent, watering the bed will be necessary.

In summary:

For native or adapted plants to thrive with minor care in Houston, they should be actually native, adapted, indigenous, or naturalized in this climate. The planting suggestions in the SHRUBS and TREES chapters are appropriate for native shrubs and trees listed.

Native plants are so identified in charts.

Most of the suggested plants will require good drainage, at least 6 hours of sun per day, and a moderately fertile soil. Organic materials, such as rotted manure or rock phosphate, are appropriate in the soil instead of chemical or non-organic fertilizers.

Keep plants watered until they show enough new growth to be on their own.

To plant wild flower seeds:
- Match the cultural needs of the plant with the conditions available in your garden. Select flower varieties accordingly.
- Plant the seeds in a prepared bed when they are planted in a home garden. Follow the directions given in the ANNUALS AND PERENNIALS chapter or those in the SOIL chapter for the preparation of seed beds, but omit chemical fertilizers. Use organic fertilizers instead.
- Prepare the seed bed several weeks before-planting time, which usually is August to November; there are exceptions.
- Stir mixtures of seeds to mix the tiny ones with the large seeds when planted.
- Moisten the prepared bed several hours before planting so the soil will be damp.
- Rake the bed to loosen the soil to a depth no more than 1/2 inch.
- Broadcast the seeds on a windless day, or plant in rows. The method of planting depends on the effect you want when they bloom.
- Press the seeds down onto the soil and cover with a thin 1/4-inch layer of fine soil or rake gently. The purpose is to have the seeds snuggling close to their growing medium and to hide them from the ever alert, ever hungry birds. Walking lightly over the bed assures good contact between the seeds and the soil.
- Water the planted bed with a very gentle spray of water, and keep it damp until the little plants show good growth. Even after the seedlings are well out of the ground, they need to be watered if there have not been any showers.
- Wild flower seeds may be planted around small trees or shrubs, as borders, in flower beds, in bark-mulched beds, or in open fields, as long as they have a loose enough growing medium to allow the tiny roots to penetrate it and sun. Keep bed moist.
- Do not fertilize wild flowers if the soil is moderately fertile. Over-fertilizing may cause growth of foliage instead of production of flowers. The inherent urge of plants is to bloom in their effort to reproduce their kind through seeds.
- Do not remove late flowers or seed pods if you want the plants to reseed themselves. The plants may be pulled up after the seed pods are dry. Shake the seeds off onto the ground, or collect them. Discard the spent plant in the compost pile. The annuals will return from their seeds, the perennials from their roots.

With experience you will learn the bloom times of the varieties of wild flowers and will be able to plant for continuous bloom. What a delight to await!

F.T.S.

Birds & Butterflies In The Garden

"...the flowers and the birds and butterflies are all that the world has kept of its golden age-the only perfectly beautiful things on earth-joyous, innocent..."

—Ouida

*T*he very thought of birds and butterflies in the garden brings to mind an image of wondrous flight, exciting colors, and musical songs. The garden becomes more animated with their presence, more alive, more interesting.

Apart from the entertainment we derive from their presence, birds are extremely helpful in the garden. They eat insects by the hundreds. It is true that birds are sometimes indiscriminate about choosing between helpful or harmful insects, but the consensus is that birds feast on those insects which are in greatest supply, and as a rule the harmful ones are the most plentiful. Any gardener will attest to the rapid rate at which aphids, lacewings, spiders, leaf-hoppers, and mosquitoes reproduce themselves. Their damage is obvious.

Though small, hummingbirds are birds and they eat their share of insects. Butterflies help pollinate flowers by carrying pollen on their wings and bodies from blossom to blossom. However, even if these three members of the wildlife world did not accomplish any mundane or helpful tasks, their beauty, gorgeous colors, and intriguing habits are reason enough to provide them with a secure haven.

To attract birds, "hummers," and butterflies, a garden must provide them with a habitat in which they can find food and fresh water daily, a place to call home, and security from their enemies. Aren't those the same elements people search for? In return for our kindness, the beautiful creatures repay us with their cheery presence and their songs.

To attract birds and butterflies, there must be a container of water kept clean and fresh. A small pond is ideal especially when there are fish in it to keep it clean. The water container should be in the open to avoid a predator's hidden arrival. Many bird baths are on standards above the ground for that reason. Particularly during freezing weather, keep water available. Food is best provided by plants the birds and butterflies prefer. Most of them are colorful and often scented flowers. Thus both gardener and wildlife are kept happy. Birds appreciate a "dust bath" in the form of a portion of soil left unplanted or a shallow container, about 2' x 3', filled with fine soil or dust in which the birds "bathe" to rid themselves of mites. For nest-making, birds have favorite trees and shrubs. The SHRUBS and TREES charts identify many. With careful selection, the same plants can provide nesting places and berries or other fruit as well as flowers. The native plants are often favorites.

Flowering perennials provide nectar to bees, hummingbirds, and butterflies alike. Since butterflies must perch while eating, flowers having a lip, such as salvia, are better for them. Hummingbirds' ability to "hover" as they sip nectar is one of their most fascinating feats. Though they enjoy syrup hanging in a tree, the sugar water does not afford them as much nutrition as does flowers' nectar.

There are all kinds of "bird-feeders" to be had, but unless the feeding is consistent and regular the birds may starve because they become dependent on the artificial feeding system. It's the easiest, probably, and they become "addicted" to the easy way. For that reason, the natural food from flowers and plants is preferable. The object is to provide food through the various seasons. Study the planting charts for complete information.

Following is a partial list of recommended plants for birds, hummers, and butterflies. All plants are listed in the appropriate planting chart.

SOME PLANTS TO ATTRACT BIRDS AND BUTTERFLIES

A = Annual   P = Perennial   S = Shrub   T = Tree   V = Vine

Hummingbirds are attracted to most bright colors:
Azaleas S
Bee Balm P
Buckeye T
Butterfly weed P
Canna Bulb
Cardinal Flower P
Carpet Bugle P
Chinaberry T
Cleome A
Coral Honeysuckle V
Coralbells P
Crabapple T
Flowering Quince S
Four-O'Clock A or P
Hawthorn T
Impatiens A
Mimosa T
Morning Glory A V
Sages S
Snapdragon A

Trumpet Creeper V
Weigela S

Orange and Banana peels left in garden attract fruit flies which hummers snatch out of the air.

To attract birds, plant a variety. Following is a short list of suggestions, many more are in the planting charts:
Beautyberry S
Blackberries S
Cedars T
Deutzia S
Elm T
Euonymus S
Grapevines V
Hawthorn T
Hackberry T
Holly T
Honeysuckle S or V
Japanese Barberry S
Mulberry T

Oak T
Pine T
Privet S
Red Maple T
Sunflower A
Sweetgum T
Virburnum S
Yaupon S

Some plants to attract butterflies:
Aster P
Everlastings P
Butterfly Bush S
Hibiscus S
Hollyhock A
Mallow S
Spicebush S
Violets P
Wildflowers A, P
 Nettles,
 Cresses,
 Bluebonnet

P.P.

Soil &
Soil Improvement

"The greatest domestic problem facing our country is saving our soil and our water. Our soil belongs also to unborn generations."

—Sam Rayburn

Soil is a living, ever-changing element we must learn to understand if we are to garden successfully. Man is the only creature capable of modifying the soil to enable it to produce the plant life so vital to our existence.

Made up of mineral particles, water, air, and organic matter, soil is the basic element for growing any plant and plays many roles in that process. It must be loose enough to allow the penetration of the roots which support the plant, fertile enough to supply nutrients to the plant, and porous enough to retain the air and moisture essential to plant growth.

To supply these needs a soil must contain organic matter to increase its fertility, and microorganisms to change the organic matter into a form which the plant can use. Organic matter and microorganisms also act as a bank, storing surplus nutrients and moisture for the plant's future needs.

Soils are formed through a combination of five factors: parent material, climate, living organisms, topography, and time.

Parent materials are the earthy materials, both mineral and organic, from which soil is formed. It can be sediment that has been transported and deposited by wind or water. Well-developed soils are made when parent material is changed both chemically and physically over time. Parent material is broken down into finer particles by a process called weathering, which is controlled by climatic characteristics, with temperature and water being the major forces. Organic matter from plants and animals which die and decay help create a soil type. As plants and animals die, they add organic material to help form topsoil and subsoil.

Soils also vary with topography because of the influence of moisture and erosion. Low areas generally contain poorly drained soils while sloping areas are usually drier and well drained. Erosion can remove all or part of the topsoil.

The age of a soil must be considered in thousands, even millions of years. It may take hundreds of years for these elements to form one inch of soil from parent material.

[1]The soil in Harris County is thought to have been formed during the last glacial period, 10,000 years ago. We know that one of the small streams that carried and distributed our soil is Buffalo Bayou, which still winds its way through Houston. Nature's busy activity left the Houston area with a soil pattern so variable that there are 47 different soil types here, grouped into 8 soil associations.

[1]Courtesy of Houston Arboretum from their NEWSLETTER

313

Soil Testing

Before you try to alter the soil in your garden, it is important to find out all you can about the existing properties of the soil you are working with. One way to begin is to consult the nearest office of the Soil Conservation Service of the U.S. Department of Agriculture to see if a soil survey has been made in your area. These soil surveys furnish valuable information about your particular soil, such as its texture, reaction, and ability to transport or hold water and air.

Soil analysis is the only reliable method for determining the chemical condition of the soil. Always have a soil test before attempting to alter the pH; otherwise, you will be working in the dark.

pH

The letters "pH" represent a scale from 0 to 14 on which the hydrogen ion concentration is tabulated. The pH rating indicates the degree of acidity or alkalinity of the soil—a pH of 7 is neutral; higher pH numbers represent increasing alkalinity, lower numbers show increasing soil acidity. Soils which are either too acid (pH below 4) or too alkaline (pH above 8) seriously retard or kill plant growth. To be complete and really helpful, a soil test should be made by an expert. Contact your nearest County Extension Agent to get forms and procedures for having your soil analyzed. There is a very nominal charge, but you will easily recover the price by avoiding mistakes. The results of the test will indicate the materials required to modify your soil pH and the appropriate fertilizer materials for the plants you are growing. There are home testing kits available, but the results are not so accurate as a laboratory test. Home testing kits are useful for checking the results of your efforts *after* you have had an expert test made and have implemented the procedures suggested by it.

Basic Soil Composition

For home gardening purposes, soil can be divided into three simple classifications by texture: sand, clay and loam. Sand is composed of irregularly shaped particles which do not cling together and can be seen with the naked eye. Nearly all sandy soils contain some fertile clay particles. Moist sand will form a ball under hand pressure, but promptly falls apart when the pressure is released. Sand is very loose and drains so rapidly that soil moisture is not retained and nutrients are readily leached through the soil, beyond the reach of plant roots. This property makes sand quick-drying and subject to rapid heating. Sand, by itself, is not a good soil for gardening, but it can be improved by adding large quantities of organic matter and some clay. If you are not in a great hurry, green manuring, the planting of a cover crop such as legumes, later to be tilled into the soil, improves the soil structure of sandy soil. Sandy soil is especially adapted to the culture of bulbs and other plants that are very hardy, drought resistant, and deep rooted.

Clay is composed of smooth, slightly flattened particles so minute that they can be seen only through powerful microscopes. Clay particles hold nearly all of the plant nutrients in any soil. These tiny particles cling together to form a hard, cement-like soil when dry, and a sticky, cloddy soil when wet. Clay soils hold large amounts of moisture for plant use, but in wet periods they often become waterlogged and soil air is expelled. Plant roots, water, and air generally move very slowly in clay soils; yet, when clay is loosened by modifiers such as organic matter, sand, gypsum, vermiculite, or perlite, it usually becomes crumbly and easy to manage. The additives alter the soil structure, which in turn improves the aeration and drainage of the clay soils. The predominant soil found in Harris County is commonly referred to as "black gumbo."

Loam is a mixture of sand, silt, and clay, giving it the good properties of each in a satisfactory proportion. Moist loam can be formed into a ball by hand pressure, and the shape will not crumble until some pressure is applied. A loam soil is usually well drained, well aerated, and fertile. It retains nutrients, water, and air for moderate periods. Loam is generally considered to be the best textured soil for most garden plants.

The exact composition of soil changes from one location to another. There is a simple test to help determine the soil type by identifying the texture of the soil: when the soil is wet and rubbed between the fingers, a dominant texture will be obvious; clayey soils are very smooth and slick and will ribbon out when rubbed between the fingers; sandy soils feel gritty, and loamy soils feel loose and crumbly and show no dominant texture as do clayey and sandy soils.

Organic Matter and Humus

These two materials are so closely related that it is almost impossible to discuss one without discussing the other. Organic matter (plant or animal) is the material we add to the soil in any of several forms such as: manure, shredded pine bark mulch, rice hulls, compost, leafmold, lawn clippings, leaves, cottonseed meal, dried blood, bones, hair, etc. Through the process of decomposition, organic matter becomes the dark spongy substance known as humus. (Remember the term "humus." It is often referred to in discussions about soil content.)

It is generally in this final stage, as humus, that organic matter has the greatest nutritive value and the most lasting effects on the soil. In all stages, however, organic matter helps soil in several ways by:

- pushing the tiny particles of clay apart, leaving spaces or pores which can be filled with water and air;
- improving a sandy soil by adding material for the large sandy particles and water to cling to;
- adding fertility to the soil;
- improving aeration (the passage of air through the soil); and
- providing an excellent medium for the growth of soil organisms.

If organic matter is not in a well-advanced stage of decay when incorporated into the soil, microorganisms will extract nitrogen from the soil, stealing it from the growing plant during the process of decomposition. Therefore, extra nitrogen should be added when large amounts of organic matter are incorporated. With the addition of nitrogen, the microorganisms can further decompose the organic matter and the growing plant will still have an adequate supply of nitrogen.

Mulching

The covering of soil with loose material, preferably organic matter, serves many purposes by:

- promoting healthy growth of plants;
- keeping the soil surface from cracking and hardening;
- detering weeds;
- keeping the roots at an even, beneficial temperature, protecting them from temperature extremes; mulch keeps soil and roots cooler in summer and warmer in winter;
- adding organic matter to the topsoil; and
- preventing loss of moisture from evaporation

A mulch composed of a mixture of several different materials allows more aeration and better penetration of water. The variety of textures in the mixture retards compaction or packing, which prevents the entrance of water. A mulch keeps the soil crumbly and easy to work. Never till or work a wet soil. It will cause compaction which is difficult to correct.

Types of Mulch

Different types of organic mulches available to Houstonians are:

- Compost can be made at home from discarded organic matter.
- Grass clippings are always available to those who have lawns, but when fresh, they attract flies and other insects. Dry or put in compost pile before using. Alone, they become compacted.

315

- Hay is used principally in vegetable or fruit beds. It is not attractive though it might look better when mixed with some of the other mulching materials. Incorporate some nitrogen when used.
- Manure, fresh, is usually yours free for the loading and hauling away. It should be rotted before applying to planting beds to avoid burning the plants. Fresh manure gets very hot during decomposition. Fine for compost piles in reasonable amounts. Beneficial mixed into soil.
- Manure, rotted, is available in sacks. Some has been sterilized to kill weed seeds. Mix with other materials like pine needles when used as a mulch. Very beneficial to the soil.
- Newsprint paper is sometimes used to cover the ground under other more attractive materials. When cut into fine strips, it incorporates well in a mixed mulch but should be moistened. Beneficial to the soil.
- Peat moss comes in different types. The Canadian peat moss in 6-cubic-foot bales is usually considered the best. Always moisten peat moss before incorporating into a mulch or soil because it is difficult to wet through. Mix with other coarser-textured organic materials when used as a mulch. Many gardeners avoid using peat moss because once it becomes dry it gets very hard and is difficult to wet again.
- Pine bark comes in different textures. The medium size bark helps prevent compaction when mixed with finer materials. The shredded bark blows away easily if not kept damp. Mixing shredded pine bark mulch with coarser organic materials is advisable.
- Pine needles (pine straw) are an excellent mulch, especially for azaleas and camellias because they acidify the soil and they don't blow away. Everyone should have a pine tree or two nearby. Frequently you can obtain needles from those who discard them. The texture of the pine needles helps avoid compaction when mixed with finer textured

mulches. If desired, they may be cut up with a mower.
- Rice hulls should be mixed with other organic material because when used alone they mat and keep water from entering the soil.

Essential Soil Elements

Although many elements are necessary for plant growth in a fertile garden soil, the three most essential are nitrogen, phosphorus and potassium. The numbers on packages of fertilizers always refer to the percentages of those elements in that order—nitrogen (N), phosphorus (P), and potassium (K). A fertilizer marked 5-10-5 means that it contains 5% Nitrogen, 10% Phosphorus and 5% Potassium (Potash) or a ratio of 1-2-1. The other 80% of the mixture may contain a small percentage of trace elements, but most of it is a filler to facilitate application. (Some companies use gypsum as the filler.) The abundance of these elements in the soil is best determined by a soil analysis, but a careful gardener is always alert for plant symptoms signaling deficiency or excess.

Nitrogen in the soil:
- accelerates the growth of stem and foliage;
- gives a healthy green color to plants;
- initiates root growth;
- stimulates rapid early growth;
- improves the quality and crispness of leafy crops; and
- is especially beneficial when plants are making buds.

Nitrogen *deficiency* is indicated by a yellow-green leaf color, sometimes causing premature development. Nitrogen *in excess* delays maturity, reducing the development of flowers and fruit, and is symptomized by flaccid, unhealthy growth.

The principal inorganic sources of nitrogen are:
- sodium nitrate,
- ureaform,

- ammonium sulfate, and
- calcium nitrate.

Some organic sources of nitrogen are:
- compost,
- organic material,
- dried blood or blood meal,
- bone meal, and
- cottonseed meal.

Phosphorus is called by some the "master key" to agriculture because in the soil it:
- stimulates root growth; thickens cell wall;
- gives plants a vigorous start;
- hastens maturity;
- promotes abundant seed and flower formation;
- increases the proportion of seed and fruit to stalk; and
- hardens plants to winter injury.

Virtually all plants need soil with phosphorus to maintain flower and fruit production, and it is generally recognized that organic material in the soil increases the amount of phosphorus available to the plant.

A phosphorus deficiency in the soil is usually indicated by:
- low vigor in the plant;
- weak stems; and
- few flowers.

The principal inorganic source of phosphorus is normal or triple superphosphate, produced from raw rock phosphate.

An organic source of phosphate is raw or steamed bone meal.

Potassium, commonly called potash:
- strengthens plants;
- enables them to resist diseases, insects and winter damage;
- promotes the production of starches, sugar,

and oil in the plants; and
- improves the quality of the crop yield.

The main inorganic sources of potash are:
- potassium chloride,
- sulfate of potash, and
- potassium nitrate.

An organic source of potash is wood ash.
A mineral source is granite dust.

Other elements plants use, such as magnesium, calcium, sulphur, boron, etc., are not generally needed in the soil in the quantities of the principal three, so they are usually grouped under the term "trace elements." This term is printed on the package of some fertilizer mixtures as being present in the filler with which the elements are mixed for convenient use.

All trace elements are needed in the soil for plant health, but in small amounts. Their benefits and where to find them are:
- *Boron:* helps plants assimilate calcium and formation of seeds; found in borax. Deficiency causes thickened leaves and poor production.
- *Calcium:* helps in cell formation; found in dolomitic limestone and gypsum.
- *Copper:* for stimulation of enzymes and promotion of vitamin A; found in copper sulfate or copper chelate. Deficiency shows in stunted plants and dieback of tips of twigs.
- *Iron:* needed for chlorophyll to stimulate green color; found in iron chelate, iron sulfur, and copperas. Excess of iron tends to reduce soil's ability to absorb manganese.
- *Magnesium:* in chlorophyll; found in magnesium sulfate (Epsom Salts) or dolomitic limestone.
- *Molybdenum:* works together with nitrogen to aid protein function; found in ammonium or sodium molybdate. Deficiency causes burned leaf edges and rolling or cupping of leaves.
- *Sulfur:* necessary for plant proteins and cells; found in gypsum, superphosphate, ammo-

nium sulfate, and elemental sulfur.

- *Zinc*: helps regulate growth and size; found in zinc chelate or sulfate. Deficiency shows in rosettes of leaves at branch tips.

A "complete, balanced fertilizer" usually refers to one with equal ratios of the top three—nitrogen, phosphorus, and potash, such as 1-1-1 or 13-13-13 on the bag.

A "complete fertilizer" usually refers to one including all three (NPK) nutrients, but not necessarily with the same ratio of each, such as 3-1-2, or, as printed on the bag: 15-5-10.

There also are slow-release fertilizers. A special way of processing the granules allows the fertilizer to dissolve gradually into the soil. The use of these slow-release fertilizers, such as Osmocote, reduces both the frequency of application and the danger of over-dosage which can cause burning of the plants.

It is helpful to change brands of inorganic fertilizers because each has different percentages of trace elements and the principal elements often have been obtained from different sources. By interchanging brands, a build-up of any one chemical may be avoided and a broader range of trace elements may result. However, bagged fertilizers rarely contain enough of the micro-nutrients (trace elements) to correct a real deficiency. The micro-nutrients can be obtained separately if necessary.

We speak of fertilizing plants, but actually it is the soil which must be fertilized or made fertile because plants derive their nutrition from the soil and from water through their roots.

Commercial Fertilizers.

To be highly productive, soils should contain a blend of all three essential elements. The inorganic or chemical sources of the elements are more rapidly available to the plant, but they do not improve the soil's tilth or texture. Before applying inorganic fertilizers, always water the soil first, and again immediately following application.

"Organic" gardeners try to obtain all the necessary soil elements from organic or natural mineral sources. Elements from natural or organic sources give slower results but they also:
- improve the soil's texture;
- remain in the soil longer; and
- expedite the availability of fertilizing elements to the plant by promoting the growth of micro-organisms, retaining moisture, and giving the soil body.

Although the organic and inorganic fertilizers have different functions, they complement each other when wisely used. Each has its purpose, and it seems sensible to combine them as needed. The principal caution is to follow the manufacturer's directions, resisting the impulse to use quantities greater than specified. It is rarely wrong to use dosages *smaller* than recommended. Plants absorb fertilizers slowly. It is also important to follow the dictum: *Never fertilize a dry plant, and always water a fertilizer in thoroughly*. Inorganic fertilizers cannot become available to the plant without water.

Foliar Feeding with Inorganic Fertilizers

The use of fertilizers in a water solution sprayed on the leaves of plants, is based on the ability of a plant to absorb nutrients through its leaves. Fertilizers are usually dug into the soil to allow a plant's roots to absorb them, but leaves also have the ability to absorb. Most liquid or soluble fertilizers have a high concentration of nutrient salts which may burn the foliage if used in concentrations stronger than recommended. Moreover, *in the hot summers of Houston*, it may be wiser to dilute 50% more than the proportions recommended by the manufacturer to avoid defoliating or even killing your plant. For example: when plants like azaleas, camellias, and any others that like acid soil begin to show an iron deficiency (possibly indicated by the yellowing of the leaves between the veins), a foliar spray of iron chelate in solution is often recommended. In our hot weather, use 50% more water than is recommended on the label. Spray is best applied to fresh-looking foliage because the leaf surface has maximum absorption when fresh, not wilted.

Manure, Organic Fertilizer

Barnyard manure in the soil is very useful as a fertilizer and especially as a soil conditioner because it:

- promotes the growth of soil organisms;
- adds nutrients to the soil; and
- helps change minerals into forms more available to plants.

Fresh, or "hot," manure is apt to burn plants when touching them, but well-rotted manure is an excellent mulch, particularly when mixed with other organic materials such as pine needles, pine bark mulch, compost, or old hay. An old but still accepted way of using manure is to make "manure tea." Steeping a burlap bag of manure in a barrel of water for at least two weeks results in a liquid manure. When diluted to the color of weak tea, it can be applied to plants as a quick stimulant. The soil around the plants should be loosened and moistened before application, and watered again after application. Chrysanthemums are encouraged into good bloom by this treatment, as are many other plants in bud.

Other Organic Fertilizers

Bone meal, containing both nitrogen and phosphorus, is one of the safest and most efficient fertilizers. It is slow-acting and tends to make the soil alkaline.

Cottonseed meal has a somewhat acid effect, is rich in nitrogen, contains small amounts of phosphorus and potassium, and is especially fine for lawns and bulbs.

Activated sewage sludge and tankage are good soil conditioners with slowly available nutrients. They improve the physical condition of mixed fertilizers, but should *not be used on edible plants*.

Organic matter is indispensable to soil conditioning.

WARNING: In all gardening activities, the safety of the gardener must always be foremost. Protection from overexposure to sprays and chemicals is advisable. Wash your hands after handling chemicals. If you use manure, check with your physician as to the advisability of tetanus shots.

Soil pH

Most garden plants, vegetables and ornamentals prefer a slightly acid soil, while most herbs prefer a slightly alkaline soil. Most soils in Houston are slightly alkaline.

Soil acidity may be increased by the addition of:

- organic matter,
- iron sulfate (copperas),
- agricultural sulphur,
- gypsum (calcium sulphate), or
- magnesium sulphate, used according to directions. Magnesium sulphate is quicker-acting, but the other materials are longer-lasting.

Agricultural gypsum (calcium sulfate) is a mineral which does wonders as a soil additive. It loosens the soil by causing the clay platelets to join together, thus developing larger air spaces, a condition which improves plant vigor and increases root production. The looser soil allows better penetration of water and other nutrients throughout the plant's structure. Recent findings indicate that gypsum is more effective in soils with a salt content. If the pH of the soil is 8.5 or higher, gypsum will be helpful. Gypsum also adjusts the pH and thus aids bacterial growth.

Organic matter serves the many purposes discussed earlier. Three or four inches of organic material worked into the soil are helpful to most soils. The same material used as a two-to-four-inch mulch tends to maintain an acid soil condition.

Soil alkalinity is increased or neutralized with the addition to the soil of lime, wood ashes, limestone sand, or bone meal. The greater the quantities of the above additives, the more alkaline the soil becomes. Again, information from your soil test will include the pH of your soil and will suggest what additives your soil needs.

Compost

Composting is the process used to speed decomposition of organic matter into humus. Because carbon is the principal element of all plants, it is the principal constituent of compost.

The goal in composting is to encourage the growth of more bacteria to decompose the carbonaceous materials. Since the bacteria or microorganisms must have nitrogen to carry out the decomposition process, it is helpful to add some form of nitrogen to your compost pile.

Raw rock phosphate is also a desirable additive. The weak acids in the organic material help break down the phosphate into forms readily available to plants.

Soil may be added to the compost to increase the nutrients, serve as a base to which the nutrients can cling, and be a host for microorganisms.

The compost should be aerated because air is necessary for the bacteria to carry out the work of decomposition. To speed the decomposition process, the pile should be turned regularly or built around a wire chimney or flue. Moisture in the compost keeps the bacteria activated and prevents the compost heap from becoming a fire hazard. Build the compost pile to at least three to four feet high to build up heat, but it may be of any design you choose as long as you assure the presence of the necessary elements. Composting, as well as other recommended gardening practices, is aimed at making the soil environment more favorable to the all-important soil micro-organisms.

Suggestion for Compost Pile.

Make it in layers of:
- 1" good soil or 4" manure; and
- 10" organic matter mixed with some soil.
- Alternate layers up to 4-5 feet height.
- Top with 2-4" dirt, and shape top into shallow basin to catch rainfall.

- Chemical additives may be added, particularly if the manure content is low:
  — 20% superphosphate, at the rate of 1/2 cup per bushel of compost; and
  — Epsom Salts, at the rate of 1/2 tablespoon per bushel.
- If the compost is primarily dried leaves, add:
  — a 5-10-5 fertilizer, at the rate of 1-1/2 table spoon per bushel; and
  — Epsom Salts, at the rate of 1/2 tablespoon per bushel.

Preparation of Soil in Planting Beds for Vegetables or Flowering Plants:

For growing most plants, the planting area should receive at least 6 hours of sunshine and be well drained.

To prepare a 100-square-foot bed:
- Remove all grass, rocks, or any other debris.
- Till or dig up the soil to about an 8" depth for shallow-rooted plants, breaking clods as you go. The soil should be fairly fine texture when finished.
- If the soil is typical Houston gumbo clay, cover the tilled surface with agricultural gypsum, wet it, and allow to sit for a week or so.
- Till or dig again until texture is workable, *BUT NEVER TILL OR WORK WET SOIL.*
- Over the entire surface spread about:
  — 20-25 lbs. of agricultural gypsum if soil is clay-gumbo; use less (15 lbs.) if it is sandy loam
  — 1 yard (25 cu. ft.) of topsoil and sharp sand
  — 15 lbs. of composted manure, preferably sheep or steer - for nitrogen
  — 5 large wheelbarrows of well-rotted compost or humus - or more
  — 10 lbs. granite dust - for potash
  — 5-10 lbs. of bone meal or ground rock phosphate—for phosphorus
  — 5 lbs. of a 5-10-5, 12-24-12, or 13-13-13 complete commercial fertilizer

Dampen all additives and mix. Water well and allow bed to rest and settle for at least three weeks, watering it once a week. Cultivate bed again until soil particles are fairly fine for planting plants, finer for seeding.

It is no longer recommended to turn each spadeful of soil over because weed seeds are then exposed, allowing them to germinate.

Soil for Hanging Baskets

The mixture should be fertile, well-draining but water retentive, and not too heavy.

- 2 parts organic matter, like fine shredded pine bark or rotted compost
- 1 part mineral matter, such as soil, sand, perlite, or vermiculite, or a mixture of those
- and a small amount of slow-release fertilizer *or* equal parts of sand, loam, and dampened moss.

Mix in a small amount of slow-release fertilizer.

For More Alkaline Soil

The soils in Houston are usually on the alkaline side and Houston's water is alkaline; but if there is a need to make the soil more alkaline (raising the pH one point), add 7-8 pounds of ground limestone per 100 square feet of soil whether it be loam or heavy clay. The action is more rapid if the limestone is finely ground. Mixing the additives into the soil, thoroughly, is necessary for effectiveness.

For More Acid Soil

To lower the pH one point, making it more acid, add 1 to 2 pounds of ground agricultural sulfur per 100 square feet. The addition of humus (well-rotted organic matter) may not be the most rapid method but it is the best and longest lasting way to acidify soil.

For Soil Which is Too Sandy

If the soil is too sandy, incorporate large quantities of organic matter, such as compost or humus, and perhaps perlite, into the sandy soil to create a better water-retaining texture.

The addition of organic matter improves soils in every way. It is a necessary ingredient in clay soils when adjusting the pH. Save all healthy leaves, prunings, and grass clippings in containers or in a compost pile. It is not only excellent nourishment for the garden soil, but is a fine mulch also. Composting helps the garden and your pocketbook.

To form a "picture" of the soil in your garden, follow this procedure: Place a handful of soil in a glass jar. Add water to above the level of the soil. Allow the mixture to stand until the soil particles have separated and settled into layers at the bottom of the jar. These layers show the composition and proportion of each component type: sand at the bottom, silt in the middle, and clay on top.

In measuring soil components or fertilizers, it might help to know that:
> a 2" clay pot = 1/3 cup
> 3" clay pot = 1 cup
> 4" clay pot = 2-1/2 cups
> 6" clay pot = 8 cups or 2 quarts

Basic measure units:
> 3 teaspoons (tsp.) – 1 Tablespoon (Tb.)
> 2 Tbs. = 1 fluid ounce (oz.)
> 12 ounces liquid measure = 1 pound (lb.)
> 1 pint water = 1 pound
> 43,560 square feet = 1 acre
> 27 cubic feet = 1 cubic yard (yd.)

Fertilizer bags usually contain 2 or 3 cubic feet.
> 9 fertilizer bags, each
> containing 3 cubic feet = 1 cubic yard

Raising the level of soil:
To determine the number of cubic yards required to raise your soil level by 4 inches, divide the square measure of the area by 73. The quotient (answer) represents the number of cubic yards needed.

Example:
> 10 feet x 25 feet = 150 feet divided by 73 = about 3 1/2 cu. yds.

Water & Watering

R.J.B.

"Water is the adorner and refresher of the world."
—Charles Mackey

Without water there can be no life. Although there is as much water on the earth today as there ever was—or ever will be, our demand for it is constantly increasing. All water comes from rain, melted snow and ice, and evaporation from the oceans. As the earth's population grows, some areas may face a water shortage if their water supplies are not managed wisely.

Water is the single most important element for plant growth. Water is the primary means for transporting life-giving nutrients in the soil to the roots of plants. It is to our advantage and, indeed, for the protection of all living creatures to practice water conservation in our daily lives, especially in our gardens. Without plants, mankind could not exist.

The Houston area has a heavy annual rainfall of approximately 45 inches. Much too often our rains come in the form of unfortunately heavy downpours, and the majority of this life-giving liquid flows into the city drains. How we wish for that wasted water as day after day passes without rain! The lack of water is particularly harmful in the heat of summer when we face drought conditions along with a severe shortage of city water. It behooves us to turn our attention to ways of conserving water.

Choosing the appropriate method to drain away excess water is very important. To a great extent the texture and composition of the soil affects its drainage capacity. If the water in a water-filled hole fails to drain out within 30 minutes, the soil texture is probably too dense. Sometimes that indicates the presence of an impenetrable hard-pan layer beneath the topsoil. See DRAINAGE chapter.

Creating a soil texture which encourages water absorption and drainage is part of the solution. To accomplish this, incorporate into the soil a layer, at least 4 inches thick, of a combination of decomposed (rotted) organic materials and the mineral, gypsum, mixed into the soil in such quantities as to create a texture hospitable for root growth and water absorption. See SOIL and DRAINAGE chapters for more detailed suggestions for achieving water-conserving drainage.

Water travels downward through the soil pores, carrying with it oxygen and nutrients as well as moisture. While the soil's structure must be loose enough to allow roots and water to penetrate, it must be dense enough to hold some water in reserve for future use and to steady the roots which support plants. Roots extend from a few inches to several feet below the earth's surface. The deeper the roots, the more drought tolerant the plant.

During periods of drought, the soil should be soaked thoroughly to prevent roots from seeking the surface in search of moisture. Shallow roots are vulnerable to damage from heat, dryness, insects, and disease. Soaking a properly prepared soil allows it to retain moisture, thus encouraging deeper root growth. Appropriate texture and soaking protect roots and plants during periods of extended drought. Deep watering also helps the gardener because the need for frequent watering is reduced.

Shady areas require less water because they receive less sunlight and heat and, therefore, lose less moisture to evaporation.

To conserve water and also time, energy, and money:
- Improve the texture of the soil. As discussed above, the amendments add nutrition to the soil so roots penetrate deeper, making the plants less susceptible to drought and reducing the need for frequent watering.
- Apply and retain a 2-inch thick mulch around all plants. The mulch delays evaporation of moisture while also feeding the soil as it decays. When the mulch becomes thinner, it should be augmented to retain the 2-inch height. For mulching use a mixture of well-rotted organic material, such as compost, manure, strips of newspaper, chipped twigs, pine needles and leaves, well-dried grass clippings, and any other rotted but once-living material. Mixing several materials avoids compaction and creates a well-aerated mulch which will accept and retain water. An organic mulch feeds and replenishes the soil and lessens wasteful run-off of rain or other water. Beds kept mulched are warmer in winter and cooler in summer and need much less watering than those without mulch. There are two warnings about mulching: Do not mulch over poor soil, and do not use green or fresh, undried material because the decaying process will rob nitrogen from the soil during the process of decaying.

- Remove all weeds and other undesirable plants from the root areas because their roots steal water and nutrition from the desirable plants, sapping their strength.
- Keep ground cover away from the root area of shrubs for the same reason as for removing weeds.
- Group together plants of similar water requirements for easier watering. Roses require 2 inches of water per week; shallow-rooted plants, like azaleas, wilt if their roots dry out. As a general rule, plants with waxy, needled, thick, or leathery leaves or needles, plants with taproots and plants adapted or native to *your area* are usually drought tolerant; they need much less water.
- Repair any leaky hoses or faucets. "A small leak will sink a great ship." Replacing washers may be the simple answer.
- Restrain yourself from washing driveways and walks with the water hose. Use a blower or a broom instead. (Sweeping is excellent exercise.)
- Set automatic sprinkler systems to water between 4 and 6 A.M., the time when your town's water demand is at its lowest. Otherwise, water in the morning. Evening watering may encourage disease.
- Don't allow sprinklers to waste water on concrete. It won't grow anything.
- Water slowly for better absorption and less evaporation but never on a windy day.
- Use a timer; it will remind you to turn off a forgotten hose.
- Set an empty wooden barrel or a plastic garbage can out where it can catch rainfall. It's still an excellent way to save water for a dry day.

In addition to normal maintenance watering, there are times when plants need special watering:
- Recently transplanted plants should be watered immediately and thoroughly. Check their moisture every day for a week. Roots require water to establish themselves. Fur-

rows should be dug around newly transplanted shrubs and trees. Keep the furrows filled with water for slow, deep watering. This waters the plants while conserving water and is helpful during drought.

- Plants about to bloom need extra water.
- Seed beds and seedlings must be kept damp with gentle sprays of water while the seeds are sprouting and until the plants have at least four true leaves. Watch thereafter; do not let the plants become totally dry.
- Lawns need to be watered when there is a shortage of rain. When blades of grass turn grayish-dull and footprints remain visible (indicating weakness of the grass blades), water repeatedly to attain deep watering. Deep watering encourages deeper root systems and more drought tolerance.
- Plants should be watered before they are fertilized or sprayed with chemicals. Watering the soil before fertilizing plants allows more efficient penetration of the fertilizer. Watering the soil and rinsing off the foliage after fertilizing prevents fertilizer burn. Always follow the directions on the label. *MORE IS NOT BETTER!*
- Hanging baskets and potted plants usually require daily, thorough watering. Double-potting with pebbles in between the pots keeps container plants moist longer, as does a mulch of compost or pebbles.
- Plants need to be watered when a freeze is predicted. Water in the roots and stems of plants protects them from freeze to a certain extent if the freezing weather does not last more than a day or two. Wet soil decreases frost damage. Be sure to water after a freeze to remove frost before the sun's rays reach the foliage. This prevents freeze burn.

Adapted From: Ways to Conserve Water and Special Times to Water by Chris S. Corby, Editor/Publisher of THE TEXAS GARDENER, May/June 1987.

Plants have their way of showing us when they need water: Leaves lose their glossiness, taking on a dull, grayish look. Flowers look weary just before they droop. A wilted or droopy appearance in the heat of the day is not unusual, but the same appearance at late dusk or early morning is an obvious call for water. Though watering in the middle of a summer day, or at night, is not recommended, such a wilted plant needs emergency treatment. Water the roots, but keep the water off the foliage. When the sun's rays are shining on the foliage, water can scald the leaves. Allowing plants to wilt causes harmful stress which in dire cases may cause the plants' demise.

Weather conditions affect the amount and the frequency of watering. Hot, dry winds rob the soil of moisture through evaporation much more rapidly than cool, humid air does. Ample rainfall precludes the necessity for watering as frequently as during drought conditions.

Watering equipment:
- Watering can - a very efficient method for a courtyard or other small garden because it puts water exactly where it needs to be.
- Watering wand - especially useful for hanging baskets.
- Mister bottle - fine for house plants and ferns.
- Watering hose - one for each faucet, with turn-off and spray connections.
- Rotating sprinkler - the most efficient kind throws drops of water out in a pattern horizontal to the ground. Mists and high water thrusts invite evaporation before the water ever touches the plants.
- Soaker hoses - the best ones let water ooze out on all sides. Those with holes on only one side must be kept turned down with the hole side toward the ground. Both kinds may be buried under mulch or light soil.
- Drip irrigation - most efficient watering method, using small plastic tubing directed to the roots of each plant. This system can be extensive and may be automatic with a timer.
- Perforated plastic pipes with small adjustable watering heads - popular for rose beds. The

water spray can be adjusted to water close to the ground, not wetting the foliage. Very efficient and easy to install. The pipe easily attaches to a hose.

- Automatic sprinkler system - underground pipes leading to sprinkler heads at ground level or on upright pipes, depending on the area to be watered. Unless carefully and efficiently installed, these systems are wasteful of water and often do not reach every plant or bed that should be watered. Discuss the system *in detail* with the sprinkler company, including information on the speed with which the company can repair broken heads and pipes. Lawnmowers are notorious for breaking sprinkler heads and pipes, thus putting the entire system out of use. Breaks seem to happen in the hottest weather in the middle of the longest drought. Inquire carefully about the method the company uses to install the pipes to avoid leaving the grounds in a real mess, taking months to recover. Make sure the sprinkler will not be wasting water from run-offs or on paved areas. If there are beds of water-demanding plants, such as azaleas or roses, plan a separate system of sprinkler heads especially for them.

A predominantly clay soil is especially difficult to water thoroughly because its texture slows the entrance of water into the soil pores. Leave a sprinkler on until puddles form. Turn it off until the water seeps in the ground; repeat the procedure. To find out the depth the water penetrated, push a trowel or rod into the soil. If it enters easily, the soil is wet. The dampness on the tool shows the depth of moisture in the soil. If at least 6 inches of dampness shows, you've watered enough. If less, water again. If you record the time it took to water deeply, you will know how long to leave the sprinkler on in the future.

Test the amount of water put out by a sprinkler by setting several empty coffee cans in the watering area. Turn the sprinkler on and check the time. After twenty minutes turn the sprinkler off and check the depth in each can. Follow with the tool test described above. Then you can judge how long it takes to water to that depth, helpful information for future waterings. Deep watering is a key to successful gardening and to water conservation.

Container plants, especially hanging baskets, profit from soaking in a tub of water with the level of water up to but not over, the rim of the container. Water that is over the surface of the soil will wash away the soil in the container. Adding water-soluble fertilizer, according to the manufacturer's directions, serves a double benefit—watering thoroughly while also fertilizing. As soon as moisture appears on the surface of the soil, remove the plant from the water. Overly long soaking can cause root-rot; twenty minutes is about the maximum time. The water in the tub will be even more beneficial if allowed to sit several hours to allow the chlorine in our city water to evaporate. Chlorine is not beneficial to plants. (Even better, use rain water.) Soaking may decrease watering, but potted plants still may need watering in summer heat.

During a drought when watering is more frequent, foliage may turn yellow between the veins of leaves, usually an indication of a chlorotic condition probably resulting from the heavy use of our alkaline city water. Agricultural sulphur, aluminum sulphate, iron sulphate, or copperas, sprinkled around roots (not touching the trunk or stems) or dissolved in water and poured around roots should counteract the chlorosis. Repeat, if necessary, in 2 or 3 weeks. Follow manufacturer's directions.

WATER IS VITAL TO PLANTS. PLANTS AND WATER ARE VITAL TO PEOPLE. CONSERVE WATER. USE IT WISELY AND HELP ALL LIVING CREATURES.

T.F.

Drainage

*"Good order is the foundation
of all good things."*
—Edmund Burke

Because drainage is such an important facet of gardening, this chapter should be written in headlines. Without appropriate removal of excess water from planting areas, especially in our low coastal country, gardeners are defeated before they even begin.

If the soil is well drained, water will disappear from a planting hole in just a few minutes. Water standing as long as an hour indicates the soil is slow draining and corrective measures must be taken to allow successful plant growth.

Plants, like people, suffocate without oxygen. Standing water prevents oxygen from entering the soil. Proper drainage allows water to carry oxygen and nutrients into the soil. On the other hand drainage can be too rapid. This also is detrimental because the quickly draining water not only carries away valuable minerals required for growth but also prevents the retention of reserve water, necessary in times of drought.

Shaded planting areas require even more rapid drainage than those in the sun because evaporation is slower and the soil is cooler in the shade. With excess water standing for any length of time, the soil tends to become waterlogged and unproductive. As long as water is moving down into the soil, even though slowly, it is rarely harmful because it is drawing air (oxygen) and nutrients into the root area with it.

When you are faced with poor drainage, first ascertain if the problem is caused by the quality of the soil. Tight clay may fail to absorb any water at all, or, in the presence of standing water, can become water-soaked. Sandy soil may allow excessively rapid drainage carrying away nutrients. Both types of soil can be rendered productive. The SOIL AND SOIL IMPROVEMENT chapter gives suggestions for remedying difficult conditions.

If the quality and texture of the soil are not causing the drainage problem, check at various locations by digging holes to see if there is a hardpan layer of soil under the top soil. This condition may arise following the driving of heavy equipment over wet ground during construction, compacting the soil into such a hard layer that neither water nor roots can enter it. If some plants are growing improperly, dig them up and examine the roots. If the roots indicate downward and abruptly horizontal growth, they have probably encountered an impenetrable soil layer. This condition may have been hidden and aggravated by the use of a tractor to spread the sand often used to level the ground following construction. The failure to incorporate the sand into the existing soil causes problems.

There are two solutions:
1. Dig down deep enough to break up the hardpan and mix into it great quantities of gypsum, organic matter, and sand so as to form a homogenous soil, which should then become well-drained and, therefore, productive.
2. Lay drainage pipes underground leading downward to a drain outlet. An automatic sump pump can be attached to drain pipes.

Though the latter solution may seem too difficult or too expensive an operation, it may be a more permanent solution to the problem. The laying of drainage pipes usually calls for expert and professional assistance.

Another way to provide adequate drainage is to build raised beds whose surfaces are at least eight inches above ground level. You might build them to be high enough to avoiding stooping over when working in them. Raised beds can also ensure good drainage when filled with just the right mixture of loose soil. Another benefit: They seem to deter some insects. When attractively coordinated with other landscaping, raised beds give a refreshing change from flat terrain.

In Summary

There is a chain reaction. Poor drainage leads to insufficient aeration of the soil, and both conditions encourage spore development of disease organisms and consequent infection of the plants. The plants sicken and die. The objective of effective drainage is to reverse the order. Well-drained soil promotes adequate aeration of the soil and allows the soil to maintain reserve moisture and necessary nutrients. The plants are nourished and thrive.

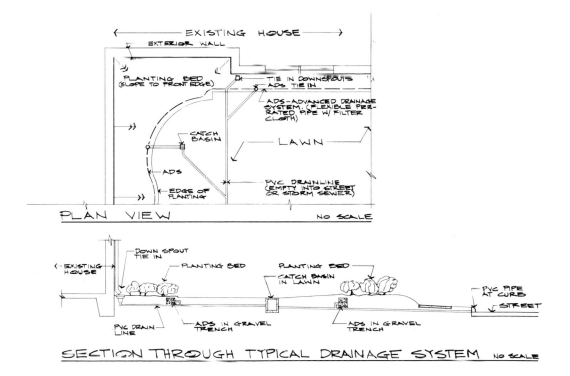

SECTION THROUGH TYPICAL DRAINAGE SYSTEM   NO SCALE

G.C.

Pruning

*"You see a thing for the
first time only once."*
—Theodore White

Pruning is the removal of parts of a plant. There is no more important function in gardening. In truth, pruning is an art-form which should be dictated by the plant's natural growth shape rather than the pruner's whim. There are types of pruning which disregard the plant's natural growth habit to achieve a particular effect. Examples of these types are hedges, espaliering, topiary, and bonsai. They will be discussed later in this chapter.

Purposes accomplished by pruning a plant are to:
- Improve its health, as in removing dead or damaged parts
- Renew growth
- Restrain growth
- Direct and encourage growth
- Improve appearance and restore order in a garden
- Stimulate the production of more flowers or fruit, and
- Allow more air and light to filter through.

Pruning tools should be carefully selected. Choose the proper type and size of tool for the type of pruning to be done. Do not try to force-cut a branch of a larger diameter than will fit into the blades of the half-opened tool. Instead, use another larger blade tool. Tools should be kept cleaned, oiled, and well sharpened to facilitate pruning and to minimize injury to the plant tissues. Always disinfect pruning tools with a 10% clorox solution or alcohol after pruning diseased wood to avoid spreading the disease.

Knowledge of a plant's structure and growth pattern is a prerequisite for appropriate and successful pruning.

Study the plant's growth habit, including its size and shape at maturity before you prune, or better yet, before you buy it. While you are looking for plants for your garden, visit public and private gardens. Take careful notice of the shape of plants and how they grow and mature. That knowledge will help you decide which plants you want in your garden. You also will learn their growth habits. With keen observation of plants, you will develop a picture in your mind's eye of the purpose of your pruning. It is understood, of course, that a garden is not a still life and that plants change day by day. Proper pruning encourages the plants' natural beauty. You, the gardener, are the best judge of whether or not a plant needs pruning.

There are special times and ways to prune certain plants. The pruning of roses, azaleas, and camellias is discussed in their separate chapters.

A plant's season of blooming, fruiting, and growing usually determines when it may be pruned, but there are exceptions. One indisputable criterion is that dead wood may and should be removed by pruning whenever it appears.

If mature deciduous shrubs and small trees are pruned early in the spring *before* they flower, most of their flower buds will be removed and flowering will be sparse.

The three methods used to prune mature deciduous shrubs and small trees are: thinning, renewal or rejuvenation, and heading back or shearing.

Thinning
- allows for growth and development of side branches;
- prevents excessive or unsightly branch formation at the top of the plant; and
- maintains the natural growth pattern.

Thin out the oldest and tallest stems first. Make the cut where the branch is attached to the main stem, the least conspicuous of all pruning methods and the best for reducing density of foliage.

To develop the outward-growing branches, remove inward-growing branches by pruning 1/2 inch above a bud or branch facing outward and angled slightly away from the bud. Plants can be maintained for years at a given height and spread by this method of thinning. Use well-sharpened hand pruning shears, not hedge shears.

Renewal or Rejuvenation
Mature, deciduous shrubs or small trees which have become too large or contain too much unproductive wood may be renewed by cutting the oldest branches at ground level, leaving only the newest stems. If there are only a few new stems, remove the older wood gradually, over a 3-year period, to maintain the overall shape of the plant. To encourage strong branch development, the new shoots should be cut back to various lengths by the thinning method described previously to encourage strong branch development. Plants which are very overgrown, severely weakened, or otherwise unhealthy can be cut back completely to the soil in late winter. They may not bloom for a year or two, or they may not even live.

Pruning camphor trees and photinia Fraseri encourages their rosy-tinted new foliage.

Heading Back or Shearing
These terms are synonymous and refer to cutting back a branch anywhere along the length of the stem, above a bud, or beneath a bud, or only a stub, to concentrate vigorous, new, upright growth below the cut. If every branch or twig is headed back, more growth develops than was removed and the natural form of the plant is changed by the extra growth. Hedges are pruned by heading back or shearing. Use well-sharpened hedge shears.

Pruning Deciduous Shrubs and Small Trees when Transplanting
Bare-rooted or balled and burlapped (B&B) deciduous shrubs and small trees should be lightly pruned when transplanted. Prune away damaged or dead roots and branches. Inspect the root system before planting. If there are roots girdling the root-ball, either remove them or score the root-ball with a sharp knife on 3 or 4 sides to a depth of 1/2 or 1/3 inch. Be sure to cut deep enough to sever the girdling roots. If severe root cutting is required, prune the branches and foliage to compensate for the loss of the portion of the root system cut or damaged in the original digging and that portion removed at transplanting. Pruning cuts should be made on a slant, preferably at a joint or crotch. Do not cut into the branch collar of the tree. Try to leave as small a wound as possible to allow for rapid healing. Cut the branches just above a bud or

joint pointing in the direction in which you want the plant to grow.

When removing a protruding branch, cut well inside the plant, even to its base, as with nandinas and other shrubs with the same growth habit.

Narrow-leaved evergreens produce new growth in the spring and fall, growing little in the summer. Prune about the middle of April. An exception is pines, which should be pruned when the candle-shaped growth develops in the spring. Prune evergreens according to their growth habit. Do not try to shape them. Shearing not only ruins their natural form, but prevents the penetration of light into the heart of the plant, causing foliage drop. Pest control becomes difficult because of the density of the foliage. Start pruning evergreens when they are small. If they are pruned a bit each year, severe and harmful pruning will be unnecessary. Remove dead branches whenever they occur. Do not cut into bare wood behind the foliage on the tips of narrow-leaved evergreens because the plant may be irreparably damaged. It is much better to select a compact or dwarf form of narrow-leaved evergreen than to prune a larger form.

It is normal for the foliage on narrow-leaved evergreens to turn brown in the fall. It is their natural pruning process and is comparable to the dropping of leaves by deciduous plants. Extensive periods of hot, dry weather also contribute to this loss of leaves or needles.

The pruning of large mature trees should be left to professional tree men. Knowing the mature size and shape of trees *before* buying and planting is of extreme importance. When a tree's size and form are appropriate for the space in which it is planted, there are few pruning problems. Thinning is sometimes recommended for trees, but much less frequently when the tree fits its space. Thinning judiciously allows light into the heart of the foliage and into the area under the tree's canopy. It also emphasizes the branch structure and reduces breakage during storms. The thinning should be done by reputable, registered tree companies. The ideal time to prune trees is during their dormant season before new growth begins.

Topping trees is recommended only under unusual circumstances. One of those circumstances is trees growing into power lines. Pruning around power lines should always be handled by professional tree companies. The best solution to the problem is to avoid it by not planting a large growing tree under the lines. If the tree has already grown into the lines, there are two remedies: top the tree, that is, cut it all across its canopy; or prune a "window" around the lines, a remedy which will probably require repeating in a year or two but it does give the tree a better appearance than the topping does.

Most flowering trees which bloom in the spring should be pruned immediately after flowering unless there is desirable fruit. In that case, delay pruning until just after the fruiting. There are exceptions. If in doubt, look in the TREES chart or ask your nurseryman.

There are differences of opinion about the use of wound or pruning paint. Some think that nature will take care of the pruning cuts in time and that the paint holds moisture in the wound. Others think that the wound-dressing is necessary to prevent the entrance into the open cut of disease and insects which may be carrying diseases. Still others prefer the paint for cosmetic reasons. Take your choice.

Root Pruning

Several weeks before transplanting a large shrub or small tree, root-prune (cut) around the plant, about 2 feet away from the trunk with a sharp spade to a depth of 6 or 8 inches, depending on the size of the plant. The purpose is to cut some of the roots before the actual moving or transplanting to diminish the shock of moving and probable cutting of the root system. With gradual root-pruning, the plant becomes accustomed to the transplanting.

Wisterias which have not bloomed well sometimes respond to root-pruning alone.

Pruning a Shrub into Tree Form

Several attractive blooming and non-blooming shrubs, such as Banana Shrub (michelia), ligustrum, cleyera, pittosporum, guava, and crape myrtle may be pruned into tree form. After considering the size and growth habit of the shrub, remove the lower branches on the main trunk up to an attractive height. If a multi-trunked tree is preferred, or is more suitable to the shrub, trim branches off several trunks. This procedure is most favorably accomplished during the dormancy of the shrub, or as the new growth is just beginning. Shoots which appear later along the trunks can be removed easily, perhaps by rubbing off the new tender growth. These small trees are often in pleasant proportion to small gardens. Many suitable shrubs bloom or fruit or have interesting foliage or bark, which can be appreciated better with the removal of the lower foliage.

Damaged Plants

When shrubs or small trees have been badly damaged by cold, they may be cut back—after all possibility of freezing weather. (The average date of our last frost is February 10, but there have been many disastrous freezes after that date). Incorporate rotted manure and compost into the soil around the shrub and water deeply. You may find your shrub rejuvenated in a few weeks. Try to protect your plants from such damage during the next winter. See WINTER PROTECTION chapter.

Generally speaking, most vines should be pruned during the dormant season. When pruning woody vines, such as wisteria and trumpet creeper, cut interfering branches back below the point of interference or at the juncture with the main stem. Prune away the top 1/3 of overgrown or elongated stems. Stems which are old, mature, or weak should have at least 1/2 of their length removed. Do not prune wisteria extensively during its dormant season because it encourages rampant vegetative growth the next spring. Instead, in July prune out the long straggly growth, leaving those branches which the vines need for climbing. This and root-pruning often stimulate wisteria to bloom. Cutting shoots back 1/2 to 1/3 their length encourages the production of short spurs on which the next season's flower clusters are borne.

Disbudding, Pinch Pruning and Finger Pruning

All three terms refer to a very useful type of garden pruning. The terms refer to the pinching off (removal) of the main tip (or apical or terminal shoot) of young stems to encourage the formation of side buds. The flowering period may be delayed, but the reward is compact, bushy plants with increased bloom. Annuals and some perennials respond beautifully to finger-pruning. In the ANNUALS AND PERENNIALS chapter, this type of pruning is recommended when the young plants put out their first bud. Pinch-pruning those buds multiplies the number of sprouts and buds, increasing flowers.

Dead-heading is the removal of spent flowers or seedpods, usually between finger and thumbnail. These last two terms probably motivated the term "green thumb" for those gardeners who practice both types of pruning have not only a tell-tale green thumbnail but also an abundance of growth and flowers in their gardens.

When annuals like Sweet Alyssum and Phlox Drummondi have passed their peak of bloom, shear them back with hedge shears to within 2 inches of the ground. Water and fertilize the plants and look forward to more flowers. All blooming plants benefit from the removal of faded flowers, a practice which encourages their natural urge to produce blooms which in turn form seedpods. It is through the seeds that plants reproduce themselves...once again, the miracle of the seed. "All the flowers of all the tomorrows are in the seeds of today."

Pruning for Arrangements

When cutting garden evergreens for decorative purposes in the home, keep in mind that you are pruning as you cut. When properly and thoughtfully pruned, the plants will be strengthened and renewed. To encourage evergreens to spread out, cut the top buds or shoots. To encourage upright growth, clip the lateral branches. Conifers need little pruning, but pinching out the terminal buds will lead to symmetry and density. Refer to the ARRANGEMENTS FROM YOUR GARDEN chapter for methods of prolonging the life of cut materials and hints for arranging them.

Hedges require regular pruning because of their formal shape, which is unnatural to the plants. To encourage thick, dense growth, prune hedge plants into a trapezoidal shape. The top surface must be narrower than the base of the hedge to allow sunshine to reach all parts of the plants, fostering even growth throughout the plants. When the hedge shrubs are first planted, pinch-prune the tip of every branch to encourage additional growth on each plant for thickness. Clip hedges regularly enough to avoid cutting too much growth at a time. Regular shearing also creates a more attractive appearance.

Espaliered plants are attached to flat surfaces, such as walls, and trained in patterns, usually along wires for guidelines. Once begun, an espaliered pattern must be pruned frequently to avoid an unkempt appearance.

Topiary pruning, the close shearing of plants into ornamental shapes, often animal forms, requires repeated clipping to be attractive. The pruning must begin when the plant is young and clipped carefully with the final shape clearly in mind.

Bonsai is the artful pruning of plants into a dwarf form. It takes a skilled, patient pruner who is familiar with the plant's natural habit of growth to be successful with bonsai. The dwarfed plant is usually grown in a complementary container, though some bonsais, 4 or 5 feet in height, are placed in gardens.

Pruning Times

Among those shrubs and small trees which bloom on the previous season's growth and which should be pruned immediately following bloom are:

Bottlebrush (Callistemon)
Deutzia*
Dogwood (Cornus)
Huisache (Acacia)
Some Hydrangeas*
Flowering Quince (Chaenomeles)
Jasmines
Mock Orange (Philadelphus)
Photinia
Pittosporum
Redbud (Cercis)
Spiraea
Viburnum

Among the shrubs and trees which bloom in late summer into fall and should be pruned while dormant in winter are:

Abelia
Althea*
Beautyberry (Callicarpa)
Butterflybush (Buddleia)*
Buttonbush (Cephalanthus)*
Chaste Tree (Vitex)*
Crape Myrtle*
Elderberry (Sambucus)
Flowering Fruit Trees*
Hibiscus
Oleander*
Parkinsonia*
Plumbago
Poinciana*
Pomegranate
Salt-Cedar (Tamarix)*

*Should be pruned to increase blooming

Most of the information in this PRUNING chapter is from publications prepared by Robert E. Moon, former Extension landscape horticulturist, and Everett Janne, Extension landscape horticulturist, The Texas A & M University System, courtesy of the Texas Agricultural Extension Service.

J.M.K.

Propagation

"And for all this, nature is never spent; there lives the dearest freshness deep down things."
—Gerard Manley Hopkins

To propagate plants is to multiply or to reproduce them. They can also be caused to reproduce themselves. Propagation methods include layering, grafting, budding, divisions, cuttings, and seeding. The latter three ways are the simplest.

Seeds

Since most plants produce seed and many reseed themselves, propagation from seed is the most frequently used method of reproduction. Think of the wild flowers in the field which reseed and reproduce themselves with no help from us. However, gardeners realize that many seeds require care to germinate. Sunshine, fertile fine-textured soil, moisture, and fresh viable seeds are essential for success. In our warm humid climate, the fungal disease "damping off" is a notorious killer of seed sprouts. It causes the stem of the tiny plant to turn black and rot off at the soil line. The condition can be discouraged by planting in raised beds which are well drained and sunny. When buying seeds, look for those which have been pretreated to be resistant to the disease. Seeds may be dusted prior to planting with a special disinfectant available at garden supply shops or nurseries.

Very early spring and fall are the seasons when seedlings are most susceptible to damping off. When the weather is warm and relatively dry, there is less chance of difficulty. If you find any seedlings with the symptoms, the bed can be dusted with fungicides such as Terrachlor or Zineb to prevent the spread of the disease. Aerosol methods are not very successful.

Planting Seeds

Check the date on the packages when buying seeds. Fresh seeds are most likely to germinate well. Follow the directions given for the planting depth and for the cultural requirements of light, soil, and water. Take note of the mature size of the plant, the color of its flowers, and the season it blooms. Some plants, like sweet peas, are planted in October but do not bloom until spring. Notice also whether or not the seedlings of each variety prefer to grow where they are planted. Some varieties do not tolerate transplanting.

Plant seeds thinly in moist soil, usually twice their depth, with the soil pressed firmly above them. Extremely fine seed should be mixed with sand and pressed lightly but not covered. A common fault is to sow seeds too deep and too thick; crowded seedlings are more susceptible to the damping off disease.

Germination of many seeds may be hastened by dusting them with hormone powder. Hard-coated seeds and seeds which are naturally slow to sprout, such as parsley, may be soaked in tepid water and planted before they dry out. Bluebonnet and Texas bluebell seeds should be planted when ripe, otherwise they will become hard and need to be soaked. Buy from reputable seed companies or save your own in a dry place. The growth of certain hard seeds, such as canna, coralbean, and mountain laurel, can be accelerated by clipping off an end of the hard seed coat, permitting moisture to enter the inner part of the seeds without delay. The seeds of many flowering shrubs germinate in the first year after sowing, but there are numerous garden shrubs and trees which commonly require two years or more before the seeds germinate. Nuts, if not planted as soon as ripe, should be stratified (stored in moist peat moss or sand) to simulate the usual conditions under which they sprout.

Although the seeds of bulbs take three or four years to bloom, a single choice bulb yields dozens of fertile seeds. Agapanthus, hybrid spurias, and hybrid amaryllis may be produced in great quantity by planting the seeds. To insure the true color of amaryllis, tie cheesecloth or a paper bag around the bud before it opens and pollinate it artificially. Allow the seed pods to ripen and dry on the stalk. Fertile seeds contain a kernel.

Fill a wooden box four to six inches deep with friable soil. Press each seed into the soil one inch apart, bearing down strongly with your finger. Sprinkle 1/4 inch of soil over the entire surface, but do not press down. Place four sheets of newspaper the same size as the box directly on the soil, and weight the edges with narrow strips of wood. Wet the paper thoroughly, then cover all with a pane of glass. Place the box in semi-shade and sprinkle the paper lightly whenever it seems to be drying out. After a few days, when the sprouts are 1/4-inch tall, remove the paper

and replace the glass. Keep soil moist but not sopping wet. Seedlings may be planted in the open ground when they are seven to twelve inches tall. Too much shade makes spindly seedlings. Careful weak fertilizing and gentle watering will bring them to the earliest possible bloom.

Open Beds

The following formula for planting seeds is also appropriate for plants. The only exception is that the soil need not be as fine for plants as it must be for seeds, but it should be deeper for perennials' long roots.

To prepare a seeding bed:
- Select an area which receives at least four hours of sun, preferably six hours.
- With a shovel or fork break up the soil, removing weeds and their roots as you go. *never* work, till, hoe, or use heavy machinery on wet soil. The resulting compaction is very difficult to correct.
- Till or hoe the soil until the clods are broken up. If the soil is very dry, moistening it a little may help. If the soil is typical "gumbo" clay found in Houston, wet it, then cover it with gypsum and let it set for several days. Gypsum helps break up the clods. Otherwise, add sandy loam to your soil.
- Even with the addition of loam, the soil will benefit from a layer, 2 to 4 inches thick, of a combination of:
  1. Well-rotted compost with aged manure and pre-dampened peat moss make the soil more hospitable to the all-important soil micro-organisms. It will also improve aeration and moisture retention, and increase the friability (the ability of soil to crumble). See SOIL chapter.
  2. Bonemeal, cottonseed meal, blood meal, and phosphorus for nutrition.
  3. Gypsum to loosen the soil.
  4. Sulphur to acidify the usually alkaline soils in Houston. A test of your garden soil by the nearest County Extension office is the

only sure way to know the composition and needs of your garden soil.

5. Sand for improved texture and porosity.
6. Balanced fertilizer (2 pounds to 100 square feet of area) to feed the plants.

- Work or till the soil to mix it thoroughly into a homogenous whole.
- Water the bed thoroughly to help the additives meld.
- Covering the bed with plastic discourages weeds.

Several days before planting, remove plastic, work the soil again, rake and moisten it. Plants should thrive in such soil.

Planting seed beds should be watered sufficiently before sowing to avoid further watering until the seeds germinate. When ready to plant, loosen the top 2 or 3 inches, rake smooth again, and with your finger form drills (little ditches) to the depth suggested on the seed packet. If the seed is very fine, you may mix it in a salt shaker with sand and shake the seeds into the drills. Cover seeds with the loose soil. Press soil firmly and water with fine spray, enough to get the moisture down to the seeds. Mark the rows with the name of the annuals you planted. (You think you'll remember, but you won't). All you do now is keep the soil damp and watch for the sprouts to push up through the soil. The first two leaves are cotyledons. The "true" or typical leaves will follow shortly. Until you gain experience in identifying the leaves, don't pull up anything green. Wait until you're sure which is a weed and which is an annual.

Seeds of bedding plants, especially those which do not transplant easily (such as poppies, phlox, and larkspur) may be broadcast where they are to bloom. Seeds of bedding plants, such as sweet alyssum, may be sown in shallow rows or drills. When planting in open beds, mix the seed with sand to insure thin sowing and to reduce the labor of thinning out excess plants. Newly planted seeds may be protected from hard rains by covering the ground with cheesecloth or thin burlap.

Flats

Flats are generally used to sow seeds for later transplanting because the flats are easily handled and moved for protection from rain and extremes of temperatures. For the majority of the year, warmth for germination is simple to find in our climate, but during the cold months flats can be placed on top of water heaters, in sunny windowsills, or in a greenhouse with good ventilation. The wooden flats are seldom used now though they may return to favor if the move to abolish the non-biodegradable plastic items increases in fervor and influence. The usual dimensions for wooden flats are 3" deep, 12" wide, and 18" long. Plastic flats or trays with perforated bottoms may be filled with a growing mixture just as they are, but the flats with open squares should be lined with 6 or 8 pages of newspaper to hold the soil. If shallow foil containers are to be used as flats, puncture enough holes in the bottom for good drainage. The flats may be filled with a combination of equal parts of perlite or vermiculite and well-dampened, fine peat moss, thoroughly mixed and dampened before seeds are planted. There are various soil-less mixes available at a garden supply store or a nursery.

An old favorite soil mixture is:
- 1 part very fine-textured, fertile loam to supply food;
- 1 part coarse sand to improve drainage; and
- 1 part well-moistened peat moss to retain moisture.

As an extra precaution against fungal disease such as damping off, the soil mix may be sterilized by heating it in a 160° oven, but do not place plastic flats in a conventional oven.

Seeds may also be sown in pots filled with a starting soil as described above, but they should first be soaked in and scrubbed with a chlorine-water solution to combat fungus. The best method of watering the pots is to set the pots in water almost to the rim until the soil is moistened. Be careful not to leave them in the water after the soil's surface is moistened. Flats should be watered with a very fine spray.

Cold frames and hot beds are seldom used in Houston because our temperate climate does not require them. Our plants, especially seedlings, can be damaged just as much by being left in a closed greenhouse on a warm sunny winter day as by frost. Our rapid temperature changes even during a morning are unpredictable. When constructing a greenhouse, try to place it where it will receive summer shade and winter sun. An exhaust fan is practically a must in our climate. There is a trick to keeping the greenhouse warmer in winter and cooler in summer. Keep the glass windows clean during the winter to let in all the winter sun, warming the greenhouse. During the summer, allow the windows to remain coated with dust to *reduce* the amount of sunlight entering the windows.

Transplanting

When the small seedlings have from two to four or more "true" leaves, they should be carefully "pricked out" with a knife tip or sharp stick and transplanted to stand farther apart in other flats or set in permanent beds. The flats should be well watered before seedlings are removed to the new moist soil. Some species, pansies for instance, do better if reset and transplanted twice to develop stronger root systems and sturdier plants. Seedlings that grow too quickly need to be thinned out before they become leggy, to allow the plants to develop shorter, stronger stems and a well-balanced top growth.

In any transplanting, pressure of the soil against the roots is necessary to anchor the plant and bring the roots into closer contact with the soil so they can absorb moisture and food and to rid the soil of air pockets. Many plants have highly developed taproots, as well as a system of fibrous roots. Great care should be exercised to prevent injury and breakage of the root system. Handling the seedlings by the leaves and stem avoids injury to the roots. Bare-rooted plants may be dipped in a rooting hormone solution to speed growth. The roots should be spread out to their natural position, leaving the bits of earth clinging to them to avoid tearing off their hair roots. To prevent decay, badly bruised or damaged roots should be snipped off with clean shears.

Plants transplanted on a cloudy day or late in the day do not wilt as easily and take almost immediate hold in their new surroundings. If transplanting is done on a sunny day, wilting may be avoided by inserting sprays of evergreens among the plants to provide shade. Summer transplanting is generally considered risky, but it can be done safely if the roots are well encased in a ball of earth and the plants are watered liberally and provided with temporary shade.

Division

Vegetative propagation without using seed is carried out by dividing into sections those species which form bulbs, corms, tubers, rhizomes, or crowns. Varieties which do not reproduce seed, or do not reproduce true to color or form because the seed-producing flowers have been cross-fertilized, may be perpetuated by this reliable method.

Many of the bulbous plants, such as narcissi, tulips, and hyacinths, propagate naturally by the division of the bulbs into small bulbs or bulblets. When naturalized, these should be separated as they become crowded. Some other species, such as the Tiger Lily, form aerial bulblets in the leaf axils. The bulblets may be planted in the same way as those produced on the underground parts.

Scaly bulbs, such as those of many lilies, may be propagated readily by removing the loose outer scales and planting them in the same way you plant seeds.

Corms are bulb-like structures popularly classed as bulbs. They proliferate in much the same way as bulbs by producing one or more tiny corms, known as cormels, on top of the parent corm. Gladioli form cormels around the base of the new corm. Cormels are planted in essentially the same way as seeds. If properly cared for by transplanting when they become crowded, they will grow into corms of flowering size in one to four years. Corms may be broken apart with the hands or cut with a sharp spade into root-bearing sections which, when replanted, form new plants. Crowns must be planted slightly above soil level.

Tubers are thickened stems with eyes below the soil, such as potato and Jerusalem artichoke. Tubers are easily propagated by planting whole or cut in sections. Each section must possess an eye, from which a new plant will sprout. Tuberous roots have eyes in the stem. Dahlias and daylilies are examples. For propagation purposes, the roots should be cut with a portion of stem attached to each division.

Rhizomes are underground or partially underground stems which (if cut into portions, with each portion having a growth bud) rapidly increase the plants. Usually such divisions are made when plants are dormant (cannas, for example), but in the case of Bearded Iris most gardeners prefer to do this soon after the plants have bloomed.

Runners are slender shoots that run along the surface of the ground, rooting and developing into a succession of new plants. These may be separated from the parent stock and set in new locations. The strawberry is propagated by this means.

Stolons are underground suckers or trailing branches peculiar to some species. They take root when they come in contact with the soil. Stolons may be severed with attached roots and transplanted. Some azaleas and many grasses, such as St. Augustine, may be propagated in this manner.

Clumps should be lifted and divided at intervals if the plant's vigor is to be maintained and new plants secured.

Layering

Several methods of layering are used to multiply new stock from plants which are difficult to propagate by other means. Simple layering is the easiest method. Strong, young branches, notched on the underside, may be pegged firmly to the ground, preferably at a joint or near an eye. The cut portion should be buried about two inches deep so that calluses will form at the cuts, on which roots will develop. When layering woody or semi-woody plants, strong shoots should be slit part way and a wedge or pebble inserted to keep the cut open. Layers are usually made in the early spring, allowing roots to develop by fall, when they may be severed from the parent plant and transplanted. Many plants, including azaleas, jasmines, pink magnolias, holly, dogwood, and most hardwood shrubs may be easily propagated in this way.

When *serpentine* or *continuous layering* is employed, several plants may be obtained at the same time from one long flexible shoot, such as grapes, ivy, and some roses. In serpentine layering, a long shoot is undulated and the lower loops are covered with earth. In continuous layering, the long shoot is pegged down and covered lightly with earth along its length.

In *mound layering*, the parent plant should be cut back to promote the production of quantities of young shoots near the ground. A layer of earth is mounded over the center of the plant until the stems root. These rooted shoots are cut off at normal ground level and planted. The parent or mother stock plant is then allowed to produce another crop of shoots that are in turn mound layered. This method is used mainly with low bushy shrubs, such as azaleas, hydrangeas, Japanese quince, and spirea.

Trees and shrubs whose branches cannot be conveniently brought into contact with the earth may be propagated by *air layering*, often called Chinese layering. A notch should be cut in the branch, or the bark girdled, and kept open at the point where root formation is desired. A ball of well-saturated sphagnum moss should be bound firmly with plastic over the wound. The moss will stay moist until sufficient roots have formed, when the rooted branch may be severed and planted. This method, commonly applied to rubber plants, crotons, dracaenas, and similar foliage plants, causes the old plant to leaf out and become more shapely. Camellias may also be propaged by air layering.

Cuttings

Cuttings are sections of plants that are rooted in shallow boxes or pots of sand, soil, wet peat moss, or one of the patented, root-growth mediums. There are several methods of taking cuttings from roses and many perennials and from most shrubs and trees, both deciduous and evergreen. Cuttings of root, leaf, or stem may be made at any time of the year, but the early spring months are considered best. Azaleas may be propagated from cuttings.

Cuttings may be soaked in root-inducing chemicals for better propagation. Synthetic plant hormones, marketed under various trade names, are very successful in stimulating root growth of plants heretofore considered difficult to propagate. Follow directions explicitly, as success depends mainly upon the correct strength of the solution and the proper duration of treatment for each particular plant. Fungal attacks on cuttings, which often cause them to rot, may be prevented by dipping the ends in fungus-preventing products developed for this purpose.

Stem cuttings, the type usually employed by amateur gardeners, are made of non-flowering shoots of either half-ripened wood (softwood cuttings) or of dormant shoots (hardwood cuttings). Make all cuttings with a sharp knife, just below an eye or bud, into lengths containing three or four eyes. Cuttings should be stripped of all surplus leaves except the upper two leaves which should be cut in half. The cut end of the cutting should be dipped into a root hormone such as Rootone. Then make a hole in the soil using a pencil or smooth stick to prevent knocking off the rooting powder. Put the cutting in the hole and press soil around it.

Important factors in the success of cuttings are:
- a root stimulant,
- a good rooting medium,
- adequate shelter from wind and sun, and
- sufficient moisture but not too much.

The roots develop from a callus formed on the cut surface. When several leaves appear, repot the cuttings or place them in good garden soil, water gently, and protect from sun and wind for several days.

Although hardwood cuttings usually take longer to form roots than those of softwood, they may be rooted more successfully in the open ground. Hardwood cuttings of shrubs and trees may often be rooted where they are to remain if they are planted in holes the size a posthole digger makes and filled with a rooting medium. If kept constantly moist, the roots of the cuttings soon go through the medium and into the soil, making transplanting unnecessary. When cuttings are taken in quantity in the late fall, they may be tied in bundles for convenience, buried completely in moist earth or sand, and mulched. In the early spring the majority will have callused or rooted, and these may be planted in beds for further development. Some cuttings, as those from oleander and willows, root easily in jars of water.

Heel cuttings are made to retain a small portion of the older stem at the base of each cutting. Although this type of cutting is more damaging to the parent plant, it roots more readily than one cut off below the node.

Leaf cuttings taken from certain plants, generally those that are fleshy or succulent, soon form roots and new plants. Rex begonia leaves should be cut across the larger veins and pegged down in damp sand, while leaf sections taken from sansevieria plants should be simply cut into sections and stuck in moist sand.

Root cuttings are the easiest of all in the case

of crape myrtle, blackberry, and many trees and perennials. When cut into sections and covered with earth, the roots soon form new plants.

Grafting and Budding

The word "graftage" is used to include both grafting and budding. The difference between the processes is slight; both are used to unite the growing tissues of two plants which are botanically related. Many varieties of citrus fruits are rendered hardier by being grafted or budded on the native orange stock known as *Citrus trifoliata*, which becomes dormant and practically frost hardy in winter. Many varieties of ornamental trees, camellias, and other shrubs are grafted or budded on stocks having a very strong root system.

In grafting, the base of the shoot, known as the "scion," is shaped and inserted into a previously prepared incision in the stem or branch of a rooted plant, known as the "stock." Good contact between the soft outer tissues or cambium layers of scion and the stock is essential. The two are bound tightly together to maintain the close contact, and the graft is often covered with a grafting wax to insure that the juncture does not become dry before the union is established. Shoot roots growing from below the point of grafting continue to produce their own characteristic leaves, fruits, and flowers. To give all possible strength to the new and desirable growth, all the suckers coming from below the point of union should be cut off. There are numerous types of specialized grafting practiced by experienced gardeners, mainly cleft, whip, bark, splice, saddle, veneer, side, and shield grafting.

Budding involves the same essential processes as described above except that the scion consists merely of an axillary bud together with a small portion of the outer tissues of the stem on which it was borne. The practices of grafting and budding require accuracy and skill, and there is much to learn from authoritative writers and nurserymen.

Clones

A clone is the original selected plant and the aggregate of the plants descended from it by vegetative (asexual) propagation. Most so-called "varieties," "cultivated varieties," "horticultural varieties," "named varieties," and "garden varieties" are clones. Clones may be selected from species, varieties, or forms of species. Plants grown from seed are not identical as are members of a clone, but if you raise a plant grown from seed and propagate it, then that plant and all the individuals descended from it form a clone. "Clone" is a horticultural rather than a taxonomic term.

R.J.B.

R.J.B.

Helpful denizens
in your garden;
protect them.

Clockwise:
Chameleon,
Toad,
Ladybug.

R.J.B.

Diseases, Insects, & Weeds

"There are some remedies worse
than the disease."

—Horace

*E*ven in Eden there was a snake. And as long as this Earth turns around, there probably always will be. The answer to coping with diseases, insects, and weeds is clear. There has to be a reasonable compromise. It is self-defeating to fight the pests with substances so toxic as to threaten our environment. Understanding the risks to people before thoughtlessly using chemical controls which have dangerous side effects is mandatory. Continual widespread and careless application of broad-spectrum pesticides as a control is unnecessary. Why kill the beneficial insects and plants when the actual target is usually only one pest? When the natural enemies of harmful pests are destroyed, the pests have a greater chance to multiply. Nature's control is disturbed.

Suggestions for reasonable control:
• Employ natural and biological controls first.
• Healthy plants are the best defense against diseases and insects which attack unhealthy or weak plants first. Place the plants in the location and soil they prefer.
• Keep your garden clean with all debris removed. Various insects hide and breed in debris. Diseases often begin in or spread from diseased foliage left carelessly in the garden.
• Maintain a healthy garden by following thoughtful procedures, such as:
  1. Correct any drainage problems. Refer to the DRAINAGE chapter. Follow suggestions in the WATER AND WATERING chapter for proper watering methods and times appropriate to our warm, humid climate.
  2. Build and maintain a fertile soil, cultivating it to remove pests which overwinter in the soil and weeds which serve as host plants to pests. Refer to the SOIL chapter.
• Diversify your plantings to maintain nature's control system. Different pests and diseases attack different plants. With diversification, not all plants will be susceptible to the same attacks.
• Plant resistant varieties and also plants native *to your locale*. They are usually stronger, hardier, and more tolerant to disease, drought, heat, and our unpredictable winters.
• Interplant aromatic herbs and other plants with strong-smelling leaves, such as the French and African marigolds, among vegetables, annuals, and perennials. The pungent odors not only

confuse but sometimes repel pests.

- Encourage birds, toads, frogs, lizards, and harmless snakes. They consume millions of insects per day. Learn to recognize the few poisonous snakes. A visit to the Museum of Natural Science will allow you to see examples of each.
- Be alert for insect and disease damage by examining your plants frequently, observing the leaves, both top and under side and the axils (the beginning of the leaf stem from the stalk or branch), places pests often attack first.
- Mulch all plants to discourage weeds and allow easier pulling up of those which venture through.
- Pluck harmful insects off foliage and destroy them, preferably in early morning or late afternoon, the times most likely to find insects. Wear gloves and carry a bag to deposit the bugs.
- Wash aphids and other insects off foliage with a strong force of water; repeat every few days to upset their mating schedule. Black ants eat aphids.
- Examine carefully every plant you intend to bring into your garden or home for symptoms of disease or insect damage. Do not add to the pests already present.
- Before using chemical sprays, try soapy, not detergent, water, or blend hot peppers, garlic, or onions in a blender and combine with water to use as a spray.
- Saucers of beer placed in the evening wherever you suspect slugs entices them to drink and die.
- Wipe garden tools carefully with alcohol or a clorox solution after using, especially after pruning diseased foliage, to avoid spreading disease. For the same reason, wash garden gloves after each use.
- Keep all mowing and pruning blades sharp to cut stems cleanly. Ragged cuts are harmful and invite disease and insects.
- Before re-using a container for planting, scrub it well in clorox and water solution to prevent spread of disease.
- Sprinkle wood ashes, sharp sand, diatomaceous earth, or flour around young transplants to discourage worms and caterpillars. The rough materials hurt their stomachs when crawled over; the flour covers the slime on which they need to crawl.

Pesticides are poisons. For safety first: *READ EVERY WORD ON THE LABEL OF ANY PESTICIDE YOU CONSIDER USING.* Follow suggested precautions to the letter. Avoid the broad-spectrum pesticides which kill the beneficial insects as well as the harmful pests. With their enemies decimated, the harmful pests multiply more rapidly.

The solution to maintaining a wholesome environment seems to be to employ natural and biological controls first. A hole or two in a leaf does not spell a disaster! Then, if absolutely necessary, resort to chemical materials with the greatest caution.

Know the enemy. Try to learn not only the identification of each pest but also its habits. The descriptions in this chapter should acquaint you with those pests most frequently found in Houston. Please refer to the ROSES chapter for more information.

A Poisonous Creature in the Garden

One of the most painful stings is inflicted by the Puss Caterpillar, often incorrectly called an "Asp." It is a fuzzy creature which changes color as it progresses from a larva to an adult, from whitish to tan to grayish with darker markings. Among the fuzzy hairs are numerous short spines which discharge a vicious venom upon contact. The pain is intense and reddening and swelling begins soon. The inflamation may spread and eventually affect the lymph nodes or cause a headache. Contact a doctor.

These caterpillars are often found on trees, bushes, or plants. *Before* you touch any bark, branch, or leaf, look closely on the underside as well as the top. They do not appear in enough numbers to damage a plant, but it takes only one puss caterpillar to create agony for a person.

At first cursory glance, the puss caterpillar (or "asp") appears to be a small lump of dirty cotton or fluff, about an inch or 1-1/2 inches long and puffy. If possible, knock it to the ground with a stick or tool and kill it. When found in profusion, spray or dust with products containing *Bacillus thuringiensis* (Dipel, Thuricide, Bio Spray) or carbaryl (Sevin).

Not all natural and biological controls are safe for people. Nicotine can be very dangerous. Some pesticides derived from plants, such as rotenone, pyrethrum, and ryania, are considered environmentally safe, but they are broad-spectrum materials which kill beneficial as well as harmful insects. However, they do have good traits for a pesticide: low toxicity to wildlife, safety in application, and rapidity in breaking down.

Biological controls include:

- Diatomaceous earth, often sold as a filter for swimming pools, relies on its physical features to destroy pests. It is a powder with razor-sharp particles from sea-dwelling plants called diatoms. In powder form, it causes the insect to dry out and die. *Care must be taken to avoid inhaling the dust.*
- Dormant and summer oils suffocate the insects themselves, their eggs, and their larvae. These oils are considered to be non-toxic *unless* pesticides, such as ethion, are added to them. Do not use dormant oil if the temperature is over 85°F. or under 45°F.
- Insecticidal soaps are made principally of fatty acids. They can be effective against soft-bodied insects, *but* they are harmful to fish and should not be used near lakes, ponds, or streams.
- *Bacillus thuringiensis* (Bt) and *Bacillus popiliae* are bacteria which, with their variants, are used to control insects such as mosquitos, caterpillars, cutworms, and leafrollers.

Gardeners must come to the realization that, by and large, insects are not so harmful as we sometimes think. If there is an infestation which seriously affects a crop, apply or spray with a substance which is the least toxic to the fewest members of our terrestrial sphere.

Beneficial Insects and Diseases:

GLOWWORM or FIREFLY is a beetle identified by a light on the terminal segment of its body. Glow worms, together with their larvae, are voracious eaters, feeding especially on slugs, snails, and cutworms.

LADYBUG or LADY BEETLE, one of the most effective beneficial insects, is about 1/2-inch long, almost spherical in shape with a convex back. The varieties most commonly seen here are the red, the spotted, and the convergent lady beetle, which has 12 black dots on its reddish wings and 2 convergent white lines on its thorax. Other ladybugs are red or tan with black spots, or black with red spots. The larvae, also helpful predators, are flat and carrot-shaped with a warty grayish-black coloring and blue or orange spots. The eggs, usually orange, stand on end in large clusters attached to a leaf. Ladybugs and their larvae eat aphids, mealy bugs, and scales.

LACEWING has gauzy green or brown wings. Its larvae, called aphid lions, are 1/3-inch long, yellow or gray mottled with brown or red. Their flat bodies taper at both ends. The lacewings and the larvae suck juices from aphids, cottony-cushion scales, mealy bugs, thrips, and mites.

PRAYING MANTIS and its relatives have the habit of holding their front legs in a praying position as they devour their insect prey.

CATERPILLAR HUNTER BEETLE is an iridescent ground beetle which cannot fly but instead scurries along the ground. Its name suggests its purpose.

TRICHOGRAMMA WASPS lay eggs which become minute parasites inside the eggs of other insects, particularly caterpillars. Most wasps are

342

beneficial predators, but human beings should stay well away from them.

BACILLUS THURINGIENSIS is a non-harmful bacterium which paralyzes and kills the insects which eat it. *Bt* is sold under various names and is especially successful in controlling caterpillars and worms.

BACILLUS POPILIAE or MILKY SPORE DISEASE is a bacterial organism fatal to some grubs and to the Japanese Beetle, a damaging pest. It is sometimes sold under the name DOOM.

Chemical Pesticides:

The mild, humid climate in this locale is inviting to diseases, insects, and weeds. Some chemicals are at present approved by the appropriate national authorities as safe *WHEN PROPERLY USED ACCORDING TO LABEL INSTRUCTIONS.* From time to time some are withdrawn by said authorities as inadvisable. It is the decision of each gardener whether or not to use chemical pesticides. *USE WISELY AND CAREFULLY.*

If chemical controls are used, the following precautions are of utmost importance:

1. Use the product for the particular purpose for which it is intended. Do not mix with any unauthorized material. Do not store in any container other than the one in which it was sold. Do not store leftover, diluted material.
2. *Store well out of the reach of inquisitive children and in a dry place.*
3. Do NOT use any poisonous product or systemic chemical on or near food crops. Systemic materials enter the structure of the plant and the soil.
4. Read all the directions on the label and follow them to protect yourself and the environment. If needed, use a magnifying glass. A product which has a crossbones sketch on it is extremely poisonous. Try to avoid that kind.
5. The product may lose its effectiveness with age. Toxicity ratings are printed on the label.
6. Dispose of empty containers as safely as pos-

sible, according to direction on label.
7. Protect yourself while using chemical controls, especially when spraying or dusting. Use a face mask and wear a long-sleeved shirt, long pants, heavy shoes, and a protective hat. Avoid contact with skin and eyes. Immediately wash with soap and water any portion of your body which has been exposed to a chemical pesticide.
8. Do not flush material down a toilet. Do not pour down household or storm drains. Do not bury in the yard.

For answers to your questions, contact your County Extension Agent.

Being able to identify a weed before digging it up may not be a requirement, but recognizing the enemy is helpful. Weeds are divided into two categories: the broadleaf and the grassy. Broadleaf weeds include those which usually invade lawns: chickweed, henbit, spurge, buckhorn, clover, dock, mustards, dandelion, and plantain. The grassy weeds include: crabgrass, Johnson grass, sandbur, nutgrass, annual bluegrass, goose grass, and Dallis grass.

Herbicides and weed-killing chemicals should be used only as a last resort, and even then with great caution and according to directions, because the chemicals are poisonous to many desirable plants and can be harmful to people and wildlife. Herbicides remain in the soil up to 18 months. Most herbicides are harmful to ornamentals, and few are recommended for use on St. Augustine grass or centipede grass. Neither herbicides nor any other weed killing chemical should be used on or anywhere near food crops. If herbicides are used, follow directions explicitly.

Weeds should be removed from a garden because they steal nutrients and moisture from garden plants. They offer shelter to insects and harmful disease spores. Tall weeds prevent smaller plants nearby from getting their share of the sunlight. If permitted to go to seed, weeds multiply manyfold and present an even more exasperating problem to the gardener.

Light cultivation with hand and hoe remains the safest method of weed eradication. But when you are confronted with a large, weed-filled space, as is possible when beginning the preparation of a new bed, hoeing, scraping, or tilling will help. If an area is small enough for hand digging and pulling, water the ground thoroughly two or three days before weeding. Be sure to wear your gardener's gloves! Use a pointed trowel or long, thin, forked tool or "weeder" to dig each weed out, being sure to remove all the roots, especially those of Bermuda grass. It will return to haunt you if you leave any root nodes. The dampness of the soil allows the roots to come up with less disturbance to surrounding soil and plants. A narrow-pointed hoe may be used, but do not cultivate deep enough to expose roots of garden plants to drying wind and sun. Carefully cover with soil any accidentally exposed roots. It is best to work on a cloudy day or late in the afternoon, so there will be less possibility of injury to garden plants.

Once a bed is weed-free, mulch the ground at least two inches deep to suffocate future weeds (see Mulching in the SOIL chapter). If weeds do grow through the mulch, they will be much easier to pull out. Try to pull weeds when they are still very small, before their root systems get widespread.

A sterilized fertilizer may prevent weeds to some extent, but it is an expensive prevention and may not last for long, since birds, animals, and wind scatter and spread weed seeds anyway. The truth is that there is no complete escape from weeds. Think of weeding chores in a positive way. Enjoy the exercise, the fresh air, and the sure knowledge that you are helping your garden thrive.

Poisonous Plants

Common Poison Ivy (*Rhus radicans* or *R. toxicadendron*) is a native vining plant which is poisonous on contact. It may be identified by its three-part leaflets and its small, white, berry-like fruit. Poison Oak (*Rhus diversiloba*) is a similar species with similar effects. Identify red fall foliage before touching; it may be Poison Ivy or Poison Oak. Smoke from a fire in which Poison Ivy is burning may also be irritating. A good home remedy to employ very shortly after you have touched the ivy is to smear a paste made of brown laundry soap on the affected area. If the irritation has already begun, consult a physician.

A related plant with an even more poisonous effect is Poison Sumac (*Rhus vernix*), a tall shrub with reddish twigs and leaflets of seven to thirteen leaves and small white fruit. Treatment is the same as for Poison Ivy.

To eradicate these poisonous plants, wear thick gloves and clothing that covers you well, and dig up their deep roots. Salt placed in the heart of the plant will kill Poison Ivy, but it may severely injure other plants nearby.

Do not eat any part of any plant with which you are not completely familiar. Many are poisonous.

Be watchful of any small child in a garden or near indoor plants. Many are beautiful, but many are also poisonous.

If symptoms of headache, nausea, or convulsion appear, see a physician and try to take part of the plant with you to show. See POISONOUS PLANTS chapter.

PLANT PROBLEMS

Diseases and Insects		Possible Controls	
Name	Symptons and Effects	Biological Control	Chemical Control (according to label directions)
ANTS (Insects)	Harmful because they spread Aphids. Stir up ants' hills of fine soil before applying control.	Tanglefoot banding; steamed bone meal scattered on ground, a pepper spray, or tansy plants nearby.	Diazinon, Dursban, or Orthene.
APHIDS (Insects)	Tiny, green or brown, soft-bodied insects grouped in masses along stems and leaves. Leaves become stunted, discolored, and curled. Aphids suck juices primarily from new plant growth, excreting a honeydew which attracts ants and forms the medium for a fungus, a black sooty mold. Aphids spread Fire Blight, Mosaic, and other viruses. They cause the leaves to wrinkle, thicken, and turn yellow or brown.	Repeated strong sprays of water on all parts of leaves and stems or spray with Dormant oil or Insecticidal Soap. Black Ants eat Aphids. Spray with soap and water early in the growing season.	Orthene, Malathion, Cygon or Diazinon.
ASP OR PUSS CATERPILLAR- See Poisonous Creature in chapter text.	1-1 1/2" long cottony looking caterpillar. Vicious stingers.	*Bacillus thuringiensis*	Dipel, Sevin, Thuricide
AZALEA PETAL BLIGHT (Fungus Disease) See AZALEA chapter	Small translucent, soggy spots, brown on white flower petals, white on colored petals; spots enlarge and spread rapidly from bush to bush, flower to flower, destroying all azalea blooms in a few hours. The blight's severity depends on warmth and humidity of weather. Wind and bees spread fungus spores.		Spray entire plant with fungicide such as Bayleton, Benlate (Benomyl), and Zineb immediately. Prevent by spraying when first flowers open. Repeat 2 or 3 times a week during blooming season. Spray causes white dots on petals.

PLANT PROBLEMS

Diseases and Insects		Possible Controls	
Name	Symptons and Effects	Biological Control	Chemical Control (according to label directions)
BAGWORMS (caterpillar-like Insects)	Carry bag-like homes to attach to a twig by a thread while they eat.	Remove bags and burn. Trichogramma wasp is natural enemy. *Bacillus thuringiensis* spray is effective.	Pierce bag, put sprayer nozzle in hole, and spray with Orthene, Diazinon, Dursban, Malathion, or Sevin.
BARK BEETLES (Insects) Also: SOUTHERN PINE, ENGRAVER, and BLACK TURPENTINE BEETLES	Bark beetles very harmful to trees. Their pitch-tubes are yellowish or reddish-white masses of resin on bark entry of beetle into trees. Leaves turn light green.	Have a person from a reputable tree company come to inspect tree. Prevention is to keep trees healthy and be vigilant for early signs of beetle attack.	
BLACKSPOT (Fungus Disease) (often on roses)	Causes small black spots on foliage which gradually become larger, yellowing and killing the leaf. If not controlled, it spreads rapidly and defoliates the bush. Without leaves, the plant cannot manufacture its food effectively and it may die.	Provide sufficient aeration around bush by allowing ample space between plants, keeping bush trimmed into open vase form. Remove infected and fallen leaves and burn. Plant resistant varieties.	Spraying every 7 to 10 days with a fungicide, such as Funginex or Black Leaf 40, is good prevention and control.
BORERS, various (caterpillars or grubs (larvae) of moths and beetles)	They invade plant tissues, especially newly planted or weakened trees. Injuries to leaf or bark, poor soil, drought, sunscald, and poor drainage all weaken trees. Pitch or sawdust on bark at borer's entry hole is first symptom.	Keep trees healthy. Protect from injury. Vigilance and immediate attention needed. Call professional tree man. He may be able to cut borers out or remove limbs.	Spraying with Malathion or Methoxychlor might prove helpful.

PLANT PROBLEMS

Diseases and Insects		Possible Controls	
Name	Symptons and Effects	Biological Control	Chemical Control (according to label directions)
BOTRYITIS BLIGHT (Fungus Disease) (Madonna Lily is susceptible)	Brownish-red spots on leaves, bloom, and stem; sometimes water-soaked and discolored. Thread-like gray mold may cover blooms.	Remove and destroy infected parts. Mites spread disease. Space plants for air circulation. Avoid high humidity and low light planting locations. Plant resistant varieties.	Spray with a fungicide, such as Benlate (Benomyl), adding a spreader sticker according to directions.
BROWN PATCH (Fungus Disease)	Shows in discolored, yellow ring in lawn grass. Disease can spread throughout lawn if uncontrolled.	Keep grass healthy. Provide good drainage. Avoid excessive moisture and excessive nitrogen. See LAWNS chapter.	Treat with a fungicide, such as Terraclor.
CATERPILLARS (larvae of moths and butterflies)	Worm-like, soft-bodied, sometimes hairy or spiny. Eat foliage voraciously.	Sprinkle sharp sand, wood ashes, or Diatomaceous Earth around plants to discourage insects. Scratchy substances hurt their soft bodies. *Bacillus thuringiensis* paralyzes and kills caterpillars when they eat it. Biological sprays kill pests.	Dipel or Thioride.
CHINCH BUGS (Insects)	Small black insects, often attack St. Augustine grass in hot, dry weather, causing irregular brown patches in the lawn. See LAWNS chapter.	Keep grass healthy and well watered, especially in hot weather.	Pesticides, such as Diazinon, Ethion, or Dursban, may be sprayed on area affected and beyond it. Water lawn before spraying. Granular application is also appropriate. Follow label directions.
CHLOROSIS (a deficiency)	Yellowing of foliage, especially between veins, indicates the lack of usable iron in the soil.	Have the soil tested. Call your County Extension Agent for instructions about soil testing.	Incorporate iron sulfate or iron chelate into soil and water in.
CONIFER BLIGHT (Fungus Disease)	Browning of foliage. Attacks especially: Arizona cypress, junipers, arborvitae, and native cedars.	Keep plant healthy to avoid disease.	Spray with a fungicide, such as Zineb or Bordeaux.

347

PLANT PROBLEMS

Diseases and Insects		Possible Controls	
Name	Symptons and Effects	Biological Control	Chemical Control (according to label directions)
CUTWORMS (caterpillar larvae of various night-flying moths)	Surface cutworms most damaging, feeding on foliage, cutting stems at ground. They are fat, soft, smooth worms. Some climb on plant; others stay in soil feeding on roots.	Ring plants with cardboard collars pushed an inch or two into soil. Mulch lightly with wood ashes or sharp sand to discourage insects.	Cutworm bait, Sevin, Diazinon, or Dylox.
DAMPING OFF (Fungus Disease)	Causes seedlings to rot at soil line and fall over.	Avoid planting same plants in same location successive years. Sterilize soil by baking 3 to 4 hours in 160° oven. Use species resistant to this fungus and seeds treated against fungus. Eliminate excessive soil and plant moisture. Do not water at night.	Captan or Zineb, following label directions.
DIE-BACK (Fungus Disease)	Browning or blackening of leaves; stems or branches die from tip, progressing down to larger branch. Most destructive of young wood, but may attack old wood, too.	Remove affected parts of plant.	Captan or Benlate.
EARWIGS (Insects)	Distinguished by pincers on their rear. Not usually harmful; they eat decaying tissue.	Nicotine sulfate, if necessary.	Baygon Bait, if needed, or Diazinon.
FIRE BLIGHT (Bacterial Disease)	Browns and kills leaves and stems, giving burned appearance. Spread by insects and rain. Bacteria winter in bark. Pear trees are especially susceptible.	Plant resistant varieties. Prune infected branch a foot past infected area back to healthy wood. Disinfect pruning tool between cuts with 10% clorox in water solution, or with alcohol.	Apply fungicidal sprays, such as Zineb, Bordeaux, or Strepomycin, several times.

PLANT PROBLEMS

| Diseases and Insects | | Possible Controls | |
Name	Symptons and Effects	Biological Control	Chemical Control (according to label directions)
GALL (Bacterial Disease)	Usually on roots but also on other parts. Large, ball-like, woody swelling. Bacterium enters through wounds or natural openings.	Select healthy plants. No known cure.	
GRASSHOPPERS (Insects)	En masse, they wreak havoc, stripping plants.	Eggs laid in fall in uncultivated soil can begin hatching in March. Nymphs or hoppers are big eaters. Pick adults off and destroy. Keep all soil cultivated. Try Nicotine Sulfate, Pyrethrum, or Rotenone.	Diazinon.
IRIS BORERS (caterpillars' larvae)	Make pinpoint holes in Iris blades and work downward to rhizome, on which they feed. Leaf becomes ragged and water-soaked in appearance. Borers carry a bacterium which causes vile-smelling soft rot.	Remove all old foliage and debris and burn. Try killing borers by pressing them on leaf between thumb and finger, while wearing gloves.	Difficult to eradicate. Malathion or Methoxychlor may help.
JUNE BUGS (Beetles)	Large brown or black beetles appear from March to June, flying around lights at night, hiding in daytime under debris. Eggs laid in soil hatch in 2 or 3 weeks. Fat, white, repulsive grubs feed on grass' roots, damaging them badly.	Keep garden clean, without debris. If grass shows damage, cut portions, roll back, and leave for birds to eat grubs. Use "bug lights," which don't attract beetles.	Diazinon, Sevin, and Dursban may control. Read label carefully.

PLANT PROBLEMS

Diseases and Insects		Possible Controls	
Name	Symptons and Effects	Biological Control	Chemical Control (according to label directions)
LACE BUGS (Insects)	1/8-inch long, tan with clear, gauze-like wings, difficult to see. They suck sap from underside of leaves, leaving brown excrement, draining plant of vigor. Attack azaleas, pyracantha, and chrysanthemums, giving leaves a mottled appearance.	Pyrethrum, Rotenone, or Nicotine Sulfate.	Sevin, Orthene, Cygon, or Malathion.
LEAFHOPPERS (Insects)	1/4-inch long. Feed on all types of foliage by sucking under leaves, hopping away quickly when startled. Leaves become yellow and stippled. Leafhoppers carry many diseases.	Ladybugs feed on Leafhoppers. Rotenone or Pyrethrum, as directed on label.	Bordeaux mixture.
LEAFMINERS (Insects) (many species; larvae of tiny black and yellow flies)	Feed under the epidermis of leaf surfaces, leaving long, serpentine tunnels.	Once the miner is in the leaf and the tunnels are visible, the only remedy is to remove the affected portion of the leaves each day.	Control with Malathion spray while flies are swarming.
LEAFROLLERS (Caterpillars)	Feed while rolled up in leaf, cutting slits in it. Infestation can prevent formation of pods.	Biological spray as directed. *Bacillus thuringiensis.*	Control with Thuricide, Dipel, Metasystox, Orthene, Sevin, or Diazinon.
MEALY BUGS (Insects)	Oval-shaped insects covered with white powdery wax cluster in axils and on undersides of leaves, multiplying rapidly. Indoor plants very susceptible. Plants become weak and covered with a honeydew mealy bugs secrete.	Outdoor plants are helped by natural enemies of these insects. Strong sprays of water, or touching each bug with cotton tip dipped in alcohol. Give indoor plants some time outdoors.	Diazinon, Orthene, or Dursban.

350

PLANT PROBLEMS

Diseases and Insects		Possible Controls	
Name	Symptons and Effects	Biological Control	Chemical Control (according to label directions)
MILDEW, POWDERY (Fungus Disease)	Causes powdery, white, mold-like growth on leaves, buds, and young twigs, stunting and often killing them. Crape myrtles and roses very susceptible.	Try to improve air circulation and intensity of light. High humidity encourages mildew. Dust weekly with dusting sulfur.	Phaltan, Benlate, or Funginex.
MOSAIC (Virus disease)	Light green, mottled foliage or twisted leaves and/ or deformed flowers. Spread by insects. Disease pervades plant tissue and kills plant. Destroy plant.	Plant resistant varieties.	
NEMATODES (Eel worms)	Worms feed inside root fibers, causing root knots. Plants become stunted and wilted. Severely infected plants must be removed and burned.	Marigold's roots poison nematodes. Lime and fish fertilizer repel them. Small amount of cane sugar worked into soil and watered seems to help. Consistent use of humus and fertilizer in the soil.	Nemagon, as directed.
PILL or SOW BUGS (Insects)	Small, oval, dark gray or black insects which usually curl up in a ball when touched. They eat tender growth, like seedlings. They hide in damp dark places as under boards or bricks.	Remove their hiding places. Frogs are natural predators. Sprinkling of lime repels bugs.	Mesurol, Baygon Bait, Sevin, or Dylox.
ROSEBUGS or ROSE CHAFERS (Beetles)	1/2-inch long, tan beetles with reddish-brown heads, long spiny legs, appear in swarms. They feed on plants just before breeding. Grubs are white and feed on roots. They over-winter in soil.	Hand pick off plants and destroy. Cover plants with cheesecloth temporarily, during beetles' breeding season. Cultivate soil often.	Methoxychlor or Carbaryl.

PLANT PROBLEMS

Diseases and Insects		Possible Controls	
Name	Symptons and Effects	Biological Control	Chemical Control (according to label directions)
RUST (several Fungus Diseases)	Causes rusty brown patches or pustules on leaves, stems, and buds on a wide variety of plants. Disease is spread by wind and insects. Encouraged by warm, humid weather.	Dusting or spraying with sulfur checks spread. Plant resistant varieties.	Fungicides, such as Funginex or Zineb.
SCALES (various Insects)	1/8 to 1/16-inch in size. They secrete a waxy house over their bodies. Newly hatched crawlers feed on young succulent growth. Parents suck leaf juices causing yellow spots on top sides of leaves, which later fall off. They also secrete a honeydew in which a black, sooty mold grows.	Because scales multiply rapidly, begin control early. Dormant or summer oils are often used, but oil sprays damage foliage if used when temperature is over 85° or under 40° within 48 hours of spraying. Spray in late winter or early spring before new growth begins, and again in 10 days.	Malathion, Cygon, Dursban, Kelthane, or Diazinon.
SLUGS and SNAILS (Mollusks)	A slug is a snail without a shell, about 1-inch long with thick, slimy bodies. They feed at night making rasping holes in leaves.	Eliminate their dark hiding places under boards, pots, etc. They are attracted to saucers of beer in which they drown. Scatter wood ashes or sharp sand on soil around plants. Flour and salt kill them, but salt used in excess can also damage roots and plants. Diatomaceous Earth kills slugs and snails.	Metaldehyde.

PLANT PROBLEMS

Diseases and Insects		Possible Controls	
Name	Symptons and Effects	Biological Control	Chemical Control (according to label directions)
SPIDER MITES (Insects)	Red, yellow, or black infinitesimal bugs which cause tremendous damage by puncturing a leaf and sucking the juice out. Since there are hundreds of mites on each leaf, the plant is quickly harmed. Leaves take on mottled, grayish look. If the mites can't be seen, hold a sheet of white paper under leaves and tap leaves. Tiny insects will be visible on the paper. Begin control immediately.	Knock mites off with strong sprays of water. Repeat every 2 or 3 days or until they are gone. Be vigilant.	Kelthane, Ethion, Dursban, Orthene, or Malathion. Read label carefully. Some sprays are harmful to gardenias, schefflera, and other plants.
TARNISHED PLANT BUG (Insect)	Small, 1/4-inch with yellow, white, and black blotches and yellow triangles on each side. Nymphs are greenish-yellow with 5 black dots. They suck out plant juices causing deforming or discoloring injuries to many plants, including vegetables and fruits. They over-winter in debris.	Remove all debris. Keep garden clean.	Malathion is spray control.
THRIPS (Insects)	Almost invisible insects which scar fruit, foliage, and flowers with their scraping mouth parts. Rosebuds turn brown and fail to open, or open in a deformed way with brown edges on the petals. They seem to prefer light or yellow flowers. Difficult to eradicate.	Remove infested buds and blooms at once. Use Pyrethrum according to directions.	Malathion as directed on label.

PLANT PROBLEMS

Diseases and Insects		Possible Controls	
Name	Symptons and Effects	Biological Control	Chemical Control (according to label directions)
WHITEFLIES (Insects)	Sucking insects which fly out in clouds when an infected plant is shaken or disturbed. They secrete a honeydew on which a black sooty mold feeds and grows. Especially bothersome to citrus, gardenias, hollies, ligustrum, viburnum, and sometimes lantana and boxwood.	Frequent forceful sprays of water applied to undersides of leaves may discourage the pests.	Helpful are sprays such as Cygon, Malathion, Orthene, Diazinon, or Thiodan.

IMPORTANT

Insecticide label clearances are subject to changes, and changes may have occurred since this printing. The pesticide USER is always responsible for the effects of pesticides on his own plants or household goods as well as problems caused by drift from his property or plants. *Always read and follow carefully the instructions on the container label.*

The information given herein is for educational purposes only. References to commercial products or trade names is made with the understanding that no discrimination is intended and no endorsement by the River Oaks Garden Club or A GARDEN BOOK FOR HOUSTON is implied.

G.C.

Winter Protection

*"A change in the weather is enough
to renew the world and ourselves."*
—Marcel Proust

*T*hough December 10 and February 10 are approximate dates for first and last freezes, there is no certainty that winter will keep its suggested frost dates in Houston. Experienced gardeners are seldom surprised by such lack of punctuality. They accept winter when they feel the cold weather.

Plants are not as prepared. Their "cooling systems" need some time to get ready for cold, time to respond gradually, and time to attain a dormancy when the sap drains down into their roots. Unexpected freezes following balmy temperatures catch plants off guard and leave them easy prey to Old Man Winter unless gardeners follow certain gardening practices to protect them.

If deep, thorough watering has been practiced, there is less to worry about when a freeze strikes. Deep watering encourages deep root growth, and the depth in turn protects the roots from cold, as well as from heat and drought. If the roots are properly protected, the plant itself should be able to grow back even if the stem and foliage suffer damage. The only danger in watering exists if there is a lack of sufficient drainage, which allows water to stand in the root zone. Roots standing in water will kill a plant every time. The DRAINAGE chapter tells you how to check the drainage and how to improve it.

The best protection is to know your garden. The areas most exposed to cold north winds and freezes are the low spots. Like water, cold settles in low places. It makes sense then to position the plants most susceptible to cold in higher places. Protect them from the cold with a wall, fence, or grouping of dense-foliaged shrubs. Plants on the south side of a building suffer less from cold, but they may be exposed to hotter summer sun there. Be careful in your placement of plants; find out in what location the plant thrives *before* you plant it.

Two practices, severe pruning and fertilizing with a high nitrogen fertilizer in the fall, encourage new growth, which is very sensitive to cold damage. Delay extensive pruning until early spring and fertilize with a high potash ratio fertilizer to encourage cold resistance.

Maintaining a 3-inch mulch composed of a mixture of decayed organic materials is known to protect plants from cold as well as heat and drought. See the SOIL chapter.

Plan ahead by accumulating bricks, old sheets, and boxes large enough to cover your small-to-medium-sized plants. Plastic is not recommended because it transmits cold to the plant so quickly.

Even when practices to strengthen plants' cold resistance are followed, gardeners should take the weatherman at his word if he predicts a freeze:

Begin last minute protective procedures:
- Water deeply.
- Apply extra mulching around plants to protect them from cold. Well-aerated materials like pine needles and tree moss mixed with leaves, mounded around the roots of plants and dampened to avoid blowing away, offer protection.
- Cover and wrap larger plants with old sheets or similar material. Try to keep the covering from touching the plant. If there is a hard freeze, the foliage touched by the covers may get frost bite, but the main part of the plant will probably survive. Hold the covers down with bricks or stones because high strong winds often accompany freezes. It is advisable to tie the cover around the plant.
- Cover smaller plants with boxes weighted down with bricks.
- If the foliage becomes covered with frost or ice, spray it with water in the morning before the sun's rays reach it to reduce frost damage.
- Water, then cover seedlings with burlap, boxes, or mounds of dampened leaves, pine needles, or tree moss. Remove covering as soon as the hot sun comes out.
- Move pots of tender plants into the house or garage. It helps to leave a light on in the garage and close the door. Be sure the plants are watered well.
- Use greenhouse to protect plants if it can be closed or if it has some source of heat. Be careful to ventilate it soon after the weather warms. Temperatures rise very rapidly in a closed greenhouse when the sun shines on it.

Freezes are usually of short duration in the Houston area, but wait until the freeze season is positively over before carefully cutting away damaged foliage. Cut or prune gradually, down to firm, vigorous portions of the stem or stalk. You will soon see fresh new growth, demonstrating once again the eternal cycle of the spring awakening of the plant world.

Poisonous Plants

*"Learning without thought is useless,
thought without learning is dangerous."*
—Confucious

Poison Ivy in fall foilage.   R.J.B.

*C*hildren are inquisitive. They often seek oral satisfaction and frequently put objects in their mouths.

Adults decorate their homes with attractive plants. It is a way of bringing the outdoors in.

Combine the two tendencies and trouble can ensue because children touch and examine everything they can reach. Their curiosity includes putting the object in their mouths to chew on it. If they can reach a leaf of a plant, they will pull it off, and pop it in their mouths. Unfortunately some plants, attractive as they may be, were not intended to be eaten—"ingested" is the medical term. Some plants are poisonous. If a curious child decides to chew on a leaf of a plant, there can be difficulty. The health of the child may be endangered.

Homemakers must be aware of the danger and of these simple precautions:
* Keep plants out of reach of toddlers.
* Know the names, common and botanical, of the plants in your house. Write the name on each container.

If you are concerned about a leaf or flower your child has eaten, call the Texas State Poison Center. Someone there can help you, especially if you know the name of the plant involved.

Texas State Poison Center[1]
The University of Texas Medical Branch,
Galveston, Texas 77550-2780,
Houston (713) 654-1701;
Galveston (409) 765-1420.

[1]All information courtesy of the Texas State Poison Center, Houston Branch.

SOME POISONOUS PLANTS

The following list is not a complete list but it does include quite a few common plants which may be harmful especially when ingested.

Plant	Toxic Parts	Symptoms
AZALEA *Rhododendron* spp.	All parts	Vomiting, muscle weakness, breathing difficulty; heart depressant. May be fatal.
BLUEFLAG IRIS *Iris* spp.	Bulb	Severe vomiting and diarrhea.
CALADIUM *Caladium* spp.	All parts	Irritation, swelling, and intense pain of the mouth, lips, cheeks, throat; may block breathing or swallowing.
CASTOR BEAN *Ricinus communis*	Bean (seed)	Nausea, vomiting, diarrhea, intestinal colic, thirst, convulsions. May be fatal.
CHERRY LAUREL *Prunus caroliniana*	All parts	Contain cyanide-producing substances. Difficulty in breathing, coma. May be fatal.
CHINABERRY *Melia azedarach*	All parts	Breathing difficulty, vomiting, constipation or diarrhea, paralysis, weakened heart.
DAFFODIL *Narcissus* spp.	Bulb	Vomiting, diarrhea, trembling, convulsions.
DELPHINIUM *Delphinium* spp.	All parts	Tingling of mouth, nausea, vomiting, diarrhea, low blood pressure, weak pulse, convulsions. May be fatal.
DIEFFENBACHIA *Dieffenbachia* spp.	All parts	Irritation, swelling, and intense pain in the mouth, lips, throat, cheeks; may block breathing or swallowing.
ELEPHANT EAR *Caladium* spp.	All parts	See Caladium and Dieffenbachia.
ENGLISH IVY *Hedera helix*	All parts	Diarrhea, excitement, labored breathing, coma.
HOLLY *Ilex* spp.	Berries	Nausea, vomiting, diarrhea, stupor.
HYACINTH *Hyacinthus orientalis*	Bulb	Nausea, vomiting, diarrhea.
HYDRANGEA *Hydrangea macrophylla*	All parts	Contain cyanide-producing substances. Vomiting, dizziness, headache, diarrhea, fast heart rate, respiratory stimulation, convulsions.

SOME POISONOUS PLANTS

Plant	Toxic Parts	Symptoms
IRIS *Iris* spp.	Bulb	Nausea, vomiting, diarrhea.
JAPANESE/CHINESE TALLOW *Sapium sebiferum*	Leaves; berries, green or black	Nausea, vomiting, diarrhea, abdominal pain.
JAPANESE/ CHINESE YEW *Podocarpus macrophylla*	Berries	Nausea, vomiting, diarrhea, abdominal pain.
JASMINE	All parts	See Jessamine.
JASMINE, CAROLINA or YELLOW *Gelsemium sempervirens*	All parts	Muscular weakness, double vision, sweating, convulsions, respiratory paralysis. May be fatal.
JERUSALEM CHERRY *Solanum Pseudocapsicum*	Red berries	Nausea, local irritation, slowing action of the heart.
JESSAMINE, NIGHT-BLOOMING *Cestrum nocturnum*	All parts	Muscle and nerve irritability, elevated temperature, dry mouth, dilated pupils, shortness of breath, rapid heart rate.
JESSAMINE, YELLOW (WILD) *Gelsemium sempervirens*	All parts	Muscular weakness, double vision, sweating, convulsions, respiratory paralysis. May be fatal.
JONQUIL	Bulb	See Daffodil.
LANTANA *Lantana* spp.	All parts	Muscle weakness, vomiting, dilated pupils, slow breathing, circulatory collapse, coma. May be fatal.
LIGUSTRUM *Ligustrum* spp.	All parts	Gastric irritation, pain, vomiting, diarrhea.
LILY-OF-THE- VALLEY *Convallaria majalis*	All parts	Vomiting, dizziness, headache, dangerously slow and irregular heart beat, fall in blood pressure.
MISTLETOE *Phoradendron serotinum*	All parts	Vomiting, diarrhea, slowed pulse, circulatory collapse. May be fatal.
MOONFLOWER *Ipomoea*	All parts	Nausea, vomiting, thirst, delirium, dilated pupils, hallucinations. Usually not fatal.

SOME POISONOUS PLANTS

Plant	Toxic Parts	Symptoms
MORNING GLORY *Ipomoea*	Seeds	LSD-like chemicals. Hallucinations, visual disturbances. Suicide has occurred under the influence of these chemicals.
MOUNTAIN LAUREL *Sophora secundiflora*	All parts	Excitement, high then low blood pressure, rapid heart rate, delirium
NARCISSUS	Bulb	See Daffodil.
OAK *Quercus* spp.	Young shoots, acorns	Constipation, bloody stools, gradual kidney damage. Rather large amounts are needed for poisoning.
OLEANDER *Nerium oleander*	All parts	Nausea, vomiting, depression, slowed and irregular pulse, dilated pupils, bloody diarrhea, paralysis. May be fatal.
PEACH *Prunus persica*	All parts of plant, not fruit pulp and skin	See Cherry.
PHILODENDRON *Philodendron* spp.	All parts	See Dieffenbachia
PLUM *Prunus americana*	All parts but fruit pulp and skin	See Cherry.
POINSETTIA *Euphorbia pulcherrima*	All parts	Burning in the mouth and throat, vomiting, diarrhea, intestinal irritation.
POISON IVY *Toxicondendron radicans*	All parts	Itching, oozing sores, swelling of throat and mouth, weakness, fever, reduced urine output.
POISON OAK *Toxicondendron quercofolium*	All parts	See Poison Ivy.
POISON SUMAC *Toxicondendron vernix*	All parts	See Poison Ivy.
POKEROOT or POKE SALAD *Phytolacca americana*	All parts	If improperly cooked, symptoms include: burning in mouth, intestinal cramps, vomiting, diarrhea, sweating, salivation, weakened respiration and pulse. May be fatal.
PRIVET	All parts	See Ligustrum.

SOME POISONOUS PLANTS

Plant	Toxic Parts	Symptoms
SWEET PEA *Lathyrus odoratus*	Seed	Weak pulse, depressed respiration, paralysis, convulsions.
VIRGINIA CREEPER *Parthenocissus quinquefolia*	All parts	Abdominal pains, vomiting, weakness, muscular cramps, death due to tetanus, kidney failure.
WISTERIA *Wisteria* spp.	Seeds (pods)	Nausea, vomiting, diarrhea, abdominal pain.
YAUPON *Ilex vomitoria*	Berries	Vomiting, diarrhea, stupor, dizziness.
YEW, JAPANESE/CHINESE *Podocarpus macrophylla*	Berries	Nausea, vomiting, diarrhea, abdominal pain.

Remember, these plants are not the only plants that could be harmful to you and your family. If you have questions about any plants, cultivated and wild, please call the Texas State Poison Center for prompt, professional advice.

If your child eats one of the poisonous plants listed above:
- Call the Texas State Poison Center or your family doctor.
- For children over one year and for adults, if vomiting is indicated:
  – Give one tablespoonful of Syrup of Ipecac (available at your local pharmacy).
  – Immediately give 8 to 16 ounces of any fluid except milk (water, Kool-Aid, soda pop, fruit juice, etc.).
- If you take your child to your doctor or emergency room, be sure to take a sample of the plant (the bigger the sample, the better).

Plant Nomenclature

"The thing is, not to stop questioning."
—Albert Einstein

*L*innaeus sat thinking. His beloved plant world was in total confusion. The numerous colloquial names referring to each plant made coherent discussion impossible. He must find a common denominator for successful communication. What language was common to all educated people? In 18th century Europe it was Latin. Of course, that was the answer! The Swedish botanist Carl Linnaeus devised a new plant language using Latin genera (nouns) for names and species (adjectives) for description. His binomial nomenclature brought order out of chaos. In time its use spread world over and remains the botanic terminology understood by all. There have, however, been additions to the original names. For further and more precise description and identification, the genera were divided into Families and the additional descriptive terms: variety, forma, hybrid, and cultivar were added.

Garden literature, catalogs, and nurseries rely on the Latin botanical names for clarity, so it is beneficial to familiarize yourself with the accepted nomenclature, especially for the purposes of discussion and purchase. The botanical names serve as more than mere labels, often describing the appearance, structure, original habitat, and other pertinent, integral characteristics.

Binomial nomenclature is divided into:

FAMILY: a broad classification of plants resembling each other in appearance or characteristics more closely than those in other Families. Each Family is composed of one genus or many genera. The Family name is usually composed of the name of one of its genera plus the suffix *"aceae,"* meaning "belonging to." There are exceptions.

GENUS: Plant within a Family and written as first word in name. Example: *Iridacea* Family includes the genus *Iris,* but also includes many more genera (plural) including: *Crocus, Moraea,* and *Watsonia,* all sharing the family traits of being bulbous and having sword-shaped leaves originating from the base of the plant. Each genus may be modified by several different descriptive terms:

SPECIES (spp., both singular and plural): second word in plant name; follows and modifies genus in

gender; ending of species word usually agrees with gender of the genus:
- a = feminine
    example: *Camellia japonica*
- us = masculine
    example: *Podocarpus macrophyllus*
        (JAPANESE YEW)
- um = neuter
    example: *Acer rubrum* (RED MAPLE)

The capital letter L. after the species name indicates Linnaeus named that plant.

SUBSPECIES: a variation of a species.

SPECIFIC EPITHET: refers to either a species or to the two-word (genus plus species) botanical term.

Species designate plant's characteristics, native habitat, cultural preferences, person being honored, or other pertinent information. In the examples above, "*japonica*" indicates "from Japan;" "*macrophyllus*" indicates "large-leaved;" "*rubrum*" means "red," referring to foliage. A plant whose name honors a person is "*Buddleia Davidii*" (BUTTERFLY BUSH), honoring "David."

VARIETY (var.): a subdivision of species and a descriptive term following species, usually referring to a limited geographic location, particularly one in the wild.

CULTIVAR (cv. = contraction of "cultivated variety"): a variety originating under cultivation (as opposed to in the wild).
    Example:
        Firmiana simplex cv. 'Variegata' =
        Genus/species/cultivar/leaves mottled white.

FORMA (f): another descriptive term; when used, it follows species.

HYBRID (X or hyb.): indication of product of cross between two or more species, usually in same Family. Follows species.
    Example:
        Abelia chinensis x A. uniflora = GLOSSY ABELIA.

Sometimes non-Latin names are used for varieties of plants, usually enclosed in apostrophes. For example: *Azalea* 'Red Ruffles,' *Camellia* 'Purple Dawn,' and *Rose* 'Brandy.'

Authorities differ on rules for pronouncing botanical names. Though there are many exceptions, generally speaking the rules are:

1. Vowels are long.
2. Accent first of two syllables. Example: *frágrans* = fray-grans; fragrant.
3. Accent middle of three syllables. Example: *chinensis* = chin-nén-siss; of China.
4. Accent second of four syllables. Example: *ibericus* = eye-béer-ik-us; of Spain or Portugal.
5. Accent penultimate (next to last) of five or more syllables. Example: *horizantalis* = hor-i-zan-táy-lis; dwarf.
6. When preceded by another vowel and perhaps a consonant, pronounce final *e* as separate syllable; often in Family names. Example: *Labiatae* = La-bi-a-ta-e; a genus in the *Mentha* Family.
7. When in doubt, pronounce all syllables equally.

Once you get the hang of it, botanical nomenclature is not only interesting but the only way to make yourself clearly understood when referring to a particular plant.

You may not realize how many Latin names you already use:

ajuga	*aucuba*	*hibiscus*	*peperomia*
agapanthus	*begonia*	*kalanchoe*	*petunia*
ageratum	*cacti*	*narcissus*	*spathyphyllum*
aspidistra	*gardenia*	*oxalis*	*zinnia*

On the other hand, don't forsake the common names entirely. You certainly wouldn't ask the grocer for *amalus* when you wanted an apple, would you? The colloquial names are sometimes descriptive, often quaint, and comprise a fascinating part of our folklore heritage. Keep both types of names in mind. They enrich your gardening knowledge.

Some of the Most Commonly Used Specific Names
(The gender of the specific name agrees with that of the generic name.)

aggregatus (ag-reg-gay-tus) - clustered
alatus (al-lay-tus) - winged
alba (al-ba) - white
albi-plenus (al-bee-pleen-us) - double white-flowered
alternifolius (al-ter-nif-foh-lee-us) - with alternate leaves
angustifolius (an-gus-tif-foh-lee-us) - narrow-leaved
arborescens (ar-bor-ress-ens) - becoming tree-like, woody
argenteus (ar-jent-ee-us) - silvery
aurantiacus (aw-ran-tye-ak-us) - orange-red
aureus (aw-ree-us) - golden
australis (ost-ray-liss) - southern
azureus (az-yew-ree-us) - sky blue
baccatus (bak-kay-tus) - berried
bellus (bell-us) - handsome
biennis (bye-en-niss) - biennial, living two years
botryoides (bot-rye-oy-deez) - in clusters, grape-like
bullatus (bul-lay-tus) - swelling, puckered
caeruleus (see-rew-lee-us) - dark blue
campanulatus (kam-pan-yew-lay-tus) - bell-shaped
canescens (kan-ess-sens) - downy gray
cernuus (ser-new-us) - bent, nodding
chinensis (chin-nen-siss) also *sinensis* - of China
chrysanthus (kriss-anth-us) - golden-flowered
ciliatus (sil-ee-ay-tus) - hairy fringed or margined
coccineus (kok-sin-ee-us) - scarlet
contortus (kon-tort-us) - twisted
cornutus (kor-new-tus) - horned
crenatus (kren-nay-tus) - scalloped

deciduous (des-sid-yew-us) - with parts falling (as leaves)
dentatus (den-tay-tus) - toothed, dentate
digitalis (dij-it-tay-liss) - finger-form
dioecious (dye-oh-ik-us) - having male and female flowers on separate plants
divergens (div-verj-ens) - wide-spreading
elatus (ee-lay-tus) - tall
exoticus (ex-ot-ik-us) - foreign, not native
ferox (fee-rox) - very thorny
filicifolius (fil-iss-if-foh-lee-us) - fern-leaved
flavus (flay-vus) - yellow
floribundus (floh-rib-bund-us) - flowering profusely
foetidus (feet-id-us) - ill-smelling
fragrans (fray-grans) - fragrant
glabrus (glay-brus) - smooth
glaucus (glaw-kus) - "bloomy," grayish
gloriosus (gloh-ree-oh-sus) - superb
gracilis (grass-il-iss) - slender, graceful
grandiflorus (gran-dif-floh-rus) - large-flowered
guttatus (gut-tay-tus) - spotted, speckled
herbaceus (her-bay-see-us) - fleshy stemmed, not woody
hirtus (hert-us) - hairy
horizantalis (hor-i-zan-tay-lis) - dwarf
humilis (hew-mil-iss) - low-growing, dwarf
ibericus (eye-beer-ik-us) - of Spain or Portugal
ilicifolius (il-iss-if-foh-lee-us) - holly-leaved
inermis (in-err-mis) - thornless
japonicus (jap-pon-ik-us) - of or from Japan
labiatus (lay-bee-ay-tus) - lipped
lancifolius (lan-sif-foh-lee-us) - pointed-leaved
latifolius (lat-if-foh-lee-us) - broad-leaved
leucanthus (lew-kanth-us) - white-flowered
longifolius (lon-jif-foh-lee-us) - long-leaved
macranthus (mak-ranth-us) - large-flowered
macrophyllus (mak-roh-fill-us) - large-leaved
microphyllus (mye-kroh-fill-us) - small-leaved
nanus (nay-nus) - small, dwarf
niger (nye-ger) - black
nocturnus (nok-turn-us) - night-blooming
nudiflorus (new-dif-floh-rus) - naked-flowered
odoratus (oh-dorr-ay-tus) - fragrant
opacus (oh-pay-kus) - pale

palustris (pal-lust-riss) - marsh-loving

parviflorus (par-vif-floh-rus) - small-flowered

patens (pay-tens) - spreading

phlogiflorus (floj-if-floh-rus) - flame-flowered

plenus (pleen-us) - full, "double" (denoting many petaled flowers)

polyanthus (pol-ee-anth-us) - many-flowered

praecox (pree-cox) - very early

purpereus (pur-pew-re-us) - purple

quercifolius (kwer-sif-foh-lee-us) - with leaves like an oak

racemosus (ras-em-moh-sus) - with racemes as compared to panicles, spikes, etc.

radicans (rad-ik-anz) - rotting (along stem)

repens (reep-ens) - creeping (also *reptans*)

reticulatus (ret-ik-yew-lay-tus) - netted, net-veined

roseus (roh-zee-us) - rose-red

rotundifolius (roh-tun-dif-foh-lee-us) - round-leaved

rubens (roo-bens) - red or ruddy

rubrus (roo-brus) - red

sempervirens (sem-per-vye-renz) - evergreen

serratus (sery-ray-tus) - saw-toothed

sessifolius (sess-if-foh-lee-us) - stalkless-leaved

stellatus (stel-lay-tus) - star-like

stenophyllus (sten-oh-fil-us) - narrow-leaved

striatus (strye-ay-tus) - striped

sylvestris (sil-vest-riss) - of woods and forests

tardiflorus (tar-dif-floh-rus) - late flowering

trifoliatus (trye-foh-lee-ay-tus) - three-leaved

umbellatus (um-bell-lay-tus) - with clusters of flowers whose stems rise from a common point

vegetus (vej-et-us) - vigorous

versicolor (ver-sik-kol-or) - variously colored

virens (vye-rens) - green

viridis (vihr-id-iss) - green

xanthocarpus (zanth-oh-karp-us) - yellow-fruited

Often Used Prefixes and Suffixes

PREFIXES

semper- - always, ever

pauci- - scanty, few

multi- - many

atro- - dark

leuc- - white

SUFFIXES

-carpus - fruit

-ferous - bearing

-florus - flowered

-folius - leaf

-phyllus - leaf

Books for continuing the fascinating study of plant names are available in libraries and bookstores. Suggested here are only three:

A Gardener's Dictionary of Plant Names, by A. W. Smith, revised by William T. Stearn.

How Plants Got Their Names, by L. H. Bailey.

The Self-Pronouncing Dictionary of Plant Names, by Ralph Bailey.

Garden Terms

"...language charged with meaning."
—Ezra Pound

ACIDITY, ALKALINITY: Referring to the soil's chemical reaction, or to the type of soil condition a particular plant needs. See pH and the SOIL chapter.

ANNUAL: A plant that completes its entire life cycle within one year.

B&B (BALLED-AND-BURLAPPED): Shrubs and trees dug with a ball of dirt around the roots, wrapped in burlap, and tied to hold together, thus protecting roots.

BIENNIAL: A plant that usually completes its life cycle in two years.

BONSAI: Japanese term for training plants on a miniature scale, usually in containers.

BRACTS: Modified leaves that turn a showy color and seem to be flowers (e.g., poinsettia, bougainvillea, shrimp plant).

BUD: A small projection or swelling on a stem, from which growth develops.

BULB: Generally used to refer to any thickened underground stem, but a "true bulb" is only one type of such stem, which is almost round and is made up of fleshy leaves or scales that store food and protect an embryo plant inside (e.g., Tulip).

CAMBIUM: The very important thin green layer of living tissue just beneath the bark which channels food to leaves and roots and pro-duces protective covering for wounds.

CHILLING FACTOR: The degree and the number of hours of cold weather certain plants need for dormancy to develop flowers and fruit properly. Gardeners in mild winter areas should select plants, especially fruit trees, which do not require long cold winters.

CHLOROPHYLL: The substance in leaves which makes them green. It is necessary for photosynthesis.

CHLOROSIS: Refers to the yellowing of leaves, signifying that the plant is unable to absorb the elements necessary to make chlorophyll. May be corrected by adding iron chelate, a combination of iron and a complex organic substance which allows the plant to absorb the iron in the soil. Acidifying the soil with one part agricultural sulphur and two parts copperas sprinkled lightly around plant and immediately watered in may also free iron to the plant's roots.

COMPLETE FERTILIZER: Plant food containing the three necessary nutrient elements: nitrogen, phosphorus, and potassium, listed in that order, with the percentage of each in numeric form. 12-24-12 signifies 12% nitrogen, 24% phosphorus (phosphate), and 12% potassium (potash), making 48% of the total. The other

52% might consist partially of important so-called trace elements including: iron, manganese, copper, zinc, or boron, with any remaining percentage of the whole being a filler for easy mixing and spreading. It is wise to use various fertilizers with varying percentages of the elements, from different sources, combining ample organic materials. "Balanced fertilizer" is a common but ambiguous term, probably referring to a mixture balanced for the needs of certain types of plants, or to a fertilizer containing equal or "balanced" amounts of each of the three principal nutrients, such as 13-13-13.

COMPOSTING: The practice of heaping healthy garden refuse to speed its decomposition for use as a soil additive or a mulch. See SOIL chapter.

CORM: A type of short fat bulb which stores food in its center rather than in its scales (e.g., Gladiolus). See BULBS chapter.

DECIDUOUS: Plants which shed all their leaves at one time each year, usually in the fall.

DIOECIOUS: Types of plants having male and female flowers on separate plants, often requiring planting one of each for fertility to produce blooms and fruit.

DIVIDING: Digging up and pulling apart the developing roots and top growth of clumps of plants, particularly when they have multiplied to a crowded stage.

DRIPLINE: The imaginary circle drawn around a tree under its outermost tips.

EPIPHYTES: Plants, like orchids and bromeliads, which grow on other plants, perching on trees to attain light and moisture. Since they do not take food from the host plant, they are not parasites.

EVERGREEN: Plants that do not lose all their leaves at one time, though they shed the old leaves intermittently as new leaves come out.

EYE: A growth bud, as on a cutting or a tuber, which eventually produces new growth.

GUMBO: A heavy black-brown clay soil often found in Houston. Though difficult to break up, it is usually productive when properly handled. See SOIL chapter.

HARDY: Indicating a plant's tolerance to freeze or frost.

HEAVY SOIL: A dense soil, such as clay, made up of tiny particles which pack closely, preventing aeration and penetration of water and even of roots. See SOIL chapter.

HERBACEOUS: A soft, fleshy plant, such as an annual, perennial, or bulb, as opposed to a woody plant, such as a tree or shrub. The term may also refer to a "herbaceous perennial," which retains leaves all year.

HEELING IN: A method of temporarily storing plants by covering their roots with soil or mulch to prevent their drying out before planting.

HORTICULTURE: The art or science of growing plants.

HUMUS: A soft black or brown substance from completely decomposed animal and/or vegetable matter. In common usage it may refer to incompletely decomposed matter, such as pine bark mulch. Humus is of extreme importance to the soil in which plants are grown. Humus is very helpful also for its ability to retain moisture and to encourage growth of micro-organisms in the soil.

HYBRID: The result of crossing two species or varieties of plants to form another plant.

LEACHING: Repeated watering of plants to drain out and remove excess salts accumulated in the soil.

MONOECIOUS: Plants with male and female flowers on the same plant, though separate.

MULCH: Loose, porous material, usually organic matter, to cover soil. See SOIL chapter.

NATURALIZE: Acclimation of a plant to an environment to which it is not indigenous (native); to become established and grow as its kind does in its native habitat. Also to plant so as to give the effect of natural wild growth.

NITROGEN: An element in soil which increases growth of stem and foliage, gives green color, and stimulates rapid growth.

NORTHER (or BLUE NORTHER): Strong cold north wind which may cause the temperature to drop to freezing or below within a few hours. Characteristic of the upper Gulf Coast area, including Houston.

ORGANIC MATTER: A general term referring to animal and vegetable materials in any state of decomposition. It is not only beneficial, it is essential to every soil. See SOIL chapter.

PERENNIAL: A plant which lives more than two years, but which may die down each winter and grow again in the spring.

pH: A scientific term denoting the hydrogen ion concentration, by which soil acidity or alkalinity is measured on a scale of 14, with 7 being neutral, below 7 acid, and above 7 alkaline. A soil test is necessary to determine the pH rating. Generally, sulphur increases acidity and lime increases alkalinity. See SOIL chapter.

PHOSPHORUS (PHOSPHATE): An element which stimulates root growth, gives plants a vigorous start, promotes greater seed and flower formation, and hardens plants to cold weather.

PHOTOSYNTHESIS: A process, yet to be duplicated by man, by which plants combine chlorophyll, sunlight, air, moisture, sugars, and starches in their leaves to make food for themselves.

PINCH-PRUNING (also called FINGER-PRUNING): The pinching off, with thumb and forefinger, of tender new growth at tips of branches to increase growth, promote greater bushiness, and, often, more blossoms.

POTASSIUM (POTASH): An element which strengthens plants, enabling them to resist diseases, insects, and cold damage; it promotes production of sugar, starches, and oil for food.

RHIZOME: A thickened underground stem, long and slender or fleshy and thick, which spreads by creeping roots underground (e.g., Iris).

STANDARD: A plant trained into tree form, often supported by a rod or stake.

STOLON: A runner or horizontal branch, growing either above or below ground, from the base of a plant, producing new plants from buds at the tip (e.g., Strawberry Plant).

SYSTEMIC: Anything introduced into the system of a plant by application to the soil or by spraying.

TAPROOT: The main anchoring root growing straight down.

TENDER: Indicates a plant's lack of tolerance to frost or freezing temperatures.

TERRESTRIAL: Plants growing in soil, as contrasted to epiphytes, which grow in the air perched on other plants.

TILTH: The quality of a soil attained by tilling and amending it with organic matter until it has a texture to make it hospitable to plants and seeds.

TUBER: An underground stem, thicker and shorter than a rhizome, which bears buds (e.g., Caladium).

TUBEROUS ROOT: A root that is a thick underground storage structure, with the growth buds at the base of the plant (e.g., Daylilies).

UNDERSTORY TREE: A tree small enough to grow under a larger tree.

Metric Conversion Chart

Handy approximate conversions to metric measurements.

Linear
1 inch = 2.54 centimeters
1 foot = 30.48 centimeters or .31 meter
1 square foot = 929 square centimeters
1 square yard = .84 square meter

Liquid
1 teaspoon – 5 milliliters
3 teaspoons - 1 tablespoon = 15 milliliters
2 cups = 1 pint = 16 ounces = 480 milliliters or
    about one-half liter
1 quart = .9463 liter
4 quarts = 1 gallon = 3.79 liters

Dry
1 pint = .55 liters (a bit over one-half liter)
1 quart = 1.1 liters
8 quarts = 1 peck = 8.81 liters
4 pecks = 1 bushel = 35.24 liters

Weights
1000 grams = 1 kilogram (kilo) = 2.2 pounds
1 avoirdupois ounce = 28.35 grams
1 avoirdupois pound = .45 kilograms

Table of Measurement

Liquid
1 level tablespoon	= 3 level teaspoonfuls	
1 fluid ounce	= 2 tablespoonfuls	= 29.57 milliliters
1 cupful	= 8 fluid ounces	
1 pint	= 2 cupfuls	= 16 fluid ounces
1 quart	= 2 pints	= 32 fluid ounces
1 gallon	= 4 quarts	= 128 fluid ounces

Weight
1 ounce	= 28.3 grams	
1 pound	= 16 ounces	= 454 grams
1 ton	= 2,000 pounds	

Dilution Tables
Number of ounces of wettable powder to use in small sprayers when amount per 100 gallons is known

100 gals.	10 gals.	5 gals	2 gals	1 gal.
0.5 lb.	0.8 oz.	0.4 oz.	0.2 oz.	0.1 oz.
1 lb.	1.6 oz.	0.8 oz.	0.3 oz.	0.2 oz.
2 lbs.	3.2 oz.	1.6 oz.	0.6 oz.	0.3 oz.
3 lbs.	4.8 oz.	2.4 oz.	1.0 oz.	0.5 oz.
4 lbs.	6.4 oz.	3.2 oz.	1.3 oz.	0.6 oz.
5 lbs.	8.0 oz.	4.0 oz.	1.6 oz.	0.8 oz.

Emulsifiable Concentrates

100 gals.	10 gals.	5 gals.	2 gals.	1 gal.
1 pt.	1.6 fl. oz.	0.8 fl. oz.	0.3 fl. oz.	0.2 fl. oz.
1 qt.	3.2 fl. oz.	1.6 fl. oz.	0.7 fl. oz.	0.3 fl. oz.
2 qts.	6.4 fl. oz.	3.2 fl. oz.	1.3 fl. oz.	0.6 fl. oz.
1 gal.	12.8 fl. oz.	6.4 fl. oz.	2.6 fl. oz.	1.3 fl. oz.

(Read label on all pesticides and herbicides before using.)

Courtesy of Cornelius Nurseries, Inc.

Bibliography

The New American Landscape
Phebe Leighton and Calvin Simonds, Rodale Press, Emmaus, Pennsylvania

Landscape Gardening; Annual Bulbs and Perennials
Books of The Time-Life Encyclopedia of Gardening Series by James Underwood Crockett and the editors of Time-Life Books, Time-Life Books, New York

Exotica
Alfred Byrd Graf, Roehrs Company, Inc., E. Rutherford, New Jersey, U.S.A.

Western Garden Book
Editors of Sunset Magazine and Sunset Books, Lane Magazine & Book Co. , Menlo Park, California

Landscaping with Native Texas Plants
Sally Wasowski and Julie Ryan Texas Monthly Press, Austin, Texas

Houston Garden Book,
John Kriegel and the editors of Houston Home & Garden Magazine, Bayland Publishing, Inc.

Landscaping with Perennials:
Emily Brown, Timber Press, Portland, Oregon

All About Perennials (Ortho Books)
A. Cort Sinnes, Publisher: Robert L. Iacopi, Chevron Chemical Co.

Taylor's Encyclopedia of Gardening
Edited by Norman Taylor, 4th Edition, Houghton Mifflin Co., Boston

A talk on landscaping given to the River Oaks Garden Club
Johnny Steele of McDugald-Steele, Landscape Architects & Contractors

Neil Sperry's Complete Guide to Texas Gardening
Neil Sperry, Taylor Publishing Co., Dallas, Texas

Bartlett's Familiar Quotations
John Bartlett, Little, Brown and Co., Boston, Toronto

Planning the Home Landscape
William C. Welch, Landscape Horticulturist, Texas Agricultural Extension Service

Botanical names and their spelling
Hortus Third: initially compiled by Liberty Hyde Bailey and Ethel Zoe Bailey; revised and expanded by staff of the Liberty Hyde Bailey Hortorium, MacMillan Publishing Co., New York

Trees for Southern Landscapes, Southern Flower Gardening, Shrubs and Vines for Southern Landscapes
William D. Adams, Pacesetter Press, Houston Publishing Co.

Herb Gardening in Texas
Sol Meltzer, Lone Star, Gulf Publishing Co.

How to Grow Herbs
Editors of Sunset Magazine and Sunset Books, Lane Magazine & Book Co., Menlo Park, California

Annuals, How to Select and Enjoy
Derek Fell, HP Books, Tucson, Arizona

Southern Lawns and Groundcovers
Richard Duble and James Carroll Kell, Pacesetter Press, Gulf Publishing Co., Houston, Texas

Gardening in Containers
Editors of Sunset Magazine and Sunset Books, Lane Magazine & Book Co., Menlo Park, California

Southern Gardener's Soil Handbook
Dr. William S. Peavy, Pacesetter Press, Gulf Publishing Co., Houston, Texas

Azaleas
Fred C. Galle, Callaway Gardens, Georgia, Osmoor House, Inc., Birmingham, Alabama

Great American Azaleas
Jim Darden, Greenhouse Press, Clinton, North Carolina

The Complete Guide to Growing Bulbs in Houston
Sally McQueen, River Bend Co., Houston, Texas

Pruning
Robert L. Stebbins and Michael ManCaskey, HP Books, Tucson, Arizona

Simon & Schuster's Guide to Garden Flowers
Guido Moggi and Luciano Giugnolini, U.S. Editor: Stanley Schuler, Simon and Schuster, New York

Plants for the South, A Guide for Landscape Design
Neil G. Odenwald and James R. Turner, both with Louisiana State University, Claitor's Publishing Division, Baton Rouge, Louisiana

Forest Trees of Texas: How to Know Them–Bulletin 20
John A. Haislet, Texas Forest Service, College Station, Texas, a part of the Texas A&M System

Native and Adapted Trees for the
Houston-Harris County Area
The Species Selection Committee of The Park People's Coalition; Sandra Thorne-Brown, Urban Forester; Bill Adams, Horticulturist, Texas Agriculture Extension Service; John Koros, Mercer Arboretum; Lee Marsters, Garden Columnist; Bill Basham, Landscape Designer

Forty Thousand Quotations
C. N. Douglas, Halcyon House, New York

KIT: Sun Angles in the South, Designing for People.

Periodicals, newspapers, and magazines.

Informative Bulletins by Teas Nursery, Houston, Texas

Articles by May Del Flagg and Lee Marsters
The Houston Post

Bob Flagg's Gardening Newsletter

Houston Metropolitan
City Home Publishing, Houston, Texas

Horticulture
Editor: Thomas C. Cooper, Horticulture Associates, Boston, Massachusetts

American Horticulturist
Especially "Refining the Front Yard," by Dr. Henry M. (Marc) Cathey, February 1988

Neil Sperry's Gardens & More
Taylor Publishing Co., Dallas, Texas

Newsletter by The Houston Arboretum & Nature Center

The Newsletter by National Wildlife Research Center, Austin, Texas

Simon & Schuster's *Complete Guide to Plants & Flowers*
Edited by Frances Perry, Simon & Schuster, Inc., New York

Rodale's *Organic Gardening*
Editor: Robert Rodale, Publisher: Thomas Stoneback, Rodale Press Inc., Emmaus, Pennsylvania

Texas Gardener
Editor and Publisher: Chris S. Corby, Suntex Communications, Waco, Texas

Index

(Cornflower) *Centaurea cyanus,* 2-29, 231
Bagworms, 346
Bald Cypress *(Taxodium* spp.), 94
Ball Cactus *(Notocactus),* 69
Balloon-flower *(Platycodon* spp.), 12, 15, 17, 19, 226
Balsam *(Impatiens* spp.), 2-29, 226-227, 286
Bamboo, 43, 50, 134, 135
Bamboo Palm *(Rhapis humilis),* 63
Bambusa spp. (Bamboo), 43, 50, 134, 135
Banana, *(Musa* spp.), 9, 12, 22, 24, 50
Banana Shrub *(Michelia Figo),* 135
Barbados, Cherry *(Malpighia glabra),* 2-29, 135
Barbados, Winter-Green *(Berberis Juliana),* 135
Barberry, Japanese *(Berberis Thunbergii* spp.), 135, 312
Barrel Cactus *(Ferocactus),* 69
Basil *(Ocimum),* 80
Bauhinia (Orchid Tree - Anacacho), 7, 51, 94
Bay, Loblolly *(Gordonia lasianthus),* 107, 135
Bay, Sweet *(Laurus nobilis),* 107, 136
Bead Plant *(Crassula),* 70
Bean, Scarlet Runner *(Phaseolus coccineus),* 15, 17, 19, 288
Bear Grass (Texas Sotol) *(Dasylirion texanum),* 12, 136
Bear's-breech *(Acanthus mollis),* 47
Beaucarnea spp. (Pony Tail Palm or Elephant-foot), 64
Beaumontia grandiflora

(Easter Lily Vine - Herald's Trumpet), 291
Beautyberry *(Callicarpa americana),* 136, 312, 332
Bee Balm *(Monarda didyma),* 80, 312
Beech, American *(Fagus grandifolia),* 94
Beetles, 16, 167, 346
Begonia spp., 2-29, 43, 227, 338, 363
Belamcanda spp. (Blackberry Lily), 2, 4, 6, 15, 17, 29, 257, 266
Belladonna Lily, 19
Bells-of-Ireland *(Moluccella laevis),* 6, 21, 227
Berberis
    B. Juliana (Barbados, Winter-Green), 135
    B. (Mahonia) trifoliolata (Agarito), 7, 132
    B. Thunbergii (Barberry, Japanese), 135, 312
Betula nigra (River Birch), 116
Biennial, 366
Bignonia capreolata (Crossvine), 7, 10, 12, 17, 19, 22, 25, 288
Billbergia (Vase Plant), 6,14,17
Bird's Nest Fern *(Asplenium nidus),* 61, 302
Bird-of-paradise Flower *(Strelitzia reginae),* 7, 24, 48
Birds, 3, 13, 36, 88, 109, 121, 127, 151, 168, 311-312, 341, 344
Bishop's Cap *(Astrophytum myriostigma),* 69
Black Cherry *(Prunus serotina),* 94
Black Gum *(Nyssa sylvatica),* 94
Black-eyed Susan *(Thunbergia alata),* 288-289

Blackberry, 21, 123, 312, 339
Blackberry Lily *(Belamcanda* spp.), 2, 4, 6, 15, 17, 29, 257, 266
Blackhaw, Southern or Rusty *(Viburnum rufidulum),* 94
Blackspot, 5, 8, 11, 23, 214, 346
Blanket flower, 2-29
Bleeding Heart (Glory Bower) *(Clerodendrum Thomsoniae),* 289
Bletilla striata (Orchid, Ground), 280
Blight, 3, 7, 18, 187, 188, 199, 345, 347, 348
Blood Lily *(Haemanthus katharinae),* 4, 6, 9, 14, 19, 254, 273
Bloodleaf (Iresine), 14, 17
Bloom times (Month by Month), 2-29
Blue Cardinal Flower *(Lobelia x Gerardii),* 227, 238, 312
Blue Daze *(Evolvulus nuttaliana),* 227
Blue Gum *(Eucalyptus leucoxylon),* 100
Blue Lace Flower, 14, 237
Blue Sage *(Salvia farinacea),* 246
Blue-eyed Grass *(Sisyrinchium iridifolium),* 2-29, 257, 266
Bluebell, Texas *(Lisianthus),* 2-29, 249
Bluebonnet *(Lupinus subcarnosus* and *L. texensis),* 2-29, 43, 228, 312
Blunt-lobed Woodsia Fern *(Woodsia obtusa),* 302
Bois D'Arc (Osage Orange) *(Maclura pomifera),* 95
Boltonia asteroides, 22, 25, 228
Bone meal, 2-29, 76, 130, 195, 212, 253-257, 259,

Flamevine of Brazil *(Pyrostegia venusta)*, 20, 292

Flats, 5, 8, 19, 21, 75, 77, 335, 336

Florida (Purple) Anise *(Illicium floridanum)*, 101, 142

Flower arranging, 38-43

Flowering Tobacco *(Nicotiana)*, 2-29, 240

Fluffy Ruffles Fern *(Nephrolepis exaltata)*, 303

Foliar feeding, 8, 23, 200, 318

Forget-me-Not *(Myosotis palustris semperflorens)*, 2-29, 234

Forma, 363

Forsythia, 43

Fountain (CORAL) Plant *(Russelia equisetiformis)*, 142

Four-O'clock *(Mirabilis jalapa)*, 2-29, 235, 312

Foxglove, Wild or Common *(Penstemon Cobaea)*, 4, 11, 13, 27, 28, 235

Fragaria spp. (Strawberry), 3, 23, 26, 125, 180, 337, 368

Frangipani *(Plumeria)*, 48

Franklinia, 25, 101

Fraxinus spp. (Ash), 93

Freesia, 2, 24, 27, 29, 271

Frikartii *(Callistephus chinensis)*, 226

Fringe Tree (Grancy Graybeard) *(Chionanthus spp.)*, 7, 101

Fruit trees and fruits, 43, 90, 120-125, 184, 339
chart, 123-125
chilling hours, 121, 366
Month by Month, 3-28
pruning, 328-332

Fungicides, 5, 8, 11, 23, 26, 168, 188, 199, 200, 216

G

Gaillardia pulchella (Indian Blanket), 4, 17, 237

Galanthus nivalis (Snowdrops), 5, 281

Gall, 187, 349

Galphimia glauca (Thryallis), 158

Galtonia candicans (Summer Hyacinth), 9, 256, 271

Garden terms, 366-368

Gardenia, 11, 13, 23, 26, 65, 143, 363

Gardens, public, 37, 210, 221

Garlic, 25

Garlic Vine *(Pseudocallima alliaceum)*, 292

Gasteria, 70

Gay Feather *(Liatris)*, 2, 4, 18, 20, 21, 238

Gazania, 10, 235

Gelsemium sempervirens (Carolina Jessamine), 175, 295, 359

Genus, 183, 193, 362, 363

Geranium *(Pelargonium spp.)*, 2-29, 43, 81, 235

Gerbera jamesoni hybrida (Transvaal Daisy), 2-29, 43, 235

Germander *(Teucrium)*, 82

Germination, 8, 18, 223, 321, 333, 334, 335

Ginger Lily (Hidden) *(Cucurma spp.)*, 6, 9, 262, 271

Ginger, Shell *(Alpinia Zerumbet)*, 2, 4, 6, 9, 12, 25, 262, 271

Gingko (Maidenhair) *(G. biloba)*, 101

Gladiolus Hortulanus, 2-29, 43, 253, 257, 260, 272, 336

Gleditsia triacanthos (Honey Locust), 104, 286

Globe, Amaranth *(Gomphrena globosa)*, 2-29, 235

Globe thistle, 20

Gloriosa rothschildiana (Climbing Lily - Glory Lily), 2-29, 256, 257, 272, 292

Glory Lily *(Gloriosa rothschildiana)*, 2-29, 272, 292

Glory of the Snow *(Chionodoxa)*, 267

Glow worm (firefly), 342

Godetia spp. (Clarkia), 7, 10, 12, 13, 15, 24, 28, 230, 236

Gold Dust Plant *(Aucuba japonica)*, 47, 134, 363

Golden Barrel *(Echinocactus grusonii)*, 70

Golden Dewdrop *(Duranta repens)*, 13, 15, 17, 19, 22, 141

Golden Trumpet *(Allamanda)*, 15, 17, 19, 22, 288

Golden Vine *(Mascagnia macroptera)*, 292

Golden Wonder *(Cassia splendida)*, 138

Goldenrod *(Solidago spp.)*, 20, 22, 236

Gomphrena globosa (Globe, Amaranth), 235

Gordonia spp. (Franklinia), 101; (Loblolly Bay), 107, 135

Gorse *(Ulex europaeus)*, 10

Gourd *(Cucurbita spp.)*, 9, 12, 293

Grafting, 5, 194, 198, 199, 201, 333, 339

'Grand Duke' *(Jasminum sambac)*, 65

Grape Hyacinth *(Muscari)*, 7, 22, 24, 27, 29, 257, 272

Grape Ivy *(Cissus rhombifolia)*, 62

Mexican or Wild), 115, 122

P. persica (Peach, Flowering), 5, 7, 39, 112, 121, 124, 360

P. serotina (Black Cherry), 94

Pseuderanthemum alatum (Chocolate Plant), 230

Pseudocallima alliaceum (Garlic Vine), 292

Psidium littorale (Strawberry Guava), 143

Pteridium aquilinum (Bracken Fern), 302

Pueraria lobata (Kudzu Vine), 296

Punica Granatum (Pomegranate), 11, 13, 16, 18, 20, 22, 25, 125, 154, 332

Purple Coneflower (Rudbeckia) *(Echinacea purpurea)*, 20, 245

Purslane *(Portulaca* spp.), 12, 14, 244, 286

Pyracantha coccinea (Fire Thorn), 11, 154-155

Pyrostegia venusta (Flamevine of Brazil), 292

Pyrus spp. (Pear), 3, 7, 18, 113, 121, 124

Q

Queen Anne's Lace *(Daucus Carota)*, 2-29, 245

Quercus spp. (Oak), 87, 110-112, 312, 360

Quince, Chinese *(Cydonia sinensis)*, 115

Quince, Japanese Flowering *(Chaenomeles japonica)*, 3, 5, 7, 11, 16, 155, 312, 332

Quisqualis indica (Rangoon Creeper), 18, 298

R

Rain Lilies *(Habranthus brachyandrus)*, 2-29, 254, 255, 272-273

Rain Lily *(Cooperia* spp.*)*, 2-29, 254, 255, 281

Rain Tree, Southern Golden *(Koelreuteria bipinnata)*, 25, 115

Raised beds, 3, 36, 46, 74, 121, 122, 183, 195, 196, 198, 207, 208, 211, 212, 225, 257, 327, 333

Rangoon Creeper *(Quisqualis indica)*, 18, 298

Ranunculus asiaticus, 2-29, 43, 281

Raphiolepis indica (Indian Hawthorn), 10, 13, 146

Rebutia (Crown Cactus), 70

Red Hot Poker Plant (Tritoma) *(Kniphofia* spp.*)*, 276

Red Spider Lily *(Lycoris aurea)*, 2-29, 254, 255, 279

Redbay *(Persea borbonia)*, 115

Redbird Cactus *(Pedilanthus tithymaloides)*, 65

Redbud *(Cercis canadensis)*, 3, 7, 115, 332

Resurrection Fern *(Polypodium polypodioides)*, 305

Rhamnus caroliniana (Carolina Buckthorn), 95

Rhapis spp. (Slender Lady-palm), 50, 64; (Bamboo Palm), 63

Rhipsalidopsis Gaertneri (Easter Cactus), 61

Rhizomes, 21, 253, 336, 337, 368 (see also Bulbs)

Rhododendron, 183 (see also Azalea)

Rhus spp. (Poison Ivy), 169, 344, 357, 360; (Poison Oak), 169, 344, 360;

(Sumac, Flameleaf), 157; (Sumac, Smooth), 117

Rice Paper Plant *(Tetrapanax papyriferus)*, 3, 155

Richmondensis cv. (Begonia), 227

Ricinus communis (Castor Bean), 6, 9, 12, 14, 17, 19, 219, 229, 358

River Birch *(Betula nigra)*, 116

River Red Gum *(Eucalyptus camaldulensis)*, 100

Robinia spp. (Locust, Black), 10, 107; (Rose Acacia), 16, 155

Rock Rose *(Cistus* spp.*)*, 19, 22, 155

Rocket *(Eruca* spp.*)*, 11, 84

Rocket Salad *(Rugula)*, 84

Root rot, 25, 68, 188, 257

Rose, 43, 206-217, 337, 338
  beds, 210
  buying, 212
  care, 214, 323-325
  classifications, 208
  climber, 298
  list, 217
  miniature, 214
  Month by Month, 2-29
  planting, 212

Rose Acacia *(Robinia hispida)*, 16, 155

Rose Mallow *(Hibiscus moscheutos)*, 16, 20, 155-156, 245, 312

Rose of Sharon (Althaea) *(Hibiscus syriacus)*, 15, 17, 19, 22, 132-133, 332

Rosebugs or Rose Chafers, 351

Rosemarinus officinalis (Rosemary), 4, 11, 84

Rosemary *(Rosemarinus officinalis)*, 4, 11, 84

Rotation planting (vegetables), 75